EDUCATION POLICY-MAKING IN ENGLAND AND WALES

THE WOBURN EDUCATION SERIES
General Series Editor: Professor Peter Gordon

EDUCATION POLICY-MAKING IN ENGLAND AND WALES

The Crucible Years, 1895–1911

NEIL DAGLISH

Victoria University, Wellington

Routledge
Taylor & Francis Group

NEW YORK AND LONDON

First published in 1996 *by*
THE WOBURN PRESS

This edition published 2013 by Routledge
711 Third Avenue, New York, NY 10017, USA
2 Park Square, Milton Park, Abingdon, Oxfordshire OX14 4RN

First issued in paperback 2016

Routledge is an imprint of the Taylor & Francis Group, an informa business

British Library Cataloguing in Publication Data
Daglish, Neil D.
Education Policy-Making in England and
Wales, 1895–1911: Crucible Years. –
(Woburn Education Series)
I. Title II. Series
379.42

ISBN 13: 978-1-138-96841-7 (pbk)
ISBN 13: 978-0-7130-0200-3 (hbk)

Library of Congress Cataloging-in-Publication Data
Daglish, Neil D.
Education policy-making in England and Wales, 1895–1911: the
crucible years / Neil D. Daglish.
p.   cm. – (The Woburn education series)
Includes bibliographical references and index.
ISBN 0-7130-0200-X
1. Education and state–England–History–19th century.
2. Education and state–England–History–20th century.
3. Education and state–Wales–History–19th century. 4. Education
and state–Wales–History–20th century. 5. Education law and
legislation–England–History–19th century. 6. Education law and
legislation–England–History–20th century. 7. Educational law and
legislation–Wales–History–19th century. 8. Educational law and
legislation–Wales–History–20th century. I. Title. II. Series.
LC93.G7D34   1996
379.42'09'041–dc20   95-44531
                                           CIP

Typeset by Regent Typesetting, London

Contents

Preface

The significant contribution that education can make to the development of society has been well acknowledged over many centuries in the history of Western society, if, at times, more by individuals than governments. In *The Republic*, one of the earliest and most influential expositions of this concept, Plato argued that it was essential if a just society was to be achieved. But for the majority of individuals in nineteenth-century English society, that is the working class, the reality of life demonstrated not only the omission of any substantial education provision but also the absence of a just society. As far as their education was concerned, the only concept of *The Republic* that applied was the least desirable, namely a class-based stratification of the education system. G.M. Young characterised the absence of any substantial education provision for much of the century as the 'great Victorian omission' but towards the close of the century substantial efforts were made by some education policy-makers to remedy the educational and social problems it had engendered. Recent scholarship has revealed the dominance of Platonic concepts in the influential social idealist philosophy which helped shape the aims and views of some of the key civil servants and politicians of the time.[1] It is with the efforts of the education policy-makers to create their vision of a more just society that this book is primarily concerned.

One of the most striking changes they achieved was the replacement of most of the *ad hoc* administrative structures, which had characterised the nineteenth century, by a more rationalised system. The establishment of a unified central government education department, the Board of Education, in 1899 and the creation of a uniform, national system of local education authorities (LEAs) three years later heralded the beginning of a dual partnership between local and central government. This partnership, described by one Permanent Secretary of the Department of Education and Science as *the* characteristic feature of the twentieth-century education system, provided the successful basis for the development of the nation's schools and other educational institutions until its effective dismemberment by the Thatcher government in 1988.[2] These major alterations to administrative structures and functions were but one part, however, of the policy innovations achieved, for they were matched by others no less significant. The enunciation of clearly defined educational goals for both elementary and secondary schools, a rationalisation of the funding of elementary schools, the provision of school meals, medical inspection and treatment, as well as reform of the inspectorate and the pupil-teacher training system were other policy changes that directly affected the activities of the schools, the teachers and, most importantly, the welfare of the nation's children. The magnitude and the durability of these changes would appear to provide justification for labelling this period the crucible years for twentieth-century English education. One aim of the detailed analysis of the genesis of these changes that follows is that it will contribute to the history of education.

To ascribe these achievements solely to efforts of the Unionist and Liberal governments in power during this period, however, would be to overlook both the real nature of the 'state in education' and the complex processes involved in policy-making. The myopic concept of 'L'état, c'est moi' may have served the needs of Louis XIV and Charles de Gaulle but in reality the state is a much more complex corpus. Dale acknowledges that government is a most important component, being the most active and most visible part of the state, but it does not represent its totality. Equally important are what he labels the 'state apparatuses' or what McLennan describes as a set of 'agencies, departments, tiers and levels, each with their own rules and resources and often with varying purposes'.[3] The consequences for policy-making are considerable, Grace noting that while the government and the minister of education may represent 'the formal embodiment of the state in education at the highest level' the power relations between these two levels

> can and do change over time as a result of wider political developments; the energy and ideological commitments of particular ministers and the experience, skills and vested interests of the senior officials.[4]

Not surprisingly then, as Rose has commented, policy-making can be at times as much a matter of individuals as policies.

Sutherland has observed that 'anyone who devises the simplest of schemes for the education of the next generation is offering comments on his society, as he sees it and as he wants it to become'.[5] The validity of this view is borne out by examination of the policy changes effected during the crucible years. Equally important, however, is the need for as complete an understanding as possible of the ways in which, and by what individuals, policy-making is carried out in a (theoretically) democratic society, given that many may be, and are, affected by policy aims over which they may have little control or input. The recent, disturbing trends towards exclusion in education policy-making and the ascendancy of a set of values based firmly not on consensus between central and local government but upon highly centralised state control (and involving a virtual reincarnation of various nineteenth century educational models) are not the province of this study but do highlight this need. Dale argues that in order to understand the source and nature of the control exerted over both education and schools it is necessary to focus on the state, for in the analysis of the state one 'may begin to understand the assumptions, intentions and outcomes of various strategies of educational change'.[6]

This study focuses, then, on the roles of the education policy-makers within the state, notably the interaction between the key politicians and civil servants, in an attempt to reveal the aims underlying the changes made during these crucible years. Although it may be debatable whether one can define a certain number of years as a period, given the continuity of change within a society, in this instance the change of government and the advent in 1895 of two key education policy-makers, Sir John Gorst and Sir Robert Morant, provides a useful start. The year 1911 has been chosen as the end for after Morant's transfer from the Board of Education none of the major figures of this study remained members of the 'state in education'.

Musing upon the roles played by some of her friends in the governance of society before the Great War, Violet Markham was worried about how they would be recorded by posterity:

> Good, bad and indifferent, the actors who have played any part on the stage are all swept at death into the pit, there to be sorted out at leisure by the Posterity Assessors.[7]

What she could not foresee was the paucity of material that might befall the assessors. While Plato may have stipulated that the minister of education should be accorded the highest position among the holders of supreme office in the state, this was not a view held by the majority of either the Unionist or Liberal governments of Salisbury, Balfour, Campbell-Bannerman and Asquith.[8] Consequently, even prominent education issues did not always feature in the correspondence of the government members whose collections of letters remain, those of Balfour and Runciman being notable exceptions. The lacunae

tion, or partial curtailment, of some individual's collections by themselves (McKenna), by their families (Gorst) or by enemy action in the Second World War (Morant). Furthermore, there is the absence of any collections or memoirs for a great many other individuals (especially the civil servants in the Board of Education). This has meant that there has had to be substantial reliance upon official documents, although wherever possible this has been balanced by other material. Two points need to be made about the documents cited in the text. The first is that where abbreviations were used by the authors these have been expanded for ease of reading, and the second is that, unfortunately, there is no way effectively to reproduce the variety of emphases used by Robert Morant in his inimitable handwriting: consequently the italics employed here fail to convey the sheer force of ink and line to which some of his correspondents were subjected.

An important component in the determination of the aims and content of education policy is the interaction (or contestation) that usually, but not always, occurs between the state and society. Dale has observed that 'State policy-makers do not possess perfect knowledge of the State's needs or of how to meet them through education or any other means at their disposal'.[9] The variety of agencies existing in society, at both local and national levels, and espousing a multitude of secular and sectarian interests ensures that sufficient views abound and all invested with an ability to overcome any such shortcomings on the part of the policy-makers. The variety and, inevitably, conflicting nature of this advice in most instances ensures that the interaction will never be easy. The state in education's interaction with local government bodies and other agencies of interest is, consequently, an integral component of this study although no attempt has been made to provide a detailed consideration of the various agencies of interest such as teachers' unions, trade unions, Fabians, religious bodies, and so on, since most have been the subject of extensive analysis and narrative.[10]

The point has been made by some educationists that there is a need to differentiate between 'education' and 'schooling' since the former refers to 'all forms of learning, the second to that specific historical form which involves specialised institutions and professional practitioners'.[11] While this is a useful distinction, the limitations implied in the term 'schooling' overlook the effect that the achievement of literacy, an integral component of education, can have upon an individual, even if it is acquired in a specialised institution. As Lerner indicates, the acquisition of literacy provides training in vicarious thinking and, beyond the ability to read and write, it produces a capacity in the individual to think of him/herself in another role.[12] The term education system is used here, therefore, in the sense of a social system brought into existence to act out some phase of the institutional order concerned with educating. The exigencies of space have meant that this study has had to be confined to an examination of the policy issues affecting schools coming directly under the aegis of the state in England and, to a lesser extent, Wales. Consequently, the public schools and post-school institutions are for the most part not covered.[13]

Silver has stated recently that history constitutes 'the recording and analysis of change' and consequently, for historians, the 'selecting from and giving real or apparent coherence to the human record is their sole mission'.[14] Only the reader can decide whether the analysis provided here gives a real rather than apparent coherence to the policy changes of the crucible years but, even so, perhaps the final decision rests with one of the key persons from this period:

> Documents scarcely deserve the implicit reliance which is placed upon them. It is true that the words actually written down at the time may be faithfully preserved. But the motive with which they were written, the effect which they were designed to produce upon the person to whom the document was addressed, the facts and considerations omitted, because necessarily present in the mind of the recipient – all these things and many more, may be unknown or forgotten. Written as well as spoken words are sometimes used to conceal thoughts. From all this it results that history, however carefully compiled, must inevitably reflect to a very considerable extent the imagination of the historian, and that the real truth about events, even recent, even contemporaneous, cannot always be discovered.[15]

NOTES

1. J. Harris, 'Political Thought and the Welfare State 1870–1940: An Intellectual Framework for British Social Policy', *Past and Present*, 135 (May 1992), pp. 125–31. See also M. Richter, *The Politics of Conscience: T.H. Green and His Age* (1964); P. Gordon and J. White, *Philosophers as Educational Reformers: The Influence of Idealism on British Educational Thought and Practice* (1979).
2. W. Pile, *The Department of Education and Science* (1979), p. 4.
3. R. Dale, 'Education and the capitalist state: contributions and contradictions' in M. Apple (ed.), *Cultural and Economic Reproduction in Education* (1982), pp. 138–9; G. McLennan *et al.*, *State and Society in Contemporary Britain* (1984), p. 3 cited in G.R. Grace, 'Teachers and the State: A Changing Relation'

in M. Lawn and G.R. Grace (eds), *Teachers: The Culture and Politics of Work* (1987), p. 196.
4. Grace, op. cit., p. 196.
5. G. Sutherland, *Policy-Making in Elementary Education, 1870–1895* (1983), p. 1.
6. Dale, op. cit., pp. 129–30.
7. Violet Markham, *Friendship's Harvest* (1956), p. 206.
8. Plato, *The Laws* (1976), p. 241.
9. Dale, op. cit., p. 134.
10. See, for example, A. Tropp, *The School Teachers* (1957); P.H.J.H. Gosden, *The Evolution of a Profession* (1972); C. Griggs, *The Trades Union Congress and the Struggle for Education 1868–1925* (1983); E.J.T. Brennan, *Education for National Efficiency: The Contribution of Sidney and Beatrice Webb* (1975); M. Cruickshank, *Church and State in English Education* (1963); B. Sacks, *The Religious Issue in the State Schools of England and Wales 1902–1914* (1961); G.I.T. Machin, *Politics and the Churches in Great Britain 1869–1921* (1987); D.W. Bebbington, *The Nonconformist Conscience* (1982).
11. Education Group (Centre for Contemporary Cultural Studies), *Unpopular Education: Schooling and Social Democracy in England since 1944* (1981), pp. 14–15.
12. D. Lerner, *The Passing of Traditional Society* (1958).
13. For details of these schools see eg J. Roach, *Secondary Education in England 1870–1902: Public Activity and Private Enterprise* (1991); B. Simon and I. Bradley, *The Victorian Public School* (1975); J.R. de S. Honey, *Tom Brown's Universe: The Development of the Victorian Public School* (1977).
14. H. Silver, *Education, Change and the Policy Process* (1990), p. 1.
15. John E. Gorst in H.E. Gorst, *The Fourth Party* (1906), pp. vii–viii.

Acknowledgements

Two major debts of any historian are to other historians and to the conservers and controllers of archives. Although the first debt is so wide-ranging as to prevent any detailed acknowledgements tribute must be paid to the pioneering works in this area of educational history of Eric Eaglesham, Brian Simon and Gillian Sutherland. I am especially indebted to Ann Low-Beer, Professor David Hamer, Professor Peter Gosden, Professor Peter Mellini, Dr Bill Stephens and the late Richard Goodings for their advice and encouragement over the years. The research for this work was enriched by the generous hospitality, advice and access to their private collections of family papers and records provided by the late Miss Joan Clarkson, Mrs Kitty Thomas, Mr Paul Lysley and Mr and Mrs Lionel Jebb. The unstinting co-operation, correspondence and hospitality of the late Mrs Margaret Bailey, Sir Robert Morant's daughter, in the past decade has been undoubtedly one of the most pleasant aspects of my research.

For access to the archive material in their care I am grateful to the librarians and staff of the British Library; Public Record Office; Bodleian Library, University of Oxford; Cambridge University Library; Churchill Archives Centre, Churchill College, Cambridge; Brotherton Library, University of Leeds; Department of Education and Science Library; William R. Perkins Library, Duke University; Durham County Record Office; Eastbourne Public Library; Hatfield House Library, Hatfield; Hereford and Worcester Record Office; India Office Library; Lady Margaret Hall Library, Oxford; National Library of Scotland; Scottish Record Office; University of Liverpool Library; Greater London Record Office; Lancashire Record Office; Gloucestershire Record Office; Lambeth Palace Library; New Zealand National Library, Wellington; University of California Library, Los Angeles; University of Auckland Library and the University of Newcastle upon Tyne Library.

For permission to quote from copyright material held by them I wish to thank the Controller of Her Majesty's Stationery Office (for material held in the Public Record Office and India Office Library), the Earl of Balfour, the Marquess of Salisbury, Sir Richard Acland, Mrs Margaret Bailey, Mr R.F. Sadler and Mrs Ann Hornby, Dr

Pauline Dower, the Robinson Library of the University of Newcastle upon Tyne and the Trustees of the Trevelyan Family Papers. While every effort has been made to contact the holders of copyright material, if any oversights have occurred I must apologise and hope that this general acknowledgement will suffice.

Some of the material used in certain chapters has appeared in articles published in *History of Education* and the *Journal of Educational Administration and History*; I am grateful to the editors and Taylor and Francis Limited, publishers of *History of Education*, for their permission to use the material here.

Thanks are owed to the Victoria University of Wellington for the granting, and partial funding, of the three research leaves needed to access the above archives and to Mr Vic Elliott, the University Librarian, and his staff for all their efforts on my behalf. I wish to acknowledge the encouragement given by my colleagues in the Education Department, especially Professors Hugh Lauder and Gerald Grace. A special word of thanks is owing to Professor David Hamer for his critical analysis of a draft of the manuscript. Last, but not least, the book is dedicated to my wife Sue and son Toby for their constant support, co-operation and toleration over the years. Any errors that remain are solely mine.

List of illustrations

Abbreviations

Add.MS	British Museum Additional Manuscripts
ATTI	Association of Teachers in Technical Institutes
BMA	British Medical Association
BP	Balfour Papers
CAB	Cabinet Paper
ED	Education Department
HMI	Her/His Majesty's Inspector [of schools]
IAHM	Incorporated Association of Headmasters
ILP	Independent Labour Party
LEA	Local Education Authority
LCC	London County Council
MP	Member of Parliament
NUT	National Union of Teachers
PD	Hansard's Parliamentary Debates
PP	Parliamentary Papers
PRO	Public Record Office
TUC	Trades Union Congress

1

Education, politics and policy-makers

> . . . from our Educational Minister we look for naught paltry, partial, peddling. Faltering and piecemeal reform will make confusion worse confounded, and arouse that discontent which it should be the means of pacifying.[1]

The collapse of Lord Rosebery's Liberal government in the summer of 1895 had been anticipated for many months by observers of the British political scene. Beatrice Webb had noted a month before the government's resignation, 'the Haves thoroughly frightened' (partly because of the death duties which had been introduced the previous November), 'the Have-nots unsatisfied' (by the lack of significant social reform).[2] The dissatisfaction with the lack of progress in social reform came as no surprise to Webb for soon after the Liberals had come to power in 1892 under Gladstone she had observed that although the younger Cabinet members, including Asquith and Arthur Acland, were busy introducing administrative reforms there remained a tangible query as to whether the 'old gang will not dictate a policy of evasion to all legislative proposals'.[3] A year later her prognosis appeared to be correct when Acland, the radical Vice President of the Committee of Council on Education, privately vented his frustrations over the Cabinet's preoccupation with Ireland and the correspondingly slow progress in initiating social reform. 'Were the government', he asked the Liberal Chief Whip, Tom Ellis, 'straining ourselves and spending so much time to any real purpose? It is a miserably poor way to spend our lives unless we are really working for something which is real . . .'[4] Lord Rosebery's succession as Premier after Gladstone retired in 1894 did little to boost the Cabinet's morale, and by the beginning of 1895 Webb observed that with the exception of Acland 'none of the Ministers are doing any work'. One Liberal, R.B. Haldane, believed the Cabinet were unable to free themselves from their lassitude and problems: the 'Rot has set in . . . there is no hope now but to be beaten and then to reconstruct a new party'.[5] The

1

government lurched on for another six months until defeat over the supply of cordite for the army provided an excuse for resignation.

The change of government that followed their resignation, and was confirmed by victory in the subsequent General Election held in July, was accompanied by the usual critical appraisal in the press of the new Ministers and their future roles. Apart from having established a royal commission to investigate the administration of secondary education, the legacy of educational reform from Arthur Acland to his Conservative successor, Sir John Gorst, was small owing to the reasons cited. This meant that there was a danger that the education system would continue to trundle on into the future along well-worn grooves and impervious to the changing nature and needs of society. Thus much of the first debate on education in the new Parliament, one marked by an unusual degree of consensus, was spent in identifying key topics requiring urgent administrative or legislative resolution. The consensus view which emerged was matched by those being published in articles written by educationists and the list was substantial. The financial state of many elementary schools, the conditions of employment of their teachers, the plight of half-time pupils, the content and administration of secondary education as well as the nature of teacher training college facilities comprised the core problems.[6] The need for substantial reforms was heightened by a growing awareness in parts of society that education was becoming a critical factor in the nation's ability to survive the increasing economic competition with both Europe and the USA. This concern was intensified by a perception that the current system was not meeting the nation's needs:

> It was no longer possible to pass over the fact that a young Englishman on leaving school was intellectually two years behind a German of the same age with the consoling reflection that he made up in character what he lacked in information, and that, if more ignorant, he was better equipped for practical life. ... A nation of amateurs was being forced to recognise that they could not compete with a nation of professionals.[7]

Much was thus expected from Gorst and the Duke of Devonshire, the Lord President, for the crucial questions they faced were: just how legitimate were these perceptions of the state of the nation's education system and were the problems identified by the House and in the press the only serious ones afflicting it?

Surveying the development of the elementary education system over the 80 years since its inception, on a mass scale, in the first decade of the nineteenth century, one education administrator acknowledged that the system had been more of a growth, rather than having been created. It was, he believed,

> the resultant of the action, not always harmonious, of various forces originating in the very depths of our national existence – the outcome of which is a system differing in some of its most prominent features from any which is to be found elsewhere. [8]

One of the most active of these forces had been class and one invidious consequence had been that the provision of education for the majority of children, that is, those of the working classes, was both minimal and in accordance with the prevailing view of being for the poor. The absence of any government intervention, financial or otherwise, before 1833 meant that the provision of elementary education had been virtually the prerogative of voluntary agencies. The State's general lassitude as far as education was concerned prevailed until the mid-century when it became more interventionist, as demonstrated by Robert Lowe's Revised Code of 1862. The effects of this pattern of growth coupled with the consequences of the 1870 Education Act, whereby an alternative to the voluntary schools was created in the form of board schools, meant that for the final quarter of the century the system was characterised by certain features. The first was that the State's supervisory role was based primarily upon its financial contribution to the system, rather than 'any inherent right . . . to regulate the education of its future citizens'. Secondly, although the system was ostensibly a secular one, in reality it possessed a quite marked religious character, this being a distinctly denominational one in the majority of schools. And, finally, although there was a dual system of school management in existence after 1870 at least two-thirds of the elementary schools were controlled by private managers.[9] Consequently, by the summer of 1895, while the provision of elementary education was no longer quite so minimalist in approach or content as it had been, it still carried the stigma of being essentially for the poor working classes.

The voluntary schools were in the main the educational offspring of religious bodies and had been, and still were, the main providers of elementary education. They were funded by a mixture of voluntary subscriptions and parliamentary grants, the major force among them being the Church of England (via the National Society) with some 1,850,545 children on average in its schools in 1895. The children present in other voluntary schools run by the British and Foreign

School Society and other undenominational bodies (235,151), the Roman Catholic (230,392) and Wesleyan (129,724) authorities brought the total attending this type of school to 2,445,812. Virtually the sole providers of organised elementary education until 1870, the majority of voluntary schools had found it difficult to accept the competition provided in the subsequent 25 years by the board schools.

The growing impact of technological advances upon manufacturing processes which had previously relied on the use of child labour had, by the mid-nineteenth century, resulted in the loss of employment opportunities for many children. This phenomenon, when combined with the overall increase in numbers of school-age children as a result of the continued growth of the birth rate nationally, necessitated an increase in school places. At the same time, there was concern in some quarters of society not only about the dominance of the voluntary school organisations in the provision of elementary education and the quality of education they were providing but also about the poor attendance statistics. The need to address these problems fell to Gladstone's first government, with W.E. Forster as Minister of Education. The solution, contained in the 1870 Education Act, had been to establish *ad hoc* school boards in either boroughs or civil parishes after the voluntary agencies had been given time to remove the deficit in places. Originally intended to fill the gaps left in the voluntary school system, the board schools had not taken long to become the competitors of, rather than complementary to, the voluntary schools, especially in many urban areas. In 1883 the board schools were educating 1,028,904 pupils as against the 2,098,310 attending voluntary schools and by 1895 the gap had diminished so that 5,316 board schools contained 1,879,218 children compared with the 2,445,812 in 14,484 voluntary schools.[10] This phenomenal growth rate of 14.5 per cent per annum since 1872 was the consequence of a combination of funding, curricular emphasis and demography.

Like the voluntary schools, the board schools were eligible for parliamentary grants based upon the numbers of children in average attendance each year plus, until 1895, the pupils' academic achievements in annual examinations administered under the payment by results scheme introduced in 1862 into the Education Department's Annual Code by the Vice President, Robert Lowe. But where the voluntary schools had to make up the shortfall between their expenditure and the parliamentary grant by voluntary subscriptions, the school boards had recourse to rate funding. By 1895 the board schools were receiving an income of 19s 8d per child in average attendance from the rates while the average income per child in the voluntary schools from subscriptions was 6s 9d. As the board schools' growth rate had continued on its undiminishing path since 1872, especially in the urban areas, epithets such as 'omnivorous', 'extravagant' or even 'palatial' had been used by their opponents to describe both their expenditure and schools. But such generalisations were misleading for the rural school boards tended to be small and suffered, like their voluntary counterparts, from financial problems. This situation reflected the critical fact that a school board's rate was totally dependent upon the rating of the district in which it was located. Thus while London and Liverpool could raise £140,000 and £13,200 respectively from a penny rate, the corresponding sums for Clayhanger (Devon) and Ashen (Essex) were £7 14s and £6 3s. Differentials in government funding compounded this problem; whereas London needed to raise only £1 9s from rate aid for each pound from the Exchequer to complete its school board's financial needs, Great Bentley in Essex had to find £14 on the same basis.[11] The rate demands arising from these rural school boards' educational activities were such that if, as one HMI reported from Cheshire, the average farmer was forced to choose between the Colorado Beetle and a School Board 'he wouldn't know which way to go'.

The majority of school boards were small – out of a total of 2470 boards in 1895 some 2,293 were parish boards, and of these 1,696 had only five members each and 469 seven members each but, none the less, the majority of board school pupils lived in urban areas.[12] It was not surprising therefore, given their financial circumstances, that the creation and growth of a new type of secondary school, the higher grade school, offering a more vocational and modern type of secondary education than that of the traditional secondary schools, should have been almost entirely the preserve of the urban school boards. But at the same time, and following the rationalisation of local government authorities which had been instituted by the Local Government Act of 1888, both the composition and attitudes of some of the school boards had become a source of concern in some parts of society. The substantial rate demands of many boards, the increasing unwillingness of some to be publicly accountable for their expenditure and demands, the absence of any special qualifications needed by candidates for board elections, triennial elections and the use of the cumulative vote had reinforced the increasing division in society between those in favour of collectivisation and those wishing to maintain *ad hoc* bodies in local government. This was reinforced by the

5

London School Board election of 1894 in which an acrimonious dispute over the religious instruction provided in the Board's schools dominated. The responses of the factions involved, including the teachers, the Anglicans and the Nonconformists, had revealed some of the tension that existed about the elementary school curriculum and the place of religion in it.[13] Of equal importance was the fact that the dispute reinforced the feelings of the opponents of school boards that

> ... the *ad hoc* election of School Boards ... is now regarded by a considerable body of public opinion as no longer the most satisfactory arrangement for constituting a local authority for the oversight of elementary education.[14]

This notwithstanding, the voluntary schools felt that the financial differential with the board schools severely affected their continued attempt to preserve their dominance in elementary education. This funding plight had been exacerbated in 1892 by the Education Department Circular 321 under which the Inspectorate were required to report on the condition of the facilities and buildings of every school they inspected. This, coupled with changes made to the Annual Code between 1890 and 1895, represented Acland's attempt to ensure that the parliamentary grant was only secured by schools which were efficient both educationally and structurally. One effect had been to force some Anglican voluntary schools in areas of Birmingham, Chester and London, plus parts of urban Lancashire, Yorkshire and South Wales, to claim that they could no longer cope with the 'intolerable strain' placed upon them, a claim which had led Lord Harrowby to complain that there had never before been a government 'so determined to bring about the destruction of the Voluntary Schools'. As a result, the Church Parliamentary Committee had been formed in 1893 to try to protect the voluntary schools' interests in Parliament while two committees, one Anglican (under the chairmanship of Lord Cross) and the other Roman Catholic (under Cardinal Vaughan), had been set up to report on the condition and needs of their schools.

If the board schools in urban areas were able, in general, to provide better schools in terms of buildings, teachers and equipment because of their superior funding, and thereby attract more pupils, one aspect of their curriculum was an important contributory factor also in the competition with the voluntary schools. Under Clause 14 of the 1870 Act, the Cowper-Temple clause, board schools had to be non-sectarian, that is, 'no religious catechism or religious formulary which is distinctive of any particular denomination' had to be taught in them. For Nonconformist parents these schools provided a welcome alternative to the Anglican voluntary schools, if the choice was available. In most urban areas it was, and this aspect of the schools' work helped to reinforce their potential for providing a more democratically controlled and community-responsive elementary school system than existed in the voluntary sector, which tended to be dominated by parson or priest and the church. For all this, the board schools were still very much part of the elementary system and affected by all the social connotations applied to it:

> 'Board school' was a term of contempt in my 'middle-class' suburban milieu; and one said 'board school boy' much as Swift's houyhnhnms used the term 'yahoo'. The products of these establishments were looked down upon as being shabby and dirty urchins, who shouted in the street and could not speak the Queen's English; whereas we were 'sons of gentlemen' and knew how to behave (or thought we did). It would have been considered an unspeakable disgrace if one of us had had to be transferred to an 'elementary' school.[15]

In rural areas the Anglican voluntary schools were dominant – even in those areas such as Wales where the population was predominantly Nonconformist. Furthermore, the growth of a militant faction within the Church of England during the 1890s had been linked to a determination not to relinquish denominational religious instruction in their schools while also pressing for its inclusion in other schools. This did not ease tension over elementary schooling, as was seen in the 1894 London School Board election, especially as these views were accompanied by demands for additional state funding of the voluntary schools without the important corollary, as far as many Nonconformists were concerned, of public control over expenditure of that funding. But it was not only Nonconformist parents who felt aggrieved about schools in rural areas, for questionable conditions, physical and educational, prevailed among both board and voluntary rural schools.

One Chief HMI was critical of the quality of the teachers in rural schools, observing that the schools

> ... do not secure in the open market the ablest and most inventive and independent-minded of teachers; and it is not every inspector (even when possessed of many special gifts and abilities) who can awaken and develop and lead a sleepy village, and

7

a nervous managing body and a timid schoolmistress for a march along comparatively unbeaten Code paths.[16]

Another HMI, A.P. Graves, was more sympathetic and commented that while the elementary schoolteachers he had met in Cheshire were not so sophisticated as their urban counterparts he had learned more from them educationally. They realised, he claimed, that qualifications were only the means, and not the end, of self-improvement and they diligently continued their studies at their own pace.[17] While both views were valid, given the very broad spectrum of teaching ability present within rural schools, what neither mentioned were the poor conditions under which many of these teachers had to work, especially in those schools located in areas where there was little support for education among the inhabitants. An NUT pamphlet describing some village schools in various parts of the nation in 1897 was a depressing litany of unhygienic, overcrowded conditions and HMI Sneyd-Kynnersley confirmed this when he recalled his experiences of the variations which had existed among Cheshire schools:

> On Monday I had a town school of 400 boys in a black hole: on Tuesday a suburban school of 150 girls in a beautiful building with a lavish supply of teachers: on Wednesday I drove 10 miles to a country village, where the whole 45 lambs of the flock were collected in what an esteemed inspector called 'a third class waiting-room and a jam cupboard'.[18]

The burdens which arose from such working conditions were not eased by the additional tasks which were the lot of many rural voluntary schoolteachers, as one advertisement in 1891 for a certificated headmistress revealed. Not only was she expected to run a school of 50 pupils but she had to be a Churchwoman, be prepared to take the Sunday-school and play the harmonium. For this she was paid £30 a year plus half the school pence and half the government grant and also had the use of a furnished cottage. Furthermore, security of tenure was not a right and in many cases depended on the satisfactory performance not only as a teacher but in these extraneous duties. Tenure could be lost swiftly, as one head teacher discovered when he refused to chastise a seven-year-old child for failing to curtsey to the vicar's wife and found himself dismissed instantly despite having held the post for 20 years.[19]

By 1895 the majority of elementary schoolteachers were women although most head teacher positions were occupied by men; in 1880 there had been twice as many female as male pupil-teachers and by

1895 the ratio had become four to one. This gender imbalance was not helped, as far as the women were concerned, by the fact that the majority of Assistant Teacher positions in schools were also held by women. Assistant (or Uncertificated) Teachers constituted the bottom rung in the teacher hierarchy and were ex-pupil-teachers who had failed to gain entry to a training college and thus lacked a Teacher's Certificate. The rapid growth of this sector of the teaching force after 1870 had been caused by the dearth of qualified teachers once the board schools had been established coupled with the inability of many voluntary and some board schools to pay the salaries of trained teachers. Thus by 1895 only a quarter of the teachers in elementary schools were the products of training colleges. Concern had been expressed about the deterioration in standards that would accompany the increase in Assistant Teacher numbers and this was mainly because of the low esteem accorded pupil-teachers, who constituted another quarter of the teaching force.

The pupil-teacher system had been introduced in 1846 by the first Secretary of the Education Department, James Kay-Shuttleworth, as a temporary expedient to alleviate the shortage of trained teachers and consisted of a five-year apprenticeship for selected elementary pupils over the age of 13. In return for assisting in the teaching of the school, the pupil-teacher was to receive a grant from the Education Department – which increased from £10 in the first year to £20 in the fifth – plus additional personal education for up to 90 minutes per day, either before or after school hours. Shuttleworth had envisaged, correctly, that the majority of apprentices would be derived from the working classes. The remuneration offered was sufficient in rural areas, in comparison with other available wages, to attract both males and females to become pupil-teachers, while in towns and cities the terms and career opportunities remained sufficiently attractive for many girls from both the working and lower middle classes to be articled by their parents. In 1862, however, Robert Lowe's Revised Code had terminated the system of grants to pupil-teachers and their schools, being part of a government cost-saving exercise. Thereafter pupil-teachers had to reach their own agreement with the school managers as regards payment while a school's staff were now expected to instruct the apprentices as part of their normal duties. The effects of these changes were significant, with cheapness of hire becoming a predominant factor in the recruitment of pupil-teachers while the quality of instruction afforded the trainees now became very dependent upon the conscientiousness of the teachers responsible.

9

F.H. Spencer, articled to a Swindon board school in 1886 at the age of 14, remembered his academic training as:

> . . . largely a fraud . . . .things varied according to the conscientiousness of the various masters, of whom the more intelligent were, as a rule, the less conscientious.[20]

Many pupil-teachers found the burden of their load oppressive and one, who subsequently became the successful headmistress of a London school, regarded the five years as the hardest period of her life. Spencer tellingly observed: 'You sank or swam. Either you could "hold" a class of thirty, fifty or sixty boys or you could not'.[21]

Criticism of the limited perspectives and examination-orientated approach which marked the pupil-teacher system after 1862 mounted during the 1860s and 1870s. Innovations introduced by Liverpool in 1874, and subsequently developed by the London School Board, established centralised classes for the apprentices with the classes being held on two evenings from 6 to 8 pm and on Saturday mornings from 9 am to 12.30 pm. The pressure this put on the pupil-teachers, given that they were also teaching each day, led to a reduction in the number of hours of teaching they had to give, to two and a half days a week, while the classes were provided during the mornings and afternoons in purpose-built pupil-teacher centres. The London and Liverpool models were copied by other major urban school boards so that by the turn of the century there were 292 centres educating two-thirds of the 31,000 pupil-teacher force. Unfortunately, it was beyond the resources of many rural communities to make similar provision and their pupil-teachers remained trained under the old methods. Despite these changes, by the time the Cross Commission reported in 1888 on the nation's elementary education system, the continuance of the pupil-teacher system was being questioned.

The Majority Report of the Commission remained in favour of the system but in their Minority Report some of the Commissioners argued that the pupil-teacher system was 'the weakest part of our educational machinery, ...in general . . . the pupil-teachers teach badly, and are badly taught'.[22] Furthermore, far from wanting the system to be maintained, they were worried that the temporary expedient planned by Kay-Shuttleworth had become a permanent feature of the elementary education landscape. Their fears were not to be allayed, however, for little effective reform was initiated after the appearance of the Commission's reports. The pupil-teacher system continued unchecked and with it the concomitant of a low status in society for

10

elementary teachers. The lot of teachers was not improved either, in some cases, by the relationship with the Inspectorate over the conduct, approach and content of their work.

Established on rather tentative lines by Kay-Shuttleworth in 1839, the Inspectorate had grown from an initial establishment of two to over 300 by 1895. By then they were differentiated into Chief HMIs, HMIs and Sub-Inspectors (First and Second Class) plus two inspectors of music and two women inspectors. Although the inspectors were appointed by the Sovereign in Council, patronage was not an unknown factor in their selection. Sir George Kekewich, the Permanent Secretary of the Education Department and originally appointed to the Education Department under patronage, noted that for a considerable period the sole qualification required for an inspector was 'Latin, Greek and Mathematics' and the majority lacked any knowledge of education or experience of elementary schools.[23] Above all, the inspectors 'were most emphatically gentlemen', especially as they were supposed to be on the same social and academic scale as the Department's Examiners.[24] Although Kay-Shuttleworth had viewed the inspectors' role not 'as a means of control, but of affording assistance', the implementation of the payment by results system after 1861 had altered this dramatically:

> For a third of a century 'My Lords' required their inspectors to examine every child in every elementary school in England on a syllabus which was binding on all schools alike. In doing this, they put a bit into the mouth of the teacher and drove him, at their pleasure, in this direction and that. And what they did to him they compelled him to do to the child.[25]

In some instances, the defects introduced by this system were reinforced by the personalities and actions of some of the Inspectorate for, as in any organisation, there were the competent and the incompetent. One major weakness of some of the Inspectorate was irresponsibility:

> The income is moderate, but sufficient and certain. In the dim and distant future looms a pension, assuring bread and butter. The standard of comfort, therefore, is assured; unfruitfulness of honest work does not threaten poverty.[26]

One HMI discovered, on taking over the West Somerset district, that he was faced with 'an immense accumulation of inefficient schools'. His predecessor was renowned for his prowess as a fox-hunter and had often visited the area's schools

> . . . in pink, looked at the registers, school accounts and log-book, chatted with the managers, and then rode off to the hunt, leaving his sub-inspector to do all the examination work alone.[27]

The poor sub-inspector was not only unable to cope with the workload placed upon him but he also lacked any authority to improve matters. But the problems created by such an attitude were nothing compared with those left in the wash of the almost vindictive manner adopted by some inspectors in their annual examination of a school's pupils. This approach could strike terror into the heart of a teacher whose career depended on the results obtained, for if a child failed an examination then the chief portion of the parliamentary grant available for him/her was lost by the school. The first president of the NUT, James Runciman, had experienced such men and declared that

> . . . sooner than teach in an elementary school, under any one of some score of inspectors whom I could name, I would go before the mast in a collier, or break stones in a casual ward – or, better than all, die.[28]

The net effect of this experience, repeated across the nation and provoking condemnatory statements from the NUT during the 1880s and 1890s, was to ensure that strained or even sour relations existed between many teachers and inspectors for decades. Even with the abolition of payment by results the legacy of the past had become so ingrained that this poor relationship remained for a long time to come. Thus the state of the elementary education system in 1895, when viewed from almost any aspect, was not good. While there were good schools, good teachers and good inspectors they tended to be rather thin on the ground and their efforts were overshadowed by the problems and faults pervading the rest of the system. Unfortunately, the secondary school system was in a comparable state.

Reviews of secondary schools had been conducted by two Royal Commissions in 1864 (Clarendon) and in 1868 (Taunton) but delays in the implementation of their recommendations after 1869, partly because of the slow, methodical continuing survey and reform of the endowed schools engendered by the Taunton Report, meant that the reform of secondary education became essentially a piecemeal operation and the chance for a new national structure of secondary education was lost sight of.[29] Michael Sadler, Acland's protégé, believed that the subsequent movement for the reorganisation of secondary education in the 1890s resulted from two factors. The first was the power of the new county and county borough councils to aid secondary and technical education and the second was the growing impact of international economic competition, especially from Germany.

The creation of county and county borough councils as new local authorities under the 1888 Local Government Act had provided the Welsh with the basis for a rationalisation of their local secondary education administration. Under the Welsh Intermediate Education Act of 1889, the councils were utilised as the locus for Joint Education Committees to oversee existing as well as future secondary, or 'intermediate', schools. But in England the new bodies, empowered to levy a one penny rate for technical education by the Technical Instruction Act (1889) as well as apply the so-called 'whisky money' for educational purposes (under the Local Taxation (Custom and Excise) Act, 1890), only increased the congestion and competition existent in the field. The absence of well-defined boundaries between elementary and secondary and technical education meant that by the beginning of the 1890s secondary education was being offered by the endowed grammar schools, private and public schools, higher grade schools and technical institutes. Acland had been instrumental in securing the funding for local council work in education under the 1889 and 1890 Acts and he was alarmed by the deleterious effects of this unco-ordinated activity. Sadler, in turn, identified three major points of concern affecting secondary education, the first being the 'insufficient provision of first-rate intellectual instruction in cheap and easily accessible secondary day-schools'. The second was a 'very insufficient provision of the highest kinds of technical, scientific and professional training, deliberately and skilfully adjusted to the most recent needs of modern life', while the third was the effect of the nation's comparative neglect of secondary education for nearly a century. Although there was debate about education in society he claimed that in general there was a demonstrable lack of interest

> in methods of instruction, in the choice of curricula, and in the direct application of the results of scientific study to the organisation of industry, to the development of commerce, and to the administration of public affairs.[30]

To try to remedy this Sadler organised a two day conference on secondary education held at Oxford under the auspices of the university in October 1893. The conference members, nearly 200 in all, agreed that government action was necessary to overcome the problems and their deliberations resulted in a memorial being sent subsequently from the university to the government advocating the establishment of a Royal Commission to examine secondary education. This was accepted by the government, with the proviso from Acland that the Commission should be swift in the execution of their task so as not to delay the formulation of legislation to provide public control over secondary education. The members of the Commission started their labours in March 1894 under the chairmanship of James Bryce and completed their report 17 months later.

They acknowledged that the organisational problems bedevilling the system reflected the fact that problems in secondary education had been approached 'from different sides, at different times, and with different views and aims..'. Not surprisingly, then:

> This isolation and this independence, if they may seem to witness to the rich variety of our educational life, and to the active spirit which pervades it, still nevertheless prepare the observer to expect the usual results of dispersed and unconnected forces, needless competition between the different agencies, and a frequent overlapping of effort, with much consequent waste of money, of time, and of labour.[31]

In their attempt to formulate a satisfactory reform of the local administration of secondary education the Commission found the plethora of existent bodies a hindrance. They believed that of the two major contenders for the role of local secondary education authority, that is, the county/county borough councils and the school boards, the latter were essentially concerned with elementary education. It was only through the existence of their higher grade schools that the boards had any claim to the role and, even so, it was contentious.

The Commission acknowledged that these schools occupied one of the strata of secondary schools, having 'stepped into the educational void which the Schools Enquiry Commissioners . . . had proposed to fill by what they termed "secondary schools of the third grade"'.[32] The Commission identified three distinct types of higher grade school. The 'pseudo' type, making up some ten per cent of the total, was dismissed as educationally insignificant as it differed from the public elementary school only in charging a higher fee. The majority, or 'normal' type, like those run by the school boards of Birmingham, Hull and Sheffield, provided classes for Standards V–VII and at least two years of ex-Standard classes after Standard VII. The third type of higher grade school differed from the 'normal' in providing schooling in all of the elementary school standards as well as ex-Standard classes.[33]

Conan Doyle likened the higher grade schools' double- or triple-storied buildings to lighthouses amidst the urban, working-class environment and Sadler believed they appeared to gratify 'the ambitions of the clerks and chairmen of the new progressive School Boards and to have been wedged into practice'.[34] He did concede that for many parents of higher grade school pupils the schools' modern curriculum was more congenial than that of the traditional grammar schools with their emphasis upon study of the classics. None the less, ambiguity clothed the name higher grade school:

> To the ambitious School Boardmen, it meant intellectually superior; to the affronted ratepayer it meant a higher fee; to the poor struggling clerk it meant a socially higher grade of school; to the Education Department . . . it seemed to harmonise two things: (a) grading of schools according to the Schools Inquiry Commission; (b) keeping the ordinary elementary school cheap and nasty.[35]

Witnesses before the Cross Commission had believed that the higher grade schools were catering for 'the class who are earning weekly wages', 'workingmen's children . . . going to manufactories'; or the 'thoughtful and better-to-do' working class and lower middle class.[36] The signatories of the Commission's second minority report perceived the schools to be of 'the greatest value to the more intelligent artisans', and advocated the opening of similar schools for 'the lower ranks of the commercial classes'.[37] If this was done then the higher grade schools would cater for the educational needs of 'an entirely different class from those who desire really secondary education'.[38]

A critical factor in the development of these schools had been the age limit of 14 years placed on the earning of parliamentary grants for elementary education in 1879 by the Education Department. The effect of this limit, which had been an attempt to restrain the schools boards from 'entertainment of educational proposals of a more ambitious character' than prescribed by the 1870 Education Act, had been to force those higher grade schools requiring funding for their ex-Standards classes over and above rate aid and school fees, to turn to the Science and Art Department as a source of revenue.[39] This had resulted in the development of 'schools of science', covering the ex-Standards classes within the higher grade schools, having a curriculum with a scientific bias. Such schools were recognised by the cognoscenti as 'true' higher grade schools, while their curricular bias was of great significance in determining their educational and social roles, as well as the social composition of their pupils. This notwithstanding, the higher grade schools offered a curriculum which in some ways appeared to resolve the major criticism about secondary education being generated by the economic competition from Europe and the USA. Unlike the curriculum of many established secondary schools, grammar and public, with its emphasis upon the classics, the higher grade school curriculum was vocationally oriented and supported by efficient teaching methods and purpose-built facilities. But the criticism made by some smaller secondary schools about the unfair competition being generated by these schools had inevitably raised questions about their legal status, who should have access to secondary education and, of course, what was secondary education?

The Bryce Commission perceived the higher grade schools to be 'really secondary in character' since they defined secondary education as

> ... the education of the boy or girl not simply as a human being who needs to be instructed in the mere rudiments of knowledge, but it is a process of intellectual training and personal discipline conducted with special regard to the profession or trade to be followed.

All secondary schools, they believed, therefore, 'in so far as they qualify men for doing something in life, partake more or less in the character of institutes that educate craftsmen' and secondary education 'inclusive of technical, may be described as education conducted in view of the special life that has to be lived with the express purpose of forming a person to live it.'[40] The Commission concluded that higher grade schools were doing much needed work in meeting the demands for secondary education from the 'lower social strata, and the region of its special activity is the space, left practically vacant, between elementary education and the second grade secondary school'.[41] More importantly, they appeared to pose no direct threat to the established secondary schools.

If the higher grade schools provided the school boards with a claim to be considered as the local authority in a rationalised (secondary) education system, the claim of the county and county borough councils rested upon the work of their technical instruction committees. Although still in their relative infancy their expertise had been gained from work in secondary and technical education. Some councils' committees were both politically powerful and educationally progressive bodies, such as the London Technical Education Board established in 1893 and guided by Sidney Webb and William Garnett, the latter as Secretary to the Board. But progress in this field was not limited solely to large urban authorities, the inspectors of the Department of Science and Art identifying Cheshire, Hampshire, Somerset, Surrey and the West Riding of Yorkshire as notable county authorities. Their financial contributions to secondary schools included grants for equipment, apparatus, buildings and the provision of scholarships, the latter allowing significantly more pupils to attend these schools.[42] These developments impressed the Bryce Commission, and they proposed that in their areas the county councils should form the new secondary education authorities, and separate from the technical instruction committees. In the case of county borough areas the Commission tried to reach a compromise, with their recommendation that the county borough councils and the school boards should each be allocated one-third membership of the authority, the remaining third being derived from local higher education institutions and co-opted members. But in July 1895 these were merely recommendations under formulation and the chaotic organisation of secondary education remained.

The content and methodology of education in both the elementary and secondary school systems of the nation were thus legitimate areas of concern not only for parents and employers but also for the incoming government. Devonshire noted that the local control and organisation of both systems also left much to be desired and was in need of reform although the vested interests of the bodies involved guaranteed that this would not be an easy task:

> We have School Boards under the Education Acts, County and Borough authorities under the Technical Education Acts, Committees and Managers under regulations of the Committee of Council. Some of these dispense considerable sums raised locally, others considerable funds given to them by Parliament, and they will not be easily displaced.[43]

But of equal significance was the fact that during the century the state had become progressively more involved in the funding, content and direction of education, more so at the elementary level but, none the less, also in the secondary field. How then had this relatively chaotic state of affairs been allowed to develop? The simple answer was that the administration at central government level was in little better shape than that at the local level. The educational agencies were physically scattered around London and in only two cases were they nominally related: the Education Department in Whitehall and the Department of Science and Art in South Kensington both had the Lord President and the Vice President as their political heads. Even then this had not prevented them from maintaining overlapping functions in both elementary and secondary education.

The Education Department was primarily responsible for the nation's elementary schools in respect of curriculum content and the disbursement of parliamentary grants whereas the Department of Science and Art retained responsibility for some aspects of secondary and technical education. The Charity Commissioners in Chancery, on the other hand, oversaw the application of charitable trusts and endowments chiefly, but not exclusively, in respect of secondary schools. The higher grade or organised science schools were thus the recipients of curricular advice and administrative control from both Whitehall and South Kensington. But between these departments there was virtually little or no communication, let alone with the other government agencies involved with particular aspects of the education system such as the Local Government Board (Poor Law schools), the Board of Agriculture (agricultural colleges), and the War Department. This situation reflected the fact, as Devonshire remarked, that the central bodies had never 'been accustomed to look at educational problems as a whole, or to work together for the co-ordination of educational agencies'.[44] Central government control of the nation's education system was thus diverse and disjointed and in these aspects closely resembled the local government situation. It was perhaps little wonder, then, that by 1895 the nation's schools were equally diverse in both educational and organisational terms. As Michael Sadler aptly pointed out:

> A national system of education involves, implicitly or explicitly, a definite theory as to the right ordering of national life. The establishment of educational unity presupposes general agreement as to national aims, and as to the best form of social organisation. Where two ideals of national organisation and of social welfare are in conflict, and those in sympathy with the one ideal are fairly well balanced by those in sympathy with the other, there tends to be an educational deadlock so far as systematic unification is concerned.[45]

Agreement and unity had been, and still were, two conspicuously absent elements within the educational, political and religious circles of the nation. The policy tasks ahead of Gorst, as Vice President, and the eighth Duke of Devonshire after the election of 1895 were daunting yet necessary if the children and, ultimately, the nation were to benefit. Before 1900 and the establishment of the Board of Education the brunt of this policy formulation was to fall upon the Education Department.

The Department was one of the largest in central government and its offices were scattered over central London, a situation which created problems, as Gorst graphically illustrated to the House of Commons:

> I do not think the House really knows where the Education Department is. [Laughter] Hon. Members fancy it is in Whitehall, but there there are only the secretarial staff and certain heads of department. A great part of the Department is housed in Canada Buildings, in King Street; another part is in the old Census offices; another in Northumberland Avenue, and the staff of the Director of Special Inquiries are now wandering about looking for a new home. [Laughter].[46]

Compounding these problems was the administrative effort required of the staff in their dealings with the large number of schools under their aegis. The sheer drudgery involved affected both the morale and outlook of the Department and consequently, as one inmate noted, it

> . . . seems never to get a glimpse of the width of the problem which it ought to be solving, and of which it is really touching the mere surface or edges. The dry old office gropes along, busy with minute details of doles of state money, only wearisomely giving in now and then to persistent pressure from outside and then only letting a few isolated new ideas and ways have a chance.[47]

Presiding over this somewhat scattered empire of buildings and civil servants in 1895 was Sir George Kekewich, the Permanent Secretary. Kekewich had been appointed Permanent Secretary in 1890 on the death of Patric Cumin. The Lord President, Viscount Cranbrook, had noted in his diary that the appointment had been well received outside the Department since Kekewich was seen as being 'perfectly familiar with the work & in touch with all the people. Kekewich is a Churchman, a Conservative but with liberal ideas on Education combined with fair views on Voluntary schools'. Inside the Department the appointment had caused friction among the Examiners from whose ranks Kekewich had been plucked but his political superiors were satisfied with their choice.[48] Acland was also favourably impressed by Kekewich, even before his sojourn as Vice President, telling his father: 'I liked what I saw of him quite different in manner from Cumin & really interested in his work'.[49] The two men worked well in harness during Acland's Vice Presidency, with Kekewich's encouragement of the board schools matching Acland's reforming views, and they remained on close terms after Acland's departure from office. Kekewich was opposed to the rigidity of the nation's education system, and although he was responsible for the administration of the Annual Code he wanted the system to become more flexible in both its structures and curriculum content. He opposed what he called the 'Procrustean theory of education' and he thus welcomed Gorst's appointment, knowing of his reforming views, and in the first few years the two men strove to continue with the reform of the education system. But, as will be seen, they eventually diverged on how this was to be achieved, Kekewich objecting to the constraints being placed upon the work of the school boards. By then Kekewich's role as an effective contributor to policy formulation was virtually finished, his place having been taken by a young Examiner.

The majority of the civil servants in the Department were classified as clerks, assistant, second or first class, and bore the brunt of the administration relating to the schools under the Department's aegis. Although they were theoretically the least involved in policy decisions one observer saw them as the most meritorious of the Department's officials:

> Their mission in life was to keep the examiners in the straight path, and at times they treated both them and the younger inspectors much as a caddie treats a beginner at the game of golf .... Their merit was accuracy and trustworthiness; their foible was pedantry.[50]

Sutherland has shown that the clerks were 'the conscience of the Department, that they played a far greater part than the Examiners in supplying the elements of continuity and often fairness and justice in the implementation of policy'.[51] Numbering some 224 by 1900, the clerks were selected on the basis of open competition, mainly from the the ranks of the upper working and lower middle classes, and had to possess some form of secondary education. Gender discrimination and segregation of the clerks were established practices of the Department (and were maintained by the Board of Education). While women clerks carried out duties comparable with those of the second division clerks they received only half the salary as well as being provided with little in the way of promotion prospects. Even by 1912 an officer of the Board saw little chance of any change within another generation.[52]

Next in the staff hierarchy were the 26 Examiners (18 Junior and eight Senior), a very different social group. The majority were Oxbridge graduates, with a notable preponderance of classicists, a feature which had worried Acland for, although he acknowledged that they had had 'a good education of a certain type, . . . I think it is very narrow'. The Education Department was unique among government departments in retaining patronage for these (and inspectorial) appointments, so that the Examiners (and Inspectors) were the appointees of the Lord President. The persistence of this method of selection was justified on the grounds that

> . . . [for] our particular work, which is extraordinarily contro-
> versial, which runs up against religious, social, and political
> controversies at every turn, which has, as a matter of fact, been
> complicated by legislation and attempted legislation, to a very
> great extent, it is particularly important to recruit the office with
> men of rather greater age than ordinarily enter the Civil Service
> and of rather more varied experience and character.[53]

Whether the qualifications they possessed were absolutely necessary for the tasks for which they were engaged was debatable, and in several instances the Examiners had applied for the post in order to be able to pursue interests outside education. E.K. Chambers, the Elizabethan scholar, joined the Department as a temporary Examiner in 1892, becoming a Junior Examiner in 1895 and Senior Examiner in 1903. When asked how he had managed to maintain his Elizabethan scholarship with his post he had replied that before 1903:

> . . . the burden of the department was so light that . . . he could
> spend the greater part of the day at the [British] Museum; calling
> just at the office to dictate a few letters or write the brief minutes
> required, and then hurrying to the Museum, which he only left in
> time to sign his correspondence for the post.[54]

Other Examiners with literary talents included J.W. Mackail, the biographer (and son-in-law) of William Morris and subsequently Professor of Poetry at Oxford, F.T. Palgrave and W.J. Courthope – two other holders of the Oxford poetry chair.[55] A corollary of the Examiners' social class, educational background and qualifications was that the majority lacked any substantial experience of the elementary schools they had to administer: 'they sit and work on paper and comment and write, but they do not know enough about schools'.[56] It was perhaps not surprising either that some of them did not hold elementary education in high esteem and found much of their work boring, involving as it did the determination of each elementary school's annual government grants based upon the inspectors' reports. Sutherland believes that by 1895 the Examiners constituted rather an 'arrogant intellectual coterie' who could by no means be considered innovators in educational policy. They were prepared to accept the irritation arising from the boredom of their work as a necessary evil in return for financial security and the ability to pursue their other, predominantly literary, interests.[57] None the less, the Examiners were the effective interface of the Department with the schools, the Inspectorate and the local education authorities:

> It used to be told of one of the best known of the Whitehall officials, F.T. Palgrave, of Golden Treasury fame, that a school manager once interviewed him on some grievance, and, getting little satisfaction, enquired whether he might ask whom he had the honour of addressing.
>
> 'Oh, certainly,' said he, 'my name is Francis Palgrave.'
>
> The visitor thanked him, but explained that he rather wished to know the official's rank: for instance, was his opinion final? 'Not at all,' replied Palgrave airily; 'I am what they call a Senior Examiner: above me are the three Assistant Secretaries, Mr. A., Mr. B., and Mr. C.: above them is the Secretary, Sir Francis Sandford: above him the Vice President, Mr. Forster: above him the Lord President, Lord Ripon: and above him, I *believe,* the Almighty.'[58]

Palgrave's answer revealed quite clearly not only the senior hierarchy of the Department but also the path along which serious or difficult problems arising in policy implementation outside of established precedents were likely to be passed. Any investigations arising out of such problems usually became the task of one or more Examiners but in 1895 a new research section came into being with the establishment of the Department of Special Inquiries and Reports.

In his first year as Vice President, Acland had written to Sadler about the problems facing him in the Education Department and had stated that he wished 'it were possible to stir into it with a great spoon some of the newer hopes and the fresher spirit which all the work that you have been engaged in brings to one [*sic*] mind'.[59] But it was not until 1894 that Acland was able to bring forward the idea of a research centre for the Department, having found Kekewich favourable to the concept of 'one little centre in our great department devoted exclusively to obtaining and supplying information; especially at first from abroad'. He asked Sadler if he was interested in the post of director as it presented, he believed, 'a great opportunity for us to combine in laying the foundations quietly for a great modification of the attitude of the State to National Education'.[60]

Although only 33 when he accepted Acland's offer, Sadler's educational credentials were substantial. Educated at Rugby and Trinity College, Oxford, Sadler had been greatly influenced by the views of T.H. Green, Arnold Toynbee and John Ruskin whom he had heard and met while an undergraduate. He claimed later that it was from Green's *Prolegomena* that 'I got my religion'.[61] His subsequent membership of Acland's 'Inner Ring' of Fellows and undergraduates, a group which met to explore economic, political and social topics, had exposed him to Acland's influence. This appears to have inspired Sadler to something akin to hero worship, given their mutual interest in social and economic issues and Acland's commitment to the university extension movement.[62] And it was partly through Acland's influence that Sadler had been elected in 1885 as his successor to the secretaryship of the university's extension lectures sub-committee. But it was Sadler's prodigious efforts and achievements in this position during the next decade, his unswerving commitment to education and his seminal role in the convening of the Oxford conference on secondary education that resulted in his appointment to the Bryce Commission. In addition he was the steward of Christ Church College, so that when Acland's offer came Mary Sadler noted in her diary that they had decided he should accept; 'he is so overworked there seems no help for it'.[63]

On meeting Kekewich for the first time Sadler found him remarkably amiable as well as frank about the state of the Department: 'hardly any of the older men in the department care for education in its wide sense . . . we are all groovy – we want someone to help us out of our grooves'.[64] Kekewich thus fully supported Acland's initiative as well as his choice of Sadler. To aid Sadler in his seemingly monumental task, Acland had secured Treasury approval for an assistant who had to be 'a man of high academical and intellectual qualifications', and by May 1895 Sadler had drawn up a list of the five shortlisted applicants for Acland's perusal. At its head was the name of Robert

Morant, Sadler having been asked by Canon Barnett of Toynbee Hall to interview him. Morant shared Sadler's enthusiasm for Green's idealist philosophy but at their first meeting in the Spring of 1895 what struck Sadler was Morant's

> . . . dim halo of Buddhist austerity . . . He was very tall, clean-shaven, clerical (episcopal) looking, intensely sympathetic, nervous in gesture, persuasive in negotiation . . . and entirely disinterested.[65]

He was taken also by Morant's 'exciting' experiences tutoring the Crown Prince of Siam and his sudden departure 'after the breakdown of some brilliant but inconclusive intrigue'. Unfortunately Sadler had no means of checking the veracity of this nor of discovering the real reasons that lay behind Morant's return from Siam. He was convinced, none the less, that Morant was the best man for the job.

Educated at Winchester and New College, Oxford, Morant as a student had suffered considerable privation owing to the financial difficulties experienced by his mother after the premature death of his father. His social life at Oxford had been the antithesis of Sadler's. While Sadler was President of the Union, a member of the Palmerston Club and Browning Society, Morant was preoccupied with running a Sunday school at Hinksey, a 'Brotherhood' religious study group in his college and a weekday service initially at Marston and then in St. Aldate's parish. These activities had led to an invitation to join the Strafford Club but he was unable to reconcile his views with those of the majority of Church and Conservative members and soon resigned. Much of his vacations was spent in paid employment as a tutor to the children of various families, yet in 1885 he obtained a First in Theology. This success was somewhat hollow as far as his career was concerned, for in his last year he had given up all ideas of entering the Church although he appears to have remained committed to the idea of a career involving service to others. While he had considered joining the university settlement in the East End of London, Toynbee Hall, Morant was unsettled about his career after graduation and in the event accepted the offer of a teaching post at a preparatory school in East Sheen. After a year there he still remained unsure about his future and welcomed an appointment in Siam as tutor to three young royal princes and secretary to their father. His subsequent appointment to the tutorship of the Crown Prince in November 1888 resulted in his also becoming involved with Prince Damrong, King Chulalongkorn's half-brother and the Minister of Public Instruction, in planning the reforms proposed for the national education system. But when he had returned from leave in 1892 Morant found it impossible to adapt to the government changes that had taken place in his absence. His refusal to accept the reality of his new, lowered status, owing partly to his loss of Damrong's patronage, and his failure to achieve any satisfactory progress with the Crown Prince's education were contributory factors in his dismissal from the court by Chulalongkorn in 1894. Far from being a palace conspiracy against him, it was Morant's own self-deceit and intriguing which had alienated Chulalongkorn and had led Prince Devawongse, the Foreign Minister, to comment in his letter of dismissal:

> . . . You entirely misunderstand your situation, the conditions of your appointment, your rights and your duties. Your situation is not so exalted, it is not so exclusive . . . as you think fit to describe it.[66]

Though granted six months' salary and a testimonial, Morant was barred from any entry to the royal palace.[67] The trauma of the dismissal was reflected in Morant's demeanour, as Sadler noted, and the artist W.B. Richmond, one of Morant's employers while he had been at Oxford, used his gaunt appearance as the model for his mosaic of Christ the Redeemer on the ceiling above the high altar in St. Paul's Cathedral.

In the first few years after Morant's appointment Sadler found him to be 'as near a saint as might be a sadhu or a Buddhist monk, with just a touch of the Curé d'Ars as like a French priest he always wore a black frock coat'.[68] Sadler's view was perhaps influenced by the similarity of ideas which he and Morant shared, not least being their adherence to the tenets of Green's idealist philosophy, with both men committed to serving society and the State through the medium of education. At the same time, they were both conscious of the limitations of the education system and wanted to see significant improvements made. How these were to be achieved was to lead subsequently to a divergence of views and Sadler, late in life, believed his choice of Morant had been 'fateful' because of the effect of Morant's personality, having in it 'a vein which made me think of the Italian Renaissance'.[69] A friend of his, Fitzgibbon Young, recalled that Lady Bryce used to say that Morant 'looked like an "escaped Jesuit priest"! He certainly had a curious hunted look as though he was fleeing from Justice, human or divine, or both.'[70] Such views were undoubtedly coloured by the interpretations put on the reasons for the split between the two men, and there is no doubt that Morant's powerful and complex personality was to have considerable consequences for Sadler's and others' careers as well as for the development of the nation's education system, but in the summer of 1895 both men were preoccupied with preparing themselves for their new role in educational research. Educational policy formulation rested with the political heads of the nation's education system, the Lord President and the Vice President, and there were sufficient problems afflicting the service needing resolution. But while all these problems required attention they could not be dealt with simultaneously and priorities had to be accorded, a process which was to prove to be dependent on other non-educational factors, not least of which was politics.

Lord Salisbury, the leader of the Conservative Party, had become convinced after the General Election of 1892 that if the party was to stand any chance of remaining politically viable in the future it would have to be formally linked with the Liberal Unionists, not least because he and other party members believed that the electorate remained fundamentally Liberal in persuasion. Although the idea of having Joseph Chamberlain and the Duke of Devonshire as colleagues in the councils of power was distasteful to him, a loose alliance with the Unionists had taken place gradually after the latter had split from the main Liberal Party over the issue of Home Rule for Ireland in 1886. But before 1895 it had remained just that, for the Liberal Unionists expected that once Gladstone had gone the breach between Liberals would be healed. However, by 1895 this possibility was virtually non-existent but the political accommodation likely to be necessitated by a more formal alliance had led Chamberlain to tell another leading Liberal Unionist, Sir Henry James, that

> If a Unionist Government is to be formed my personal inclinations would lead me to stay outside in an independent capacity.
> . . . But, if, for any reason, it appears desirable or necessary that I should serve in a Cabinet which I assume will be formed by Lord Salisbury, then it is evident that I must make terms both as to Policy and as to Personnel.[71]

A subsequent discussion between Chamberlain and Devonshire about the formation of such a government revealed that Devonshire's reaction, if asked to join, would be 'Aut Caesar aut nullus'.[72] The reality, however, proved to be somewhat different. When Lord Salisbury received the Queen's commission to form a government in June, he was so determined to create a coalition as far as possible on his terms that his sheer speed of action effectively prevented Devonshire and Chamberlain from hammering out a concordat with him based on their declared aims. Devonshire angrily confided to James that not only was Salisbury 'extraordinarily precipitate in his arrangements' but he had 'a curious way of making his own assumptions of what people will like without consulting them'.[73]

This notwithstanding, Salisbury did offer Devonshire and Chamberlain the choice of any of the Cabinet portfolios, apart from that of First Lord of the Treasury, which was reserved for his nephew, Arthur Balfour. Devonshire chose the Lord Presidency and Chamberlain, somewhat surprisingly to his colleagues, the Colonial Secretaryship. And during the subsequent distribution of the minor government offices Balfour had to warn Salisbury that they were 'in danger of bringing the wrath of the Tories down upon our heads by giving an unfair share of the spoils to the Liberal Unionists'.[74] The Vice Presidency of the Committee of the Council on Education thus went, with Devonshire's concurrence as Lord President, to the prominent Tory Democrat, Gorst. And when the government-making was complete, Salisbury believed that he had achieved the best possible results for his party in the circumstances. His enthusiasm was to be short-lived, for when the results of the General Election were complete he discovered that the Conservatives, having won 341 seats, had a working majority and no need of Liberal Unionist support. His precipitate actions meant that the coalition character of the government had to remain a reality and it would, consequently, 'be invited to enter upon a legislative ocean that is unknown to us – and the steering may be difficult'.[75] This was to be especially so in the case of education.

While other Cabinet ministers were members of the Committee of the Privy Council on Education in association with the Lord President and Vice President, the practice in most governments had been that the Lord President and the Vice President were the *ab initio* educational policy-makers of the government.[76] The working relationship between the Lord President and the Vice President was very much dependent upon the personalities of the two incumbents but the fact that the Lord President was invariably a peer with a seat in the Cabinet while his colleague was in the Commons and rarely in the Cabinet negated the original concept of the Vice President as the effective Minister of Education. For while the Vice President may have been a 'much more real' person as far as the Education Department was concerned there were constraints upon his role, as one civil servant noted:

It was his duty to defend the Office, and the Inspectors against the attacks of numerous enemies, and once a year, late in the Session, when the House was getting thin, he was allowed to move the Estimates, and to make a nice long speech. For anything I know to the contrary he may have thought that he both reigned and governed.[77]

None the less, Salisbury had told Gorst that although Devonshire would be his nominal chief he would be able to enjoy 'an independence more than usually complete' in solving the 'difficult but urgent' education questions as Devonshire's hands would be 'full of other matters'.[78]

Spencer Compton Cavendish, the eighth Duke of Devonshire, spent his formative years as a child and adolescent at Holker Hall, the family home in North Lancashire. He was tutored there, mainly by his father (who had been a second Wrangler in the mathematical tripos as well as having read for the classical tripos at Cambridge) before entering Trinity College, Cambridge, in 1851 to read for the mathematical tripos. His father had observed that his son was rather indolent as far as academic matters were concerned owing to his extreme fondness for society. This was confirmed by Cavendish's devotion as an undergraduate to the pleasures of the turf and his membership of the Athenaeum Club [of Cambridge], the latter being described by one member as an 'idle set . . . manly in pursuits and ideas, insouciants, taking life easily as it came, without ambition, and with but little culture'.[79] Unlike the majority of the club, however, Cavendish possessed sufficient ability and application to obtain a second class honours degree. Yet throughout his career Devonshire's notable strain of indolence meant that 'work' was always only done from a sense of public duty: this trait, accompanied by the 'hereditary taciturnity' of the Cavendishes, was a characteristic many found unsettling in their dealings with him. It was perhaps apposite that a new composition by Dr Hubert Parry played at Devonshire's installation as Chancellor of Cambridge University in 1892 should have been a setting of the Choric Song from Tennyson's 'The Lotos-Eaters'.

Entering the Commons in 1857 as the Member for North Lancashire and a supporter of Lord Palmerston, Cavendish also became Marquess of Hartington the following year when his father succeeded to the Devonshire title. Five years later Palmerston appointed him to the position of Under Secretary at the War Office and when Earl Russell succeeded Palmerston as Premier, Hartington became Secretary of State for War. His marked ability in the Commons and his subsequent progress through the ranks of the Liberal Party, now under Gladstone's leadership, led him to become its leader for five years when Gladstone retired from political life in 1875. Gladstone's return, however, meant that Hartington had to decline the Queen's offer to form a government in 1880. The subsequent pursuit of a policy of Home Rule for Ireland proved to be the breaking point between Hartington and Gladstone, and in 1886 Hartington found himself linked with Chamberlain and other dissatisfied Liberals in the breakaway Liberal Unionist Party. He was once characterised by Arthur Balfour as a 'lukewarm and slippery Whig whom it is so diffi-cult to differ from and so impossible to act with' but Salisbury, noted for his rash statements, discovered that 'in spite of his blunt manner and ungrammatical sentences there's no man who weighs his words more carefully than Hartington or has more "intention" in what he says'.[80] Devonshire's political ability and practical commonsense have led to his nomination by Vincent as the 'best Prime Minister England never had'.

Although Devonshire was to become a major influence in educa-tional policy formulation, he did not make a favourable impact upon Sir George Kekewich, who remembered him as

> . . . dull, silent, and impassive . . . from the day he assumed that position [Minister of Education] to the day he vacated it, he was profoundly ignorant of the system the Department had to administer, of its routine, and of its duties. . . . He gave me the impression of being so wrapped up in his own dignity and family pride, that he regarded commoners such as myself as people to be kept at a distance. He was a living wet blanket.[81]

Kekewich's views have to be taken with some caution, however, given his enforced premature retirement from the Board of Education in 1902: his comments usually reveal more about him than their subject. Sir Almeric FitzRoy, able to observe the Lord President more closely, first as his private secretary and then as Clerk of the Privy Council, claimed that:

> . . . he was the most considerate of masters, as well as the most loyal of chiefs. He gave his confidence without reserve, and once given it was not lightly withdrawn . . . .There was an extra-ordinary simplicity and depth of human nature about him which perhaps came out in his relations with subordinates more effec-tively than in any other connection.[82]

Sir James Yoxall, MP and NUT executive member, likened him to a sheet anchor: 'he keeps us riding safe; I don't know what would become of the Board of Education without him'.[83] This said, Devonshire's previous accomplishments in the educational field were minimal for, apart from being the Chancellor of Cambridge University, his only other notable achievement had been to hold the presidency of the National Association for the Promotion of Technical and Secondary Education. But he had been fully exposed to the conundrums of denominational and non-denominational education policies as Irish Secretary and he did bring to the Department a reputation for sagacity, objectivity and fairness, useful attributes given the nature of the problems then facing the education system. Indeed, for the majority of the public Devonshire 'embodied practical sanity'.[84] Despite his reputation for indolence, Devonshire could also work extremely hard, although he was, by nature, a believer in delegation. This last feature was to have several important repercussions in educational policy formulation in the years before 1901. More immediately, his personality and the common-sense nature of his views enabled him to achieve a very good working relationship with his new colleague, Sir John Gorst.

Gorst was only two years younger than Devonshire and there were certain similarities between the two men's upbringing. Both grew up in Lancashire, both had lost their mother while young, neither had attended a public school (Gorst was educated at Preston Grammar School) and both had read for the mathematical tripos at Cambridge, Gorst being a student of St John's College. But there the similarities ceased, for while Devonshire was the eldest son of an aristocrat Gorst was the second son of a Preston solicitor, albeit deputy Clerk of the Peace for Lancashire, and belonged firmly in the urban middle classes. Although both men had read for the mathematical tripos Gorst had emerged as Third Wrangler and had been awarded a college fellowship as a result. In personality Gorst was the very antithesis of his chief being, Kekewich commented, Puck to Devonshire's Jupiter, whereas Michael Sadler characterised him as 'a sort of democratic firebrand nailed to a country gentleman's mansion which won't catch'.[85]

By 1895 Gorst was firmly wedded to Tory Democracy as his political creed and had also become well known for his advocacy of social reform. Such characteristics were a far cry from those he had demonstrated shortly after he had entered Parliament in 1866, for then he had been a 'convinced anti-democrat to an extent unusual among Conservative backbenchers . . . .[and] his interest in social reform was,

1 Sir John Gorst with General William Booth of the Salvation Army, *circa* 1903. In the background are Lady Gorst and her eldest daughter, Constance Mary. (Photograph by courtesy of Miss Joan Clarkson)

relatively, very small'.[86] This early outlook had reflected his failure to come to grips with the social and racial problems of New Zealand's bicultural society during his stay in the new colony between 1860 and 1863. While his probity and ability had brought him progress through the positions of inspector of Maori schools, principal of a technical school for Maoris in Te Awamutu, resident magistrate for the Upper Waikato and, finally, civil commissioner for the Waikato, his somewhat naïve acquiescence in Governor Grey's plans had led to his eviction from the Waikato by Rewi Maniapoto and his followers. His subsequent political transformation from convinced anti-democrat to radical Tory and social reformer had been initiated by his work as Conservative Party Agent under the aegis of Disraeli between 1870 and 1874.

There is evidence, albeit limited, to suggest that Gorst was in an unsettled state of mind and was rethinking his ideas following the loss of his seat in the General Election of 1868. His acceptance of the offer of the position of Party Agent in 1870 was indicative of this, not least because the offer was not made solely on his personal abilities but because he had by now 'shown a keen interest in the problems of urban Conservatism . . . . He was a genuine believer in working class Conservatism'.[87] Gorst had already gained first-hand experience of the grim plight of the working classes in London both from his work as the secretary of a local branch of the newly formed Charity Organisation Society and from teaching evening classes in a slum area of Lambeth.[88]

His success in revitalising dormant or depressed local Conservative party organisations and promoting the creation of new ones was mirrored in the Conservatives' electoral victory of 1874 and Gorst may have seen it as reflecting popular support for Disraeli's view of Tory Democracy as the underlying principle of the Conservative Party. On both counts, his exclusion from the spoils of victory was a bitter disappointment and he never forgave what he called thereafter the 'Old Gang', that is, the landed aristocracy, for their self-aggrandisement and neglect of the rest of the party. The irony of his view was that he conveniently overlooked the significant snub he had received from Disraeli in 1874, possibly because of his reverence for his old chief but also, no doubt, because it would have undermined his advocacy of Tory Democracy which he was able to propagate initially through his membership of a small guerrilla Conservative group in the Commons, the Fourth Party.[89]

His activities with Lord Randolph Churchill, Sir Henry Drummond

Wolff and Arthur Balfour between 1880 and 1884 allowed him full rein for his political ideas, although his concern with the creation of a Conservative base among the working class ultimately produced a situation whereby his 'idea of where the Fourth Party might go, like his ideas about the ultimate destination of the party at large, were not those of his colleagues'.[90] Disraeli believed that these views marked Gorst as the 'only dangerous Fourth Party member' and it was somewhat ironical, therefore, that by 1882 Gorst was convinced that the group's successes had created a political milieu that appeared to be 'ripe for the rise of the Democratic Tory party, which was always Dizzy's dream'.[91] Although Churchill initially collaborated with him in promoting this concept, his accommodation with Lord Salisbury and the party hierarchy after the 1884 National Union conference meant that in return for Salisbury's reneging on the Central Committee he sacrificed Gorst who suddenly found himself isolated politically.[92]

Ostrogorski has pointed out that ultimately such a concept as Tory Democracy, by establishing 'a new kind of plebiscitary Caesarism exercised not by an individual but by a huge syndicate', would lead to the demolition of the inequalities upon which the very existence of the Tory party was based.[93] The potentially damaging career consequences of the serious pursuit of such a goal by a Tory MP were obvious, yet after 1884 Gorst remained ineluctably wedded to his view of the concept that

> ... all government exists solely for the good of the governed; that ... all ... public institutions are to be maintained so far, and so far only, as they promote the happiness and welfare of the common people; that all who are entrusted with any public function are trustees, not for their class, but for the nation at large; and that the mass of the people may be trusted so to use electoral power, which should be freely conceded to them.[94]

This ideological commitment was also mirrored by his pursuit of the goal of political devolution, an activity which also resulted from his negative experiences of the 'Old Gang'. His commitment to social reform, on the other hand, appears to have been crystallised by his attendance at the Berlin Labour Conference of March 1890 as the head of the British delegation.

The aim of the conference convened by the young Kaiser was to try to achieve agreement in Europe on conditions of work both in certain sectors of industry and for women and children. Gorst's participation reflected, as Hennock has indicated, extreme caution by Lord Salisbury's government, for Gorst's ministerial position 'had no official connection with any of the departments dealing with labour questions'.[95] Unfortunately for Salisbury and his colleagues, as subsequent events were to prove, Gorst found the conference 'one of the most interesting and instructive tasks I ever was engaged in'.[96] His agitation on his return from Berlin for the establishment of a Royal Commission on Labour contributed not only to its establishment but also to his membership of it from 1891 to 1894. This, his membership of the Local Government Board Departmental Inquiry into the Poor Law schools of the Metropolis (1894–95) and his frequent stays with Canon and Mrs Samuel Barnett at Toynbee Hall in Whitechapel from 1890 onwards provided him with numerous examples of the plight of the working class, especially their children, and reinforced his belief in the necessity for social reform legislation.

In 1894 he used his election to the Rectorship of Glasgow University to publicise his support for the role university settlements could play in the resolution of contemporary social problems, having gained first-hand experience of Jane Addams's work at Hull House in Chicago as well as of Toynbee Hall. He believed that it was necessary for the settlements, and society, to find ways to guide the ideas of the masses 'into channels in which the common good of all is the prevailing influence'.[97] As to the actual resolution of the problems afflicting the poor, Gorst felt that this was best tackled via the line of least resistance in a neighbourhood, that is, the children, and by utilising the medium of education. But he was at pains to emphasise that the process of true learning is a dialectical process between learner and teacher in which the teacher is also the learner, or as the residents discovered, they learned more than they taught. Such a process could help to resolve current social problems through interaction between the two social classes: the masses, with their 'latent interest' (in resolution of the problems afflicting them) and 'latent power' (at the polls), and the cultured, with their 'latent knowledge' and 'latent ability'. His overriding aim was that not only should better living and working conditions be achieved for the poor but that there should be a redressing of the social distortion and deprivation derived from the class imbalance in the governance of society.

Henrietta Barnett believed that Gorst was entitled to consideration as the Home Secretary since he 'really knows and really cares for social reform and is known by the workman [sic] all over the country'.[98] But Balfour and Salisbury's scepticism about social reform, with the latter convinced that 'these social questions are destined to break up our party – but why incur the danger, before the necessity has arrived?' as well as their distrust of Gorst precluded this possibility.[99] Furthermore, any claims Gorst might have had to high office had been marred the previous year by the legal decisions in the New Zealand Loan Company case, in which the company directors, of whom he was one, were reprimanded for their laxity since it contributed significantly to the company's collapse. The public opprobrium was enough to make one director, A.J. Mundella, resign his position as President of the Board of Trade and *The Times* did not forget the affair when it commented in moderately favourable terms upon Gorst's appointment as Vice President in 1895, adding the rider that it would have preferred office not to have been given to any of the politicians associated with the company.[100] But Gorst's views, his unparalleled knowledge of both the Conservative Party and Parliament, plus his somewhat tetchy nature and tendency to bear grudges, made him a person Salisbury preferred to have inside rather than outside his administrations.

Gorst's advocacy of social reform earned him Kekewich's approbation on his appointment, for he was seen as 'educational as our excellent late V.P. [A.H.D. Acland] and he has good broad views'.[101] Kekewich also enjoyed Gorst's frequent sallies against his government colleagues for whom 'he entertained a whole-hearted and probably justifiable contempt . . . [since] he was far abler than most Cabinet Ministers'.[102] None the less, they, and some Department officials, were to be responsible for curbing Gorst's enthusiasm for reform once he had demonstrated just what he was capable of. Policy formulation, in the final analysis, is about the exercise of political power, and in the summer of 1895 Gorst was not prepared to waste what was possibly his last chance of wielding it.

NOTES

1. J.J. Davies, 'The new Minister of Education and his work', *Westminster Review*, 144 (Sept. 1895), pp. 336.
2. B. Webb, *Diary* (typed version), 15, pp. 1392–3, 27 May 1895.
3. Ibid., 14, pp. 1276, 24 Dec.1892.
4. A.H.D. Acland to T. Ellis, 23 Dec. 1893 cited in D.A. Hamer, *Liberal Politics in the Age of Gladstone and Rosebery: A Study in Leadership and Policy* (1972), p. 215.
5. B. Webb, op. cit., 15, pp. 1367, 20 Jan. 1895.
6. *4 PD*, 36, c.1021–41, 28 Aug. 1895.

7. E. Halévy, *History of the English People: Epilogue: 1895–1905* (1939), pp. 44–5.
8. E.M.Hance, 'Elementary Education in England' in *Subjects of the Day, No.1: State Education for the People* (1890), p. 25.
9. Ibid., p. 31.
10. By 1901 the gap was even smaller with 5857 board schools teaching 2,344,020 pupils (on average) while the 14,294 voluntary schools taught 2,546,217: *Whitaker's Almanack* (1895), p. 607; G. Sutherland, *Policy Making in Elementary Education, 1870–1895* (1973), p. 350; *4 PD*, 107, c.623, 5 May 1902.
11. T.J. Macnamara, 'The local support of education', *The Nineteenth Century and After*, XL (Dec. 1896), pp. 922–3.
12. Sutherland, op. cit., p. 353.
13. Lord G. Hamilton, *Parliamentary Reminiscences and Reflections*, II (1916), pp. 232–5; J.E.B. Munson,'The London School Board Election of 1894: A Study in Victorian Religious Controversy', *British Journal of Educational Studies*, XXIII, 1 (Feb. 1975), pp. 7–23.
14. Sadler Papers, MS Eng misc c.551, fo.26, M.E. Sadler, 'On the possible consequences of the acceptance of the principle of Sir A. Rollit's amendment to the Education Bill, June 11, 1896', p. 3.
15. H.C. Barnard, *Were Those the Days? A Victorian Education* (1970), p. 57.
16. Board of Education, Annual Report for 1899–1900, *PP* 1900, XIX [Cd.390], p. 247.
17. A.P. Graves, *To Return to All That* (1930), pp. 178–9.
18. E.M. Sneyd-Kynnersley, *H.M.I. – Some Passages in the Life of One of H.M. Inspectors of Schools* (1910), p. 108.
19. P. Horn, *The Victorian and Edwardian Schoolchild* (1989), p. 175: P. Horn, *Education in Rural England 1800–1914* (1978), pp. 191–3.
20. F.H. Spencer, *An Inspector's Testament* (1938), p. 76.
21. Horn, *The Victorian and Edwardian Schoolchild*, p. 167; Spencer, op. cit., p. 75.
22. Minority Report of the Royal Commission on Elementary Education (1888) cited in the Report of the Departmental Committee on the Pupil-Teacher System, *PP*, 1898, XXV1 [c.8761], pp. 3–4.
23. G.W. Kekewich, *The Education Department and After* (1926), p. 28.
24. Sutherland, op. cit., p. 56.
25. E.G.A. Holmes, *What Is and What Might Be* (1911), p. 7.
26. Sneyd-Kynnersley, op. cit., p. 162.
27. Graves, op. cit., pp. 218–19.
28. J. Runciman, *Schools and Scholars* (1887), p. 129 cited in M. Hyndman, *Schools and Schooling in England and Wales: A Documentary History* (1978), p. 33.
29. See J. Roach, *Secondary Education in England 1870–1902: Public Activity and Private Enterprise* (1991), especially pp. 3–69.
30. M.E. Sadler, 'The Unrest in Secondary Education in Germany and elsewhere', Board of Education, *Special Reports on Educational Subjects*, 9 1902 [Cd.836], pp. 6–7.
31. Royal Commission on Secondary Education, *PP*, 1895, XLIII [C.7862], pp. 17–18.
32. Ibid., p. 10.
33. Ibid., pp. 52–3.
34. L. Grier, *Achievement in Education* (1952), p. 71.
35. Ibid., pp. 71–2.

36. Royal Commission on the Working of the Elementary Education Acts, England and Wales, *PP*, 1887, XXIX, p. 180; 1888, XXXV, pp. 180, 469.
37. Ibid., 1888, p. 317.
38. Ibid., p. 319.
39. Report of the Committee of Council on Education 1879–80, *PP*, 1880, XXII, p. ix.
40. Royal Commission on Secondary Education, *PP*, 1895, LXIII, [C.7862], pp. 135–6.
41. Ibid., pp. 67–8.
42. Roach, op. cit., pp. 107–11.
43. PRO ED 24/8, Memorandum by Duke of Devonshire, 28 Jan. 1898, p. 4.
44. Ibid.
45. M.E. Sadler, 'The Unrest in Secondary Education in Germany and Elsewhere', Board of Education, *Special Reports on Educational Subjects*, 9 1902, [Cd.836], p. x.
46. *4 PD*, 39, c.538, 31 March 1896.
47. Haldane Papers, MSS 5905, fo.176, R.L. Morant to J.B. Haldane, 25 May 1902.
48. N.E Johnson (ed.), *The Diary of Gathorne Hardy*, 17 Jan. 1890 (1981), p. 754.
49. Acland Papers, MS Eng lett e.100, fos.111–4, A.H.D. Acland to C.T.D. Acland, 17 May 1890.
50. Sneyd-Kynnersley, op. cit., p. 55.
51. Sutherland, op. cit., p. 53.
52. See evidence of E.B. Phipps, 13 June 1912, Royal Commission on the Civil Service, Appendix to Second Report, *PP*, 1912, XV [Cd.6535], p. 247.
53. Ibid., pp. 241–3 – evidence of L.A. Selby Bigge.
54. J. Dover Wilson Papers, MS 14357, fo.104.
55. See Sutherland, op. cit., pp. 35–44.
56. Evidence of A.H.D. Acland, 9 May 1912, Royal Commission on the Civil Service, Appendix to Second Report, *PP*, 1912, XV [Cd.6535], p. 78.
57. Sutherland, op. cit., p. 341.
58. Sneyd-Kynnersley, op. cit., p. 113.
59. Sadler Papers, Eng misc c.550, fos.115–117, A.H.D. Acland to M.E. Sadler, 8 Oct. 1892.
60. Ibid., fos.117–20, A.H.D. Acland to M.E. Sadler, 17 Oct. 1894.
61. M.E. Sadler, *Diary*, 4 Nov. 1940 cited in E.J. Higginson, *Selections from Michael Sadler: Studies in World Citizenship* (1979), p. 203.
62. M. Sadleir, *Michael Ernest Sadler* (1949), p. 68.
63. M.A. Sadler, *Diary*, 23 Nov. 1894, cited in Sadleir, op. cit., p. 126.
64. M.E. Sadler to M.A. Sadler, 21 Jan. 1895, cited in Sadleir, op. cit., p. 136.
65. Sadler Papers, MS Eng misc c.550, fo.10, M.E. Sadler, 'Note A: The Department of Special Inquiries and Reports on Education: Robert Morant'.
66. Scott Papers, Prince Devawongse to R.L. Morant, 15 Jan. 1894.
67. For further details see N.D. Daglish, 'The Morant–Chulalongkorn Affair of 1893–94', *Journal of Educational Administration and History*, XV, 2 (July 1983), pp. 16–23.
68. Sadler Papers, Eng misc c.550, M.E. Sadler, 'Note A: The Department of Special Inquiries and Reports on Education: Robert Morant.'
69. M.E. Sadler, *Diary*, 4 Nov. 1940, cited in Higginson, op. cit., p. 205.
70. Lynda Grier Papers, R. Fitzgibbon Young to L. Grier, 27 Nov. 1952.
71. James Papers, M45/1744, J. Chamberlain to Sir H. James, 11 Dec. 1894.
72. Ibid., M45/1747, J. Chamberlain to Sir H. James, 9 Jan. 1895.

73. Ibid., M45/1757:1760, Duke of Devonshire to Sir H. James, 25 and 26 June 1895.
74. Salisbury Papers (3M), A.J. Balfour to Lord Salisbury, June 1895.
75. Lord Salisbury to Lord Cranbrook, 23 July 1895 cited in A.E. Gathorne Hardy, *Gathorne Hardy, First Earl of Cranbrook* (1910), II, p. 351.
76. Sutherland, op. cit., pp. 14–19; D.G. Paz, 'The Composition of the Education Committee of the Privy Council, 1839–1856', *Journal of Educational Administration and History*, VIII, 2 (July 1976), pp. 1–9.
77. Sneyd-Kynnersley, op. cit., p. 114.
78. Salisbury Papers (3M), Lord Salisbury to J.E. Gorst, 1 July 1895.
79. Lord Welby cited in B. Holland, *Life of the Duke of Devonshire 1833–1908* (1911), I, p. 15.
80. Cited in J. France, 'Salisbury and the Unionist Alliance' in Lord Blake and H. Cecil (eds), *Salisbury: The Man and his Policies* (1987), pp. 240–1.
81. Kekewich, op. cit., pp. 92–6.
82. Holland, op. cit., II, p. 421.
83. J.H. Yoxall, 'Our Educational Dux', *New Liberal Review* (Dec. 1901), p. 681.
84. J.R. Vincent and A.B. Cooke, *The Governing Passion: Cabinet Government and Party Politics in Britain, 1885–86* (1974), p. 10.
85. Sadler Papers, MS Eng misc c.551, fo.205, M.E. Sadler to P. Hartog, 17 Sept. 1901.
86. J. Vincent, '"A Sort of Second-Rate Australia": A Note on Gorst and Democracy, 1865–68', *Historical Studies (Australia and New Zealand)*, 15 (1973), pp. 539, 543.
87. R. Blake, *The Conservative Party from Peel to Churchill* (1970), pp. 144–54.
88. J. Rutherford, *Sir George Grey, KCB, 1812–1898: A Study in Colonial Government* (1899), p. 584.
89. R. Shannon, *The Age of Disraeli; the Rise of Tory Democracy* (1992), pp. 392–3.
90. R.F. Foster, *Lord Randolph Churchill* (1982), pp. 70, 79.
91. Churchill Papers, J.E. Gorst to Lord R. Churchill, 10 Sept. 1882.
92. Shannon, op. cit., pp. 392–3.
93. M. Ostrogorski, *Democracy and the Organisation of Political Parties* (1902), I, p. 283.
94. *The Times*, 30 Dec. 1906.
95. E.P. Hennock, *British Social Reform and German Precedents: The Case of Social Insurance 1880–1914* (1987), p. 30.
96. Salisbury Papers (3M), J.E.Gorst to Lord Salisbury, 31 March 1890.
97. J.E. Gorst, 'Settlements in England and America' in J.M. Knapp (ed.), *The Universities and the Social Problem* (1895), p. 6.
98. Sandars Papers, MS Eng hist. c.726, fos.27–8, H.O. Barnett to A.J. Balfour, 28 Jan. 1895.
99. BP Add MS 49690, fo.66, Lord Salisbury to A.J. Balfour, 26 July 1892.
100. *The Times*, 3 July 1895.
101. Sadler Papers, MS Eng misc c.550, fo.129, Sir G.W. Kekewich to M.E. Sadler, 20 Nov. 1895.
102. Kekewich, op. cit., pp. 100–1.

2

Tory democracy and education

'What passed for ideas in many men's minds were often fragments rather than systems, tangled up with half-stated assumptions and prejudices, sometimes inconsistent with each other – but none the less powerful for all that'.[1]

The Vaughan and Cross Committees established by the Roman Catholics and Anglicans, respectively, to investigate the plight of their elementary schools after the effects of the Education Department Circular 321 had begun to take effect, completed their investigations by the end of 1894. The beginning of 1895 saw both churches, now armed with their committees' findings, moving onto the offensive in support of the needs of their schools, but using diametrically opposed strategies. The Catholics opted to produce a draft Education Bill in which the main aim was to achieve parity of funding for all public elementary schools from the rates. Their Bill ignored the complexities which would arise from the concomitant need for public control where rate aid was concerned but recognised the impracticality of trying to achieve, however desirable 'in the abstract', a uniform school system given the widespread and various religious beliefs held within society. The unity of purpose which marked the public presentation of the Bill by the Catholics contrasted strongly with the divisions among the Cross Committee made public by the Church's decision to publish their report in its entirety. Furthermore, the Committee had rejected the idea of rate aid for voluntary schools, a majority preferring to press instead for increased government subventions. In spite of these different strategies, the two churches were, none the less, united in their desire for increased funding of denominational schools and their historical right to provide elementary education in accordance with the religious wishes of parents as well as in their communication of the sense of injustice being felt among their members living in school board districts at having to pay rates which ultimately helped to contribute to the maintenance of the competition between board and voluntary schools. While they both knew that there was very little likelihood of Rosebery's government responding to their views, they were as keenly aware as anyone of the current political situation and the increasing possibility of the not-too-distant advent of a Conservative government. A fairly rapid public response by Balfour appeared to validate their perceptions.

Addressing a meeting of his constituents in East Manchester a week after the publication of the Cross Committee Report, Balfour emphasised his support for the voluntary schools, especially the ability of their sectarian teaching to transform their pupils into true 'English citizens', an achievement he believed was denied board schools by the limitations of their secular instruction. He also supported them on more pragmatic grounds, noting that their existence provided financial relief for many ratepayers, a condition that would disappear if there was a uniform board school system. His main concern, therefore, was to ensure the continuance of sectarian teaching as an 'important part of the great machinery of education', and he believed that government aid should be forthcoming so as to prevent the potential submission of voluntary schools to board schools.[2] His remarks were given added weight by his uncle's subsequent public comments.

Where Balfour was an 'undogmatic but sincere' Christian with evangelical sympathies his uncle was profoundly religious and much more firmly opposed to educational secularism and school board expenditure than his nephew.[3] Although not very interested in education, believing that character was superior to intellect, Lord Salisbury believed in the power of the Church

> . . . to halt that slow slide towards chaos and anarchy, a movement which he considered to be the inevitable consequence of the advent of democracy. . . . In this context, the voluntary schools, with their correct moral stance, would be the bulwarks of Church stability.[4]

In two speeches, one in Limehouse in March and the other before the Anglican National Society in June, Salisbury revealed that he had finally lost patience with the religious compromise of the 1870 Education Act. Undeterred by the religious controversy which had surrounded the London School Board election in the previous year, Salisbury believed that the public increasingly shared his feelings and he was convinced that the board school was 'losing its hold on the affection and opinion of the people'. In such circumstances he felt justified in warning opponents of voluntary schools that nothing was eternal, 'not even a compromise'.[5] In his speech to the National Society Salisbury exhorted his audience and their colleagues to go forth and capture the school boards, pledging them at the same time 'a better law which shall place you under no religious disability'.[6]

At face value Salisbury's pledge augured well for voluntary schools should the Conservatives win the next general election, but it was also intended as a warning to the Church's leaders – who had introduced an Education Bill into the Lords to try to make Rosebery's government heed their schools' plight – to leave policy-making to the politicians. At the same time, and keenly aware of the Nonconformist adherents within the Liberal Unionists, Salisbury abstained from any declarations on educational policy during the general election, as did most of the two parties' leaders. Devonshire did no more than stipulate that social legislation should be a government's priority but Balfour indicated that the Conservatives intended to intervene in education should they win the election.[7] He argued that parents should have the right to have their children educated in accordance with their religious beliefs and, accordingly, the preservation of the voluntary schools was a question of the first magnitude. This view made its mark among Anglicans, Catholics and Wesleyans and the sweeping victory of the Conservatives in the election reflected this. The new government thus had to decide how best it could achieve effective implementation of Balfour's promise.

In August *The Times* started a campaign on behalf of the voluntary schools and maintained it for much of the parliamentary recess by the judicious use of articles and letters. Lord Cranborne, leader of the Church Parliamentary Committee and Lord Salisbury's heir, availed himself of this useful platform and publicly sought Balfour's assistance, as Leader of the House, in procuring legislation for the relief of the voluntary schools. Balfour confirmed his electoral promise with an acknowledgement that something 'effectual' must be done to relieve the 'intolerable strain' of the schools.[8] In private Balfour told his cousin that he found the Archbishops' Bill of the previous session completely unsuitable as the basis for any legislation and any effective solution to the problem would have to come from Gorst and himself. He added, however, that he did want to be kept informed of current Church thinking on the matter, and Cranborne, for whom the conflict between board and voluntary schools was a 'contest between the forces of darkness and light', readily acceded to this request.[9]

Devonshire, following *The Times*'s campaign, was not sure whether it amounted to much apart from indicating 'what is expected of us'. Kekewich thought the letters 'very poor stuff', and wrote to Sadler, currently examining the German education system at first hand, expressing the view that any forthcoming bill would be a 'very little one', and as such it would undoubtedly be a considerable disappointment to the Church.[10] His presentiment appeared to be confirmed by the duke's subsequent comment that the proposed Education Bill would probably only provide an indication of goodwill by the government towards the managers of voluntary schools. For his own part, Devonshire was willing to grant whatever additional aid was required by schools, provided there was equality of treatment between voluntary and board schools. He was perplexed as to how this could be actually achieved while, at the same time, ensuring that those schools who were in actual need received the aid. While he pondered the question, he asked Gorst to prepare a discussion document for the first meeting of the newly formed Cabinet Committee on Education, to be held on 19 November.[11]

Gorst gladly undertook the task, having spent a good part of the recess in becoming better acquainted with the problems facing the education system. His membership of the Local Government Board's Departmental Committee of Inquiry into the Metropolitan Poor Law Schools had led to his staying frequently at Toynbee Hall with Canon and Mrs Samuel Barnett, the latter a fellow committee member and both opponents of Salisbury's educational views. Their discussions on education had also involved another resident, Morant, who revelled in the opportunity to discuss educational problems and research with the political head of his department. Morant, who was supposed to be learning German, had deliberately stayed on at Toynbee Hall so as to be able to cultivate Gorst, telling the absent Sadler:

> ... as you left almost without seeing him [Gorst], I rather feared lest our Section might lose ground, through losing the strong personal contact that had existed between Acland and yourself: and so I thought I had better make every effort to renew the same relations with Acland's successor, as far as possible.

The outcome clearly matched his expectations:

> In Educational matters however it has been invaluable, as a source of knowledge. The machinery of Education, both Whitehall & Kensington is a fearfully complicated thing to really know & understand, unless one has grown up in it like the Officials here, or *worked* it like the School Board Members & Managers. It is in the latter direction that I score at Toynbee. Gorst is quaintly ignorant of the whole machinery. He comes to me for all sorts of things: & as my own similar ignorance is so recent &

so vivid in my memory, I am perhaps able to enlighten him better than some of the Officials might, who wd be unable to realise this condition of ignorance.[12]

A few days later he was delighted to be able to inform Sadler that Gorst and Devonshire fully expected their section to act as the 'intelligence Department' for the Committee of Council and not just a research unit of the Education Department. He also added the rider that 'Gorst has declared himself very strongly' and hoped that Salisbury 'won't try and smash him for it'.[13]

Morant's comment referred to Gorst's speeches during his round of public engagements in the autumn, the contents of which revealed how much he had benefited from the discussions at Toynbee Hall. His speeches ranged far and wide, encompassing many of the educational issues requiring attention and not only substantiated Kekewich's assessment of him as an educationist but drew praise also from one Bryce Commissioner:

> Gorst . . . is working hard at 'great questions' and makes a profound study of our Report. He has been speaking a good deal, and not at all in a reactionary way.[14]

But Gorst was vitally aware of the gulf which existed between his educational views and those of Balfour and Salisbury, as well as his restricted ability to achieve reform. One theme he constantly used, therefore, was his discontent with the ineffectiveness of government and Parliament to achieve substantial social reform. He advised his audiences to start developing the considerable but under-utilised powers already possessed by local government bodies if they wanted to see effective reforms achieved. Addressing one audience on the problems besetting the nation's secondary schools, he counselled them, and any interested in the subject, that they would have to 'influence and organise public opinion' if they wanted to see governmental action on the Bryce Report when it was released.[15] And speaking at Cambridge he appeared to make a broad hint that members of the Bryce Commission should 'stump the country in favour of legislation'.[16] These radical proposals, completely at variance with those held by his party, led *The Times* to reassure its readers that they were not indicative of a rift over education within the government, but rather reflected a discussion 'in unimpeachable generalities about the necessity of not stopping the progress and development of education'.[17]

At the same time as Gorst was publicising these views and preparing the Cabinet committee paper, the Church of England was embroiled in discussions over the planning of educational proposals for presentation to the government. After a minor crisis, in which the Archbishops' Bill was finally abandoned as the basis of the Church's scheme, the Archbishop of York and a small committee were charged with the drafting of a suitable memorial. In the course of this task, the Archbishop had received a friendly overture from Cardinal Vaughan, suggesting the possibility of a joint approach by Anglicans and Catholics to the government. The Archbishop viewed the idea favourably but one of his team, Canon Scott of Manchester, was so totally opposed that the idea had to be abandoned. York informed Benson, the Archbishop of Canterbury, of the potential danger of Scott's attitude, stressing that unless there was a united front from the supporters of religious education and the voluntary schools 'we shall fail of obtaining the influence which we ought to have'.[18] Benson was disturbed by this but became alarmed when he learned that Vaughan, because of Scott's action, intended approaching the government '*at once . . .* to make sure of getting his scheme under the notice of Government before we submit ours'.[19] He hastily arranged with Salisbury for the government to receive a deputation on 20 November and for the memorial to be published on 16 November, but even then Vaughan had pre-empted him, the Catholics' memorial having being forwarded three days earlier.

The Anglicans' memorial, with its reiteration of almost traditional claims and views about denominational education, was perceived by Kekewich as a 'shortsighted policy'. Amid the almost ritualistic language, however, lay a new claim which proposed that any state subvention be administered 'in such a manner as will prevent what is harmful in the competition between voluntary and board schools'.[20] The vague language employed cloaked a plan for checking school boards' expenditure, draft schemes for which had already been forwarded to Balfour by Cranborne. But beyond this checking function there was no limit laid upon school board expenditure except for the proviso that any future growth should be shared by both board and voluntary schools. This, Cranborne believed, would provide potential control of the rate expenditure by school boards although it would not yield the funding increase desired by the voluntary schools of five shillings per child, or £1,000,000 altogether, in order to put them on an equal, and competitive, footing with the board schools. Funding of this magnitude would have to come from an increase in the parliamentary grant.[21]

Support for a limitation upon school board expenditure had been provided independently by the Permanent Secretary of the Scottish Education Department, Sir Henry Craik, who had been invited by Balfour to provide critical comments on all aspects of the planning of the Education Bill.[22] He believed that educational expenditure:

> . . . is only profitable when it is wise: and much of our present expenditure is not only not wise, but profligate in extravagance. To help the Voluntary Schools the first thing is to check the extravagance in Board Schools. . . . Much of the so-called Technical Education is nothing but a delusion, which will not raise, but lower, the children.[23]

None the less, in a scheme which he prepared for Balfour, Craik was not in favour of increasing the parliamentary grant of 17s 6d. He believed that in the long term any increase would only compound rather than overcome the competition between the voluntary schools and the board schools, and what he advocated, instead, was that the school boards should have to find any sums required over a nominal parliamentary grant of 7s 6d per child from the rates. The voluntary schools, if demonstrably efficient, would receive, however, the same grant of 7s 6d plus the existing fee grant of ten shillings per child. The overall effect would be to lessen the 'severe' competition from 'lavishly managed' board schools faced by many voluntary schools.[24] Balfour reacted favourably and put this plan to Devonshire before the first Cabinet Education Committee meeting as a possible basis for helping the voluntary schools out of their problems while 'preserving the appearance of fairness to Board schools'.[25] Cranborne, unaware of Craik's plan and unsure of Balfour's reception of his scheme, believed that the Church's best chance for securing its aims lay now with its deputation to the government.

Devonshire and Salisbury met the huge deputation, led by the Archbishop of Canterbury, in the Foreign Office on 20 November. After listening to the submissions, Devonshire conceded that it would be possible to make changes to the 17s 6d limit on parliamentary grants and to the rating of schools. At the same time he was unequivocal that the Department would not depart from the principles of the 1870 Act. Voluntary subscriptions would thus have to remain a major component as far as voluntary schools' income was concerned. As for recent agitations by more militant members of the Church for the provision of denominational religious instruction in all public elementary schools, he applied a cold douche to such aspirations. Although Anglicans might be unhappy with the undenominational religious instruction provided in board schools, the Nonconformists, Devonshire noted, were 'well satisfied' with it, and, he added, 'I do not grudge them, and I hope they will always have that facility.'[26] Devonshire was later to make the point to Lord Cranborne that he believed there was 'some defect in my intelligence which renders me incapable even of understanding the apprehensions of the advocates of denominational education. If I could only understand them, I might try to do something to remove their objections.'[27] The chill induced in the deputation by these views was partly relieved by Salisbury's statements, in which he charmed the deputation with his churchmanship and his claim that the chief educational problems before the government were those of religious education and the want of control over school board expenditure. His final counsel – 'what we can do, we must do quickly and not despair if it takes time to prepare the sinews of war' – was gratefully accepted by most of his listeners, but Benson was puzzled by his quotation from Bacon:

> Does this mean we shall have a small measure of relief . . . and have to wait for anything like a real subvention? If so we shall not get it, for the House of Commons will never take two Education Bills this year – and I shall 'despair'.[28]

Unperturbed by such worries, Devonshire and Gorst had been closeted away from departmental routine during November in order to develop their ideas for the Bill. At the beginning they concentrated on the voluntary school problem but soon moved to others including Gorst's aim for an administrative decentralisation of the school system utilising new local education authorities. He took support from the Bryce Report's advocacy of rational, decentralised local education authorities and by 20 November Kekewich was able to tell Sadler that 'it is just on the cards, and only just, that we may attempt to deal with Secondary Education and Primary Education in a single Bill'.[29] But as the plans for the Bill developed and Gorst wanted to shape the Bryce Report's recommendations into a more comprehensive form he became annoyed that Sadler, with his intimate knowledge of the Bryce Commission, remained in Germany and was unable to provide the necessary input to help shape policy. Morant, vitally aware of the problems Sadler's continued absence could create for their section, desperately tried to convince Sadler of the need to return but Sadler remained unmoved, only acceding when he received Kekewich's command. Kekewich had, at the same time, relayed the state of progress of the planning:

> . . . the scheme we are trying to get the Govt. to assent to is that of a County & County Borough Educational Authority, to be used at first perhaps only for primary education (except so far as the Technical Edn. Committees will be merged in it) but to be used hereafter for Secondary Educatn. also . . . . My idea is that for primary schools the Dept. should give what I may call a 'living wage' to all schools, leaving the *Local* authority to aid out of a state subvention, possibly increased by a rate, specially necessitous schools. It is only so that we can get all schools up to a fully efficient level . . . .I want to see a bigger policy than the abolition of the 17/6 limit, exemption from rates, & general increases of grants, the latter of which will involve a certain waste of public money.[30]

Morant hastened to Harwich to meet and brief Sadler on the journey to London, but a delay caused by stormy weather in the North Sea meant that Sadler reached the Education Department only in time to find that Gorst had just forwarded his draft proposals for the Bill to Balfour.

If Sadler was dismayed by this, Balfour shared his feelings when he read Gorst's draft and the more detailed, accompanying memorandum from Kekewich. He felt Gorst had disregarded the policy agreed upon by the Cabinet committee to support the voluntary schools, while Kekewich's memorandum included topics 'which were never even discussed'.[31] Balfour was unwilling to accept Gorst's draft as the basis for the Bill but thought Kekewich's memorandum might serve. Unwilling, however, to upset Gorst at this juncture he asked Salisbury to get Gorst to have both documents drawn up as bills for comparison. Although Salisbury was unable to perceive any difference between their aims he acceded to his request but Gorst responded by indicating that no difference was intended between the two documents and, furthermore, he had obtained the committee's agreement to the principle of decentralisation being incorporated in the Bill. He had arranged, therefore, for Sir Hugh Jenkyns, the Parliamentary Draftsman, to prepare only a single draft Bill.

Gorst's draft had emphasised the need for the creation of new local education authorities both to rectify the administrative chaos prevalent at the local level and to provide the only effective means of resolving the necessitous schools problem. The new authorities, to be committees of the county and county borough councils, should, he argued, be responsible for the distribution of government and other education funds in accordance with their assessment of local conditions and needs. The flexibility that would accrue from this type of funding distribution would ensure that the schools in need received whatever aid was required yet, at the same time, permit economies to be made in central government administration. While he was willing for rate aid to be used for all elementary schools, provided there was the necessary concomitant of public control over its expenditure, he shared Kekewich's view that abolition of both the 17s 6d limit (on parliamentary grants) and the rating of schools was not the solution to the necessitous schools' problem because it could not generate sufficient funding. Similarly, the granting of an additional state subvention would not curtail the detrimental effects of the rivalry between board and voluntary schools. He also believed Balfour would find, on further consideration, that his checking clause was impracticable.[32]

The draft Bill of 26 clauses which emerged from Jenkyn's office on 20 December reflected the committee's polarisation of views on educational policy with the first 14 clauses, devoted to the structure and roles of the proposed new education authorities, representing Gorst and Devonshire's views. The remaining clauses, including provision for a new state grant to necessitous schools, the abolition of the 17s 6d limit and school rating, a checking clause on school board expenditure, plus repeal of the Cowper-Temple clause of the 1870 Act, emanated from Balfour supported by Salisbury and Cross.[33] At this stage, then, policy for the Bill was being formulated primarily by Gorst and Balfour. But any further development was suddenly threatened by the unexpected, and dramatic, intervention of Chamberlain.

Devonshire had accepted an invitation from Chamberlain to stay at his Highbury home while fulfilling some public engagements in Birmingham in mid-December. Sharing one of these engagements with Chamberlain, Devonshire had been perturbed by some derogatory comments made by Chamberlain in his speech about the local education authorities proposed by the Bryce Report. The proposals had upset the town councils and school boards and one consequence was that Birmingham was 'very angry, and Chamberlain . . . told them they are right to be angry'.[34] Devonshire warned Salisbury that it looked as though Chamberlain was 'rather uneasy about Education' but decided, none the less, to leave Gorst and Kekewich's drafts for the Bill with him when he left for Chatsworth a few days later.[35]

At the time of the general election, Chamberlain had indicated his willingness to support any reasonable plan for the relief of the voluntary schools, in spite of his reputation as a champion of the school boards.[36] But the proposals left by Devonshire exceeded the parameters of his concession and produced a paroxysm of anger. He was incensed by the 'deadly blow' they aimed at the 1870 compromise and he prophesied that they would do more 'to reunite a solid Liberal opposition and also shatter the Unionist coalition than could be accomplished by any other means'.[37] He acknowledged the compromises necessitated by membership of a coalition government but felt, none the less, that he would be unable 'to hold up [his] head for a day' if he agreed to the proposals.[38]

Devonshire accepted Chamberlain's views as 'vital, and political rather than educational' but was prepared to jettison the Bill's contentious clauses rather than risk the destruction of the coalition and government. Balfour, when he learned of the situation, was willing also to sacrifice the same clauses, as long as the Bill managed to save the voluntary schools for he would '*not* be content if we fail in this object'. At the same time, he took the opportunity to reiterate his view that the Bill should concentrate solely upon relieving the voluntary schools 'and no extraneous provisions should be introduced into it except with the object of smoothing the passage of an effective measure through the House'.[39] Gorst was rather more sanguine, believing that Chamberlain could be brought round on most of the essential points, although he was moved sufficiently by the tone of Chamberlain's memorandum to produce a long memorandum for the Cabinet countering Chamberlain's points. He was adamant that the Bill should cover both elementary and secondary education, arguing that many Radicals 'would swallow the proposal' of giving aid to the voluntary schools if it, in turn, was accompanied by a resolution of the problems facing secondary education. He was, furthermore, unwilling to yield on the creation of the new education authorities as they were the linchpin for educational progress. He did, however, support Chamberlain's objections to the checking clause and was willing to postpone the repeal of the Cowper-Temple clause.[40] Salisbury was not convinced, however, and believed that Chamberlain was intent upon some drastic changes being made to the Bill; changes which he viewed with 'perfect dismay. Randolph [Churchill] at his wildest could not have made a madder suggestion.'[41]

The concessions offered by Devonshire and Balfour proved sufficient to avert the threatened catastrophe and the Cabinet agreed at its meeting on 18 January that the Queen's Speech for the opening of Parliament should include the promise of a Bill 'for the assistance of the voluntary schools'. But the delay in reaching this decision, partly owing to Lord Salisbury's ill health, led the Cabinet to retain the draft Bill of 20 December as the basis for further discussion. Gorst was delighted by this but the chances of the measure actually reaching the Statute Book receded as additional discussions about the measure took another two months by which time pressure on the parliamentary timetable had become acute. The major cause for the delay was Balfour's determination to secure the best possible financial provision for the voluntary schools, and in this he received the full support of Craik.

A centralist as far as educational administration was concerned, Craik was highly critical of Gorst's policy, arguing that 'if devolution is to mean unguided or misguided effort like this, it would be well to think twice before carrying it further'.[42] He was unhappy about the proposed autonomy of the new local authorities and the lack of detailed prescription for the new state grant to necessitous schools. The grant, prescribed by Clause 4 of the Bill, was 'to be paid to an education authority without regard to special needs although it is to be distributed to schools only on the basis of special needs'.[43] Craik believed that any parliamentary grant should be given only on a fixed basis to schools, and under terms determined by the Education Department. Gorst would not accept this view, however, since it would clearly destroy one of the chief advantages to be derived from the creation of the new local authorities. If there had to be a new state subvention then, he contended, it should be distributed locally and on the basis of local assessment of needs.[44] Balfour was unhappy with both views, as neither provided the clear-cut preferential treatment of voluntary schools which he desired, and he feared that Gorst was not 'lending his energies to this problem'.[45] Balfour was to become more optimistic, however, when Craik forwarded a new scheme, for it seemed to be closer to his desired aim.

Craik's plan, based 'partly on average attendance and partly on some poverty test', advocated awarding all voluntary schools a grant of four shillings per child (on average attendance figures) as well as an increase to the grant received by poor school boards under Clause 97 of the 1870 Act owing to the low rating power of their districts (the poverty test). Any increase to this grant, denied to all voluntary schools, even by only a small sum such as half-a-crown, would enable Balfour to claim that Clause 4 provided parity of treatment for all necessitous schools while enabling the voluntary schools to be the main beneficiaries. The plan had the additional advantage that the finance required – £66,000 for the school boards and £489,000 for the voluntary schools – was tolerably close to the Education Department's original estimate of the sum needed for the Bill's financial require-ments.[46] Satisfied by this, Balfour seems to have gone out of his way to prevent Gorst from interfering with this possible realisation of his goal for Jenkyns had to check constantly with Balfour's private secre-taries to ascertain whether Gorst was allowed to see subsequent drafts of the relevant clauses.[47] It was to be the intervention of Sir Michael Hicks Beach, the Chancellor of the Exchequer, and not Gorst, how-ever, that upset Balfour's plans.

Zealous in his hopes for maintaining a projected budget surplus of some four million pounds for the forthcoming financial year, Hicks Beach had been upset to discover that the Education Department had overlooked, in its planning of the Bill's financial needs, the effect of abolishing the 17s 6d limit. The shortfall of £54,000 which would result from this omission, plus the £55,000 by which Craik's scheme would actually exceed their total estimate, led him to refuse to countenance Clause 4 providing more than 3s 6d and 1s 6d for voluntary and poor board schools respectively. Balfour attempted to circumvent this obstacle at the next Cabinet meeting by proposing that the provision of Clause 4 should cover only the voluntary schools. Gorst was dismayed, Kekewich pronounced it 'unworkable', and Balfour received 'very grave' objections from others. None the less, it required Chamberlain's intervention at the next Cabinet to force a return to the clause's original aim of aiding all necessitous schools. At this point, Devonshire decided to apply pressure to Balfour.

Claiming to be confused by all the changes being proposed or made, but clearly irritated by the delay in completing the Bill being caused by Balfour's activities, Devonshire sent Balfour a Minute embodying both his and Kekewich's views on the Bill's clauses. They included a reversion to the sums originally suggested for Clause 4, together with evidence demonstrating that their achievement was possible within the Department's original financial estimate. This rebuttal of Hicks Beach's assertion, and hint of annoyance with Balfour's procrastination, was accompanied by a thinly veiled warning that Devonshire would not accept much more tinkering with an Education Bill.[48] Balfour, recognising the possibility of a new strain on the coalition, as well as being under increasing pressure from the Commons to introduce the Bill, yielded to Devonshire. Clause 4 reverted to Craik's original sum for the voluntary schools while the grant for poor school boards was to be allocated by the new local authorities. Four days later the Bill was ready for Gorst to introduce it into the Commons.

In his introduction Gorst stated that the Bill's principal aim was the establishment of a 'paramount' education authority in every county and county borough. At the same time, he provided a comprehensive analysis of the Bill's features and was at pains to indicate the rationale for each, an effort which brought him congratulations from all sides. Michael Sadler noted that the House was staggered by the 'bigness' of the Bill and the *Revue Pédagogique* believed the Bill's main feature to be 'une attribution nouvelle', but Edward Hamilton thought that the Bill was a 'drastic measure, and looks as if it were intended to elbow out School Boards'.[49] His views were shared by the Opposition and their supporters; Dr A.M. Fairbairn, a leading Nonconformist and Bryce commissioner, felt that the Bill contained 'so many clauses and provisions that can be worked insidiously against both Education and Nonconformity' that it was not surprising that the majority of Liberals and Nonconformists opposed it.[50] The proposed grant for the voluntary schools and the checking clause on school board expenditure as well as Clause 27, the latter because of its potential for destroying the Cowper-Temple compromise, were arousing the ire of these groups. For many Nonconformists the Cowper-Temple clause of the 1870 Education Act constituted one of the essential components of the board schools' curriculum and any attempt to interfere with it was thus viewed as an attempt to undermine the very foundations of these schools. The point was emphasised in the provocative and partisan articles that flowed from the pens of the Rev. John Clifford, Lyulph Stanley and Fairbairn and were designed to stir supporters of the schools into action against the Bill. The Liberal Opposition now found itself with a cause which allowed it to discard the dispirited and listless behaviour that had characterised its parliamentary performance since the general election. Major attacks were thus launched against the contentious parts of the Bill in the Second Reading and the Opposition utilised all the political and religious rhetoric at its command.

Asquith rather than Acland was entrusted with the Opposition's reply to Gorst's speech on the Second Reading and with the incisive skill that underlay his success in the law courts he exposed those parts of the Bill which he believed would have the effect of

... revolutionising the foundations, of dislocating the machinery, of impoverishing the results, and embittering the spirit of our whole system of national education.[51]

His coruscating attack upon the Bill's underlying principle of decentralisation was matched by an analysis of the implicit attack being made against the school boards. He used this last point to try to drive a wedge into the coalition by playing upon the discomfiture Chamberlain must have felt in making a speech a short while before at Birmingham, in which he gave his first (and only) public support for the Bill and its preservation of the voluntary schools:

> I read that speech . . . with something akin to the same sense of admiring bewilderment which overtakes us when at an earlier stage of our life we first make the discovery that it is equally easy for an accomplished acrobat to stand upon his head or his heels.[52]

Such biting cynicism was characteristic of his speech and none of the government leaders remained exempt from it as he highlighted their contributions to the measure: the generosity of the financial provisions for the voluntary schools thus drew an acerbic comparison with the 'penurious aspirations' of Lord Salisbury. The ferocity of this and subsequent attacks by other Opposition Members upon the government's policy, coupled with the incessant invocation of religious shibboleths when reference was made to either the school boards or voluntary schools, led both Gorst and Bryce to try to steer the debate to the educational issues at stake, but with little success. Matters were not helped by the absence of a united government front bench in the face of this relentless onslaught on the Bill. Chamberlain and Hicks Beach were conspicuous by their absence while Balfour's statement at one point that ultimately he would like to see the complete municipalisation of educational administration threatened the viability of the proposed LEAs. Gorst's attempts to postpone the consideration of detailed aspects of the Bill until the Committee Stage annoyed some government backbenchers and added to their discontent with the measure. After five nights of heated debate the Second Reading was passed, in this instance the government's majority being swollen by the support of the Irish MPs who had been coerced by their bishops into voting for the measure despite the rupture it caused with the Liberal Nonconformists.

The government's decision not to introduce Closure resulted in 1,335 amendments being tabled for the Committee Stage and urgent discussions on strategy took place over the Whitsuntide break with

Gorst, excluded from the Cabinet deliberations, taking counsel with Sadler, Llewellyn Smith and Sidney Webb. All the discussions had to consider the implications of the widening rifts being caused by the Bill among both government backbenchers and supporters. Anglicans in the north of England had recently denounced the four-shilling grant as insufficient and at their York Convocation had voted for rate aid – a move opposed by the Archbishop of Canterbury, the Bishop of London and others. There were also murmurs of discontent about Clause 27's aim of allowing parents to obtain in *all* schools the religious teaching they required for their children, some clergy having realised the full implications of such an aim. Thus, embarrassingly for the government, the Church of England now represented a body divided over a Bill designed to aid its schools. Discontent also existed among the ranks of the Nonconformist Liberal Unionist MPs, for they opposed the potentially detrimental effects the Bill could have upon the school boards and the compromise of 1870.[53]

Discontent was not confined solely to the religious or school board issues raised by the Bill, for it was becoming clear before the Committee Stage that some county councils were beginning to have doubts about becoming responsible for the administration of the Bill should it become law. At the same time, however, they would not countenance the smaller municipal authorities assuming the powers contained in Clause 1. The municipalities and their representatives, led by Sir Albert Rollit on the government backbenches, in their turn, were furious at being excluded from the Bill's scheme of decentralisation, and in their bid to try to rectify this omission they had the growing support of many county boroughs and, seemingly, Balfour. His statement during the Second Reading about municipalisation had compounded the issue, however, for it had alienated many county supporters and other government backbenchers who perceived him to be too closely under Rollit's sway. In these circumstances, it was hardly surprising that Clause 1 proved to be the sticking point when the Bill went into Committee.

Six years later, when the same situation arose over the 1902 Education Bill, the solution to these administrative problems was to make the municipal boroughs authorities for elementary education only, that is, Part III authorities. An identical solution existed in 1896, contained in an amendment drafted by Sir Richard Jebb and upon which an agreement appears to have been reached privately between Gorst and Jebb, the two Cambridge University MPs.[54] Before Jebb's amendment could be reached, however, Gorst had first to achieve the rejection of a preceding amendment from Rollit designed to place municipal council authorities on the same footing as county borough councils and in charge of elementary *and* secondary education for their areas. Gorst had given his reasons for rejecting Rollit's amendment, including the huge increase in the number of authorities that would result if it was accepted, when Balfour strolled nonchalantly into the chamber. When appealed to by backbencher Mark Oldroyd to honour his earlier statement about municipalisation by accepting Rollit's amendment, Balfour did so, and thus overthrew Gorst. This was a disastrous decision politically, for it reinforced the Opposition's determination to press more amendments upon the government, as well as undermining the Bill's policy. The effect of his action was like the opening of flood gates, with the Bill submerged under the inrushing flow of amendments. The Liberal leader Sir William Harcourt remarked gleefully to his wife:

> The Lord hath delivered them into our hands. I have never known a Government so soon and so completely discredited. The chariot wheel will drag heavily and the horse and his rider will be cast into the sea.[55]

The *Revue Pédagogique* summed up the general feeling at the time:

> L'attitude de M.Balfour, traitant aussi cavalièrement le chef du département d'éducation et acceptant, au nom du gouvernement un amendement que Sir John Gorst venait de déclarer inacceptable, était très commentée au lendemain de la séance du 11 Juin et trouvait peu d'approbateurs.[56]

Realising his error, Balfour tried to save what he could, and at a special meeting of the Unionists proposed an autumn session so as to provide enough time for dealing with all the amendments. His suggestion only alienated those members anxiously awaiting the delights of the glorious twelfth while Edward Hamilton noted that the Bill was 'getting more and more into a tangle. The Unionists are all "at sixes and sevens over it"; and it looks as if the Bill will have to go or else Gorst.'[57] A week later, with only two lines and 14 words of Clause 1 passed, the Cabinet decided to abandon the measure, despite a plea from the Queen to reconsider their decision. Salisbury, angered by his colleagues decision yet having to acquiesce in the collective nature of Cabinet decision-making, refused to chair the meeting to inform the parliamentary party of the decision.[58] The impact upon Gorst was dramatic also, Mary Sadler recording that he was in 'great straits' while Herbert Gladstone observed him 'wandering "like a disembodied spirit", anywhere except on to the Treasury Bench'.[59] Perhaps not surprisingly then, when Balfour moved the abandonment of the Bill to a House

> . . . packed from floor to topmost range of galleries; the same throng at the bar; the same long lines in the side galleries; Press crowding entrance to their seats, like mob at pit or gallery of Haymarket Theatre when *Trilby* is on; the same electric air vibrating through crowded chamber. All the same, and yet a universe of difference . . . [60]

Gorst was nowhere to be seen.

The comprehensive nature of the Bill had ensured that in its passage through the House the debates were marked by the fact that 'each champion fought more or less for his own hand'.[61] It was left to Gorst and Balfour to defend the Bill against attacks, but each used his own conflicting terms; a repetition in some ways of the planning stage in which Michael Sadler had observed 'different ministers indifferent each to every part of the Bill but that in which they took special interest'.[62] Balfour's defence rested on a commitment to the voluntary schools and hostility towards the board schools whereas Gorst chose to concentrate upon the issue of decentralisation and ignored many of the details of the Bill, details which were 'to the majority of his party the very key of the position'.[63] Arthur Acland thought such a stance 'most perilous when one knew how really in earnest men of full responsibility like Balfour took the Bill'.[64] The conflicting interests and inputs into the planning were not exceptional but the subsequent absence of a unified government front bench during the Bill's passage in the House, plus the role played by Balfour, were. Although he was forced to allow Gorst free rein over the Bill's introduction thereafter he adopted an interventionist role, culminating in his overturning of Gorst on the Rollit amendment. These interventions, especially the last one, effectively destroyed both Gorst's position and the Bill. Why Balfour did this, given his considerable input into the Bill's formulation, is unclear but there are several possibilities.

Contemporary observers overwhelmingly indicted him for ineptitude, including Hamilton, who noted the growing dissatisfaction with Balfour among the Unionists:

> . . . he does not sit sufficiently enough in the House . . . He sits in his room; and then when difficulties arise he is called in, with the

result that not having his fingers on the pulse of the House he is at a disadvantage when he gets on his legs.[65]

Another possible explanation for his action was his awareness of the Pandora's box opened by Clause 1. Not only was there doubt among the supporters of the Conservative Party about the new authorities but both municipal authorities and Liberal Unionist supporters regarded the proposed new education authorities as 'an unjustifiable attack on the existing system'.[66] This and additional opposition rendered the likelihood of the Bill's passing and achieving relief for the voluntary schools highly unlikely. The acceptance of Rollit's amendment may well have killed the Bill but, at the same time, this fate could provide the necessary rationale for a simpler measure concentrating solely upon aid for the voluntary schools. And compounding the issue was his dislike of both Gorst and his political ideology. None the less, Balfour's subsequent comments concerning this episode in his career were always gloomy and he remained apprehensive of any possible repetition where educational legislation was concerned. This suggests that the episode of the Rollit amendment was not planned but an impromptu reaction. There is evidence that Balfour was going through something of a personal crisis with Lady Mary Elcho at the time of the committee stage: a letter of hers included the statement that she could not 'bear to see you sitting back in that chair more depressed than if the Education Bill had gone wrong instead of me'.[67] At that moment, then, Balfour was clearly not anticipating any major problems with the Bill but one consequence of his action, in precipitating the failure of the measure, was that his reputation as Leader of the House plummeted to its nadir.

Balfour stated publicly after the Bill's débâcle that there would be a change in the government's approach to educational policy, but the government did not completely abandon the policy contained in the Bill, despite Salisbury's misgivings:

> The commonest error in politics is sticking to the carcasses of dead policies. When a mast falls overboard you do not try to save a rope here and a spar there in memory of their former utility; you cut away the hamper altogether and it should be the same with a policy. But it is not so. We cling to the shred of an old policy after it has been torn to pieces.[68]

In a speech to the United Club, Balfour acknowledged that the comprehensive nature of the Bill had imperilled the provision of relief for the voluntary schools 'on which our hearts were most especially set' but promised the voluntaryists a new bill in the near future. His statement that the measure would be limited solely to the relief of these schools revealed also that the government's future educational policy would be formulated on a piecemeal basis.[69] Gorst remained convinced, despite being blamed by some – including Balfour – for the Bill's failure, that 'if a bill is demanded by the country, he must be used to draw it up' and made his views clear during the parliamentary recess.[70]

In an address to a ruridecanal conference at Colchester in mid-September, his message to the Church about its schools was that it should look to the local authorities rather than government sub-ventions as the main hope for help. Church advocates of rate aid saw this as support for their views and began to exert pressure for it to be adopted as Church policy. But Hicks Beach and Sir Matthew White Ridley (the Home Secretary) both intervened on the eve of the National Society's meeting, the former to try to persuade the Church to adopt the opposite view to Gorst's, the latter requesting them to be 'prudent in their desires'. The Society opted for both possibilities, however, pressing for state aid in the form of a *per capita* sum of six shillings for all elementary schools plus rate aid for voluntary schools located in school board districts. The subsequent joint Convocation of Canterbury and York, presided over by the Archbishop of York but greatly influenced by the Archbishop of Canterbury designate, Temple, voted unanimously in favour of the same approach, having accepted Temple's plea of the necessity for a united front in facing the government with its demands. Even while these demands were being formulated, Balfour had already started work on a new Bill.

In the early stages of his preparations on the Bill Balfour had received some advice from Edward Talbot, the Bishop of Rochester, to

> face the points to be met, determine on a solution, refuse pro-posals which are not solutions; and then having your Bill well in hand use your power as Leader, and the additional force lent by the fact that Gorst is not a Cabinet Minister, to fight it strongly and steadily through.[71]

Balfour was to follow Talbot's exhortations and, in a confidential reply to a letter from Cranborne advocating rate aid for voluntary schools, Balfour made it quite clear that although he was sympathetic to the idea he thought it would be difficult to gain both Cabinet and Commons approval for it. The problem was the thorny issue of public representation on the managing bodies of voluntary schools in receipt of public moneys, and Balfour was convinced that 'if we plunge into this bottomless subject, we shall get thoroughly bogged'. He was concentrating, instead, upon the production of a measure containing the four-shilling grant from the withdrawn Bill, and already had a draft prepared by Jenkyns. He was willing to let his cousin see it but warned him: 'The Education Department know nothing of my proposals as yet'.[72] This reflected Balfour's unwillingness to follow the additional advice he had been given by Talbot concerning Gorst:

> . . . tho' he does not care much for our Church views in themselves, [he] does see the whole position pretty well, and would like to deal with it in a broad and vigorous way. It would be a great thing if you could come into close personal accord with him.[73]

Instead, he told Devonshire that Gorst's handling of another education bill was unacceptable.

Devonshire's response was to try to protect Gorst's career, informing Salisbury that he would 'be very sorry to suggest any change which would injure his political prospects', but, if a new government position could be found for him, then he was quite content to have a new Vice President, suggesting as possible replacements the Liberal Unionists Hobhouse or Wodehouse.[74] Salisbury was unwilling to agree to any transfer of Gorst, however, and at the first Cabinet meeting to consider the Bill in November it was agreed that Balfour would be responsible for it and that it would be one of the first Bills of the new session. Devonshire informed Gorst of this, adding that he (Gorst) would not 'be held responsible for its deficiencies' and, to sweeten the blow, asked him instead 'to prepare and take charge of a Secondary Education Bill'.[75] Gorst, obviously piqued by this exclusion, could not resist the chance of including in his address to the Metropolitan Division of the National Union a few days later the view that the government 'stood greatly in need of . . . guidance and information' on the education issue. *The Times* commented acidly that Gorst's own conduct could have been improved 'by a clearer perception of what is wanted by those who are interested in the preservation of voluntary schools' and went on to remark that although he was the Vice President 'he is not a member of the Cabinet, and has, therefore, to speak with marked reserve'.[76] Balfour thus appeared to be well on the way to achieving a free hand in the shaping of the legislation to redeem his election and United Club speech promises.

The draft proposals Balfour had mentioned to Cranborne intended that the Bill should provide relief for the voluntary schools only, thereby excluding the possibility 'of moving a vast number of amendments which a Bill of more extended scope might permit, and even justify'.[77] In addition to a special aid grant of four shillings, Balfour proposed the abolition of both the 17s 6d limit and the rating of voluntary schools. The only problem lay, therefore, with the distribution of the grant. While this would be under the supervision of the Education Department, he advocated the grouping of schools into federations 'by which their varying needs may be most successfully supplied out of the common funds which are to be fed from the special aid grant'.[78] Control of the federations would be a matter for their respective religious bodies.

Devonshire's response was to make clear his concerns about the nature of the measure, contending that the manner in which the Bill was presented to Parliament was of equal importance to the actual contents of the Bill, and he took care to emphasise his belief that it had to be presented only as a temporary measure. He noted that although the supporters of school boards had definite views about the future of elementary education, the country as a whole did not and was 'hopelessly divided, or indifferent' as to how the voluntary schools should be preserved. Such a state of affairs meant, he believed, that the Bill should only provide provisional relief and not attempt to formulate any permanent educational principle. The latter could only be achieved when 'the constituencies' were in a position to decide finally whether the schools were 'to be permanently maintained, and on what conditions'. While his specific proposals for the provision of relief were very similar to those of Balfour's original draft, he differed in that he proposed associations of schools to which the grant would be paid as well as postulating a grant to help the poor school boards.[79] Balfour countered by arguing that he had excluded consideration of the school boards on the basis of the Cabinet's earlier agreement to deal with educational policy 'not in one but in several Bills'. The treatment of the voluntary schools alone, he argued, 'forms a natural and convenient fragment of that policy'.[80] Chamberlain was not convinced, however, by any of Balfour's arguments and sent Salisbury a copy of his own proposals the day after the Cabinet meeting.

Like Devonshire he was in favour of a grant for both poor voluntary and board schools but preferred distribution to the voluntary schools to be by the Education Department, based upon the recommendations of the inspectorate. He rejected the concept of associations/federations as well as Balfour's attempt to limit the Bill solely to the relief of the voluntary schools. To this end he advocated the administration of secondary and technical education being placed in the hands of the county and county borough councils while the schools boards were 'strictly confined' to elementary education.[81]

Balfour acknowledged Chamberlain's objection to associations/federations at the next Cabinet meeting, observing that the concept appeared to have 'too ecclesiastical a flavour' for some of them. But he was not prepared to jettison the concept, worried that the Department's involvement could lead to an imbalance in the awarding of the grant to different denominations. He advocated the Department being responsible, instead, for planning the division of the country into areas suitable in size for the establishment of associations of voluntary schools, and also for distributing the grant to the associations. The associations were to remain responsible, however, for the allocation of the individual grants to schools within that organisation, albeit being under the jurisdiction of divisional controlling bodies made up of equal numbers of representatives from the schools and the Inspectorate. But this did not satisfy Devonshire who wanted greater public control of the associations/federations, citing as one reason the growing concern within the coalition about the role of these bodies in the spending of public funds. Balfour subsequently received confirmation of Devonshire's view from his cousin Lord Hugh Cecil, who revealed that the evidence from Lancashire, London, the West country and the Midlands pointed to considerable opposition to rate aid for voluntary schools. Relaying this information to his uncle, Balfour added that he could not detect any feeling of support likely to ensure the passage of a rate aid bill through the House.[82] But as the problems grew, so too did Salisbury's uneasiness about the likely fate of the Bill, and he felt constrained to lay his objections before Balfour.

He acknowledged the impossibility of rate aid, given not only Chamberlain and Devonshire's opposition but also that of the party. He also accepted that there would have to be a collective rather than an individual allocation of the grant but felt none the less that, as framed, the Bill did not meet the needs of the people for whom it was intended, and would not relieve the 'intolerable strain'. There were, he believed, three major groups jockeying for mastery of the education system – the economists, the religionists and the educationists. While the religionists played a crucial role in the general election, if the Bill was passed dominance would rest with the educationists, and in particular the Education Department since it would determine the conditions under which the grant would be given. This disturbed him, for it was staffed by educationists:

> Now we know from Acland's brief reign that their demands are practically unlimited . . . and there is no apparent ground for believing that if the demands of today were satisfied, a new or more costly ideal . . . would not speedily spring up . . . .The educationist is one of the daughters of the horse leech: and if you let him [*sic*] suck according to his will he will soon have swallowed the slender increase of sustenance you are now tendering to the voluntary schools.[83]

The remedy he proposed was the use of as simple a scheme of distribution as possible, not involving the inspectorate yet ensuring that the local associations had an 'absolute veto on any conditions'.

Balfour concurred with his uncle's estimate of educationists but pointed out that the inclusion of the inspectorate had arisen from the objections raised by Chamberlain as well as Salisbury's low estimation of the Church's ability to administer the associations. Although the Education Department did not want to be involved in the associations the Church was insistent that it be involved. He took care to stress also that the voluntary schools suffering most under the 'intolerable strain' were the urban ones, and their problems had arisen partly from the effects of the implementation of the 1891 Education Act – a measure which Salisbury had played a major role in formulating. While he was able to refute Salisbury's points, Balfour was by now becoming somewhat disheartened by his task, confiding to Lady Elcho that he was 'oppressed at this moment with many cares, the lightest of them being the total impossibility of devising a generally acceptable Education Bill. I have expended treasures of ingenuity on this most thankless task.'[84] His problems were to be increased, moreover, as a result of Salisbury's next move which was the presentation of more formal objections to the Bill framed within a long memorandum prepared for the next Cabinet meeting.

Highlighting the point that the Bill's original purpose had been to provide for schools on the basis of their needs rather than because of their performances, Salisbury reiterated his strong objections to both its contents and structure; the latter because most of the contentious proposals were to be included in a Departmental Minute rather than the Bill. His objection to the contents of the Bill centred on the fact that it did not 'put the relief of poverty' as its avowed aim, being concerned instead with improving the efficiency of voluntary schools in the hope that this would be sufficient to attract more pupils to these schools and, because of the financial consequences of such a migration, thereby relieve the strain on them. What was required, he argued, was that the Bill should include a definition of poverty so as to help ensure an efficient distribution of the special aid grant. He was highly critical also of the proposals relating to the associations, not least because he felt that the Bill's wording left the creation of such bodies to be formed by 'spontaneous generation'. His final objection was reserved for the potential powers of the Divisional Committees to be formed from the Associations and Department representatives. He estimated that these powers would so deter voluntary school managers from surrendering their independence that less than half of them would be willing to join the associations. Consequently, the difficulties before them appeared to him to be of 'formidable magnitude'.[85] There were other points troubling Salisbury which he did not, wisely, cite:

> In our house we were all for including the *poor* school boards in the money grant. But I think the Educationists are going too fast in the great towns – London of course especially – . . . . At present as far as I understand the national system is only one for elementary education and should not be carried beyond it – Why should we pay for London boys learning the piano and have country boys with only an imperfect knowledge of the three Rs if we can screw up enough money even to pay for that – The whole thing seems to me to be greatly a schoolmasters question and I am sure the more that very pushful class is kept in order, the better.[86]

Balfour's rebuttal of his uncle's and Chamberlain's views was ready a week later and his memorandum was an elegant demolition of them as a result of demonstrating the practical difficulties that would face the Department and the Education Minister should their clauses be accepted, not least being the fact that schools would have to be virtually bankrupt in order to qualify for any assistance under the required definition of poverty. As he noted, 'I do not think it would be easy to devise a plan for more effectively putting a premium both on bad management and on bad education'.[87] After reiterating the reasons for maintaining his own proposals Balfour commented that Salisbury's estimate regarding managers agreeing to come under the associations was unduly pessimistic, and he preferred to opt instead for a figure closer to 90 per cent. He continued to reject any inclusion of aid to poor school boards in the Bill, despite 'a considerable body of opinion' being in favour of it, arguing that such an inclusion would render the Bill subject 'to discussions and amendments on all sorts of miscellaneous subjects' and thus lead to a possible repetition of the fate of the 1896 Bill. His final statement, 'I very distinctly prefer the policy of dealing with the relief to Voluntary schools alone', left the Cabinet in no uncertainty as to his feelings on the Bill. This was sufficient to ensure that the Bill retained its restricted aims although the nature of the aid to be provided was not resolved.

Chamberlain and White Ridley remained opposed to rate relief being provided by legislation and wanted to see what could be achieved by a government subvention. When Balfour tried to meet their objections he discovered that very little information actually existed in the Department about the rating of schools and it would have to be collected 'piecemeal as best we can from Inspectors and Local Authorities'.[88] A week later, however, Kekewich was able to produce a report collated from these and other sources. Furthermore, with the removal of any form of rate aid to the voluntary schools, Devonshire felt able to support Balfour's draft of the Bill, although he had to confess that it was so long since the last Cabinet meeting on the measure that he could not recall many of the decisions made.[89] Two days later Salisbury was able to inform the Queen that the Bill was almost ready, being 'short and simple, and raises few difficult questions'.[90]

Introduced to the House on 1 February, the three-clause Bill now promised a five-shilling per head subvention to the voluntary schools in addition to relief from rating and the abolition of the 17s 6d limit. Balfour revealed that the Bill would be subject to the process of closure in the Committee Stage, a disclosure which greatly annoyed the Opposition. This limitation also meant that the only really uncontrollable variable that remained as far as the passage of the measure was concerned was Gorst, especially as he had caused quite a stir with the publication of two articles on education a few months earlier. In the first he had claimed that

> the chief obstacles to the progress of education in England are party spirit and religious intolerance . . . . English statesmen will postpone reform indefinitely if they can see their way to secure a party advantage thereby.[91]

His advocacy of rate aid for voluntary schools, with the concomitant of public control over its expenditure, in his second article led to one observation that 'whatever breath has been left in the high and dry old Tories after they have read his American manifesto, will be taken away by this'.[92] Not surprisingly then, Kekewich's comment to Balfour that Gorst had expressed a wish to know the Bill's contents as soon as possible 'as he would of course have to sit on the Front Bench and give all the support he could' may have brought a chill to Balfour who could not be sure, given Gorst's articles, as to the form this support would take.[93]

Gorst, in fact, remained true to his word, his contribution during the Second Reading being short and, in general, supportive of the Bill. At the same time, he could not resist the temptation to fire a few salvoes in the direction of his Front Bench colleagues. He adopted the position of that of the official representative of the Committee of Council on Education in the House, thereby distancing himself from Balfour; a point which he reinforced later in his speech:

> I am quite certain that the Government – I do not know that I have a right to speak for my right hon. Friend the First Lord of the Treasury, who is not here at present – [Opposition ironical laughter] – but I can speak as far as the Committee of Council is concerned – any Amendment which really goes to secure that this State aid grant shall be used really for the purpose of promoting and improving the education of the country will be welcomed by the Government.[94]

While he would have preferred the Bill to cover both necessitous voluntary and board schools Gorst hoped that the provision of the grant would result in improvements to both the teaching materials available in the schools and to the salaries of the teachers. His query about the efficiency of 'poorly-fed and poorly-clad' men and women in exercising 'one of the most important functions to society' was received sympathetically by the House and led John Morley to observe that the difference between Gorst's and Balfour's approach to education was that of the difference between an expert and an amateur.[95] These points notwithstanding, the application of closure ensured that the Bill reached the Statute Book and the politically contentious topic of financial aid for the voluntary schools appeared to have been disposed of. For Salisbury and Balfour the promise made at the election had at last been fulfilled, and to their satisfaction, as well as Lady Salisbury's:

> . . . I am glad the Education Bill is over! Arthur seems to have

kept his men well together this year, through all his rather high handed proceedings! Nothing succeeds like success![96]

But Gorst and Devonshire remained outside the happy Salisburian circle, not least because of the Bill.

During the passage of the Bill Sir Henry Campbell-Bannerman had highlighted the magnitude of Gorst's exclusion and alienation:

> They could not speak of the Vice President because they did not know where to find him, either in a physical or in a moral sense. [Laughter.] He was now here and now there – now in one part of the House and now in another; now writing in one magazine or in another, but never, until last night, taking any part in the explanation of this Bill to the House. ['Hear, hear!'] He had become, in fact, a sort of parliamentary will-o'-the-wisp. [Laughter.][97]

Gorst tended to shrug off such criticism, telling Beatrice Webb instead:

> The newspapers say this is a humiliation for me, the Education Bill. But it's the Duke [of Devonshire] who is humiliated. . . . The Duke is quite as much against this Bill as I am. He told the Cabinet so: and when they insisted he shrugged his shoulders![98]

None the less, Gorst had reached the low point in his tenure of the Vice Presidency and he was to confess to Kekewich that, apart from their friendship, his position in the Education Department

> would be quite intolerable. Besides the difficulty of conducting part of the affairs of a Department, in which you have no power, . . . there is the ever present consciousness of being surrounded by Balfour's spies, who as the Psalmist says "lay wait for my soul".[99]

Devonshire's position was, in some respects, little better, having been effectively usurped by Balfour for the second time in the planning of an Education Bill. But with the Bill passed most of the Cabinet were relieved to abandon any remaining educational policy issues to Devonshire. The experiences of the previous year had made Devonshire appraise Gorst's preoccupation with decentralisation issues although he was still prepared to support his Vice President. Both men thus embarked in 1897 on campaigns which were to lead to changes to the nation's education system, changes which Salisbury, Balfour and the rest of the Cabinet could not possibly have foreshadowed. In achieving them they were to be aided by a junior Department staff member who, as a result, would soon come to dominate educational policy formulation. Robert Morant's ascent to power was about to begin.

NOTES

1. G. Sutherland, *Policy-Making in Elementary Education 1870–1895* (1973), p. 1.
2. *School Board Chronicle*, 53 (26 Jan. 1895), p. 95.
3. J.R. Fairhurst, 'Some Aspects of the Relationship between Education, Politics and Religion from 1895–1906', unpublished D.Phil thesis, University of Oxford, 1974, p. 36.
4. A.I. Taylor, 'The Church Party and Popular Education 1893–1902', unpublished D.Phil thesis, University of Cambridge, 1981, p. 110.
5. *School Board Chronicle*, 53 (30 March 1895), p. 352.
6. *The Times*, 13 June 1895.
7. Ibid., 9 July 1895.
8. Lord Cranborne to A.J. Balfour, 20 Aug. 1895; A.J. Balfour to Lord Cranborne, 22 Aug. 1895, *The Times*, 20 Sept. 1895.
9. Salisbury Papers (4M), S(4) 19/172, A.J. Balfour to Lord Cranborne, 12 Sept. 1895: A.I. Taylor, op. cit., p. 41.
10. Kekewich Papers, Duke of Devonshire to Sir G.W. Kekewich, 7 Oct. 1895; Sadler Papers, MS Eng misc c.550, fo.25, Sir G.W. Kekewich to M.E. Sadler, 13 Nov. 1895.
11. In addition to Devonshire and Gorst the members of the committee were Salisbury, Balfour and Cross. See Sandars Papers, MS Eng. hist c.727, fos.74–6, S.K. McDonnel to A.J. Balfour, 7 Nov. 1895.
12. Sadler Papers, MS Eng misc c.550, fos.16–17, R.L. Morant to M.E. Sadler, 19 Nov. 1895.
13. Ibid., fo.18, R.L. Morant to M.E. Sadler, 23 Nov. 1895.
14. Bryce Papers, UB 74/N.1., W.N. Bruce to J. Bryce, 3 January 1895. The date should be 1896 but Bruce had clearly forgotten the change to the new year.
15. *The Times*, 21 Oct. 1895.
16. Bryce Papers, UB 74/N.1., W.N. Bruce to J. Bryce, 3 Jan. 1895.
17. *The Times*, 26 Nov. 1895.
18. Archbishop E.W. Benson Papers, 173, fos.194–5, Archbishop of York to E.W. Benson, 16 Oct. 1895.
19. Ibid., fos.217–18, J.S. Brownrigg to E.W. Benson, 29 Oct. 1895.
20. *The Times*, 16 Nov. 1895.
21. BP Add MS 49757, fos.14–25, Lord Cranborne to A.J. Balfour, 28 October 1895.
22. Craik's role is particularly interesting in that he appears to have been a poacher turned gamekeeper, having in 1890 been involved by Kekewich in supporting the Department's views against those of Salisbury. Lord Carlingford's assessment of him as a 'clever, disagreeable, intriguing man' seems to have been justified: see Lord Carlingford's *Journal*, 17 June 1885, cited in Sutherland, op. cit., p. 24.
23. BP Add MS 49851, fo.17, H. Craik to A.J. Balfour, 25 Jan. 1896.
24. BP Add MS 49781, fos.20–30, B. Mallet to A.J. Balfour, 18 Nov. 1895.
25. BP Add MS 49781, fo.33, B. Mallet to A.J. Balfour, 22 Nov. 1895.
26. *Annual Register* (Nov. 1895), pp. 196–7.

27. B. Holland, *Life of the Duke of Devonshire, 1833–1908* (1911), II, p. 272.
28. A.C. Benson, *The Life of Edward White Benson, sometime Archbishop of Canterbury* (1900), II, pp. 627–8.
29. Sadler Papers, MS Eng misc c.550, fo.128, G.W. Kekewich to M.E. Sadler, 20 Nov. 1895.
30. Ibid., fo.17, G.W. Kekewich to M.E. Sadler, 30 Nov. 1895.
31. BP Add MS 49690, fo.124, A.J. Balfour to Lord Salisbury, 6 Dec. 1895.
32. BP Add MS 49791, fo.24, 'Memorandum by Sir J. Gorst'. The date of February 1896 assigned by the British Library to this document is incorrect; it should be 5 December 1895.
33. BP Add MS 49781, fos.42–55, Draft Education Bill, 20 Dec. 1895.
34. Bryce Papers, UB 74/N.1., W.N. Bruce to J. Bryce, 1 Jan. 1896.
35. Salisbury Papers (3M), Duke of Devonshire to Lord Salisbury, 17 Dec.1895.
36. Hicks Beach Papers, D2455 PCC/86, J. Chamberlain to Sir M.E. Hicks Beach, 20 July 1895.
37. Devonshire Papers, 340.2670, J. Chamberlain to Duke of Devonshire, 15 Dec. 1895.
38. Ibid.; BP Add MS 49773, fos.86–8, J. Chamberlain, 'Memorandum on Draft Scheme for an Education Bill', 16 Dec. 1895.
39. BP Add MS 49781, fo.57., A.J. Balfour to B. Mallet, 21 Dec. 1895.
40. BP Add MS 49791, fo.10., 'Cabinet memorandum by Sir J. Gorst'.
41. BP Add MS 49690, fo.137, Lord Salisbury to A.J. Balfour, 27 Dec. 1895.
42. BP Add MS 49851, fo.17, H. Craik to A.J. Balfour, 25 Jan. 1896.
43. BP Add MS 49781, fo.105, H. Craik, 'Criticism of the general principle of the Bill', 12 Feb. 1896.
44. BP Add MS 49791, fos.11–13., Sir J. Gorst, Memorandum, 12 Feb. 1896.
45. BP Add MS 49834, fo.260, A.J. Balfour to Lord Salisbury, 26 Jan. 1896.
46. BP Add MS 49781, fos.155–6, H. Craik to B. Mallet, [late] Feb. 1896.
47. BP Add MS 49851, fos.32–3, Sir H. Jenkyns to J.S. Sandars, 17 Feb. 1896; BP Add MS 49781, fo.123, Sir H. Jenkyns to B. Mallet, 20 Feb. 1896; see also fo.121, G.W. Kekewich to B. Mallet, 20 Feb. 1896.
48. BP Add MS 49769, fo.82, Duke of Devonshire to A.J. Balfour, 19 March 1896; Add MS 49781, fos.231–4, 'Minute on Education Bill', 19 March 1896.
49. *Revue Pédagogique*, May 1896, p. 422; Hamilton Papers, Add MS 48669, fo.14, *Diary*, 31 March 1896.
50. Bryce Papers, UB 21, A.M. Fairbairn to J. Bryce, 3 May 1896.
51. *4 PD*, 40, c.569, 5 May 1896.
52. Ibid., c.577, 5 May 1896.
53. BP Add MS 49769, fos.89–93, A. Pye-Smith to A.J. Balfour, nd; See also fos.84–8, J. Boraston, 'Memorandum on the Education Bill 1896', 22 [?Oct.] 1896.
54. Sadler Papers, MS Eng misc c.551, fo.26, M.E. Sadler, 'Memorandum on the amendments to the Education Bill', 11 June 1896.
55. Harcourt Papers, WVH 7/6–8, Sir W. Harcourt to Lady Harcourt, 16 June 1896.
56. *Revue Pédagogique*, July 1896, p. 40.
57. Hamilton Papers, Add MS 48669, fo.71, *Diary*, 12 June 1896.
58. P. Marsh, *The Discipline of Popular Government: Lord Salisbury's Domestic Statecraft, 1881–1902* (1978), p. 254.
59. M. Sadleir, *Michael Ernest Sadler*, p. 148; C. Mallet, *Herbert Gladstone: A Memoir* (1932), p. 158.
60. *Punch*, CXI, 4 July 1896, p. 11.

61. *Journal of Education*, XVII (July 1896), p. 344.
62. Sadler Papers, MS Eng misc c.204, fo.106, *Diary of Sir M.T. Sadler*, 20 April 1896.
63. *Journal of Education*, XVII, July 1896, p. 343.
64. Sadler Papers, MS Eng misc c.550, fo.249, A.H.D. Acland to M.E. Sadler, 1 Nov. 1896.
65. Hamilton Papers, Add MS 48669, fo.74, *Diary*, 17 June 1896.
66. BP Add MS 49769, fo.87, J. Boraston to J. Chamberlain, 22 Oct. 1896.
67. M. Elcho to A.J. Balfour, 6 June 1896 cited in J. Ridley and C. Percy (eds), *The Letters of Arthur Balfour and Lady Elcho* (1992), pp. 135–136. The cause of this crisis may have been Lady Elcho's confession that her daughter, Mary, born the previous October, had been fathered by Wilfrid Blunt, not Lord Elcho; rather a devastating confession for her to have to make to her lover.
68. Earl of Middleton, *Records and Reactions 1856–1939* (1939), pp. 105–6.
69. BP Add MS 49760, fos.88–96.
70. Barnett Papers, F/BAR/143, S. Barnett to F. Barnett, 11 July 1896.
71. BP Add MS 49789,fos.74–5, E. Talbot to A.J. Balfour, 3 Sept. 1896.
72. BP Add MS 49757, fos.54–60, Lord Cranborne to A.J. Balfour,19 Oct. 1896; fos.61–3, A.J. Balfour to Lord Cranborne, 22 Oct. 1896.
73. BP Add MS 49789, fos.74–5, E. Talbot to A.J. Balfour, 3 Sept. 1896.
74. Salisbury Papers (3M), Duke of Devonshire to Lord Salisbury, 13 Sept.1896.
75. BP Add MS 49769, fo.112, Duke of Devonshire to A.J. Balfour, 7 Nov. 1896.
76. *The Times*, 13 Nov. 1896.
77. PRO CAB 37/43, A.J. Balfour, Memorandum, 10 Oct. 1896.
78. Ibid.
79. PRO CAB 37/43, Duke of Devonshire, Memorandum, 7 Nov. 1896.
80. Ibid., A.J. Balfour, Memorandum, 8 Nov. 1896.
81. Salisbury Papers (3M), J. Chamberlain to Lord Salisbury, 11 Nov. 1896.
82. Ibid., A.J. Balfour to Lord Salisbury, 18 Nov. 1896.
83. BP Add MS 49690, fos.181–2, Lord Salisbury to A.J. Balfour, 22 Nov. 1896.
84. A.J. Balfour to Lady Elcho, 28 Nov. 1896 cited in J. Ridley and C. Percy (eds), op. cit., p. 152.
85. PRO CAB 37/43, Lord Salisbury, 'Memorandum on the Education Bill', 3 Nov. 1896.
86. James Papers, M75/894, Lady Salisbury to H.James, 3 Feb. 1897.
87. PRO CAB 37/43, A.J. Balfour, Memorandum, 7 Dec. 1896.
88. Salisbury Papers (3M), A.J. Balfour to Lord Salisbury, 6 Jan. 1897.
89. BP Add MS 49783, fos.56–7, G.W. Kekewich to A.J. Balfour, 12 Jan. 1897; Add MS 49769, fos.146–7, Duke of Devonshire to A.J. Balfour, 12 Jan. 1897.
90. PRO CAB 41/24/1, Lord Salisbury to Queen Victoria, 14 Jan. 1897.
91. J.E. Gorst, 'Prospects of Education in England', *North American Review*, 163 (Oct. 1896), p. 427.
92. *Review of Reviews*, 14 Nov. 1896, p. 429.
93. BP Add MS 49783, fo.157, G.W. Kekewich to B. Mallet, 12 Jan. 1897.
94. *4 PD*, 46, c.488–9, 15 Feb. 1897.
95. Ibid., 47, c.861, 17 March 1897.
96. James Papers, M45/907, Lady Salisbury to H. James, 28 March 1897.
97. *4 PD*, 46, c.585, 16 Feb. 1897.
98. B. Webb, *Our Partnership* (1948), p. 137.
99. Kekewich Papers, J.E. Gorst to G.W. Kekewich, 1 Jan. 1898.

3

A Swiss model for England?

... though broadly speaking, policy is the concern of Ministers and administration the concern of Civil Servants, policy and administration are, in so large and complicated a service as that of Education, so mixed up that the line between them is very indistinct.[1]

A recurring criticism of the 1896 Bill in the debates both in and out of the House had been of the omission of a unified central government education authority. The Bryce Report had included such a proposal and had advocated that the new body should come under the aegis of a Minister of Education advised by an Education Council, in addition to his permanent officials. The Minister would also be responsible for both elementary and secondary education. Gorst's response during the debates had been to state, correctly, that such a central authority existed already in the Committee of Council on Education, given that it had 'the most perfect jurisdiction over the Education Department and Science and Art Department, and can mould and combine those Departments as it pleases'.[2] But his subsequent cynical refutation of the benefits to be derived from a Minister of Education being a permanent member of the Cabinet minimised the effect of his earlier point. Gorst's advocacy, instead, of the devolution of central authority power to the proposed new LEAs had been seen by many as too radical and had raised the fear, articulated by Asquith for the Opposition, that it would produce 'a spectral and disembodied' central authority.[3]

With the drafting of the Voluntary Schools Bill almost completed by the beginning of 1897, Devonshire used the opportunity presented by his having to give an after-dinner speech to the Drapers' Company to signal his views about future education policy. He acknowledged the need for there to be efficient local education authorities, being careful to cite the Bryce Report's recommendations as supporting evidence, but stated that any future developments should be accompanied by a reorganisation of the central government education authorities. His ideas were to bear fruit some two and a half years later but what he could not have envisaged in 1897 was the impact that the intertwined yet separate activities of Sadler and Gorst were to have upon them. Sadler went so far as to state, once the Board of Education Bill was passed in 1899, that he was thankful

> ... that we were able to fight our fight last summer. We stopped much which, if done, would have caused grave mischief, and, if it hadn't been for you, there would have been no Board of Education Act. As long as we live, we shall have the satisfaction of knowing that we laid some of the chief foundations. It is certain that no one but ourselves will ever know . . . what was involved in it all, and why it was such a great struggle and what we were empowered to do for England. But, in big things like this, privacy is far best.[4]

It was Gorst's activities immediately following the withdrawal of the 1896 Education Bill, however, that initiated the struggle Sadler referred to, and the key factors in this were the Department of Science and Art and the nation's higher grade schools.

In the summer of 1896 Sir John Donnelly, the Permanent Secretary of the Department of Science and Art, gave vent to his irritation about the continued criticism in the press of his Department's art courses and had written to Devonshire suggesting the establishment of a committee of distinguished artists to examine, and where necessary, to make recommendations about the courses. Aware of Gorst's despondency over the recent demise of the Education Bill, Devonshire welcomed his offer to look into this problem and 'other questions relating to Science and Art Instruction' during the parliamentary recess.[5] The outcome was the establishment a few months later of a committee consisting not of distinguished artists but of a group of three ex-Bryce commissioners, Professor Richard Jebb, Sir Henry Roscoe and Mrs Eleanor Sidgwick, together with members of the Department, Treasury and the Irish National Gallery as well as Lord Balfour of Burleigh. Gorst chaired their investigations into the whole issue of art and science courses funded by the Department, an investigation started in October and completed by the following April. A visit by Gorst to Toynbee Hall just after the committee had started work left Canon Barnett observing that the task of the 'strong' committee was 'to overhaul South Kensington'. At the same time, aware of the sensation being caused by the frank appraisal of the nation's education system contained in Gorst's latest article, Barnett could not help feeling that Gorst was 'playing with edged tools'.[6]

If the committee's formation had passed largely unremarked, the release of their report was the reverse with considerable public attention being focused on it. In the course of their work the committee had revised the Department's regulations contained within its annual Directory and had inserted a new clause based upon a recommendation of the Bryce Report. Clause VII enabled county and county borough councils 'possessing an organisation for the promotion of secondary education' to apply to the Department for control of the science and art instruction within their areas, the aim being to curtail the overlapping in secondary education provision. The only new schools or classes that would be recognised henceforth by the Department for funding would be those which came under the aegis of these local authorities.[7] To all intents and purposes, therefore, implementation of the clause would permit the creation of local authorities for secondary education. This possibility was unpalatable to the school boards, however, for it possessed the potential to hamper the development of their higher grade schools and this, in turn, would undermine any claim that they, the boards, might have to be considered as local education authorities for both elementary and secondary education. The higher grade schools thus became a pivotal point in the struggle over policy formulation.

Gorst made it clear after the publication of the 1897 Directory that he hoped 'concert and union' would prevail between school boards and council committees in the formation of the new authorities, rather than 'discord and rivalry'.[8] He had hoped that any new local education authorities could be established by enlisting local knowledge and zeal, for one result of this could be the creation of schools directly responsive to community needs. He was consistently conciliatory, therefore, in his approach to the school boards and the work of their higher grade schools and the *School Board Chronicle* noted with some surprise that the Science and Art Department was following Gorst's directions, requiring in county boroughs 'not only the consent but association of the School Board' in the formation of the new Clause VII authorities. Even the *Spectator* felt obliged to note that Gorst was 'more disposed to favour the machinery of School Boards than most of his colleagues'.[9]

This approach notwithstanding, Gorst was inclined towards the county and county borough councils as the basis of any future LEAs, partly because he felt that the school boards' *ad hoc* basis prevented the effective formulation of a more coherent and comprehensive community policy by the main local government bodies. The other reason for his preference was a belief that the only effective local government bodies were those that had absolute command of local finance, for with this, he argued, came not only full responsibility to ratepayers but also the strength necessary to resist central government, and it was this that *ad hoc* bodies lacked. The only bodies involved in local education provision that met all his criteria were the county and county borough councils and Gorst recognised the wider potential these bodies offered as far as achievement of his ultimate goal was concerned – the establishment of 'one sole authority responsible to the people and possessing its confidence which would arrange the whole of the education, elementary and secondary'.[10] What Gorst found particularly attractive about the operations of the county and county borough councils under the Technical Instruction Act was that the fairly vague wording of the Act had enabled councils to be virtually autonomous since it was 'not directed by Act of Parliament what to do, but left to find what to do for itself'.[11] While he acknowledged that there had to be some central government agency in any national system of education, he believed its role should be minimal as far as policy formulation was concerned since such an authority

> . . . could make no distinction between one school and another. They could only distribute any Parliamentary grant to all alike. They could make a great waste of public money by giving it to some schools that did not want it, while they would be withholding it from some schools that required it, and that would fail to ensure efficiency.[12]

And it must be noted that Gorst's choice for the future LEAs also reflected his scepticism about the quality of the majority of school board personnel, at both management and teaching levels. His scepticism was to become tainted with hostility when it became clear that the boards were unwilling to participate in his scheme and constantly obstructed his plans; a hostility that was reciprocated.

For Sadler with his close ties with the universities and established secondary schools there were several problems associated with Gorst's Clause VII policy. If it was successful one possible consequence might be a smudging of the hitherto relatively distinct educational and social demarcation between elementary and secondary schools, especially if the school boards accepted Gorst's advocacy of their involvement in the new authorities. Furthermore, the institution and development of Clause VII authorities would not only strengthen the powers of the county and county borough councils but reinforce the control exerted by the Science and Art Department over secondary education. This latter state of affairs was already deplored by some secondary schools because of the bias it had produced in their curriculum as a consequence of the Department's regulations on funding. Compounding this situation was Gorst's known support for the South Kensington Department and its officials, a feeling which had strengthened after the failure of the 1896 Bill since all the official advice in the planning of that measure had come from the Education Department. The development and control of secondary education thus appeared to be moving increasingly towards a position in which the role of the established secondary schools would be minimalised and accompanied by a possible loss of their 'freedom, elasticity and variety' of action, which Bryce had claimed should be maintained. This state of affairs was unsatisfactory not only for Sadler but also for many head teachers of the lesser endowed secondary schools, not least because they regarded the activities of the higher grade schools in secondary education as akin to trespass. Morant was equally worried by these developments, sharing the sentiment that the higher grade schools represented a major threat to certain types of secondary schools.

Morant had publicised his views on these developments in a survey of French higher primary schools in 1897 and in it he was critical of the aspirations of some higher grade schools:

> In how many towns and villages in England is money – hardly earned and with difficulty spared – being unwittingly wasted in giving to a boy either an education which is quite unsuited to his capacities and which will leave him stranded and out of employment at the end of it, or else a base, fraudulent, and spurious imitation of education, which is far worse in its effects upon him than if the lad had gone out immediately to the work of life on leaving the elementary school. Nothing but good can come from the popular realisation of the clear distinction, for instance, between (1) schools intended to give a definite trade apprenticeship (such as the écoles pratiques), and (2) schools intended to give a general educative training in industrial, commercial, or agricultural methods, to pupils who have just left the elementary schools and have at most three years at their disposal, and (3) schools giving true secondary education – whether modern, classical – to scholars whose education is intended to last approximately from 7 to 18 years of age.[13]

Morant's concept of a tripartite system of schools at the post-elementary level not only mirrored, at a general level, the views of the Bryce Report but in their specifics also presaged the system to be postulated in the twentieth century by the Hadow, Spens and Norwood Reports.[14] Equally important was the fact, however, that at the time he wrote this, Morant was aware that the possibility of achieving such a system, incorporating delimitation of the higher grade schools, could arise from a secret conference being held at the Education Department under Kekewich's chairmanship.

The establishment of the conference may have been initiated by a memorial forwarded to Devonshire in the autumn of 1896 from the Incorporated Association of Head Masters, one of whose honorary secretaries was R.P. Scott. Claiming that 'mischief' was one effect of the overlapping between higher grade and secondary schools, the memorial included a plea for the institution of some effective local control of secondary education. Subsequently, representatives from the headmasters' associations of both the secondary and the higher grade schools were invited to attend the conference in May in an attempt to reach a consensus on the roles of their schools. Meeting intermittently until November one participant recorded that as a result of the meetings 'a good many misconceptions on both sides were cleared away'.[15] Although a degree of mutual trust was established by mid-July the meetings were, none the less, often strained, and this reflected the preoccupation of both sides with whether the higher grade schools' 'potentialities and actualities are intended to be curbed or not'.[16] In the event the answer was in the affirmative, for although the Joint Memorandum issued at the end of the conference acknowledged that the two types of school taught similar courses and subjects it also emphasised the differences between the schools and thus established a concept of delimitation. Distinctions were held to exist between the aims and curricula of the two types of school, and these, in turn, were reinforced by 'those broad conditions of school life which lie outside the class-room'.[17] This last point substantiated some data about the clientele of both types of school collected by Sadler and Morant for the conference.

The two men had analysed and presented their findings based on data obtained from 43 higher grade schools in 22 English towns and cities (out of a total available sample of 63 schools in 36 English and Welsh towns and cities) and an equivalent number of secondary schools. Their classification of parental occupations was not unique but appeared to demonstrate conclusively that each type of school had a substantially different social class of clientele (see Table 3.1).

TABLE 3.1
OCCUPATIONS OF PARENTS OF PUPILS AT HIGHER GRADE AND
SECONDARY SCHOOLS IN ENGLAND, 1896-7, GIVEN AS
PERCENTAGES[18]

Occupation of Parents	Higher Grade schools		Secondary schools
	Girls	Boys	Boys
1. Persons of independent means	1.9	1.6	4.9
2. Professional men (eg. doctors, clergy and ministers, lawyers, military and naval officers, architects, etc.)	3.5	3.4	16.9
3. Teachers	1.8	1.3	3.2
4. Manufacturers and whole-sale dealers and merchants (ie heads of firms)	5.2	6.0	17.1
5. Manufacturers and whole-sale dealers and merchants (ie managers)	5.5	4.8	6.0
6. Farmers (not including paid farm labourers)	1.3	1.2	1.8
7. Retail tradesmen, restaurant keepers, etc.	15.9	15.1	15.5
8. Commercial travellers, etc.	4.8	4.1	4.3
9. Salesmen, shop assistants	3.3	2.5	1.7
10. Clerks, bookkeepers, accountants, warehousemen, etc.	9.4	9.4	11.0
11. Subordinate public officials, post and telegraph service, etc.	3.2	3.5	3.1
12. Foremen of industrial concerns, responsible railway service men, etc.	6.3	5.9	2.3
13. Workmen at skilled trades and handicrafts	23.3	26.8	5.8
14. Unskilled workmen, labourers, carmen, etc.	7.8	7.3	1.0
15. Others	6.8	8.8	4.2

For the historian the basis of their classification of parental occupations is fraught with problems, one arising from the fact that contemporary observers appear to have found it difficult to perceive distinct breaks in the class structure at the centre of society although the more well-to-do parents of higher grade school pupils were 'obsessive over socio-economic status', a factor readily appreciated by most pupils:

> Even in a Board School there were social grades. My feeling of inferiority was probably caused by the fact that my boots were of the cheapest kind . . . and that my clothes were made by my mother.[19]

It could also be argued that Sadler and Morant's analysis was constructed in such a way that by disregarding these points the overall effect of their data was to make a definite point which favoured the established secondary schools in terms of the socio-economic composition of their clientele. This notwithstanding, their analysis appears to have been accepted by the conference members, not least the higher grade school headmasters who would have been able to make their own judgments based not only on the running of their schools but also upon the careers taken up by their pupils.

If the higher grade schools enjoyed the support of certain social classes because, as one headmaster claimed, they gave them 'what they want', the careers chosen by, or available to, their pupils tended to demonstrate the pupils' (and/or parents') social aspirations and class, as well as the constraints induced by the standing of these schools in society (see Table 3.2).

TABLE 3.2

CAREERS AND TRAINING UNDERTAKEN IN 1897 AND 1900
(AS PERCENTAGES)[20]

Careers and/or additional training	Higher Grade schools		Secondary schools
	1897	1900	1897
Secondary education	7.3	4.83	17.8
Technical education	1.5	2.55	2.5
University education	0.4	0.81	7.3
Pupil-Teacher	2.7	4.14	1.4
Commercial life, clerks, etc.	37.1	36.08	37.7
Industrial occupations	22.6	29.63	8.7
Small shops, at home, etc.	7.1	5.12	N/A
Errand boys	1.6	3.1	N/A
Other	15.1	13.82	14.7

Significant differences did exist in the careers chosen by higher grade and secondary school pupils; for example, the number of boys becoming clerks or accountants was almost identical for each type of school (and allowing that there could well have been significant social differences within these categories) but three times as many higher grade school pupils became skilled or industrial workers as did secondary school pupils. Furthermore, almost ten times as many secondary school boys passed on to universities or technical institutes as those from higher grade schools. Given that nationally all occupations increased between 1881 and 1911 by 48 per cent, and non-manual occupations by 72 per cent, then the careers chosen by higher grade school pupils reflected to a considerable extent their social class, and the dominance of the working and lower middle classes in the higher grade schools. These career patterns thus tended to reinforce Sadler and Morant's analysis as well as the Bryce Report's view that the higher grade schools' role was training for 'the higher handicrafts, or the commerce of the shop and town'.[21]

This fact was reinforced by the statement made in the Joint Memorandum that the curriculum of the higher grade schools had to bear 'some direct relation to manual and industrial employments', and thus gave a 'high place to immediate utility'.[22] Such a statement effectively ensured that this bias of the higher grade schools' curriculum would remain uppermost in society's mind for, despite the apparent economic needs of the nation, 'the weight of prejudice was heavily against the compatibility of liberal education (increasingly *the* mark of a gentleman) and utility'.[23] At the same time, this bias also meant that the higher grade schools would no longer pose any direct threat to the established secondary schools.

Kekewich's private secretary recalled that as the conference meetings had progressed his superior had become impatient with the constant consultation with R.D. Swallow and R.P. Scott, the two secretaries of the IAHM brought in by Sadler, and he had decided to 'cultivate his roses'. Since Sadler and Morant were acting as secretaries to the conference, Kekewich's action undoubtedly helped to strengthen their influence over the outcome of the conference.[24] The subsequent acceptance of the Joint Memorandum by the annual meetings of both headmasters' associations appeared to mark the achievement of a *modus vivendi* on higher grade schools, and a definite prescription of their educational and social roles, 'by making them give up trying to be what they cannot, and also what they are not required to be'.[25] Professor Richard Jebb privately described the conference memorandum as the 'Delimitation Memorandum' and believed that it represented a great achievement.[26] The possibility of any further invasion of 'true' – that is, liberal – secondary education by the higher grade schools appeared to have been forestalled and the rights of each class of English society to its particular species of secondary education proscribed. Such a state of affairs was not to be permanent, however, owing to Devonshire's initiation of new educational policy at the beginning of 1898 as well as developments arising from Gorst's Clause VII policy.

During the course of the Department conference Jebb had had a meeting with Kekewich at the Athenaeum Club to discuss education matters, including the contents of an Education Bill creating new local authorities for secondary education and intended to reinforce the change introduced by Clause VII. Kekewich felt that the Bill had by then taken on a 'workmanlike shape' and he believed that overall it was good although the problems which had bedevilled the proposed education authorities in the 1896 Bill, that is the role, if any, to be played by municipal authorities, still remained. This notwithstanding, Kekewich was in favour of the measure being allowed to lie on the table in the House during the current Session so as to permit discussion during the recess, and thus provide a better chance for success on its introduction in the following (1898) Session. Jebb noted that 'S[adler]'s Delimitation scheme' could not be incorporated into the Bill as a secondary school could only be defined, for all practical purposes, as a 'school in which the greater part of the education given is higher than elementary'. Therefore, he observed, 'a rigid line would be unworkable'.[27] Jebb's comment revealed the gap between the educational accord being forged at the Department conference and the exigencies of politics but another major obstacle in the path of achieving reform in secondary education was Devonshire's uncertainty about the new Bill, partly owing to the strong opposition to Kekewich's views from other government advisers, including Sir Hugh Jenkyns. Seven months were to pass before Devonshire decided to raise the topic of a new Education Bill with the Cabinet and even then, from Sadler's and Morant's perspective, the outlook was not hopeful.

In a Cabinet memorandum presented in late January 1898, Devonshire acknowledged that the 1896 Bill's failure to provide for a central education authority while proposing new LEAs was 'not only a tactical mistake, but also a mistake in principle'.[28] He also expressed his doubts as to whether, in the event of that Bill having been passed and the new LEAs established, the requisite 'authoritative guidance or advice' could have been provided by the existent, disparate central education authorities especially as the central bodies, 'have never, so far as I know, been accustomed to look at educational problems as a whole, or to work together for the co-ordination of educational agencies'.[29] Considering the problems currently bedevilling secondary education, plus the fact that Parliament was providing not less than one million pounds annually in support of what was essentially a malfunctioning system, Devonshire found it 'indefensible' that there had never been policy formulation on the aims or content for either this or elementary education by any previous President or Vice President. As a solution he proposed the implementation of the relevant Bryce Report recommendations including the creation of a Minister of Education of Cabinet rank, overseeing a unified central education authority and advised by an education council. If this could be achieved in such a way as to inspire public confidence then, he believed, the path would be clear for the necessary rationalisation of local educational administration, although this phase would have to be achieved by leading rather than driving existing local education authorities towards acceptance of the necessity for such a change.

Devonshire envisaged that the creation of a new central Board of Education from the merger of the three existent central education authorities – the Education Department, the Science and Art Department and the Charity Commissioners – would be accompanied by a simple transfer of their powers to the new body by an Order-in-Council. There appears to have been little dissent within Cabinet to this proposal but the subsequent statement in the Queen's Speech for dealing with secondary education was rather tenuous, and noted that the Bill's proposals would be only laid before the House 'in case the time at your disposal should permit you to proceed with them'. A conversation between Jebb and Kekewich revealed just how tenuous the Cabinet's acceptance of Devonshire's proposal was:

> The new scheme is tentative – an experiment, and is framed so as to avoid the risk of friction at the start. It will be introduced after Easter, but when is unknown. The Government presumably do not care very much about passing it this year. Next year, if it does not pass this year, it will probably be reintroduced.[30]

Morant, on the other hand, was horrified to hear rumours that the government's policy also included making 'Clause vii statutory & for Secondary . . . unless strong reason be shown to the contrary' and he asked Sadler, 'if this be *really* the project', if he could not get the Head Masters' Conference 'on to a protest or a suggestion of what ought to be done'.[31] Events were to prove this unnecessary, for when Devonshire had to respond to repeated questions from Lord Norton in the House of Lords about the date of introduction of the new measure he had continually to postpone making an announcement due to 'some points of difficulty'. These difficulties derived mainly from the proposed transfer of the Charity Commission's powers to the new Board, but also from the creation of the Education Council.

Compared with the lineage of both the Education Department and the Department of Science and Art that of the Charity Commission was extensive, its origins being traceable to the mediaeval period, although the Board of Charity Commissioners which was responsible for educational endowments, among other charities, had only been established in 1853. Vested with certain judicial powers, the independence of the Commission from public control had, over time, created sufficient adverse comment to ensure that in the 14 years up to 1898 it had been the subject of seven Parliamentary investigations. That it was not a popular body was quite clear and the reasons for this had been enunciated by James Bryce in 1883: 'It was so to speak hidden away in a dark corner. It was not amenable to public opinion; and there were no means of ascertaining what it did, or what it did not do, or what were the grounds of its action.'[32] When, in 1893, a departmental committee of the Treasury, in the course of scrutinising the rationale for the Commission's continued existence, had come to examine the Commission's likely role should there be some future central authority for secondary education they had been unwilling to accept it as a possible candidate. At the same time, they were not prepared to place the Commission under the aegis of a Minister of Education. Such an arrangement, they concluded, would not only contradict the original policy concerning the Commission's role *vis-à-vis* endowed secondary schools but would also 'be open to all the disadvantages attending the union of judicial and administrative functions'.[33] And while the Bryce Commission had accepted the need for a state central authority for secondary education to control the endowments affecting secondary schools, they had shied away from stating explicitly how the necessary transfer could be made given the judicial component of the Commission's work. By the time of his second Cabinet memorandum on the creation of a Board of Education, Devonshire and Courtenay Ilbert, the Assistant Parliamentary Counsel, had come to appreciate the magnitude of this particular problem and the section of the memorandum dealing with the Charity Commissioners now limited the important transfer to 'some of the powers now exercised . . . in regard to education' although stipulating that the powers the Commissioners retained would be either in co-operation with, or as agents of, the Board.[34]

Devonshire's next memorandum indicated that the problems related to the transfer remained unsolved and, consequently, the wisdom of Parliament would be sought on the latest proposal by including it in the Bill and not by relying on an Order-in-Council. This proposal was that none of the Commissioners' powers should be transferred except those which related to the administration of schemes completed by them; even then there had to be concurrence between the Board and the Commission. More significantly, the Commissioners were to retain their right to frame schemes for endowed schools. When he discussed the matter in the Lords a few days later, Devonshire's tactful description belied the magnitude of the problem as well as the intransigence of the Commission:

> Logic and symmetry might perhaps appear to require that the whole of the powers of the Charity Commissioners, so far as they relate to educational endowments, should be transferred to the Education Department [sic]. But the subject of endowments is so delicate, the distinction between charitable and educational objects and charitable trusts, the extent to which the necessities of special cases are to be regarded, the sectarian questions which they involve, are all so difficult and controversial in character, that we have hesitated to propose to transfer all such questions from a quasi-judicial to a political authority.[35]

Another key feature of the Bryce Report in connection with the establishment of a rationalised, central government education department had been a proposal for the establishment of an advisory education council. Furthermore, the appropriate recommendations, unlike those pertaining to the Charity Commission, had been a model of clarity, delineating precisely both the composition and function of this body. Devonshire acknowledged that Bryce had seen the prime function of this body as consultative but he was only prepared to commit to it *in toto* one educational topic, that is the registration of teachers. Beyond that all else was tentative for while he acknowledged the pressure being exerted by the teachers' organisations to provide the council, and thus themselves, with a 'more statutory and important position' in educational policy formulation he also knew that such a possibility was totally opposed by the government.[36] Because of this, the Bill introduced into the Lords on 1 August made the creation of the council (renamed the Consultative Committee) optional, with the registration of teachers being consigned to a separate Bill.

Concern about the delay in the appearance of the government's Bill, and whether it would include an educational council, had been mounting among some secondary school headmasters, including Edward Lyttelton of Haileybury College. When he had learned from Jebb of the Bill's likely contents in March he had agreed with him that patience was required of the schools, at least until the Bill was published, before they assailed the government with their views. None the less, he had been worried when he heard about the subsequent dropping of teacher registration from the Bill, since it jeopardised the establishment of 'our Educational Council', and he suggested a meeting of the Head Masters' Conference in June to formulate action. But Jebb, who had learned by then of the tentative nature of the Bill and that the way it was being framed was an attempt 'to avoid the risk of friction at the start', counselled patience.[37] The non-appearance of the Bill by June, however, snapped the secondary schoolteachers' patience. They attempted now to pressure the government into hastening its policy decisions by the introduction into the Commons by Colonel Lockwood of a Private Member's Bill for secondary education. *The Journal of Education* noted that although this Bill was

> . . . obviously not drawn to pass . . . The object . . . we take it, is to concentrate and rally the most enlightened professional opinion throughout the country, to give the Government a lead, and so prepare the way for a Government measure . . . it embodies and interprets the main aspirations of secondary teachers.[38]

A meeting of the MPs supporting this Bill was addressed by R.P. Scott, representing on this occasion not only the IAHM but also the Head Masters' Conference, the Head Masters' and Head Mistresses' Associations and the Conference of Catholic Schools: the organisations in fact sponsoring Lockwood's introduction of the Bill. The *School Board Chronicle* criticised this sponsorship, observing that in the Bill, 'the cloven hoof of Delimitation seems to make itself apparent to a degree which must prove fatal'.[39] This assumption was correct for the key aspect of the Bill was the creation of a large (72-member) and powerful education council which would have referred to it all questions relevant to the nature and limits of elementary, secondary and technical education as well as those matters relating to the classification, inspection and efficiency of secondary schools.[40] Neither Kekewich nor Gorst was pleased by the introduction of the Bill, and if it had been intended as a signpost for government policy its sponsors were to be disappointed.

The appearance of the Board of Education Bill late in the Session meant that the measure had to be left to lie on the table but Devonshire was quite satisfied with this and utilised the situation to appeal for widespread public discussion of the measure before the next Session. His appeal was not ignored, interest in the Bill having been heightened by the decision of the London School Board to challenge the application of the London County Council to become the Clause VII authority for London. This move appeared to challenge not only the principles agreed upon in the Joint Memorandum but also to raise the possibility of new challenges to the secondary schools arising from the Clause VII policy. The professional organisations of secondary school teachers were quick to respond and by November had established a joint committee, chaired by Scott, charged with conducting a media campaign 'for the purposes of placing before the country the claims of Secondary Education to national aid and recognition'.[41] By March of the following year, the committee had published a thick volume of papers and articles presented in the interim and entitled *What is Secondary Education?* But in some respects their thunder had been stolen by the publication in the previous October of a report ostensibly on Swiss education but in reality presenting a blueprint for English education. The author was Morant.

Based on his inspection of the Swiss education system in December 1897, Morant's report has usually been seen by historians as a vehicle to launch an indictment on the illegal secondary education provided by the higher grade schools. Such a view, however, overlooks the essential theme of his report, as well as certain other important points. First, the visit to Switzerland had enabled him to clarify his views about English education, for as he informed Sadler at the time '. . . this Swiss trip is shaking me all over the place: & I seem to see things very clearly, which were vague before'. Rather significantly, he noted in another letter, 'I'm not being rubbed the wrong way, here, in spite of the democratic basis: for here too, a man counts: counts tremendously'.[42] Second, albeit fortuitously, it afforded him the chance to formulate publicly the principles he believed were essential for a new administrative structure for English education. The timing may have been fortuitous but Morant's aim was not, for as he confided to Sadler, his experiences made me feel more clearly than ever the need of making the unimaginative English folk somehow realise what is meant by organisation & what wld be the definite advantages, & what the methods of actual & complete organisation. And it is this which, after endless muddling about, I have at last succeeded in making a pivot of my Swiss stuff as now written.[43]

Morant claimed that writing the report had been 'a long nightmare to me for weeks past: . . . feeling desperately keen to say certain things which are intensely felt, but madly impotent to put them into word, & phrase & sentence' but he need not have worried.[44] The *leitmotiv* of the report was strong enough to be picked up, as one reviewer observed:

> Mr Morant's Switzerland is plainly meant for our imitation, and very close imitation, too . . . .It is quite the most important contribution to current educational politics which has yet appeared.[45]

What then were his views on the Swiss education system, and what did he postulate for English education?

Morant accepted in principle the concept of a dual system of administration for education, that is the sharing between the local authorities and the central authority of both the control and development of the system, as exemplified by the Swiss Cantonal system. He believed that one advantage of decentralisation was that everyone in a locality was able to understand the details and the structure of the system. Furthermore, local authorities were able to both perceive and control the overall, but at the same time individual institutional, working of the system. These aspects, together with the strong spirit of local patriotism, as he termed it, helped to provide an education system, 'really complete and really organic in every point of structure, material and design, and of a character and scope directly suitable to, and complete in itself' required by the community. But, at the same time, Morant saw also a very clear role for a central authority. For him, its strength lay not only in the control of finance and regulations across all grades of education, but also because

> the knowledge and wide experience of the Centre, with its constant watchfulness for the good of the whole community, practically prevents the rise of undue overlapping, or, on the other hand, of real defects or inefficiency of supply.[46]

The achievements of the Swiss central authority appealed greatly to his sense of administrative order and more so when contrasted with the 'amorphous and incomplete condition of any English County in respect of public educational provision'. What the Swiss had managed to achieve with their educational system was a harmonious marriage between the roles of the local and central authorities. The local authority possessed the freedom to raise rates for education and to spend its own money 'as freely as it pleases on educational provision of all kinds (an arrangement which is only what one would expect in a thoroughly democratic country)'. The central authority, on the other hand, provided the overall guidance for the system; a control, Morant argued, that was recognised by the Swiss as 'the very essence of rational democratic government'.[47] The seminal value of this relationship was that it appeared to overcome the fears expressed in the Bryce Report about the potential dominance of the State over secondary education. Thus, he argued:

> A central control of this nature over the aim and curriculum of each school is not often conceived of in England, and yet in itself it is eminently rational and in no way contrary to the requirements of 'freedom, variety and elasticity'.[48]

Morant developed his own ideas about the ideal central authority in the course of his analysis of the Swiss model. For the control exerted by a central authority to be effective, the authority should, he postulated, ideally be

> an aristocracy of brains, – of picked men of educational (as well as of administrative) knowledge, wisdom and experience, chosen as such by the democracy for this express purpose, and invested accordingly with the supreme power over public education, . . .

Such a body, with more than a passing resemblance to Plato's Philosopher Kings, was essential, he argued, not only for the provision of a rational education system but also for national survival, for

> without this 'control by knowledge' in the sphere of public education of all grades just as in other spheres of national life, a democratic state must inevitably be beaten in the international struggle for existence, conquered from without by the force of the concentrated directing brain power of competing nations, and shattered from within by the centrifugal forces of her own people's unrestrained individualism.[49]

A strong central authority was thus a Morantian prerequisite for a truly efficient education system. Not only had it provided the comprehensiveness and intelligibility of the Swiss education system but it could provide the necessary data about how and where central and local educational efforts were being expended. For any nation's statesmen the advantage of this was obvious for it would enable them to ensure that 'each grade, each type, has its due share, and that no one portion of the educational field is too highly developed at the expense of and to the detriment of the other'.[50] And only with such an authority could effective systematisation of a nation's education system be achieved.

Morant's report in some respects bore a striking resemblance, in its advocacy of a central authority, to the draft Board of Education Bill but it differed, however, in the role postulated for that authority. Devonshire and Gorst saw the Board as playing no more than a supervisory role in relation to that to be undertaken by efficient local authorities for secondary education. Morant was unhappy with such a view and in an address to civil servants in the 'Education Club' he emphasised the desperate need in England for an authority, 'which shall watch, consider and advise upon all our national educational arrangements of all grades, of every type, as one whole'.[51] In spite of the efficiency of the Swiss Cantonal system, Morant envisaged the Education Department/Board of Education as the arbiter of English educational policy. His belief in this concept had already been noticeable in 1897 when he had commented to Sadler that if the central authority could glean information from all schools in receipt of public grants, then that authority would gain an 'immense hold' over the schools which by careful manipulation, could be used to make them improve their standards. In this, he had contended, there was nothing which, 'the most democratic could object to, or which the educationists could have the face to condemn or resent'.[52] It was the possibility of the government's educational policy reflecting Gorstian, or decentralist, lines plus the revelations provided by the Swiss system which convinced him of the correctness of his view; but it also meant that he was now close to the point of breaking with Sadler. The latter was wedded to the secondary schools playing a seminal role, via the Education Council, in educational policy decisions, a view publicised in the closing part of his report on Prussian education, published simultaneously with Morant's. That Sadler was aware of this possibility became clear a few weeks later when he did not try to dissuade Morant who was tempted to apply for the headship of the new Gordon College at Khartoum; he even offered to get Lord Rosebery to act as a referee for him.[53]

The views espoused in the Swiss Report explain also, at least partly, why Morant accepted an offer from Gorst to work on the Board of Education Bill. Gorst wanted him, in the first instance, to act merely as 'a drudge, to cram me with facts in his possession, and to fetch and carry for me while the committee is going on'.[54] Morant's effectiveness impressed Gorst sufficiently, however, for him to offer the position of his private secretaryship when the incumbent left to fight in the South African war. Despite his avowed contempt for Gorst's 'rotten ideas', Gorst was still a powerful force in the Department and this position could provide Morant with his entry into policy formulation at the highest level. Kekewich who, with good reason as will be seen, viewed private secretaries as 'the dark forces behind the throne, [who] have to be reckoned with as such', noted that for

> a private secretary in the complete confidence of his chief (especially if that chief is a Minister), and is clever enough to know exactly how to handle him, and to ingratiate himself with him, the temptation to intrigue is very strong.[55]

Morant's activities in his new role undoubtedly provided a major, if not the chief, reason for this comment. But at the time of the offer Morant discussed the implications with Sadler and Scott and the trio agreed that, 'in the interests of educational progress', he should accept.[56] Sadler, although a party to this decision, soon forgot the agreement and came to view Morant's transfer to Gorst's service as almost repugnant, seeing it as desertion; it was not to be long before the links between the two men were to be all but severed. The Board of Education Bill was thus to mark the beginning of the subsequent rise of Morant and the fall of Gorst and Sadler in educational policy formulation.

In the early planning stages of the Board of Education Bill Devonshire had begun to consider the steps necessary for its implementation, most especially those associated with the reorganisation of the Education Department and the Department of Science and Art. He appears to have decided initially that there should be two administrative branches of the Board, one handling elementary education and the other secondary education. Leakage of this proposal, with the corollary that the staff of the Department of Science and Art would be primarily responsible for the latter, ruffled the secondary schools. Their response was that such an arrangement for secondary education would be 'too ghastly for words' unless there was a 'new Kensington without Donnelly and the right man at the head of it'.[57] While there were some grounds for this critical view of Donnelly's regime, not least the bias in the curriculum of many secondary schools caused by the Department's preferential funding of science subjects, the leak appears to have been generated by the Education Department and marked the beginning of an internal power struggle with South Kensington for dominance in the new Board. Devonshire was on the side of the Education Department and in his response to a memorandum from Donnelly, arguing the case for a tripartite system of administration with the third branch to be responsible for technical education, he noted that while it was worthy of consideration, 'it will be certainly said and perhaps will be the fact that the Third or Technical Education Division will be nothing but the Science and Art Department under another name'.[58] Such a possibility did not please him given his view of the Science and Art Department's administration as 'extremely cumbrous' and he hoped that reorganisation would produce some streamlining in that quarter.

Of equally pressing concern was the sensitive topic of the inspection of secondary schools. The Charity Commissioners had had the power to appoint inspectors of such schools, since the 1887 amendment of the Charitable Trusts Act, and they had embarked upon an inspection of selected schools, albeit focused more on the administrative than the educational aspects of the schools.[59] Yet even the transfer of these powers to the Board was not a simple issue, however, for there had been the development of local authority education inspectorates following the creation of county and county borough councils in 1888. The Bryce Commissioners, cognizant of this, had advocated the inspection of secondary schools by local authority inspectors, albeit with the proviso that they should be subject to regulations issued by central government. The first (1898) Board of Education Bill had not followed this recommendation and, instead, would have permitted inspection either by officers of the Board or by the universities. Devonshire decided, on reflection, that it might be wiser to test the waters first and sent Sadler on a fact-finding mission among the secondary schools early in 1899. Just before Sadler's departure Morant had attended a meeting of the Joint Board (the Oxford and Cambridge Schools Examination Board) on the role the universities might play in inspection. While he had found the universities concerned about issues such as funding and which schools were to be inspected they were 'in thought, all over the place'. He believed Sadler would discover similar problems but tactfully added: 'If anyone can bring them in, it is you'.[60]

Sadler tackled his task with relish, undoubtedly buoyed by the knowledge that he had just been offered the Vice Chancellorship of Birmingham University as well as having heard that there was a rumour 'of a circumambient kind' that he was likely to be made the head of the Board's secondary education branch.[61] Furnished with introductions by Ilbert, Sadler interviewed the head teachers of 17 major public schools within eight days, his progress being smoother than he had anticipated. He found the headmasters '. . . splendid men. So wise, and cautious and self restrained, not bragging or cynical, but rather stern and more easily touched by pity than any other sort of appeal'. Warre of Eton, Fearon of Winchester and Moss of Shrewsbury he found more impressive than Rendall of Charterhouse, a rather repellent personality and 'a little squeaky on the slate', Walker of St. Pauls, 'friendly but fierce – and cynical rather', or James of Rugby with his 'rough sense and not very subtle mind'.[62] But, significantly, Sadler found himself fully in accord with their desire to save their schools from the ' "many-headed beast" and bureaucratic impertinences'.[63] Furthermore, the rapport he had established during his visits enabled him to secure virtually unanimous consent to his proposal that any school, apart from those under the sole control of the proprietor or shareholders, could be inspected by either the Board's inspectors or university personnel approved by the Consultative Committee. The inspections would be general and not concerned with curriculum details while the reports produced would remain confidential to the Board and the school concerned. The secondary schools, however, wanted the costs of inspection to be borne solely by the state and Devonshire was horrified by the likely costs of such an exercise, believing that neither the Chancellor of the Exchequer nor the Commons would agree to them. While Sadler had been away, Devonshire had also had second thoughts about his earlier view that the schools to be inspected should be those that would have been under the Charity Commission or that wished recognition for their efficiency. Now he envisaged that the inspection should be just sufficient 'to enable the Local Authorities when created to organise the Secondary Education of their district'.[64]

As the Bill had progressed through the final planning stages Devonshire had become more assertive about its contents and, unusually for him, kept having meetings with Ilbert about the drafting of the measure. He rejected an earlier decision that the Board's political heads should be virtually the same as those for the Education and Science and Art Departments, preferring instead that the President

90

should have a Parliamentary Secretary 'distinctly his subordinate, instead of a Vice President with a sort of dual authority'.[65] This change, given Gorst's activities, would undoubtedly have been greeted with a sigh of relief by most of the Cabinet, not least Balfour and Salisbury. The new Board was to consist of the President, the Lord President (unless he was the President of the Board), the Principal Secretaries of State, the Chancellor of the Exchequer and the First Lord of the Treasury. Gaining Cabinet assent to this modification meant that the only outstanding problem remained the transfer of the Charity Commissioners' powers. In the third draft of the Bill it had been proposed that 'more elastic powers of transfer' should be adopted, with the only power to be immediately subsumed by the Board being the inspection of schools.[66] This, as Ilbert had indicated, was all that was really necessary at this stage because it allowed the final resolution of the issue to be postponed but when reached it could be achieved by an Order in Council. Devonshire was happy with this, especially after Sadler's report, and the Cabinet's approval allowed the final (and fourteenth) draft of the Bill to be introduced into the Lords five days later, on the Ides of March.

The passage of the Bill through the Lords was quite rapid, receiving its Third Reading on 15 May. Three days later Gorst introduced it to the Commons where its reception was rather more critical. Although Bryce had to concede that the government's aims were satisfactory he was highly critical of the Bill's lack of detail, finding it 'somewhat vague, somewhat obscure, and rather in the nature of a blank cheque'. Lord Cranborne attributed the Bill's structure and content to the Education Department, ' . . . a remarkable Department. It is sometimes loquacious, as in its Code; it is sometimes extremely reticent, as in this Bill; but it is always obscure'.[67] Cranborne disliked the possibility of the new Board subsuming any of the Charity Commissioners' work and tried to convince Balfour, on behalf of the Church Parliamentary Committee, of the need for an amendment allowing any Order in Council from the Board to be subject to the control of the Lords or Commons, otherwise 'all our endowed voluntary schools will be more or less at the mercy of the new Board of Education'.[68] Devonshire objected strongly to this, arguing that giving the Lords 'the power to paralyse the administration of a Department, without responsibility' appeared to him most objectionable. His reaction had the desired effect but it was now becoming debatable whether there was sufficient parliamentary time left for the Bill to pass. This, combined with a general lack of interest in the measure among the bulk of members –

demonstrated by the question about the existence of a quorum having to be raised in both the Second and Third Readings – worried Jebb, among others, and he half suspected that 'the High Church party have been giving the Government hints to drop the Bill'.[69] His fears proved groundless and the Bill passed into the Statute Book on 9 August, to take effect from 1 April 1900. There still remained the outstanding and not inconsiderable problem of deciding on the type of reorganisation to be undertaken in order to create the new Board.

Shortly after the introduction of the Bill, and while Sadler was overseas, Morant had been asked to provide an analysis of the initial responses to it. He noted that Devonshire's changed position on inspection had caused alarm among the major public schools as well as the universities of Oxford and Cambridge because it jeopardised the necessary and outstanding reform of secondary education. Morant also recorded that Devonshire's vacillations about the type of administrative organisation to be employed in the Board were also giving rise to concern, although his current support for a tripartite scheme found much favour in the secondary schools and universities. They were opposed to the concept of a bipartite organisation within the Board because such a move would lead to an 'undesirable technicalising of Secondary Education and to the gradual ousting, to some extent at least, of Liberal Education in favour of more technological courses'.[70] Sadler shared these views, telling his father that he believed the alterations Devonshire had made to the Bill meant that 'a fine chance has been lost'.[71]

On 26 June Gorst forwarded to Devonshire a copy of a letter which Kekewich's predecessor, Cumin, had written about a decision taken by the Committee of Council on Education not to continue with the idea of amalgamating the Education and Science and Art Departments. Gorst appended to it his comment that it was a pity the reasons behind the decision were not known as 'they would be very useful just now, as teaching us what to avoid'.[72] Mindful of this, Devonshire ordered a departmental committee to be appointed to consider the necessary changes in staffing and organisation required to bring the Education and Science and Art Departments into 'closer relations to each other'. Under the chairmanship of Sir Hugh Walpole of the India Office, Kekewich and the two Principal Assistant Secretaries of the Education and Science and Art Departments, W. Tucker and Captain W. de W. Abney respectively, were joined by Spring Rice from Treasury and later by D.R. Fearon, the Secretary to the Charity Commission, and the Secretary to the Board of Agriculture, T.H. Elliot. Jebb was disappointed to learn that the committee consisted solely of civil servants, refused to accept evidence from outside organisations and were not to consider the whole organisation of secondary education. His feeling was shared by W.N. Bruce, a member of the Charity Commission, who thought that the committee 'will not inspire confidence in the minds of those who fear that Sec. Education is to occupy a subordinate position in the new organisation'.[73] He believed that Kekewich, who was to be the Board's Permanent Secretary, intended to do nothing until forced either by the Consultative Committee or by a change of government in the forthcoming election. In the event Bruce's prophecy was not far off the mark, except that Kekewich wanted all civil servants in the Board to be responsible to the Assistant Secretaries and 'he hoped that the exception made in Mr. Acland's time in the case of the Director for Special Enquiries might be terminated'.[74] This point reflected the bitter struggle that was taking place both in and out of the Department over the organisation for the Board in spite of the existence of the Walpole Committee.

In the same week as the committee was created, Dr Warre, the headmaster of Eton, had approached Sadler for his views about the reorganisation. Sadler had replied that a bipartite system of organisation was the one currently favoured because of the pressure being exerted on the government by the secretaries of the county council technical instruction committees, led by H. Macan of Surrey, and on the grounds of economy by the Education Department. He felt that the Walpole Committee would also support this scheme and it therefore behoved those in support of a tripartite system 'to say clearly what they think'. He told Warre that only the tripartite system he had sketched in a memorandum for the Duke would provide the 'proper recognition and status and official influence of Higher Secondary Education' since the bipartite scheme would give the Department of Science and Art power over all secondary schools, with the possibility that the established ones might 'be muzzled'. He was worried that if a decision about the scheme to be adopted was deferred until the autumn it would become the province of another departmental committee which would decide in favour of the bipartite scheme. He told him that he had informed Kekewich that, in his judgement, 'the Great Public Schls & Oxford & Cambridge ought to refuse to have anything to do with the new system unless this [tripartite] organisation was definitely promised in the House of Commons before the Bill passes'. Furthermore, he had made it clear that he would most likely resign if any other form of organisation was adopted.[75]

After receiving Sadler's views, Warre saw Devonshire and warned him that the secondary schools felt that reorganisation was too big an issue to be left solely to the Walpole Committee. Instead, they wanted the government to make a statement on the form of organisation to be employed while the Bill was still in the Commons.[76] At the same time the headmasters of other public and secondary schools individually bombarded Kekewich with letters about reorganisation and one, Dr Fry of Berkhamsted, informed him that there would be agitation if a tripartite scheme was not adopted. Devonshire, warning Kekewich that unless they were able to satisfy Warre there would be problems in the Commons, pressed him for the paper on reorganisation he had earlier requested of Sadler.[77]

Sadler's memorandum, ostensibly analysing both the bipartite and tripartite systems of administration, was in essence an advocacy of the latter. He contended that under the bipartite scheme proposed, that is:

Permanent Chief Secretary to the Board of Education

Principal Assistant Secretary for Elementary Education	*Principal Assistant Secretary for Higher Education*
	Sub-Secretary for Technological Education · *Sub-Secretary for Secondary Education i.e. scientific and literary alike*

it would be impossible to find a person who possessed the knowledge of both secondary and what he termed 'technological' education required in order to be competent and fair as the Principal Assistant Secretary for Higher Education. In view of this, he argued, the ideal organisational structure for the Board could only be a tripartite scheme, that is:

Permanent Chief Secretary to the Board of Education

Principal Assistant Secretary for Elementary Education	*Principal Assistant Secretary for Technological Education i.e. applied to the furtherance of industrial and other processes*

*Principal Assistant Secretary for Secondary Education
i.e. scientific and literary alike*

He refuted the claim that defenders of the tripartite scheme were against the county councils as education authorities, arguing that the need for local secondary education authorities was accepted as a *sine qua non* provided there was a strong central authority:

> . . . strong, that is, not by the exercise of coercive powers but strong by being always well-informed, always up-to-date in its knowledge and appreciation of the value of educational experiments, and by its hold on the confidence of those locally concerned in educational work.[78]

He concluded by warning that the strength of public opinion behind the great public schools and the universities was greater than that which supported an organisation of the Board on lines which would both weaken the influence and impair the efficiency of the Board.

Sadler's memorandum provoked a swift response from Abney on behalf of the Science and Art Department. He disputed Sadler's allocation of roles for the two non-elementary Principal Assistant Secretaries in the tripartite scheme (which were the same as for the sub-secretaries in the bipartite scheme), correctly perceiving that Sadler's division, with scientific education distinct from technological, was fallacious. He also hoisted Sadler with his own petard by asking how this division, with literary and scientific education under one secretary, could be construed as being different from the role Sadler conceived impossible for the Principal Assistant Secretary for Higher Education in the bipartite scheme. If scientific education had to come under secondary education then the officer appointed, given the established nature of science education as opposed to literary instruction which was 'in an embryonic stage', should be 'the one who is now responsible for Science and Art instruction' (Abney himself), with the other non-elementary Principal Secretary chosen for his technological qualifications. Abney added, somewhat waspishly, 'I scarcely think that this is the result that Mr. Sadler contemplated'. Rather than incurring further partisan debates Abney counselled the avoidance of creating permanent divisions within the new Board until it was able to gauge 'the requirements of the future and the materials which will be at its disposal to meet those requirements'.[79]

Abney's paper made its point, and although Sadler enjoyed the cut and thrust over the Bill he was 'angry with the present Education Department who are plotting to put secondary education with – almost under – technical'.[80] But Devonshire, still mindful of the warnings of Warre and others, asked Sadler to prepare a paper on the role of a secondary education department, which he promptly did. At the same time, Acland wrote to Kekewich about the Board's organisation, not wishing to trouble Devonshire, but clearly expecting Kekewich to convey his views to him none the less. Taking an opposite position to Sadler, he was at pains to stress the seminal role played by the Science and Art Department in secondary education and to negate the idea that it was only associated with technical education. Not surprisingly, therefore, he found the idea that 'the University and public schools can dictate the appointment of an assistant secy. for technical [education] (Abney to be labelled technical) for this is what it means + one for secondary at once is absurd'. If this came to pass, he warned, it would impair relations between the county councils and the Board in the future although he was confident that 'no pledges as to this will be given at present'.[81] Acland's views carried little weight with Devonshire, however.

On 17 July, Gorst was asked in the Commons, by both Jebb and Bryce, for clarification about the organisation to be employed in the Board. He replied that while the final system would not be determined until after the Board came into existence in 1900 there was no intention of placing secondary education under either of the existing departments. Instead, there would be 'a third official, whose responsibility will be distinct from and equal to that of the two existing secretaries', and the Walpole Committee would be given instructions to this effect.[82] Devonshire was pressed, four days later, in the Lords to give his views on the topic despite the 'altogether satisfactory' answer provided by Gorst.

Devonshire's response revealed that he had now accepted Sadler's arguments in preference to those of Abney and Acland. Reiterating the case for a tripartite system of organisation, he stated that 'secondary education proper' could not be 'properly and advantageously' entrusted to the Science and Art Department. Thus the third division to be established would be 'independent of and equally responsible to the Permanent Secretary as the divisions charged with Primary Education and Science and Art and Technical Education'.[83] Morant gleefully told Sadler the next day that Kekewich was 'furious at the Secondary pressure having been continued and so persistent'.[84] And Jebb found himself buttonholed in the Commons a few days later by Gorst 'in a vile temper' because of Devonshire's decision to bypass the Science and Art Department in the control of secondary education, and he found himself addressed

> in a bullying way, as if he was angry with me, and I had a glimpse of what he could be like when he wanted to be disagreeable. I had some difficulty in keeping my temper, and left him as soon as I could.[85]

2 Michael Sadler *circa* 1902, from M. Hartog, *Philip Hartog: A Memoir* (1949)

Gorst's anger reflected the fact that Devonshire's decision threatened to undermine any future progress towards the development of new LEAs based on the county and county boroughs which could be achieved by utilising the regulatory powers of the Science and Art Department. Sadler's contribution to the decision, and through it the maintenance of the secondary schools' autonomy, earned him Gorst's enmity. As he told his wife, 'Gorst is (I hear) violently abusive of me personally', but he added that it was 'not at all ungrateful hearing'.[86]

The day after the Board of Education Bill passed into the Statute Book, R.P. Scott had written to Sadler:

> You think, and plan and inspire, I act (adapting as needs arise) along the line traced out by yourself. And if the result pleases you look beyond me for the cause.[87]

Sadler's response has been cited at the beginning of this chapter and reflected his belief that the struggle over the control of secondary education had been won. Yet only a few months later he was totally disillusioned, being firmly convinced that the organisation of secondary education by the Board was going to represent a golden opportunity missed because of the 'office obstruction hopelessly strong against it'. His position within the Department was by then almost that of a pariah. His activities had caused 'serious personal friction with the heads of the present Department', so that it was not surprising that the prime aim in the Department appeared to be to exclude him from gaining

> control of the Secondary Ed. department for which the voice of the Great Schools and Universities designate him and partly because it will tend to make him the eventual head of the whole department.[88]

Sadler had believed that if he was offered the headship of the secondary branch he ought to take it, 'for England's sake'. But after a conversation with Kekewich in August about the possible membership of the Consultative Committee he had to recognise the possibility of disappointment. As he told his wife, 'I think he wants to know my mind on this (the last remaining part) of the question, before they proceed to appoint some one else Secy!'[89] Scott had started organising a campaign to get Sadler appointed and was alarmed that Sadler's mood might lead him to jeopardise his chances of appointment. In the event Scott's activities rebounded unfavourably on Sadler, Kekewich pointing out that civil servants were dependent upon their own merits for promotion. He chastised him (Sadler) for not preventing the memorials organised by Scott from being sent to the Duke of Devonshire and added: 'Such memorials are unwise, and show a regrettable ignorance of the proprieties of official life'.[90] This response deepened Sadler's feeling of depression for only the previous week he had received a note from Morant indicating that he had accepted the position as Gorst's private secretary, ostensibly for Morant 'one of the most uncomfortable and difficult situations in my life'.[91] Thus by the end of 1899 in which he had managed to achieve a substantial policy decision beneficial for the future of 'proper secondary education' Sadler felt certain he was to be deprived of the opportunity to implement it, while the staffing of his own research section was now virtually halved. His premonition was correct for Devonshire vetoed any claim which he might have had on the position, contending that Sadler's 'educational goal would probably lead him into extreme councils'.[92] Consequently, W.N. Bruce of the Charity Commission was appointed to head the secondary branch.

In the time that it took Devonshire to reach a decision about Bruce's appointment instead of Sadler's but also aware of the impending implementation date for the new Act, Abney tried to seek a reversal on the organisational structure to be employed in the Board. His argument to Kekewich was that if the tripartite scheme went ahead there was a danger that the status of the Technical Branch would be degraded by the secondary schools' insistence that the head of the Secondary Branch should be someone whose educational background was literary or classical in type. This degradation would be reinforced by their other desire that science education should come under the aegis of this branch as well. Consequently, the Technical Branch would be deprived of any influence over secondary education and he felt that the schools would either 'drift away from modern to literary education, or the grant would be fruitlessly expended'. The only reasonable structure for an effective tripartite organisation would be a division, therefore, into elementary, liberal and technical education, the second to include classical and literary education while the third would consist of modern and technological education. As he pointed out, the issue was too serious for personal considerations to apply:

> It is a question whether the fruits of the victories of the war waged during the last 25 years between modern and literary education shall be disallowed to the former. The present national needs point distinctly to the fact that a larger and not a smaller share of modern education should be available for the middle

classes and any false step in the constitution of the New Board may have disastrous effects.[93]

In a subsequent memorandum to Devonshire, Abney attempted to strengthen his argument by referring to the changed perspective of the secondary schools' headmasters who now appeared to support a bipartite system of organisation. His plan accommodated this change by having a tripartite division within the Secondary Branch and having the branch under the control of two Principal Assistant Secretaries, each having equal access to the Permanent Secretary.

After discussing the matter with Devonshire, Gorst submitted a plan of organisation for the Board involving three Principal Assistant Secretaries, one each for elementary, secondary and technical education, and in which science and art education was recognised as being fundamental to the work of both the primary and secondary branches.[94] Gorst's continued support for the Department of Science and Art which was implied in his submission did not prevent Devonshire from both admiring its logic nor from pronouncing it 'a fairly practical division of the work of the Office at which we might aim'. But, he added, the major snag was that Abney would have to be taken away from those functions for which he was best fitted and, furthermore, he did not know how to justify a third Principal Assistant Secretary at a salary of £1300 per annum but with only very limited functions assigned to the role. He decided to opt, therefore, for a bipartite scheme along the lines suggested by Abney but with the proviso that it was to be temporary and to last only until such time as Gorst's scheme could be implemented. He did not, moreover, envisage 'much difficulty in retracting our pledges' about the Board's organisation.[95]

The effect of these changes was effectively to negate Sadler's earlier achievements, and by May he had been released from consultations on questions of policy. His father observed that he seemed to have determined 'to take no more active part in Sec Ed arrangements'.[96] Sadler explained his reasons to his wife:

> It has really been a struggle between two incompatible ideals of administration. I never more deeply believed that the view which I have been fighting for is the right one and absolutely necessary to the future welfare of the country. It is a privilege and an honour to have been allowed to suffer for it. But it is no good disguising the fact that I have been utterly and overwhelmingly beaten on my own ground.

Aware that what was really at stake was 'the intention with which the colossal power of the State shall be brought to bear on the spiritual side of Education', he continued:

> ... much of last year's Act, much of the new constitution of the Consultative Committee are due to our work, feathers borrowed from our cockades. But we should deceive ourselves if we flattered ourselves by thinking that, because they have stolen the form of our plans, they are any the more likely to give effect to them in our spirit. And it is the spirit which matters, and controls the form, while the latter though it may facilitate the operation of the right spirit cannot create it or take its place.[97]

Perhaps not surprisingly, he now felt that he would like to be free from the Department and his father noted how much his outlook had changed, owing to 'experience of men and affairs'.[98] In fact, he was to remain for another three years before he felt compelled to resign when confronted by a difference of interpretation over his section's role in the Board, that interpretation being furnished by the new Permanent Secretary, Robert Morant.

If Sadler's important contribution to the organisation of the Board of Education did not result in a success career-wise, in a similar way Gorst found himself partially thwarted in his aims for the Act. The only personal beneficiaries of the successful passage of the Act, in fact, were Devonshire and Morant. Devonshire had been able, for the first time since the government came to power, to dominate the planning of an education policy measure although he was willing, as has been seen, to listen to other points of view and modify his own subsequently. The Act was his and by virtue of this control over educational policy reverted to the Education Department. If his Swiss Report had not swayed Devonshire or Gorst, the combination of the 'open cheque' nature of the Act plus Devonshire's subsequent unwillingness to implement the Board's organisation (before his resignation in 1902) meant that when Morant gained the Permanent Secretaryship at the end of 1902 he had a free hand to implement his scheme of administration for the Board. As will be seen later, as each successive component was established after 1902 it became quite clear that Morant had utilised the ideas embodied in his Swiss Report. But this had involved the existence of a rationalised system of local education authorities and, once more, it was to be Gorst who, in order to establish this vital component, initiated the events that were to culminate in changes that dramatically altered the face of English education.

NOTES

1. L.A. Selby Bigge, *The Board of Education* (1927), pp. 70–1.
2. *4 P.D.*, 40, c.557, 5 May 1896.
3. Ibid., c.570.
4. Sadler Papers, MS Eng misc c.551, fo.89, M.E. Sadler to R.P. Scott, 18 Sept. 1899.
5. PRO ED 23/4, Sir J. Donnelly to Duke of Devonshire, 26 June 1896; Duke of Devonshire to Sir J. Donnelly, 9 Aug. 1896.
6. Barnett Papers, F/BAR/152, S. Barnett to F. Barnett, 24 Oct. 1896.
7. Report of the Committee appointed to inquire into the Distribution of Science and Art grants, *PP*, 1897, XXXIII [C.8417] pp. 421–30.
8. *4 PD*, 64, c.350, 5 Aug. 1898; see also *The Times*, 18 Nov., 21, 24 Dec. 1897: *4 PD*, 59, c.603, 17 June 1898.
9. *School Board Chronicle*, 59 (5 Feb. 1898), p. 143; *Spectator,* 78 (20 Feb. 1897), p. 261.
10. *The Times*, 29 Oct. 1898.
11. *School Board Chronicle*, 67 (3 May 1902), p. 446.
12. Ibid., p. 447.
13. Education Department, Special Reports on Educational Subjects, 1896–7, *PP*, 1897, XXV [C.8477], R.L. Morant, 'The French System of Higher Primary Schools', p. 335.
14. For these developments see G. McCulloch, *Philosophers and Kings: Education for Leadership in Modern England* (1991).
15. W. Dyche, 'Presidential Address at the Annual Meeting of the Association of Head Masters of Higher Grade Schools and Schools of Science', *School Board Gazette*, II (July–Dec. 1899), p. 359.
16. Jebb Papers, Servanda, XIII, p. 55: Jebb's note of a conversation with 'K' [Kekewich], 14 July 1897; Sadler Papers, MS Eng misc c.550., fo.92, R.L. Morant to M.E. Sadler, n.d. but late 1897.
17. 'Joint Memorandum on the Relations of Primary and Secondary Schools to one another in a National System of Education', *PP* 1898, XXV, p. 537.
18. Higher Grade Board Schools and Public Secondary Schools (Statistics), *PP* 1898, XXV [C.8447] p. 530.
19. G. Rowles, unpublished autobiography in J. Burnett (ed.), *Destiny Obscure: Autobiographies of Childhood, Education and Family from the 1820s to the 1920s* (1984), p. 155; W.E. Marsden, *Unequal Educational Provision in England and Wales: The Nineteenth-century Roots* (1987), p. 68. Other problems arose from the salary limit applied as the division between occupations in the middle middle and lower middle classes; teachers could be classified as members of either class and, even so, there would be other teachers on a purely salary consideration, who could be classified as working class. See F. Musgrove, 'Middle-Class Education and Employment in the Nineteenth Century', *Economic History Review*, NS 12 (1959–60), p. 99; J. A. Banks, 'The Social Structure of Nineteenth Century England as seen through the Census' in R. Lawton (ed.), *The Census and Social Structure* (1978); W.A. Armstrong, 'The Use of Information about Occupation' in E.A. Wrigley (ed.), *Nineteenth-century Society: Essays in the Quantitative Methods for the Study of Social Data* (1972).
20. Higher Grade Board Schools and Public Secondary Schools (Statistics), *PP* 1898, XXV [C.8447] p. 529; *School Board Gazette*, IV, 5 (Nov. 1900).
21. Royal Commission on Secondary Education, PP, 1895, LXIII [C.7862], pp. 67–8. See also H.J. Perkin, 'Middle-Class Education and Employment in the Nineteenth

Century: A Critical Note', *Economic History Review*, NS 14 (1961), p. 130; J. Roach, *Secondary Education in England 1870–1902: Public Activity and Private Enterprise* (1991), pp. 113–15.

22. 'Joint Memorandum on the Relations of Primary and Secondary Schools to one another in a National System of Education', *PP*, 1898, XXV (381), pp. 535–6.
23. M.J. Wiener, *English Culture and the Decline of the Industrial Spirit 1850–1980* (1981), p. 19.
24. Sadler Papers, MS Eng misc c.552, fo.242, Interview with Sir Hugh Orange by Lynda Grier, 1946.
25. Ibid., Eng misc c.550, fo.93, R.L. Morant to M.E. Sadler, n.d. but Dec. 1897.
26. Jebb Papers, Servanda, XIII 1898, Memorandum by R.C. Jebb, 18 March 1898.
27. Ibid., XII, 'Wed. Jul 14, 1897. K. The Athenaeum', p. 55.
28. PRO ED 24/8, Duke of Devonshire, Cabinet memorandum, 26 Jan. 1898.
29. Ibid.
30. Jebb Papers, R.C. Jebb, 'Note of conversation with "K" ', 18 March 1898.
31. Sadler Papers, MS Eng misc c.550, fo.44, R.L. Morant to M.E. Sadler, March 1898.
32. A.S. Bishop, *The Rise of a Central Authority for English Education* (1971), pp. 212–14, 241.
33. Ibid., p. 249.
34. PRO CAB 37/47, Duke of Devonshire, Memorandum, 15 July 1898.
35. *4 PD*, 63, c.677, 1 August 1898. It was not until 1914 that the Board of Education gained the complete transference of all the relevant educational powers from this body.
36. Kekewich Papers, Duke of Devonshire to G.W. Kekewich, 16 Dec. 1898.
37. Jebb Papers, Servanda, XIII, 1898, E. Lyttelton to R.C. Jebb, 7 March 1898, p. 99; Memorandum by R.C. Jebb, 18 March 1898.
38. *Journal of Education*, XX (1 July 1898), p. 391.
39. *School Board Chronicle*, 59 (18 June 1898), p. 679.
40. H. Steedman, 'Michael Sadler and the Campaign for an Educational Council, 1893–1903', *Research in Education*, 2 (Nov. 1969), p. 79.
41. R.P. Scott (ed.), *'What is Secondary Education?' and Other Short Essays* (1899), p. v.
42. Sadler Papers, MS Eng misc c.550, fos.35 and 89, R.L. Morant to M.E. Sadler,14 and 16 Dec. 1897.
43. Ibid., fo.47, R.L. Morant to M.E. Sadler, 14 March 1898.
44. Ibid.
45. H. Macan, Secretary of the Surrey County Technical Instruction Committee, cited in J.R. Fairhurst, 'Some aspects of religion, politics and education 1895–1906', p. 151.
46. R.L. Morant, 'The National Organisation of Education of all grades as practised in Switzerland', Special Reports on Educational Subjects, 3, *PP*, 1898, XXV [C.8988], pp. 21–2.
47. Ibid.
48. Ibid., p. 23.
49. Ibid., p. 24.
50. Ibid., p. 64.
51. B.M. Allen, *Sir Robert Morant:A Great Public Servant* (1934), p. 126.
52. Sadler Papers, MS Eng misc c.550, fo.35, R.L. Morant to M.E. Sadler, 14 Dec. 1897.
53. Ibid., fos.61–2, R.L. Morant to M.E. Sadler, 2 Dec. 1898.

54. Kekewich Papers, J.E. Gorst to G.W. Kekewich, 30 June 1899.
55. Kekewich, *The Education Department and After*, p. 121.
56. A.C. Twentyman, 'Some Memories of Sir Michael Sadler' cited in H.J. Higginson, 'My Life in the History of Education: II: Rescuing Sadleriana', *History of Education Society Bulletin*, 52 (Autumn 1993), pp. 39–40.
57. Sadler Papers, MS Eng misc c.550, fo.44, R.L. Morant to M.E. Sadler, Thursday morning, March 1898.
58. Kekewich Papers, Duke of Devonshire to G.W. Kekewich, 8 Dec. 1898.
59. Bishop, op. cit., pp. 246–8.
60. Sadler Papers, MS Eng misc c.550, fo.67, R.L. Morant to M.E. Sadler, 25 Feb. 1899.
61. Ibid., fo.58, T.B. Strong to M.E. Sadler, 3 Feb. 1899.
62. M.E. Sadler to M.A. Sadler, 27,28 Feb., 1 March 1899 cited in M. Sadleir, *Sir Michael Sadler* (1949), pp. 188–9.
63. M.E. Sadler to M.A. Sadler, 27 Feb. 1899 in M. Sadleir, op. cit., pp. 188.
64. Kekewich Papers, Duke of Devonshire to G.W. Kekewich, 6 March 1899. When Devonshire outlined these parameters in his introduction of the Bill to the House of Lords on 14 March, Morant was angry: '. . . some of it [Devonshire's speech] makes me feel furious, and none of it is satisfying, for *such* a chance': Sadler Papers, MS Eng misc c.550, fo.69, R.L. Morant to M.E. Sadler, 15 March 1899.
65. Salisbury Papers (3M), Duke of Devonshire to Lord Salisbury, 6 Feb. 1899.
66. PRO CAB 37/38, C.P. Ilbert, Memorandum, 27 Feb. 1899.
67. *4 PD*, 73, c.630–1 (26 June 1899).
68. BP Add MS 49575, fos.113–16, Lord Cranborne to J.S. Sandars, 23 July 1899.
69. Jebb Papers, R.C. Jebb to C. Jebb, 7 Aug. 1899.
70. PRO ED 24/8, R.L. Morant, 'Précis of opinions recently expressed by persons or bodies of weight on the Board of Education Bill', April 1899.
71. Sadler Papers, MS Eng misc c.204, Diary of Sir M.T. Sadler, 16 March 1899.
72. PRO ED 24/8, J.E. Gorst to Duke of Devonshire, 26 June 1899.
73. Bryce Papers, UB 74/H 49, W.N. Bruce to J. Bryce, 22 July 1899.
74. PRO ED 24/62, Minutes of Meeting 3 Nov. 1899.
75. Sadler Papers, MS Eng misc c.550, fo.68, M.E. Sadler to E. Warre, 5 July 1899.
76. PRO ED 24/64, E. Warre to G.W. Kekewich, 7 July 1899.
77. Ibid., Duke of Devonshire to G.W. Kekewich, 7 July 1899.
78. Ibid., M.E. Sadler, 'Memorandum on the future organisation of the internal departments of the Board of Education', 7 July 1899.
79. Ibid., W. de W. Abney to G.W. Kekewich, 11 July 1899.
80. Sadler Papers, MS Eng misc c.204, Diary of Sir M.T. Sadler, 14 July 1899.
81. Ibid., MS Eng misc c.550, fo.70, A.H.D. Acland to G.W. Kekewich, 13 July 1899.
82. *4 PD*, 74, c.1006, 17 July 1899.
83. Ibid., c.1528, 21 July 1899.
84. Sadler Papers, MS Eng misc c.550, fo.71, R.L. Morant to M.E. Sadler, 22 July 1899.
85. Jebb Papers, R.C. Jebb to C. Jebb, 27 July 1899.
86. Sadler Papers, MS Eng misc c.550, fo.73, M.E. Sadler to M.A. Sadler, 4 Aug.1899.
87. Ibid., MS Eng misc c.551, fo.80, R.P. Scott to M.E. Sadler, 9 Aug. 1899.
88. Ibid., MS Eng misc c.204, Diary of Sir M.T. Sadler, 14 and 17 July 1899.
89. Ibid., MS Eng misc c.550, fo.73, M.E. Sadler to M.A. Sadler, 4 Aug. 1899.
90. Ibid., MS Eng misc c.551, fo.107, G.W. Kekewich to M.E. Sadler, 27 Nov. 1899.

91. Ibid., MS Eng misc c.550, fo.77, R.L. Morant to M.E. Sadler, 21 Nov. 1899.
92. PRO ED 24/64, Duke of Devonshire to G.W. Kekewich, 25 Jan. 1900.
93. Ibid., W. de W. Abney to G.W. Kekewich, 22 Feb. 1900.
94. Ibid., J.E. Gorst to Duke of Devonshire, 8 March 1900.
95. Ibid., Duke of Devonshire to G.W. Kekewich, 15 March 1900; Duke of Devonshire to J.E. Gorst, 26 March 1900.
96. Sadler Papers, MS Eng misc c.205, Diary of Sir M.T. Sadler, 18 Feb., 25 and 27 May 1900.
97. Ibid., MS Eng misc c.551, fo.84, M.E. Sadler to M.T. Sadler, 4 July 1900.
98. Ibid., MS Eng misc c.204, Diary of Sir M.T. Sadler, 7 Dec. 1899.

4

Administrative pincers

Kekewich observed that Gorst's exclusion from the planning of the Board of Education Act had generated 'increased friction' yet Gorst's reaction was understandable since one of the most contentious issues affected by the measure was secondary education and Devonshire had asked Gorst in 1897 to prepare a bill covering secondary education. Despite this anomaly Gorst hoped that he would still be able to determine secondary education policy through implementation of Clause VII but in this aim he was consistently opposed by the Association of School Boards. In July 1898 the Association had forwarded a petition to the Commons decrying the policy represented by the clause and this action was reinforced by individual school boards and their supporters mounting increasing pressure on the government to repeal the clause. Gorst's response was to lose patience with the boards; the first warning sign had appeared when he spoke in Liverpool in late October 1898 and stated that Clause VII had been 'much misrepresented and much misunderstood, sometimes purposely'. He had regretted that so many school boards had opposed its implementation, and when he had addressed the London Technical Education Board annual prizegiving meeting a few weeks later his comments were tantamount to a challenge to the boards, especially his statement that they 'must give up the position that they were the exclusive authority, chosen by the people, to manage education'. His anger manifested itself further in condemnatory remarks about school board elections and electorates, the former being derided as a 'kind of field day' for local party organisations while the mass of the electorates were deemed 'incompetent' to select people to manage education.[1] His anger increased yet again when he learned of the London School Board's decision to oppose the London County Council's application under Clause VII, for the Board's pre-eminence in the school board world meant that such a move, and its outcome, would be carefully scrutinised throughout the country.

The origin of the LCC's application was a consequence of the 1898 spring elections for the Council. The loss of the Progressives' majority saw the chairmanship of the Council's Technical Education Board pass from the Fabian Sidney Webb to the Moderate Edward Bond, sometime assistant Charity Commissioner and now the Conservative MP for Nottingham. Where Webb had not pursued the idea of a Clause VII application, for fear of alienating the School Board, Bond indicated to Garnett straightaway his belief that the Council should apply. A dinner party at Toynbee Hall with Bond as one of the guests revealed a possible reason for his views on this matter:

> There was talk of education and as Bond is Chairman of the Technical Education Board, the talk was with knowledge. Opinion went against School Boards – 'Why should they not control education?' said the School Board man. 'Because of the elementary teacher' said Bond and Gorst. The answer was convincing. An *ad hoc* board must fall under the army of its own officials . . .[2]

But Garnett was not ready to pursue such a course until the summer, despite Taylor's evidence that by 1897 Garnett

> had displayed a willingness to take the L[ondon] S[chool] B[oard] on in public and attempt to discredit their work in advanced education.[3]

Tantalisingly brief comments in some of Morant's correspondence with Sadler during this period indicate their concern with the state of affairs in London and Garnett's views, especially his passionate dislike of the School Board's evening classes. In a note to Sadler in March 1898, Morant wrote:

> I feel Kekewich is right about London H[igher] Grade. How neatly he puts the real obstacles. The only thing is, perhaps London can do it without raising the question. Shall I talk it over with Johnny?[4]

Whether 'Johnny' (Gorst) discussed the matter with Morant and then took it up with Bond is not known. During a visit to Tyneside, Morant observed that all the people he had met in the shipyards and elsewhere emphasised the value of evening classes, noting, 'Higher Primary theories rot. But *what* a contrast the whole atmosphere is to London'.[5] At a conference on commercial education held in July both Gorst and Garnett presented papers, Bond, Sadler and Morant being present in the audience. Gorst was at pains to stress the need for a general education forming the basis of elementary education but Garnett was careful to indicate his deliberate eschewing of any discussion about the authority to control the subjects of his paper, continuation and evening classes. Thus, whether Garnett's delay in concurring with Bond was occasioned by his waiting for the publication of the Board of Education Bill, and the possible provision of new local authorities for secondary education, is uncertain. Even after agreeing with Bond in the summer to proceed with the application he was clearly unsure about the reception it would receive and he decided to circularise all the educational institutions coming under the Council's aegis and likely to be affected by the application. The majority of responses revealed that his doubts were groundless, a feeling shared by the General Purposes and Finance Committee of the Technical Education Board when they resolved at their October meeting that his report proposing the application be forwarded to the full Board.

Kekewich undoubtedly knew of Bond and Garnett's plan by the time he made a speech at the opening of the Ferndale Organised Science School by the Ystradyfodwg School Board in mid-October and he used the opportunity to indicate very clearly his support for all the post-elementary activities of school boards. Not only did he contradict Gorst's and Devonshire's denunciations of the boards, by stating that a 'good deal of nonsense had been talked of overlapping', as well as denying that higher grade schools should be regarded as luxuries, but he argued also that evening continuation schools, properly organised, 'would become the centre of social life of the locality'.[6] The considerable tension which developed between Gorst and Kekewich over this was manifest in Gorst's subsequent reprimand. Gorst not only reminded him of his position but added:

> . . . as much as I value any assistance you are able to give in carrying out our policy, I cannot allow you to intervene between me and the Lord President, nor to hamper my initiative, whenever I think it right to make enquiries for the purpose of suggesting matters of policy to him.[7]

Kekewich's speech, however, undoubtedly strengthened the resolve of the London School Board representatives on the LCC Technical Education Board to oppose further progress being made on the Clause VII application.

The full Technical Education Board meeting of 14 November endorsed the findings of their sub-committee on Garnett's report and, in turn, sought the approval of the County Council for the application, forwarding a report of their findings and recommendations to the General Purposes Committee's meeting of 6 December. The London School Board, apprised of these developments by their representatives on the LCC, discussed the likely consequences on their own position. Dr T.J. Macnamara made the salient point that while it would be useless to 'clamour for this new authority when the Municipal Councils were going on with the work' the School Board 'had got to be there' as a nucleus, not a fraction, of such an authority through the process of educational co-ordination.[8] Lyulph Stanley, Vice President of the Board, concurred with Macnamara's view and cited several recent precedents in the development of secondary education. These included Gorst's repeated request for voluntary co-ordination in the creation of Clause VII authorities as well as Kekewich's evidence to the Bryce Commission that school boards, through their dominance in the provision of evening continuation schools were, 'to a certain extent, a secondary education authority'. Stanley contended that the Board had a right to apply as the Clause VII authority but believed that co-operation with the LCC should form the basis of the Board's actions. The Board concurred with these sentiments and requested a meeting with Council representatives to discuss the application. The Council complied and the meeting was held on 14 December.

The School Board representatives, led by Lord Reay (Chairman) and Lyulph Stanley, advocated a postponement of the application until such time as the government had resolved the issue and composition of local secondary education authorities. Indicating their belief that if the application was proceeded with as it stood it could seriously prejudice the subsequent creation of an LEA for London by legislation, the Board's representatives did not sway the views of those of the Council. In their subsequent report of the meeting, the Council representatives urged the whole Council 'not to neglect this opportunity of acquiring useful powers which affect technical education, and which will simplify the co-ordination of schools'.[9] The Council accepted this recommendation, stating that the application 'can in no way prejudice the question of the future local secondary education authority'.[10] This rider did not satisfy the School Board. They requested an inquiry by the Science and Art Department into the application and, at the same time, forwarded a lengthy memorial to Devonshire, invoking his, Gorst's and the Department's statements in support of the right of the Board to be a constituent member of the authority. The events set in train as a result of the claims made by the Board's representatives, notably Stanley and Macnamara, at the inquiry held at South Kensington under Donnelly's chairmanship on 1 February were not only to dash the Board's ambitions but ensure the complete implementation of Gorst's decentralisation policy.

In their memorial to him, the Board had referred Devonshire to the fact that under the Education Code (1890) Act school boards had been freed from the limitation of providing chiefly elementary education in their evening continuation schools and the Board had thus queried his statement that they lacked any statutory authority to be recipients of grants from the Science and Art Department. They accepted that no local authority or group of managers possessed such a right, for the power, albeit questionable, lay with that Department and its ability 'to work by minutes, which are not laid before Parliament, like the Education Code'.[11] But, as Stanley argued before the inquiry, under the terms of the Act, all school boards were entitled to apply unlimited rate funds to 'all grades and subjects of Education, including University and Technical Education'.[12] As such, then, not only was the Board in a superior position to the Council *vis-à-vis* the right to be the Clause VII authority but there was also the implication in his argument that Gorst's policy support for the county and county borough councils, with their limited educational experience, was flawed. Macnamara's comment that the Board would, if the Council's application was approved, open more new institutions in the vicinity of those under the Council's aegis and thus increase the overlapping problem, can hardly have assuaged Gorst's feelings as he listened not only to this refutation of his policy but also contravention of the spirit of the 1897 Joint Memorandum. Garnett, for the Council, refuted the Board's claims concerning the interpretation of the Act but they had left their mark on Gorst as Canon Barnett's letter to his brother a few days later indicated:

> Gorst spent the night with us. He is as despondent as ever and is now angry that Stanley and the School Board people are blocking his attempts to establish educational authorities under his Science and Art Department.[13]

As soon as the inquiry had concluded, Gorst had discussed the School Board's claims in private with Donnelly, Kekewich and Garnett. Agreeing that the LCC's application, subject to Cabinet agreement, should be approved, the rest of the meeting focused on the best method of ascertaining the legal validity of the Board's claims concerning the provisions of the 1890 Act. Garnett claimed subsequently to have provided the necessary information, a rather curious claim for a scientist given that he had been discussing the matter with a barrister and one-time Solicitor-General – Gorst. Furthermore, Gorst had been examining previous cases of school board illegalities during the previous year and he was also aware of the points made about them in Morant's Swiss Report, not to mention the fact that Roscoe, one of the members of his 1896 Departmental Committee, had been responsible for raising the queries made by the Bryce Commission concerning the legality of school board activities in post-elementary education. It would thus appear that some 30 years after the event Garnett had forgotten the reality of the situation, which was that Gorst had been using him as a sounding board for his own ideas. This notwithstanding, it was decided that the best chance of obtaining the requisite legal action was to 'obtain a surcharge on the School Board by the District Auditor, against which the School Board would be sure to appeal'.[14]

There were certain problems associated with this scheme, not the least being the need to find a cheque drawn by the School Board which was solely for an illegal payment since there appeared to be an established procedure among Local Government Board district auditors that 'unless the precise amount of illegal payments were ascertained, no surcharge could be made on the signatories of a cheque', a fact well known amongst school boards. Another problem was that only a ratepayer could appeal to the district auditor so that any member or members of school governing bodies affected by the School Board willing to initiate an appeal had to act in their private capacity. This was, as Garnett recalled, 'a very invidious and troublesome task', a remark no doubt recalling an earlier case of one ratepayer who had challenged his local school board's expenditure and had had two tons of books deposited before him to peruse. Garnett, however, did know one person who was able and willing to place a challenge before a district auditor. That person was Francis Black, the owner and headmaster of the Camden School of Art, and a personal acquaintance of Garnett's. Gorst informed Bond who, in turn, contacted Black.

Two cheques in the School Board's accounts for the payment of local fees, by members of the Board, for the examination of School Board pupils by the Science and Art Department, that is to say for subjects not covered by the Education Code and, therefore, technically of a non-elementary nature, were located by Black. He enlisted the aid of F.W. Hales, a solicitor and member of his school's governing body, and the two men brought the issue to the attention of the district auditor, T. Barclay Cockerton, in March, shortly after responses had been made in the House by Gorst and Henry Chaplin, President of the Local Government Board, to orchestrated questions about school board accounts. Gorst, in reply to a question from Bousfield, the Member for

Hackney and ex-London School Board member, stated that the Committee of Council on Education 'have always been of opinion that the school fund cannot legally be applied to supply instruction which is not under the day school or evening school Code of the Education Department'. He added that this view had been communicated to the London Board some 11 years earlier.[15] When asked by Lord Evelyn Cecil, also a member of the London School Board, about district audit procedures, Chaplin replied that the auditing of the previous half year's accounts was in progress and, 'moreover, the auditor would be willing to make a special appointment to hear any . . . objection'.[16] An anonymous article in *Education* discussing the illegality of school board expenditure so convinced Hales of the validity of his and Black's case that he decided to challenge the total expenditure on evening schools by the Board. Cockerton thus had not one but two issues to decide upon and he required three further appearances from Black and Hales before reaching his conclusions. Hales's action was rejected but he found against the Board in connection with the two cheques located by Black and thus surcharged the Board members involved for the expenditure which they had illegally sanctioned. As Gorst and Garnett had surmised the Board took the bait, lodging an appeal in the Queen's Bench against Cockerton's decision rather than pay the few hundred pounds involved. Gorst was determined that his plan should succeed, making the point to Kekewich that it was important for the Department 'that the point raised should definitely be settled by a decision of the High Court' and took the steps necessary to ensure that Cockerton not only employed an eminent barrister but that he should be one of the government Law Officers.[17] But the inception of the court case created a problem for Gorst, in that he had either to await its outcome before proceeding any further with his plan for new administrative or legislative measures or, if he proceeded with the latter, he had to live with the uncertainty about the outcome of the case. But he was not the only one aware of this consideration.

Three of Lord Salisbury's sons, Evelyn, Robert and James (Lord Cranborne), were fully aware that all subsequent policy decisions were critical for the way in which the development of the nation's secondary education system took place. They had considered initiating their own surcharge case against the Board before a district auditor but, as Evelyn Cecil commented, even if they were successful, 'Where are we? It may take a year or two to decide, and will probably cost some £600; and by that time a Radical Government may be in power and pass legislation to nullify the decision in our favour'. A cheaper and possibly more positive outcome could be achieved, he believed, if they took it upon themselves

> to stiffen the backs of the Duke of Devonshire and Gorst to bring in a sufficiently comprehensive measure as to local secondary education authorities so as to determine that the policy is to go in our direction rather than pay £600 for a delay which will enable Radicals to start off the policy in their direction.[18]

Cranborne preferred, however, to introduce a Private Member's Bill in 1899 to try and accomplish their aims but it was unsuccessful owing to the pressure on parliamentary time. Evelyn had tried to convince a meeting of members of the Association of Directors and Secretaries for Technical and Secondary Education of the viability of the Bill's aims but by then the die was being cast with the successful passage of the Board of Education Bill and, unbeknown to them, decisions taken by Gorst and Devonshire over subsequent policy measures.[19] The introduction in 1900 of a modified Code for elementary schools and a Higher Elementary Schools Minute revealed the outcome of these decisions as well as the fact that Gorst and Devonshire were not prepared to wait for the result of the Cockerton case before embarking upon any new policy measures. In the autumn of 1899, Devonshire had asked Balfour whether there was likely to be any time available in the forthcoming Parliamentary Session for the final part of the legislation concerning secondary education, that is the creation of local authorities. He had added that if time could be found there were 'some steps which I should like to take before long in the way of preparation'. The 1900 Code was part of this preparation.

The Code was in some respects a radical departure from previous departmental practice for it incorporated a new, fixed block grant of 22s per child to replace the variable amounts previously earned by elementary school children under the complicated system of government grants which had evolved from Robert Lowe's Revised Code of 1862. The new grant was greater, on average, than the annual amounts earned previously by a child in board or voluntary schools. Under it the voluntary schools stood to gain nearly £191,000 annually, whilst the board schools' income would increase by almost £68,000. Increased grants made to pupil-teachers in the Code meant that the elementary schools would receive additional funding totalling £274,566 annually.[20] Furthermore, the principle behind the block grant was that there should be a greater degree of liberalisation, locally determined, in the form and content of the elementary school curriculum. Canon Barnett believed that the Code was 'really for the good of education' although he noted that Gorst 'would have liked more variety' but had to give way to Cabinet pressure, notably from Hicks Beach.[21] As it was, all schools were required to provide a common core of subjects, including English, arithmetic, geography, history and physical education, as well as offering supplementary subjects from a list which included algebra, Euclidean geometry, mechanics, chemistry, physics, animal physiology, hygiene, botany, horticulture, Welsh (only in Wales), German, Latin, French, bookkeeping and shorthand. There were some technical subjects included for which additional grants could be earned – for example, cookery, laundry work, dairy work, and household management (for girls); manual instruction, gardening and, in seaport towns, cookery for boys.[22] These changes effectively consigned the concept of payment by results, which had continued to dominate elementary school teaching despite its abolition in 1895, to the past and this, together with the enhanced funding provided, ensured that the Code received warm support from various quarters. *The Schoolmaster* believed it represented 'a first class piece of administrative wisdom' while the NUT Executive heartily welcomed it, and even Dr T.J. Macnamara conceded that this particular component of government policy fulfilled what the London School Board had been advocating for several years.[23] The Leader of the Opposition, Sir Henry Campbell-Bannerman, admitted in private that he was glad to see an end to Lowe's system, 'which stopped or checked the friends of parsons, but which froze up real education'.[24] But the full implication of the funding changes was soon perceived by school board proponents who provided a chill counterblast to this acclaim.

Their criticisms focused on the fact that under the new Code many of the large urban school boards would suffer financial cuts. The cause of this lay not only with the block grant of 22s. being the fixed earning capacity of any child but also because Article 13 of the Code imposed an age limit of 14 years on the earning of the grant. The schools that would suffer most, therefore, under these limits would be the higher grade schools. Thus while the Leeds School Board would lose overall some £7000 annually, its Central Higher Grade School stood to forfeit 9s 6d and 6s 9d for each boy and girl, respectively. Or, in the case of a small urban board like Swansea, the higher grade school would lose 4s 6d per pupil compared with the board's overall loss of 1s 5d per head.[25] As the *Journal of Education* noted, the Code 'was generally taken to imply a further menace to what are called "higher-grade schools"'.[26] The *School Board Chronicle*, 'raging furiously', denounced the Code as further evidence of the Government's 'hostility and animus to Board schools and School Board work', and pondered whether 'the virus of Clause VII' was about to be introduced into 'the organism of the Code?'[27] The National Education Association felt the Code came down with a 'vigorous blow upon all the best School Boards' and constituted the 'most revolutionary step' in education since Lowe's Revised Code.[28] Kekewich's fear that Article 13 would be seen by the boards as a 'stronger declaration of war against Higher Grade Schools' thus appeared to be justified and this was reflected in another memorial received by Devonshire from the Association of School Boards.[29]

The memorial levelled substantial criticism at the government's policy on higher elementary education. Not only was the implementation of Clause VII singled out but the claim was made that only the Science and Art Department had any doubts about the legality of the higher grade schools.[30] Asked by Devonshire to respond to these criticisms, Abney defended the record of his old department, but conceded that the Association's views were essentially an accurate statement of the difficulties confronting the boards. He supported the idea of the boards being allowed to continue with their work in higher elementary education and argued that the loss of this type of education would be a 'national calamity'.[31] Devonshire was not assuaged by these comments, being worried that the Association's views and its political clout might generate enough of a reaction to jeopardise his and Gorst's plans for the reform of the education system. He counselled Balfour that assent to the Code represented approval only of the principle of the block grant rather than of detail, and added that 'a promise to reconsider the position of the Higher Grade Schools will remove all serious opposition'.[32] This Balfour did shortly afterwards, and concern about the Code's contents was put aside not least because of the education world's preoccupation with another new policy measure, the Higher Elementary Schools Minute, published on 6 April.

The aims and general contents of the Minute had been presented by Gorst to the Treasury in a memorandum detailing a scheme of grants for a new school, the higher elementary. The main aim was to achieve a welding together in the new school of the higher Standards of the elementary school with the lower classes of the school of science, and financed by a consolidated grant under the Code. One result envisaged by Gorst was that the new school would have

> . . . a definite top limit to its scope, and putting that limit lower than hitherto; at the same time arranging that only such children should be admitted to it and get the benefit of the higher work as are really qualified to profit by it.[33]

The reason he cited for this limitation was that it would ensure that this type of State-provided education would be available for working-class children and not be 'a cheap resort for middle class children'.[34] To reinforce this, only pupils who had been in attendance at a public elementary school in the previous year were to be eligible to attend this new school. At the same time, the nature of the curriculum to be offered was clearly defined:

> This type of school should be distinctly marked as an Elementary School, and so prevented from posing as a Secondary School. The education it is to give, the class of boy and girl for whom it is to be suited, the character of its staff, and the limits of its scope, alike, make this point very important.[35]

The aims and terms of Gorst's memorandum thus clearly mirrored those of the 1897 Joint Memorandum, the difference being that with the Minute of 6 April the Board of Education possessed the means to achieve practical results and was no longer being dependent upon the co-operation of higher grade school head masters. Furthermore, it was to be the Board of Education, and not the school boards, who would determine the necessity for such schools. Mowatt, the Permanent Secretary to the Treasury, observed that while the scheme would certainly 'restrain any rapid increase' in both the numbers of these schools and the pupils attending them there was the danger that the managers of higher schools would 'cry out against their curriculum being curtailed'. Although Gorst argued that only 1,250 students out of a total of 12,579 would be disadvantaged by the changes, the new curriculum, as representative of the highest work now to be permitted under school boards, had been shorn of most of the secondary component found in higher grade schools and, furthermore, terminated at the earlier age of 15. That the Minute would be a Procrustean measure was made clear from Gorst's behaviour over its implementation.

The first stage in implementation of the new policy was to try to convince the education world of the Minute's value, and this took place in a debate upon both the Code and the Minute in the Commons on 3 May. In this Gorst played second fiddle to Jebb, who had engineered the debate at Balfour's request.[36] Jebb argued that the two measures were conducive to the interests of education, and refuted the criticisms which both had generated. In doing so, he was careful to stress that the measures had to be considered together, not in isolation, since the Minute dealt only with elementary, and not secondary, education. To support his view Jebb invoked the 1897 Concordat, and the agreed definitions of elementary and secondary education, laying stress on the 'immediate utility' of elementary education and its leaving age of 'fifteen at the latest'.[37] He believed that general acceptance of both measures plus the effects of a soon-to-be-introduced Bill creating new secondary education authorities would produce the desired clarity of structure and function for the nation's education system. Jebb's eminence as an educationist and the clarity of his argument, plus Gorst's assurances that the Board of Education would apply the Minute intelligently, and modify it if needed, seemed to achieve the necessary placation of potential opponents, for most commentators, in and out of the House, appeared to accept the Minute as a progressive and beneficial measure. Henry Hobhouse claimed not only that the Minute was a step towards the co-ordination advocated by the Bryce Report but also that thanks were owed to Gorst 'for laying the foundation of a new and far-reaching reform in our national education system'.[38] The main Opposition speaker, J.H. Yoxall, made the important point that he would only criticise the Minute in respect of its details, not its principle, while *The Journal of Education* saw the Minute as a trump card played by Gorst amid the growing dissent over the Code and hoped that it would 'put an end to the internecine warfare, which continues in spite of the concordat signed some three years ago'.[39] Buoyed by this achievement, Gorst pressed for immediate implementation of the Minute as it stood but had first to surmount the problem of Kekewich, given his public support of the school boards. To achieve this Gorst secured Devonshire's agreement that all applications under the Minute had to receive the approval of both the President and Vice President. Gorst then notified Kekewich that the Minute's prescriptions were not to be relaxed.[40] When Kekewich signalled his acceptance, Gorst appeared to his friends to be 'happy with his success in moving on education'.[41] But it was not long before problems arose over the Minute.

The London School Board sent a deputation to the Board of Education to explore the possibility of the age limit in the Minute being extended only a few days after Gorst had introduced the measure. Kekewich tried to circumvent Gorst's directives, and appealed directly to Devonshire but he referred the matter to Gorst who, still annoyed by the Board's role in the Cockerton case, negated

117

the idea of making concessions 'to a body . . . which is avowedly trying to get the Secondary Education of London into its hands'.[42] This
refusal to modify the Minute was seized on by school board supporters
as a reneging on Gorst's assurances to the House, and a blistering
attack on the government's policy was made in Manchester by G.J.
Cockburn, the President of the Northern Counties' Education League.
At the same time, the *School Board Chronicle* lambasted the Board of
Education for its 'narrow, hard and rigid limitations as never were
dreamed of under the most reactionary administration known'.[43] Gorst
remained undeterred, for although he had accepted that the Minute
might have to be modified after it had been in operation for some time
he was not prepared to surrender at the first summons, and in this he
received Devonshire's support. But, in a similar vein, the London
School Board were not prepared to relinquish the pursuit of their
claims.

While Gorst was holidaying in the Tyrol, the School Board submitted an application for recognition of 79 of their higher grade
departments under the Minute and Devonshire asked Kekewich to
investigate the nature of the education provided by these departments.
The subsequent analysis revealed that although 46 such schools had
received the Education Department's approval in 1890 to concentrate
upon teaching in Standards V to VII, not only had the number grown
but in 1899 it had become clear, from an inspection of the higher
grade schools in Chelsea, that 'considerable extensions have been
made to the curriculum of instruction' and the schools were now going
well beyond the limits of the Code. Although Kekewich had directed
that further investigations be carried out they had not yet been concluded. Gorst was appalled to discover this state of affairs on his
return and ordered that the School Board be informed that their application for such a large number of schools was inconsistent with the
spirit of the Minute. He was not moved by the Board's subsequent
appeals for consideration on the grounds of population size or
previous support by the Department, and his anger about the latter – as
evidence of the cumulative effect of Kekewich's influence – led him
to minute the Board's letter:

> The representatives of the Education Department do not appear
> to have reminded the London School Board that their expendi-
> ture of the School rate on these Schools had been pronounced by
> the Education Department to be irregular.[44]

Gorst also remained adamant that the schools recognised under the

118

Minute should offer an education with a scientific bias, and not a commercial one as was being requested by the London Board and supported by Kekewich.

His opposition rested on a belief that commercial subjects were technological in nature and therefore not suitable for elementary schools, despite the fact that both the old and new Codes had included bookkeeping, shorthand and typing as special subjects. He believed also that higher grade schools with a commercial curriculum were 'of a very inferior type, having a pretentious name, a poor curriculum and a very inadequate staff'.[45] Consequently, when William Garnett submitted a memorandum putting forward a case for relaxing the Minute's strictures and including commercial subjects in the curriculum, his views drew Gorst's ire. Comparing the roles of secondary and higher elementary schools Garnett likened the latter to the 'training of non-commissioned officers of the Industrial and Commercial Army'.[46] Gorst objected strongly to this analogy, stating that the fundamental aim of any school must be 'Education (the development of faculties) not Training (the development of tricks)'.[47] Garnett's subsequent argument for a much more vocational approach in the teaching methodology used in the higher elementary school only weakened his case in Gorst's eyes, the latter being firmly convinced about the effects this would have on secondary schools:

> . . . parents would eagerly send their children to learn, gratis, tricks which would for some time to come increase their money value – the secondary schools would be deserted by all except those children who were sent on social grounds.[48]

Both men's views reflected their feelings about the relative strength of higher grade schools and the secondary schools, with Garnett's being the more confident because of his expectations of the outcome of the Cockerton case. Gorst, on the other hand, was more cautious as well as concerned for the secondary schools, no doubt because of the impact of the continued opposition he had had to face from the school boards in most of his work since assuming office. If some of his statements manifested almost a siege mentality in their rigidity of outlook as far as the London Board was concerned, he did not neglect the opportunity presented a month later in the House to expound his criticisms of the work of the higher grade schools in general.

The major problem besetting these schools, he contended, was that they were tainted with the defects of the elementary system, putting far too much emphasis on drill and training and not enough upon originality of thought or the development of children's characters.[49] His comments reflected his disdain for elementary and higher grade school teachers, a feeling he had already displayed at the Toynbee Hall dinner which Bond had attended, and were shared by his friend Canon Barnett:

> The teachers themselves reflected the worst aspects of modern society; they were too determined to secure material advancement, too uninterested in more enduring human values, too indifferent to the individual character and needs of their students.[50]

Gorst's views also mirrored closely those contained in a report recently sent to to him by Owen Owen, the Chief HMI for Wales. Owen believed fervently that the low percentage of graduates in higher grade schools 'shows the necessarily and inevitably great inferiority of the Board School work judged from the intellectual standpoint'. Although these views were too general and simplistic, given the supportive comments of other observers of school board teachers, Gorst claimed that one corollary was that the retention of pupils beyond Standard VII in the higher grade schools was actually preventing these pupils from receiving a good secondary education. As Owen had put it:

> Our enemies attack our present policy as being class legislation . . . *On the contrary*, we are endeavouring to stop the short-sighted policy of those who *are* keeping the clever boys of the 'masses' *out* of the Secondary Schools, and who *are* restricting them to what cannot in the nature of things be so good an education or intellectual stimulus and training . . .[51]

Although these views naturally alienated the school boards, higher grade school staff and their supporters, they indicated Gorst's intention to stand firm on the Minute. Equally significant was the fact that by the summer of 1900 his policies for secondary education had created a situation closely resembling that of containment as far as the school boards' aspirations towards becoming local education authorities were concerned. His actions had, in effect, resulted in a pincer movement being mounted against the school boards. The Cockerton case, on one flank, constituted a legal challenge to the post-elementary education being given in board schools while the Code and the Minute, on the other flank, were administrative devices designed to ensure that any elementary school provided only an elementary

120

education of a type deemed suitable for the children of the working classes. His chances of remaining in a position to ensure the completion of his aims were temporarily disturbed, however, by the general election of 1900.

The so-called 'Khaki Election', because of the impact of the Boer War upon the nation's sensibilities, returned the government with a reduced majority, despite one observer's belief that the country had gone 'Khaki-mad'. Salisbury, aided by Balfour, became preoccupied with the 'difficult and disagreeable' reconstruction of his Ministry. Balfour acknowledged the public belief that 'fresh blood is required to regenerate our worn-out system' but he did not subscribe to it, preferring instead to opt for promotion 'both within and into' the government.[52] One member of the government who remained, but without promotion, was Gorst. The lack of promotion was not unexpected, for an earlier request for transfer to another department, when the Board of Education Bill had passed, had been turned down by Salisbury. Among other reasons Salisbury had given at that time, he had cited the antagonism Gorst had generated within the party by his derogatory comments on both voluntary schools and certain supporters of the party. As Salisbury charitably put it:

> . . . when you are defending the policy of the Government, you give both to friends and foes the impression that you are attacking it. Your manner of fencing seems to involve a, not infrequent, backhander, aimed at those who are standing by your side, or behind you. You are evidently yourself unconscious of this peculiarity in your manner – but the impression that it exists prevails largely.[53]

Although Jebb and Anson had both been mooted as a possible replacement for Gorst in Balfour's and Salisbury's discussions about the new government, Gorst's retention of his position partly reflected their belief that he would be safer within rather than without the government fold. When Edward Hamilton raised the topic of the government changes, and Gorst's position in particular, with Devonshire while staying at Sandringham, another reason became apparent:

> Gorst had evidently played his cards better of late. Indeed the Duke spoke in quite approving terms of his Vice President. He said, he had almost got to like Gorst, who was accordingly going to remain on.[54]

Gorst privately acknowledged that it was 'mortifying to be passed over' but claimed that it was partly because he had not brought himself to Salisbury's attention and partly because 'I persuaded myself, like the fox in the fable, that a seat in the Cabinet was not an object to be desired'.[55] The questionable validity of his views notwithstanding, Gorst's retention of the Vice Presidency was greeted with acclaim in some quarters:

> This is . . . very satisfactory . . . to those who recognise him as almost the only Conservative who has any interest in education other than that of securing the maximum of public money for the denominational schools.[56]

More importantly, he could now continue to pursue his policies and in this he was aided by the judgment of the Cockerton Case.

The Queen's Court found against the London School Board, not only in its use of rate moneys for classes held under the Department of Science and Art regulations but also for similar expenditure on evening school classes. Mr Justice Wills and Mr Justice Kennedy maintained that the Board was bound by the Elementary Education Acts in both the application of rate money for education and in the principal part of the education it provided. They judged, furthermore, that the Education Code (1890) Act did not empower the Board to provide adult education at the expense of the rates as it only related to the obtaining of grants from the Education Department. For these conditions to be changed would require an Act of Parliament and not the 'stroke of a pen of a Government department'.[57] Thus, while some of the work of school board higher grade schools had been pronounced illegal, so had the majority of the education given in their evening schools. The judgment had not included a definition of childhood but had indicated an upper age of 16–17 years. Under this limit just over half the number of evening school pupils could not continue with their studies as the schools stood constituted, while if the age was lowered to 15, then nearly 70 per cent of the pupils would be affected.

As a response to the Cockerton judgment, and the London School Board's decision to appeal against it, Morant drafted a memorandum on evening schools because of the serious administrative and educational consequences if the Court of Appeal upheld the lower court's decision. In his penetrating analysis of the development of these institutions, and their illegal work, he apportioned a major part of the blame to the Education Department, and by implication Kekewich, for trying to keep them within the elementary system despite their blatantly secondary character. Morant castigated the

Department's policy as one of drift following the line of least resistance. Highlighting the fact that a parliamentary solution to the problem had to be found in the very near future, Morant argued that one section of the Board should have responsibility for all evening schools and classes under a new set of regulations. At the local level he supported the concept of the county and county borough councils as the new education authorities and advocated their control over these schools and classes. As this would mainly affect the county borough councils – the majority of rural evening schools being administered by the counties under the Technical Instruction Act were not affected by the Cockerton judgment – he was prepared to let the school boards act as agents for the councils if this would overcome any serious political objections. Gorst concurred with his views and brought the matter to Devonshire's attention, making the point that although the Higher Elementary Schools Minute effectively catered for any problems connected with the day schools of science, no provision had been made for the 'catastrophe' which would occur in evening schools should the Court of Appeal's decision uphold the earlier judgment. If this was not rectified the government could, he claimed, find themselves on the horns of a dilemma through having either to close a number of evening schools or 'beg the School Boards to carry them on illegally, with a promise of indemnity when Parliament meets'.[58]

The Court of Appeal reached its verdict on 1 April and in supporting the Queen's Bench judgment reached against the School Board, the Master of the Rolls emphasised the fact that the education to be provided by it and other school boards had to be elementary. He defined a child, using Section 48 of the 1876 Elementary Education Act, as one between the ages of five and 15 years.[59] This confirmation of the illegality of parts of higher grade and evening school work placed the government in the position Gorst had forecast and the necessary changes to the law had to be made and made quickly, despite the anticipated appeal by the School Board to the House of Lords. This need was confirmed when the School Board decided not to pursue the case any further and ministers soon became the recipients of a barrage of letters entreating them to preserve the evening schools. One working-class writer made the point that the evening classes were

> . . . the only means of advancing my knowledge, and to crush them I consider the Government is acting in direct opposition to the wishes of the people who put them in power. In my trade, imported foreigners are surely and quickly taking the place of

British labour, and it is only by attendance at such classes that I have been able to maintain my position among the host of Germans who surround me. Surely this action of the Government cannot be called patriotic, and I urge you to vindicate its patriotism in this matter.[60]

Morant was unimpressed by this and similar letters, claiming that they were being organised by persons

who knew the 'ins and outs' of the matter: hence the answers that are sent will be scanned by experts and used (as I know they are being used) at further public meetings, to get up further agitation. This letter is an example of the political danger of the situation. These adult scholars at Evening Schools have votes.[61]

None the less, he did concede that while technically the Cockerton judgment was the responsibility of the courts the resolution of the difficulties lay with the government and if it did not act through legislation then 'the Government *do* injure the man's opportunities'.[62]

Parliament rose for the Easter Recess shortly after the Court of Appeal's decision had been made public, but on the last day before the break Balfour and Gorst were subjected to intense questioning from Macnamara and Yoxall about how the government intended to rectify the current situation. Gorst answered by stating that the fortnight's break would provide a useful period to think about the judgment and he reminded the House that their chance to achieve a solution would come with the introduction of a new Education Bill. Naturally this did not stop attacks being mounted against the government's educational policies during the recess and one Liberal MP, Francis Channing, decried them for being subservient to the demands of the 'two great groups of obscurantists to whom Lord Salisbury's administration owes so much, the clerics . . . and the old Tories'.[63] The speeches made at the NUT's annual conference also contained a considerable degree of militancy, one speaker claiming that the government's policies were a conspiracy 'against the advanced instruction of the working classes, and it was largely a conspiracy of one family in the country'.[64] Unperturbed by such claims, Gorst, Morant and Abney had started work on drafting a new set of regulations for evening schools and they finished their task by the end of the month.

The regulations capitalised on the opportunity presented by the Cockerton judgments to reorganise both the administration and educational role of these schools. At the central level, control of the schools was to rest with the Secondary Branch of the Board, for the schools were to be recognised, using one of Kekewich's phrases, as 'secondary education for the masses'. Local administration of the schools was to be the same as proposed in the Bill – by the county and county borough councils – as this would ensure that in the future funding of all the work done in the schools and classes would be legal. The minimum age of entry for pupils to the schools was to be 12 years and they were not to be in attendance at either an elementary or secondary day school. Devonshire sanctioned the regulations although he wanted an accompanying memorandum to be provided indicating their genesis and to show how they would work in relation to the Bill, contending that 'it might give the Bill a leg-up, if it were shown how throughout the Regulations it is assumed that the Bill will pass'.[65] The regulations were issued on 3 July and the destruction of the school boards' work in secondary education was now complete, for in addition to the Cockerton judgments and these regulations, the Higher Elementary Schools Minute had recently come into operation. All that now remained outstanding to complete Gorst's aims was the establishment of new local education authorities.

The Duke of Devonshire had originally signalled his appreciation of the need for new local secondary education authorities in the course of his Drapers' Company speech at the beginning of 1897. The subsequent development of the Board of Education Act had precluded achievement of this goal but while the Act had been before the Commons, Balfour had commented that the measure should only be regarded as an instalment of some further Bill which would place secondary education on a more satisfactory footing. Planning of this 'further' Education Bill started in January 1900 when Gorst and Devonshire met Ilbert, the Parliamentary Counsel, to discuss their ideas, and Devonshire then floated the main points to be contained in the Bill before Salisbury. Describing its main proposal as making the county and county borough councils the nation's secondary education authorities with responsibility for establishing and aiding secondary schools in addition to their current roles in technical education, Devonshire claimed that the only potential problem he could envisage was the 'denominational difficulty'. This, he believed, could be overcome given the precedents provided by the Technical Instruction Act of 1889 and the Endowed Schools Act of 1869, but Salisbury was quite perturbed by the possibility of denominational religious instruction being excluded from public funding of these schools while undenominational instruction was not, and he made his thoughts plain to Devonshire.[66] Devonshire thus had to return to the drafting board with Ilbert and when questioned subsequently in the Lords about the date of the Bill's introduction, he indicated that although it had been 'under very careful consideration for some time' it would not be brought in until after April. Further conversations with Ilbert on over-coming the denominational instruction problem convinced him that the best solution was for the Bill to be drafted along the lines of the 1889 Technical Instruction Act.[67] He thus sent Salisbury not only a copy of the draft Bill and a memorandum by Ilbert but his own memo-randum detailing the principal points 'in less technical language'.[68]

Salisbury's reply indicated his unease with two aspects of the draft, namely the financial implications of the proposed extension of the councils' rating powers and, again, the denominational issue. No doubt irritated by the Premier's limited view of the State's role in education, Devonshire took great pains to indicate the likely outcome of his objections in the first case. Although he conceded that an increase in the councils' rating powers was not vital, he did make the observation that no sector of education had ever been self-supporting. 'If it had', he pointed out:

> endowments or Government subventions would have been unnecessary for our Universities, University Colleges and Secondary Schools. We can scarcely rely on fresh endowments meeting the educational wants of the future, and unless Secondary schools can receive some assistance, either from the taxes or the rates, I am afraid that we shall remain permanently behind other countries.[69]

The only other realistic possibility before them was to use govern-ment funding, one which Devonshire felt the Chancellor of the Exchequer would oppose as well as being 'a more doubtful policy than that of allowing County authority (Councils – not Education Committees) to spend such sums out of their own funds as they thought necessary in the circumstances of their own districts'. As to the recurring topic of denominational education, Devonshire stressed that the most effective way of surmounting the problem was to main-tain the provisions of the Technical Instruction Act which had worked 'without friction of any kind for 10 years, [and] have not prevented strictly denominational institutions from receiving aid from the County Authorities'. He was confident that they would work 'equally smoothly' in the case of most, if not all, secondary schools, and Salisbury gave way before these points so that Devonshire was able to present the Bill to the Cabinet.

COOL PARLIAMENTARY LARDER

THE DEVONSHIRE CREAM.

Martha Balfour (house-keeper). "THERE, DON'T 'EE CRY, DUKEY DEAR! I'VE PUT IT AWAY, AND IT'LL KEEP BEAUTIFULLY TILL NEXT YEAR. AND I'VE GIVEN YOU SOMETHING TO GO ON WITH!"

3 'The Devonshire Cream': One view of the control being exerted over education policy by Balfour and the Duke of Devonshire. (Cartoon in *Punch*, CXXI, 3 July 1901, p. 15)

His memorandum on the draft measure covered similar territory to that of his correspondence with Salisbury, but he devoted a major part to the questions likely to arise from the choice of the local authorities to be recognised as the new local secondary education authority, given the relative plethora of local bodies currently recognised as rating bodies for the purpose of aiding technical education. He made it clear that the size of the authority was of paramount consideration where the efficient administration of the schools to come under the new authority was concerned. This criterion had been recognised by the 1890 Local Taxation Act and the precedent provided by it reinforced the decision to restrict the new authorities to the county and county borough councils. The Bill allowed the new authorities to aid and develop both secondary and technical education and it was envisaged that each council should establish an education committee, to be sanctioned by the Board of Education, while the 'whiskey' money provided by the 1890 Act would be used for broader educational purposes. Devonshire's arguments appeared to have convinced the Cabinet, Gorst reporting to the Barnetts shortly afterwards that, 'a sort of promise from the Great Joseph that the Secondary Bill shall be brought on' had been obtained.[70]

It was to be late June, however, before Devonshire could introduce the Bill into the Lords and while he hoped that it might proceed during the remainder of the Session he did acknowledge that at this late stage there was little likelihood that this could be accomplished. Although he did confess in his introduction that the Bill contained 'very little' beyond the secondary education proposals of the 1896 Bill, he was at pains to establish the credentials of the new measure, invoking not only the 1890 Act but also the Bryce Report.[71] He also took care to point out that there was nothing in the Bill which precluded the representation of school boards on the education committees to be established by the councils, a conciliatory gesture yet one which also covered the government should the Cockerton case not produce the desired result. Time was the enemy in this particular instance, the Bill having to be dropped after achieving its Second Reading in the Lords, and Devonshire thus had to resort to the same tactic he had employed with the Board of Education Bill in 1898, asking all interested in the new measure to think about it before the next Session. The *School Board Gazette* soon came to the conclusion that it was nothing more than a 'very little measure for dealing with a very large subject, and one conceived in a spirit quite unworthy of the object professedly in view'.[72] And the general election a few months later ensured that public interest was firmly focused on other issues, not least the progress of the Boer War, rather than this latest government venture in educational reform.

Gorst returned to a consideration of the contents for the new Bill in November 1900 and he produced several lengthy memoranda for Devonshire to consider. They argued the need for the county and county borough councils to be the new education authorities, for he rejected the use of *ad hoc* bodies as their existence was 'an anomaly and inconsistent with the true principles of local government'. To make the councils effective authorities it was necessary that they should have conferred upon them not only the same powers of rating and management enjoyed by school boards councils but also 'the most extensive powers of combination and of contribution'. To overcome the problem of the non-county borough and urban councils, Gorst advocated the use of Clause 10 of the 1896 Bill which practically forbade the local authority to be the manager of any schools and compelled them to delegate their authority to bodies of local managers; thus these smaller authorities could be utilised by the new LEAs as their agents. He also detailed the obstacles posed by the school boards which would confront these new authorities and, if not resolved, would render them 'little more than a feeble competitor'. He suggested, therefore, that the powers of the school boards be transferred to the new authorities. This arrangement would resolve the question being increasingly asked in the nation about the need for

> . . . two educational authorities in one district. I feel sure that if the Government took a bold line and proposed such a measure they would meet with very general support in the Country and only a few School Board enthusiasts like Mr. Stanley would be likely to oppose them very strongly.[73]

He argued that the new authorities should administer by means of an education committee to whom all powers except that of rating could be delegated. Similarly, an authority's agents would carry out their administration by means of a statutory committee. While the rating for secondary education would remain the preserve of the county or county borough councils, all the councils involved within an authority would have the power to employ rate aid for any elementary school in their district. To overcome the continuing voluntary school problem of funding, Gorst argued that the authorities should also have the power to aid these schools from the rates. Having outlined the need for comprehensive, and not just secondary education only, education authorities, Gorst warned Devonshire that if the government did not implement such a plan the hydra-like activities of the school boards would exacerbate the problems already afflicting both secondary and elementary education.

Support for Gorst's ideas had recently come into existence with the publication a few months earlier of Sidney Webb's Fabian tract, 'The Education Muddle and the Way Out'. Webb's document had had a prolonged birth as a result of the opposition it had encountered within the Fabian Society, especially from Graham Wallas and Stewart Headlam. It had been first presented to the Society in May 1899 and, like Morant's Swiss report, had been obviously intended to guide government policy. Although necessarily modified for publication two years later, Webb's intention remained the same. His succinct analysis of the faults still bedevilling the education system led him to advocate local administrative unity as a key component in their resolution. Worried that the proposed government Education Bill would follow the line of 'least resistance and least thought', Webb resolutely dismissed *ad hoc*ery as a possible basis for the local education authority and firmly advocated instead the county and county borough councils. But while he wanted administrative unity within the counties, including the transfer of all school board functions and schools, in the county boroughs Webb proposed retention of the school boards, leaving the councils to control all other education in their areas. Gorst was sufficiently impressed by the similarity of these arguments to his own to have had 50 galley pulls circulated through Whitehall.[74]

Devonshire's response, however, indicated that he was beginning to have second thoughts about the measure and that he was uncertain whether the county councils would be willing to undertake these new duties. In addition, he was not sure whether he understood the proposals concerning rating powers. Unless these points could be clarified, he felt the opposition that the proposals would generate would seriously limit the chances of their being accepted. Of equal importance was the need to secure the support of the county councils.[75] Gorst replied that there was sufficient evidence to indicate that the councils were ready to take on this task but that he would check with Sir John Hibbert, well known for his involvement in county council educational affairs and an ex-president of the County Councils' Association. Hibbert's response was, however, rather more qualified than Gorst expected, and stated that in the case of the county boroughs there would be some who would be opposed 'to the bitter end' to Gorst's plan and he felt that it would be better to try to reach an agreement over the proposals rather than force them through, pointing out that he did not wish to see a repetition of the 1896 Bill. As far as the counties were concerned, there might be some differences of opinion, and the smaller ones might baulk if new or increased rating was involved, but on the whole he was confident that there would be concurrence with the proposals. The recent judgment in the Cockerton case, however, compounded the matter, for he believed it created a 'most difficult' situation in which there would have to be some *modus vivendi* in urban areas between the school boards and the new secondary education authorities.[76]

While the Cockerton judgment reverberated through the educational world and generated an outcry from some sectors, others believed it represented the catalyst for major change:

> Now is the opportunity for the Duke of Devonshire. Things cannot remain as they are. Fresh legislation is inevitable. Either the School Boards must have further powers given them, or they must be absorbed in the one Educational Authority, whose advent seems at last near . . . The Duke must go back to the principles of Sir John Gorst's Bill of 1896.[77]

If such exhortations helped to strengthen Devonshire's resolve, Balfour was not so sure and remained apprehensive about a forthcoming visit to Chatsworth during the Christmas break, fearing that

> Devonshire is sure to talk to me at length upon his educational schemes. I confess they alarm me: not because they are defective but because they are too complete. I fear a repetition of our parliamentary experience of '96.[78]

And on his return from Chatsworth Balfour consulted Ilbert about the current state of the Education Bill and this was followed, two days later, by a long meeting between Devonshire, Gorst and Ilbert. One outcome was that Gorst informed Ilbert two weeks later that the second part of the Bill, relating to elementary education, was to be dropped. For Ilbert this change raised the question of whether it was still intended to create single, comprehensive LEAs, for if it was then he foresaw no legislation being forthcoming during the current Parliamentary Session.[79] But only a few days later Devonshire told Gorst that in his forthcoming speech on Supply to the Commons, 'it would do no harm to hint at the possibility of creating an authority for all education', although he added the rider that it would have to be made in such a way 'as if it was the V.P.'s own suggestion, and the Government should not of course be committed in any way'.[80]

Gorst was more than happy to oblige with this request and used his speech to mount a critical analysis of the illegal work of the school boards, including their evening schools, 'the most chaotic part of the whole of our chaotic system'. Condemning the competition this illegal work had engendered with other, legitimate educational institutions, Gorst's picture of the boards as educational agencies was painted in the darkest of hues. The solution was, he believed, relatively simple:

> . . . we shall never have anything like a proper system of education in this country until we make up our mind what is to be the authority, until we have one authority, and until schools of every kind of every grade are placed under that one authority. Then there will be no more overlapping, no more trouble about the particular kind of school, or the particular course of education to be given in it . . . .You would have education carried on in a sensible and business-like kind of manner, and you would get rid of the chaos which exists at present.[81]

Support for this view came from both sides of the House but Bryce counselled the government that for their Bill to be successful it should be free of anything likely to arouse sectarian passions.

Observing the activities of his colleagues with a detached frame of mind, Michael Sadler was not sanguine about the need for any further educational legislation, being convinced that the country was 'not ripe for a satisfactory measure. Conservatives depend too much on reactionary vote, Liberals on the democratic school board vote'. He believed that the best scheme would allow the county councils to control secondary education and the school boards elementary education. Unimpressed by the educational work of the non-county borough and urban district councils, he believed that any municipalisation of education would be disastrous and would lead to the development of 'inefficient secondary education on school board lines'.[82] Canon Barnett was more concerned about the government's likely approach to the Bill, doubting in his 'heart of hearts . . . if the government has [the] backbone to push it through against the certain opposition of many'.[83] The Cabinet had taken cognizance of the increasing public concern over the effects of the Cockerton judgment, however, and had decided 'to press through all its stages an Education Bill which is urgently called for'.[84] The chief problem was deciding on the best time for its introduction since there would have to be a delay before the Second Reading could be held, owing to the time required for the budget and the new civil list arising from Edward VII's accession to the throne. On 3 May they decided not to postpone the matter further and Devonshire was asked to direct Gorst to introduce it four days later.

Devonshire sent his instructions about the introductory speech only a few hours before Gorst was due to deliver it, wanting him to stress the government's unanimity on the need for the establishment of one local comprehensive authority. Gorst needed no prompting on this point, being glad to reiterate the reasons underlying the choice of the county and county borough councils as the new education authority. He hammered home the theme of the need to achieve an effective decentralisation of educational administration by the establishment of authorities who could not only meet the educational needs of their localities but who would also be able to provide the local unity of control to resolve the problems afflicting the education system. Small counties would be allowed to combine if they wished, in order to become a more effective education body, while non-county borough and urban district councils could remain distinct from the county by acting as its agent for secondary education. But the limitation of the measure was that it did not create truly comprehensive authorities, elementary education remaining outside the new authorities' purview, apart from being able to empower school boards to maintain any school whose income was impaired by the Cockerton judgment. As one government MP observed, Gorst's speech 'said so little but hinted at so much'.[85] The consensus view of the Opposition was that a larger measure, creating truly comprehensive authorities, would have been welcome and, given the acknowledged shortage of parliamentary time, it should have been preceded by a limited measure legally empowering the school boards to continue for a year.

Henrietta Barnett felt that Gorst's speech had dwelled too much on clauses and difficulties which 'the mass do not understand' but her husband believed that there were signs of a favourable reaction to the Bill owing to a 'curious change in opinion – people are now much more ready for county council management'.[86] R.P. Scott contacted Kekewich shortly after the Bill's introduction to ask about the possible line of support the IAHM could provide while further support for the measure came from the County Councils' Association, the Association of Municipal Corporations and various denominational bodies. Eleanor Sidgwick told her brother, Balfour, that Henry Hobhouse's view that an amendment to the Bill was urgently required so as to enable the Board of Education 'to bring local authorities together with a view to their amalgamation' was sufficiently worthy of his attention. She supported Hobhouse because

> . . . there is not sufficient (?motive) power to make local authorities take the initiative as to uniting, and overcome the initial difficulties of doing so and yet it is believed that a very little pressure would bring desirable combinations about.[87]

The school boards did not hesitate, however, to make their displeasure with the measure known to the Board of Education and Acland was equally critical in his response to Sir Henry Campbell-Bannerman's request for his views about the Bill. He was cautious about the concept of single secondary authorities for although Gorst had made 'a magnificent exordium' on the subject the Bill failed to provide any information on certain issues, including how the school boards in large cities as well as rural voluntary schools were going to be treated. At the same time, he rejected the claim of some of the more radical members of the Liberal Party for single authorities based on school boards, not only because of public concerns about the sectarian squabbles which had increasingly dominated school board elections but also because the county councils would not yield the 'whiskey money'. In general, his position was very much what it had been in 1896 – that is, 'it is premature to force elementary education as well as secondary education upon the County Councils (which is supposed to be the intention of this Bill)'. As a postscript he noted that one Conservative and ex-Vice President, Sir William Hart Dyke, was 'quite disgusted with the Bill . . . He suspects the Cecil influence in making the Bill such a fiasco'.[88]

The reaction of the Conservative and Liberal Unionist MPs to the measure was remarkably muted and one observer commented that:

> The reception the Bill has met with so far is of the wet-blanket and shower-bath order. The Bill has hardly any friends, Sir John has hardly any sympathisers. He wanders about and waits about and shows his anxious face in vain. Not even the Bill of 1896 got such a douche on its First Reading. The fighting spirit of party was at first behind the 1896 Bill; the fighting spirit of party is conspicuous by its absence to-day . . . the Bill is practically still-born; "it is not worth the while to bother about it" seems to be the verdict of the average M.P. Anything more chilly, more discouraging, more cold-shouldery, cannot be imagined.[89]

The subsequent postponement of the Second Reading was thus seen by political and educational commentators as an ominous sign and as time went by the chances of the Bill's being passed became more remote. Edward Talbot felt constrained to contact Balfour at the beginning of June, asking him to stick 'quietly but tenaciously' to the Bill, arguing that since Balfour had indicated that the measure was the first and correct initial step towards a more substantial reform of educational administration, it would make it easier, if successful, for the subsequent measure to pass. He believed that the opposition to the Bill stemmed partly from 'the old intolerant fiercely undenominational' views of school board supporters but added: 'The Church may not appear very warm in support – because they cannot see your whole plans'. He warned Balfour that abandonment of the Bill would seriously affect the government because its 'worst enemy is an impression that it is weak or languid'.[90] Before Balfour had time to send a reply he had to receive a deputation of government back-benchers about the Bill, including Jebb, Anson, Lockwood, Hobhouse and Talbot.

Jebb, acting as spokesman, outlined their view of the situation, including the belief that in order to pass, the existing measure would require the House to sit into September or that there be an autumn Session. The alternative was to pass a single-clause Bill authorising county and county borough councils to license school boards to carry on higher grade schools as the councils saw fit. They were opposed, however, to a simple Bill merely suspending the Cockerton judgment because they believed the school boards would use the year to entrench themselves more firmly in secondary education and it would be virtually impossible to dislodge them subsequently. Balfour agreed that without an autumn Session the Bill could not be passed but when Jebb intervened to urge that in that case there should be the promise of a Bill brought in early in the next Session, Balfour 'to our surprise rather demurred'. When pressed on the need for such a promise the deputation found him indifferent to the loss of prestige that the government would suffer by dropping the Bill, and indignantly denied that any complaint would be justified, seemingly forgetful of the fact that both he and the Duke had declared publicly that the Bill 'must pass'. All that he would promise them was that no decision would be taken before the Cabinet at the end of the week but Jebb was not convinced, telling his wife, 'of course they will drop the big Bill, and bring in the small one', despite the fact that the rank and file of the party were now against dropping the Bill and a petition had been started to save it. The outlook for education, he felt, was not good and some of the deputation

135

> . . . were much impressed by the singular indifference to the subject of Education which A.Balfour showed: he does not seem to realise that the question is of urgent national importance, and that the country is now keenly interested in it.[91]

Balfour's attitude to the deputation was in reality a mask for his anger about the educational problems engendered by the Cockerton judgment, a situation which he found 'tiresome' and over which 'Gorst has got us into a mess'.[92] One crucial factor in the situation, as he told the Bishop of Coventry, was parliamentary time, for

> . . . I never anticipated dealing with the Education Question this session: nor should I ever have permitted any Bill even to be introduced had it not been for the Cockerton judgment. It was quite evident, with the war going on in South Africa, with the enormous amount of financial work . . . in connection with the Budget, etc., a less convenient season for original legislation could not well be imagined. The Cockerton judgment renders it necessary to do something to this end, and the Education Bill was read a first time. It has provoked a degree of opposition which seems to be wholly irrational, and which indeed is only worth consideration because it involves an expenditure of Parliamentary time which it may be impossible to find before next year. I do not know what view upon this the Cabinet will take, but if they hold that it is impossible to ask that the measure should pass as it stands in the present Session, they will probably decide to deal with the immediately pressing problem of Continuation Schools on the lines laid down in Clause 8 of the Bill, and thus embody, though in a provisional form, the very principle to which the opposition seem most to object. Such a clause would no doubt be as controversial as the whole Bill, but, being only a clause, the question of time ceases to be the dominant consideration.[93]

Three days later, Edward Hamilton learned that the Cabinet had decided to drop the Bill and replace it with a temporary measure.[94] The reason Lord Salisbury gave to the monarch for this decision was the Cabinet's belief that the government backbenchers were unwilling 'to incur the discomfort involved in regular attendances at the House' which, in turn, meant that they had to substitute a smaller Bill for 'so complicated a measure as the Education Bill'. The short, replacement Bill would deal with 'the immediate difficulties raised by the Cockerton judgment' but there would also be a public statement of the government's hope to introduce another Bill at the beginning of 1902.[95] A small Cabinet Committee, consisting of Balfour, Devonshire, Gorst, Long and Morant, was quickly established to draft the new Bill and then Balfour, Devonshire and Gorst met Unionist MPs in Committee Room 10 of the House on 4 July to explain why the original Bill was being dropped, Balfour providing the reasons and Devonshire the details of policy which were implicit in the shorter, replacement measure. Devonshire indicated his disappointment with the turn of events but hoped that now the school boards were to be limited to the provision of elementary education, it would be possible to pass a larger measure in the next Session. Gorst's displeasure with the abandonment of the Bill soon became apparent during his response to questions in the House, one observer going so far as to claim that he was sulking, partly because he was having to bring in a measure 'to set right legislatively the mischief he had administratively induced'.[96]

The new, one-clause 'Cockerton Bill' was introduced under the ten-minute rule which effectively curtailed any possible obstruction. The clause enabled county or county borough councils and other authorities coming under the terms of the Technical Instruction Act to empower school boards to use the rates to maintain schools or classes declared illegal as a result of the Cockerton judgment for a period of one year. Gorst's minimal introduction of the Bill did not minimise, Bryce asserted, the objection felt by the Opposition to the use of the rule and to the contents of the clause. Curtailed by the rule in what he could say, Bryce contended that the Bill's proposed subjection of 'one popularly elected body, elected for a particular purpose, to another popularly elected body, elected for another purpose, and for such a course as that I think there is no precedent in our legislation'.[97] But if Gorst had been unusually terse in his introduction in the Second Reading he gave vent to his feelings of frustration as well as rebutting charges made that he had, during the course of his introduction of the earlier Bill, laid false charges against the school boards about their use of government funds. He not only substantiated these earlier charges but calmly proceeded to introduce new ones, backing them up with comments from reports made by the inspectorate. As his speech developed the tension in the House increased, with Liberal members becoming incensed when he claimed:

> Are we to keep up in this House the farce that school boards are elected for educational purposes? Everybody knows that educational purposes are the very last ideas in the minds of the members of school boards. [Opposition cries of 'Oh'] I have

heard that they are elected, some on religious grounds, some on party grounds, but I have never heard of anyone being elected on educational grounds.[98]

As to the charge that the new one-clause Bill would maintain the status quo as far as the boards were concerned, he agreed, but it was a status of 'competition, of waste, of extravagance' and would, he claimed, prevent the arrival of a better state of things.[99] The press cartoonists had a field day, usually depicting Gorst as a jester, and *The Spectator*, although supporting Gorst's approach, could not forbear to comment that the Opposition had often wished Gorst could be unmuzzled in the House, 'to show what a good educationalist he is. Their prayer has been granted; we wonder how they like the answer'.[100] *The Schoolmaster* thought that as his speech had progressed so 'the cloven hoof began to peep out' while Gorst's cynicism had offended the moral sense of the House; the combined effect of his speech and manner had been 'almost enough to make angels weep'.[101] Acland wrote despairingly to Asquith: 'What a Mountebank Gorst is. I wish you would chastise him.' But he had to add, 'no one cares much about education in the country. What do they care about in the matter of politics?'[102]

The reaction Gorst had provoked did not help smooth the passage of the Bill, the Opposition putting up a determined resistance during both the Second Reading and the Committee Stage. The absence of 'Jemmy' Lowther, the Chairman of Committees, owing to an attack of gout, meant that closure could not be applied during the Committee Stage and the Opposition 'simply revelled in obstruction at their own sweet will', the debates being a 'réchauffé' of the Second Reading.[103] None the less, the Bill passed its Third Reading on 30 July; one Liberal MP believed that Balfour, irritated by the opposition, 'solaced himself by violently thrusting through a small, inconclusive and harmful Bill by sheer force of numbers, not argument'.[104] The respite gained by this success was only temporary for the government was now faced with the task of drawing up a new educational measure for the next session. Although Gorst had been effectively barred by Balfour from any major role in the formulation of educational legislation since 1896, he had used all the administrative means available to him to ensure that the government would have to re-examine the issues he had first raised six years earlier. What he could not have foreseen was that his influence over the new Bill would soon be curtailed as Balfour, Devonshire and Morant increasingly assumed control.

NOTES

1. *School Board Chronicle*, 60 (26 Nov. 1898), p. 597.
2. S.A. Barnett to F. Barnett, 1899, quoted in H.O. Barnett, *Canon Barnett* (1918), II, p. 27. See also E.J.T. Brennan, *Education for National Efficiency: the Contribution of Sidney and Beatrice Webb* (1975), p. 51; B.M. Allen, *William Garnett: A Memoir* (1933), p. 70.
3. A.I. Taylor, 'The Cockerton Case Revised: London Politics and Education 1898–1901', *British Journal of Educational Studies*, XXX, 3 (Oct. 1982), p. 333.
4. Sadler Papers, MS Eng misc c.550, fo.46, R.L. Morant to M.E. Sadler, March 1898.
5. Ibid., fo.59, R.L. Morant to M.E. Sadler, 20 Aug. 1898.
6. *Glamorgan Free Press* cited in A. Jones, *Lyulph Stanley: A Study in Educational Politics* (1979), pp. 120–1.
7. Kekewich Papers, J.E. Gorst to G.W. Kekewich, 14 Jan. 1900.
8. *School Board Chronicle*, 60 (26 Nov. 1898), p. 587.
9. Department of Science and Arts: Accounts and Papers, *PP*, 1899, LXXV (121), pp. 1024–5.
10. Ibid.
11. Ibid., p. 1035.
12. W. Garnett, 'A Retrospect: How the County Council became the Local Education Authority for London', *Educational Record* (April 1929), p. 753.
13. Barnett Papers, F/BAR/183, S.A. Barnett to F. Barnett, 5 Feb. 1899. Barnett dated the letter 1898 but the contents and context of the letter indicate a new year writing error on his part.
14. Garnett, op. cit., p. 755.
15. *4 PD*, 66, c.101 (16 Feb. 1899).
16. Ibid., c.1446 (20 Feb. 1899).
17. PRO ED 14/25, J.E.Gorst to G.W. Kekewich, 6 Dec. 1899; J.E. Gorst to Duke of Devonshire, 2 Jan. 1900; J.E. Gorst to R.L. Morant, 20 March 1900.
18. Salisbury Papers (4M), 37/124–5, E. Cecil to Lord Cranborne, 31 Dec. 1898.
19. For a detailed discussion of the work of the Cecil brothers see A.I. Taylor, 'The Church Party and Popular Education 1893–1902', unpublished D.Phil thesis, University of Cambridge, 1981, pp. 267–91.
20. *Teachers' Review*, III, 4 (April 1900), p. 76.
21. Barnett Papers, F/BAR/215, Canon Barnett to F. Barnett, 24 March 1900.
22. Report of the Board of Education, 1899–1900, *PP*, 1900, XIX [Cd.328], pp. 10–11.
23. *The Schoolmaster*, LVII (31 March 1900), p. 584.
24. Bryce Papers, UB 21, H.Campbell-Bannerman to J. Bryce, 7 May 1900.
25. *School Board Chronicle*, 63, 24 March 1900, p. 584.
26. *Journal of Education*, XXII (May 1900), p. 290.
27. *School Board Chronicle*, 63 (17 March 1900), p. 276.
28. National Education Association, 'Save the Higher Grade Schools', Special Leaflets, Higher Grade Schools, No.5 (1900), p. 1.
29. PRO ED 24/71, Sir G.W. Kekewich to Sir J.E. Gorst, 27 Feb. 1900.
30. PRO ED 12/91, E. Maclure to Duke of Devonshire, 14 March 1900.
31. Ibid., Memorandum by W. de W. Abney, 30 March 1900, pp. 7–9.
32. BP Add MS 49769, fo.177, Duke of Devonshire to A.J. Balfour, 30 March 1900.
33. PRO ED 24/39, J.E. Gorst, 'Scheme for New Grants under the Code to Higher

Elementary Schools', 2 April 1900, p. 3.
34. Ibid., p. 5
35. Ibid.
36. Jebb Papers, R.C. Jebb to E. Jebb, 4 May 1900.
37. *4 PD*, 82, c.596–605, 3 May 1900.
38. Ibid., c.609.
39. *Journal of Education*, XXII (May 1900), p. 290.
40. PRO ED 24/39, J.E. Gorst to Duke of Devonshire, 4 May 1900; J.E. Gorst to G.W. Kekewich, 6 May 1900.
41. Barnett Papers, F/BAR/218, S. Barnett to F. Barnett, 12 May 1900.
42. PRO ED 14/102, J.E. Gorst to Duke of Devonshire, 14 May 1900.
43. *Manchester Guardian*, 18 June 1900, p. 11; *School Board Chronicle*, 63 (30 June 1900), p. 736.
44. PRO ED 14/102, London School Board to Secretary, Board of Education, 29 June 1900.
45. PRO ED 24/40, J.E. Gorst to Duke of Devonshire, Nov. 1900.
46. PRO ED 24/40, W. Garnett, 'Curricula of Higher Elementary Schools distinct from Secondary Schools', Feb. 1901.
47. Ibid.
48. Ibid.
49. *4 PD*, 90, c.613 (5 March 1901).
50. S. Barnett to F. Barnett, 24 March 1900, cited in E.K. Abel, 'Canon Barnett and the First Thirty Years of Toynbee Hall', unpublished PhD thesis, University of London, 1969, p. 77.
51. PRO ED 24/38, 'Comparison between Higher Grade and Secondary Schools as to Staff'. For more sympathetic views of the teachers see J. Burnett, *Destiny Obscure: Autobiographies of Childhood, Education and Families from the 1820s to the 1920s* (1984), pp. 158–204.; T. Thompson, *Edwardian Childhoods* (1981), pp. 92–3; 116–17.
52. Sandars Papers, MS Eng hist c.732, fo.35, A.J. Balfour to Duke of Devonshire, 16 Oct. 1900.
53. Salisbury Papers (3M), Lord Salisbury to J.E. Gorst, 27 Sept. 1899.
54. Hamilton Diaries, Add MS 48677, fo.45, 6 Nov. 1900.
55. H. Lucy, *Nearing Jordan* (1916), pp. 250–1.
56. *Review of Reviews*, 22 (Dec. 1900), p. 529.
57. Cited in E.J.R. Eaglesham, *From School Board to Local Authority* (1956), p. 131.
58. PRO ED 24/83, J.E. Gorst to Duke of Devonshire, 15 March 1901.
59. PRO ED 114/26, Judgement of Court of Appeal, 1 April, 1901. Rex v T.B. Cockerton, pp. 4–5.
60. BP Add 49835, fo.67, G. Williams to A.J. Balfour, 28 March 1901.
61. Ibid., R.L. Morant note, 18 April 1901.
62. Ibid.
63. F.A. Channing, 'The Liberal Solution of the Education Problem', Northern Counties' Education League, April 1901, Box Education 38, John Johnson Collection of Ephemera.
64. *The Schoolmaster* (13 April 1901).
65. PRO ED 24/83, R. Walrond to R.L. Morant, 20 May 1901.
66. Salisbury Papers (3M), Duke of Devonshire to Lord Salisbury, 21 Jan. 1900. Lord Salisbury to Duke of Devonshire, 21 Jan. 1900 cited in Holland, *Life of the Duke of Devonshire*, II, p. 271.

67. C.P.Ilbert, *Diary,* 28 March 1900.
68. Salisbury Papers (3M), Duke of Devonshire to Lord Salisbury, 11 April 1900.
69. Ibid., Duke of Devonshire to Lord Salisbury, 21 April 1900.
70. Barnett Papers, F/BAR/ 218, S. Barnett to F. Barnett, 12 May 1900.
71. *4 PD*, 84, c.1040, (26 June 1900).
72. School Board Gazette, IV, 1 (July 1900), p. 5.
73. PRO ED 24/29/11, J.E. Gorst, Memorandum, Nov. 1900.
74. E.J.T. Brennan (ed.), *Education for National Efficiency: The Contribution of Sidney and Beatrice Webb*, p. 86; A.M. McBriar, *Fabian Socialism and English Politics, 1884–1918* (1962), pp. 212–13.
75. PRO ED 24/29/11, Duke of Devonshire, Memorandum, 6 Dec. 1900.
76. Ibid., J. Hibbert to J.E. Gorst, 21 Dec. 1900.
77. *Journal of Education* cited in *School Board Chronicle*, 65 (5 Jan. 1901), p. 13.
78. Salisbury Papers (3M), A.J. Balfour to Lord Salisbury, 5 Jan. 1901.
79. Ilbert Diaries, 9, 11 and 27 Feb. 1901, House of Lords Library. I am extremely grateful to Dr Glenn Swafford for these references.
80. PRO ED 24/15, R. Walrond to R.L. Morant, 5 March 1901.
81. *4 PD*, 90, c.613, (5 March 1901).
82. Sadler Papers, MS Eng misc c.205, p. 56, Diary of Sir M.T. Sadler, 19 April 1901.
83. Barnett Papers, F/BAR/236, S. Barnett to F. Barnett, 4 May 1901.
84. PRO CAB 41/26/8, A.J. Balfour to H.M. King, 26 April 1901.
85. A.S.T. Griffith-Boscawen, *Fourteen Years in Parliament* (1907), p. 200.
86. Barnett Papers, F/BAR/237, S. Barnett to F. Barnett, 11 May 1901.
87. BP Add MS 49832, fos.137–8, E. Sidgwick to A.J. Balfour, 14 May 1901.
88. Campbell-Bannerman Papers, Add MS 41236, fos.107–10, A.H.D. Acland to H. Campbell-Bannerman, 5 June 1901.
89. 'Our Note-Book at St. Stephen's', *The Schoolmaster*, 59 (18 May 1901), p. 879.
90. BP Add 49789, fos.125–7, E. Talbot to A.J. Balfour, 6 June 1901.
91. Jebb Papers, R.C. Jebb to C. Jebb, 25 June 1901.
92. Salisbury Papers (3M), A.J. Balfour to S. McDonnell, 6 June 1901.
93. BP Add MS 49854, fos.119–20, A.J. Balfour to Bishop of Coventry, 25 June 1901.
94. Hamilton Papers, Add MS 48678, fo.70, *Diaries,* 28 June 1901.
95. PRO CAB 41/26/15, Lord Salisbury to H.M. King, 28 June 1901.
96. 'Our Note-Book at St. Stephen's', *The Schoolmaster* (29 June 1901), p. 1127.
97. *4 PD*, 96, c.613, (2 July 1901).
98. Ibid., c.1180, (8 July 1901).
99. Ibid.
100. *The Spectator*, 87, 13 July 1901, p. 48.
101. 'Our Note-Book at St. Stephen's', *The Schoolmaster* (13 July 1901), p. 49.
102. Asquith Papers, Vol 10, #25, A.H.D. Acland to H.H. Asquith, 15 July 1901.
103. Jebb Papers, R.C. Jebb to C. Jebb, 16 July 1901.
104. Trevelyan Papers, CPT 35, 'Pictures from Parliament', 31 July 1901.

5

The 1902 Education Act
– stage one

Arthur Balfour professed a dislike of educational affairs but he had nevertheless ensured that he had played a key role in the formulation of nearly all of the government's educational measures since 1895. His position as Leader of the House and First Lord of the Treasury might have demanded no less and, it could be argued, his additional role in 1901 more than justified it being maintained:

> The truth is he was the *de facto* Prime Minister long before he had that office *de jure*. Lord Salisbury was frequently difficult to find – he would stay at Hatfield for days together; and A.J.B. had frequently to take decisions in his absence.[1]

None the less, his actions had, at times, completely superseded those of Devonshire and Gorst, the two political heads of the education system. While Devonshire managed to retain a moderately phlegmatic approach towards his role the same could not be said of Gorst. But at the crucial first stage in the planning of the 1902 Education Bill, Gorst was somewhat under a cloud owing to his performance during the passage of the two 1901 Bills. Liberal MP Yoxall characterised him as the 'evil genius' of the Board while an article in *Truth* portrayed him as 'simply pantaloon in a screaming harlequinade'.[2] It was not without significance, therefore, that the initial planning meeting for the Bill took place in Balfour's rooms in the House of Commons.

The Cabinet Committee consisted of those who had drafted the Cockerton Act: Balfour, Devonshire, Gorst, Long and Morant, with the addition of Kekewich, Ilbert and Sandars.[3] Morant had prepared a memorandum for the committee, detailing his opinion of the main questions to be considered before the drafting of one of two possible Bills. His memorandum not only highlighted many of the problems associated with establishing secondary education only authorities but also contained an analysis of 'the infinitely more difficult and interesting question of whether Elementary Education is to be included in the next Educational Measure'.[4] Morant acknowledged that the creation of comprehensive local education authorities might lessen school board opposition but he pointed out that if it was believed that the only way to overcome school board opposition was by the inclusion of rate aid for voluntary schools, there was none the less the fact that the new authorities could not be 'saddled with undenominational conditions'; and this would not 'bring peace in the House of Commons'. Furthermore, the other problems associated with the creation of comprehensive authorities, including the educational and administrative divisions between elementary and secondary schools and the possible roles to be played by non-county borough councils (including rating powers), led him to argue that the resolution of the education system's problems could only be

> . . . based on the varying functions of each of the various types and grades of Schools, as arranged on educational principles: while the various Local Authorities . . . must be established on sound principles of local government, having regard to the very varying area which is supplied by the respective types of schools.[5]

These solutions could not be produced, he believed, by establishing a local authority for all education in every area. His presentation of the two options before the committee portrayed them as being fraught with difficulties and in which neither of them was a clear candidate on either educational or political grounds.

Mindful of the limited duration of the Cockerton Act, the committee considered both options but concentrated on the issue of comprehensive education authorities and the related topic of the role to be played by smaller, existent authorities, not least with respect to the voluntary schools. Gorst suggested that a double system of schools could operate under each borough council, those which would be rate-supported and maintained in keeping with the provisions of the Cowper-Temple clause, and those which would be rate-aided but, as a result of terms agreed between the council and the school's managers, without the Cowper-Temple restrictions. Mention of the fact that Sir Charles Dilke and the extreme Radicals in the Liberal Party would baulk at a repeal of the Cowper-Temple clause brought to light the fact that Chamberlain would most probably join them. In view of this, Balfour suggested that Gorst's plan could be amended so that schools were either rate-aided or rate-supported, the latter to be subject to Clause 27 of the 1896 Bill. Kekewich raised the possibility of the voluntary schools being transferred to the authority of the school boards, under Section 23 of the 1870 Act, which would provide the aid required for them, but this was hardly in keeping with the form desired by either the government or the schools. The two-hour meeting proved to be little more than 'a rambling preliminary conversation, without much in the way of definite conclusions' and Balfour decided that a draft Bill should be prepared so as to focus future discussion on the seminal points which had been raised.

Ilbert found his notes of the meeting too scanty to be suitable for the basis of a draft and wanted more specific directives to be provided by the Board, contending that there was a limit 'to one's powers of making bricks without straw'.[6] Gorst took it upon himself to prepare the draft and had it completed and printed only two days after Balfour had issued his command. In it he stuck to his principle of comprehensive education authorities based upon the county councils, as in the first 1901 Bill, but with the proviso that they should be able to promote both elementary and secondary education as they saw fit. In addition, he stipulated that there should be the 'amplest power of division and com- bination' so that an urban district council, for example, could be made an education authority independent of the county authority in whose area it was located. Furthermore, these small authorities would not only retain the right to raise a penny rate for secondary education, under the Technical Instruction Act but they should also be able to raise a rate for elementary and evening schools, in order both to aid voluntary schools and to take over the role of school boards with respect to the latter. He acknowledged that this concept of division could lead to problems of overlapping but he could see no other solution apart from 'common sense and mutual forebearance' providing an acceptable *modus vivendi*. He did suggest that the smaller authorities might agree to remain under the county's aegis while the larger ones could either opt to be independent or become the managers for all education in their area as agents of the county. Failing this, a limitation of the areas of opera- tion of the county and non-county/urban district councils could be made and this might remove any problem of overlapping.[7] Riversdale Walrond, Devonshire's private secretary, was not impressed by this draft and complained to Morant that Gorst should have taken a few days longer and produced 'a rather less "loose"' version. He thought that Ilbert and Lindsell (the Board's legal adviser) would have to 'knock it about a good deal. Gorst has a mania for brevity, which generally means inaccuracy'.[8] Even so, Gorst's proposals were to be jeopardised as a result of a meeting between Balfour and Salisbury at Hatfield.

Balfour told Devonshire that Salisbury had expressed a desire to have a Bill in print by the time the Cabinet met on 5 November and he had promised there would be two draft proposals: '(a) one dealing with secondary education, (b) one dealing with secondary education plus primary education'.[9] Balfour thought it might also be worthwhile to prepare a third draft dealing completely with secondary education but only abolishing the cumulative vote for school boards plus introducing Clause 27 of the 1896 Bill as far as elementary education was concerned. The drafts, he believed, would provide sufficient material for discussion by the committee after the parliamentary recess, but if anything further occurred to him in the meantime, he asked that he be allowed to contact Morant directly whenever Devonshire was away from the Board. It had not taken Morant long, once he had become directly involved in education policy formulation, to appreciate the significance of Balfour's role in the process and he had engineered an invitation from Edward Talbot, the Bishop of Rochester, whom he had known from his Oxford days, to his home in Kennington on Palm Sunday, 1901, in order to meet Balfour. The latter usually visited the Talbots on that day to mark the anniversary of the death of May Lyttelton, Mrs Talbot's sister and Balfour's intended wife. Talbot had believed, correctly, that Morant would support the educational views of the Church but the meeting produced a notable interaction between Balfour and Morant once the latter had expounded his plan for the reform of the nation's education system. Impressed by this exposition, Balfour allowed Morant to contact him henceforth on educational matters and Morant was to acknowledge subsequently that 'from that day "everything" has dated for me'.[10] His role in policy formulation was now to develop significantly given Devonshire's assent to Balfour's request.

Devonshire's response to Balfour's news was to refuse to be hustled over the Bill and he reminded him that they had Gorst's draft to consider, one he believed to be 'tolerably comprehensive [and] to contain most of the points which we shall have to decide'.[11] Thus, while Devonshire forwarded Balfour's requests for three draft Bills to Gorst, he also indicated that he still retained a preference for his original draft. Chamberlain, getting wind of these preparations, told Salisbury that although he had no idea what was envisaged for the Bill he believed that they would have great trouble with any Bill and only wished that Devonshire 'could be persuaded to do more and that Gorst did less'.[12] Devonshire had, in fact, queried some of Gorst's proposals, including the control of elementary education. On this issue it appeared to him impossible to deprive any considerable Borough or Urban district of the control over its elementary education either through a School Board or its council, and I do not understand that it is necessary to bring the County Council in for purposes of Elementary Education except in those rural districts which have inefficient School Boards, or in those which have no School Boards but where the Voluntary Schools would like to put themselves in connection with the County Authority.[13]

He also wanted it made clear that the county authorities were to be ultimately responsible for all secondary education in their areas although it could be that they could delegate this duty to the smaller authorities. This, he believed, would not only satisfy the educationists but, more importantly, would act as an inducement to the counties to 'stimulate rather than repress the zeal of the boroughs'.[14]

Gorst accepted most of Devonshire's points as being more liberal than his, and was prepared to jettison his idea of compulsory and limited delegation of a county's secondary education duties to the smaller authorities. He admitted, however, that he would be unhappy if a county authority did not have the possibility of assuming control over elementary education and he also took the opportunity to express his doubts about Balfour's first and third proposals for the Bill. He felt that the introduction of a measure based purely on a secondary education authority would be met with considerable opposition from both sides of the House but the third proposal worried him the most, for he thought it would be difficult to select any other points touching on elementary education which were 'less necessary or more mischievous to deal with'. The abolition of the cumulative vote for school boards would be bitterly opposed by the Roman Catholics, supported by the Irish MPs, while the government MPs would see it as a declaration of permanency in connection with the school boards. As far as the religious question was concerned, they both knew it had no relevance to the practical running of schools and was only 'an object for Parliamentary conflict'. As such, it should only be introduced either to establish a major principle or to please the government party; Clause 27 of the 1896 Bill would achieve neither. But having thus 'delivered his soul', Gorst promised his 'most loyal and hearty assistance' in the preparation of all three draft Bills.[15] That said, a few days later, he reported the discovery by Morant of a precedent in the Local Government Act of 1888 supporting his proposal for the compulsory delegation of a county council's secondary education duties to a municipal council. He proposed that in view of this his clause should remain, as it would not be difficult to pass and it did provide 'a perfectly effective provision against duplication of authority and overlapping'.[16]

At the first planning meeting with Gorst and Morant after their holidays, Devonshire was concerned with achieving some clarification of the issues at stake and they started with a consideration of the proposed transference of school board powers to the councils. This led to a discussion about rate aid for voluntary schools and Morant may have mentioned a note he had received a few days earlier from Evelyn Cecil indicating not only his support for a comprehensive bill but also the fact that 'Hatfield [Lord Salisbury] . . . would be willing to support rate-aid to associations of voluntary schools, . . . abolition of the Cowper-Temple clause, and support the principle of Clause 27 of the Bill of 1896'.[17] This notwithstanding, the trio's exploration of the problems associated with providing the aid and various schemes involving the school boards met with little success and Devonshire was led to conclude that if the voluntary schools could not get rate aid 'without extinguishing School Boards the Bill will provoke a fight in almost every School Board District. It would be almost better to summarily suppress School Boards altogether'.[18] After this meeting Morant went to stay with Balfour at Whittingehame, his family home in the Lammermuir Hills of East Lothian, and to discuss the current stage of the Bill. One of Balfour's nieces later recalled the spectacle of the two men walking around the wooded grounds of the house, deep in conversation about Devonshire's and Gorst's proposals: 'Morant was a giant, with a large pale face, and glowing eyes, set in deep hollows. Beside him Balfour, tall as he was, looked small in frame.' More importantly, the effect of their discussions was that Balfour 'never inspired a deeper devotion in a subordinate and the zeal of another never had more influence on himself'.[19] Learning Balfour's views of the Bill from Morant, Gorst drafted a new version – a task which took considerably longer than his first effort. None the less, Ilbert's detailed scrutiny of the draft revealed certain ambiguities in various clauses and two subsequent meetings between Gorst, Devonshire and Long generated the need for a new draft.

The major problem lay with the role of the smaller, municipal authorities and alternative drafts of the respective clause were required. The first was to follow as closely as possible the principles of section 11 of the 1888 Local Government Act – that the county authority was to maintain its suzerainty by levying a rate over all its district and to give to urban districts either the complete sum required for elementary education by the districts or such amount as the county thought fit. The second was to follow Gorst's draft, that is, there would be greater autonomy for urban districts but it was now to be limited to non-county boroughs with a population greater than 10,000. Devonshire was emphatic that this version of the clause had to give these smaller authorities complete powers over elementary education, and not merely those of school boards, so as to ensure that there would be no further Cockerton problems. Devonshire also requested alternative versions of the clause providing for the full maintenance by the new authorities of any school, except that provided by a school board, as he wanted the issue to be fully discussed by the Cabinet. No doubt mindful of Salisbury's views, Devonshire asked for the drafts not to be 'saddled with any reference to the cost of religious instruction'. Apart from these alterations, the draft would remain substantially that produced by Gorst, and Devonshire was quite happy with this. His additional request to Ilbert to produce drafts corresponding to Balfour's first and third schemes for the Bill was made 'very unwillingly, but feeling that he is compelled to do it, because Mr Balfour and Hatfield have definitely required it'.[20]

While Ilbert was engaged on his task, Gorst began to have second thoughts as he had become convinced that it would be impossible to deprive the larger non-county boroughs of their autonomy in elementary education and felt that if the government tried to do so it would probably not be able to withstand the storm of opposition which would be generated by the proposal. And, in what amounted to a volte-face, he was worried about the proposed abolition of the school boards, believing that while public opinion was ready to accept the loss of the smaller, inefficient ones he was not sure that the same held true for the abolition of the larger boards. He proposed, therefore, that a population size of 10,000 be established as the determining factor between the abolition or survival of school boards. But before they could meet to discuss these points, Devonshire delivered a speech in Liverpool which was to have important repercussions.

At the opening of the new Central Technical School, the duke responded to a criticism that the government was demonstrating 'indifference or supineness' on the continued absence of effective local educational authorities. Observing that where substantial measures of reform were concerned there had to be significant public consensus if any measure was to succeed, he claimed that the government found itself confronted by public apathy and a lack of support from educational authorities. He recognised, correctly, that a request by him for a more definite expression of public wishes might be seen as 'whistling for a wind' but he none the less hoped that it would be forthcoming. He attempted to reinforce his theme by reference to the negative impact of jargon on discussions of educational topics but the nature of his comments undermined the seriousness of his endeavour:

> . . . I have occasionally to listen in the House of Lords to speeches by educational experts, sometimes not one word of which, I am bound to acknowledge, I can understand (Laughter) . . . I acknowledge – and it is a very sad and humiliating confession – that after being several years in the Education Department I am unable to understand the language of the experts on this subject, however technical it may be. What I want to impress upon you is that probably I am a fairly average specimen of the man in the street – (Laughter) – at all events. It is the man in the street – the public generally – you want to convince, and it is no use addressing him in terms which are intelligible only to the initiated and the expert.[21]

Sadler was furious that Devonshire, by adopting this approach, had thrown away a golden opportunity to indicate the government's educational policy, especially as he had been provided with 'a careful reasoned argument . . . but would not or could not make use of it'.[22] Macnamara believed the speech implied that the government would let educational matters drift unless pulled up sharply by the public, while the *Church Quarterly Review* claimed that if the government only had 'the courage of its convictions, and would believe that the problem demands to be attacked seriously, it might pass a useful, even a great measure'.[23] But while the hapless duke was lampooned for his comments, Asquith was worried about the political consequences of the increasing clamour for a single authority:

> It has become the shibboleth of three distinct educational parties who have nothing really in common viz.
> (1) the Board School extremists (Channing and Co.):
> (2) the Teachers Trade Union (Macnamara and Co.):
> (3) the more astute Denominationalists (Jebb and Co.)[24]

He feared that Devonshire would not be strong enough to confine the Bill to secondary education and if, consequently, he had to try to establish comprehensive LEAs it would cause 'infinite confusion and division' among the Opposition. But the duke's reaction to being covered with ridicule was to make him determined to have an education Bill of significance passed.[25]

An indication of the duke's new resolve manifested itself when he met Gorst on 29 October and they discussed the latter's concerns about the Bill. Morant felt that the ensuing discussion was more fruitful than usual and tried to flatter Balfour by querying whether he had perhaps raised some questions earlier with the duke which had stimulated him. Devonshire also took the relatively unusual step, for him, of instructing Ilbert personally about new drafts to be prepared of the Bill, 'one drastic, the other one his own lines of local option'.[26] At the same time, Morant's activities in connection with earlier instructions from the duke, to take soundings about the Bill among various influential MPs, including Henry Hobhouse, Sir Albert Rollit, Sir John Hibbert and Sir John Dorrington – all well versed in local government affairs – as well as Cardinal Vaughan, the Bishop of Rochester and Lord Hugh Cecil as church representatives, and personal friends who were members of the LCC and London boroughs, were starting to yield results.

Hobhouse indicated a preference for the creation of secondary education authorities although he could see the logic in dealing with both elementary and secondary education issues in one Bill, provided the government ensured adequate time for debate. If there was to be a comprehensive Bill then, he stipulated, there should be efficient control exerted by county councils albeit in conjunction with sufficient delegation of their powers. Rollit's response, however, revealed the likely obstacles that such county suzerainty could face. His declared hatred for rate aid to voluntary schools proved mild compared with his views relating to the role to be played by small local authorities. He was steadfastly committed to the achievement of educational autonomy for non-county boroughs, making the point that these boroughs

> ... resent and detest the over lordship in any form of the County Councils, and the suggestion to give the latter either administrative or financial powers, or rights to contribution, would ... be felt to be an extension of the present over lordship, and, as such, most obnoxious.[27]

A subsequent letter, strenuously reinforcing his position, led Morant to despair. He wondered if the concept of county suzerainty should not be dropped and be replaced by 'some Equalisation of Rates Clause, for all Counties, on the lines of that now existing in London', for he believed that Rollit's stance on rate aid to voluntary schools meant that Devonshire's plan of local option would please no one.[28]

Some of the political problems likely to be generated within the Liberal Unionist Party by the inclusion of rate aid to voluntary schools in the Bill were brought to Devonshire and Chamberlain's attention by a report from J. Powell Williams, a key figure in the party's organisation. His monitoring of the state of feeling among party members about the introduction of a new education Bill had revealed unencouraging signs, partly due to a belief that the government was too considerate about the claims of the Church party. If rate aid was included, he was certain large numbers of party supporters would be lost and it 'might even be fatal to the L.U. Party'.[29] Morant claimed Devonshire and Chamberlain received a fright from this report but Devonshire's Cabinet memorandum of 2 November accompanying the drafts of the Bill emphasised the point that, although the concept of rate aid for voluntary schools 'has never been decided on and . . . scarcely discussed by the Cabinet', the question would be raised on any Bill purporting to cover elementary education. He argued that it would be better for it to be covered by the Bill rather than be added as a result of some amendment passed in the House and possibly based on the resolutions passed by the Church the previous summer at the joint convocations of York and Canterbury.[30] He also pointed out that the dissatisfaction among government MPs and supporters at the time of the withdrawal of the first 1901 Bill had only failed to become serious because of the expectation that there would soon be a replacement, comprehensive Bill. This point was accepted and a proposal from another member to limit the measure solely to secondary education was defeated. But on rate aid to the voluntary schools Devonshire's arguments failed to move the Cabinet and they voted decisively against any such aid being provided. FitzRoy observed that although Chamberlain would have found a pretext for leaving the government if Devonshire's view had prevailed, the reason which swayed the Cabinet was a dislike of the increase in urban and rural rates that would accompany such a provision.[31] Despite this, little progress was made on the Bill and it was decided to appoint a new Cabinet Committee with Devonshire, Balfour and Long being joined by Hanbury, Lord Selborne and Lord James.[32] An apparently surprising omission was Gorst, especially in view of the substantial nature of his contribution to the development of the Bill since August, and Devonshire's almost renowned protection of his deputy.

Shortly after Devonshire's 'whistling for the wind' speech, Yoxall had published a somewhat surprising but veritable eulogy of Devonshire as President of the Board of Education. At the same time he had taken the opportunity to contrast, and condemn, Gorst's role in educational policy formulation, characterising him as 'Flibbertigibbet, "that fiend of mopping and mowing", who antics round the ruin he has wrought in English education'. If Devonshire's 'patience, tolerance, magnanimity, *grand-seigneur*-ism . . . towards his freakish junior Minister' was laudable, it did appear to Yoxall as though he had 'rather fallen into the habit of thinking and saying very much what Sir John suggests he should think and say . . . No great man ever had a more dangerous adviser'.[33] Whether the Cabinet agreed with this analysis and wanted to minimise Gorst's future contribution, given the increasingly uncomfortable similarity between the proposals in the draft Bill and those of the 1896 Bill, is not certain. But Devonshire had complained privately to Edward Hamilton, at the beginning of October, that not only was the Board of Education in an 'extremely unsatisfactory state', with Kekewich rarely in Whitehall and 'of little use', but 'Gorst was most difficult'.[34] Unfortunately Hamilton only recorded this comment and not the reason for it, but it may explain why Gorst was not included in the new committee, lacking Devonshire's usual protection, and it may also account for Devonshire's increasingly personal involvement with all stages in the development of the measure, Morant noting that he was now not only personally directing Ilbert but was writing all his Cabinet memoranda on the Bill as well.[35] Gorst was not barred from making further contributions but they were as an adjunct to Devonshire's activities rather than being equal to them.

Meeting twice before the next Cabinet meeting on 19 November, the new committee made little progress and had nothing prepared for the Cabinet to consider, thus leaving the whole sitting to be devoted to a discussion of the Boer War. Balfour's subsequent absence through illness led to a further postponement of any discussion at the next Cabinet meeting on the 25th. This lack of progress on the Bill was compounded by Ilbert's increasing antipathy towards the measure. As early as May he had congratulated the Liberal MP Charles Trevelyan upon a speech on 'this vile Education Bill' but now he was not only writing the drafts in 'a highly horrible spirit' but openly admitted that they could not be implemented as written.[36] Just before Christmas, therefore, Ilbert was tactfully relieved of his position by Balfour and replaced by Thring.[37]

Waiting for Balfour to recover from his illness, Morant, worried by the loss of valuable planning time as well as the lack of progress on the Bill, was glad to be able to visit the Webbs and discuss the measure with them, Sidney having been sent a copy of responses made to the draft Bill by Oliver Lodge, the Vice Chancellor of Birmingham University, at the request of Chamberlain.[38] Gorst also used the hiatus to discuss the Bill with Ilbert before contacting Devonshire about some of the major flaws in the current draft. His prime concern lay with the Bill's inability to ensure that the elementary sector would become more uniformly efficient because of the insufficient provision being made for the improvement of voluntary school finances. On one hand, this reflected the limited powers proposed for the municipal councils plus the fact that it was only optional for managers of voluntary schools to transfer their schools to the local authority; an option which he did not envisage Roman Catholic schools, for example, taking up. On the other, it would be impossible for the counties to fund all the elementary schools from the county rate. This would be exacerbated by the limitations that would result from the counties taking over the rural school boards in their area. Thus although the voluntary schools educated more than half the children in the elementary education sector the new authorities would have their powers so constrained that they would be unable to help them. This position would not, he believed, commend itself to either the public or to the county councils who would have to accept the additional responsibility for elementary education while being expected to improve their efficiency.[39] Devonshire accepted the wisdom of these points and decided to raise the issue first with Chamberlain and then with Balfour.

Chamberlain was well aware that education was a very delicate topic as far as the Radical Liberal Unionists were concerned and any attempt by the Bill to promote rate aid to voluntary schools would, he thought, 'lose Birmingham and the Birmingham influence, whatever that may be worth, to the Unionist Party'. He knew that the government's earlier educational legislation still rankled with this section of the party and that it would be unwise to ignore their feelings.[40] Consequently, the outcome of his discussion with Devonshire as to whether he would consent to 'any proposal . . . in any form' on rate aid to voluntary schools was a statement that while he might assent to a permissive power for such aid being given to the local authorities he believed it would be an extremely unwise proposal. The duke was inclined to concur and felt that the only alternative – obligatory rate aid for voluntary schools – would mean that they would either have to drop the Bill or see the government disintegrate. But while he could see the logic of permissive rate aid Devonshire was not sure whether it could be carried. None the less, this discussion, along with Gorst's points, inclined him even more to the conclusion that the Bill could not be defended unless it contained some proposals for rate aid. He told Balfour, therefore, that although the Bill purported to establish local authorities for elementary as well as secondary education, in reality it did not. And if the Cabinet would not agree to rate aid then 'we had better revert to the Secondary Bill and leave Elementary Education alone'.[41] Balfour was not left in any doubt about this issue for Morant supported Devonshire's point:

> . . . Is the new County Borough to be the Authority for all Education in the Borough? Yes.
>
> Is it to set the standard of efficiency of the Town Schools? Yes; for if not, it is not *the* Authority.
>
> But if it may not finance the non-Board Schools it cannot bring them up to proper efficiency. Obviously, and therefore it *must* be able to finance those schools when necessary.[42]

Morant tried to convince him that if rate aid was made only permissive it would lead to a 'crash in the middle of the Session' but if compulsory rate maintenance of voluntary schools was accepted it would eliminate all the difficulties associated with the special aid grant (of 1897) and the section 97 grant (of the 1870 Act). He went on to state that a recent conversation with the duke had revealed that he was still 'quite fluid' about the Bill and had not thought out 'any *one* of the various plans. And this *must* mean a collapse in Parliament must it not?' To prevent this he suggested that the committee 'put the Bill on one side, and go step by step through the various points which are of vital importance and formulate their views, and their reasons on each'. This would enable them to identify the points which had to be resolved 'before any Bill however drafted can be passed' although he added the rider, 'Am I too absolutely utopian in it all?'[43]

Balfour acknowledged these points by his acceptance of the fact that a politically acceptable measure could not be formulated within the limits set by the Cabinet and the next scheduled meeting of the Cabinet was postponed until Friday, 13 December. Before then, Morant was despatched to Highbury to discuss the issue of rate aid with Chamberlain as an attempt to minimise the 'strongest strain' to which the Unionist alliance had yet been exposed.[44] In trying to con-

154

vince Chamberlain of the viability of this view Morant was on much more difficult ground, despite the fact that the Cabinet Committee had by now accepted that some form of rate aid was required to make the Bill politically viable. The discussion at Highbury was vigorous but although Morant's notes for Balfour – the only extant copy of the conversation – favourably portrayed the points made by their author, he was not sanguine that he had converted Chamberlain. His view was confirmed on the next day when, at the Cabinet meeting there was a division over the Bill and a majority (of 10) led by Chamberlain and Salisbury succeeded in restricting the Bill to secondary education. As a contingency measure, a Bill dealing with elementary education was ordered to be prepared, although it would not be mentioned in the King's Speech.[45]

This victory, Chamberlain realised, was purely Pyrrhic since he could ultimately be the loser, politically, whatever measure was introduced. A secondary education-only Bill could rupture the alliance whereas a comprehensive measure would lose him the Radical Unionist support. He accordingly wrote to Devonshire the day after the Cabinet meeting, not only offering sympathy to him in his 'almost hopeless task' but also sending constructive comments for a comprehensive Bill. Although he confirmed his belief that government policy should be an indication 'in plain and unmistakable language' that there was no intention to deal with elementary education in the forthcoming Session, he acknowledged the growing movement within the party for a comprehensive measure. If, as he carefully put it, Devonshire was convinced that this was the right path, then he suggested that the Bill should contain the abolition of school boards, the creation of municipal authorities for education and, if necessary, the abolition of the Cowper-Temple clause, 'although I would rather not raise this thorny issue if it could be avoided'. In return for these concessions, given they had been part of the draft just rejected, he wanted the new, comprehensive authorities 'to make such grants to such schools for such times and under such conditions as may be agreed upon between the new authorities and the Managers of any Voluntary School in its district'.[46] In this somewhat circuitous manner he signalled his recognition of the need for some form of optional rate aid and believed that the wording he had provided for this would enable him 'to draw the sting of Nonconformist criticism'.[47] His final comment revealed the make-or-break nature of his offer; 'It may be worthless as a practical suggestion and then I fear we must confine ourselves to Secondary Education only.' Three days later, at a meeting at Chatsworth, Devonshire, Selborne, James and Gorst discussed these suggestions in connection with the latest draft of the Bill. Clause 3 now provided optional rate aid for voluntary schools on conditions very similar to those suggested by Chamberlain although Devonshire had directed that an alternative clause drafted by Balfour be added to the Bill, but only in parentheses.

Lord Salisbury, in the meantime, gave signs of altering his own position, possibly as a result of reflecting on a letter he had received from the Bishop of Rochester. In it the bishop had made it very clear that

> the palliative of 1897 is exhausted (in many places), and the strain is now at *breaking point*. Putting it practically, I mean that if the schools are not in some way relieved in this next Session, many will go within the year – enough greatly to weaken the cause, and by creating the impression that the 'game is up,' to bring down others in increasing numbers and at an accelerating rate. I am speaking of what I know.[48]

Salisbury's subsequent Cabinet memorandum focused on the plight of the voluntary schools and stated that while the debate about the other issues contained within the Bill could be maintained for many years, these schools could not wait:

> They are all of them hard pressed, many of them are on the brink of starvation, and if nothing is done to satisfy them, they will strike out with all the vigour and all the recklessness of very hungry men.[49]

He complained, somewhat bitterly, that the extra funding acquired by the schools under the 1897 Act had been virtually ineffectual in relieving the 'intolerable condition' of the schools because of the 'theoretic perfection' contained in the demands made upon the schools by the inspectorate and the Board of Education. He was now in favour of a minimalist approach to the issue centring solely on the removal of the financial problems facing the voluntary schools.

Balfour noted on his copy of Salisbury's memorandum, 'we have gone too far in the direction of pledging ourselves to a single authority', and he accordingly produced a memorandum countering Salisbury's recommendation as well as dissecting the Cabinet decision of the previous week. If the Bill remained confined to secondary education, then there would have to be serious consideration of the Cockerton judgment although it had not been 'even remotely touched upon' in the previous discussion. The draft of the secondary education authority-only Bill did not abolish the school boards, yet the judgment prevented them from providing any form of secondary education. Unless the draft was altered, a definition of both elementary and secondary education would have to be included and this would generate, in the case of elementary education with the continued existence of the school boards, a serious although unnecessary controversy and create 'the elements of a very pretty quarrel' between urban councils and school boards. The whole exercise would place the government in a ludicrous position, especially when the school boards came to be abolished under a second, later Bill for elementary education. This position would be exacerbated by the fact that the composition of the borough councils under the first Bill would differ considerably from that required if they became comprehensive education authorities under the second Bill. As to Salisbury's suggestions, the very wording of Balfour's comments indicated how strongly he disagreed with his uncle's views. They so completely negated policy implicitly accepted by the Unionist Party that not only would they, if adopted, provoke a hostile vote in the first week of the Session but, more importantly, they failed to resolve the chaos prevalent throughout the education system:

> Two local authorities will, without mutual consultation, raise rates for Elementary Education. Two local authorities will have to settle the proper standard of Education, of buildings, of salaries.[50]

In the Cabinet meeting on 19 December, Balfour went one stage further when he declared that he would not accept responsibility for any Bill that dealt with the problems 'on narrow and half-hearted lines'. For full measure he added the comment that if his colleagues were 'disposed to prefer the parliamentary conduct of Sir J. Gorst, they will know what to expect'.[51] The nature and tone of Balfour's views, coupled with Chamberlain's concessions, produced something approaching a change of policy on the Bill and the Cabinet 'inclined more' towards the comprehensive measure. Salisbury felt the difference in opinion was 'still considerable, and a definite agreement had not been reached when the Cabinet adjourned' but FitzRoy noted that 'the door is still left open for the adoption of the bolder and more enlightened policy'.[52] Balfour was confident that his threat had been accepted, as his sister-in-law, Frances, recorded, '. . . good talk with Arthur on Procedure, Education, the last to be comprehensive'.[53]

Morant was instructed to draft a Bill creating comprehensive LEAs, repealing the Cowper-Temple clause and allowing rate aid to be optional 'on any terms, to any School, and to any amounts'.[54] The draft was to be ready by 9 January but, even so, there still remained a considerable degree of uncertainty about the Bill's future, not least because of Balfour's recurring ill health.

Afflicted by influenza just before Christmas, Balfour found himself unable to put parliamentary and party matters to one side while he tried to recuperate. On Christmas Eve, Hicks Beach forwarded his development of an idea originally made by Lord Balfour of Burleigh that any voluntary schools seeking rate aid should have to provide half of the sum required in excess of the parliamentary grant.[55] Although Hicks Beach was trying to curb government expenditure due to the escalating costs of the Boer War, the contents of his letter were at complete variance with the latest Cabinet agreement. One contemporary believed Hicks Beach's obstruction over education was based on hostility rather than financial reasons while Balfour felt that as long as he remained the Chancellor, he would go on dropping 'little grains of sand into the wheels of every department in turn'.[56] But no sooner had he disposed of this potential hazard than Balfour received 12 closely covered foolscap sheets in Morant's scrawl, sent ostensibly to be of help for his forthcoming visit to Chatsworth.

Morant had done this because he believed Devonshire, as he told Sandars, 'is so immersed in the Education problem just now that he won't be able to resist telling A.J.B. about it'. But Morant, equally, was unable to resist going through all the major issues raised by the Bill, prefacing his remarks with the critical comment that

> up until now the Cabinet has come to (?varying) decisions on separate points, without any comprehensive outlook upon the state of things, as a whole, which the Bill is to bring about; and that someone must 'vanger' the whole thing, if we are to do anything but drift aimlessly along and end in no definite scheme at all.[57]

What was required, he told Sandars, was to

> get more members of the Cabinet to understand the situation and the problem, & to withdraw their obstruction even if they won't give us their support. The views held by Hicks-Beach & the Prime Minister are fundamentally incompatible with any scheme that AJB c[oul]d defend.[58]

4 Robert Morant, *circa* 1907. (Photograph by courtesy of Mrs Margaret Bailey)

But this time Morant had presumed too much in his relationship with Balfour and his comments earned him a reprimand, reminding him that his position was that of an adviser not that of a policy formulator. The next letter from an apparently chastened Morant brought a copy of the Bill altered to comply *more closely* with the new detailed instructions which both Thring and I are very glad to receive from you'.[59] Privately Morant held to his views, telling Sidney Webb that

> . . . we are in great difficulties still. The differences within the Cabinet are acute. The difficulty of getting a Bill thro' this Cabinet are even greater than getting a Bill thro' Parliament.[60]

Public debate and speculation about the Bill mounted during the Christmas period, and resolutions plus requests for financial assistance from voluntary schools and their supporters started to flood into the Board of Education. Unhappiness among some government back-benchers about the 'pottering helpless way' in which the government was carrying on its business had led Sir William Anson, Unionist MP for Oxford University, in association with some other government backbench MPs, such as Talbot, Foster and Gray, to initiate the formulation of an alternative measure. They hoped that this would lead to the establishment of an educational party which, in turn, might be able to exert some influence over the planning of the government Bill.[61] Devonshire, oblivious to this, was more preoccupied with the role of the proposed education authorities, having been rather perturbed to discover that the West Riding County Council had stated that while it was willing to take over the control of secondary education in its area, it was not interested in directing elementary education. A brief comment made by Balfour about overcoming this problem if it was likely to become more general confused Devonshire and he sought clarification.

Balfour confessed that it had been more of 'an *obiter dictum* than a well thought out scheme' but decided to elaborate it given the potentially embarrassing situation for the government if some councils did not undertake the prescribed duties in the Bill on the due date. He thus advocated a scheme which allowed councils to opt out of the Bill's requirements until they were prepared to adopt it. One advantage of this arrangement would be that the Bill would be implemented initially, and effectively, by the progressive local authorities. The resultant 'lighthouse effect' would, he believed, spur the less progressive or more timid authorities into undertaking implementation of the Bill while, at the same time, providing them with efficient models to simulate. He foresaw no disadvantages in such a 'piebald' system operating in the first instance, provided that it was a requirement of acceptance of the Bill by an LEA that the authority carried out all its duties.[62] But he appeared to have overlooked the multi-faceted and disparate administrative system that would exist until all authorities undertook to implement the Bill, not to mention the administrative chaos that would ensue – not least for the Board of Education with its responsibility for the disbursement of parliamentary grants. That he had rejected his uncle's proposals for similar reasons seems to have escaped him also but as his sister, who lunched with him on the day he forwarded his ideas to Devonshire, observed, 'he (A.) did not believe in Education – and whatever line he took the Bill would be torn to pieces, and there was really no satisfactory line to take'. Since Balfour had informed his sister that the Cabinet 'insisted on his conducting the Education Bill in the Commons – they would not have Gorst at any price', it is perhaps little wonder that Michael Sadler believed the government were in serious difficulties over the Bill.[63]

Sadler's fears were reinforced by the first Cabinet meeting of the new year when very little progress was made on the Bill, Salisbury noting that there was still a very marked difference of opinion about each of the contentious issues. The vexed question of rate aid to the voluntary schools still troubled the Cabinet and even Salisbury now believed that the demands of the Church party were 'very high' given that they wanted the aid but were not prepared to yield sufficiently enough on the issue of public control to satisfy the Nonconformists.[64] Alfred Cripps, the Webbs' 'little jewel of an advocate', was busily liaising with both Balfour and Chamberlain to try and arrange a compromise over the Bill because of Chamberlain's opposition to state aid, 'fearing the recrudescence of the church-rate crusade. Balfour felt the force of the Church's cry "Now or never"'. After his efforts had achieved little, Cripps was inclined to leave the House to resolve all the 'knotty points', an attitude which Beatrice Webb thought was a 'counsel of despair when the knots are so complicated'.[65] But at the next meeting of the Cabinet Devonshire was to surprise his colleagues.

He produced a memorandum providing a solution for the rate aid problem and supported by a detailed comparative analysis of the strengths and weaknesses of the proposals for optional and complete rate aid. In many ways the situation had become similar to the later stages in the planning of the 1896 Bill, where Balfour had taken a major role in its planning but had started to procrastinate when faced with the apparently insoluble difficulties involved whereas Devonshire had achieved the full measure of them and had planned accordingly. Devonshire was now close to producing a rationally planned and constructed measure capable of resolving all the outstanding issues. Even so, the strain of the planning was beginning to tell on him, for when he was informed of a recent suicide he asked grimly if the person had had anything to do with the Bill.[66]

The duke had come to accept the view that if the Bill was to provide a resolution of the administrative chaos at the primary and secondary level through a rationalisation of the local education authorities, with a concomitant simplification in financial provisions at local and central government level, then the compulsory rate maintenance of schools within an LEA's area was essential. For what was needed by the nation was not just new authorities but authorities with the necessary controlling power and financial resources to ensure that all elementary, and secondary, schools within their area would operate efficiently; the *quality of educational provision* was *au fond* the critical factor, as Gorst had correctly argued earlier. The comparative analysis Devonshire provided revealed the immense difficulties that would confront the new authorities trying to maintain this educational efficiency if they were hampered by the constraints of optional rate aid and also through not possessing, by virtue of the continued existence of voluntary subscriptions, the requisite control to ensure achievement of this paramount goal. Similarly, voluntary schools could find themselves, he believed, in the position of having to play the local authority off against the Voluntary Schools Association (established after the 1897 Act to distribute the special aid grant) and playing both off against the Board of Education in order to achieve the necessary funding, thus being rather like 'a hungry mendicant dealing with a different patron round each of three different corners'. Compulsory rate aid, on the other hand, overcame these problems by creating

> . . . a real local authority . . . at once and permanently beyond question, in the position of being really responsible for the efficiency of *every* school in its area . . . and of having full authority and power, as well as the absolute duty to control every one of its schools, to see that its staff is adequate, and that the secular education it gives is efficient.[67]

By being able to budget adequately for all the educational needs of its area, each authority would be able to ensure that as well as meeting the requests of all its schools there would be a uniform contribution from the community for education. Since the LEA would be the arbiter of educational policy for all schools one important corollary was that it did not matter if there was an imbalance in the composition of school managerial bodies as, for example, in the case of voluntary schools, because all managers would be subject to the directions and control of the authority. And where there were distinct imbalances in the type of school provision, for example in Wales where in largely Nonconformist populations Anglican elementary schools predomi- nated, the LEA could redress these imbalances by establishing non- denominational schools. He believed that unless the government signalled that the proposed LEAs were to be comprehensive bodies in respect of their powers and duties, then they would fail to gain the acquiescence they needed from the county and county borough councils. At the same time, it was only by the adoption of such a concept that they could logically justify the abolition of the school boards. Devonshire had clearly accepted the message relayed to him by Almeric FitzRoy from the Whips that they were not only in favour of a comprehensive measure but also that it would be 'hazardous to ignore the feeling of the great bulk of the party in favour of rate aid to voluntary schools, for the sake of removing the scruples of a few Radical Unionists in the Midlands'.[68] And his delivery of his views to the Cabinet was so powerful and his resolution so unexpected that not even Chamberlain's interruption disturbed him. Salisbury did not call for a formal conclusion on the proposals, believing that a negative out- come might have produced Devonshire's resignation.[69]

Balfour's response followed the next day and represented an attempt at mediation between Devonshire's concept and the objections still maintained by Chamberlain and Hicks Beach. He identified the general acknowledgement of the plight of the voluntary schools but the existence, at the same time, of a reluctance 'among us' to compel local authorities to support these schools. This reluctance reflected a belief that ratepayers would object to the increased rate demands if rate aid to the schools was introduced and a fear that county and county borough councils would refuse to be associated with the denominational controversy. To alleviate these components of the 'great difficulty' they faced over the Bill, he proposed both a simple and a more complicated solution. The first put all teachers' salaries on the county rate, with the council determining their general employ- ment and conditions, including control of secular education, although the managers of schools would still appoint them, subject to the authority's approval. In addition, he advocated a one-third:two-thirds composition of school managing bodies with the one-third of the members being provided by the local authority and the remaining two-thirds by the owners of the school. This plan would undoubtedly aid the voluntary schools but it did, he believed, remove any rating difficulties and made the local authorities responsible for all secular education in their area without involving them directly in the denominational issue. His more complicated scheme still entrusted the control of secular education to the local authority and gave it the power to ensure that any school within its area met its specified standards of teaching and accommodation. The local authority would contribute annually, however, towards the costs of the voluntary schools, providing 'any sum by which the average per scholar of those school expenses exceeds the average of the last three years before the improvements were made'. Though subscribers to voluntary schools would not be relieved of their contributions under this scheme, it did contain an element of compulsory rate aid in so far as the authorities had to contribute to any improvements they deemed necessary; at the same time, the authorities' contributions would remove the financial problems of the voluntary schools. The plan would also overcome Nonconformist grievances – for although the locality as a whole was made responsible for the standard of all schools within its area, there was the concomitant of public representation on the managing bodies of all schools in receipt of rate aid. In addition, ratepayers would welcome the continuation of voluntary subscriptions and educationists would approve the LEA being in touch with every school in its area.[70]

The Cabinet was not convinced by this latest effort, the 'extreme difficulty of every proposal was only brought more strongly into light as the debate went on', and the discussion was adjourned for another week. But there were signs that Devonshire's plan was gaining ground, partly because Balfour, as well as Chamberlain and the Bill's other opponents, had failed to devise acceptable alternative plans. Balfour sensed this but was still unhappy about the possible political fall-out from the rates increase likely under Devonshire's scheme; so he proposed yet another variation. Retaining the management proposals made in his previous memorandum his new scheme offered slightly different proposals on finance. Voluntary school managers were to be financially responsible for the maintenance of their school and all management costs while the authority would assume responsibility for the teachers' salaries and for the costs involved in any improvements it required of the managers. He acknowledged that there appeared to be some evidence that subscriptions might not be able to be maintained at their current level and he did not know whether the Chancellor of the Exchequer, given his adherence to Balfour of Burleigh's idea concerning subscriptions, 'would find it in his heart to meet this difficulty by a small increase in the [1897] Aid Grant. If he did', he added, 'the passage of the Bill would, no doubt, be greatly smoothed'. If he could not then there was the other unknown factor – whether Chamberlain would consent to local rate contributions being made to the Aid Grant.

Balfour believed that with this proposal he came closest to meeting the conditions of Balfour of Burleigh and Hicks Beach's position on the maintenance of voluntary subscriptions and the minimalisation of rate increases, as well as Chamberlain's on the issues most likely to engender Nonconformist opposition, while not losing sight of the essential components of Devonshire's scheme. Devonshire, on the other hand, had been busy having clauses drafted so as to allow the practical implementation of his proposals and he presented them in time for the Cabinet meeting on 14 February. The result of this move was that he gained enough support within Cabinet for a new draft of the Bill to be made incorporating his proposals. But shortly afterwards Balfour was struck down by another bout of illness and he was confined to his bed until early March. Devonshire was quite alarmed by this development and worriedly contacted Sandars to ascertain if there was any chance that Balfour would be able to attend the first meeting of the reconstituted Cabinet Committee, established to consider the case of London *vis-à-vis* the Bill. Gorst shared Devonshire's concern, especially as Parliament was already well into the Session; his distress was visible to Barnett when they lunched together:

> . . . there is no Bill as yet ready and he thinks there never will be one – Joe insists it should be optional on Councils to take over education but none can agree to let the LCC have such option. Possibly a secondary Bill will be presented but more probably the government will break up.[71]

The Bill's future was jeopardised further when the new Cabinet Committee, chaired by Ritchie, the Home Secretary, met on 4 March. FitzRoy attended the meeting in Devonshire's room and noted Ritchie's 'extraordinary energy in enforcing his opinions . . . his use of a quill pen, as an instrument of oratory, was conspicuous'. But if Ritchie's urging of 'some pet object' was made with a degree of complacency which even Chamberlain's 'pallid countenance . . . could not disconcert when lit up with its most sardonic smile', it was Chamberlain's actions which were to be decisive. His statement of his views was so vigorous that Devonshire felt constrained to ask Morant to join the meeting and requested Chamberlain to repeat his argument. He then asked Morant for his comments and this 'he did with such success that Chamberlain admitted the case against him unanswerable'. Not surprisingly, the meeting concluded in 'some heat, the duke only just preventing a resolution hostile to anything touching elementary education being adopted'.[72] None the less the committee resolved to raise at the next Cabinet meeting the possibility of dropping the Bill. Balfour was alarmed to learn of this development, commenting that the committee's hope of using his illness as an excuse for their decision was 'quite a new use to which to put a leader of the Party!' Although he admitted to doubts about the Bill he did not see how it could be dropped or, 'if we do, what measures we are to take up in its place'.[73]

Sandars told him that the party aspect of the decision alone had so alarmed him that he had called together the party agent and the two whips to discuss it. They concluded that:

1. We were adverse to an Autumn Session.
2. Any Bill dealing with Education, if introduced, *must* be passed during the Session.
3. In view of
(a) the size of our present programme, (b) the Coronation holiday period, (c) the chances of unexpected debates in connection with the War, it seems hardly possible to find time for the Comprehensive Bill to be passed within the limits of the present Session.
4. Procedure by Resolution is inexpedient.
5. The question of proceeding with a Bill dealing only with Secondary is open to more question, and requires careful consideration.[74]

Sandars went on to state that having considered the problems associated with a secondary education-only measure the best that could be hoped for, the larger measure could only be an introduction before the Easter recess. But with all the other pressures on the parliamentary timetable, including the necessity of making progress on the revision of the procedural rules for Parliament, Hicks Beach's demand for the budget to be taken on 14 March, 'then the Water Bill will be coming downstairs. Then there is the Coronation –', he felt constrained to ask, 'How shall we ever be making progress with a very controversial Education Bill, when only interstices of time are ours?'

He conceded that he had presented the picture in the darkest of hues but added that while Middleton, the party agent, believed the party would be disappointed if a comprehensive measure was not forthcoming, '*any* result is preferable to the failure to pass a Bill, which has once been introduced'.[75] Balfour's recovery shortly afterwards, plus the pressure of the crowded parliamentary timetable, forced the Cabinet to make a decision about the fate of the Bill.

On 18 March Salisbury was able to inform the King that the Cabinet had agreed that the Bill would be introduced six days later but while it would omit any reference to London, the Cowper-Temple clause would remain and rate aid for voluntary schools was to be made optional.[76] Since the Cabinet had agreed principally to Devonshire's proposals, as the Bill that Balfour introduced made clear, Salisbury had confused the one issue where a major compromise had had to be reached on these proposals, that is the control of elementary education. Under the final version of the Bill reached on 22 March, assumption of this control was to be made optional for the new authorities. If they accepted it the school boards and attendance committees would be abolished in their area with the schools transferred to the LEA. The authority could delegate this control, in turn, to non-county borough and urban district councils with populations greater than ten and twenty thousand respectively. This compromise bridged the differences between Devonshire and Chamberlain without sacrificing the full potential of Devonshire's plan, but Parliament was to be the arbiter. Although Balfour and Devonshire thought 'the question will wreck the Government' they did manage to secure the Cabinet's assent to the House sitting for any length of time if the Second Reading was passed.[77]

After eight months of vigorous debate and dissension, the Bill agreed to reluctantly by the Cabinet was very much a political compromise, an outcome which reflected both the fragile nature of the Alliance and the strength of the opposing forces within the Cabinet. FitzRoy believed the problem resided in

> . . . the large mass of ill-informed and fluctuating opinion . . . encountered on almost every subject of importance: on the Education Bill no one is entitled to speak as an expert, and the difficulty is aggravated by the indifference of some and the covert hostility of others.[78]

This was correct, and Devonshire's aim of achieving the creation of comprehensive LEAs was potentially weakened by the damaging limitation placed upon the authorities' powers by Chamberlain's insistence on the inclusion of optional control of elementary education. Created by political and not educational considerations, this vital flaw was quickly identified by at least one Member as he listened to Balfour's introduction of the Bill to the House:

> . . . a most revolutionary Education Bill. Sweeps away School Boards. Creates the County Council the educational authority for the County and puts the Boards schools and the Voluntary Schools under it . . . Up to the present I rather like the Bill. It is quite as much as one would expect from a Tory Government – in fact, more than anyone could anticipate.
> Whole thing destroyed by making the whole Bill optional – it is left entirely to discretion of each County Council! What a miserably weak thing this Government is.[79]

David Lloyd George was to change his opinion about the measure although the changes that were made to the Bill as it passed through the House improved it educationally. At the same time, the Bill's successful passage was to engender significant problems in connection with its implementation while substantially affecting the political situation.

If political necessity drove Balfour to be involved in educational policy and legislation there were others who, while equally involved by virtue of the positions they held, shared his dislike of it. One was the leader of the Opposition, Sir Henry Campbell-Bannerman. For him, education was

> . . . much what the French call a 'terrain vague' – weeds, broken bottles, no fence; 'rubbish shot here', are suggested by its impact. And I have a notion it is the same to everybody. One must cover its vagueness by an excess of platitudinous zeal.[80]

He was all for 'standing under the old banners both as to sugar and as to schools' but he was to find that the passions aroused by the contents of the Education Bill during 1902 were not only to generate some of the most violent political clashes over education in the nation's history but also to lead to a unification of his party after its disastrous division over the Boer War.

NOTES

1. Chandos Papers, CHAN I 3/6, Sandars' note on A.J. Balfour as First Lord of the Treasury, p.1., no date but post-1910.
2. J.H. Yoxall, 'The Education Bill and the Minute', *Picture-Politics* (July–Aug. 1901), p. 11; 'Chaos in the Education Department', *Truth* (15 Aug. 1901) cited in G.W. Kekewich, *The Education Department and After* (1926), p. 336.
3. Taylor argues that Devonshire and Long were not present, using as evidence the minutes taken by Morant and Ilbert. Ilbert's diary entry for the day, however, confirms their presence. See A.I. Taylor, 'The Church Party and Education, 1893–1902', unpublished D.Phil thesis, University of Cambridge, 1981, p. 315; Ilbert Papers, MS 46, Diary, 8 Aug. 1901, House of Lords Record Office.
4. PRO ED 24/14, 'Some questions to be considered before drafting Education Bill for 1902', 1 Aug. 1901, p. 7.
5. Ibid., pp. 12–13.
6. PRO ED 24/16/81, Sir C.P. Ilbert to R. Walrond, 17 Aug. 1901.
7. PRO ED 24/15, J.E. Gorst, Memorandum on First Draft of Education Bill, 1902, 19 Aug. 1901, p. 2.
8. PRO ED 24/16/79g, R. Walrond to R.L. Morant, 20 Aug. 1901.
9. Salisbury Papers (3M), A.J. Balfour to Duke of Devonshire, 20 Aug. 1901.
10. G. Stephenson, *Edward Stuart Talbot, 1844–1934* (1936), pp. 141–2; See also B.M. Allen, *Sir Robert Morant* (1934), p. 155.
11. BP Add MS 49769, fos.195–6, Duke of Devonshire to A.J. Balfour, 25 Aug. 1901.
12. BP Add MS 49691, fos.145–6, J. Chamberlain to Lord Salisbury, 23 Aug. 1901.
13. PRO ED 24/79, Duke of Devonshire to J.E. Gorst, 2 Sept. 1901.
14. Ibid.
15. Ibid., J.E. Gorst to Duke of Devonshire, 9 Sept. 1901.
16. Ibid., J.E. Gorst to Duke of Devonshire, 14 Sept. 1901.
17. PRO ED 24/16/83, E. Cecil to R.L. Morant, 19 Sept. 1901.
18. PRO ED 24/14/15, Duke of Devonshire's notes on Bill, 30 Sept. 1901; Duke of Devonshire to R.L. Morant, 1 Oct. 1901.
19. B.E.C. Dugdale, *Arthur James Balfour* (1939), I, p. 242.
20. PRO ED 24/16/95, R. Walrond to C.P. Ilbert, 21 Oct. 1901.
21. *School Board Chronicle*, 66 (9 Nov. 1901), p. 472.
22. Sadler Papers, MS Eng misc c.205, Diary of Sir M.T. Sadler, 2 Dec. 1901, p. 76.
23. 'Education in Parliament', *Church Quarterly Review*, LIII (Oct. 1901), p. 162.
24. Acland Papers, MS Eng lett d.81, # 107, H.H. Asquith to A.H.D. Acland, 30 Oct. 1901.
25. Sadler Papers, MS Eng misc c.205, Diary of Sir M.T. Sadler, 3 May 1902, p. 86.
26. BP Add MS 49787, fo.29, R.L. Morant to A.J. Balfour, 30 Oct. 1901.
27. PRO ED 24/16, A.K. Rollit to R.L. Morant, 29 Oct. 1901.
28. Ibid., A.K. Rollit to R.L. Morant, 1 Nov. 1901; BP Add MS 49787, R.L. Morant to W. Short, 31 Oct. 1901.
29. PRO ED 24/16, J.P. Williams to Duke of Devonshire, 1 Nov. 1901.
30. The Church had accepted that government or rate aid was crucial for the maintenance of its schools and it had acknowledged also the necessary concomitant of public control in the case of rate aid but, none the less, wanted LEA representation to be limited to no more than one-third of the school managers.
31. A. FitzRoy, *Memoirs*, I (1927), p. 63.
32. PRO CAB 41/26/24, Lord Salisbury to H.M. King, 5 Nov. 1901.

33. J.H. Yoxall, 'Our Educational Dux', *The New Liberal Review* (1901), pp. 681, 684.
34. Hamilton Papers, Add MS 48678, fos. 107–8, Diaries, 6 Oct. 1901.
35. BP Add MS 49787, fo.33, R.L. Morant to A.J. Balfour, 1 Nov. 1901.
36. Trevelyan Papers, CPT8, Mrs.C. Ilbert to C.P. Trevelyan, 10 May 1902; BP Add MS 49787, fo.34, R.L. Morant to A.J. Balfour, 1 Nov. 1901.
37. Ilbert had to suffer the further ignominy of being evicted from his office because the building was required for the Colonial Office but he did become, however, Clerk of the House of Commons in 1902. See BP Add MS 49854, fos.221–2, A.J. Balfour to C.P. Ilbert, 20 Dec. 1901; Add MS 49760, fo.259, J.J. Sandars to A.J. Balfour, 25 Dec. 1901.
38. Passfield Papers, II.3(i) 211, S. Webb to B. Webb, 25 Nov. 1901.
39. BP Add MS 49769, fo.199, J.E. Gorst to Duke of Devonshire, 5 Dec. 1901.
40. Selborne Papers, MS 9, fo.124, J. Chamberlain to Lord Selborne, 7 Nov. 1901.
41. BP Add MS 49769, fos.201–2, Duke of Devonshire to A.J. Balfour, 6 Dec. 1901.
42. Ibid., Add MS 49787, fo.39, R.L. Morant to A.J. Balfour, 7 Dec. 1901.
43. Ibid.
44. A. FitzRoy, op. cit., p. 66.
45. Ibid., pp. 67–8.
46. Devonshire Papers, 340.2878, J. Chamberlain to Duke of Devonshire, 14 Dec. 1901.
47. J. Amery, *The Life of Joseph Chamberlain* (1951), IV, p. 487.
48. G. Stephenson, *Edward Stuart Talbot 1844–1934* (1936), pp. 142–3.
49. PRO CAB 37/59, Lord Salisbury,'Education Bill', 17 Dec. 1901, p. 1.
50. Ibid., A.J. Balfour, 'Memorandum on the Proposal to Introduce Two Bills for Education, with a Note on the Prime Minister's Memorandum of December 17', 18 Dec. 1901.
51. FitzRoy, op. cit., p. 69.
52. PRO CAB 41/26/28, Lord Salisbury to H.M. King, 19 Dec. 1901; FitzRoy, op. cit., p. 69.
53. Balfour Papers (Whittingehame), GD 433/2, Bundle 416, Diary of Lady Frances Balfour, 5 Jan. 1902.
54. PRO ED 24/17, R.L. Morant, 'Mr.Balfour's Instructions to me, December 20, 1901 as to lines of Education Bill'.
55. BP Add MS 49695, fo.132, M.E. Hicks Beach to A.J. Balfour, 24 Dec. 1901.
56. See Passfield Papers, II (i) 169, S. Webb to B. Webb, 24 April 1901; Sandars Papers, MS Eng hist c.732, fo.80, A.J. Balfour to Lord Salisbury, 20 Oct. 1900.
57. PRO ED 24/18, R.L. Morant to A.J. Balfour, 3 Jan. 1902.
58. BP Add MS 49787, fo.53, R.L. Morant to J.S. Sandars, 4 Jan. 1902.
59. Ibid., fo.57, R.L. Morant to A.J. Balfour, 6 Jan. 1902.
60. Passfield Papers, II.4b 96f, R.L. Morant to S. Webb, 8 Jan. 1902.
61. Jebb Papers, Servanda, XVI, W.R. Anson to R.C. Jebb, 12 and 31 Dec. 1901, pp. 136–7.
62. BP Add MS 49769, fos.213–215, A.J. Balfour to Duke of Devonshire, 22 Jan. 1902.
63. Lady Rayleigh's Diary, 22 Jan. 1902 cited in R.F. Mackay, *Balfour, Intellectual Statesman* (1985), p. 95; Sadler Papers, MS Eng misc c.205, Diary of Sir M.T. Sadler, 31 Jan. 1902.
64. PRO CAB 41/27/3, Lord Salisbury to H.M. King, 31 Jan. 1902.
65. B. Webb, *Diary,* 22, p. 2115, 30 Jan. 1902.
66. FitzRoy, op. cit., p. 73.

67. PRO CAB 37/60, Duke of Devonshire, 'Free Optional Rate Aid versus Complete Rate Maintenance', 4 Feb. 1902, p. 3.
68. FitzRoy, op. cit., p. 72.
69. Ibid., pp. 73–4.
70. PRO CAB 37/60, A.J. Balfour, Memorandum, 6 Feb. 1902.
71. Barnett Papers, F/BAR/259, S. Barnett to F. Barnett, 22 Feb. 1902.
72. FitzRoy, op. cit., pp. 79, 80.
73. Sandars Papers, MS Eng hist c.735, fos. 52–4, A.J. Balfour to J.S. Sandars, 7 March 1902.
74. BP Add MS 49761, fos.13–14, J.S. Sandars to A.J. Balfour, 8 March 1902.
75. Ibid.
76. PRO CAB 41/27/10, Lord Salisbury to H.M. King, 18 March 1902.
77. FitzRoy, op. cit., p. 81.
78. Ibid.
79. K.O. Morgan (ed.), *Lloyd George: Family Letters 1885–1936* (1975), p. 131.
80. Campbell-Bannerman Papers, Add MS 41236, fo.87, H. Campbell-Bannerman to V. Nash, 16 Jan. 1901.

6

The 1902 Act – stage two

The Duke of Devonshire believed that the reception accorded Balfour's introduction of the Education Bill was 'just right, certainly without too much enthusiasm' but his view was not shared by others.[1] Sir William Anson felt the Bill was 'somewhat sketchy and half-hearted' while another observer thought that the measure 'bristles with difficulties' and would be beyond the power of the government to pass.[2] Gorst, going to Cheltenham to recuperate from a debilitating attack of influenza which had prevented his contribution to the Bill's introduction, told Jebb that he wondered if the Cabinet had the 'pluck and steadfastness' to ensure that it reached the Statute Book.[3] And Jebb, sharing Gorst's fear and with it the spectre of a possible repetition of 1896, instigated a meeting of Unionist MPs in mid-April which then forwarded a resolution to Balfour urging him to take the Second Reading as soon as possible while, at the same time, pledging him their complete assistance to ensure that the Bill was a success.

Michael Sadler was equally pessimistic about the Bill, partly because he was convinced that the government failed to appreciate all the nuances connected with education and partly because of the current state of society:

> The root difficulty is that no one is really clear what we ought to teach. The social future is so dark; changes in industry, etc., are taking place at such a headlong speed: the intellectual situation is so full of perplexities: men's minds are so full of unrest about the ultimate questions: there is so much disagreement about the ethical postulates of national and individual life – that to propose to erect a new education system is like building a big new house on an unsurveyed quicksand – with unknown tides ebbing and flowing.

He was worried also by Balfour's comments about the government's policy for the voluntary schools, being convinced that if denominational education

> means anything, it means an atmosphere which pervades the whole educational life of the school. But the tacit assumption of

the Bill is that 'religious instruction' is like stamp-edge on a sheet of postage stamps, – an affix which can be torn off and treated separately from the stamps themselves- the latter being secular education. I deny this assumption. . . . AJB speaks as though we were all agreed to accept one type of 'secular' primary education (like one type of packet tobacco) provided that something called "religious instruction" could be added or omitted to taste. The problem is far more subtle and deep seated than this.[4]

His views appeared to be vindicated by the declarations made by Dr John Clifford and other leading figures in the Nonconformist world. In a letter to the *Daily News*, Clifford warned that 'if we have collision and overlapping of authorities now we shall have "Chaos and old Night" . . . when this Bill is passed' and he claimed that the cry for 'one efficient local authority' represented hypocrisy on the part of the government for the real aim of the measure was to sacrifice children's education to denominationalism.[5] Hugh Price Hughes labelled it 'the most reactionary and clerical . . . proposed since 1832' while Hirst Hollowell thought that under the terms of the Bill the militant denominationalists had gained what both they and the Church's Committees of Convocation had asked for; the Nonconformists, on the other hand, stood to lose almost everything. Not surprisingly then, a joint meeting of the education and organising committees of the Free Churches strongly condemned the Bill for its lack of truly representative LEAs as well as for the possibility of rate aid being given to voluntary schools without any effective public control over the use of such funds.[6] William Garnett did not share these views, being convinced that the control of the elementary schools would rest ultimately with the new LEAs:

> I understand that the Bill is a sort of glorified Clause VII; not only will the local authority distribute the local rates to the public elem. schools – voluntary and others alike – but it will also have the distribution of Gvt grants: this gives to the local authority the complete control.[7]

Notwithstanding the truth of this view, Nonconformist anger had been roused by what was perceived to be an educational policy designed to reinforce the concept of a State Church and henceforward, their opposition would focus on religious rather than educational issues. Lloyd George was aware of this and in the course of a speech given in Pwllheli shortly after the Bill's introduction the thrust of his argument was that although the Bill could cause a revolution within the education system, 'Priestcraft was at the root of the evil in the educational system, and the new Bill tended to pander to priestcraft'.[8] Campbell-Bannerman was likewise not slow to scent the political potential this represented for the Liberal Party, and told Sir William Harcourt that the thrust of the Opposition's attack should be centred on the apparent lack of public control over rate money spent on voluntary schools. He believed from what he had seen of the 'scores and scores' of resolutions from the Nonconformists that

> they have a question of principle beyond the mere question of uncontrolled rating . . . .The Non.Con feeling (& Protestant feeling) is roused as it never was before, and we shall come to eternal grief if we do not play up to it.[9]

In Anglican circles the Bill was initially greeted with a sense of relief, with church dignitaries hurrying to support it through their diocesan associations.[10] But the absence of uniformity of opinion within the Church reflected the considerable divergence of views on educational as well as religious issues. Representative of many of the High Church sector, Lord Hugh Cecil was sceptical about the government's intentions and publicly expressed his fear that the part of the Bill covering elementary education might be dropped. Even if it was not, there would still remain for him and others the thorny issue of control of the voluntary schools; for although he admitted that the recent Convocation agreements could not be revoked, 'we cannot either hide from ourselves that in many cases the new [elected] Managers will be a source of friction and annoyance'.[11] His words were prophetic, for after the question of local option the most controversial part of the Bill was Clause 7, covering the managerial structure for voluntary schools.

Although untroubled by these criticisms, Balfour told Bishop Talbot that the Bill 'must pass'; a comment which mirrored his awareness of the strain that the measure had created within the Alliance and not least Devonshire's need for a successful measure, for the latter had stated that he was damned if he would be 'made a fool of as he was last year'.[12] None the less, he counselled the Church not to start any agitation, at least for the present:

> If we saw any symptoms . . . in the autumn or earlier of a formidable agitation against the Bill, a counter agitation might be extremely desirable . . . But in the meanwhile, though I should keep my powder dry, I should forbear to use it.[13]

What did preoccupy him was the almost universal condemnation by those supporting the Bill of the adoptive or option clause on elementary education. He believed that the issue could not be satisfactorily resolved until the views of the county councils were known but they could not be learned before the Second Reading of the Bill had to be taken and passed if the measure was to secure the complete support of the Cabinet.

Arthur Acland, who vehemently opposed the Bill, was worried that the Liberals were still not completely united given that the forthcoming struggle had to be taken as 'a really serious matter'.[14] Campbell-Bannerman took a more pragmatic view, arguing that there were 'so many fatal objections to the Bill that I can see no way of meeting the 2nd Reading'.[15] Sidney Webb, on the other hand, was optimistic and believed that not only was a rejection of the Second Reading out of the question but that the Bill would pass with a majority of 275.[16] In the event Webb's prognosis was the most accurate, for the Bill passed with a majority of 237, the Unionists having had the support of the Irish Members. The Cabinet was now committed to ensuring its success and the local option issue could be more thoroughly explored.

The declaration on 1 June that a peace treaty had been signed with the Boers brought an air of relief to the nation but it was not enough to stop the visible erosion of public support for the government. At the Bury by-election a few weeks earlier a Conservative majority of 849 at the general election had been converted into a Liberal one of 414 and this trend was to be repeated shortly in North Leeds. At the same time, the end of the war and the presence of the Education Bill succeeded in reuniting the previously divided Liberals:

> The sunlight of the Peace of Pretoria falls with chastened glow on the Front Opposition Bench. How good it is to see brethren dwelling together in unity! . . . Happiness of the hour accentuated by the fact that not only is the chasm in the Liberal ranks closed, but the Bill before the House chances to be one on which the Opposition would, in any circumstances, present a united front. All sound on the Education question.[17]

Faced with these problems, Balfour refused to grant the Commons a day off to celebrate the end of the war and on 2 June the House moved on to the Committee Stage of the Bill. As one Liberal MP observed, 'Mr Balfour makes no concessions. At present he looks as if he intended to have the Bill and nothing but the Bill'.[18] A month later the strain was beginning to tell on all participants, as Lucy noted:

... little do you know what a day's work on Education Bill in Committee means. Begins about half-past two in afternoon; goes on till half-past seven; surviving Members laid out in comatose state till nine o'clock, when they buckle to again and grind away till midnight. Well enough for some of them who stray away whilst speeches are made, coming back at sound of Division bell to run up their record in the Session's divisions. But for PRINCE ARTHUR, always at his post; for JOHN O'GORST, who shares his drudgery without the refreshment of occasional speech-making; .... the experience suggests comparison favourable to a term of penal servitude.[19]

But there were additional problems for Balfour in connection with the passage of the Bill and his colleagues.

Shortly after the Committee Stage had started Hicks Beach was angered by the possibility of the government introducing an amendment to provide Treasury relief for the LEAs, in order to ensure that all LEAs would pay a uniform sum for each child attending any elementary school. He claimed that this was 'a liability which you cannot promise me shall not be largely increased' but Balfour would not be deterred, pointing out that the sum required by the amendment, three-quarters of a million pounds, would not lead to a major diminution in the demands on ratepayers but it would enable the Bill to be a financially viable measure. Balfour's final comment was that there would be considerable political difficulties for the government if this plan was not adopted. His view was substantiated when Devonshire and Gorst received a deputation from the County Councils' Association later in the month, the latter presenting a resolution asking that the extra costs associated with the implementation of the Bill should not be borne from the rates alone.[20] Beach remained unmoved and after the next Cabinet meeting Devonshire learned from Long that it had been decided to present Beach with an ultimatum 'such that he was not wanted'.[21] Balfour introduced the amendment, providing rate relief of 7s 6d per child, but there was an accompanying proviso that LEAs accepting the grant had to abolish the school boards in their area. The outcry from School Board supporters, Nonconformists and Trade Unionists was soon heard but, as one Liberal journal observed, the government had 'set up a bribe for the adoption of the Bill, or, conversely, a fine for not adopting it, which it was hopeless to expect that any ordinary local authority, having a care for the interest of the ratepayers, could resist'.[22] The amendment was passed but Hicks Beach resisted all the attempts made by Balfour to get him to remain in the Ministry after Salisbury's retirement was announced three weeks later.

The postponement of the Coronation because of the King's attack of appendicitis had provided Salisbury, whose own health was rapidly deteriorating, with a valid excuse for retiring from the Premiership now that peace had been secured in South Africa. While it had long been recognised within the party that Balfour was Salisbury's logical successor, the manner in which the transfer of power was effected lacked both sensitivity and finesse. Although Balfour called on both Chamberlain and Devonshire on the day he became the new Premier, in his discussion with the latter he only mentioned accepting the King's commission almost as an afterthought to a long discussion about aspects of the Education Bill. The duke could only manage to say 'oh!' before quitting the room, no doubt hurt that his possible claims to the position, albeit very slight, had not received any consideration.[23] Devonshire soon recovered his poise, however, and was able to inform the House of Lords two days later that with one exception, that is Hicks Beach, 'an exception deeply to be regretted', Balfour had been given the promise of continued support from the Cabinet. Hicks Beach's stance led Sidney Webb to tell his wife the next day that 'we are all mainly agog for ministerial changes now that Hicks Beach is going – possibilities of Gorst going, the Duke giving up Education, and Henny being appointed – all of which I do not believe a word'.[24] On this occasion Webb's judgement failed him, for Devonshire had indeed decided to give up the Presidency of the Board of Education and Gorst, as soon as he had learned this from Devonshire, promptly tendered his resignation to Balfour. The latter was thus faced not only with finding a suitable replacement for Hicks Beach but also with filling the two key positions at the Board of Education.

Gorst's departure from the Board of Education was a source of relief in some quarters, including the *Manchester Guardian* and *The Times* – the latter hinting that it was Balfour's dissatisfaction with Gorst's contribution to the passage of the Bill that had led to his loss of office – but elsewhere there was generally disquiet about the loss. *The Schoolmaster* regretted his departure 'more in sorrow than in anger', but looked forward with anticipation to 'squalls' when he reappeared in the autumn as a backbencher. The *Journal of Education* recorded the 'shock, followed by a feeling of regret' which had been caused by the announcement, while *The Speaker* compared the appointment of Akers Douglas, the new Home Secretary, with Gorst's loss of office, to the detriment of the former, who had 'never distinguished himself intellectually in any way' whereas Gorst had discharged his duties as Vice President, 'when allowed by his superiors to do so, with an intellectual distinction quite beyond dispute'.[25] Gorst may have stepped down from office but, as will be seen, he was still to influence educational policy decisions in the future.

Sir William Anson, chosen by Balfour as Gorst's successor from a short list which had included Jebb, received an urgent summons to Balfour's room in the House on 6 August. Hurrying there, he found

> . . . a compromise under discussion with Lloyd George and Hutton to enable us to finish by Friday. After this was settled, Balfour kept me back, and asked me to take office as Secretary to the Board of Education. I said I should like it if I could do it. He said he would take that risk, so in five minutes the thing was settled, and I went away rather dazed . . . Then to bed and a sleepless night, wondering if I have done right about office.[26]

He was to confess to Charles Trevelyan shortly afterwards that he found his new role 'rather alarming and the detail one has to learn seems oppressive'.[27] While Michael Sadler characterised Anson as a 'misadventurous opportunist Whig' his appointment was greeted with equanimity by most of the educational press although his lack of detailed knowledge of elementary education was seen as a marked disadvantage. *The Schoolmaster* described him as a 'quiet, precise, good-natured, rather liberal-minded little man' and saw his strength residing in the possession of a 'large amount of that very uncommon sense – common sense'.[28] The press reaction, however, to the appointment of Lord Londonderry as the new President of the Board of Education verged on the incredulous.

The *Manchester Guardian* highlighted the problem presented by this appointment with the comment that 'few men if given fifty guesses . . . would have named Lord Londonderry'. *Commerce* was rather more frank, observing that his appointment 'would be simply comic if it were not so pitiable a comment on the Government's desire to help the country beat our rivals in Europe and America'.[29] Londonderry's marked failure in his previous position as Postmaster General did not inspire confidence about his occupancy of the Presidency even among educationists who knew of his work as a member and chairman of the London School Board. This and the other government changes made by Balfour had caused rumblings within the Conservative Party:

... the quid nuncs were growling about A.J.B.'s want of strength etc etc that he should have made a much bigger clear out – have got rid of many of us old tadpoles and tapers and have given more chances to young and brilliant men –[30]

But these views did not trouble Balfour, his reaction in such circumstances being to comment, 'They say. What say they? Let them say'.[31] For him there were more pressing matters to attend to, not least the Education Bill.

Debate on the three most contentious clauses of the Bill – those which covered the option for LEAs to administer all elementary schools (Clause 5) and the management structure and administration of elementary schools (Clauses 7 and 8) had begun with Clause 5 on 9 July. Inserted to meet Chamberlain's views about the role to be played by the new LEAs with regard to voluntary schools – that it should be optional – the clause had been welcomed initially by both supporters and opponents of the Bill. But during the early stages of the Bill's passage opinions had changed and on 9 July Henry Hobhouse moved an amendment to make this role compulsory, arguing that it was now generally agreed that what was wanted was a properly organised system of primary and secondary education:

> They did not want a mere patchwork plan, ... Above all, they did not wish to see continued a kind of chaos of different authorities, with agitation proceeding and discontent prevailing, in educational circles, even where it did not exist at present.[32]

The potential political problem presented by this amendment, given Chamberlain's declared views on the clause, was fortuitously circumvented two days earlier when the hansom cab containing the Colonial Secretary had overturned beside the Canadian Arch, pitching Chamberlain forward with such force that his head shattered the window of the cab and he received an ugly gash to his right temple. Detained overnight in Charing Cross Hospital and then confined to bed for the remainder of the week, Chamberlain was thus prevented from attending the House and voting on the amendment. Balfour signalled his own support for the amendment, arguing that the rate relief amendment passed earlier had removed the financial burden which had made county councils reluctant previously to assume responsibility for elementary education. At the same time, mindful of Chamberlain's views, he made the question a free vote, claiming that it was a matter which 'might be very properly left to the judgment of the House itself'.[33] It was carried by 271 to 102 votes, Chamberlain's son, Austen, being conspicuous among the 'Noes'. Balfour did not relish the result, however, and his sister noted that at a private dinner party the following day he claimed that 'he was beginning to hate both education and religion' as a result of the debates on the Bill.[34]

Now that all the LEAs to be created under the Bill had no choice in their role *vis-à-vis* elementary education, attention focused closely on Clause 7 and the highly contentious issue of popular representation on the managing bodies of voluntary schools. One Nonconformist, Principal Fairbairn of Mansfield College, had written to Haldane:

> I wish you could persuade our Government to lift Education out of the miserable sectarian slough into which they are about to push it further. They are certainly about to sacrifice Education on the Elementary side to the interests of the very persons who have disliked it most. I deeply deplore the present controversy but if the Bill is passed it will grow bitterer than we have ever known it.[35]

His pleas were in vain as he discovered when, addressing Balfour on behalf of a deputation of 70 Nonconformists presenting their objections to the Bill, Balfour remained obdurate and refused to make any concessions. The original clause left the management of these schools to be covered by the provisions of previous Education Acts since 1870. This was changed by an amendment introduced by Balfour on 21 July which stipulated a majority of trustee over LEA representation on voluntary school management bodies, where the number of trust managers was not to exceed four and those of the LEA two. The Opposition's main argument, that such a ratio did not provide the necessary popular control, given the financial support to be provided from local rates for these schools, did not deter him. His response was that the six managers would be equally concerned with the contentious issues connected with voluntary school management, that is, the appointment of teachers and regulation of the religious instruction. Furthermore, the managers were to be the delegates of the LEA, a body to be popularly elected and responsible for the control of school finances and secular education. He felt that the 'storm of educational controversy' about them was absurd 'considering how little under the Bill these Managers have to manage'.[36] In private, he told Lord Hugh Cecil that he was determined to save the denominational character of the voluntary schools by having a denominational majority on their managing bodies and by giving it 'unfettered discretion in all matters which do not fall under the control of the education authority'.[37]

Balfour stuck resolutely to this view despite Chamberlain's private comment that if progress on the Bill was to be achieved, it could only be done by confronting the realities facing them, not least the way the measure had turned the Nonconformists into 'active instead of merely passive opponents' and the striking effects their campaigns were having on large sections of the lower middle and upper working classes, hitherto supporters of the Unionist Party.[38] Chamberlain believed that, as amended, one outcome of Clause 7 would be an endangering rather than the preservation of the voluntary schools. He claimed that the minority of LEA representatives on a voluntary school's managing body would have a 'permanent grievance which will cause them to act on each Committee as a section apart constantly putting sand into the wheels and opposing everything that is done by the other managers'. He forecast, correctly as events were to prove, that this would be compounded by the non-payment of rates by large numbers of Nonconformists, and although he decried the latter action as 'foolish and illogical', the overall effect would be to maintain the controversy about the Bill and thereby justify the Liberals, when they returned to power, in reversing educational policy. To prevent this possible outcome meant amending Clause 7 in such a way that control over secular education was placed 'in the hands of those who find the money'. While he was willing to abide by Balfour's decision on the matter he stated that they should then 'face the situation with the full knowledge of what will happen if we continue on our present lines'.[39]

Balfour found Chamberlain's views difficult to accept, although they were reinforced by reports forwarded to him from experienced Liberal Unionist agents. He claimed to be perplexed by the whole issue given his belief that the Bill was a reasonable one, not unduly favourable to either the Church or clergy, and added that he found himself provoked 'by the extraordinary campaign of lies which has been set on foot against it, and by the total indifference to the interest of education which seems to be shown by the contending parties'. He admitted that his feelings were irrelevant if, as Chamberlain had suggested, the Bill could not be passed in its present form or, if it were passed, it created such friction as to render it 'a curse instead of a blessing'. At the same time, he hinted that a defeat of the government would be preferable to having to make concessions which would not conciliate their opponents in the long term yet at the same time would 'endanger all confidences among friends'.[40] He also pointed out to Chamberlain that although all the demonstrations made so far had been against the Bill its supporters had yet to move.

An attempt had been made in July by the Bishop of London, Winnington Ingram, in the form of a conference held at his palace in Fulham, to bring Church and Nonconformist leaders together to discuss the contentious issues of the Bill. The Bishops of Winchester and Rochester, Lord Hugh Cecil and various Nonconformist leaders, including Hirst Hollowell, were among those who attended. The Bishop of Hereford's proposal that the managing bodies of voluntary schools should consist of equal numbers of representatives of the LEA, the denomination and the parish council (or meeting) was broached by Morant, who had been sent by Balfour, for consideration as a possible compromise over Clause 7. Although Hereford's proposal was not favoured by Balfour, Chamberlain may have drawn it to his attention and Balfour could not afford to ignore it. Hereford's somewhat radical position within the Church was not accepted by many of his colleagues and it was not surprising that the bishops attending the conference found the proposal 'too great a concession towards popular control'. Some of the Nonconformists present viewed it as 'a denial of popular control and civil liberty' but they were left in no doubt by the tone of the meeting that their only hope of achieving concessions or alterations to the Bill was to take the issue to the country, and to employ more militant tactics.[41] Balfour, in the meantime, had applied closure to the passage of the Bill and using this had ensured that his amended version of Clause 7 was passed the day before Parliament broke up for the summer recess. But with the advent of this recess Dr John Clifford's derogatory catch-cry of 'Rome on the rates' was increasingly heard as it tumbled from the lips of Liberal MPs and Nonconformists addressing meetings against the Bill throughout the country.

As the public controversy over the Bill deepened so too did the discomfort within the ranks of the Conservative Party. Akers Douglas was told that not only was there growing hatred towards the Bill but hitherto stalwart supporters of it were weakening. Devonshire was not surprised by these developments, although he admitted to being perplexed as to how they could be resolved:

> . . . I daresay that we shall come to grief over the Education Bill, but I think that we always anticipated that this might happen. The Bill has not been criticised in the country much more strongly than it was in the Cabinet. We always knew that it would be fought tooth and nail by the N[on] C[onformist]s and that the L[iberal] U[nionist]s would not like it. Where we perhaps miscalculated was as to the distrust and dislike of the

clergy of many of the clauses. Educationally I believe it is right, and I don't know what else we could have done . . . I don't see at present what we can do to make concessions to the anti-clericalists which will do any good, but the genius of Morant may evolve something during the Recess . . .[42]

On this occasion Devonshire's faith was misplaced, for Morant had not only underestimated the magnitude of the Nonconformist opposition but was perplexed by the problems arising from Clauses 7 and 8 in connection with the Roman Catholics. Furthermore, he was somewhat preoccupied with the security of his own position at the Board.

Towards the end of August, Morant had gone north to Londonderry's country seat at Wynyard, near Stockton-on-Tees, in order to acquaint the new President with matters relevant to both the Bill and the Board of Education. A few days later, when he left Wynyard for London, Morant was in a somewhat bemused state, telling Sandars he found it difficult to conceive that 'anyone could be so blankly ignorant after being chairman of a big School Board and having various Cabinet discussions on our Bill'. Equally worrying was Londonderry's ignorance about office matters, especially as Morant now had no formal attachment to the new political heads of the Board, and Kekewich had taken the recent changes to represent 'a new lease of life and power for himself'. The appointment of Kekewich's protégé, Pelham, as Anson's private secretary, was seen by Morant as but one manifestation of the fact that 'the whole office feel that they must now look to K as the working director'. He was convinced that Kekewich's whole aim was to manoeuvre Anson into a position so as to be able to effectively control and direct the Board. 'The extent of the functions of a Parliamentary Secretary of a Board is, as you know,' he told Sandars:

> . . . very ill defined, and can be made in practice to include very much. I have given hints of all this to Londonderry, but of course in his profound ignorance of every subject matter under dispute it is quite impossible to tell him what matters are difficult or dangerous and also impossible for me, having no means of hearing of any proposed developments or seeing any minutes or any decisions, to exercise any preventive action.

Critically aware that his influence over subsequent policy decisions was in danger of being extinguished, Morant's letter was tantamount to a *cri de coeur* for help to redress the situation.[43] But Sandars' reaction to the 'long dreary letter . . . the colour of which is due entirely to want of holiday', apart from noting later that Morant now appeared to value more highly 'the slow digestion of the old Duke', was to ask Balfour to order Morant abroad for a holiday of at least three weeks.[44] Morant was forced to comply and took himself off to Derbyshire.

Morant's fears proved to be groundless, however, for at the same time that he was pouring out his worries to Sandars, Londonderry was extolling his virtues to Balfour. Furthermore, Londonderry was more perceptive than Morant portrayed him, telling Balfour that at the Board there was clearly some chaos and uncertainty, features which could be explained 'by Gorst being impossible and Kekewich useless'. Although he did not like having to adopt the role of being a 'new broom', Londonderry wanted someone in charge of the office to replace Kekewich, that someone being 'a really good man thoroughly acquainted with the Bill'. His choice fell on Morant, and in this he had Anson's support, the latter having described Kekewich as 'doddering' following his discussions with him.[45] Londonderry's views were implemented a few months later when Kekewich was given extended leave until the official date of his retirement (1 April 1903) and Morant became acting Permanent Secretary in his place.

Before he left for his holiday, Morant had had to admit to Balfour that after long discussions with Cardinal Vaughan and Edmund Talbot the more he examined Clause 8 the more difficult it seemed to be to find a compromise which could be accepted by the Roman Catholics. Although Londonderry, with his strong connections with the Orangemen of Northern Ireland, had remarked that he would not be adverse to the Catholics being penalised or even cut out of the Bill, not only was he speaking 'with much zeal but very little knowledge' but to pass a Bill which excluded the Catholics would have been absurd.[46] Morant had tried Cardinal Vaughan with 'every sort of bridge' as far as the control of religious education by the managers under Clause 8 was concerned, but without success. The stumbling block was that the trust deeds of all Catholic schools reserved religious instruction absolutely to the priest and/or bishop, as indeed did those of many Anglican schools. If this arrangement was altered, Vaughan had indicated that the Catholics would consider removing all their schools from the national system. Acutely aware of the consequences this would have for the Bill's policy as well as for the education system, and knowing that Bishop Davidson was due to go to Whittingehame to discuss the Bill with Balfour in a few weeks' time, Morant raised with the bishop his doubts about the Bill's policy of tampering with trust deeds. He knew that Balfour was in favour of all the managers of a voluntary school being in control of its religious instruction, as a means of diminishing the possibility of ritualist excesses by over-zealous clergy, but he believed that the outcome of such a policy would produce a 'whole huge wrangle of a new Reformation settlement . . . of a continuous unseemly wrangle in managing bodies'. For Morant the problem was best resolved by the provision of alternative schools to meet the needs of parents opposed to the teaching provided by existent schools. This solution seemed preferable to the pursuit of Balfour's view which might wreck the Bill and he could not help but wonder if it was Balfour's Presbyterian background which allowed him to permit a 'concourse of six persons' to decide 'the true doctrine of the Church of England'.[47] His scepticism about this Balfourian view may have been reinforced by the increasing agitations being mounted by the Nonconformists.

Hirst Hollowell, the indefatigable organiser of the Northern Counties' Education League, had been busy traversing the country, addressing meetings in more than 200 locations and stirring opposition to the measure ever since its introduction. His activities had been paralleled by those of Clifford, now the unrelenting, dogmatic high priest of Nonconformity, Drs Hugh Price Hughes, Scott Lidgett and Parker. But it was Hollowell who was responsible for organising the climax to the campaign in the north of England with a monster demonstration against the Bill held on Woodhouse Moor in Leeds on 20 September. Sixteen hired trains were used to convey Liberal and Nonconformist demonstrators from throughout Yorkshire to the meeting, where they swelled the numbers to an estimated 70,000 to 100,000 and were able to listen to speeches made by 16 MPs and others from five platforms arranged around the moor. Not content with this, Hollowell also composed a 'Battle Song of the Schools' for the meeting:

> England, rouse thy legions,
>   Ere it be too late,
> Foes of right, and foes of light,
>   Would storm the schoolhouse gate.
>
> CHORUS
> Children's voices call thee,
>   Call thee to the fight;
> Do thy bravest; do it now!
>   And God defend the Right!

185

Thirty years have come and gone,
    Since, with valiant hand,
Gladstone, Forster, Bright, upreared
    Free schools throughout thy land.

While our sons were over-sea,
    While the soldier fought,
Priest and traitor sought to bring
    The people's schools to nought.

Now the angel Peace returns,
    Guard thy flock at home;
Let the priestly spoilers hear
    Thy trampling millions come.

Rally, then, from sea to sea,
    England in thy might!
Win for men – more Liberty!
    Win for the child – more Light![48]

The passions engendered by the singing and the speeches ensured that a resolution condemning the Bill because of the loss of civil liberties and popular control as well as the use of rate support for sectarian dogmas was easily passed. The meeting also clearly demonstrated the strength of discontent among Liberals and Nonconformists and Balfour now admitted to Herbert Gladstone that there was a possibility that the government could be beaten during the autumn Session.[49] Campbell-Bannerman was pleased to hear this for it appeared to support his own recent observation:

> All the casual Tories I have met take our line 'Why the — did they meddle with this hornet's nest'. What the country wants is higher education and technical. Elementary was going on well enough. What tempted them to meddle with the School Boards?

He told Bryce that their party's strategy should be to denounce the futility of constant debate about Clause 7 and then 'go on a bold line; carry the stalwarts with us; shame the weakkneed and frighten them' and, he added, 'if beaten, what good ground we should be upon'.[50] This last point acknowledged that Balfour would not be prepared to give up the Bill without a fight.

Balfour, at the same time, took steps to try to assuage his colleagues' fears about the possible political consequences of Clauses 7 and 8 by formulating two possible schemes of voluntary school management for their consideration, each scheme containing three variations within it. The first scheme allowed a denominational majority on a school's managing body as in Clause 7, whereas the second gave the majority to LEA representatives. Balfour's preference was for a variation of the first scheme under which the managers were to have complete control over all school matters except those coming under the aegis of the LEA. For him its strength lay with the abolition of single-person control of elementary schools while it ensured, at the same time, that a voluntary school still belonged to the parent denomination. He accepted that this scheme would not be acceptable to the Roman Catholics, who would prefer another variation: that the control of religious instruction had to be as specified by a school's trust deeds. Although he believed that his preferred variation could be made to work, Balfour acknowledged that a variation of the second scheme, which allowed reserved subjects such as religious instruction to be the preserve of the denominational members of the managing body while all other educational matters came under the control of all the managers, shared the same 'simple, logical, intelligible' quality and might conciliate most of the opposition, although there still remained a query about the Catholics' response to it. To ascertain this, Morant was sent to Derwent Hall at the beginning of October.

The outcome of his 'huge talk' with Cardinal Vaughan, Lord Edmund Talbot and the Duke of Norfolk was that he learned that the Catholics had decided that they did not want the Bill jeopardised because of any stance of theirs and they were prepared, having examined fully the nature of the trust deeds of their schools, to accept Balfour's preferred variation, 'provided we let them protest, to save their consciences, against the principle of letting two outside (possibly atheist) managers have a voice in religious instruction'.[51] This achievement was tempered, however, by Morant's observation that Balfour, while he had indicated that he would not welcome 'any course which would absolutely undo what was accomplished in Clause 7', now 'hankers after reintroducing option into the Bill' and he was beginning to consider that there might be a need to make concessions. Furthermore, he was thinking of announcing this in the course of his forthcoming speech in Manchester, significantly his first public speech since becoming Premier.[52] Sandars was alarmed by this news and tried to draw Balfour's attention to the general agreement existent within the party that Clause 7 should remain as passed. Middleton was very nervous, he reported:

> lest there should be any undoing of that piece of work. His

message is that our only chance is to stick to the Bill as as we have gone with it, and if alterations must be introduced then they must not conflict with the general scheme of the Bill as it is now before the House. In other words, where we can help our own side, by all means try to do so: but the Noncon agitation will be placated by nothing.[53]

But Morant had already been asked by Balfour to ascertain the Duke of Devonshire's views about the possibility of changes.

Morant found Devonshire convinced that Clause 7 should not be tampered with and that Balfour should stick to the path originally chosen, 'making all the play we can with the various points you name – pupil-teachers, teachers, single school areas, lay control of religious instruction, etc. etc'. But no sooner had Morant reported this than he received an invitation from Chamberlain to visit him for a discussion before the latter's private conference with Liberal Unionists in Birmingham two days later.[54] Chamberlain, faced with the possibility of censure by a very disaffected Birmingham party, had told Devonshire of his discontent with the measure:

I told you that your Education Bill would destroy your own Party. It has done so. Our best friends are leaving us by scores and hundreds and they will not come back . . . .If we go on, we shall only carry the Bill with great difficulty – and, when it is carried, we shall have sown the seeds of an agitation which will undoubtedly be successful in the long run.

Eleven days later, his final comment in another letter was 'Damn the Bill!'[55] In view of this Morant was carefully briefed before his departure for Highbury by Sandars who took considerable pains to try to ensure that Morant would stress to Chamberlain the point that Balfour's ideas for his Manchester speech should not be anticipated 'by any soothing words at Birmingham'. Any such comments could be politically damaging by leading the Bill's Conservative supporters to construe Balfour's ideas as concessions or modifications insisted upon by the Liberal Unionists.

But Chamberlain remained convinced, even after his discussion with Morant, that the only way to ensure success for the Bill was to 'change the issue' and make it clear that secular education would not be under the control of denominational managers in voluntary schools. Reinforced in his belief by the recent condemnation of Clause 7 at a recent meeting of the Birmingham Liberal Unionists, Chamberlain did not think that such an aim was impossible and warned Sandars that 'if

Balfour nails his flag to the mast on Tuesday at Manchester, I consider that the Unionist cause is hopeless at the next election, and we shall certainly lose the majority of the Liberal Unionists once and for all'.[56] Worried by this response Sandars discussed it, and Morant's report of his meeting, with Middleton. While the latter believed the state of the nation and the party required Balfour's Manchester meeting to be of a rallying kind he conceded that given Chamberlain's views it would be better for Balfour not to make a speech. As for Chamberlain's advocacy of 'changing the issue', Sandars conveyed to Balfour Middleton's warning that it would have a severely debilitating effect upon the Conservative backbenchers who, while they may have cared little about the Bill, 'as party men they have played the game and have voted for the clause [7] . . . and defended it in their constituencies'. Sandars tactfully warned Balfour that if he felt under pressure to make drastic changes to the Bill the feeling at party headquarters was that it would be better to withdraw it; 'That,' he added, 'of course, means an election and a rout'.[57]

Chamberlain's meeting with the Liberal Unionists in Birmingham demonstrated his extremely dextrous handling of his supporters and he was at pains to emphasise not only the government's determination to pass the Education Bill but also its willingness to make concessions. These, he argued, should be made within the parameters dictated by the principle of popular control of secular education and denominational control of religious education in voluntary schools. At the end of the three-hour meeting a resolution was passed that the majority of managers in voluntary schools should be appointed by the LEA.[58] Lord Cranborne was furious on learning this, claiming that Chamberlain had 'boiled the whole show . . . What a method to adopt! Vital amendments in detail, not first proposed to Parliament nor even to the Cabinet but to the Liberal Unionist Caucus in Birmingham.' Although he tried to express himself moderately to Balfour, not least because of the awful time he believed the latter to be having with the Bill, Cranborne could not contain himself. He not only implied that Chamberlain had forced Balfour's hand on the issue but also that he had little confidence that Balfour would not be 'driven further' into making more concessions.[59] Balfour, politically more pragmatic than his cousin, was not deterred by these comments, as was demonstrated by his speech at Manchester to the party faithful attending the annual conference of the National Union.

The day after the speech, Sir Robert Finlay, the Attorney General, commented to Balfour's sister-in-law, Frances, that 'Arthur last night was simply admirable. He has effectually cleared the political horizon – our men will fight now'.[60] Finlay was correct in his observation yet the great irony about Balfour's speech was that both in essence and in argument it was incredibly Gorstian, being remarkably similar to the one Gorst had made when introducing the 1896 Education Bill to the House. Thus the 'central principle' of the Bill, as Balfour described it, was decentralisation and 'on that everything else hangs'. The only differences, this time, lay with the charisma of the speaker and the fact that the public were now ready to accept this message. Surveying the main points raised by opponents of the Bill, Balfour was careful to indicate that if parental choice was to be a valid criterion in the provision of education, justice required the continued maintenance of the voluntary schools. At the same time he tried to minimise the argument against rate aid being given to these schools by referring to them as not being totally financed by the public purse. While he castigated those who had declared that they would refuse to pay rates should the Bill become law he was at pains to stress the role to be played by school managers. He argued that much of the opposition to the clause could be removed if it was remembered that the control of education rested not with the managers but with the LEA, the managers being only the servants of the Authority. To claim that the managers were, or should be, the effective controllers of the education to be received by children was to ignore the central principle of the Bill and to this end he requested supporters of the measure to concentrate not on 'the balance of power among the managers for secular education, but to increasing the authority of the borough council or county council as the case may be'.[61]

This same point had been made a fortnight earlier by Gorst in an article published in a symposium on the Bill by the *Nineteenth Century*, an article which Sandars thought Balfour would 'have read with interest, if not surprise'.[62] But on this occasion Balfour's enunciation of this and the other points made, coupled with his telling style of delivery, not only refuted the arguments raised against the measure as far as the majority of his audience were concerned, but stirred them to greater support for him, their cheers increasing as each new point was made. That he was in deadly earnest about the Bill being carried was made plain in his scathing attack upon the extreme Nonconformists who he believed were motivated solely by political considerations, as well as by his closing comments. Here Balfour adopted the role of the disinterested statesman:

I tell you that there are at stake issues greater than the fortune of any political party; there is at stake the education of your children for a generation, and . . . if we . . . hesitate to do our duty, and to carry through this great reform, . . . we shall receive the contempt of the parents and the children living and to be born, and that contempt we shall most justly earn.[63]

He was able to leave the meeting buoyed by the loud cheers of the capacity audience of 7,000 ringing throughout St James's Hall and also by the fact that earlier in the day the National Union delegates had agreed unanimously to a resolution approving the Bill. *The Times* claimed that his speech had 'a ring of clear decision and steady purpose' but when the House reassembled two days later it was clear that this view was not shared by all government backbenchers.

Visits to their constituencies during the recess had left them with the impression that the government needed to be more conciliatory in their handling of the Bill as far as Nonconformist grievances were concerned. The government had also forfeited the support of the Irish for the Bill as the result of the recent actions of the Chief Secretary, George Wyndham, in Ireland. And the first clause to be discussed was Clause 8, another of the measure's more contentious items since it contained provisions regarding religious instruction in schools as well as the appointment of teachers. Lloyd George could not resist goading Balfour by claiming that a series of amendments would be needed to implement the views of his Manchester speech as well as the 'famous Birmingham amendment, framed with the assistance of the Colonial Secretary'.[64] But as the clause was debated, more than one MP noted the contrast between Balfour's actions in the House and the rhetoric of his Manchester speech.

While the Liberals tried to ensure, through the use of various amendments, that there would in reality be public control, through the LEAs, over all elementary schools, Balfour would make only one concession, that of the control of finance. His advocacy in Manchester of more support for LEA control was refuted by his 'refusal to put into the clause outright that the managers shall be under the dictation of the local authority. He keeps on asserting it in words, but avoids it in the Bill'.[65] This exhibition of obduracy rattled the Liberals and although they plied their amendments they were successfully repelled and it began to appear increasingly doubtful if they would succeed in preventing the measure from reaching the Statute Book. Loulou Harcourt believed that the government's success in the recent Devonport by-election would strengthen their resolve to 'cram' the Bill through.[66] Campbell-Bannerman was absent from many of the debates, both preoccupied and weary with having constantly to attend to his wife during her severe illness, but so too were other Opposition front bench members. Sir William Harcourt thought the fight had become 'too hollow' while Lloyd George, Charles Trevelyan, Alfred Hutton and other young Liberal MPs petitioned Campbell-Bannerman about the very small numbers of Liberals present in most of the Divisions on the Bill.[67]

Sir Robert Finlay also sensed the change in the atmosphere of the House, noting that there was now a distinct feeling that the government were winning on the Bill. None the less, he had to admit that progress was slow and would remain so until Clause 8 was completed:

> We shall have a great debate on Monday about the dismissal of teachers, whether it is to be subject to the vote of the local authority, and some time next week a battle royal with Linkie [Lord Hugh Cecil] who is furious at an intention of accepting Kenyon-Slaney's amendment . . .[68]

J. Pease's amendment, that the LEA and not the managers should be responsible for the appointment of teachers, was eagerly anticipated by the teaching world, for an important feature of the amendment was that it would have meant the end of teacher appointments being subject to religious tests. Balfour opposed the amendment and received support from Lord Alwyn Compton who argued that the Church ought to retain the right to control appointments in its schools by virtue of the 'valuable asset' its schools represented in the educational fabric of the nation. This was too much for T.J. Macnamara who tore Compton's assertion to shreds by pointing out that with the State's contribution to the maintenance of voluntary schools since 1833 this meant that in reality the Church's portion of the asset of its schools amounted to three shillings per child. Under the terms of the present Bill the State would be required to fund almost the entire maintenance of these schools: 'Out of a total of 60s. per child, the public paid 55s'. Although the occupants of the Treasury Bench sat 'miserably and helplessly dumb' throughout this denunciation, their authority was such that their followers, albeit 'solid, silent and sulky', voted to ensure the rejection of the amendment.

But four days later Balfour and the government appeared to yield on the amendment proposed by the Member for North Shropshire, Colonel Kenyon-Slaney. This stipulated that the religious instruction provided in a voluntary school should be in accordance with the tenor of the trust deed, if one existed, but it was to be under the control of all the managers. Kenyon-Slaney made it clear that while he did not intend the amendment to represent a slur on the clergy it was designed to prevent the 'possible abuse of the powers at present possessed by certain extreme-minded men'.[69] Anson indicated the government's acceptance of the amendment, on the grounds that it reinforced the policy contained in Clause 7, and *The Times* thought that this action 'should go far to soften some of the bitterness with which they have been attacked as the aiders and abetters of priestcraft'.[70] Under the arrangement reached earlier at the second Derwent Hall meeting, Lord Edmund Talbot gave an impassioned plea objecting to the amendment on behalf of the Catholics, a speech that received a special tribute from Balfour before he engaged in a genuine conflict with his cousin, Lord Hugh Cecil, over the likely interpretation of 'tenor' in the future implementation of school trust deeds. Lord Hugh was correct in asserting that many of the clergy would feel that Kenyon-Slaney's amendment constituted a veritable slap in the face, for many in the Anglican and Roman Catholic churches were alienated by what they perceived to be a further limitation on their rights and control over their schools. Their campaign against it, including a major Anglican demonstration in the Albert Hall a fortnight later, made no impact, however, on the government. One person deeply upset by the government's action was Lord Salisbury, as Frances Balfour discovered when she tactlessly claimed that the amendment was only an expression of what had always been the intention of the Bill:

> Uncle R [Lord Salisbury] said it never was in the Bill and if it was you [Balfour] had concealed it from him and 'basely deceived the Church and him'. I adduced arguments to show it had always been the aim of the Bill, to give the control to the Managers and that was why there had been such a contention to give the Church the majority. He again and again repeated had it not been concealed from him he would have stayed on over the Session, defeated it thus and trusted to time. At one point I th[ought] myself justified in saying – 'You did not believe the Cabinet would have held together had the purpose of the Bill been other than control given to the Managers'. I hope I did not say too much? Jim [?Lady Cranborne] argued that it never was the intention of the Government till they were pressed by the Protestant element, and then this government put this amendment into the hands of K-S. She said Jem [Lord Cranborne] had gone to her, at the end of the summer, saying there was a very dangerous amendment the Government might accept. Uncle R

got very violent with her and said he ought to have been told, and that they had waited to get rid of him to do to the Church what they could not have done had he remained for 'I should have stopped it'. I argued it was always A's [Balfour] intention. In the midst of his great agitation I heard Jim muttering under her breath to me, to stop my line of argument, and to let him think it was an amendment of the Bill forced on you by the 'Puritans' – his word. I saw his state and swung off and she said afterwards I had worked it with great tact. But before the crisis of his feeling, I said to him – 'Ask Arthur when he comes', but he put his head up and said 'Arthur is not coming' – In a tone I understood to mean 'He knows what I feel, and will avoid me' . . . he could not sleep the night of the K.S. debate . . . It is terrible to see how utterly unhappy he is. I think he is bitterly convinced the world is with you. He calls it a Puritan Wave.[71]

Lord Salisbury's threat to intervene in the Lords' debate on the Bill did not worry Balfour unduly for he knew that his uncle's health was now not sufficiently robust to allow him to take part in any debate without breaking down, and implied that Salisbury was aware of this.[72]

The amended version of Clause 8 was passed on 31 October and thereafter the Bill's passage through the Commons was rapid, the dramatic increase in its speed of progress having been achieved by the application of closure. While this procedure produced, according to one critic, 'an unedifying spectacle . . . The Government supporters more or less ashamed. The Opposition sullen and irritated', it achieved Balfour's aim.[73] Furthermore, with Devonshire in charge of the Bill in the Lords and the presence of a Conservative majority there, there was no doubt that the Bill would receive their 'fore-ordained blessing'.[74]

The Lords' discussions of the Bill, unsurprisingly, produced little debate of significance. Indeed, contemporary observers seemed determined to highlight only instances of humour in the debates, especially after what had been a rather bitter and drawn-out affair in the Commons. Devonshire's casual conduct of the debates was characterised by one instance when he was appealed to 'on the meaning of some knotty passage . . . [and] he said that any one of their Lordships was quite as competent to put a meaning on the words as he was'.[75] FitzRoy thought that Lord Rosebery's contributions resembled '*feux d'artifice*, brilliant, yet leaving the darkness all the greater when they had burnt themselves out' while Lord Londonderry's participation engendered complete bewilderment. He 'gaily met one amendment with an answer that was intended for another, and left the House in a state of complete obfuscation'. In his case, however, he was seen as being 'so pleasant, and animated with such an obvious desire to do his duty as Minister in charge of the department, that no one takes him to task'.[76] The Bill finally received the Royal Assent on 18 December and passed onto the Statute Book after one of the longest periods of debate in the annals of the Commons.

The policy enshrined in the 1902 Education Act revealed how little the educational policy aims of key government members had changed since 1895 or, to put it another way, the 1896 Education Bill had truly been a dress rehearsal for the later measure. While his emphasis upon the need for paramount local education authorities in his introductory speech acknowledged the legal problems which had generated the need for the Bill, Balfour's actions over Clauses 7 and 8 indicated that he had not deviated from his sole educational goal of achieving a permanent solution for the financial plight of the voluntary schools while not surrendering their autonomy; a goal he shared, but disagreed over details, with his uncle, Lord Salisbury. Although the LEAs would henceforward control all secular education in these schools, the provision of rate aid, added to the fact that the appointment and dismissal of teachers together with the provision of religious instruction remained the prerogative of the managers, even allowing for the terms of the Kenyon-Slaney amendment, meant that the dual system of elementary schools was made more secure by the Act. Balfour's refusal in the following six years to allow this settlement to be prejudiced, let alone altered, even when on the Opposition benches, mirrored his commitment to his original goal. Not for nothing did the Act come to be known as the Balfour Act but, at the same time, there was a certain irony in this appellation.

The antipathy which existed between Gorst and Balfour, coupled with Morant's manipulative reporting and advice, ensured that once Balfour took charge of the 1902 Bill, Gorst's contributions would be minimised. By the end of 1901 this was virtually the case as far as the detailed formulation of the measure was concerned, and even more so once the Bill had started upon its passage through the House. This notwithstanding, the most outstanding and progressive feature of the measure was the creation of a coherent national system of local education authorities armed with the powers necessary to ensure effective educational development and administration. This component was, in principle and in genesis, and without minimising the contributions made by Balfour, Devonshire and Morant, Gorst's. It is true that at the last minute Gorst veered away from the measure's instant creation of such authorities, favouring the more gradual process offered by the local option clause, but this reflected his prescience of the problems, including potential jeopardy of the measure's continued existence, that would attend such a *modus operandi*. Without Gorst's activities during the preceding seven years, and especially in view of the educational goals and beliefs of Balfour, Salisbury and Chamberlain, it is debatable whether this much needed reform would have been achieved quite so soon.

By the creation of 131 major LEAs, based on the county and county borough councils (excluding London), plus some 202 minor or Part III authorities, the Act replaced the *ad hoc* system of administration which for elementary education alone had required 2,568 School Boards and 14,238 School Attendance Committees. The establishment of the minor authorities, unwittingly prevented by Balfour in 1896, effectively resolved what had been referred to as the 'Rollit problem' while Part IV of the Act ensured a uniform management structure for each LEA by requiring the establishment of an education committee on which the majority of members would be councillors although allowing 'some persons with experience in education' to be members also. Furthermore, the new major authorities could now provide

> as much education as they choose, of whatever kind they choose, at such fees as they choose, up to whatever age they choose, with as many and as valuable scholarships as they choose, without distinction of sex or rank or wealth.[77]

The Act thus not only achieved Gorst's long cherished goal of the devolution of educational power to local communities but, equally importantly, it also established a balance of power between central and local authority, or the 'dual authority' system as it came to be known subsequently. For the first time since the State had become involved in the provision of education, the rational framework of control and administration at the local level instituted by the Act, whereby each LEA became responsible for the secular education given by all the elementary schools in its area, meant that it became possible to ensure closer parity between these schools – a situation which was to prove to be of benefit ultimately to the beneficiaries of education – the children in the schools. An additional benefit was that public control over education had been extended, not contracted, for the greater resources of the major LEAs, coupled to their powers and duties under the Act, allowed local participation in the development and institution of reforms affecting the majority of components of the nation's education system to a far greater extent than had previously existed. Although relegated to the back benches after July 1902, Gorst must have taken comfort from this signal achievement and, as his subsequent activities in promoting educational reform demonstrated, he now felt free to pursue new educational goals.

Morant once told William Dyche that he could think of nothing better for an epitaph than that day secondary schools had at last been established in the nation, 'for it was that aim that was my fundamental aim in 1902'.[78] Some would argue that a weakness of the Act was that it made the provision of secondary education by LEAs only permissive rather than compulsory. That Morant bore the major responsibility for the Act's provisions for secondary education can be in little doubt and the question has to be asked, therefore, as to why the LEAs were only empowered 'to take such steps as seem desirable to supply education other than elementary' and, furthermore, to have had a rate restriction of 2d in the pound imposed upon any funding of this activity. Some of the reasons will be made clearer in the next chapter but, in brief, Morant does appear to have wanted to ensure that the State, in the guise of either the Board or the LEAs, did not have the power to interfere with the established secondary schools. A power rather than a duty, coupled with the financial restriction, would ensure that even progressive LEAs could only effectively deal with day secondary schools and evening classes in addition to teacher training colleges and other post-elementary institutions covered by this part of the Act. Even so, he believed that only the county councils were fit to shoulder these powers and the Part III authorities, likely to be too much 'at the mercy of the ill-educated tradesmen in the small towns who know not what *good general education* means', were restricted to elementary education.[79]

In 1902 there had been a marked shift in the control of educational policy chiefly as a result of Balfour taking charge of the passage of the Education Bill, and this had not changed when the Marquis of Londonderry and Sir William Anson replaced Devonshire and Gorst at the Board of Education upon Balfour's assumption of the Premiership. This state of affairs meant that Morant, through his liaison with Balfour, was the only Board of Education member who was consistently involved with the Bill during 1902. It was not surprising, therefore, that he and Balfour were the prime recipients of numerous messages of gratitude from various individuals and organisations after the Bill's success in December 1902. For Balfour the triumph was a welcome relief after the vicissitudes of the previous nine months and it also cemented the enhanced political status he had slowly accrued within the government and his party during his conduct of the measure. For Morant the plaudits were really only the icing on the cake for his personal position had already been enhanced considerably by the announcement in the previous month that not only was he to succeed Kekewich as Permanent Secretary after Kekewich's official retirement on 1 April 1903 but that he would be Acting Permanent Secretary until then. But if both these men had gained from the Bill's success there was one who had not.

Joseph Chamberlain's standing within Liberal Unionist circles had been undermined by Balfour's abrogation of the Cabinet agreement over Clause 5. Marsh has argued that this action of Balfour's initiated the breakup of the parliamentary party for it enabled Chamberlain, on his return from South Africa in 1903, to pursue a similar freedom of action in his championing of Tariff Reform.[80] The repercussions of his action were to have considerable, and politically detrimental, consequences for both the Alliance and Balfour's own position. The division of government MPs into pro-Chamberlain Tariff Reformers and opposing Free Traders produced inter-party contortions which Balfour was unable to resolve, and after the general election of 1906 the government lost office, while five years later Balfour had to give up the leadership of his party. The ultimate irony for Chamberlain was that a stroke in 1906 prevented him from taking any further role in politics and by the time of his death in 1914 the 1902 Act remained the legislative basis of the English and Welsh education systems.

NOTES

1. BP Add MS 49769, fo. 216, Duke of Devonshire to A.J. Balfour, 24 March 1902.
2. W. Anson, *Journal*, 24 March 1902 cited in H. Henson, *A Memoir of the Rt Hon Sir W. Anson* (1920), p. 177; Browning Papers, OB1/579, S.S.F. Fletcher to O. Browning, 25 March 1902.
3. Jebb Papers, *Servanda*, XVI, p. 23, J.E. Gorst to R.C. Jebb, 25 March 1902.
4. Sadler Papers, Eng misc c.551, fo.214, M.E. Sadler to M.T. Sadler, 1 April 1902.
5. *Daily News*, 27 March 1902 cited in M.R. Watts, 'John Clifford and Radical Nonconformity, 1836–1923', unpublished D.Phil thesis, University of Oxford, 1967, p. 319.
6. *School Board Chronicle*, 67 (5 April 1902), p. 345–8.
7. PRO ED24/21, W. Garnett to R.L. Morant, 8 April 1902.
8. *School Board Chronicle*, 67 (5 April 1902), p. 347.
9. Harcourt Papers, dep 77, fos. 194–5, H. Campbell-Bannerman to Sir W.V. Harcourt, 29 April 1902.
10. D.R. Pugh, 'The Church and Education: Anglican Attitudes 1902', *Journal of Ecclesiastical History*, XXIII, 3 (July 1972), p. 221.

11. *School Board Chronicle*, 67 (5 April 1902), p. 344.
12. Harcourt Papers WV1/9, L. Harcourt to W.V. Harcourt, 24 March 1902.
13. BP Add MS 49789, fo. 153, A.J. Balfour to E. Talbot, 21 April 1902.
14. Spender Papers, Add MS 46391, fos. 105–6, A.H.D. Acland to J.A. Spender, 3 May 1902.
15. C.P. Trevelyan Papers, CPT 9, H. Campbell-Bannerman to C.P. Trevelyan,30 April 1902.
16. S. Webb to G. Wallas, 26 April 1902 cited in N. Mackenzie (ed.), *The Letters of Sidney and Beatrice Webb: Partnership, 1892–1912*, II (1978), p. 148.
17. H.W. Lucy, 'Essence of Parliament', *Punch*, CXXII (11 June 1902), p. 427.
18. C.P. Trevelyan Papers, CPT 35,'Parliament Week by Week', 14 May 1902.
19. Lucy, op. cit., CXXIII, 30 July 1902, p. 67.
20. BP Add MS 49695, fos. 142–3, M.E. Hicks Beach to A.J. Balfour, 8 June 1902; fos. 144–6, A.J. Balfour to M.E. Hicks Beach, 9 June 1902.
21. BP Add MS 49769, fos. 218–19, Duke of Devonshire to A.J. Balfour, 19 June 1902.
22. *Picture-Politics* (July–Aug. 1902), p. 8.
23. G.R. Askwith, *Lord James of Hereford* (1930), pp. 268–9 cited in P. Fraser, 'The Liberal Unionist Alliance: Chamberlain, Hartington, and the Conservatives, 1886–1904', *English Historical Review*, 77 (1962), p. 68.
24. Passfield Papers, II 3(i) 34, S. Webb to B. Webb, 15 July 1902.
25. *The Schoolmaster*, LXII (16 August 1902), p. 207; *Journal of Education*, XXIV (Sept. 1902), p. 563; *The Speaker* (30 Aug. 1902).
26. W. Anson, Journal, 6 Aug. 1902 cited in Henson, op. cit., p. 178.
27. Trevelyan Papers, CPT8, W. Anson to C.P. Trevelyan, 14 Aug. 1902.
28. Sadler Papers, MS Eng misc c.205, Sir M.T. Sadler, Diary,16 Aug. 1902; *The Schoolmaster*, LXII (16 Aug. 1902), p. 208.
29. *Manchester Guardian*, 9 Aug. 1902; *Commerce,* 13 Aug. 1902.
30. Sandars Papers, MS Eng hist c.737, fo.101, A. Akers Douglas to J.S. Sandars, 28 Aug. 1902.
31. Balfour Papers (Whittingehame), GD 433/2, Sir Sydney Parry's memories of 10 Downing Street, 1931, p. 24.
32. *4 PD*, 110, c.1234, 9 July 1902.
33. Ibid., c.1243.
34. Lady Rayleigh's Diary, 10 July 1902 cited in R.F. Mackay, *Balfour Intellectual Statesman* (1985), p. 102.
35. Haldane Papers, MSS 5905, fo.188, Principal Fairbairn to J.B. Haldane, 4 June 1902.
36. PRO CAB 37/62, A.J. Balfour, 'Voluntary Schools Management under the Education Bill', 6 September 1902, p. 1.
37. BP Add MS 49759, fos. 16–18, A.J. Balfour to Lord H. Cecil, 4 Sept. 1902.
38. BP Add MS 49774, fos. 7–12, J. Chamberlain to A.J. Balfour, 4 Aug. 1902.
39. Ibid.
40. BP Add MS 49835, fos. 99–100, A.J. Balfour to J. Chamberlain, 3 Sept. 1902.
41. A.I. Taylor, 'The Church Party and Popular Education 1893–1902', p. 380; W. Evans, *James Hirst Hollowell* (1911), p. 86.
42. James Papers, M45/1187, Duke of Devonshire to Lord James, 18 Aug. 1902.
43. BP Add MS 49787, fos. 72–77, R.L. Morant to J.S. Sandars, 28 Aug. 1902.
44. BP Add MS 49761, fos. 24–25, J.S. Sandars to A.J. Balfour, 29 Aug. 1902.
45. BP Add MS 49802, fos. 89–91, Lord Londonderry to A.J. Balfour, 29 Aug. 1902.
46. BP Add MS 49787, fo.71, R.L. Morant to A.J. Balfour, 28 Aug. 1902.

47. Archbishop R.T. Davidson Papers, Education Box #1, R.L. Morant to R.T. Davidson, 10 Sept. 1902.
48. Evans, op. cit., p. 85.
49. Campbell-Bannerman Papers, Add MS 41216, fo.230, H. Gladstone to H. Campbell-Bannerman, 23 Sept. 1902.
50. Bryce Papers, UB 32, H.Campbell-Bannerman to J. Bryce, 23 Sept. 1902.
51. Archbishop R.T. Davidson Papers, Education Box #1, R.L. Morant to R.T. Davidson, Sunday night: in all probability 5 Oct. 1902.
52. BP Add MS 49761, fos. 36–9, R.L. Morant to J.S. Sandars, 27 Sept. 1902.
53. Ibid., fos. 51–2, J.S. Sandars to A.J. Balfour, 8 Oct. 1902.
54. BP Add MS 49787, fos. 89–90, R.L. Morant to A.J. Balfour, 7 Oct. 1902.
55. J. Chamberlain to Duke of Devonshire, 22 Sept. and 3 Oct., 1902 cited in J. Amery, *The Life of Joseph Chamberlain*, IV (1951), p. 496.
56. BP Add MS 49835, fo.110, J. Chamberlain to J.S. Sandars, 9 Oct. 1902.
57. BP Add MS 49761, fos. 53–56, J.S. Sandars to A.J. Balfour, 9 Oct. 1902.
58. Hamilton Papers, Add MS 48680, fo. 33, *Diary,* 10 Oct. 1902; J. Amery, op. cit., pp. 503–4.
59. BP Add MS 49757, fos. 129–132, Lord Cranborne to A.J. Balfour, 10 Oct. 1902.
60. Balfour (Whittingehame) Papers, GD 433/2, Bundle 327, R. Finlay to F. Balfour, 15 Oct. 1902.
61. *The Times*, 15 Oct. 1902.
62. BP Add MS 49761, fo.45, J.S. Sandars to A.J. Balfour, 3 Oct. 1902.
63. *The Times*, 15 Oct. 1902, p. 5.
64. *4 PD*, 113, c.98, 16 Oct. 1902.
65. Trevelyan Papers, CPT 38, C.P. Trevelyan, 'Parliament Week by Week', 22 Oct. 1902.
66. Harcourt Papers, dep 666, fos. 267–8, L. Harcourt to W.V. Harcourt, 23 Oct. 1902.
67. Hamilton Papers, Add MS 48680, fo. 40, *Diary*, 21 October 1902; Campbell-Bannerman Papers, Add MS 41237, fos. 54–5, D. Lloyd George *et al.* to H. Campbell-Bannerman, 31 October 1902.
68. Balfour (Whittingehame) Papers, GD 433/2, Bundle 327, R. Finlay to F. Balfour, 25 Oct. 1902.
69. *4 PD*, 113, c.1313, 16 Nov. 1902.
70. *The Times*, 1 Nov. 1902.
71. BP (Whittingehame), GD 433/2, Bundle 327, F. Balfour to A.J. Balfour, 4 Dec. 1902.
72. Ibid., G. Balfour to E. Balfour, 8 Dec. 1902.
73. J. E. Ellis, *Diary*, 27 Nov. 1902 cited in A.T. Bassett, *The Life of John Edward Ellis* (1914), p. 200.
74. Trevelyan Papers, CPT 38, C.P. Trevelyan, 'The Education Bill', 9 Dec. 1902.
75. Balfour (Whittingehame) Papers, GD 433/2, Bundle 327, R. Finlay to F. Balfour, 12 December 1902.
76. FitzRoy, *Memoirs*, I (1927), pp. 113–14.
77. Fabian Tract No.114, 'The Education Act, 1902: How to Make the Best of It' (March 1903), p. 2.
78. Morant Papers, W. Dyche to Lady Morant, 15 March 1920.
79. PRO ED 24/14, R.L. Morant, 'Some questions to be considered before drafting Education Bill for 1902', 1 Aug. 1901, p. 3.
80. P. Marsh, *The Discipline of Popular Government: Lord Salisbury's Domestic Statecraft 1881–1902* (1978), p. 324.

7

New broom at the Board

If the 1902 Education Act marked the completion of the major reform of educational administration initiated by Gorst in 1895, its placing on the Statute Book also marked the return of control over educational policy formulation to the Board of Education. Lord Londonderry's ineptitude coupled with Anson's inexperience meant that Morant, as the new Permanent Secretary, would soon become the dominant member of the triumvirate. While Morant was closely involved with all of the major policy changes initiated by the Board until 1912, he was very aware, none the less, of the contributions made by others, as he acknowledged to E.K. Chambers:

> ... you were one of those ... who most earnestly and effectively 'did things' from 1903 onwards for which an absurd amount of credit has been attributed to me.[1]

Unfortunately, the passage of time has tended to obliterate this fact, as a *Times Educational Supplement* editorial in 1987 revealed. Bearing the caption '1904 and all that', the article argued that the Thatcher government's intention to institute a national curriculum in 1988 mirrored the precedent of *Morant's* 1904 Secondary School Regulations.[2] Such ascriptions can be misleading. At the end of 1902, however, Morant was under no illusion about the effect his promotion had had upon some of his colleagues within the Board nor of the magnitude of the task before him in implementing the 1902 Act, being faced with 'a rotten staff and a hostile minority in each district determined to wreck the Act'.[3] He was soon to discover that his contribution to subsequent educational reforms would not only generate successes but would also create additional opposition and this, ultimately, would deprive him of his key role in policy formulation.

Shortly after he had joined the Department of Special Inquiries and Reports, Morant had told Sadler that he felt he had to spend much of his time soaking 'in varied Educational juices' in order to cope with any questions on education that might be directed to him but he had added that he hoped the time would arrive before long when 'we can sort out all our authorities and "informations" and know where to put a hand on anything in the dark'.[4] This desire for organisation and order was matched, as his Swiss Report indicated, by a belief in the need for the subordination of individual (and therefore limited) ideas to the wider and deeper knowledge of specialised experts in the science of national life and growth. This view contained, by implication, a concept of the 'correctness' of the professional, the corollary of which Morant made quite clear to the Board's senior staff when he informed them that they were expected to attain and maintain 'a high standard of knowledge of educational problems in the widest sense'. Not only should they possess an awareness of current social, economic and political factors but

> if the best use is to be made of the influence exercised by this office, through its ordinary administration it is essential that the administration should be guided and informed by intelligence well versed in the study of both the special and general problems of education.[5]

Professionalism and organisation were thus to be the hallmarks of the Board of Education under Morant's aegis, and accompanying them was the assumption that in the dual partnership between the Board and the LEAs it would be the Board that would be the dominant partner. As revealed in the reform measures initiated in 1903, this assumption represented a marked change from the previous ethos of the Education Department which had preferred, under the legacy of Kay-Shuttleworth, to act in an advisory manner. Furthermore, the dramatic reshaping of the Board's policy concerning pupil-teachers, the educational aims for state schools and the role of the inspectorate revealed also Morant's determination to establish a truly national system of efficient schools. But in achieving this he was not to be aided by the man who could probably have helped him most, Michael Sadler.

When the staffing changes necessitated by the Board of Education Act were being completed in 1900, Sadler's morale had been lowered by the knowledge that he was not to become the new Assistant Secretary for Secondary Education. He had toyed seriously with the idea of resigning his position and he had started to take the appropriate steps, given such a possibility, to prepare himself for public life.[6] But a few months later his depression had lifted and he had shelved his plan. Two years later, with the appointment of Morant as Permanent Secretary, he decided to review this plan of resignation, setting out the pros and cons in a private memorandum. His wife did not think he could stay at the Board under Morant, which she saw as 'the triumph of evil', but Sadler believed that if he resigned now it might appear to be due to jealousy or pique.[7] More importantly, he recognised that if he resigned he would probably lose the chance to influence future educational policy. But, at the same time, he acknowledged that if he was to play such a role his department would have to be 'in very intimate relations with the Permanent Secretary'. This was the nub of his problem for he had no confidence either in Morant's 'aims or methods or in his personal loyalty to his colleagues or chiefs'.[8] This notwithstanding he decided to remain in his post, at least for the time being, and to try to carry on influencing educational policy, but in doing so he was to trigger off a chain of events which forced him to change his plan.

In mid-January 1903, a letter written by Sadler, over the pseudonym of 'Sigma', appeared in *The Times*. In it he urged the new LEAs to include in their education committees representatives from Oxbridge and the secondary schools, including the public schools, as a means of ensuring the best possible development of education in their areas under the new Act. The accolade of a supportive editorial was undermined a few days later when Sadler received a summons to see the President of the Board. Londonderry made it clear that while he would not ask Sadler officially if he was 'Sigma' he could not tolerate letters being sent to the press by officers of the Board. Sadler admitted, unofficially, that he was the author but claimed that there was nothing to link the letter with either him or the Board especially as 'nothing had been told me by any one of the mind of the office in this regard'. He went on to argue that provided a civil servant acted decorously, by not revealing departmental secrets and by using a pseudonym, it might be his duty to lay before the public 'certain general considerations which ought to be known'. The corollary of this commitment to influencing policy by whatever means were at his disposal was that he told Londonderry he would have to consider whether he could remain in his post if such contributions were forbidden. He did not believe it was in the public interest for civil servants 'to be muzzled entirely on their own subject, or that a sort of premium should be placed on surreptitious communications'. Londonderry remained unconvinced and indicated that while he would be sorry to lose him, Sadler would have to abide by the rule or resign. In view of this comment it is difficult to understand why Sadler left the interview feeling that the matter had been left 'rather vague and open: each apparently thinking on the question'. Although he did not see why he 'need necessarily take the next step', Sadler went straight to Morant's office and repeated what he had told Londonderry, including the fact that he had cited Morant's earlier anonymous letters to *The Times* as a well-known precedent for his action. Morant's reply, which included the claim that Anson was the instigator of the affair, convinced Sadler that Morant was lying and when they parted he made sure that Morant clearly understood that if he (Sadler) stayed it would be on terms 'consistent with duty and efficient education' but if he left 'I go unmuzzled and shall speak my mind'.[9]

A few days later, Sadler met with Anson to plead the case for completion of the series of Special Reports which were such a significant product of the DSIR. Ostensibly wanting approval for £30 from the DSIR budget to be spent on a report on Italian education, a sum which Anson had refused previously to authorise, Sadler was primarily concerned with his autonomy as Director of the DSIR. During their discussion Sadler rather naïvely told Anson that he did not expect to remain much longer in his post. Not surprisingly, he only managed to gain Anson's agreement to a reconsideration of the Italian report and a promise to peruse a memorandum about the other, planned reports. But when Sadler saw Morant immediately afterwards, and told him that Anson's agreement to a reconsideration about the Italian report revealed that his earlier decision had been made in ignorance of the DSIR budget, Morant was unwilling to discuss the matter apart from referring to the Board's need to economise because of the increased expenditure likely to result from implementation of the 1902 Act. Sadler persisted in putting before him the needs of his section but then observed that Morant appeared to be quite excited and not quite 'self controlled'. Just as Sadler was on the point of leaving Morant shouted angrily across the room to ask if he was being accused of deliberately misleading Anson. Sadler's reply, that he thought Anson had been 'insufficiently informed', placated Morant partially though he still 'seemed angry and said he resented insinuations'.[10]

Sadler's next move was to invite Londonderry to visit the DSIR in Cannon Row in order to see the varying work carried out by the section and his offer was accepted. The visit passed amicably enough, Londonderry being impressed by Sadler's achievements, until Sadler raised the issue of increased expenditure on the section. Sadler chose to ignore Londonderry's hint that it would be no use putting the case, since the Chancellor of the Exchequer would simply laugh at him [Londonderry], and continued to press his argument. When he raised, once more, the possibility of his resignation over the issue, Londonderry countered that the funding issue could not be altered. Sadler observed at this juncture that Londonderry's tone had changed and he felt that the odds were now heavily against him.

Unwilling to yield, he prepared next a long memorandum on the role of an intelligence branch for Imperial and British education for Londonderry and Anson. He asked also for a Treasury Inquiry to be established and told a friend that if Londonderry could not, or would not, get Treasury to act then his final step would be to appeal to Balfour to see the DSIR. At the same time he observed that while he had received an invitation for a position from Manchester University recently he had had to make it clear that there could be no obligation upon either party until his fight with the Board was final and made public.[11] Sadler's wife was worried that if he did win his case and stayed on at the Board it would turn out to be very unpleasant, for

> R.L.M.'s malignity will know no bounds if you get the better of him now. He may be smooth on the surface but he will move heaven and the other place to stab under the surface.[12]

In the event, she need not have worried for Sadler lost his struggle, as he told a colleague:

> I had either to submit to an intolerable sort of servitude, or to defend the Special Enquiries Office by advancing to the attack .... We nearly won. But, at the very end, he [Morant] played his ace, and made it a question of confidence in himself. So Lord Londonderry collapsed.[13]

What Sadler omitted to mention was Morant's stipulation that in future the DSIR would carry out research into items specified by the Board, and not continue its independent approach to educational research. While Sadler bridled at this demand from his erstwhile subordinate, the request was not novel for Gorst had made a similar one in 1895 which Sadler had been happy enough to comply with. The issue, in 1903, thus pointed up the fundamental difference between the two men, Morant the pragmatic administrator and Sadler, in effect, the academic, a difference noted by Dover-Wilson. Acknowledging that Sadler was 'a great man in his way', Dover-Wilson commented that it was a way which Morant could not have much sympathy for. This difference was highlighted by a subsequent dinner conversation at Sheffield University in late 1916 when Sadler was in the company of E.K. Chambers and H.A.L. Fisher:

> Who was to be the new President of the Board of Education, was

a question in the minds of all present. And Sadler, eager and charming as ever, began telling us what he would do if the choice fell upon him. 'What we need', the theme ran, 'is *research* in education. We ought to set aside some administrative county or county borough as our laboratory, and carry out there all sorts of experiments in teaching and organisation. For only so can we hope to arrive at positive results.' Chambers' face as this went on was an interesting study. At last he could stand it no longer. 'What would the *parents* say?' he blurted out, and the question brought the topic to an end.[14]

Sadler's approach was correct, in an academic sense, but could not be married to the realities, political, financial and administrative, facing the Board in 1903. Sadler maintained that he was willing to make the necessary adjustment but only on his terms, which were that not only would he be provided with the extra staff he required but that the Board's work should not interrupt his current research programme.[15] Such a request was unacceptable to Morant, cognizant of the topics needing research and analysis if his reforms were to stand a chance of being implemented, and he was unwilling to accommodate his old colleague. By May 1903, Sadler was thus left only with the option of resigning and, initially at least, gaining the sympathy of the media, if not of all his colleagues.

Graham Wallas believed Sadler had 'come out on the wrong issue', and while the educational press proclaimed shock at the announcement of the resignation as well as lauding Sadler's achievements and personality, the overriding concern was with the continued existence of the DSIR.[16] It fell to the *Journal of Education* to make the obvious point that it was a pity, after reading between the lines following the publication of the Blue Book on the DSIR and Sadler's resignation, that there was not 'on the one side a little more pliability without any sacrifice of principle, and on the other a little less insistence on official dignity and the letter of the bond'.[17] Whether such a compromise could have been reached, given not only the antipathy of the two men's views but also the strained nature of their personal relations, is a matter for conjecture.[18] Sadler was thus left to develop his career in the groves of academe, although cherishing for a long time the belief that a call would come for him to return to the Board in a more eminent role. He was to be disappointed both in 1911, after Morant's transfer from the Board, and in 1916, after Asquith's resignation. Like most academics, as he was by then, he found himself reduced to commenting upon rather than formulating policy. Coming as it did between the London Act and the fight to implement the 1902 Act, Sadler's action was one Morant could well have done without. The resignation and its attendant publicity were an embarrassment for him so soon after taking over as Permanent Secretary as questions were, once more, raised about his own appointment over the heads of more experienced men. Lacking any successful reform at that moment to bolster his appointment, Morant would have no doubt felt vulnerable; how keenly he felt the affair may be judged by the fact that he eschewed any contact with Sadler during the rest of his life. He was able to immerse himself, however, in initiating the reforms which were to consolidate both his reputation and position.

In March, 1903 a committee of H.M. Inspectors, plus Miss Hale, the Principal of Edge Hill Training College, Liverpool, was established under the chairmanship of Chief Inspector Legard to examine the different methods of education and training for pupil teachers. In addition to formulating recommendations as to how LEAs might improve these, now that they were responsible under the Act for the efficiency of elementary school teaching staff, the committee was charged with advising the Board on any other changes to its regulations and grants for pupil teachers that might be necessary. Their task was lightened, somewhat, by the fact that there were available to them certain analyses of the system carried out in the preceding six years. A Departmental Committee report on the pupil-teacher system had been published in 1898 and the firmly entrenched position of the system in the economy of the overall education system had made that committee acknowledge that it would be impossible either to destroy it or to make any 'violent and revolutionary changes'. None the less, they had recognised that the defects of the system had become sufficiently grave to warrant legislative or administrative measures to ensure its reform. Their recommendations had included raising the age of admission in urban areas to 15 years and then to 16 by 1900, but 14 and 15 years respectively in rural areas if the consent of the local HMI was obtained. This would reduce the period of training from the then usual four years to three. More significantly, they had stressed the importance of pupil teachers receiving a more liberal, secondary education than hitherto, and for it to be provided either by a recognised pupil-teacher centre or in a secondary school. At the same time, this committee had wanted the pupil-teacher centres, 'substitutes and supplements in an imperfect system' for secondary schools, reformed. While the best of them could easily provide a good secondary education, many were little more than classes brought together for 'cramming' their students for examinations and possessed staff who were 'imperfectly qualified and narrowly trained'.[19] The reforms they proposed for the centres were designed, in the long term, to allow conversion of the outstanding ones into secondary schools where pupil teachers, albeit in the majority, could be taught in conjunction with pupils pursuing other careers. Only by such reforms, the Committee had contended, could the quantum change needed within the system be achieved. Unfortunately, these views and proposals had generated substantial opposition both in and out of Parliament. Lord Norton had condemned the report vigorously in the House of Lords and had argued that not only would the proposals have deprived the majority of rural voluntary schools of any pupil teachers but he saw a contempt of manual labour as the theme underlying many of the recommendations.[20] The National Society had also opposed the report, fearful of the cost of implementing the proposed reforms, and by exerting pressure on the government had ensured the withdrawal of most of the changes proposed for inclusion in the 1899 Code. None the less, the changes to the entrance requirements for training colleges remained, including removal of the premium upon success in the Queen's Scholarship Examination, and in the following year's Code, the ordinary period for a pupil teachership was reduced from four to three years.

The possibility, in 1901, of a second Cockerton case, this time over the legality of rate expenditure by the London School Board on the building of a new pupil-teacher centre, had stimulated Gorst to raise queries about the system, not least the role of pupil-teacher centres which he viewed as 'highly-equipped and expensive and exclusive'. He felt that the segregation of pupil teachers in the centres was a faulty policy and preferred, instead, the scheme utilised by some Welsh school boards whereby pupil teachers were sent 'for a considerable period without break to a neighbouring Secondary School'.[21] If the centres constituted, for him, a waste of money, by being of transitory use only, he was equally critical of the whole system of pupil teachers. He told Devonshire that:

> A boy or a girl cannot be made into an efficient teacher, unless the whole period of youth is devoted to being educated. Pupil teachers should not enter schools except for the purpose of learning by practice to teach. They should not be counted on the staff. They cannot at the same time be school drudges, and be prepared for a difficult and important profession. When Education is better understood and appreciated, the present plan of preparing our Teachers will be swept away.[22]

Devonshire, embroiled in the 1902 Bill, failed to respond to his comments so, as the (second) Cockerton case started to progress through the law courts, Gorst asked Morant to produce an analysis of the problems affecting the pupil-teacher system.

The two key problems identified by Morant were the excessive use of pupil teachers by schools – as a cheap means of ensuring their 'sufficiency of staff', and thus eligibility for central government funding – and the education given to pupil teachers. Schools were limited in the number of pupil teachers who could be employed and be counted towards their staff sufficiency but it was well known that many schools, and some school boards, employed more than the minimum limit in order to fill any unexpected staff vacancies. They also had a constant supply of 'embryo pupil teachers' [probationers] on hand to replace either departing pupil teachers or those who, at the age of 18, had become certificated Assistant Teachers after having passed the (now) King's Scholarship Examination. Thus there were pupil teachers and ex-pupil teachers (waiting to take the scholarship papers after extra tuition, usually in the pupil-teacher centres) as well as probationers and all usually on the payroll of a board or voluntary school. Such high concentrations of trainee teachers on school staffs tended, inevitably, to lower the standard of education provided.

As far as the personal education of pupil teachers was concerned, Morant highlighted the problem of the gap which existed between that provided for pupil teachers in the elementary schools and what was needed to achieve success in the King's Scholarship examination. This problem was compounded, he believed, by the social class from which the pupil teachers were drawn. But it was by ignoring the educational needs of the pupil teachers, that the education provided should be free and that the pupil teachers should receive some 'slight' remuneration to offset the loss of wages undertaken by becoming an apprentice teacher that the Department had, he believed, more or less forced the boards to establish pupil-teacher centres. Their growth and development had been, consequently, haphazard. Again, this had been ignored by the Department and the problems which now existed could have been prevented if only it had 'properly grasped the *whole* problem of organising a *sound* system of elementary education for the Country'. But it had not, and had contented itself instead with

> makeshifts and with tinkering concessions (in the Code) which merely evade and slur over, instead of adequately handling, the real educational problem of the period. The Department has been spending ten millions sterling a year upon Elementary Education

without taking the most obvious steps to secure an efficient staff for its Elementary Schools.[23]

Morant was not alone in recognising the need to achieve change in the pupil-teacher system, the fact being stressed by several Chief HMIs in their annual reports for 1902. It was C.A. Buckmaster, Chief HMI for the Southern Division, who highlighted, however, the real problem besetting any attempt at significant change:

> Any drastic alterations in the present system . . . must necessarily involve a large increase in the cost of staff at any school; for if, as has been suggested, the pupil teachers were to give the whole of their time, say for three years, to secondary school studies, their place would have to be supplied at least for the next three years by a qualified staff which is at present non-existent.[24]

It was not surprising, therefore, that the establishment of the review committee in 1903 reflected Morant's concern about 'one of the most difficult and the most fundamental [problems] which educational administration . . . has to face'.[25] At the same time, he was aware that the Board had to 'boldly *make* a solution of a practical character as quickly as possible'.[26] The speed with which Legard's committee worked reflected this point and the new regulations were published in July 1903.

Designed to bring the recommendations of the 1898 Departmental Committee Report into effect, the new regulations were based on two principles. The first, that the employment of pupil teachers should be deferred, meant that henceforward pupils were not to be less than 16 years old before being accepted as pupil teachers, an exception being made for rural areas where an age limit of 15 applied. The second principle was a limitation of the number of hours of teaching to be undertaken by pupil teachers. To this was coupled the specification of a minimum number of hours of instruction (not less than 300 per annum) for each pupil teacher. This point was reinforced by LEAs being urged to take the appropriate steps to ensure that pupil teachers were provided with an uninterrupted secondary education spanning three to four years and spent, ideally, in a secondary school. This was seen to be an 'essential condition of the production of adequate results from all other expenditure upon Elementary Schools' and the regulations advocated the establishment of well-organised LEA scholarship schemes to achieve its implementation. In addition, where an LEA possessed both secondary schools and pupil-teacher centres it was recommended that steps should be taken to create closer ties between these institutions and, as far as was practicable, attempts should be made to ensure the integration of pupil teachers within the corporate life of the secondary school. Only in the absence of secondary schools was the pupil teachers' education to be provided solely by a pupil-teacher centre, the chief role of the latter being now confined to the training in methodology of the pupil teachers.[27]

With this emphasis upon pupil teachers obtaining a more 'thorough general education' up to the age of 18, the 1903 Regulations revealed a long-term goal of providing a larger cohort of students qualified to profit from the training provided by the training colleges which, in turn, would yield a corps of better qualified and certificated teachers. The Board went so far as to suggest that LEAs might wish to consider the desirability of relying totally upon the products of the training colleges for their supply of elementary school teachers especially as they were entitled to fund and support these colleges under the 1902 Act.[28] A Circular issued five months later reiterated the need for secondary schools to be used in the education of pupil teachers in order to inject some fresh blood into the pupil-teacher system. But the Circular also raised the possibility of candidates for teacher training now being drawn from the secondary schools. By the end of 1903, therefore, a concerted attempt was being made by the Board to widen not only the social catchment area from which future elementary school teachers were derived but also to bring those from the traditional catchment group of the lower middle and upper working classes under the influence of a 'wider outlook and a more humane ideal of Education'. The Board recognised that a sad reality in many secondary schools was that, owing to the prevalence of strong social class differentiation, the teachers and middle-class parents objected strongly to the presence of pupil teachers in 'their' schools.[29] It was hoped that if the pupil teachers were allowed to participate fully in the life of the secondary schools then this differentiation would cease.

This approach worried *The Schoolmaster* for while it recognised the importance of a sound secondary education for pupil teachers it believed that some of the proposals might lead pupil teachers to waste their time acquiring 'good form' and learning social shibboleths – cultural attainments which could possibly alienate them from the public elementary school.[30] These comments may have been coloured, however, by the knowledge that the Board also hoped that an additional outcome of the reforms would be the destruction of the existent 'undesirable' barrier between elementary and secondary school teachers. This barrier, as one secondary school headmaster noted, stood in the way of securing the release of the pupil teachers from the elementary schools:

> The Elementary Schoolmaster will never part with them till 14 if he can help it: he is convinced he is doing them more good than we should be. The Higher Elementary School fights hard for the boys. Having got them in it can say at 15. Here are these P.T.s. It is wasteful to change their school now. We ought to have a top department to become a Secondary school, to deal with them. The Technical School similarly holds tight to them. The end result is. I get them at 15 *homogeneous neither with my school nor with one another* to bring up to London Matric[ulation] Standard in a year and 2 years halftime. It compels expensive specialisation and the separation of the P.T.s from the rest of the school in many things.[31]

These points of difference notwithstanding, the regulations were generally welcomed by the educational press, the *School Government Chronicle* noting that there was 'much in the spirit and substance of these regulations which . . . will appeal', although it was widely recognised that their success, ultimately, would depend on the LEAs.[32]

Eaglesham has claimed that the overall aim underlying the regulations was to provide the missing element of culture from elementary school teachers; 'At the back of Morant's mind was the typical product of a pupil teacher centre: starchly clean, with a provincial accent, a brain crammed with facts, skilled in techniques, but with not a vestige of the culture that Winchester and Oxford can foster.'[33] Simon, on the other hand, believed that the Regulations represented part of a policy designed to produce segregation between elementary and secondary education: 'two systems, each with a distinct social function, were to run parallel to each other; any institutions crossing the lines must be swept away'. Morant's 1902 memorandum and the closure or transformation of the pupil-teacher centres are cited as evidence of this.[34] But Simon, like Eaglesham, has not taken all of Morant's 1902 memorandum into account, especially the indictment of the Education Department for allowing the Topsy-like growth of such an important component of education

> . . . the Education Department which ought to have been watching the growth of new needs and evolving new organisations to meet them, and which ought, either by legislation or administration, to have brought the required machinery into existence, has failed entirely to rise to the occasion, has pretended not to

'recognise' the attempts made by the School Boards to meet the rising necessities, has given no increase of grants to this most important part of the Elementary Education problem, when *all* other grants have increased enormously, and has contented itself with evasive and misleading Code 'sanctions'.[35]

Morant's policy was more productive, in fact, than either Eaglesham or Simon allow. By establishing a scheme for the better training of pupil teachers, Morant believed this would help resolve the two outstanding problems facing the elementary education system: the calibre of the teaching staff and, *ipso facto*, the quality of the education provided. More importantly, the reforms of 1903 (and sub-sequently) were based upon a longer-term goal of supplying the elementary school teaching force completely from the products of the training colleges. To achieve this would require time, in order to be able to surmount the staff shortages which would result from the abolition of the pupil-teacher system, but Morant was prepared to accept this because of the overall benefits to be gained for the educa-tion system. There was substance, therefore, in Graves's assertion that Morant was convinced that unless the quality of elementary school teachers was improved, a planned national system of secondary schools, drawing a large proportion of their pupils from the public elementary schools, would bear little fruit, since these pupils would lack the necessary educational background needed to benefit from this schooling.[36]

What had not been foreseen during the formulation of this policy was the rapid decline in the number of applicants for the scheme when the regulations were implemented. The effective deferment of the full earning capacity for pupil teachers until a later age meant that where a child's earning capacity was critical for the family's survival, work-ing- and lower middle-class parents started diverting their children away from teaching into other occupations. In 1902 there had been 29,218 entrants into the pupil-teacher system: by 1906 there were 10,900. Chambers estimated that to meet the numbers of new adult teachers required for 1909 (13,500) due to the increasing average attendance in schools, the intake should have been double this, so as to allow for staff wastage, the reduced employment possible for pupil teachers as well as failures during the training programme.[37] To surmount this problem, new regulations published in 1907 introduced a bursary scheme for secondary students aged 16 years or older, who had attended a secondary school for at least three years and had expressed a desire to become an elementary school teacher. The bursary, for one year, was to be followed either by entry into a training college or by service for one year as a student teacher. By this, the Board ensured that while the long-term aims of the 1903 Regulations were not circumvented, it had secured a large enough pool of entrants into teacher training.

Widdowson has shown that the growing acceptability of girls attending university or secondary training colleges, the effect of the 1899 Code's substitution of secondary school examinations for the Queen's Scholarship examination and the development of municipal teacher training colleges by LEAs after 1902, did have an impact, albeit gradual, upon the social class of teacher training recruits for elementary schools.[38] One consequence was that the progressive teaching style and approach of 'Egeria' [Harriet Finlay-Johnson] which had struck Edmond Holmes so forcefully when he inspected her school at Little Sompting in 1903 could become more general by the time his book *What Is and What Might Be* was published in 1911. But before the 1903 Regulations had been published, however, the Board had embarked upon the next logical policy change, which was to examine the aims and contents of the elementary school curriculum. The outcome was the Elementary School Code of 1904.

The introduction in 1900 of a block grant system of funding for elementary schools had been designed to ease the previous restrictions imposed by the Code on the curriculum. The change was needed but was impeded by the very situation it sought to help remedy, since the staff of the schools had not succeeded in freeing themselves from the legacy of payment by results, despite the system having been terminated in 1895:

> For thirty three years they had been treated as machines, and they were suddenly asked to act as intelligent beings. For thirty three years they had been practically compelled to do everything for the child, and they were suddenly expected to give him freedom and responsibility, – words which for many of them had well-nigh lost their meaning. To comply with these unreasonable demands was beyond their power. The grooves into which they had been forced were far too deep for them. The routine to which they had become accustomed had far too strong a hold on them.[39]

The 1904 Code represented another attempt to introduce significant reform into the elementary schools.

Morant has long been praised for the introductory section of the Code which outlined the aims for the schools; headed by the motto

'Manners Makyth Man', its emphasis upon character formation undoubtedly reflected his views. The aims were not uniquely his, however, for they were held by the staff in the higher echelons of the Board. Whether Morant actually wrote the introduction is a matter for conjecture but, even if he did not, it does appear that he did make a significant contribution to the final version.[40] The introduction made clear that the main aim of elementary education was

> to form and strengthen the character and to develop the intelligence of the children entrusted to it, and to make the best use of the school years available, in assisting both girls and boys, according to their different needs, to fit themselves, practically as well as intellectually, for the work of life.

In addition, children were to be trained

> carefully in habits of observation and clear reasoning . . . to arouse in them a living interest in the ideals and achievements of mankind . . . to bring them to some familiarity with the literature and history of their own country . . . to give them some power over language as an instrument of thought and expression . . . and to develop taste for good reading and thoughtful study [to] enable them to increase that knowledge in after years by their own efforts.[41]

Some historians have been sceptical of these aims, Simon, for example, seeing it as another example of the Board's policy of reinforcing educational segregation based on class while Eaglesham has described them as a policy of education for followership rather than leadership. Eaglesham did concede, however, that they represented a significant improvement over the ones which had prevailed under the system of payment by results.[42] This point was clearly appreciated by contemporary observers, one going so far as to describe the Code as 'a new Covenant' because the government education department was, for the first time, not preoccupied with grants and examinations but was concerned with 'the aims and aspirations of the school itself, its wider and deeper aspect as an integral part of the nation's life'.[43] In a similar vein, the *Journal of Education* lauded the Code's introduction for its demonstration that schools existed for the sake of children and claimed that when this new concept was accepted by the teachers and inspectorate then a new type of elementary school would exist. The *School Government Chronicle* viewed the Code as a continuation of the policy of decentralisation inaugurated with the block grant in 1900 and strengthened by the presence of universal LEAs able to implement it fully.[44] It fell to *The Schoolmaster* to point out that the Code's predecessors had contained an Article, 101d (iv), which had contained very similar aims for elementary schools, the inspectorate being abjured by it to ensure that school managers took care

> to bring up the children in habits of punctuality, of good manners and language, of cleanliness and neatness, and also to impress upon the children the importance of cheerful obedience to duty, of consideration and respect for others, and of honour and truthfulness in word and act.[45]

The only significant difference was, therefore, that in the 1904 Code this article had been expanded into 'a very fine poem', an act which was seen by the writer as somewhat ironical given the Code's conferment upon the inspectorate of the power to hold an examination in a school at virtually any time during the year. This other, and usually overlooked, aspect of the Code was reinforced by a comment in Morant's prefatory memorandum that the Board would be looking 'for a higher degree of efficiency than was possible in some areas in the past' as a result of the improved funding provided under the 1902 Act.

The curriculum outlined in the 1904 Code was in many ways not strikingly dissimilar to that of 1900. Gorst had sought then, through the introduction of block grants to replace the old, tiered system of grants, to introduce much greater flexibility and curriculum autonomy for the elementary school so as to ensure that the education provided could fit both the child and the needs of the locality. The 1904 Code stated that the 'properly co-ordinated' curriculum not only took into account the needs of the children but also indicated the intended relationship between the curricular subjects, thereby completing the demise of the nineteenth-century system of a 'relatively haphazard list of possible branches of knowledge'.[46] It could be argued, given these similarities and the existence of article 101d (iv), that the 1904 Code was not so much a revolution as an affirmation of the curriculum and assessment changes that had been introduced into elementary education during the previous decade, following the abolition of payments by results. After all, one HMI had commented in his annual report for 1896 that the centre of the school system was

> no longer the State, the Department, the inspector or the teacher. It is the child. We are beginning to study the child and to

216

acknowledge that he is master of the situation. Instead of making education conform to the views of the educator, we are endeavouring to make the educator conform his views to the nature and capabilities of the child.[47]

Leese saw the new Code as a 'remarkable synthesis between the clerkly, the chivalric and the apprenticeship traditions in English education and the new democratic ideal'. It contained, as he saw it, an 'ordered freedom' for the pupils, teachers and the inspectorate because the Code now contained a clear definition of the work and scope of an elementary school perceived as a 'living organism'.[48] This 'ordered freedom', more than anything, revealed the Morantian touch for it was a tangible demonstration of the guiding principles so clearly signalled in his Swiss Report, that while freedom to develop education could exist at the local level there had to be absolute control by the central authority 'as regards the general educational lines which every state-aided school shall follow'.[49] This was the fundamental difference also between the ideology contained in Gorst's Code of 1900 and that of Morant's Code in 1904. But no one could be uncertain, henceforth, about the Board's policy on elementary education. The generally positive response accorded the Code was repeated five weeks later when a revised set of regulations for the country's secondary schools was published.

Historians critical of the views propounded within the secondary school regulations have seen them as *the* virtual expression of Morant's educational ideology, but Banks has argued that such a view overlooks the fact that the regulations' aims were not peculiar to him but were rather more symptomatic of an unease in the Board of Education and certain sectors of society about the over-emphasis of science in the secondary school curriculum.[50] Criticisms of the secondary school curriculum with respect to the needs of both pupils and employers had been noted in the Bryce Report and the attainment of a more balanced curriculum, with less emphasis upon the grant-earning subjects of the sciences, was seen by the Commissioners as a desirable educational aim. At the same time, there had also been a growing recognition, reinforced by the work of the Endowed and then the Charity Commissioners as well as the impact made by the higher grade schools, that a modern curriculum was an essential requirement of a secondary school; a purely classics-based curriculum had little relevance by the turn of the century. This was substantiated by the fact, as Roach has shown, that many, if not the majority, of the traditional grammar schools were in a pitiable position at the turn of the century, despite the efforts of the Endowed and Charity Commissioners.[51] Whitbread has pointed out that many grammar schools still saw science as an intrusion in their curriculum whose only virtue was the income it provided by way of government grants. Consequently, these schools were not supporters of Sadler's view that 'education lacking either science or the humanities cannot be called a liberal education'.[52] In addition, there were concerns being voiced about the premature specialisation taking place in some secondary schools as a result of the impact of the Department of Science and Art grants, with *The School World* reporting complaints being made by technical teachers of the 'deplorable state of incompleteness of the general education of students preparing themselves for technical classes'.[53] Some of the technical instruction committees of county and county borough councils had contributed to a broadening of some secondary schools' curricula before 1904 and experimentation was taking place in some schools to try to achieve a satisfactory compromise between the claims of traditional and modern subjects. This exercise had generated pressure from proponents of individual curriculum subjects which, in turn, compounded concerns about overloading of the curriculum. And conspicuously absent in the state of flux which characterised the curriculum of such schools was an acceptable definition of a general secondary education, especially for the majority of pupils who left between the ages of 14 and 16. By 1904, therefore, there was a demonstrable need not only for this particular deficit to be redressed but also for the establishment of a rationalised curriculum.[54] These needs were emphasised by the implementation of the 1902 Act when progressive LEAs took up their powers for aiding secondary schools and had to consider, as the Act stated, 'both the needs of individual schools and their organization over the whole area'. As the reports sent in to the Board from the inspectorate revealed, there was considerable uncertainty among the LEAs as to what the aims for secondary schools should be. Morant was not slow to seize the initiative presented by this situation and set in motion the production of a new set of regulations.

The unsuitability of the existent regulations and directory for coping with the situation produced by the implementation of the 1902 Act was summarised by A.F. Leach, one of the Secondary Branch assistant secretaries:

> The fact is that the Directory, and the Regulations . . . were not devised for, and were never intended to be applied to schools of the Grammar School Class. They grew up in relation to

spasmodic and sporadic or fortuitous concourses of local celebrities assembled in Committees, generally of unwieldy dimensions, of amorphous constitution and unsettled functions. The creation of a Local Authority as Managers over such Classes was an administrative advance of a most beneficial kind. But the regulations are, for the most part, quite unsuited to the highly developed organisms with a long life history, and the carefully constituted governing bodies of the Endowed Schools.[55]

Morant was inclined to believe that the governing bodies of the larger, established grammar schools would not apply for their schools to become secondary day schools if they felt they were likely to be superseded by the LEAs. But, in a memorandum outlining his views, he indicated that there had been general agreement that as far as the established secondary schools were concerned an LEA would never attempt to impose its views upon these schools' curricula or 'to interfere by inspection' in the daily work of the school. He argued that there was, and should be, a fundamental difference between the LEA and established secondary schools. He accorded these schools, especially the major public ones, a very elevated position within the national educational hierarchy and claimed that their staff could not be compared with the majority of LEA representatives, especially those in the boroughs who were 'persons markedly inferior, alike in social status, educational experience, and intellectual acquirements'. He felt very strongly, therefore, that as far as secondary schools were concerned the nation could not afford to put all of them under the control '*in any full sense*' of the LEAs. To do so would be tantamount to a betrayal of the trust placed in the Board of Education for fostering 'a high Standard of Secondary Education in the true sense, and of preserving it against the strong forces of "bread and butter" studies'. The Board's grants, and the regulations attached to them, were therefore to be the means of ensuring that this goal was maintained.[56]

Shortly after circulating his memorandum, Morant was annoyed to learn that the Board's Directory Committee had had a new draft of the Secondary School Regulations printed without consulting him.[57] Sir William Abney's retirement a few days later from his position as head of the Secondary Branch enabled Morant to liaise directly with W.N. Bruce, the Principal Assistant Secretary for secondary education, over possible changes to the regulations. His note written after their meeting was, in his own words, a 'very crude jotting' of his ideas yet was sufficient to indicate how he saw the future funding of these schools:

. . . 2. The grant would be for the school as a whole and for its work as a whole. 3. No school would be eligible for grant which did not give at least (say) one-third of the total hours of instruction to Mathematics and Science together. . . . . 5. The grant would be in respect of the number of hours of instruction in all (not merely the instruction in Mathematics and Science).[58]

One consequence was that a few months later Anson informed the House that henceforward the Board was going to apply the principle of the block grant to secondary education, 'that is to say, we are paying for the curriculum and not for specific subjects'.[59] At the same time it was revealed that the Board's secondary education policy would now be to encourage LEAs to develop Division B rather than Division A day secondary schools.

The Division A secondary schools, the old 'schools of science' with a predominantly scientific curriculum funded originally by the Department of Science and Art, were to be regarded no longer as *the type* for secondary schools as far as the regulations were concerned but would become a more highly funded variant of the Division B school. The latter had also received grants from the Department of Science and Art in the past but they had offered a less specialised, or more balanced, curriculum and included among their number some of the endowed grammar schools. In 1902 there were 214 Division A schools and only 144 Division B schools (69 of which were endowed grammar schools) but by 1904 the Division A schools had increased in number by only 7 per cent whereas there had been a doubling of the type B schools.[60]

Reinforcement for this policy shift had been provided by the publication in 1903 of a report on the teaching of literary subjects in secondary schools written by a temporary Secondary Branch inspector, J.W. Headlam. His report was a depressing account of the minimalisation and degradation of the humanities which had taken place within the curriculum of the majority of more than 70 second and third grade secondary schools examined by him. This phenomenon existed mainly because of the higher grants that had been awarded for science teaching in Division A schools, for while funds, well-qualified staff and good facilities existed for the science components of the curriculum in these schools, Headlam was appalled by the obverse conditions accorded the humanities. He discovered that Greek had virtually disappeared while Latin had been relegated as an alternative to shorthand and bookkeeping in some schools. If the teaching of French provided some grounds for a little optimism, the same could not be said of English where the 'very first elements of good work' were conspicuous by their absence. The teaching of history focused solely upon English history and no attempt had been made to relate it to that of Europe, nor indeed to what was taught in geography. He acknowledged that this last point would have been difficult to achieve since in general the teaching of geography, even in the upper forms, remained 'merely an acquaintance with the names on the map'.[61] The predominance of such poor teaching, coupled with the general absence of school libraries, meant that boys of 15 to 17 years were leaving these schools lacking any acquaintance with literature, not knowing how to read for pleasure nor how to extract information from books. These defects, plus the absence of any training of the pupils' imagination in the majority of the schools, led Headlam to the conclusion that it was very difficult, despite the presence of some exceptional schools, not to lose faith 'in the possibility of making literary training useful and efficient'. This constituted a serious state of affairs, he believed, when it was remembered that the products of these schools would not only form the majority of local government staff in the future but also that in the long term this neglect would have 'a most harmful influence on the intellect and character of the nation'.[62]

When Morant first saw the report he wrote excitedly to Bruce stating that he found it '*intensely* interesting. One of the most striking documents ever issued. *What* a big buzz it will make!!' He wanted some parts altered but believed that the overall effect would be to give 'a *tremendous* impetus to *your* work and all that we hope to give you a chance of doing'.[63] Arthur Acland, on the other hand, believed it produced 'a sense of humiliation' since the report only confirmed what was already known by many acquainted with the subject.[64] By November, Bruce had become convinced that the effects of Anson's comments and the publication of Headlam's report justified making significant changes to the secondary school regulations. He noted the apparent absence of a balanced curriculum in many secondary schools and could not help but query the effect of the current Division B requirements for as they stood they would make 'the Real Gymnasium of Prussia ineligible for a grant'.[65] These limitations mirrored, in turn, the insufficient freedom in curriculum planning available to those secondary schools in receipt of government grants and he envisaged two possible solutions to the problem. The first was for the State to provide grants for any approved scheme of general secondary education while the second rested upon the provision of alternative curricula 'of sufficient diversity to meet the needs of the case'. He was not amenable, however, to the idea of the State giving up all its control over the secondary school curriculum, at least until sufficient experience had been gained by both the LEAs and the Board. What course the Board should adopt was passed initially to J.W. Mackail, Assistant Secretary in the Elementary Branch, to formulate. By mid-January 1904 Mackail had completed a very long memorandum which, while meeting its goal, was also claimed to be an outsider's approach to the issues involved in devising new regulations *de novo*.

Mackail accepted the need for a reformulation of the regulations and for recognition to be given to the fact that the schools would be funded solely on the basis of their complete curriculum and not just the science component:

> It is time also, even as regards the Treasury, to abandon the fiction that the grants are for Science teaching, with which, incidentally and as a concession to popular prejudice, there is combined something, more or less, of general education.[66]

He felt that a new set of regulations should correspond in type to those for elementary schools and, in due course, they could be merged with them to form a single Code laying down the conditions of state aid for all public education. In the interim, the secondary school regulations should aim at ensuring a co-ordinated system of secondary schools 'of varying type and of different degrees and kinds of specialisation'. But having said this he wanted the two 'great dangers' of secondary education, premature specialisation and commercialism, kept constantly in view, for he saw them 'as the substitution for education, and the support as though it were education, of something which is not, in any real or vital sense, education at all, or in other words, an organised hypocrisy'.[67]

Mackail was concerned about the overlapping that still prevailed between elementary and secondary schools as a result of the continued existence of the higher elementary schools. He argued that if secondary education was to be fully organised, a definite line of demarcation should exist between the two sectors, with entry from the elementary schools being facilitated up to the age of 10 but being progressively discouraged thereafter. But whoever made up the future clientele of the secondary schools, Mackail was insistent that they should all receive a 'sound general education . . . to which all specialised training should be rigorously subordinated'. Although he believed this criterion was operational in the elementary and some Division B secondary schools, Mackail felt that, in general, the

Division A schools promoted premature specialisation while the lower grade Division B schools' curriculum fostered commercialism. The remedy for both problems resided in an alteration of the criteria relating to grants, the current arrangements for which Mackail found both puzzling and basically unsound.

In the first instance, he wanted a 'stringent revision' of the Division A school curriculum so as to ensure that in future it contained an adequate general education. But when he attempted to produce some classificatory principles relating school type to curriculum content he confessed to finding the existent system 'neither bird or beast. It is essentially a stop-gap system, full of anomalies and ambiguities, and leading in practice to great difficulties of administration'. The whole issue of curricular content was not only complex but also contentious and he acknowledged that whatever course was adopted it would be 'sharply and suspiciously criticised'.[68] Although he felt that the lower and middle grade secondary schools, that is those whose pupils would leave at the age of 14–16 years, should concentrate on providing a general education conforming to a specified type while the upper grade secondary schools (with pupils up to the age of 18 or 19 years) could be granted more flexibility as well as providing some degree of specialisation within their curriculum, Mackail was uncertain how far a specified number of hours' instruction per subject per week would achieve these goals. He was certain, however, that whatever action was taken it would create 'accumulating and irreversible consequences', for the foundations being established were not those of a building but of an organism and when established 'they forthwith take root and grow'. Thus it was paramount that no erroneous changes should be made, even in a temporary form, for it would immediately create 'fresh interests, to clothe itself in flesh and blood, and to be a yearly increasing obstacle to the introduction of what should replace it'.[69] Acutely aware, then, of the responsibility accompanying any proposals for change, Mackail opted for three types of secondary school curricula. In the first, for Division A schools, he maintained the minimum requirement of 11 hours per week for science and mathematics instruction. In the case of the second and third types, applicable to Division B schools, he specified three major curriculum components , those being foreign languages, of which Latin had to be one, English subjects (including scripture, geography, history, English grammar and composition) and science and mathematics. The third curriculum differed from the second in that Latin was not insisted upon. All three curricula had to ensure adequate provision, however, for drawing, manual instruction, singing and physical education. Six months after he had penned these views, the new regulations were promulgated and their contents reflected an amalgam of his ideas with those of Morant and Bruce.

The two main components of the new regulations were the definition of a secondary school and the requirement that such a school must provide a general education for pupils up to the age of 16 years and beyond. In his prefatory memorandum, Morant claimed that the definition was necessary to ensure a proper differentiation of functions among those institutions covered by the 1902 Act as offering 'education other than elementary'. A secondary school education was henceforward to be general and provided by 'a complete graded course of instruction'. Whereas Mackail had presented the case for a general education as a means of preventing premature specialisation or commercialism, Morant argued from the perspective of faculty psychology ie that such an education would develop all the faculties and must be provided in such a way that

> ... the habit of exercising all these faculties has been formed and a certain solid basis for life has been laid in acquaintance with the structure and laws of the physical world, in the accurate use of thought and language, and in practical ability to begin dealing with affairs.[70]

A further stipulation, that the instruction had to be both complete and graded, was designed to eliminate both the superficiality and repetition currently common in the treatment of curriculum subjects. These, and the additional requirement that a school provide a course lasting for a minimum of four years, had to be complied with if the school was to be eligible for a government grant. The regulations specified the division of the curriculum into subject hours and in this followed Mackail's suggestions for the Division B school both in content and in the proviso that, apart from its general nature, schools were to have greater freedom than hitherto to frame their curriculum so as to be able to meet local conditions and needs. Morant made it quite clear in his memorandum that while the Board desired to develop harmonious working relations with LEAs in the field of secondary education, it was to be understood that the work of headmasters and mistresses should not be subject 'to any unnecessary interference in matters of school administration for which he or she is primarily responsible'. Thus, the LEAs' control over these schools was to be exercised only through the schools' governing bodies.

The Schoolmaster responded to the regulations with a leading article entitled 'How Not to Organise Secondary Education'. Pointing out that Morant allowed class and professional prejudices 'now and again to load the dice in favour of the middle classes and the so-called "secondary" teacher', the article castigated the regulations for being a serious breach of faith with the public.[71] They represented, it was claimed, merely a continuation of the delimitation policy initiated by Gorst against the higher grade schools and thus were designed to prevent the secondary schools from becoming the democratic second storey of the education system. This theme has been taken up and developed subsequently by some historians including Simon, Eaglesham and Wiener. Simon has argued that the definition of a secondary school justified the lack of end-on educational provision in the state sector and Morant, by trying to preserve secondary education for an élite, that is the middle classes, was therefore an agent of class conflict.[72] Eaglesham reiterated the point made in R.F. Young's historical introduction to the Spens Report of 1938, namely that the Regulations checked any tendency towards a technical or vocational bias in secondary schools and, consequently, made them schools fit only for a selected few.[73] Wiener has stated, in what could be considered a summation of the critical view of the Regulations, that the day secondary schools

> developed a curriculum, an outlook, and forms of organisation in line with the ideals of the education of the gentry. This moulding of State education . . . was a legacy equal in importance to the continued direct education in public schools of the bulk of the country's elite. Through one or the other route, the late-Victorian public school outlook continued to shape British attitudes and values in the twentieth century.[74]

There was, on the other hand, considerable contemporary support for the regulations as has been clearly demonstrated by Banks, Whitbread and others, and it appears that Mackail, Bruce and Morant were prepared to formulate a policy designed not only to overcome the major faults of the curricula but also to be in line with the prevailing views about the needs of society. Much has been made by critics of the Regulations of the class-based views which permeated them and the position accorded Latin within the curriculum. What tends to be overlooked, however, is that the Board's underlying aim was to try to create order out of the chaos prevalent in the secondary sector, both educationally and administratively, by prescribing *minimum* standards while, at the same time, providing the means whereby secondary schools, without financial hardship, could adapt to meet more easily the needs of their locality. This was a necessary step given both the state of this sector of the system and the limitations of the 1902 Act. This said, it has to be admitted that Morant's concept of a national system of secondary schools did not admit of a single system of schools, nor of ease of access for children from the working and lower middle classes. The Secondary School Regulations might prescribe the operational structure and aims for the desired type of secondary school but on a more covert basis it was also intended that there was to be a double tier of secondary schools. The lower was to be occupied by the LEA-controlled day schools and old third grade schools while the second and first grade secondary schools would occupy the upper tier and remain relatively unfettered by the controls of the State. In this sense, the 1904 Regulations had modified but not destroyed the legacies of the Taunton and Bryce Commissions. None the less, the regulations were not, as Whitbread correctly states, a straitjacket, and one long-term effect, combined with the impact of the 1903 Pupil Teacher Regulations, the bursary scheme and the 1907 Free Place Regulations (discussed in Chapter 13), was to produce a change in the social composition of the LEA secondary schools mainly as a result of the entry of increased numbers of children (including a greater proportion of girls) from the elementary schools.[75]

Morant was well aware, however, that if these and other educational reforms were to be implemented successfully there had to be effective links between policy-makers and policy implementers and the agents to help achieve this were the inspectorate. He was not the first to recognise that with the changes introduced by the Board of Education and 1902 Acts there was a pressing need for the inspectorate to be reorganised. Gorst had argued the case in 1900, when faced with the implementation of the Board of Education Act, and his views were reinforced by his substantial knowledge of the work of the inspectorate. In the summer of 1902, frustrated by Devonshire's lethargy on the matter, he had taken the opportunity to make his views clear to the Commons. In what was to be his last presentation of the Education Estimates, Gorst had stressed the importance of the role of the inspectorate in the further development of the school system. He had stated that not only should there be a unified inspectorate but that it should consist of members

> who possess great qualifications, great knowledge of teaching
> methods, not only in England but in other parts of the world,

who have wide sympathies with teachers of various classes and various powers, who shall be independent of any kind of influence exercised upon them, either from the central office or from the Association of Teachers or any body of that kind, and who shall be brave and honest enough to speak the truth about the schools they visit.[76]

Such requirements represented, as those familiar with the inspectorate were only too aware, a new order for some of the inspectors. Kekewich had been cognisant of the dubious calibre of some of the HMIs and had conceived a scheme for gradually effecting an earlier retirement age among them. This had gained Devonshire's approval but by 1903 certain incompetent individuals were still members of the force. Morant was keen to accelerate the process begun by his predecessor and shed them as quickly as possible through enforced early retirement. He was very conscious of the fact that both the divisional and district inspectors would have to be tactful in their dealings with the new LEAs as the latter 'would very strongly resent any such handling as our Inspectors have hitherto (very often quite rightly) had to use in connection with recalcitrant Managers of individual schools'. But he was also mindful that Londonderry wanted the inspectorate to have greater freedom of action than hitherto, a freedom he believed some of the older inspectors would be incapable of utilising for the benefit of either themselves or the Board. He tried, therefore, to cull the inspectorate of those out of sympathy with his (Morant's) views, arguing that it would demonstrate to the LEAs that the Board was determined to increase the efficiency of both its administrative and inspectorial staff. His frank characterisation of individual inspectors as being, for example, 'extremely lethargic in temperament' or 'he has always been notorious as "a fool"' or 'he has sunk into a rut so deep that he will never again see over the edge' had the desired effect, the men in question being retired within the year. He did not get his way completely, however, with two of his targets proving to be rather more obdurate and remaining in their posts until 1905 and 1906.[77]

This notwithstanding, the main problem as far as the reorganisation of the inspectorate was concerned resided in the existence of two distinct branches of inspectors, those originally based on Whitehall (the HMIs) and those of South Kensington. Furthermore, variations in the organisational structures of the two branches had developed over the years with the Whitehall inspectorate being grouped in districts, each under a Chief HMI. Although much smaller in number, the South

Kensington inspectorate had much more extensive duties than the HMIs and Gorst had viewed them as a well-organised body, being

> under a Senior Chief Inspector . . . who is responsible directly to the Principal Assistant Secretary and has under him Chief Inspectors, Inspectors and Junior Inspectors. These have their districts and functions assigned; it is said that they are periodically transferred from district to district; and each is responsible to and receives orders from his immediate official superior. All instructions from the Principal Assistant Secretary are transmitted to the inspectorate through the Senior Chief Inspector and by him to the inferior officers.[78]

Specialists in their subject areas, and all having had teaching experience, the inspectors had increased in number as a result of Acland's reorganisation of the Science and Art Department in 1890. Their numbers still remained sufficiently small, however, for them to be referred to as 'Acland's twelve apostles'.[79] Although the Whitehall inspectors were organised in an overtly similarly manner, Gorst had believed this was illusory:

> The Senior Chief Inspector, whose office was only created in 1890, has no authority over the Inspectors generally: nor have the Chief Inspectors authority over the Inspectors of their districts: the Inspectors however have authority over their Junior Inspectors and Sub-Inspectors. So far as there is any organisation of the inspectorate it is at present carried out through the Chief Clerk, presumably under the direction of the Secretary, though it is no part of the proper official duties of the Chief Clerk.[80]

The problem caused by this organisational difference was compounded by the overlapping that existed between the work of the inspectors of both branches and those of the LEAs. Gorst had discussed the matter in some depth with Abney and both had agreed on the need for an amalgamation of the two central branches. Gorst had believed that one chief officer should be appointed, and from outside the inspectorate, so as to avoid any likely accusations of impartiality, and he should be charged with achieving amalgamation. He had made the additional point that in the reorganisation that would follow amalgamation, it would be important to ensure that every LEA should be in contact with only one inspector. Otherwise

> If the new Authority is to deal with a number of Inspectors for different parts of their areas, and different kinds of Schools –

some responsible to a Chief Inspector at South Kensington, some responsible to a Chief Clerk at Whitehall, these two Chiefs acting independently of each other – it is not difficult to foresee that the administration of the Act will prove a fiasco. Nor do I think it possible to plunge the new Authority into such a chaos, in the hopes of bringing order out of it hereafter. We should begin as we intend to go on with one Inspector for a Local Authority to deal with.[81]

Gorst conceded that the new LEAs should be able to maintain their own, limited, inspectorate but he believed that a complete and impartial inspection of schools could only be achieved through an inspectorate based on the Board of Education. In view of his declared contempt for Gorst's 'rotten ideas' Morant's approach to the reorganisation of the inspectorate in 1903 was remarkably similar.

By early 1903 the Board of Education staff had been reorganised into three branches, elementary, secondary and technical, each under the charge of a Permanent Assistant Secretary. Morant reinforced this structure by the creation of three corresponding branches of the inspectorate, each having a chief inspector and each being directly responsible to the Permanent Secretary. There were two other branches which covered teacher training and art education and they were controlled also by chief inspectors. To complement this central structure Morant created nine inspectorial divisions within England – Wales being a completely separate division – with each division's district inspectors being under the direction of a divisional inspector. It was intended that within this chain of command the district inspector would provide the link, in the first instance, with the new LEAs. To ensure that the interchange between the Board and the LEAs afforded by this link was as efficient as possible, the Board's Elementary Branch was subdivided into three groups A, B and C, each of which was responsible for the liaison with three inspectorial divisions – for example Group A covered the North, North-Eastern and North-Western divisions. These changes were in place by the end of 1903 but a similar reorganisation of the Secondary Branch took place only in 1907, its work-load and duties before then being considerably less than that of the Elementary Branch.

A memorandum on the reorganisation was sent to all LEAs in July 1903 in which both the changes made to the inspectorate and its future *modus operandi* were outlined. Stress was placed upon the intention to make one inspector responsible for each LEA and it was emphasised not only that the inspector's district would be smaller than previously but that he would either reside in the area of the LEA or, if not, at least in a conveniently close location. Additional stress was placed upon the supervisory role to be played by the new divisional inspectors, most of whom would be the old chief inspectors.[82] Lord Londonderry, going over the principles of the reorganisation at a meeting of the new divisional inspectors three months later, made it clear that one of their key roles was to ensure that 'an understanding of the broad features of the educational policy of the Board should be in the possession of the whole body of the inspectorate'.[83] Each divisional inspector was expected to liaise with his district inspectors frequently by both personal contact in the field and at divisional conferences. In addition, interviews and conferences were to be maintained at the chief and divisional inspector level so as to ensure a two-way flow of information and policy between the Board and the inspectorate. The intended outcome of this organisation was that there should be a uniform representation of the Board's policy in any dealings by the inspectorate with LEAs or any other relevant party. A corollary was that the inspectors should play a key role in gathering field intelligence so as to aid the development of future policy. While this did not represent a dramatic change in their role, for the inspectorate had previously possessed the power to contribute to policy-making, it was now very clear that this was to be a significant component of their work.[84] The achievement of such a rationalised structure was not to be without its problems, however, as Morant was to discover when, late in 1904, he initiated the formation of a secondary school inspectorate.

One of the responsibilities transferred from the Charity Commission to the Board under the Board of Education Act was the inspection (by invitation) of secondary schools. This was carried out before 1904 by officers transferred from the Commission and some of the South Kensington inspectorate and the number of schools inspected increased from 35 in 1901 to 130 in 1903; an increase derived partly from the LEAs' implementation of their powers in secondary education under the 1902 Act. The Board soon found itself lacking the necessary number of staff to cope with this increase and as a temporary expedient occasional inspectors were employed, usually men with experience of either university or public school. Morant, in the meantime, pressed ahead with the establishment of a proper secondary school branch of the inspectorate and in 1904 W.C. Fletcher, the headmaster of Liverpool College, was appointed chief inspector while four appointees to the branch included J.W. Headlam and R.P. Scott. Morant's close relationship with the latter ensured that he would retain close links with developments both in this branch and in the world of secondary schools.[85] Morant planned that the remaining nucleus of this new branch was to be derived from the transfer of well-qualified and experienced men from the ranks of the elementary schools inspectorate while the vacancies left there would be filled by promotions from the junior inspectors. But in this plan he had underestimated the commitment of Cyril Jackson, the Chief Inspector for Elementary Education, to his staff and he found himself engaged in a struggle which was to last four months.

A memorandum from Morant to Jackson in December 1904 detailing the proposed changes was accompanied by the comment that he had tried his best 'to rob *you* as *little* as possible' yet Morant revealed that he wanted to remove eight HMIs from, as well as suppressing three vacancies for HMIs in, Jackson's branch. In exchange he offered Jackson 16 South Kensington junior inspectors, four of whom 'with good qualifications for your purposes' he intended to promote to HMI.[86] He went on to argue that by removing '7 [*sic*] H.M.I.ships I give you 10 J.Insps more than you have at the moment so that I after all deplete you *very* little indeed'. If this change plus the alterations to the work load of all the elementary schools inspectorate were taken into account then Jackson's staff would have, he calculated, 'some sixty thousand days for Inspection & Conferences which seems a very ample allowance for 20,000 schools'. Morant concluded that these changes would not impair the work of the Elementary inspectorate and, furthermore, by making them he would have 'welded all the parts of the Board's inspectorate much more closely together'.[87] Jackson acknowledged this, and Morant's responsibility for the arrangements pertaining to all the branches, but he was unhappy about the loss of some of his most experienced HMIs and the potential increase to his already swollen ranks of junior staff. He believed that if Morant's scheme was implemented it would be construed that the elementary schools were to be neglected.

Faced with this reaction, Morant discussed the problem with Bruce and Ogilvie of the Board's Secondary Branch before amending some of his proposals. He calculated that Jackson would have two more staff than he had a year earlier and claimed that not only had Jackson's branch benefited from the changes but that he 'ought to have no difficulty in manning your districts adequately'. At the same time he warned him that in two months' time there would be a rearrangement of five of the Elementary Branch's divisions – North Central, West Central, East Central, East and South East. This would result in one division less but, more importantly, would ensure that Jackson's divisions 'coincide neatly with Office administration, with Ogilvie's Divisions and Districts, and with Bruce's Districts'. Morant was convinced that these fine tunings would prove to be an *'immense improvement and advantage in co-ordinating the work of the various branches of Inspectors with that of one another and also with that of the various branches of the Office'*. His final comment, that 'we have now reached finality as regards 1905', was ignored by Jackson who immediately challenged the proposed changes not only because of the deleterious effect they would have on the work and travel arrangements of the inspectors but also because of the unbalanced nature of the district arrangements within some of the new divisions.[88]

Morant was forced to acknowledge that his planning had been done 'in the large' and had not considered the details raised by Jackson but he felt that they were not insurmountable. He disputed several of Jackson's points and contended that the new North division's undesirable small size was due solely to Jackson's unwillingness to pension off the divisional inspector before his official retirement date. He was clearly unwilling to yield to Jackson and stated that 'the infinite advantages to be derived from the extreme simplicity and, so to speak, visual obviousness of the new Divisions, fully justify their adoption from April 1st next'.[89] The inevitable request for further discussion by Jackson was blocked by the reply that while it might be desirable, the whole matter had now become one of 'relative urgencies: and every penny that can be squeezed must be devoted to Secondary School Inspection for a time as it has been so neglected'.[90] Jackson persisted, however, with his resistance and managed to gain a concession from Morant when he pointed out to him that his [Morant's] initial generosity in allocating 16 staff to the Elementary Branch had in reality only amounted to ten. He also questioned all the alterations the policy change would cause, rightly stating that if the alterations to the districts were enforced on 1 April, they would disrupt the relations newly forged between the inspectorate and the 14 LEAs involved. Jackson was, however, primarily concerned with the fate of his staff whereas Morant, as the publication of the Secondary School Regulations in the previous year had demonstrated, was determined not to lose the chance to establish a more efficient organisation of secondary education. In a tactful, but forceful, memorandum Morant reminded Jackson of their difference of perspective by emphasising the fact that not only had he (Morant) to consider the needs of the Secondary and Technical Branches but that the basic administrative unit under the 1902 Act was the county. Consequently, he found it 'impossible to continue an arrangement by which individual Boroughs or Urban Districts . . . are inspected (for Elementary purposes) by an Officer whose main Inspection work is in a different Administrative County'. He was trying to implement a policy of unification with regard to inspectorial areas and he believed the time was ripe to rectify 'these particular anomalies'. In addition, there was the need 'to balance advantages and disadvantages from several, not merely from one, points of view' and he believed the advantages produced by the changes outweighed the disadvantages. Jackson was requested to arrange the changes 'as conveniently and with as little friction as possible'.[91] Jackson complied, so that by 1905 Morant had completed the establishment of a secondary school inspectorate, but at the end of the year, angered by Morant's actions, Jackson resigned and was replaced by Edmond Holmes.

Robert Blair, who knew Jackson well through their work on the London County Council, described him as a sufferer from insomnia and a person whom it was not 'easy to get on with'.[92] While Jackson was undoubtedly zealous as far as the interests of the members of his branch were concerned, his memoranda to Morant did reveal a person who preferred change on an incremental rather than dramatic scale. Morant's approach was thus difficult for him to accept, especially when it became clear that Morant was determined to achieve his aims regardless of any inconvenience they caused to others. Unfortunately their antagonism did not end with Jackson's resignation for it was hinted that relations between the Board and the London County Council suffered subsequently while Jackson was chairman of the education committee (1908–10), Morant being seen by Jackson as determined 'to attack me always and everywhere'.[93] There was one development while Jackson was Chief Inspector which he and Morant agreed upon, however, and that was the creation of the women inspectorate.

Two women had been appointed to the inspectorate by the Education Department in 1883 and 1890, both on a temporary basis and both in connection with the teaching of domestic subjects only. The first two permanent appointments, of R.A. Munday and S.J. Willis as sub-inspectors, had been made by Gorst in 1896 and by 1904 there were six women as members of the inspectorate, including Edith Deverell and Kitty Bathurst, the latter being related to Gorst.[94] All of the women were attached to district inspectors and were expected to act in a subservient role but this did not prevent either Deverell or

Bathurst from making their views known to their superiors, the latter in a frank and outspoken manner. This characteristic resulted in her being moved on from division to division in a relatively brief period of time and at one stage Gorst felt constrained to counsel her:

> ... if you break out prematurely everything will be spoilt and the last hope of any good being done by women inspectors will be gone. No one, other than a quiet young person who knows all the routine, will ever be appointed again under the present regime .... You are the last hope of the lady inspector idea. If you have patience to go through the ordeal of the sub-inspectorship without breaking forth, you may do a great work. Please therefore be silent . . .[95]

Bathurst ignored this advice but, fortunately, her subsequent actions did not result in Gorst's fears being realised.

In 1901 Gorst had arranged the promotion of all the women inspectors to the newly created rank of junior inspector, a rank that would not only ensure their equality of treatment with men of the same grade but would provide women members of the inspectorate with an equal chance of becoming an HMI. Morant held a different view, as he made clear to both Anson and Londonderry in 1904, arguing that the rank of HMI carried with it the responsibility for districts and he believed it was impossible 'for all the work in a given district to be done, or even to be directed by, a woman'. Using this premise, he argued the case for making a separate section of the inspectorate which would not alter their salary but would 'obviate the difficulty of their relative positions' to the rest of the inspectorate. In addition, Morant believed the women should be regarded as having a brief for 'special purposes' covering a wide area but especially those 'in which women as such are likely to be specially useful'. They would be allotted to divisional inspectors in urban areas, mainly because of the difficulties of travel and suitable accommodation in rural areas, and they would be given topics to tackle by the Board in addition to normal inspectorial duties, while their reports would be in accordance with a form to be drawn up by Jackson. The first topic Morant had in mind was an investigation of the arrangements made by elementary schools for the teaching of children aged 3–5 years, and in assigning Kitty Bathurst to Sneyd-Kynnersley's division (North West) he felt she would find 'plenty of scope for her energies and abilities'.[96] These arrangements were proposed by way of an experiment, with Jackson to be responsible for monitoring the outcome, but Morant had little doubt they would be accepted and had already started looking for someone to head the section.

By December 1904 Morant confessed that he found it difficult to be precise about the qualities he envisaged for the position of Chief Woman Inspector. He did hold that it was essential that she should have sufficient breadth of vision to ensure that the work of the women inspectors should be 'correlated, one with another, and brought each into due submission to a proper whole, and into proper relation with education as a whole'.[97] He was obviously worried that the poor relations which had developed between the women inspectors and their HMIs were jeopardising the possibility of women playing a supervisory role in the national education system for the 'inspectorate generally pray that no more Women Inspectors be appointed, and to be quit altogether of those they have'. Somehow the problem had to be resolved and he believed a Chief Woman Inspector whose 'name stands high in the world of women's work and of general estimation' could be the solution by giving prestige to the work of the women inspectorate. The right appointee could, he felt, inspire

> a new and proper sense of the real importance of *their* work; and further to show Local Authorities generally . . . that the Women inspectorate is intended to be, and is going to be, recognised as on a really high plane of efficiency – not merely, and not so much, in auditing the results of the teaching in the ordinary school subjects . . . but efficiency in the sense of securing proper aims in the work of the Elementary Schools, and of the training of the teachers . . .[98]

He was quite prepared to give the person a free hand provided she could achieve these goals within the next two years. Although he had originally thought of Philippa Fawcett for the post, just before Christmas he told Edith Marvin (previously Deverell) that the Honourable Maude Lawrence was now being seriously considered.[99]

The youngest daughter of Lord Lawrence of the Punjab, one-time Viceroy of India, Maude Lawrence had been a member of the London School Board from 1899 and on its abolition had been asked to become one of the co-opted members of the LCC's Education Committee. This notwithstanding, she lacked any formal qualifications and teaching experience but did possess a commanding personality.[100] She was appointed to the post at the beginning of February 1905 and the *Morning Post* commented that she was a lady 'of great practical experience' and would have 'ample scope for the employment of her special capacity'.[101] In the event, neither Morant's nor the *Post*'s beliefs were misplaced for Lawrence achieved the desired cohesiveness and efficiency in a very short time, as was demonstrated with the publication of a powerful report on the teaching of cookery in elementary schools published in 1907. The contrast between the style and impact of this report on the educational world and that of the first report compiled from the work of the five women inspectors before Lawrence's arrival could not have been greater, for the 1905 report had reflected the disparity of outlook between the five women, each having provided a different interpretation of the terms of reference. Kitty Bathurst's report was so contentious and outspoken that it was published in a minuted form, some of the minutes having been written by Morant. It had led to a demand from Londonderry for her resignation, a demand she complied with, unfortunately to the disadvantage of elementary school children.[102] The report also reinforced Morant's view about the unsuitability of Bathurst as a member of his team of experts. With her resignation he believed he had achieved also a purging of the last link with Gorst but this error of judgement was to be revealed before the end of 1905. But by then there was no doubt that he had successfully established the structure of administration and inspection he deemed necessary both to complement the implementation of the 1902 Act and to support the substantial educational reforms which had been initiated in 1903. This was a not inconsiderable achievement, as Anson acknowledged when he commented on Morant's stupendous powers in reforming the office at the very time they were in danger of being engulfed by major problems arising from the implementation of the 1902 Act.[103]

NOTES

1. J. Dover-Wilson Papers, MS 14357, fo. 95.
2. *Times Educational Supplement*, 31 Aug. 1987, p. 2.
3. B. Webb, *Diary* (typed version) 23, p. 2177, Dec. 1902.
4. Sadler Papers, MS Eng misc c.550, fo. 20, R.L. Morant to M.E. Sadler, 19 Nov. 1895.
5. PRO ED 23/216F, R.L. Morant, 'Confidential Memorandum on Office Organisation', 1907 cited in P.H.J.H. Gosden, 'The Board of Education Act, 1899', *British Journal of Educational Studies*, II (1962), p. 60.
6. Sadler Papers, MS Eng misc c.205, Sir M.T. Sadler, *Diary*, p. 32, 27 May 1900.
7. M.A. Sadler, *Diary*, 4 Nov. 1902 cited in M. Sadleir, *Sir Michael Sadler*, p. 185; Sadler Papers, MS Eng misc c.551, fo. 223, M.E. Sadler, 'Private memorandum dated November 1902 setting out the reasons against and for resignation from the B/E.'

8. Ibid., fo. 226.
9. Ibid., MS Eng misc c.552, fos. 19–24, Note by M.E. Sadler, 26 Jan. 1903.
10. Ibid., fos.25–30, Note by M.E. Sadler, 6 Feb. 1903.
11. Ibid., fo. 48, M.E. Sadler to H.J. Mackinder, 2 March 1903.
12. Ibid., fo. 89, M.A. Sadler to M.E. Sadler, 1 March 1903.
13. Ibid., fo. 226, M.E. Sadler to H.W. Orange, 23 June 1903.
14. Dover Wilson Papers, MS 14357, fos. 99–101. Fisher, despite his admiration for Morant, kept quiet during the discussion, 'smiling his Chinese smile', and it was only a few days later that his guests learned from the papers of his appointment as the new President.
15. M.E. Sadler to *The Times*, 15 May 1903 cited in *School Government Chronicle*, 70 (23 May 1903), p. 447.
16. Sadler Papers, MS Eng misc c.552, fo. 172, Mackinder Diary, 12 June 1903; *School Government Chronicle*, 70, 16 (23 May and 13 June 1903), pp. 424, 447 and 510; *Journal of Education*, XXV (June 1903), pp. 397–8.
17. Ibid., July 1903, p. 454.
18. Morant found in Sadler's successor, Dr Frank Heath, one who could make the DSIR, without additional staff, what he wanted – 'an extremely *practical* office'. In little more than ten months he claimed that it had become an integral component of the Board by the simple expedient of bringing 'all its information to bear directly on our daily work, instead of storing it up in St. Stephen's House, or putting the frothy part of it into Reports for the public to talk on'. See PRO ED 23/588, R.L. Morant to J. Bromley, 4 Dec. 1904.
19. Report of the Departmental Committee on the Pupil-Teacher System, *PP*, 1898, XXVI [C.8761], p. 8.
20. *4 PD*, 55, c.1628–9, 1 April 1898.
21. PRO ED 11/2, J.E. Gorst to Duke of Devonshire, 16 Aug. 1901.
22. PRO ED 24/68a, J.E. Gorst to Duke of Devonshire, 25 Aug. 1901.
23. PRO ED 24/76, R.L. Morant, 'The Education of Pupil Teachers, Candidates and Probationers and the Deficient Supply of Good Teachers', 26 Feb. 1902.
24. C.A. Buckmaster, General Report for 1902 in General Reports on Higher Education; with Appendices for the Year 1902, *PP*, 1903, XXI [Cd.1738], p. 2.
25. R.L. Morant, 'Prefatory Note' in General Report on the Instruction and Training of Pupil-Teachers, 1903–1907, *PP*, 1907, LXIV [Cd.3582], p. iii.
26. PRO ED 11/2, R.L. Morant to J.R. Dasent, 4 April 1903.
27. In 1905 the regulations were amended to ensure that pupil-teacher centres would possess a curriculum occupying 'a definite position between the secondary school or higher elementary school courses and that of the training college'. See Annual Report of the Board of Education for 1904–5, *PP*, 1905, XXVIII [Cd.2783], p. 37.
28. Annual Report of the Board of Education for 1902–3, *PP*, 1903, XX [Cd.1763], p. 13.
29. E.K. Chambers, 'Memorandum on the History and Prospects of the Pupil-Teacher System' in General Report on the Instruction and Training of Pupil-Teachers, 1903–1907, *PP*, 1907, LXIV [Cd.3582], p. 17.
30. *The Schoolmaster* (9 Jan. 1904) cited in O. Banks, *Parity and Prestige in English Secondary Education* (1955), p. 47.
31. Headlam-Morley Papers, ACC 727, Box 23, F.H. Chambers to [?W.C.] Fletcher, 7 Feb. 1905.
32. *School Government Chronicle*, 70 (11 July 1903), p. 32.
33. E.J.R. Eaglesham, *The Foundations of 20th Century Education in England*

(1967), p. 56.

34. B. Simon, *Education and the Labour Movement, 1870–1920* (1965), pp. 245–6.
35. PRO ED 24/76, R.L. Morant, 'The Education of Pupil Teachers, Candidates and Probationers and the deficient supply of good teachers', 26 Feb. 1902, p. 13.
36. J. Graves, *Policy and Progress in Secondary Education* (1943), p. 56.
37. E.K. Chambers, 'Memorandum on the History and Prospects of the Pupil-Teacher System' in General Report on the Instruction and Training of Pupil-Teachers, 1903–1907, *PP*, 1907, LXIV [Cd.3582], p. 17.
38. F. Widdowson, *Going up into the Next Class: Women and Elementary Teacher Training 1840–1914* (1983), pp. 44–6.
39. E.G.A. Holmes, *What Is and What Might Be* (1911), p. 111.
40. See D.E.S. File 56/1518Y, E.J.R. Eaglesham to N.E. Worcester, 2 Oct. 1958. Eaglesham cited Dover-Wilson's attribution of the introduction to 'someone like Mackail' with Morant's share probably being the 'constantly putting in [of] his oar'.
41. Board of Education, Code of Regulations for Public Elementary Schools, *PP*, 1904, LXXV [Cd.2074], p. vii.
42. Simon, op. cit., p. 240; Eaglesham, op. cit., p. 53.
43. C. Brereton, 'Revolution at the Board of Education', *Monthly Review*, 15 (June 1904), p. 59.
44. *Journal of Education*, 35 (June 1904), p. 39; *School Government Chronicle*, 71 (25 June 1904), p. 611.
45. *The Schoolmaster* (14 May 1904), p. 1082.
46. Annual Report of the Board of Education for 1903–4, *PP*, 1904, XXV [Cd.2271], p. 15.
47. Annual Report of the Committee of Council on Education, 1897–8, pp. 254–5 cited in F. Smith, *A History of Elementary Education, 1760–1902* (1931), p. 340.
48. J. Leese, *Personalities and Power in English Education* (1950), pp. 242–3.
49. R.L. Morant, 'The National Organisation of Education of All Grades as Practised in Switzerland', *PP*, 1898, XXV [C.8988], p. 22.
50. See O. Banks, 'Morant and the Secondary School Regulations of 1904', *British Journal of Educational Studies*, III (1954), pp. 33–41, and *Parity and Prestige in English Secondary Education: A Study in Educational Sociology* (1963), pp. 31–50.
51. J. Roach, *Secondary Education in England 1870–1902: Public activity and private enterprise* (1991), p. 69.
52. M.E. Sadler, 'Secondary Education in its Bearings on Practical Life' cited in N. Whitbread, 'The early twentieth-century secondary curriculum debate in England', *History of Education*, 13, 3 (1984), p. 222.
53. *The School World* (Oct. 1900) cited in Whitbread, op. cit., p. 223.
54. Ibid., pp. 221–233.
55. PRO ED 24/265, A.F. Leach, Memorandum, April 1903.
56. Ibid., R.L. Morant, Minute of 5 April 1903. His loyalty to his type of school was commendable though debatable. Why he should have felt so strongly on this issue is open to conjecture but the role played by Winchester College in the special circumstances of his family may have been significant.
57. The committee consisted of Chief Inspector C.A. Buckmaster, Assistant Secretary J.C.G. Sykes and Senior Examiners J.L. Casson (South Kensington) and J.G. Milne (Whitehall).
58. PRO ED 24/265, R.L. Morant to W.N. Bruce, 24 April 1903.
59. *4 PD*, 125, c.173, 9 July 1903.

60. A. Kazamias, *Politics, Society and Secondary Education in England* (Philadelphia, 1966), p. 132; M. Smith, 'Curricular Priorities in Secondary Schools: regulations, opinions and school practices in England, 1903–4', *British Journal of Sociology of Education*, 1, 2 (1980), p. 157.
61. J.W. Headlam, 'Report on the Teaching of Literary Subjects in Some Secondary Schools' in General Reports on Higher Education; with Appendices for the Year 1902', *PP*, 1903, XXI, [Cd.1738], p. 63.
62. Ibid., p. 66.
63. Headlam-Morley Papers, Acc.727, Box 33, R.L. Morant to W.N. Bruce, n.d.
64. *School Government Chronicle*, 70 (19 Sept. 1903), p. 239.
65. PRO ED 24/265, W.N.Bruce, Memorandum, 5 Nov. 1903.
66. Ibid., J.W. Mackail, Memorandum, 16 Jan. 1904, p. 1.
67. Ibid., p. 3.
68. Ibid., pp. 9–11.
69. Ibid., pp. 14–15.
70. R.L. Morant, Prefatory Memorandum to Regulations for Secondary Schools, *PP*, 1904, LXXV [Cd.2128].
71. *The Schoolmaster*, LXVI (27 Aug. 1904), p. 358.
72. B. Simon, op. cit., pp. 240–1.
73. Eaglesham, op. cit., p. 59.
74. M.J. Wiener, *English Culture and the Decline of the Industrial Spirit 1850–1980* (1981), p. 22.
75. Whitbread, op. cit., pp. 227–8.
76. *4 PD*, 108, c.563, 26 May 1902.
77. PRO ED 23/424, R.L. Morant to Lord Londonderry, 16 Feb. 1903. See also R. Betts, 'Robert Morant and the Purging of H.M. Inspectorate, 1903', *Journal of Educational Administration and History*, XX, 1 (Jan. 1988), pp. 54–9.
78. PRO ED 24/66, J.E. Gorst, Minute of 18 Oct. 1901.
79. D. Lawton and P. Gordon, *H.M.I.*, 1987, p. 16.
80. PRO ED 24/66, J.E. Gorst, Minute of 18 Oct. 1901.
81. PRO ED 24/67, J.E. Gorst to Duke of Devonshire, 11 July 1902.
82. PRO ED 24/1675, R.L. Morant, 'Reorganisation of the inspectorate', July 1903.
83. *The Times*, 15 Oct. 1903.
84. G. Sutherland, *Policy-Making in Elementary Education, 1870–1895* (1972), p. 54.
85. Leese, op. cit., p. 263.
86. PRO ED23/128, R.L. Morant to C. Jackson, 4 Dec. 1904.
87. Ibid.
88. Ibid., R.L. Morant to C. Jackson, 5 Feb. 1905.
89. Ibid., R.L. Morant to C. Jackson, 13 Feb. 1905.
90. Ibid., R.L. Morant to C. Jackson, 14 Feb. 1905.
91. Ibid., R.L. Morant to C. Jackson, 10 April 1905.
92. R. Blair, 'C. Jackson', *Dictionary of National Biography 1922–1930* (1930), p. 446.
93. Runciman Papers, WR 44, C. Jackson to W. Runciman, 27 Jan. 1911.
94. Mary, Gorst's wife, was the cousin of Kitty Bathurst's mother: See P. Gordon, 'Katharine Bathurst: A controversial woman inspector', *History of Education* 17, 3, (1988), p. 194.
95. Ibid., p. 195, J.E. Gorst to K. Bathurst, 8 April 1899.
96. Marvin Papers, MS Eng misc c.257, fos. 20–3, R.L. Morant to W. Anson and Lord Londonderry, 9 Feb. 1904.

97. PRO ED 23/152B, R.L. Morant, Memorandum on the 'New Post of Chief Woman Inspector', Dec. 1904, p. 1.
98. Ibid., p. 2.
99. Marvin Papers, MS Eng misc c.227, fo. 41, R.L. Morant to E. Marvin, 23 Dec. 1904.
100. M.Z., 'Maude Lawrence', *Macmillan Dictionary of British Women's Biography* (1982), p. 249.
101. *Morning Post*, 2 Feb. 1905.
102. For further details see Gordon, op. cit., pp. 201–5.
103. W. Anson, Journal, 1903, cited in H.H. Henson (ed.), *A Memoir of the Rt. Hon. Sir W. Anson* (1920), p. 181.

8

Some little local difficulties

The formulation of educational policy contained in the 1902 Education Act had not been without considerable problems, but the opposition to the passage of the measure had revealed also that policy implementation was unlikely to be easy. But just as the Board came to grips with the problems relating to this in 1903, it had to deal also with those connected with the formulation of another Education Bill since the 1902 Act had failed to make any provision for an LEA for London. The city had been included in the Education Bill prior to February 1902 and was to have been treated no differently from any other major urban centre. It would have had, therefore, the London County Council (LCC) as its LEA. Such a proposal, however, was not welcomed by certain members of the Cabinet, including Lord Salisbury and Walter Long, and their feelings were reciprocated by many of the London Unionist MPs. For them, the County Council was the *bête noire* of the local government world.

Lord Salisbury had initially approached the reform of local government in the early 1880s with a great deal of caution, but after 1884 he viewed the subject in a different way, telling the National Union that the aim of local government was to give to the people the power previously exercised by central government. He supported Ritchie's 1888 Local Government Bill but took exception to the creation of the London County Council on the grounds that it was a potential centralist rather than decentralist organisation. He felt that his view was justified by the subsequent activities of both the Progressive and Moderate Parties in making the metropolis a new political power base, not least being the pursuit of municipal socialism by the Progressives. Once, when he had agreed to give a speech to a London audience before a local council election – ostensibly to validate the campaign of the Moderate Party candidates – Salisbury had condemned the council as the place 'where Collectivist and Socialistic experiments are tried. It is the place where a new revolutionary spirit finds its instruments and collects its arms'.[1] The London Government Act of 1899 represented an attempt by Salisbury to decentralise the council by the creation of 28 boroughs within the county of London. Although the Act contained

241

the proviso that none of the council's powers was to be transferred to the boroughs without its consent there was nothing to prevent the return at some subsequent election of candidates prepared to curtail the council's authority.[2] This opposition to the county council was also mirrored in the London Water Bill, introduced during the 1902 Session, for it represented a further step in the process of decentralisation by entrusting the management of the county's water supply not to the council but to an independent Metropolitan Water Board, upon which there was to be strong representation from the borough councils.

Walter Long, the President of the Local Government Board and described by one historian as combining 'boneheadedness with hypersensitivity', had chaired the committee charged with looking at the London issue in connection with the Education Bill during the early months of 1902.[3] As author of the Water Bill, he was naturally opposed to the County Council becoming the LEA for London and preferred, instead, a similar body to that proposed for the Water Board. Support from Salisbury on this issue meant that when Ritchie, the Home Secretary, had produced a memorandum in early March arguing the case for the retention of London in the Bill, there was insufficient support within Cabinet for his case and it was decided to exclude the capital from the measure although a separate Bill would be introduced in the future to cover London education. Morant believed that the drafting of this separate measure would constitute an 'awful onus' for the government, since their previous actions had prevented retention of the School Board, while the logic of the 1902 Bill dictated that the LCC should be made the new LEA. But as the Liberal opposition to both the Education and Water Bills slowly crumbled during 1902 there came to the fore an 'intense hatred of the London C.C. and a desire to magnify the Borough Councils, which are regarded with paternal feelings, at the expense of the C.C'.[4] Fully aware of the problems this view presented for the council, Sidney Webb had started a campaign of permeation and persuasion on behalf of the LCC as the new LEA only a month after Balfour introduced the 1902 Bill.

Webb, like other Fabians, was opposed to the concept of *ad hoc* bodies as a result of detailed investigation of their functioning and this belief eliminated any support from him for possible retention of the School Board as the LEA. Unlike other Fabians, Webb had supported the 1902 Education Bill because its principles permitted the new LEAs to fund:

(a) The best possible primary schools available to all.

(b) The largest possible scholarship system.

(c) The best possible evening instruction.

(d) The most efficient secondary schools and University colleges.

(e) The most thorough provision for postgraduate study and research.[5]

Accepting the necessity, especially in large LEAs, for some decentralisation of control Webb was not averse to the concept of the borough councils being involved in the administration of London's ex-board schools or to the influence maintained by religious bodies over voluntary schools under the 1902 Act. But the guiding, central organisation of the system, and retaining financial control, had to be the LCC. The government's antagonism towards this possibility stimulated him, and his wife Beatrice, to try to change the Cabinet's view by enlisting 'all the forces we have any control over – our friends in the Church, University educationalists, Permanent officials and anyone having influence over ministers'.[6] Morant was thus invited by Sidney at the beginning of May 1902 to discuss both Education Bills. As far as the London Bill was concerned the emphasis of their discussions was on how they could influence the Cabinet so as to achieve what they believed to be the best LEA for the capital. They decided that the best plan would be to circulate copies of the report of the Council's Technical Education Board accompanied by personal letters and to set in motion 'quiet agitations' among members of the Church and other Conservative circles.

Gorst, one of the recipients of this persuasion campaign, warned Webb that the government, beset with the numerous problems surrounding the passage of the 1902 Bill, had not really considered the London Bill in any detail. He did think that Webb's warning about the undue influence which would be exerted by the National Union of Teachers (NUT) over the borough councils, should the Water Board model be adopted, would probably sway the Cabinet away from their preference for this model more than any other argument. He suggested that in these circumstances a 'desperate attempt' could be made to amend Clause 20, when it was reached in the debates, by striking out the words 'on, except as expressly provided to London', for this, if accepted, would make the LCC the LEA for London. But for the amendment to be successful would require pressure to be exerted upon the government by a majority of the London Conservative MPs and he thought that if London Churchmen could be made to 'realise the miserable condition in which the London Voluntary Schools would be left' if the LCC did not become the LEA then he was confident that there would be sufficient support for the council to be made the LEA.[7] Sidney accepted Gorst's ideas and discussed them with the Bishop of London. He was planning to see prominent London Conservative MPs as well as the Bishop of Islington, but a speech by Balfour on 19 July at Fulham revealed that London would be dealt with in a separate Bill in 1903, and this ruled out the possibility of Gorst's proposed amendment.

By late November, one member of the Liberal Party observed that the government's decision to replace the School Board in London with a new educational authority pointed increasingly to an authority elected by the borough councils and he viewed the creation of such a body as disastrous both for London government and for elementary education.[8] Webb and his wife responded by intensifying their efforts at permeation and persuasion, and Beatrice did not hesitate to seize 'every opportunity to insinuate sound doctrine and information as to the position of London Education' when she was Balfour's partner at a dinner party in the home of Mrs Horner a few days later.[9] Sidney thought she had managed her task skilfully but when Morant came to dinner alone shortly after the Education Bill had been passed, the news was that there was little change in the Cabinet's view over the London measure. Morant had drafted a two-clause Bill applying the new Act to London, which would have satisfied the Webbs' aims, but Long, 'elated with his triumph over the constitution of the Water Board, says he will be damned before he sees the LCC the education authority'. Furthermore, Morant was dubious whether there was sufficient interest in the issue after the strains caused by the passage of the Education Bill to achieve a change of view:

> . . . the Church hesitates as to the worth while, the Unionist members are terrified at the N.U.T. on the one hand, and the Tory Political worker on the other – no member of the Cabinet is keen to enhance the dignity of the L.C.C. though all except Long realise that the Borough Councils would be impossible. But Long is a loud voiced persistent creature who talks his colleagues down at Cabinet and Committee Meetings and is in touch with the commoner kind of obscurant Tory. So matters look dark and the present unsatisfactory situation is likely to persist . . .[10]

Webb was alarmed by Morant's news and contacted another Fabian, Graham Wallas, with a plan to try to remedy the situation, prefacing it with the comment: 'If you will act, and act promptly, and unquestioningly, you can do a good stroke.' Webb wanted Wallas to see Lord Londonderry immediately in order to convince him of two points:

> ... that a London Bill is imperatively urgent, and cannot be postponed without the gravest evil to education, and the gravest discontent among ratepayers etc. Second, that there is no practical alternative (assuming *ad hoc* election out of the question) to an L.C.C. Committee; as Borough Councils are the devil, under the control of N.U.T., etc.[11]

Webb was adamant that it was Londonderry who had to be convinced as he believed Anson to be of little use in this crisis. His hypothesis appeared to be correct for when a deputation from the London School Board met Londonderry and Anson at the end of January, the former was effusive in his charm and bonhomie, understandably so, given his former chairmanship of the Board, but unwilling to commit either himself or the government to any of their proposals despite the best efforts of Lord Reay, Lyulph Stanley and Dr T.J. Macnamara to argue the case for preservation of the School Board as the LEA. Webb preferred, however, to leave nothing to chance and his next action was to approach the owners and editors of the national daily press. One result was that Harmsworth handed over to him the direction of a campaign on the London Education Bill in the *Daily Mail*, which augured well as Haldane reported that the Cabinet remained in a state of indecision with Long still holding out for an authority based on the borough councils or, at the very least, a majority of borough councillors on an education committee of the LCC.[12]

Sidney thus seized the opportunity presented a few days later when he met Balfour's sister, Eleanor Sidgwick, at a meeting for the signing of a petition by Senate members of London University in favour of the LCC becoming the LEA, to expound his views about the LEA hoping, correctly as it turned out, that she would report them to Balfour. When she asked him why there could not be borough representatives on the education committee of the LCC, Webb's response was that while there could be some if they all sent one representative, the committee would become too unwieldy. He also reiterated the point he had made to Gorst and others about the possibility of the borough councils being manipulated by the NUT although he did acknowledge that there should be considerable delegation of elementary school management to the borough councils. Sidgwick promptly asked why this should be so, given his fears about the NUT, and was told that under this arrangement the councils would not have the necessary financial control over teachers' salaries as that would come under the aegis of the LCC. He added that if the LCC possessed the necessary rating power but could not appoint the majority of the Education Committee, this would circumscribe the committee's work. Sidgwick forwarded this news to her brother but told him that she had not signed the petition, claiming that she did not fully understand all the issues.[13]

A few days later Webb told Edward Pease, the secretary of the Fabian Society, that the outlook was not encouraging since a majority of the Cabinet still preferred the 'Water Board plan'. None the less, there were some cheering signs:

> ... a fight is being made against it in the Cabinet, and the combination of forces against it outside is very strong – all grades of education, the church and the RC's, all Liberals and Progressives, will unite against it – about 1/3 of the London Conservative MP's, are against it also.
>
> It may yet be stopped – either now or later – but the moment is now, before the Government are publicly committed; and the method is to put pressure on the London Conservative MPs, who are wobbling.[14]

A week later Webb was even more optimistic for, although the Unionist MPs still appeared to be obdurate, their meeting to discuss the Bill had been postponed 'by the friends of the LCC to allow time for conversions'. Furthermore, he thought that the London clergy were being adequately attended to, and 'stoked up', by their own leaders and doubted whether there was now anything more the Fabians could do to influence the Cabinet.[15] He and Beatrice decided, none the less, to try to persuade Anson although Beatrice was not confident of the help likely to be received from this 'subtle-minded Don'. Her lack of confidence in him had not been bolstered by the revelation on meeting him at the home of her brother-in-law, Alfred Cripps, that not only did he appear to be 'singularly out of place in an administrative position' but that he was

> far more interested in discussing the relation of the Privy Council to the local authorities of the seventeenth and eighteenth centuries than the proper authority for dealing with London's education. Indeed one felt he knew so little of the elements of the latter subject that it was barely worthwhile talking to him.[16]

This discovery only served to increase the despondency she felt because of what she termed the 'slump in Webbs' within the LCC Progressive Party but, given the precariousness of their position, she accepted that he ought to be invited to dinner in order to try and ensure that he, too, was not 'agin us'.

Sidney's support for the 1902 Education Bill had alienated him from his Progressive colleagues on the LCC while his activities in connection with the London Bill compounded the rift. 'Wily Webb's' links with Conservative ministers, his preference for impartiality on the 'religious difficulty' plus the fear that he was willing to advance technical and higher education at the expense of elementary education induced distrust in a clique of Progressives led by Ramsay Mac-Donald. Bitterly opposed to the 1902 Act and preferring the School Board as London's LEA, MacDonald's group were in danger, Beatrice observed, of 'steering straight into a "Water Board" authority'.[17] Aware of these fundamental differences which divided the Progressives, Sidney was prepared to stand for re-election as chairman of the Technical Education Board, in order to facilitate negotiations with the government, but would only do so with the complete consent of the party; this MacDonald was determined to prevent. The ill-timed circulation of a report prepared by Dr William Garnett, the secretary of the Technical Education Board, without Webb's consent, indicating that not only could the LCC take on the work of the School Board but also providing a detailed scheme showing how it could be done, damned Webb's cause for he was believed to have been party to it.[18] On 15 March he was ousted from the chairmanship of the Technical Education Board.

Webb's defeat, and thereby the credibility of the LCC as the potential LEA, could not have occurred at a worse moment. The government, shaken by two by-election defeats at Woolwich and Rye early in March, was now concerned about the possibility of a stiff political fight over London, given the escalating amount of Nonconformist NUT agitation in the capital. They had reached the point of considering, by mid-March, the possibility of creating an *ad hoc* body as the LEA. The possibility of an LCC debate upon a resolution put down by Hubbard, a Nonconformist councillor, calling for the establishment of such a body, generated considerable interest among the government as well as activity by LCC members. The leaders of the Progressive Party, McKinnon Wood and Collins, were concerned about the likely outcome of the debate on this resolution, preferring that the LCC should become the authority. At a meeting of the party

Collins managed to secure a small majority for a resolution in favour of the LCC as the LEA, but also condemning the principles of the 1902 Act, and an overwhelming one in favour of adjourning Hubbard's resolution. At Haldane's instigation, Webb met with Sandars and Acland-Hood, the Conservative Chief Whip, to try to get them to induce the Cabinet to introduce the London Bill with the LCC as the new authority. One consequence of this meeting was that Londonderry's private secretary sought permission for himself and a shorthand writer to attend the LCC debate on Hubbard's resolution while Morant begged Webb to let him know the result as soon as possible. In the event, the whole council extended their discussion of other business to prevent Hubbard's resolution from being taken. On learning this the Cabinet demurred from making the LCC the LEA unless they could be guaranteed the support of the Progressives. This effectively required the rejection of Hubbard's resolution by the Progressives, a requirement which Webb felt, somewhat despondently, it would be almost impossible to achieve.[19]

Webb had underestimated, however, the consequences of his counsel with Sandars and Acland-Hood upon a Cabinet who were now, according to Haldane, 'panic-stricken'. The by-election results and the mounting Nonconformist opposition to the 1902 Act appear to have convinced the Cabinet of the truth of Webb's assertion that an *ad hoc* LEA for London would soon be dominated by people of the ilk of Dr John Clifford and T.J. Macnamara and that its creation could also help fan Nonconformist opposition into permanent resistance to the 1902 Act. They were prepared, therefore, to curb their hostility to the LCC and Anson asked Webb to meet him to discuss the date of implementation of the Act.[20] Four days later Anson introduced the Bill into the House.

The Bill established the LCC as the new LEA but with an education committee consisting of 36 LCC members, 31 nominees of the metropolitan borough councils and 25 persons to be nominated by the council in accordance with its scheme for implementation of the Act plus, for the first five years, five members of the School Board. Although the LCC would have virtually unlimited powers over post-elementary education, this would not apply to elementary education. Voluntary schools were to come under virtually identical provisions to those of the 1902 Act, except that the LCC would provide only one-sixth of the managers of the schools, the other LEA manager being reserved for appointment by the borough council in whose area the school was located. Only the LCC, however, would be responsible for

*Sir W*m. *Ans-n.* "I'm afraid *this* is about all we're teaching the children just now!"

5 Sir William Anson's denunciation of the 1906 Education Bill as 'this "omnibus Bill", by way of distinguishing it from the private episcopal brougham of 1902' caught the attention of *Punch*, if not of the House. (Cartoon in *Punch*, CXXX, 16 May 1906, p. 356)

the financial provisions required of the LEA. In the case of the ex-School Board schools, these were to be managed by the borough councils, or their education committees, including the appointment of teachers, albeit in accordance with regulations determined by the LCC. The LCC was denied, however, any vetoing power over the management of these schools, it being proposed that the Board of Education would act as the adjudicator in any issue concerning their management. As the LCC's Parliamentary Committee aptly commented, while the Bill professed to make the Council the local education authority for London 'it does not give the Council a free hand in the control of education'.[21]

Anson's inept introduction, with its undue emphasis upon the demise of the School Board, plus the Bill's provisions, earned a cold reception from the House. Beatrice Webb, observing the proceedings from the Speaker's Gallery, noted that while the Opposition jeered the measure the government backbenchers were 'gloomily silent'. She thought the measure a bad one as it stood but was prepared to accept it rather than have either the *status quo* preserved or an *ad hoc* body established. She felt that the borough council representatives on the central education committee had been 'stuck in to be knocked out' and believed that the LCC's control over the decentralised administration of elementary education could be strengthened in the Committee Stage. If these changes were achieved then the Bill would be 'much what Sidney would have himself drafted'.[22] Others were critical also of the Bill, one educationist believing it to be a measure lacking any guiding principle and drafted 'not so much in the interest of Education but with a view of destroying the London County Council'.[23] The London Progressives, on the other hand, greeted the measure with 'contemptuous disapproval – almost delight because it is considered so bad that it will not pass', while it was condemned by the NUT at its Easter conference.[24] Sandars was not worried by this general reaction for he observed astutely that the criticism was only levelled at the 'machinery' of the LEA and as the Bill was 'nothing but machinery, . . . it can therefore be turned inside out to meet pressure from whatever side it may come'.[25] The Second Reading revealed that the government was prepared to be flexible in its view of the measure and this fact was quickly absorbed by the LCC Progressives, Beatrice Webb noting that they were now rapidly coming round to the idea of the LCC as the LEA, 'the natural desire of a public body to increase its dignity and power overcoming the party feeling in favour of an Ad Hoc authority'.[26]

Just before the Committee Stage, a memorandum prepared for Anson by Walrond, a Senior Examiner, conceded that the general public feeling was in favour of the LCC having a majority on the education committee of the new LEA. Walrond, furthermore, saw problems associated with either complete centralisation or decentralisation within the capital's LEA: '. . . Centralisation is waste of superior capacity on inferior duties, that of devolution of an absolute kind of ignorance of the nature and conditions of those duties.'[27] The solution was to ensure, therefore, that adequate representation and linkage existed between both central and local units. To this end he not only concurred with providing majority status for the LCC on the education committee but also advocated replacing the borough councils with local education committees coming under the aegis of the LCC. Membership of the local committees would consist of borough council representatives, elementary school managers and at least one LCC representative. Walrond was aware that such advice conflicted with Balfour's declared preference in the Second Reading for the borough councils but he concluded that even in the case of this position being maintained there should be a change necessary to ensure better links between the LEA and the boroughs than were proposed in the Bill.

Balfour had in his pronouncement about the borough councils also overlooked the possibility of a change of attitude within the Conservative backbenchers about the LCC. By the time the Bill reached the Committee Stage in late May it was clear that a change in attitude had occurred, with all but Long and a small group of London Unionist Members now in favour of the LCC as the LEA. This change appears to have been caused, first, by a growing awareness of the real nature of the metropolitan borough councils – that they were little more than glorified vestries – and, second, by an increased sensitivity to the growing opposition among English and Welsh LEAs to total implementation of the 1902 Act. Anson's proposal to amend the Bill so that there would be a reduced number of borough councillors as a result of 'grouping the councils together, so that each borough would be represented by a vulgar fraction of a member', was laughed out of the House. Balfour had to rescue the government by accepting the changes to the structure and functioning of the LEA suggested by Macnamara and Lloyd George, coupled with those of Gorst, Cripps and Peel from the government back benches, changes identical to those which Beatrice Webb had forecast.[28] FitzRoy, like Haldane, was surprised that it had taken the government so long to reach this stage:

The Bill now stands in the form that we were agreed three months ago was the only possible way out of the tangle, and after numberless drafts and redrafts, and the most damaging criticism to which any legislative measure was ever exposed, the Government have accepted the inevitable.[29]

In the Bill finally agreed upon by the House, the LCC effectively became the new LEA with the borough councils' role being relegated solely to the appointment of three-quarters of the managers of council schools. Furthermore, the managers were to be the servants of the LEA and the appointment of teachers was to be determined by a scheme to be devised by the new LEA. Beatrice Webb noted delightedly in her diary that the Bill had thus passed 'in almost exactly the shape Sidney would have given it' although she did note that he felt the measure was more liberal in the powers accorded the LCC than he felt wise since it would be difficult to persuade the Progressives 'with their enormous majority and strong non-con. element, to be fair and sane about the outside interests'.[30] Webb's concern arose, in part, from the signs of increasing discontent among mostly Nonconformists in some areas of England and most of Wales with the provisions and implementation of the 1902 Act. In August he warned fellow Fabian Edward Pease that one consequence of the disruption might be the capture of the Progressive Party in London by the Nonconformists while he told Graham Wallas that the Nonconformists on the LCC were all for declaring the council to be in accord with the opponents of the 1902 Act.[31] Webb's discomfiture from this state of affairs was to be but nothing, however, compared with that facing Morant and Balfour in the implementation of their educational policy.

Opposition to the 1902 Act within society had manifested itself in two forms by early 1903, both being based upon a rejection of the use of rate moneys to support voluntary elementary schools without the corollary of direct popular control over their expenditure. At what might be termed the grassroots level there was the refusal by individuals, predominantly Nonconformists, to pay the portion of their rates to be allocated to denominational education and this developed into a national campaign of passive resistance. At a second level there were LEAs determined not to comply with the Act as far as the voluntary schools were concerned and these included Cambridgeshire, the West Riding of Yorkshire, Durham and most of Wales. The latter's actions soon generated what became, in effect, a rebellion by the Principality against the Act.

The practice of passive resistance was not novel to the Nonconformists, the stratagem having been employed by them against the payment of Church rates in the 1840s. But Dr Joseph Parker's advocacy of its use shortly after the 1902 Bill had been introduced, if the Bill were not amended in a manner satisfactory to Nonconformists, stirred the Nonconformist world and, like the Bill, caused schisms within it. The Wesleyan and Presbyterian church councils refused to support the use of passive resistance when the National Free Church Council mooted the idea in October 1902, although they were prepared to allow individual members of their churches to become resisters. This stance was not repeated in the other Nonconformist churches and the National Council thus took steps to establish a National Passive Resistance Committee of 46 members under the charismatic leadership of Dr John Clifford. Once the Act came into operation on 1 April 1903 (except in Wales and, of course, London) the campaign got under way with individuals, and some corporate bodies, refusing to pay the portion of their rates allocated to denominational education.

From the outset, the campaign was a reflection of the outrage felt by most Nonconformists about the Act and was intended to be 'a witness to conscience and democratic conviction'.[32] One of the most ardent advocates of passive resistance apart from Nonconformist ministers was Sir George Kekewich and he argued that passive resistance was a perfectly legal option for opponents of the Act as no man was bound to pay rates upon demand – 'he may have many and various grounds of objection, and the law permits him to urge those objections before a court of justice'.[33] He also contended that the Act

> was an insult to the consciences of half the people of the nation
> . . . . it was the duty of the Act's opponents to not only engage in
> passive resistance but also to actively promote and spread
> knowledge of the injustice of the measure.[34]

But in July the first distraint sale of goods of three passive resisters for rate default took place at Wirksworth in Derbyshire. Thereafter the movement began to gain ground and the legal system found itself faced with an increasing load of cases as a result of the number of passive resisters being brought before the courts. In July there were 300 cases, in August 1,448 and by the end of 1903 some 7,000 cases had been heard. By November 1905 the total number of prosecutions had reached 65,481.[35]

Members of the legal system, especially magistrates, found themselves divided over these prosecutions although, as the chairman of

Brentwood magistrates remarked, their actions had nothing to do with principle but the carrying out of the law. This notwithstanding, some magistrates were sympathetic or at least courteous in their treatment of the prosecuted and usually received a vote of thanks from them at the end of their cases. In other instances the magistrates made their hostility and displeasure felt in no uncertain manner although some were made to feel the effect of their zeal and 'user pays' mentality in their assessment of costs when they found themselves prosecuted subsequently for their excesses. MPs, mayors, a Lord Mayor (Sheffield), members of the judiciary and even some rate collectors were among the passive resisters brought before the courts but their impact, either individually or collectively, upon the government was minimal. A letter from Balfour published in the national press indicated his belief that the passive resistance movement was inspired by sectarian rather than constitutional interests. He viewed the resisters' actions as illogical, because they ignored not only the precedent of the 1870 Education Act but also the current functioning of the Scottish and Irish education systems, and he asked: 'Are we to suppose that the immutable principles of morality are thus inextricably involved in the technical peculiarities of English finance?'[36]

Londonderry reiterated these points during an address to a Primrose League meeting in his constituency a few months later. Throughout his speech he professed himself unable to comprehend the motivation of the passive resisters as well as the likely outcome of their actions.[37] Such comments, coupled with the government's failure to respond to their grievance, served only to harden the resolve of the passive resisters and their campaign continued beyond the remainder of the life of the government. Ultimately, the campaign's effect was to force Campbell-Bannerman's Liberal government in 1905 to commit themselves to a redressing of the Act's imbalances but it had no effect upon Balfour's government. What did make his government react, however, was the serious problem arising from LEA opposition to implementation of parts of the Act for this resistance constituted a grave threat on both political and educational grounds.

An indication that the Act would not be implemented in complete accordance with the desires of the government and the Board of Education was revealed with the publication of the schemes by local authorities for the composition and constitution of their LEAs. The first scheme published was that of Hertfordshire County Council, drafted in the presence of Alderman Lord Salisbury. This, perhaps not unnaturally, augured well for the Act in that the council's scheme allowed for nine of the 22 co-opted members to be representatives of denominational interests, of which six were to be from the Church of England. But it was the next published scheme, Surrey's, which in fact was more indicative of the trend soon to emerge. Of the total Surrey LEA membership, only seven seats were to be for co-opted members and these were to be appointed by the county council on the recommendation of the education committee. Denominational interests, *per se*, were not seen to be of sufficient merit for inclusion in the criteria applied to the election of co-opted members. Lancashire, a Conservative-dominated authority and one of the strongholds of voluntary schools, only permitted denominational interests the 'privilege' of making recommendations for six of the 72 seats on the LEA while Gloucestershire, also a Tory-dominated council with a pre-dominance of voluntary schools in its area, allowed only one of the 60 seats to be filled by a representative of denominational interests. These variations upon a theme of minimalisation of denominational interests, or even the complete rejection of them, continued as the schemes were published for both county and county borough LEAs. But even worse was to follow, as far as the government was concerned, as the Welsh LEAs decided on their course of action.

A warning that there could be problems within Wales over the implementation of the Act had been signalled at the beginning of October 1902 when, at a meeting of the Carmarthenshire County Council, a resolution was passed informing the government 'respect-fully and plainly' that unless the Bill included a satisfactory form of public control over all rate-aided schools the council 'would not carry out the provisions of the Bill in and for the County of Carmarthen-shire'.[38] This intransigent stance was reiterated by 11 other Welsh county councils by the end of December 1902 with only Brecon and Radnor, both authorities having Unionist majorities, refusing to conform. The religious, educational and political attitudes which prevailed in this opposition were soon to be immersed in a more complex political situation devised by David Lloyd George.

Lloyd George's hostility to the Act was well known and his adversarial tactics in the House during the passage of the measure had earned from Balfour the generous compliment that he had not only played a 'most distinguished part' but had also 'shown himself to be an eminent Parliamentarian'.[39] In early November, in an interview published in the *British Weekly*, Lloyd George had revealed his dislike of passive resistance, commenting that it was a useless waste of enthusiasm. He preferred, instead, to see the Act made inoperable by the refusal of county and county borough councils to implement it. Such an action would be legal, he believed, in view of the advice given by an eminent lawyer that councils could not be compelled to operate the Act.[40] A few days later he took steps to ensure that such an action could become a possibility in Wales when he engineered the acceptance by Welsh MPs of an amendment to the Education Bill making county and county borough councils the education authorities in Wales. The amendment, put forward in the name of Alfred Thomas, the chairman of the Welsh MPs, was accepted unhesitatingly by Balfour, and Lloyd George now had the means with which to attack the Act and, at the same time, lay the foundations for his wider campaign for Welsh Home Rule.

By 17 January 1903, Lloyd George had completed writing a manifesto to the Welsh people and it was laid before a meeting of the the Welsh National Liberal Council held in Cardiff four days later. Revolutionary action was not, he claimed, the course to be pursued as it would alienate too many otherwise potential supporters and disrupt at least one generation of children's schooling. What was required instead was to turn the Act in on itself and make it self-defeating. Developing the theme originally enunciated in Acland's Circular 321, Lloyd George argued that the LEAs should have thorough inspections made of the physical condition of all voluntary schools in their area and if any were unsatisfactory the LEA should refuse to accept them until they had been brought up to standard. Efficiency was to be the keyword as far as LEA involvement with the voluntary schools was concerned. Even then, the LEAs should not accept responsibility for the schools unless it was accepted that there was to be full public control over them and any religious tests for teachers employed in them foregone. If these requirements were not met then there should be no rate aid for the voluntary schools. Developing this theme at the Cardiff meeting he claimed that he would work only within the framework of the law and he would give 'the pound of flesh – just one pound, and not a drop of blood. We should put a premium on popular control . . . For popular control – cash and cash down. No popular control – no cash'.[41] What he was unwilling to reveal publicly at this stage, however, was his concurrence with Gorst's view that if enough parents at a school demanded its provision then there should be religious instruction of the type demanded, that is Nonconformist teaching in a Church of England voluntary school or Anglican instruction in an LEA-provided school. He was thus deceiving his supporters not only about his true intentions but also about the legality of their possible actions, for his comments were well outside both the spirit and letter of the law. Spurred on by the ecstatic response to his rhetoric (as well as by his long-term goals), Lloyd George seemed convinced at this stage that might (in this case the Welsh people) would be right.

Having provided the impetus for a Welsh rebellion to get under way, Lloyd George then became a key player in attempts to reach a concordat between the LEAs and the Church over their schools. A fortuitous meeting with A.G. Edwards, the Bishop of St. Asaph, on a train journey from Chester to London on 4 February, revealed that the bishop was on his way to a meeting with Morant to press for a settlement of the Welsh problem.[42] Such was the bishop's conviction on this issue that he was willing, according to Lloyd George, to act as an emissary for the latter with Morant six days later. The reply from the latter was not encouraging, however, as far as Lloyd George's own campaign was concerned for Morant indicated that if the Welsh LEAs followed it 'there would be deadlock'.[43] Lloyd George subsequently took all the steps at his command to ensure that a conference of Welsh LEAs called by Swansea for the end of the month at Llandrindod Wells not only would occur but would also consider the possibility of achieving a compromise over the voluntary schools.

The Llandrindod Wells meeting was very well attended, with representatives from virtually all authorities in the Principality, and heard Lloyd George outline the necessity for a compromise while ensuring that the education system would be 'completely under the control of the people who provided it'. Lord Kenyon, attending as representative for the voluntary schools, accepted Lloyd George's speech as an olive branch but nevertheless raised the fundamental problem for the Church of the possible loss of control over their schools under such a scheme. The meeting agreed in principle with Lloyd George's views on religious teaching in schools, referred to as the 'colonial plan', with the right of entry of clergymen into council schools being granted on two days a week but with the day shortened so that technically the classes were held out of school hours. The meeting agreed also that a compromise should be sought and invited the authorities for Welsh voluntary schools to a conference to consider its implementation. The Bishop of St. Asaph's diocese accepted and the meeting was held at the Westminster Palace Hotel in London on 24 March.

Lloyd George and the bishop worked very hard during the meeting to achieve a compromise between the two organisations on the issue of religious instruction in schools and the composition of voluntary school managing bodies. What Lloyd George wanted from the meet-

257

ing was a concession from the Church on managing bodies but it was not forthcoming, the agreements reached being solely on what might be termed variations of the 'colonial plan'. One tentative agreement was that teachers could give, if they were willing, denominational instruction in council as well as in voluntary schools. Despite this considerable concession by the LEAs, St. Asaph was unable to gain the necessary support from within his own diocese, let alone the Principality, partly owing to the opposition of J. Owen, the Bishop of St. David's and an informant of Morant's.[44] St. Asaph's compromise approach, once it had been broadcast through the Church by Davidson after he had received the details from Morant, aroused considerable antagonism for what was seen as a betrayal of the Church's position. Similarly, Lloyd George now faced the task of trying to explain away these meetings with the Church to his supporters, for he was rather belatedly becoming aware of the magnitude of hostility among his supporters to any form of religious instruction in council schools.

While these meetings had been taking place, the Board of Education had been monitoring the Welsh situation closely. One officer acknowledged 'that the Welsh policy will certainly raise difficult questions and the less we commit ourselves beforehand with regard to them, the better'.[45] None the less, an enquiry directed to Morant via Bishop Owen from the Clerk to Carmarthenshire County Council about the legality of his county's resolution led to a question being raised in the House. A.S.T. Griffith-Boscawen queried Anson about the resolutions being passed by Welsh LEAs on the treatment of voluntary schools and Anson responded that under the Act it was the duty of every LEA to maintain and keep efficient all public elementary schools within their area. Unfortunately for the government, Anson also went on to state that unless there was a special educational reason a uniform standard of efficiency should be maintained in all schools. Lloyd George seized upon the phrase 'special educational reason' to justify the refusal by the Welsh LEAs to 'squander public money' on schools which were not directly under their control, a tactic which flummoxed Morant. The unanswered question was thus: what was the Board to do as the appointed day for many of the Welsh authorities, 30 September, came inexorably closer?

On 3 June, Lloyd George addressed a large meeting of representatives from trade unions, Liberal organisations and the Nonconformist churches opposed to the Act at the Park Hall, Cardiff. Resolutions urging LEAs to withhold rate aid from schools not under public control as well as the individual non-payment of rates to those LEAs which would not conform were passed unanimously. Six weeks later, Carmarthenshire County Council met to consider the report of its education committee on the voluntary schools in the area. The council agreed to decline 'for the present' the use of rate aid for any school neither provided by the council nor under its full control. And seven days later, but in England, Cambridgeshire County Council recommended that its education committee should not support from the rates any voluntary school 'so long as the majority of the managers are privately appointed, or any religious test for teachers is required, or any denominational teaching is given by paid teachers'.[46] These actions had a ripple effect and Sidney Webb told Graham Wallas that the Nonconformists on the LCC, 'as elsewhere, want to declare for the Lloyd George – Wales – Cambridgeshire policy of refusing aid to the Voluntary Schools'.[47] Sandars described the effect as one of 'infection' while Morant faced in Lloyd George a foe of comparable skill and cunning.

Carmarthenshire's 'no rate' resolution of July was supplemented in October by another resolution allowing only the payment of the parliamentary grant to the voluntary schools so that the authority had now adopted a position of practically disclaiming responsibility for any voluntary school which did not meet its conditions. Thus teachers who made enquiries of the LEA about their salaries were referred to the managers while managers who wrote requesting information about the books to be used received replies indicating that the LEA did not care.[48] This policy was quickly adopted by other LEAs, including Merionethshire, Mountain Ash, Rhondda and Pontypridd, but Caernarvonshire formulated a different policy which, while not as overtly hostile as that of Carmarthenshire, was none the less committed to achievement of the same goal. It ignored the managers of the voluntary schools completely and assumed control of these schools, dealing directly with the teachers as their employer. The parliamentary grants earned by the schools were pooled for their maintenance, the council using its bulk purchasing power to save money for coal, stationery, and so on. The Board of Education, faced with increasing complaints from managers about their constrained financial circumstances, discovered that they could not circumvent the LEAs and pay the parliamentary grants directly to the managers. One irony, given the circumstances, was that under Section 7(4) of the 1902 Act a school which was not maintained efficiently could lose its grant. The Board thus found itself having to resort to a policy of delay and subterfuge in order to avoid the additional problems this could raise.

Letters of complaint from managers of voluntary schools were re-directed to the LEA, with an accompanying query about the LEA's actions, while evidence of an LEA's failure to maintain a school received the response that the Board was giving it 'careful considera-tion'. At the same time, private assurances were obtained from volun-tary school supporters that not only would the schools be kept open until at least April 1904 but that managers would be discouraged from complaining to the Board.[49] Thankful that it was not receiving any complaints from Caernarvonshire, not least because of Lloyd George's close association with the area, the Board adopted a hands-off policy there, being 'glad to be able to ignore one large area'.[50] Yet the Carmarthenshire problem in particular, and the wider rebellion in general, still remained.

By mid-October Sandars notified Balfour, holidaying at Whittinge-hame, that Morant was anxious for his opinion 'upon a question which is agitating his mind and it must be dealt with very soon'. Outlining the main elements of the Welsh problem, Sandars indicated that plans for a new compromise were afoot, this time involving the archbishops and the Welsh bishops. Given the intransigence of the Welsh Nonconformists Morant wanted to know 'on which side [he] is . . . to throw his influence? The issue is mandamus or compromise'. Sandars firmly believed that the matter should be brought before the Cabinet for there was not only Wales to consider but also the 'question of how far the infection of the Welsh example may spread in England' includ-ing its effect upon London. The problem was compounded, he con-fessed, because 'C' [Londonderry] was 'quite useless'.[51] Lloyd George claimed, after an interview with Morant at this time, that Morant had 'practically given up the fight in Wales' and was willing to provide educational autonomy for the country in return for which Lloyd George should leave English education alone.[52] But Balfour remained unperturbed by these claims, observing that the same problem had existed at the end of the last Session and he favoured maintaining the position he had adopted then, when discussing it with Lloyd George and the Bishop of St. David's, of not committing himself. He did con-cede, however, that if the problem had been confined to Wales, given the discrepancy which existed between the Nonconformist majority of the population and the predominance of Anglican elementary schools, he would have been inclined towards a compromise. In the meantime he wanted Morant to provide a memorandum setting out all the issues.

Primed by Morant's analysis, Balfour held a meeting on the Welsh situation immediately following his return to London in early

November. Sandars, reporting the meeting to Gerald Balfour, President of the Local Government Board, who was confined to bed through illness, believed that the chance of compromise had now passed. The government was being forced to consider either legislation or the application of mandamus under Section 16 of the Act. Both expedients would be politically embarrassing and Sandars mentioned the hope that the Welsh voluntary school teachers might start legal proceedings against their managers for payment of their salaries. If this occurred it was believed that the managers and the LEA would become the defendant and the probability was, according to the government's advisers, that the judgment would find against the LEA. Sandars did concede that 'to put a County Council in prison, especially in Wales, is of course a serious business' but he believed it might have the effect of bringing the LEAs to their senses before the necessity of applying mandamus became inevitable.[53] Fortunately for the LEAs but unfortunately for the government, the teachers did not undertake this action and the Welsh revolt remained the major item on the next Cabinet agenda with the discussion centred on two possible solutions. The first, Sandars told the still unwell Gerald Balfour, was to let the managers sue the LEAs for 'teachers' salaries and anything else on which they can found an action at law'.[54] The second was the production of a Bill to permit the direct payment by the Board of the parliamentary grant to the managers of those schools neglected by their LEAs. The Cabinet agreed to steps being taken by the Board of Education which would lead towards the application of mandamus but at the same time a one-clause Bill would be ready so that its rapid enactment would prevent the need actually to apply mandamus, and with it the possibility of imprisonment if any council proved recalcitrant.[55]

The Cabinet appear to have been persuaded in their decisions by two legal opinions obtained by Morant on the issues arising from the actions of the Welsh LEAs. The first, by Sir Hugh Owen, examined the relations between an LEA and voluntary school teachers under the Act whereas the second, by Claud Schuster of the Board's Legal Department, analysed the position of the Board in relation to defaulting LEAs. What emerged from these opinions, substantiated by the Crown's Law Officers, was that in the case of a defaulting LEA the Board of Education was required by the 1902 Act to compel the authority to fulfil its duty. This could be achieved by the issuing of an order under Section 16 of the Act but only after the holding of a public inquiry. In the event of the order being ignored mandamus could then be applied to enforce it. The decisions taken by the Cabinet meant that what was required now was a case which would allow:

(1) that the facts should be clearly proved for Parliament and the public by a semi-judicial inquiry, both sides being heard and witnesses being cross-examined in public;

(2) that the length and futility of the remedies in the Act for dealing with the Welsh situation might be demonstrated, and the necessity of further powers be proved;

(3) to gain time and protract the matter till Parliament were in a position to interfere and provide increased or improved powers.[56]

By mid-December Morant had received a third legal opinion, prepared by three learned counsel, on the brief of the National Society, of the case for legal action against Carmarthenshire under section 16 of the Act.[57]

At this juncture Anson requested detailed information from nine voluntary schools in Carmarthenshire which had lodged complaints against the LEA while the Board also instituted a financial survey of all the voluntary schools in the county. The HMIs were instructed to visit each of them ostensibly by way of an ordinary visit but in reality to determine if the school was still operational and, if so, whether the school was being maintained in an efficient manner or whether there were indications of diminishing efficiency owing to a lack of funds. After a year of observation and monitoring, it looked as though the Board – under Morant's direction – was starting to move on to the offensive but Anson was not satisfied that all other possible avenues had been explored. He had already attempted to broach the idea of establishing a Welsh branch of the Board which would not only allow the Board to supervise more effectively the Joint Committee which had been established by the Welsh LEAs but would also help to diffuse tension over a default Bill 'if Welsh nationalist feeling were conciliated by the creation of a special branch of the office, located in Wales, for the transaction of Welsh business'.[58] He was unable to make progress with his colleagues on this scheme, however, so he then turned to the pursuit of compromise as a possible solution and sent his views on this to Randall Davidson, newly appointed Archbishop of Canterbury. He was careful to stress not only the problems present in Wales but also those in England:

In Durham County and the West Riding of Yorkshire efforts are being made to bring about a *Concordat*. If these should fail there may be difficulties here also; and these difficulties may be extended as the result of the next County Council election in districts such as the Kesteven and Lindsay divisions of Lincolnshire where nonconformity is strong. I may add that the attitude of the London County Council is not reassuring.[59]

He raised the spectre of disaffection with the Act spreading and commented that either the application of mandamus or use of a specific Bill could not be guaranteed to ensure obedience by LEAs. The final outcome might be that 'another government may settle it with a rougher hand' and could use disaffection with the religious difficulty to exclude religious instruction from schools during school hours. The prevention of such a possibility, he thought, could come from the Church adopting a more lenient attitude and accepting 'general religious teaching in all schools, and special dogmatic religious teaching in all schools where it was wanted'. This would require supplementary legislation along the lines of a concordat, including making the Act adoptive. The contents of such a measure would include Church schools being transferred to LEAs on payment of a rent and undenominational religious teaching being given in all schools, council and voluntary, except in those schools where denominational instruction was desired by the parents. In such instances, the instruction would be given within school hours but would be paid for by the denomination.

Davidson saw Anson's missive rather as a more formal proposal than a private letter and conceded that the Church would be prepared to accept some measure should the government believe it necessary 'for the national peace and well-being'. As far as Anson's proposed measure was concerned, he would personally accept it 'loyally but reluctantly' although he believed that a great many of the Church's clergy would oppose it. Anson replied by indicating that the Church was not the only body to be considered in achieving the necessary concordat with the LEAs and hinted that the legislation he had proposed might be a definite possibility.[60] Morant, alarmed by this apparent *volte face* on Anson's part, warned Davidson not to take Anson's views too seriously, claiming that his political superior was unaware of parliamentary difficulties and possibilities and 'quaintly innocent of the present parliamentary situation in *other* matters'.[61] He tried to make light of Anson's proposals by claiming that they merely represented, like all Anson's conversations, an attempt to clarify his mind and ascertain, in the abstract, how matters stood. He added that Anson had been 'very much overdone' before he left for a brief holiday in the south of France and had had, consequently, to 'unload himself' before his departure. What Morant wanted was half an hour's talk with the Archbishop, especially in view of Lloyd George's recent declaration against 'inside facilities' (that is, religious teaching in school hours), so that they could begin formulating 'what is possible and best'.[62]

Lloyd George's declaration about facilities had been made to a meeting of the Caernarvon Liberal Association five days earlier. Directing attention towards the forthcoming triennial council elections in March, he had argued that the days of a possible concordat had passed and the need now was to obtain substantial Liberal majorities in every Welsh county council. These comments were designed to distance himself publicly from the revelations about the Westminster Palace Hotel conference agreements recently published in an article by the Bishop of St. Asaph, not least the one about teachers providing denominational instruction in council schools.[63] The article, Lloyd George said, 'might be misunderstood'. At the same time he was careful to acknowledge, as a result of warnings from other Liberal MPs, the efforts of English Nonconformists in their campaigns against the Act and he highlighted what their plight might be if the Church's demands for 'inside facilities' were accepted.[64] Lloyd George knew that negotiations had recently been started by the Duke of Devonshire with the Liberal MP Lord Charles Spencer towards achieving a compromise on education, including such facilities. Thus, while the language and content of his speech was a rallying cry for his audience before the crucial local elections, it also demonstrated the point he had made to the new Liberal MP Winston Churchill a few days earlier that he had to knock on the head any idea which he knew would not have the support of his people, and that included 'inside facilities'. But he had also told Churchill privately that he still accepted the compromises reached at the Westminster Palace Hotel meeting although the chance of these being accepted was diminishing rapidly.[65]

After his return from France, Anson had an interview with J.S. Brownrigg, the Secretary of the National Society, with Morant in attendance. Their discussions revolved around the legal opinion obtained by the Society concerning the possibility of it being able to take legal action against Carmarthenshire County Council, on behalf of the voluntary schools in the area. Anson was quite insistent that the Society should proceed without delay to arrange for a test case to be brought against the Council, and a week later the Society's Standing Committee agreed to this request.[66] In the interim, Anson had asked the Board to carry out a survey on the conditions and degree of implementation of the Act in Wales. He had then written to Carmarthenshire County Council stating the nature of the complaints made against it and the problems arising from its treatment of the voluntary schools in violation of Sections 6(2) and 7(1) of the Act. The council was asked to give its consideration to these complaints and provide a reply. The council decided, in turn, to postpone any decision or reply until its next meeting on 17 March – after the local authority elections.

The landslide victories by the Progressives (Liberals) in the Welsh elections, with their candidates gaining majorities in all the councils, were seen as a triumph for Lloyd George's campaign as well as an indication that the rebellion would continue. But at a meeting with English Nonconformist leaders shortly after the completion of the elections, Lloyd George found himself being taken to task over the Westminster Palace Hotel Conference agreements. He was told in no uncertain terms that no compromise could exist over religious teaching in council schools as such a step would cause the dissenters to lose heart.[67] Somewhat chastened by this, Lloyd George's next step was to move for a reduction in the Education Vote in the Estimates debates a fortnight later and to dispute Anson's comments of the previous year that the Act was working without friction. Claiming that Wales was probably the most law-abiding part of the King's dominions, Lloyd George stated that the Welsh rebellion was neither an outbreak of anarchy nor a desire to break the law but rather 'a strong and emphatic protest against an Act which they considered to be unfair'.[68] Once more he pleaded the case for a compromise, although in making it he could not resist an indirect jibe at Balfour who had once replied, when asked for his views on Tariff Reform, that he had no settled convictions on the subject:

> Did the Secretary to the Board of Education really think that, having regard to the state of public opinion, this was a case in which he should proceed to extremities? Was it not rather a case in which a broad and statesmanlike view should be taken, and an attempt made to effect a settlement? These gentlemen in Wales had taken a conscientious stand, and it was as difficult to persuade men with strong convictions on a particular subject to abandon their position as to persuade a Government with no settled convictions on any subject to abandon its position.[69]

All that was required, he continued, was an amending Bill. Unexpected support for this plea came from Gorst who highlighted one of the ironies of the conflict between the Board and the Welsh when he pointed out that the underlying principle of the 1902 Act was decentralisation, one which the Welsh had welcomed from the start and were now implementing. But although he was prepared to support the case for an amendment to the Act, he was highly critical of the disruption to the education of the children in the Welsh schools being caused by the Welsh councils in their pursuit of such an amendment. Having made this point, Gorst went on to advocate the establishment of a concordat between the LEAs, the Church and the Board as a temporary solution and felt bound to congratulate Lloyd George on his earlier attempts to achieve this.[70]

Lloyd George's advocacy of an amending Bill was based on the knowledge that the Bishop of St. Asaph intended to introduce such a measure in the Lords, a move which had received Morant's support.[71] But the day after the Commons debate the Cabinet accepted a defaulting authorities Bill drafted by Balfour and agreed to its introduction after the Easter recess.[72] The Bill was designed to allow the Board of Education to fund voluntary schools directly from the parliamentary grant, the sums involved being deducted from the amount paid to the LEA. The Bill did not, however, override the 1902 Act or prevent LEAs from implementing it but it did give the Board the power to appoint managers and approve the employment of teachers. Furthermore, its appearance marked Balfour's determination to try and halt Lloyd George's campaign and successes against 'his' Act. And a few days later the Board of Education moved onto the offensive by instituting a public inquiry into the educational role of Carmarthenshire County Council, under the chairmanship of A.T. Lawrence, KC.

Lawrence, supported by Claud Schuster and R.P. Hills from the Board's legal department, listened to the case of the 48 voluntary schools who had complained to the Board about the Council's actions. The schools were represented by John Rawlinson, KC, and Edwardes Jones, lawyers appointed by the National Society, while the Council were represented by Abel Thomas, KC (the leader of the Welsh MPs in the Commons) and Llewellyn Williams. The charges brought against the Council by Rawlinson were that as the LEA, it had failed to be responsible for, or to control, secular instruction in the voluntary schools; it had not appointed the manager/s for these schools; it had not maintained or kept efficient the schools, nor had it controlled the expenditure needed for this purpose and it had withheld its consent to the appointment of teachers on non-educational grounds.[73] Throughout the inquiry Thomas failed to respond to the charges, claiming that there had not been sufficient time for the Council to have collected all the relevant evidence. This point made little impression on Lawrence and at the end of the two days he found the Council guilty on all four counts. The way was now clear, if the Board wished, to apply mandamus. The government remained committed, however, to their earlier decision and on 26 April, one week after Lawrence's report of the inquiry was published, the Education (Local Authorities Default) Bill was introduced into the House. Although essentially a one-clause measure, the Bill did not reach the Statute Book until 15 August and this slow progress provided the Welsh LEAs with time to contemplate their opposition to the Act. Similarly, the Board did not hasten into action against Carmarthenshire with the application of an order for the costs of the public inquiry.

Hills noted that with the introduction of the Bill and the findings of the inquiry there was a change of policy among some of the Welsh authorities, their decision being that they would drop the Carmarthen plan and adopt instead the Caernarvon scheme, and thereby evade the Default Bill. He told Morant, in response to Lloyd George's claim that it was only Carmarthenshire which had broken the law, that 'we could have held Public Inquiries about other Councils in Wales and obtained a report nearly as strong as that of Mr Lawrence'.[74] Carmarthen had been chosen because it was easy to prove the resolutions made by the council before committing illegal actions under the Act. More importantly, Caernarvon had also carried out illegal activities in their implementation of the Act, and the Board, well aware of this, could raise the issue whenever they wanted. But at the time of Hills's note the Bill was still in the Commons and the Board still lacked the powers necessary to aid the voluntary schools in Wales. When they did gain them, Lloyd George had not only seen St. Asaph's Bill rejected by the Lords but had also been elected chairman of the executive committee of the Welsh county councils. His policy would now be one of non-co-operation if the Default Bill was applied:

> Let Mr Morant schedule Caernarvonshire as a proclaimed area and declare its Council in default. The first thing we will do will be to get the managers of the seventy or eighty council schools to resign. The Education Committee of the council will resign en bloc. The whole administration of Education in Caernarvonshire will rest with Mr Morant and eighty of the schools will be without managers.[75]

Welsh matters suddenly became the focus of attention in the national press and at the centre was Lloyd George. He angrily repudiated the comments attributed to him in what had supposedly been a secret meeting and his rhetoric increased in subsequent public meetings, as did his denunciations of Morant. Privately Lloyd George was keenly aware that while he still hoped to bring about disestablishment in Wales, the way in which the campaign for achieving this was developing was putting his future career in jeopardy, given that there was the possibility before him of 'a responsibility for law and order in the near future' should the Liberals win the next election.[76] In this frame of mind he asked Bishop Edwards if he would arrange a secret meeting with Morant. Edwards complied and the meeting was arranged for 19 September.

Informing Balfour of the forthcoming meeting, at which Anson would also be present, Morant felt he had to brief him fully on all the issues at stake since he believed that the situation was not only 'extremely serious' but one that

> . . . deserves very much more careful and full consideration, if I may say so, from the whole Government point of view, not to mention its party aspect, than it has yet received, and than Anson seems capable, from his limited experience of giving it.[77]

He felt that Lloyd George appeared to acknowledge, in asking for the meeting, that his campaign was viable only in the short term. If the government stayed in office for another year, or longer, then all the signs were that the campaign could not be maintained. Morant was convinced that the '*real* objection' of the Welsh to the Default Act was that it exposed

> the sham which was being kept up – I mean the pretence that the Education Act was being observed in the letter, as Lloyd George was continually asserting, when of course nothing of the kind was the case.[78]

Morant's points notwithstanding, there still remained the very real problems in Wales of the plight of the voluntary schools as well as the possible consequences of the threatened retaliation of the LEAs to implementation of the Default Act. Their existence meant that the Board, and the government, were still facing the same policy decision they faced a year ago: to fight or compromise.

Londonderry was not at all happy with the idea of the meeting with Lloyd George but Anson reasoned that Lloyd George and the bishop had formulated another attempt at reaching a compromise and wanted to know not only if what they proposed was legal but also whether it would require legislation and if the Board 'could or would assist in the administration' of such a scheme. Anson firmly believed that, as a government department, the Board was bound to supply this information. He bluntly told Londonderry: 'I think you would not hesitate if Lord Spencer and the Bishop of Peterborough were the persons concerned' although he did acknowledge that Lloyd George would probably try to discover the government's intentions as to implementation of the Default Act. He was confident that he (Anson) would be better than Morant at 'limiting the scope of the conversation and refusing to allow certain things to be discussed in your absence'. None the less, Anson felt it was important that Lloyd George should leave the meeting clearly aware of the fact 'before the Welsh Councils take any irrevocable step' that the Default Act could not be applied to council schools.[79]

No record of the meeting exists but in his report to Balfour, Morant stressed a new problem which had emerged, namely that the Free Church Council had decided to become involved in the Welsh affair. This should not have been surprising given their promise of financial support for Lloyd George's campaign a few days earlier. But the problem arising from the council's decision was that it threatened the chance of a compromise being achieved in Wales owing to its total opposition to any denominational teaching being given in council schools, either in or out of school hours. A meeting to be held in Cardiff on 6 October to co-ordinate resistance in Wales meant that Lloyd George would now 'certainly be forced to make very loud utterances, and that as Clifford and Perks MP are to make big speeches . . . very big threats will be enunciated, and in truth intended'.[80] For Morant the policy options remained the same after the meeting as before, that is 'whether the big fight, and no concordats, is the line now to play for, or whether even a victory, on this line, would be too dearly purchased, and a concordat therefore the preferable line'. Although he inclined towards the Church reaching some concordat before Christmas, since he believed the Board would be blamed for the consequences of implementation of the Default Act as well as being put under severe administrative strain by it, what he wanted above all was for the government to take a firm line and for Balfour to provide 'very definite moral support . . . otherwise Londonderry and Anson will frequently quail, or hesitate at crucial moments'.[81]

Balfour's reply was brief and to the point, his opening comment being 'We are apparently in for ticklish times over education'.[82] He extended an invitation to Morant to visit him at Whittingehame to discuss the matter further but indicated that he did not share Morant's assessment of the political situation. Nor was he overtly worried about the fate which might befall Welsh council schools if the LEAs went ahead with their threat for he was convinced that the ensuing parental indignation would be directed against 'the true authors of the evil'. His intention at this stage, therefore, was to fight. Morant acquiesced, adding, 'if only we strike at the right time, and continuously, we'll make a good account of it, one way or another'.[83] Balfour's cousin Jem, now Lord Salisbury, when shown the correspondence, wondered perceptively whether 'Anson is as weak as he [Morant] seems to suggest or merely that he himself is in a state of mind' and added, '. . . however the truth may lie unless they can command their nerves they are likely to make a mess of it'.[84]

Morant continued with his negative portrayal of Anson as disclosed in his report to Balfour of a meeting at the Board with him and Londonderry on 3 October:

> I spent this morning in driving into Anson the many points of real difficulty in regard to the question of putting into operation the Default Act. He had in mind only the plain direct points. It is what I may call the indirect points on which decisions are really difficult but necessary. By Friday next he will have thoroughly digested these points and will then produce them as his own with his own views upon then, and we shall then know more definitely what he really thinks on the whole situation instead of merely on a part (which is all he has hitherto had in mind).[85]

But these points apart, Morant still preferred the Church to seek a concordat and believed that in the meantime the government should delay implementation of the Default Act. He hoped that Balfour would consider this possibility 'before we actually strike the match'.

Salisbury believed Morant's report compared unfavourably with a letter from Anson to Balfour which he thought contained, 'a much better impression of sense and nerve than did Morant's'. He also concurred with Anson's view that the Default Act should not be applied except in cases of clear injustice and believed that this approach indicated the way in which the government could proceed. Salisbury postulated that inquiries should be made within a county with only a small number of distressed voluntary schools as to their condition. The Board would then 'place the enemy in the dilemma of either accepting the situation viz. defeat by the Default Act, or of destroying the whole machinery of education in the large majority of schools in order to prevent the exaction of a comparatively small sum of money on behalf of the minority (if possible the *small* minority) of schools'.[86] Balfour took on board his cousin's views when writing a memorandum in response to the joint one presented by Anson and Londonderry three days later.

The joint memorandum belied Morant's views of his political chiefs. Taking up the main points which had emerged from the speeches at Cardiff on 6 October, Anson and Londonderry saw Welsh LEA policy consisting of two forms of opposition to the Act. The first was the Caernarvon policy of only supporting the voluntary schools from the parliamentary grant whereas the second was the threatened resignation of LEAs and the abandonment of implementation of the 1902 Act if the Default Act was put into operation. Mindful of the difficulties which implementation of either policy, but especially the second, would cause for the organisers of the rebellion, Anson and Londonderry had no hesitation in recommending that the Default Act should be brought into operation, where required, 'with fearlessness and promptitude'. If the Act could be applied against a hostile LEA without involving any immediate charge on the funds owing to the LEA then, they believed, it would make it more difficult for the LEA to use the second policy.[87]

Balfour's response, made after further consultation with Morant, was rather milder in approach. He believed that the Default Act should be used but only where (i) the default of an LEA was proven and (ii) when there was no likelihood that the voluntary school would, in the interim, 'make terms with the enemy'. But before the Default Act was applied Balfour wanted the Board to 'privately and confidentially' survey the situation and estimate which cases should be used for the initial application of the Act. Where Balfour differed from his cousin's approach was that he wanted the Board's inquiries to cover the whole of Wales while the Default Act would be implemented in a similar fashion, that is throughout the Principality. But, he warned, the government had to be sure that in each instance of application of the Default Act, it was made only after a thorough investigation. He remained convinced that if the LEAs tried to resort to the 'abandonment' policy they would receive little support from parents. The rebels would, he argued, 'either have to admit themselves defeated or to stand convicted of producing the greatest amount of general confusion on the flimsiest of all possible pretexts'. Balfour also made the important observation that Lloyd George had overlooked other breaches of the 1902 Act by the Welsh LEAs which did not involve finance. He wanted the Board to pursue these, albeit concentrating in the first instance on those cases which were 'as little technical in their character as possible, and appeal to the plain man in the most obvious way'.[88] He believed that the rebels should be fought 'simultaneously on these two separate lines of attack, and in more than one county at a time'. In concession to Morant's views, Balfour was willing to postpone the start of the campaign until the bishops and archbishops had met on 25 October. Balfour decided, therefore, not to circulate his paper to all the Cabinet but rather to a few selected members. Lord Selborne supported the plan as did Lord Salisbury, the latter conceding that he was not only converted to the blanket approach but also believed it to be a great improvement on his own proposal.[89]

Balfour wanted the meeting of the Church's leaders to be quite clear about the government's view of the situation in Wales, and he authorised Morant to make contact with the Archbishop of Canterbury. Knowing Morant's views, Anson wrote to the archbishop, this time arguing the case for the Church rejecting a concordat. He acknowledged that at the end of 1903 he had held the opposite view but he now believed that the current situation not only no longer warranted such an approach but also indicated that the Church would be making a fundamental error in even contemplating a concordat. The solution was to allow the application of the Default Act, for it would reveal the Welsh threats to be empty, but in order to achieve this, cases involving specific schools were required by the Board and he hoped that the Welsh bishops would not interfere to prevent managers from making such complaints.[90] The archbishop discovered, however, that the bishops were unwilling to contemplate a concordat on the issue of religious teaching in schools yet, at the same time, there appeared to be decided resistance to any implementation of the Default Act, especially in Wales. The view presented by the bishops was that churchmen in Wales were prepared to turn the other cheek and to accept 'without undue wrath, even unreasonable treatment' by the LEAs provided the treatment did not reach 'the point of outrageous wrong' to either the teachers or the pupils. If the Default Act had to be applied then the consensus was that it should be in the West Riding of Yorkshire.[91] As in 1896 and 1902, the Church had failed once more to support the government which was acting ostensibly on its behalf.

Fortunately for the government there appeared to be signs that the unanimity of the Welsh rebels was weakening in the face of its aggressive stance. Lord Cawdor informed Balfour that the passing of the Default Act was having an effect upon some of the LEAs since

Pembrokeshire was on the verge of rescinding its 'no rate for non-provided schools' resolution while Carmarthenshire was becoming more reasonable in its treatment of the voluntary schools. He believed the general feeling among the more moderate Radicals now was

> merely to save their face as much as possible as to the foolish Resolution they have been pushing – and in a little time fairly to administer the Act. . . . It is really quite amusing to note how very careful the Local Authorities are not to do anything they think can possibly bring them into Default![92]

By December Lord Reay was telling Campbell-Bannerman that Lloyd George's campaign was no longer a success not least because the schoolteachers opposed him.[93] These views notwithstanding, there were still many LEAs in a recalcitrant frame of mind, including Glamorgan and Merionethshire, and Lloyd George had no intention of giving up the fight. At the beginning of 1905 his view of the situation was decidedly roseate, and he told his brother William that there was 'a prospect of a truce *on our terms* in relation to the Education Act struggle in Wales'.[94] He was fully aware that the Board had still not applied the Default Act but he also knew of the efforts being made by H.R. Reichel, Principal of the University College of Wales in Bangor, to establish a national conference in Wales on the rebellion.

Reichel was acting on behalf of the university as convenor of the conference and Lloyd George had agreed to the idea, suggesting six men to represent the LEAs and to match the six Church representatives chosen by Lord Kenyon and Reichel.[95] When the *Manchester Guardian* hinted that the state of affairs might change in the near future *vis-à-vis* implementation of the Default Act, Anson received an urgent plea from Reichel asking him to delay any possible implementation of the Act until at least after the conference. Morant was sceptical, believing that Reichel 'though too good a fellow to *realise* it' had been set up by someone who wanted, in Lloyd George's interest, the Board to be delayed in applying the Act. He added, 'Of course, we can't' and Anson forwarded a similar reply to Reichel.[96] Reichel pressed for a few weeks' grace, pointing out that a few days' difference would not prevent the voluntary schools from receiving their funding either as a result of the conference or, if it failed, through the application of the Default Act. He stated that perhaps educationists should now be allowed to try to resolve the conflict which had entered its third year. To reinforce his point he highlighted the fact that what was being established by the conference was the first fairly representative meeting for the whole of Wales. Furthermore, the invitations had already been sent out over the signatures of the Vice Chancellor and Deputy Chancellors of the University to the six Church representatives, that is the three bishops (the Bishop of Llandaff had just died), Lords Cawdor and Kenyon, the Hon. Lawrence Brodrick and Charles Lloyd and to the six representatives chosen by Lloyd George. These were J.E. Grieves (Lord Lieutenant of Caernarvon), Herbert Lewis MP, Frank Edwards MP, Alderman T.J. Hughes, Councillor Tutton and Lloyd George. John Rhys and Sir John Williams had been invited as 'neutrophils' while Tom John, Vice President of the NUT, had also been asked to attend.

Reichel supported his plea for tolerance by providing an analysis of the current situation in Wales, making the point that perhaps the Board were being misled by the response of South Wales to the passing of the Default Act. Stating that while in the south of the country Lloyd George's policy might be largely bluff this was not the case in the north where it was 'serious business'. Parents in the southern counties, and especially in the industrial areas, were not as tied to the chapel as their northern counterparts. There was, consequently, less likelihood of southern parents obeying any order from Nonconformists to withdraw their children from the school. But Lloyd George's scheme had originated in the north and there the chapels could, if they wished, call out two-thirds to three-quarters of the children from the schools. Thus, while it was true that the southern areas had been 'half badgered and half wheedled' into accepting the scheme, if the Board applied the Default Act in the north there was every likelihood that what the Board feared most, the 'abandonment' campaign, would be put into effect.[97] Anson heeded this advice and it was not until March that the Board decided to proceed with its policy, after Reichel's conference had failed to achieve a solution.

The Board's first step was to institute an inquiry at Barry in Glamorgan about the LEA's reduction of the salary of the teacher in the sole voluntary (Roman Catholic) school from £150 to £100 after the 1904 council elections. The grounds for the Board's inquiry were dubious, for although the teacher's salary was now less than that of the council school teachers the latter were paid above the national average. Schuster had voiced his concerns before the Board established the inquiry but was overruled and sent to carry it out by Anson. Lloyd George had visited Barry earlier to try to persuade the Labour leaders to support the council but he found them a very intractable crowd – aggressive, hostile to nonconformity in general and to Welsh nonconformity in particular . . . . Some of them Catholics. After much talk, and more patient silence, I made some progress towards disarming them.[98]

He left, convinced that the council would not yield to the Board. In the event, Schuster found against the LEA on six grounds, including differential treatment for non-educational reasons. Anson and Morant did not hesitate to confirm his findings and, contrary to Lloyd George's belief, the council did rescind their decision although at no stage in the inquiry, or subsequently, was the threat of implementing the Default Act made by the Board. The mere existence of the Act, however, was not sufficient to prevent Merionethshire, one of the northern LEAs, from withholding the salaries for all voluntary school teachers since April on the pretext that the voluntary school buildings were defective.

The council's action had followed a very unsatisfactory meeting of their deputation with Londonderry, Anson and Morant in the House of Commons in March. The invitation from the Board to Merionethshire to send the deputation was taken as a sign by Lloyd George that the Board's resolve was faltering. But after listening to their claim that they were not in default of the 1902 Act, Londonderry asked the chairman of the county's education committee whether the disrepair of the voluntary schools was the sole reason for the LEA's action. When he received no reply Londonderry indicated the meeting was ended but the counsel for the committee tried to prolong it, yet refused to answer a subsequent question about the LEA's policy concerning voluntary schools. At this point Londonderry quit the meeting, declaring: 'It seems to be hopeless to expect a definite answer to a definite question'.[99] A response was forthcoming, however, five days later when a meeting of Welsh MPs, the executive committee of the Welsh county councils and the principal Nonconformist organisations was held in Shrewsbury to organise a *Sul y Casgliad* (Sunday collection) to raise £10,000 towards the campaign. After hearing Lloyd George support Merionethshire and pledge his continuance of the campaign, the meeting passed a resolution supporting both him and the county's action.[100] Three days later, the Board announced that £2000 would be withheld from the government grant to Merionethshire and although by mid-April actual implementation of this decision had not been made a meeting of Free Church and county council delegates was held at Bala on 2 May.

The meeting approved Merioneth's policy of not providing rate support for voluntary schools not under public control. Plans to implement the abandonment policy in the county were formulated, including asking Nonconformist parents to withdraw their children from the voluntary schools, and it was resolved that the Merionethshire LEA should go on strike, after arranging for emergency schools to be set up. A national fund-raising campaign was established to support the LEA. Lloyd George spurred the meeting on by making the point that with the religious revival currently being experienced in the Principality the nation would view

> with an intensified repugnance an institution that enforces the great duty of teaching religions by the machinery of Coercion Acts, Writs of Mandamus, County Court warrants and the squalid weapons of the process server and the Police Court . . . The present *Diwygiad* [revival] will make the people of Wales stronger to encounter the children of Amalek encamped in Whitehall . . .[101]

By the summer, several thousand pounds had been collected as a result of the campaign, Lord Rendel being one of the first subscribers with a gift of £500. Some of the money was used in Merioneth so that when the Board actually applied the Default Act against the authority in September 1905 the council could implement the abandonment policy. All the Liberal members of the education committee withdrew from the committee and the county council refused to accept any of the reports provided subsequently by the rump of the committee run by the Conservative minority. By the time Parliament rose in August, the Board was still not in control of the situation and was faced with having to consider applying mandamus. But it was also becoming apparent to Lloyd George and his allies that all was not in their favour. Montgomeryshire were getting ready to refuse to implement the 1902 Act but as the education committee was the county council their mass resignation from the committee would pose almost intractable problems.[102] Furthermore, the campaign funds were clearly insufficient to maintain any single LEA operating an alternative education system for any substantial period of time.[103] This seemingly difficult situation for both the Board and the Welsh rebels appeared to be resolved by the resignation of Balfour's government in early December.

The advent of Campbell-Bannerman's Liberal government did not persuade Merionethshire to relent, however, and resolution of this particular affair became one of the first tasks of the newly created Welsh Department of the Board of Education in 1907 with the final appeals being decided by the Lords in 1911.[104] But most Welsh LEAs accepted the reality of the situation *vis-à-vis* the 1902 Act which the failure of the 1906 Education Bill forced upon them and set about implementing it in full. In the final analysis, then, Morant and Balfour appeared to be the victors in so far as there was eventually implementation of their educational policy in the two nations. But this victory was not a consequence of their policies to defeat the Welsh. Here both men had met their match in Lloyd George and for both of them their success was to be tempered by personal defeat, Balfour's at the hands of the electorate in 1906 and Morant's at the hands of the teachers and Liberals in 1911. For Morant perhaps the ultimate irony of the whole affair was that when he was forced to quit the Board of Education in 1911 he became chairman of the National Insurance Commission and his political superior was David Lloyd George, now Chancellor of the Exchequer. To some extent their new relationship reflected the fact that if anyone had emerged victorious from the rebellion it was Lloyd George. At the same time it must be recognised that ultimately the rebellion was a failure. Although it committed the new Liberal government to attempts to redress the perceived imbalances of the 1902 Act, the forces that the rebellion had successfully harnessed were to prove insufficient to achieve the necessary amendments in the face of determined opposition from Balfour and the House of Lords. As Pierce has observed, the rebellion could not be construed as the 'high peak of expression of the nonconformist conscience but rather a stage in its decline as a "relevant" force in changing social and political circumstance'.[105]

NOTES

1. *The Times*, 8 Nov. 1894, cited in P. Marsh, *The Discipline of Popular Government: Lord Salisbury's Domestic Statecraft 1881–1902* (1978), p. 224.
2. B.M. Allen, *William Garnett: A Memoir* (1933), p. 107.
3. M. Bentley, *Politics without Democracy, 1815–1914* (1984), p. 356.
4. Passfield Papers, Folio II.4b,114f, J.E. Gorst to S. Webb, 24 June 1902.
5. Sidney Webb to Graham Wallas, 4 Dec. 1902 cited in N. Mackenzie (ed.), *The Letters of Sidney and Beatrice Webb* (1978), II, p. 174.
6. B. Webb, *Diary*, 22, pp. 2143–4, 25 April 1902.
7. Passfield Papers, Folio II.4b,114f, J.E. Gorst to S. Webb, 24 June 1902.
8. Viscount Gladstone Papers, Add MS 46060, fos. 84–5, W.H. Dickinson to H. Gladstone, 26 Nov. 1902.
9. B. Webb, op. cit., 23, p. 2173, 28 Nov. 1902.
10. Ibid., p. 2177, Dec. 1902.
11. S. Webb to G. Wallas, 14 Dec. 1902 in Mackenzie, op. cit., p. 175.

12. B. Webb, op. cit., p. 2187, 16 Jan. 1903.
13. BP Add MS 49832, fos. 145–6, E. Sidgwick to A.J. Balfour, 29 Jan. 1903.
14. S. Webb to E. Pease, 5 Feb. 1903 cited in Mackenzie, op. cit.,p. 182.
15. Ibid., 13 Feb. 1903.
16. B. Webb, op. cit., p. 2190, 25 Feb. 1903.
17. Ibid., p. 2192, 14 March 1903.
18. Allen, op. cit., pp. 122–4. Allen credits Garnett's action with having secured the LCC as the LEA but completely ignores the disastrous effect it had both on Webb's position and the government's attitude to the LCC.
19. B. Webb, op. cit., pp. 2196–8, 27 March 1903.
20. Ibid., p. 2199, 3 April 1903.
21. PRO ED 24/590, London County Council, 'Report of the Parliamentary Committee', 23 April 1903, p. 2.
22. B. Webb, op. cit., p. 2200, (?7) April 1903.
23. Browning Papers, OB1/580, S.S.F. Fletcher to O. Browning, 11 April 1903; *Manchester Guardian*, 8 April 1903, p. 4.
24. B. Webb, op. cit., p. 2200, (?7 April) 1903.
25. A. FitzRoy, *Memoirs* (1927), 1, p. 128.
26. B. Webb, op. cit., p. 2201, 29 April 1903.
27. PRO ED 24/590, W. Walrond, Memorandum, 3 May 1903.
28. A.S.T. Griffith-Boscawen, *Fourteen Years in Parliament* (1907), p. 262.
29. Fitzroy, op. cit., p. 133.
30. B. Webb, op. cit., 24, p. 2209, 15 June 1903.
31. S. Webb to E.Pease, 28 Aug. 1903; S. Webb to G. Wallas, 4 Sept. 1903 cited in Mackenzie, op. cit.,pp. 192–193.
32. G.I.T. Machin, *Politics and the Churches in Great Britain 1869 to 1921* (1987), p. 265. See also D.R. Pugh, 'English Nonconformity, education and passive resistance 1903–6', *History of Education*, 19, 4 (1990), pp. 355–73.
33. G.W. Kekewich, 'The Amendment of the Education Acts', *Contemporary Review*, LXXXIV (Oct. 1903), p. 459.
34. *School Government Chronicle*, 69 (20 June 1903), p. 532.
35. D.R. Pugh, op. cit., pp. 361–2.
36. 'Mr Balfour and the "Passive Resistance" Movement', *School Government Chronicle*, 70 (4 July 1903), p. 16.
37. Londonderry Papers, D/Lo/F/552, *Newcastle Journal* (14 Sept. 1903).
38. PRO ED 111/254 cited in L. Wynne Evans, *Studies in Welsh Education: Welsh Educational Structure and Administration 1880–1925* (1974), p. 118. See also G.O. Pierce. 'The "Coercion of Wales", Act, 1904' in H. Hearder and H.R. Loyn (eds), *British Government and Administration: Studies Presented to S.B. Chrimes* (Cardiff 1974), pp. 215–33.
39. *4 PD*, 115, c.1170–80, 3 Dec. 1902.
40. B.B. Gilbert, *David Lloyd George, a Political Life : The Architect of Change 1863–1912* (1987), pp. 231–2.
41. D. Lloyd George, speech at Cardiff, 21 Jan. 1903 cited in J. Grigg, *Lloyd George, The People's Champion 1902–1911* (1978), p. 41.
42. W.R.P. George, *Lloyd George: Backbencher* (1983), p. 373.
43. D. Lloyd George to W. George, 10 Feb. 1903 cited in W.R.P. George, op. cit., p. 374.
44. Ibid., p. 377, 16 April 1903.
45. PRO ED 111/252, R.J.G. Mayor to H.W. Hoare and H.M. Lindsell, 26 May 1903 cited in Wynne Evans, op. cit., p. 121.

46. PRO ED 24/1907, Memorandum by A. MacMorran K.C., 'Cambridgeshire County Council and the maintenance of non-provided schools out of the rates', 2 Feb. 1904.
47. S. Webb to G. Wallas, 4 Sept. 1903 cited in MacKenzie, op. cit., p. 193.
48. PRO ED24/1906, R.P. H[ills], 'Memorandum on the Defaulting Authorities Bill', June 1904, p. 4; Pierce, op. cit., pp. 218–19.
49. Ibid., pp. 3–4.
50. Ibid., p. 5.
51. BP Add MS 49761, fos. 123–33, J.S. Sandars to A.J. Balfour, 15 Oct. 1903. One obituary of Londonderry claimed that his role as a Minister reflected the character he had established when Irish Viceroy – 'that of an amiable well-intentioned, and painstaking titular chief, who was well content on the whole to leave the initiation as well as the development and explanation of matters of policy to more energetic minds'. *Manchester Guardian*, 9 Feb. 1915, cited in J. Diggle, 'A Study of the Ministers responsible for Education 1856–1944', unpublished M. Ed. thesis, University of Manchester, 1963, p. 268.
52. D. Lloyd George to W. George, 30 Oct. 1903 in W.R.P. George, op. cit., pp. 384–5.
53. Balfour (Whittingehame) Papers, GD 433/2, M122, J.S. Sandars to G. Balfour, 9 Nov. 1903.
54. Ibid., J.S. Sandars to G. Balfour, 21 Nov. 1903.
55. PRO CAB 37/67, Lord Londonderry, 'The Educational Situation in Wales', Cabinet Memorandum, 24 Nov. 1903.
56. PRO ED24/1906, R.P. H[ills], 'Memorandum on the Defaulting Authorities Bill', June 1904, p. 4.
57. Wynne Evans, op. cit., pp. 143–9.
58. PRO ED 24/1906, W. Anson Memorandum, n.d.
59. Archbishop R.T. Davidson Papers, Education Box 4, W. Anson to R.T. Davidson, 31 Dec. 1903.
60. Archbishop R.T. Davidson Papers, Education Box 4, R.T. Davidson to W. Anson, 2 Jan. 1904: W. Anson to R.T. Davidson, 5 Jan. 1904.
61. Morant was referring here to the aftermath of Chamberlain and Devonshire's resignations from the Cabinet over the issue of Tariff Reform.
62. Archbishop R.T. Davidson Papers, Education Box 4, R.L. Morant to R.T. Davidson, 10 Jan. 1904.
63. A.G. Asaph, 'Educational Concordats', *The Nineteenth Century and After*, LV (Jan. 1904), pp. 40–6.
64. *Manchester Guardian*, 6 Jan. 1904.
65. W.S. Churchill to Lord H. Cecil, 1 Jan. 1904 cited in Gilbert, op. cit., p. 242.
66. Archbishop R.T. Davidson Papers, Education Box 4, J.S. Brownrigg to Archbishop R.T. Davidson, 21 Jan. 1904.
67. R.W. Perks to Lord Rosebery, 1 April 1904 cited in Gilbert, op. cit., p. 244.
68. *4 PD*, 131, c.1005, 14 March 1904.
69. Ibid.
70. Ibid.
71. Gilbert, op. cit., p. 244.
72. PRO CAB 37/69, Lord Londonderry, Memorandum, 17 March 1904. Balfour's bill was based on the one originally submitted by Londonderry the previous November.
73. Wynne Evans, op. cit., p. 161.
74. PRO ED 24/1906, R.P. H[ills], 'Memorandum on the Defaulting Authorities

Bill', 25 June 1904, p. 22.
75. *The Times*, 10 Aug. 1904.
76. PRO ED 24/1906, R.P. H[ills], 'Memorandum on the Defaulting Authorities Bill', June 1904, p. 5.
77. BP Add MS 49787, fo. 100, R.L. Morant to A.J. Balfour, 17 Sept. 1904.
78. Ibid., fo. 97, R.L. Morant to A.J. Balfour, 17 Sept. 1904.
79. PRO ED 24/1590, W. Anson to Lord Londonderry, 18 Sept. 1904.
80. BP Add MS 49787, fo. 104, R.L. Morant to A.J. Balfour, 19 Sept. 1904.
81. Ibid., fo. 105, R.L. Morant to A.J. Balfour, 19 Sept. 1904.
82. Ibid., fo. 110, A.J. Balfour to R.L. Morant, 21 Sept. 1904.
83. Ibid., fo. 112, R.L. Morant to A.J. Balfour, 25 Sept. 1904.
84. BP Add MS 49757, fo. 323, Lord Salisbury to A.J. Balfour, 24 Sept. 1904.
85. BP Add MS 49787, fo. 114, R.L. Morant to A.J. Balfour, 3 Oct. 1904.
86. BP Add MS 49757, fos. 354–5, Lord Salisbury to A.J. Balfour, 4 Oct. 1904.
87. PRO CAB 37/72, 'The Situation in Wales', Memorandum by Lord Londonderry and Sir W. Anson, 7 Oct. 1904, p. 2.
88. Ibid., A.J. Balfour, 'Course to be pursued in connection with Welsh Education and the Defaulting Authorities Act', 9 Oct. 1904.
89. BP Add MS 49757, fos. 364–5, Lord Salisbury to A.J. Balfour, 20 Oct. 1904.
90. Archbishop R. Davidson Papers, Education Box 4, W. Anson to R.T. Davidson, 22 Oct. 1904.
91. PRO ED 24/590, Archbishop of Canterbury to R.L. Morant, 26 Oct. 1904.
92. Ibid., Lord Cawdor to A.J. Balfour, 26 Oct. 1904.
93. Campbell-Bannerman Papers, Add MS 41237, fos. 358–9, Lord Reay to Sir H. Campbell-Bannerman, 26 Dec. 1904.
94. D. Lloyd George to W. George, 13 Jan. 1905 cited in W.R.P. George, op. cit., p. 413.
95. PRO ED 24/590, H.R. Reichel to W. Anson, 8 Feb. 1905.
96. Ibid., R.L. Morant to W. Anson, 11 Feb. 1905.
97. Ibid., H.R. Reichel to W. Anson, 12 Feb. 1905.
98. D. Lloyd George to W.George, 18 Feb. 1905 cited in W.R.P. George, op. cit., p. 420.
99. *Manchester Guardian*, 29 March 1905.
100. Ibid.
101. W.R.P. George, op. cit., p. 426. The religious revival derived from the impact of the visionary Evan Roberts, an ex-miner, on the Principality from late 1904.
102. For a discussion of Montgomeryshire's position see G.E. Jones, 'The "Welsh Revolt" Revisited: Merioneth and Montgomeryshire in Default', *The Welsh History Review*, 14 (3, June 1989), pp. 417–38. See also Pierce, op. cit., pp. 229–31.
103. W.R.P. George, op. cit., pp. 442–3.
104. Gilbert, op. cit., p. 263.
105. Pierce, op. cit., p. 232.

9

The voice of the people?

The political advantages which accrued to the Liberal Party from the 1902 Education Bill were distinctly two-edged. Campbell-Bannerman's lack of interest in education has been noted already but it was offset by his awareness of the political significance of this particular measure and he had consistently supported Acland and Bryce in their endeavours to prime the most recent Liberal MPs about the Bill's contents and weaknesses while it was before the House. During the parliamentary recess he had received an estimate from Bryce that not only had the Bill contributed to the government being in a 'very shaky' state, with many Unionist MPs worried by the Nonconformist element in their constituencies, but there was very little evidence that the Bill could be passed as it stood and the government would have to modify it, drop it or be beaten.[1] He concurred with this assessment, condemning the Bill for trying 'to relieve Church funds while retaining Church supremacy'. What he believed was required was popular control of the nation's schools by directly elected representatives. As far as the problematical nature of the relationship between religion and elementary education was concerned, there had to be recognition that 'the people generally desire that in public schools there should be the minus of religious instruction'. If these premises were accepted, then the solution lay in one of three possibilities:

(a) an inoffensive dose of Christian doctrine in all State Schools; supplemented by peculiar teaching of tenets by the sects at separate hours;
(b) purely secular teaching in State Schools, supplemented as above;
(c) option to teach locally which of these should be applied.

He favoured option (b), believing that a statutory common creed was as wrong as a statutory specific creed but argued that the Board of Education should be able to resolve any overlapping of duties that might arise from the diversity of authorities which his options might produce. He was emboldened in his plan by the opinions expressed by the 'casual Tories' he had met recently:

281

> All . . . take our line. 'Why the . . . did they meddle with this hornet's nest? What the country wants is higher education and technical. Elementary was going on well enough. What tempted them to meddle with the School Boards?'

The party's campaign after the parliamentary recess, he believed, should be a denunciation of Balfour's scheme for local authorities and to take a bold line; 'carry the stalwarts with us; shame the weak kneed and frighten them; and then if beaten, what good ground we should be upon'.[2] Clearly buoyed by the political situation and outlook, Campbell-Bannerman was encouraged also by the unifying effect the measure was having upon his party while allowing some of the bitterness and divisiveness induced by the Boer War to dissipate.

By the time Parliament had embarked upon the autumn Session, however, Campbell-Bannerman was preoccupied with the poor health of his wife and was absent quite frequently from the House. His example was copied by others to such an extent that by the end of October 1902, when it became clear that the government were gradually acquiring more support for the Bill from their backbenchers, Lloyd George, Trevelyan, Hutton and nine other Liberal backbenchers petitioned him to exert his authority to ensure a more regular attendance by Liberal MPs, not least because of 'the immense advantage the party might reap from the popular dislike of the Bill'.[3] Their pleas appear to have had little effect and the mounting Nonconformist opposition to the Bill reflected not only discontent with the contents of the measure but also displeasure with the Liberal Party. As the Nonconformists mounted their campaign of passive resistance to the Act in 1903 one of their more moderate leaders, Guinness Rogers, issued a public warning about their

> . . . deep-rooted and intense dissatisfaction . . . [and] determination to have a larger representation of Nonconformity in Parliament . . . it would be rash and dangerous to prophesy smooth things as to the relations between the Nonconformists and the Liberal party.[4]

Campbell-Bannerman did acknowledge privately that this Nonconformist resistance meant that when a Liberal government came to power, there would have to be at least complete public control of the elementary schools and the abolition of religious tests for teachers.[5] But he was not to publicise these views until the autumn of 1905 when political events indicated that the remaining life of Balfour's government was likely to be brief. By then it was too late and, as will be seen, Guinness Rogers' prophecy was to prove correct; consequently the Liberal Party was to find itself encumbered by Nonconformist grievances and pressure about education for the following decade.

If the 1902 Act had helped, at least, to ameliorate conditions within the Liberal Party, as well as contributing to their political rapport with the Labour Party, it had had the reverse effect on the Unionist alliance. It appears to have been a determining factor in Chamberlain's decision to propound his policy of Tariff Reform, and the effects of the political reverberations produced by this policy upon Balfour's leadership have been well documented, not least his inability to prevent the dissolution of the Alliance and the collapse of his government's credibility. The failure of the government to address both fiscal and social issues successfully meant that by September 1905 consideration was being given in some quarters to the constitutional propriety of the government remaining in office. Balfour remained undeterred and held on to his position in order to allow the Conservative Party's organisation more time to marshal its forces for an election. A reprieve appeared to be offered when a schism appeared among the Liberals over the issue of Home Rule as a result of the advocacy by some party members of the need for political independence from the Irish Nationalists. Campbell-Bannerman's conciliatory speech at Stirling in November satisfied many within the party but provoked an angry public denunciation from Lord Rosebery of the party's apparent return to advocacy of a total Home Rule policy for Ireland. Balfour seized this moment to resign, apparently convinced that the current hiatus among the Liberals would not only affect the outcome of the general election but also ensure that any Liberal government returned to office would be flawed by the continuance of the old tensions within their party.[6]

Balfour's action on 4 December revealed a misjudgement of both the state of unity of the Liberal Party and the calibre of Campbell-Bannerman. The latter accepted the King's commission to form a government on 5 December and had soon formed it, quashing in the process a half-hearted attempt by Asquith, Haldane and Grey to consign him to the Lords. Campbell-Bannerman's government was seen by many as a strong one, not least because of the multi-talented nature of the office holders. In appointing Augustine Birrell as President of the Board of Education, however, the Prime Minister appeared to have overlooked the claims of stronger candidates including James Bryce, David Lloyd George and T.J. Macnamara, as well as Arthur Acland. While the latter had been offered the Presidency and a position in the

Lords unofficially by Herbert Gladstone during the period of Cabinet-making, for his part in overcoming the Regulas compact of Asquith, Grey and Haldane, Campbell-Bannerman had not authorised the offer nor did he choose to effect it. Bryce, despite his long support of Campbell-Bannerman, was seen by his leader as ineffectual in the Commons and he had decided that he should go to Ireland as Chief Secretary. Lloyd George's case was stronger for he had been one of the Liberals' most effective debaters against the 1902 Bill and had been closely involved with the Principality's successful opposition to the Act. Furthermore, he had been on the backbenches for more than a decade but Campbell-Bannerman was not impressed by his claims and only resignedly conceded to his inclusion in the Cabinet as President of the Board of Trade.[7]

As far as the presidency of the Board of Education was concerned, Campbell-Bannerman appears to have believed that 'anyone who was committed to the ideal of educational reform would be likely to support the underlying spirit of the 1902 Education Act' and would be unlikely, therefore, to willingly formulate legislation either to amend or replace the Act.[8] This effectively ruled out the otherwise logical choice of Dr T.J. Macnamara, and although he was offered the Parliamentary Secretaryship to the Board of Education he declined the offer, partly because of the problems generated during the Lloyd George-driven rebellion in Wales.[9] Birrell, on the other hand, although a writer, a barrister and the son of a Nonconformist preacher, was notable for his lack of serious involvement with, or substantial experience of, any facet of the education system. For the previous three years he had been the president of the National Liberal Federation and while this was a precedent similar to Acland's in 1892, when he was offered the vice presidency in Gladstone's government, it was perhaps this lack of educational involvement that was attractive to Campbell-Bannerman. The Premier's belief that the 'resolution of the religious question must precede educational reform' appeared to be confirmed by Birrell's subsequent election addresses.[10] They included as a dominant theme the hope that

> it would be possible to have in the public elementary schools of the country simple religious teaching for those who were content with it, and also to give facilities that those people who wanted more definite dogmatic instruction should have so that their children might enjoy the benefits of it – if it were a benefit to receive this dogmatic instruction.[11]

FitzRoy believed that the first day's results of the General Election 'sufficed to lay the rising hopes of the Unionist Party in the dust' and his prognosis proved to be correct.[12] By the end of the election, not only had 375 Liberals been returned compared with 157 Unionists, the remaining 137 seats having been won by Labour (54) and the Irish Nationalists, but Balfour had lost his seat and only three members of his government had managed to retain theirs. Reflecting on this overwhelming defeat, Balfour preferred to believe the result had nothing to do with his government's policies but was rather, 'a faint echo of the same movement which has produced massacres in St. Petersburg, riots in Vienna, and Socialist processions in Berlin. We always catch Continental diseases, though we usually take them mildly.'[13] Some of his colleagues thought otherwise, however. Sandars identified the causes of their defeat as being the swing of the electoral pendulum, 'arrested in 1900 only to come back the harder'; the issue of Chinese labour in South Africa; the organisational efforts of the socialists and, finally, the Nonconformists' activities in connection with education. Hicks Beach itemised, 'the general desire for a change: Chinese labour in the towns: Joe's corn duty in the agricultural counties: and the Education Act everywhere'.[14] This last point was reinforced by others, one noting:

> None who took part in the late elections, especially in Wales and the South of England, could fail to note the deep resentment in the minds of Nonconformists with regard to their treatment in the Act of 1902, nor their determination to secure a reversal of the policy which to them constituted an injustice of the gravest kind.[15]

Amendment of the Education Act had been the second most cited topic in Liberal Party candidates' election addresses, a feature consolidated by its occurrence in the addresses made by 79 per cent and 82 per cent of Labour Representative Committee and other socialist candidates, respectively.[16] But with the election campaign rhetoric over, the new government had to implement their promises and devise a remedy for the grievances of their supporters about the 1902 Act. The necessity to do so was reinforced by the presence in the new House of some 170 Nonconformist Members sitting on the Liberal benches.[17]

The persistent Nonconformist pressure for educational reform after 1902 had led to the appointment of an education committee at the first meeting of the Cabinet in December 1905. Chaired by Lord Crewe, the Lord President, the committee included Lloyd George, R.B.

Haldane (Secretary of State for War), Sir Henry Fowler (Chancellor of the Duchy of Lancaster) in addition to Birrell, with Morant as their secretary. At the committee's first meeting just before the election, Crewe proposed that the Bill they had to formulate should be a comprehensive measure so as to allow the key points of popular control and no religious tests for teachers to be cited as but components of a broader strategy for improving public education. His view was accepted by all except Sir Henry Fowler, but when the committee then considered how the 1902 Act's grievances could be actually redressed a wider divergence of views soon became apparent.

Crewe postulated that the creation of a national elementary school system in which there was only one type of school could be the means of achieving their goal, but Haldane, more sensitive to the political importance of the Roman Catholics, floated the idea of some schools remaining outside the new national system and receiving only parliamentary funding. This was not a novel idea, for Bryce had recognised the possibility of treating the Catholic schools separately from the Anglican ones during the passage of the 1902 Bill, given the significant differences in their denominational instruction, and had been fully aware of the political kudos which could result from such an approach, not least with the Irish MPs.[18] Despite this Lloyd George was quick to reject the idea because there would be no public control over such schools.

Crewe's proposal raised additional problems, not least how the privately owned elementary schools as well as the bulk of the currently 'non-provided' (voluntary) schools could be transferred into a new national system while ensuring that the government was not charged with the confiscation of property. Another problem arising in connection with such a transfer was whether the LEA-appointed managers would be bound by any applicable trust deeds as was the case under the current system, for if they were it would seriously hamper the establishment of a truly national, unsectarian education system. Birrell believed that any opposition from the churches, if the deeds had to be altered, could be mitigated by arranging that within the national system of schools religious instruction facilities could be given, albeit funded by the denomination concerned and also not as a component of the school curriculum. Yet another problem was the potential cost involved in the transfer of the voluntary schools, some of the committee feeling that the three-quarters of a million pounds which was likely to be required would provoke an outcry given that these schools were already part of the State system.[19] The complexity of the educational and political issues contained within these problems led Lloyd George and Birrell to meet Arthur Acland at the Metropole Hotel in Brighton after the election to try to clarify their views about them.

Lloyd George believed that the transfer of the voluntary schools should be made optional for the LEAs but compulsory if an LEA exercised that option. Birrell and Acland differed, only wanting compulsion in the case of those schools founded with National Society trust deeds or similar, that is where the school building was solely for the purpose of teaching children. On the related matter of financial compensation for the transfer, Lloyd George was the most generous of the three, advocating a rent to be paid by the LEAs in addition to full maintenance of the transferred schools. Birrell believed that the nation's current opposition to increased rate expenditure meant that it could be covered only by taxes. On the matter of religious facilities, Birrell remained true to his election comments whereas Lloyd George preferred that nothing specific should be included in the Bill, arguing that it would be insisted upon by the House of Lords. He was willing to entertain, however, the implementation of the 'colonial plan' whereby denominational teaching could be given on two days a week provided no teacher was forced to give the religious instruction.[20] It was this last point which came increasingly to dominate the committee's subsequent deliberations.

At the second committee meeting, Fowler reiterated his opposition to any large and expensive measure which would throw the nation's school system 'into the melting pot' and challenged his colleagues to indicate why a single-clause Bill only would not suffice. Crewe's response centred on his concerns about the abrogation of trust deeds but Fowler rebutted this with the claim that Church instruction in the transferred Church schools would satisfy the majority of moderate people. Lloyd George countered, in turn, that such an arrangement would not satisfy the Church unless there were equivalent facilities within all provided schools. When Fowler stated that this could be achieved by giving the facilities out of school hours, Crewe indicated that the Church would not accept this proposal. Alarmed by the possibility of obeisance towards the Church's views, Lloyd George told his colleagues that

> the Election had settled definitely that popular control must exist over all recognised schools, and that denominational teaching could not be provided out of the rates, nor permitted as part of the rate-provided curriculum.[21]

This was the sticking point for the government's Nonconformist supporters but also for the other religious bodies. When Birrell suggested leaving the matter to be decided by the House of Lords, Crewe pointed out that not only would this probably lead to the resignation of Lord Ripon (a prominent Catholic) from the Cabinet but that the Nonconformists would also object to the imposition of terms by the Lords. Furthermore, such an approach would be seen as a politically weak move by a majority government in its first Session.

Haldane attempted to secure some feeling of agreement by listing what appeared to be the irreducible minimum contents for the Bill. These were the absence of rate aid for schools not under public control after the enactment of the Bill; no denominational instruction in the rate-provided curriculum; the provision of denominational instruction in all schools in addition to Cowper-Temple religious teaching but at private cost, on two mornings per week and at the same time as the Cowper-Temple teaching; all teachers to be LEA appointees and not subject to religious tests. When Fowler interjected that he wished there were 'a strong Roman Catholic and a strong Anglican' on the committee, Crewe furnished a précis of Lord Ripon's opinions and the gulf between the committee's proposals and those of the Catholic community became abundantly clear.

The overarching Catholic stipulation was that there should only be Catholic teachers in Catholic schools. Although they were willing to surrender their schools in single school areas and would pay the cost of denominational instruction, they were not prepared to countenance Cowper-Temple teaching being given in all schools, that is those attended by Catholic children, nor would Catholic teachers be willing to give such teaching even though such a stance could possibly lead to their being debarred from teaching. Haldane proposed a concession, suggesting that in any school where 90 per cent of the parents did not want Cowper-Temple teaching, denominational instruction could be given, at the cost of the denomination, on each day of the school week, provided the LEA agreed. The only case where this should not be applied was in any school in a rural parish.[22] This concession and his list of other points gained general agreement and it looked as though progress was being achieved. The committee readily acquiesced, therefore, to a request submitted by Lord Ripon to be allowed to attend their next meeting believing that he would convey the Catholic Church's views about their proposals.

Much to the chagrin of the committee, Ripon gave only his personal views, not having bothered to consult the leaders of his Church.

FitzRoy, who had been able to observe the meeting in Crewe's room from his own, noted:

> As far as I could judge, he [Ripon] was talking incessantly, and emphasising his arguments with vehement facial contortions, swaying his body from side to side with an irregular motion which must have been very trying to his colleagues. Lloyd George was on his right and devoted himself to writing letters; one or two others whose faces were visible looked on with stupefaction.[23]

The key point made by Ripon in this singular manner was that the Catholic community wanted their children to be taught by Catholic teachers. When Fowler stated that he thought the committee had agreed to this point, Lloyd George emerged from his writing to oppose this notion vigorously since it would mean the continuation of religious tests for teachers. He reminded the committee of the concessions that had been agreed to already, including the payment of a rent and maintenance of the school fabric by the LEA for each voluntary school, facilities for denominational instruction on two mornings per week in both voluntary and LEA schools, as well as denominational instruction on each day of the week in 'four-fifths' schools. These, he argued, were sufficient and when Fowler observed, somewhat belatedly, that he thought it would be impossible to provide denominational facilities within provided schools, Birrell responded that if this proved to be the case then there would be no basis for a compromise. These points notwithstanding, attempts were made to bridge the gap between the Catholic and Nonconformist views with Crewe suggesting the possibility of moral pressure rather than any legal requirement under the Bill being brought to bear by Catholic parents on an LEA to ensure that there were Catholic teachers in Catholic schools. Lloyd George was not persuaded by this, stating that 'if such a thing were right at all, the Bill ought to require the Authority to do it and not leave it thus vague and optional, or attempt to mask it'.[24] The only possible solution suggested to this impasse was that the Bill should ensure that parents would have the right of recourse to a public inquiry, moderated by the Board of Education, should they feel their wishes were not being considered by their LEA.

The issue of denominational instruction in the schools continued to dominate the committee's subsequent meetings and included the question of provision of facilities by those LEAs whose schools did not provide religious instruction and in which secular instruction began, therefore, at 9am each day. Lloyd George wanted compulsory attendance when Cowper-Temple instruction was given, subject to operation of the conscience clause of the 1870 Education Act, but not on those mornings when facilities were being provided. Birrell and Crewe were worried that such a proposal could lead to the charge that the Bill was effectively introducing secular education, especially as the Church of England had indicated its willingness to consider any government's proposals provided they did not result in a purely secular system.[25] Crewe proposed that the issue should be left to the LEAs' discretion and this was accepted albeit with the rider that the conscience clause of the 1870 Education Act had to be interpreted so that compulsory attendance was not required during the time allotted for facilities. Although the committee agreed that it would be impossible to refuse the provision of facilities in rural schools if four-fifths of the parents requested them, they were not prepared to incorporate such a concession in the Bill until forced by pressure from the House.

At the end of their two months of discussions there were still points on which there was no agreement. Lloyd George was adamant that teachers should not be liable to give denominational instruction despite the fact that the exclusion of such a possibility would alienate the Roman Catholics. Consensus did not exist on the question of whether the owners of voluntary schools should be compensated if their schools contracted in to the State system. The issue of endowments and the possible codification of school attendance laws and elementary education acts generally, the last possibly requiring an extension of parliamentary time, were similarly not decided upon. Thus while the original aims for the Bill had been relatively simple, the complexity of devising a measure which would achieve this, yet be acceptable to all the interested parties, had not only taxed but also divided the committee. If Crewe had been the moving force in the early discussions, Lloyd George had emerged as the dominant member in the later stages and Birrell was notable only for his minimal contribution. He, on the other hand, had received numerous messages from interested individuals and organisations and in mid-February, when resolution of the outstanding problems was passed to the whole Cabinet, he took the opportunity to make his views known.

The Bill's policy was, he declared, 'to destroy once and for ever' the distinction between provided and non-provided schools so as to produce only one kind of elementary school, under complete popular control, with the teachers not subject to religious tests. The main problem before them, therefore, was how to provide accommodation for 3,500,000 children now in Non-Provided Schools without adding materially to the rates of the country or to the burdens already borne by the Exchequer.[26]

He believed that it was politically infeasible to expect rate money to be used to provide accommodation for these children so that the only possible practical solution required the use of some of the existing voluntary schools. To achieve this would require negotiation yet one corollary of using many of the Church of England schools would be the alteration of the schools' trusts. He argued that this would not be a disadvantage, for the trusts had already been altered under the 1902 Act and this Bill would complete 'the interference by removing the right to appoint the teacher, and thus finally destroys what was left of private management'. He did concede that achievement of these changes could only be through the means of some *quid pro quo* and this would have to be the granting of 'reasonable facilities' for denominational instruction in all the nation's elementary schools. Aware of the passions which would be aroused by this proposal, especially among the Nonconformists, Birrell warned his colleagues that when it came to be discussed in the House it would be 'one of the dangerous moments of the Bill'. He did believe, however, that the provision of facilities would go some way to pacifying opponents of the Bill in the Church, for the government could argue

> that in exchange for the right of use [of schools], we have allowed the Church Catechism to be taught as often as it ever was taught in a Voluntary School to *all* the children of the country whose parents express a desire to have it.[27]

On the issue of the Roman Catholic schools and teachers, Birrell thought the use of Haldane's four-fifths rule would be accepted by most LEAs but wondered whether the Catholics would 'wreck the whole scheme on this point'. None the less, the government could not ignore the Roman Catholic grievance given that the practical consequences of doing so were 'obvious enough'.

The Cabinet's reaction to these points was to request the production of a draft Bill including, where relevant, all possible options. This requirement meant that they did not start to consider the Bill in any detail until the end of February. When they did they concentrated on the first four clauses, the first two of which were accepted in principle without demur. Clause 3, providing 'ordinary' facilities for denominational instruction on two mornings a week and Cowper-Temple instruction during the remainder, was designed to cover most

291

Anglican schools but was seen as potentially difficult to implement yet was allowed to remain pending the preparation of a schedule. Clause 4, with its attempt to resolve the Catholic problem by the four-fifths majority rule yet allowing 'extended' facilities on each school day, provoked the greatest discussion. An alternative clause, allowing the four-fifths rule only in urban populations of more than 5,000, was adopted by a majority although Crewe thought the decision of 'doubtful wisdom' and Birrell was not happy with it.[28]

Clause 3 preoccupied the Cabinet for their next three meetings and progress was made towards settling the conditions under which non-provided schools could become provided. By 21 March, John Burns (President of the Local Government Board) gleefully recorded privately that there would be 'No facilities for Clericals' in any provided schools.[29] This drastic amendment of Birrell's *quid pro quo* meant that facilities would only be provided in transferred voluntary schools on two days a week and before school hours. In the provided schools only Cowper-Temple instruction would be given. The potential problems contained in these changes were due, Crewe told FitzRoy, to the Nonconformists:

> In return for their contribution to the ministerial majority, they seem determined to exact their pound of flesh, and make the Bill as crude a triumph for ultra-Nonconformity as the complaint is that the last Act was for the Anglican Episcopate. Lloyd George, who had accepted a compromise, is now pressing his colleagues to make large concessions, and the whole problem is still in the melting pot.[30]

Crewe's comment and Lloyd George's action were possibly occasioned by the recently published resolutions of the Free Churches Council which had stressed, in addition to supporting the concept of a national system of publicly provided and controlled elementary schools, in which the pupils would be taught by teachers not subjected to religious tests, the need for these schools to be completely free from any form of distinctive denominational instruction.

These last-minute problems irked not only Crewe and Birrell but also Morant, not least because he was not privy to the decision-making, telling Sir Samuel Provis, his counterpart in the Local Government Board, that it had been 'extremely difficult to gather from Birrell and Crewe what the Cabinet have decided on each occasion'.[31] The continuing conflict in the Cabinet over the details of the Bill led Birrell to repudiate, privately, the Bill as his own, claiming that it was

6 'Cerberus and his Sop': The President of the Board of Education, Augustine Birrell, addressing, from left to right, Redmond, Balfour and Bryce, representing the Roman Catholics, Anglicans and educationists respectively. (Cartoon in *Punch*, CXXX, 30 May 1906, p. 380)

'really Lloyd George's drafting forced on . . . [him] by a Cabinet majority'.[32] In this he was correct yet Lloyd George had made his intentions perfectly clear from the outset, having declared during the election that the Bill would 'redress the grievance which Welshmen felt most acutely – a grievance to their own free religion. It was going to establish religious equality in the schools'.[33] But of greater importance was the need to meet the declared needs of the Nonconformists for, the government had been warned by the Whips, any other possible course 'would result in defeat at the hands of their own supporters'.[34] Birrell did accept, however, his responsibility for piloting the Bill through the House although this worried Morant, at least ostensibly, for he told Crewe that Birrell seemed unable to appreciate

> . . . how awkward, indeed impossible, a situation will arise when he has to reply, in answer to questions across the floor at First or Second Reading . . . that he does not know, and cannot possibly foretell![35]

If this was not changed then, he claimed, the government was bound 'to be shipwrecked on the Bill'. In private he told Jack Sandars that 'Birrell does [?so] little work on the Education Bill, . . . that if we know our business we ought to give them a very bad time over the Bill'.[36]

Oblivious of these criticisms, Birrell introduced the Bill to a packed House on 9 April with a speech which pleased some of his listeners, John Morley finding it 'Most admirable! So rational, clear, persuasive, judicious, excellent strokes of humour' and John Burns held similar views.[37] One MP observed that the two Anglican archbishops watching from the gallery could not prevent themselves from smiling at some of the more brilliant passages in the speech, passages which helped to relieve the tension induced by the otherwise 'unpalatable plainness' of the policy being unfolded within the five main parts of the measure.[38] The first part dealt with the religious difficulty and the creation of a national system of elementary schools while the second covered the educational endowments involved in achieving these changes. Parts 3 and 5 contained miscellaneous and supplementary administrative provisions whereas Part 4 proposed to establish an education council for Wales. This part had been included at Lloyd George's insistence and was derived from negotiations he had been involved in with the previous government. The clauses relating to Part 1 of the Bill had so preoccupied Birrell and his colleagues that the remainder had been pre-eminently the work of the Board of

Education. One Liberal backbencher believed the Bill's proposals were 'in the main wise, courageous and acceptable to the great majority [of the House]'.[39] Such praise was soon to be tempered by more critical perspectives once the Bill's contents became public and Crewe's comment that 'One is never content in this world – our majority is going to be too large for Education Bill purposes' was soon to be proven correct.[40] Part 1 of the Bill, with its contentious Clauses 3, 4 and 7, was soon to be the subject of considerable criticism within and without the Liberal Party.

Official Nonconformist support for the new measure included phrases such as 'heartily welcomed' or 'warm approval' but in each instance their effect was dampened by accompanying criticisms or condemnations of Clauses 3 and 4. After an address to a meeting of Liberal supporters at Sleaford in Lincolnshire, one MP expressed his surprise at the strength of feeling shown against Clause 4 by a large number of Methodists present. He passed on to Birrell their warning that if the clause and the Bill were passed not only would the Liberals lose office at the next election but there would be a greater number of Passive Resisters than under the 1902 Act.[41] Condemnation of Clause 4 was not restricted to the Nonconformists, with the Catholic Association opposing the power accorded the LEA under the clause while Cardinal Bourne, the Archbishop of Westminster, and his colleagues were worried by the number of schools that would not meet the clause's criteria. Bourne argued publicly that the facilities proposed under the Bill were 'hopelessly inadequate' and could only be justified on the basis of political expediency.[42] In similar vein, Winnington Ingram, the Bishop of London, condemned the extended facilities proposed by the clause as, 'so grudging and so fenced round by conditions as to be practically useless'.[43]

The Archbishop of Canterbury publicly condemned the Bill in a letter to the National Society, concentrating his criticisms on what he saw as the silencing of teachers in respect of giving religious instruction. The following day, 11 April, the Anglican bishops met to consider their plan of campaign and, as Crewe had feared, they were highly critical of what they saw as the confiscation of the voluntary schools by LEAs, Ingram making the point that 'we did not spend £40,000,000 on building and maintaining our schools in order to get rent'. Thereafter, the momentum of opposition to the Bill grew swiftly within the Church as the bishops stoked the fires of discontent within their dioceses, the Bishop of Bristol voicing their view that the government had chosen a 'steam engine to crack a nut, and used it so clumsily that it came down with full force upon the Church conscience'.[44] The moderating voices of the Bishops of Hereford and Ripon were lost in the clamour issuing forth from the Church although Campbell-Bannerman wondered privately 'how much of it is all mere noise?'[45] Conducted at a much quieter and more private level, but of equal importance for the Bill's fate, were discussions held between Lord Lansdowne and Balfour.

Lansdowne, leader of the Unionists in the Lords, believed that compared with the 'lamentably weak' Opposition in the Commons the forces at his command were 'enormously powerful'. But he saw both as two wings of one army and felt there should be some co-ordination between them, especially as there would be major issues debated in the Lords which ought to be discussed 'with an eye to the effect . . . upon the temper of the House of Commons'.[46] Balfour concurred, noting that there had never been a period in which the Lords 'will be called upon to play a part at once so important, so delicate and so difficult'. He was aware of the need for caution, however, arguing that the government's legislation would probably be more radical than would be palatable to some moderate members, and while the Lords could amend such measures the more radical members of the Cabinet would gain grounds from the 'anticipated mutilation' of their measures for a case against the Lords. This notwithstanding, he believed that if he and his colleagues in the Commons fought all major points 'very stiffly' and the Lords became the 'theatre of compromise', then it could well be that the Lords could emerge strengthened rather than weakened by the 'inevitable difficulties of the next few years'.[47]

Unaware of this compact, Birrell found himself appalled by the quality of the debates on the Bill in the Commons in which the religious issues predominated. As in the Cabinet discussions, the debates during the Second Reading in May and the 21 day Committee Stage were dominated by discussions of Clauses 3 and 4:

> . . . never have I drawn my breath in so irreligious and ignorant an atmosphere as that of the House of Commons when debating religion. It often shocked me. 'Can there be such a thing as Board School Christianity?' 'What have the wishes of parents to do with the traditional creed of Christendom?' . . . 'What has the incidence of Rates to do with the Holy Trinity?' Questions of this sort hurtled in the air around me, but how could I deal with them without appearing to give offence? I had to hold my tongue again and again, at the expense of my case.[48]

Outside the House, the religious issues arising from the Bill dominated discussions and were discussed by Birrell with Lord Ripon, on behalf of the Catholics, and the Archbishop of Canterbury.

In addition to opposing Clause 4, the Catholics were alarmed by the changes proposed to endowments in the Bill. Birrell was at pains to assure Ripon that the only schools likely to be affected would be those whose trusts were of a purely educational nature. He was willing to make the point publicly in the Second Reading but added that one of the relevant clauses had been inserted by the Board of Education 'and I can assure you the Board of Education *at present* is a denominationally-minded body (*I don't refer to myself*)'.[49] In his subsequent negotiations with Cardinal Bourne, Ripon was not surprised to note, therefore, that he put great faith in the Board of Education as a potential arbitration body, particularly with respect to resolving differences over Clause 4. It was Ripon's negotiating skills with Bourne, none the less, that secured acceptance of amendments to Clause 4 palatable to the Catholics and also to the Cabinet during the Committee Stage in June.

Birrell appears to have been somewhat bemused by the vigour of the opposition to the Bill from the Anglicans and even by late May he seems not to have fully comprehended its magnitude. Discussing the importance of religious teaching in schools with the Archbishop of Canterbury, Birrell claimed that he did not believe that the issue of whether teachers gave the instruction or not was revolutionary. The Primate was worried that this meant that Birrell 'had hardly realised the feeling about teachers in country parishes being silenced' and did his best to 'set it before him'.[50] The discussion was prompted by the amendments before the House put forward by Joseph Chamberlain and Ramsay MacDonald and which, in their individual ways, would have achieved the establishment of a secular education system. In addition, the Cabinet had agreed that the discussions of the amendments in the Commons should not be 'unduly curtailed, in view of the great importance of the point raised'.[51] But if they saw this as a possible solution to the religious conflict over the Bill their hopes were soon dashed, each amendment being rejected by substantial majorities.

Birrell tried to achieve consensus in the House on the religious issues without destroying the Bill's main aims but his efforts made little headway. Thus when he raised the possibility of modifying Clause 3 so that ordinary facilities might be provided on five instead of two days a week, in order to try to meet the wishes of the Anglicans and the Catholics, Nonconformist MPs were horrified.[52] When he proposed a possible solution to the stringencies of Clause 4 and achieved concurrence from Redmond, for the Catholics, and Seely, for the Nonconformists, the Opposition front bench opposed it, as did some of Birrell's government colleagues. By mid-June the delays in resolving the problems surrounding the religious aspects of the Bill led the government to apply the guillotine to the remainder of the Committee Stage. They hoped that by doing so the Bill would then be able to go to the Lords by mid-July in order to achieve a Second Reading there before that House adjourned for a recession before an autumn session. The controversies surrounding Clause 4, however, led to a long discussion in Cabinet three days later. Although they determined to leave the clause as it stood, four days later they were forced to reconsider their decision as a result of conflicting submissions about the clause, including one resolution from 40 Nonconformists urging them to accept amendments which would cause the measure 'to be more acceptable to those members of the Church of England who are prepared to accept the principle of the Bill'. The Cabinet agreed that Birrell should introduce some amendments to the clause provided they did not affect its underlying principle.[53] These amendments made it almost obligatory for LEAs to take over, and to allow the provision of extended facilities to be given by voluntary schools which satisfied the conditions of the clause. A contracting-out amendment allowed the Board of Education, in the case of LEAs refusing to take over certain schools, to grant these schools state-aided status, that is, to receive only the parliamentary grant and not be controlled by an LEA.[54]

The intervention of the Premier in the subsequent debate, assuring his backbenchers that the measure was still 'an undenominational Bill, setting up an undenominational system' helped to ensure the successful passage of Clause 4, albeit with a reduced majority of 103. One Liberal MP, Sir Wilfrid Lawson, had struggled from his death-bed to attend the debates on the amendments and in what turned out to be his penultimate diary entry recorded the feelings of many of his backbench colleagues:

> My line in all this voting was to support the Government in their attempt to minimise the evils of Clause 4; but to vote against the clause when it came up, it being still very objectionable.[55]

Arthur Acland, closely following the debates, was delighted with the result, however, and believed: '*Things being as they were*, I doubt if any other available form of the clause would have got so large a

PUNCH, OR THE LONDON CHARIVARI. June 13, 1906.

NOBLESSE OBLIGE!

JOSEPHINE (*the damosel in distress*). "MY LORD, TIME WAS WHEN I HELD YOU IN SCANT ESTEEM; BUT NOW I CRAVE THE HELP OF YOUR TRUSTY LANCE AGAINST YON MONSTER!" (*Aside*) "HOPE THE OLD SPORTSMAN 'LL TAKE IT ON!"
[Mr. CHAMBERLAIN, in a recent speech at Highbury, stated his conviction that the Education Bill would not pass. He was apparently counting on its rejection by the House of Peers.]

7 'Noblesse oblige!': Joseph Chamberlain's last major involvement with education policy occurred over the 1906 Education Bill. His views no doubt account for the somewhat bemused expression of Campbell-Bannerman as the monster. (Cartoon in *Punch*, CXXX, 13 June 1906, p. 452)

majority'.[56] But the discussions surrounding the clause were not yet over for Robert Perks, a Liberal backbencher, claimed that the contents of the clause came under 'privilege' and as such could not be amended by the Lords. Lord Ripon was thrown into turmoil by this claim and told Campbell-Bannerman that if it was true all that had been said in the last Cabinet meeting on the clause 'becomes valueless, and the hopes that were held out to me are without foundation'.[57] The Premier's response, that he hoped Perks's 'indiscretion' would do no harm, did not mollify Ripon and he asked Birrell to consider raising the matter in the Commons. Birrell, however, was unwilling to do so for not only was he at the 'very end of my tether' over the clause but he knew that to do so would cause a revolt in the House. He added: 'I'm very sorry. We have had so much trouble over Cl. IV that I wish it were better worth it'.[58] He did, however, consult the Parliamentary Counsel and discovered that apart from the contracting-out part the Lords could amend the clause. Ripon, and the Catholics, were pacified for the time being.

By 30 July the final stage of the Third Reading was reached and in the course of his contribution to the closing speeches, Macnamara referred to a current rumour that the Lords would throw the Bill out but dismissed such a possibility. Balfour applied a cold douche to Macnamara's view, however, and indicated that the real fight over the Bill would take place in the 'other place'. He went on to make the point he had made earlier to Lansdowne that those who disliked the Bill but who would vote for it to satisfy their consciences would do so in the belief that it would be 'profoundly modified' by the Lords. Without this substantial modification, he contended, the Bill could not become law. This chill message was partly occluded by the reception accorded Birrell's final oration but events were soon to prove Balfour correct. The Second Reading in the Lords was carried in early August without a division and the Bill was accepted in principle, but both Lord Lansdowne and the Archbishop of Canterbury gave warnings that drastic alterations would have to be made in Committee in order to render the measure satisfactory. At this juncture a legal decision suddenly became a significant factor in the future progress of the Bill.

In March 1904 the West Riding of Yorkshire LEA had passed a resolution authorising the deduction of a moiety of the salaries of four voluntary school head teachers because of the time they devoted to religious teaching. An inquiry held by the Board of Education in July 1905 resulted in the Board ordering the LEA, under Section 16 of the 1902 Act, to pay the outstanding balance of the teachers' salaries. The

LEA refused to comply and in July 1906 the Board applied to the Divisional Court for mandamus which was granted. Acland, a member of the West Riding Council, told Birrell that although their lawyers thought the county's case 'might be pretty powerful on its pure legal merits in the House of Lords' the council had resolved not to appeal.[59] This was not, in fact, to be the case and in August an appeal was lodged in the Court of Appeal. Sandars had a discussion with Edward Carson at the Carlton Club just before the appeal was heard and learned, correctly as it turned out, that a majority of the court would uphold the LEA's action. He told Balfour that he had asked Thring and Morant what advice they would give the government if the prediction was correct and they had responded that they would 'press Birrell *hard* to take the case to the House of Lords'. What the government actually decided to do, he went on, raised important considerations in relation to the Education Bill. If the government did not appeal then this new interpretation of the 1902 Act would not only reduce the Nonconformists' grievance but would also add an unexpected financial burden on the churches. But if it decided to appeal, then should the Lords deal with the Bill before knowing the legal decision of the final court of appeal, the House of Lords?[60] Lansdowne contacted Balfour as soon as he heard the news and argued that the case handed them a powerful political weapon. Not only could it be used successfully for 'purposes of controversy' but if they found themselves

> compelled to wreck the Bill we could no doubt make plenty of capital out of the fact that it was framed in ignorance of the real state of the law, and in compliance with a 'mandate' given by the electors who were themselves not less ignorant.[61]

But any possible action hinged on the government's decision.

As soon as the court's decision, cancelling the Board's writ of mandamus, became known, Ripon started contacting other members of the Cabinet. Though ostensibly he was worried about the impact of an appeal upon the Lords' handling of the Bill, for which he and Crewe were jointly responsible, Ripon's membership of the Catholic community undoubtedly also affected his concern with the decision. The Lord Chancellor's response was that the Board should give notice of appeal and apply, at the same time, to the Lords for an early hearing. Birrell accepted the first point but, possibly mindful of the political gain to be made in connection with the Bill's aims by a delayed hearing, was not convinced by Loreburn's second point.

Campbell-Bannerman was confident that the Lords would overturn the Court of Appeal's judgment and accepted that the government could not avoid an appeal on both administrative and tactical grounds for, like Crewe, he was worried by the possibility that postponement of the Bill's passage in the Lords would lead to its loss. Faced with this consensus, Birrell gave way and before the Cabinet met after the summer recess it was announced that the government would appeal against the court's decision. Lloyd George was unhappy about this, feeling that they had lost the major tactical advantage offered by the court's decision. By their action they had helped the Church

> . . . out of a very bad hole – and it helps the Lords. Now they can amend our Bill with impunity knowing that if we are compelled to drop it the Act of 1902 will probably be reinstated . . . .When we come to consider what amendments we can accept Ministers will require all the influence they possess with Nonconformists to induce them to acquiesce. We are frittering away that influence by caving in – at least 9 months before we were compelled to decide one way or the other – to assist the clerics out of a difficulty into which their friends had landed them. The permanent officials of the Board of Education are naturally anxious for our appeal. The blunder in draftsmanship was theirs originally.[62]

When the Lords met the next day it looked at first as if both Ripon and Lloyd George's fears were unfounded. A resolution by Lord Stanmore to postpone the Committee Stage of the Bill until after the judgment in the West Riding case did not receive Lansdowne's support and, crucially, the House did not divide. The Committee Stage could thus proceed.

During the Second Reading in the Lords one observer had detected beneath the surface of the debate 'a wide-spread fear that a rejection of the Bill might precipitate the secular solution'.[63] The Archbishop of Canterbury gave voice to this feeling when he declared emphatically at the outset of the Committee Stage that he would neither propose nor support what he called 'wrecking amendments' to the Bill. To help him achieve this while treading delicately through the educational points under consideration, the archbishop had earlier enlisted the aid of Michael Sadler. He thus ensured that the educational advice he required would match the calibre of that being given by the Board to the government. The effect of this was soon to be seen as, clause by clause, amendments altered or destroyed the aims of the Bill while the substitutions clearly benefited denominational interests. Clause 2 as amended would have made it mandatory for an LEA to take over every voluntary school if required by the owners while Clause 3 was altered to ensure that in rural, single-school areas the LEA would have to provide ordinary facilities in council schools if a 'reasonable number' of parents desired them. Lord Balfour of Burleigh's amendment in favour of providing all-round facilities in all schools, which would have required a repeal of the Cowper-Temple clause, was supported by Lord Lansdowne and the bishops but withdrawn as a result of Devonshire and Lord St. Aldwyn's effective opposition. It was Clauses 4 and 7, however, which were altered almost out of recognition.

When the Bill had left the Commons, Clause 4 was almost mandatory for LEAs. The first amendment in the Lords made it mandatory while the next removed the limit of urban populations with a population of 5,000 so that extended facilities could, theoretically, be provided in rural, single school areas. In addition, the four-fifths parental majority required for the provision of these facilities was replaced by a bare majority and priority of admission to a school was to be given to children whose parents belonged to the denomination involved. Finally, a parents' committee of six would be established to supervise the religious instruction provided in each school, four of the members being parent appointees, one the appointee of the school owner and the sixth an LEA representative.

Clause 7 had been labelled the teachers' clause during the Bill's passage in the Commons for it was seen as freeing teachers, especially those in voluntary schools, from the yoke of denominationalism in the form of giving religious instruction and being subject to religious tests on appointment. Of all the Bill's clauses it directly reflected one of the mandates the Liberals had been given at the election but this did not deter the Lords who appeared to accept F.E. Smith's dictum that the government 'should get rid of confounding the Liberal party with the people'.[64] As a result of the amendments made, LEAs would now be required to allow teachers to give religious instruction in Clause 3 and Clause 4 schools and had to liaise with the parents' committees over appointments to Clause 4 schools. Furthermore, LEAs were not to be prevented from ascertaining the (religious) fitness of any teacher offering to provide Cowper-Temple teaching.

Just after the Bill had entered the Lords, the Court of Appeal had overturned the earlier decision in the West Riding County Council case and had found the council justified in refusing to pay teachers for giving religious instruction. It was perhaps not coincidental that shortly afterwards the Archbishop of Canterbury, for whom the Bill's clauses on the role of teachers formed the most significant part of the measure, initiated meetings with the Prime Minister in order to determine if there were possible grounds for a compromise. The first took place at Belmont Castle, Campbell-Bannerman's Scottish home, shortly after the funeral of the Premier's wife. The archbishop was somewhat surprised to find that Campbell-Bannerman, while apparently amenable to possible amendments, was not sufficiently well prepared to be able to discuss the Bill in detail. Davidson's pre-occupation with the Bill can be the only excuse for his ignoring the devastating effect which the last months of Lady Campbell-Bannerman's illness and eventual death had had on the Premier.[65]

When the archbishop sought a meeting in the following month with Lord Loreburn, the Lord Chancellor, to discuss the Bill in private he found himself directed, owing to Loreburn's ill health, to Campbell-Bannerman. Somewhat embarrassed by this, the archbishop made it clear that he could not attend in any official capacity 'in order to make suggestions or new proposals'. Campbell-Bannerman agreed, none the less, to meet him again and humorously told Birrell, when asking him to attend (with Crewe), that he would disclaim any significant role in the likely conflict 'although quite equal to part of bottleholder, and very faithful at that'.[66] After several hours the archbishop left the meeting feeling somewhat perturbed, notably by Birrell's comments that at this stage the government would resist any substantial amendments to the Bill.

Birrell's remarks during a speech following the Anchor Society's dinner at Bristol a fortnight later produced flutterings in political and episcopal circles, not least his comment that unless the Lords climbed down on Report – 'to an extent that we can hardly imagine their dignity will permit' one journalist present noted – then it was highly likely that the Premier would move that the Commons disagreed *en bloc* with the Lords' amendments.[67] A long memorandum refuting Birrell's claims in this speech about the Lords' amendments was circulated immediately among the Conservative Party hierarchy. The author [?Lord Balcarres] claimed, somewhat disingenuously, that the Lords' amendments were merely 'to put into the Bill what the Government either said it contained, or said it was its intention'.[68] But the possibility of a constitutional conflict arising from such an action precipitated another meeting between the archbishop and Campbell-Bannerman, this time at Windsor Castle on 18 November and at the King's suggestion. Discussing the Bill with Campbell-Bannerman

PUNCH, OR THE LONDON CHARIVARI.—November 7, 1906.

CUTTING IT UP.

(After Rembrandt's picture "The School of Anatomy.")

8 'Cutting it up': Randall Davidson wielding the scalpel, with (next to him) Lord Lansdowne, Lord Salisbury (between Lansdowne and Davidson), the Bishop of London (on Lansdowne's right), and Lord Londonderry (above the Bishop) among the onlookers. (Cartoon in *Punch*, CXXXI, 7 November 1906, p. 335)

before his meeting with the archbishop, the King was alarmed by the Premier's criticism of the Lords' actions and believed 'he evidently means war'. When Davidson met Campbell-Bannerman the next day, the Premier suddenly conceded that it might be useful to have a conference 'of some sort' before the Report Stage was reached in the Lords.[69] Nothing came immediately from this proposal, however, and at another meeting between the two men ten days later, also held at the King's behest but at Lambeth Palace, no progress was made. Davidson complained afterwards that Campbell-Bannerman was no more familiar with the Bill than he had been at Windsor whereas Campbell-Bannerman told Birrell just before the meeting that he was not in 'an arrangeable humour by any means, at the present stage at any rate'. He also asked if there was any truth in the report that Thring had been 'one of a nice little party – A.J.B., Hartington, Black Michael [Lord St. Aldwyn], etc. – and telling them exactly what we would and what we would not?'[70]

Lord Thring, an elderly Liberal peer, had attended the first of three meetings of the Conservative and Unionist leaders plus the Archbishop of Canterbury held at Lansdowne House on 23, 26 and 27 November to consider amendments on Report. He had indicated what amendments the government would be likely to accept, and on this basis, the Duke of Devonshire had managed, at the second meeting, to gain agreement to the more extreme amendments being removed. But as Davidson noted, there still remained a difference of opinion about the likely consequences of either the rejection or death of the Bill. After a separate meeting with the other key Conservatives and Unionists in the Commons, Balfour asserted his authority to prevent any further alterations being agreed which might prove acceptable to the government.

At first sight the Report Stage in the Lords appeared to reflect Balfour's concept of the Lords as the 'theatre of compromise', with a motion by Devonshire leading to Clause 2 being restored to its original form while the Bishop of Oxford's amendment to Clause 3 was dropped, so that ordinary facilities were only to be provided on two days a week. But new amendments indicated otherwise. An amendment by Lord Salisbury extended the terms covering single-school areas to urban ones and was designed to overcome the possibility (albeit highly unlikely) of a single Nonconformist child preventing a school from providing extended facilities for the majority of its pupils. Ripon's apposite comment was that this amendment struck at the very heart of the Bill while Crewe was led to complain that the Opposition had 'turned rules into exceptions and exceptions into rules'. The possibility of any compromise now seemed remote as Campbell-Bannerman's subsequent public letter to the Committee of the National Liberal Federation appeared to confirm. In it he stated that the Lords' amendments appeared to have turned the Bill

> ... into a travesty of its original form. As amended, it perpetuates, if it does not extend, the very grievances and wrongs that were fixed upon the country by the Act of 1902.[71]

Faced with a measure now resembling 'a miserable, mangled, tortured, twisted *tertium quid*', Birrell told his Cabinet colleagues that the time had arrived when they had to decide what, if anything, they were prepared to do to save the bill:

> ... Nothing is easier than to kill it – to save it is difficult – but to lose it, unless some immediate alteration is made in the existing law, is to open the door to a sea of administrative troubles of an almost intolerable character.[72]

He stated that if the Bill was lost it would reflect the government's inability to reach a compromise with the Church over Clause 3 schools, schools which were of no interest to the Catholics. Against this was the fact that the loss of the Bill would be welcomed by many of their supporters in the country as providing the basis for a conflict with the Lords, a conflict they were prepared 'to enter with light hearts'. But this point notwithstanding, if the Bill was lost he believed a new Bill would be required to prevent the administration of the 1902 Act from becoming impossible. He preferred, therefore, that the existing Bill should be saved for, whatever its faults, it would secure popular control and remove the long outstanding Nonconformist grievance in rural areas.

Birrell's arguments made little impact on some of his colleagues. John Burns proposed a rejection of the amended measure and claimed

> ... much to dejection of Birrell [to have] killed his semblance of a Bill. L.G. agreed but did not say much in support. 'Tip Top' his exclamation when I had disposed of the skeleton from the Upper House.[73]

Campbell-Bannerman told the King, however, that the Cabinet had decided that the Bill should be saved if a compromise could be achieved which did not damage its main principles. On 8 December the Cabinet agreed, after 'much anxious discussion', to a rejection of the Lords' amendments *en globo*. Birrell was charged with making a general statement about these amendments but, before moving their total rejection, was to indicate also the government's willingness to make some moderate concessions, if they would save the Bill. Four days later, the Cabinet agreed to allow amendments to Clauses 3, 4 and 7. Under Clause 4, the 5000 population limit in urban areas was waived while the requirement of a four-fifths parental majority to establish schools under the clause would be reduced to a three-quarters majority. Believing that these alterations would satisfy the Catholics, the Cabinet were prepared to allow teachers to give religious instruction in large urban schools, for at least five years, in order to satisfy the main Anglican grievance. But until the agreement of the Liberal Party was secured for these changes, seen as the necessary *quid pro quo* to secure the Bill, they would have to remain confidential.[74]

After the Lansdowne House meetings in late November Davidson had been confined to bed with an attack of gastric 'flu but on 3 December, the last day of the Report Stage on the Bill, he had written to Lansdowne stating that the Bill should pass provided certain basic parameters were met. His comments were prompted by the knowledge that there was now a strong section of the Cabinet prepared to make concessions, and in view of this he was willing to reduce or remove the amendments concerning denominational teaching in council schools and the provision of extended facilities. He argued that if the Lords did not do this, especially in respect of the last point, then they could not deny that they were in effect 'turning the Bill round'. Davidson's biographer noted that these views alarmed the Conservatives and Lord Salisbury expostulated that he wished 'Bishops would leave politics to politicians'.[75] These views may have been partly responsible for Balfour entering the Commons and sitting in the position from where he usually addressed the House, although Walter Long was supposed to be winding up the debate for the Opposition, as Birrell made his case in accordance with Cabinet instructions on the afternoon of 12 December. Balfour did contribute to the debate with a stinging rebuttal of Birrell's points, including the, of necessity, vaguely described concessions, while making his comments

> in the most defiant tones, and in language which, while throwing the responsibility for failure on the Government, showed that he, at any rate, had nothing to offer which Ministers could accept.[76]

This speech surprised and antagonised many of his followers but it was not surprising given his views at the Lansdowne House meetings and Davidson's subsequent letter to Lansdowne. It did not prevent the government from achieving a majority of 309, partly thanks to the support of the Irish Catholics, for their rejection of the Lords' amendments *en bloc*.

Five days later the Cabinet received a report from Birrell and Crewe of a meeting held with Lansdowne, Devonshire and the archbishop. Lansdowne had made a concession over the form the Lords' subsequent debate might take, despite the government's rebuff to that House, and if this was accepted by the Lords then private inter-party consultations on the Bill might take place. Birrell commented that with the Law Lords' recent overturning of the Court of Appeal's decision on the West Riding County Council case, the attitude of the Nonconformists to concessions on the Bill would be as nothing to the increase in passive resistance which would result if he was called upon to administer the 1902 Act rigorously. Faced with these facts, Crewe was authorised by the Cabinet to state explicitly the concessions which the government was willing to make in the course of his speech explaining the rejection of the Lords' amendments. Furthermore, he was to invite the Opposition to negotiate 'with a view to adjusting differences' on the measure. In the Lords that afternoon Lansdowne moved a resolution criticising the novel constitutional procedure adopted by the Commons in their rejection of all the Lords' amendments and he invited Crewe to explain the government's case in detail. This Crewe did, and as his speech unfolded some key Opposition members were struck by the substantial nature of the government's concessions. FitzRoy noted that Devonshire and Goschen were favourably impressed while Lord Percy thought that the Catholics, if not the Anglicans, would be satisfied with them. Furthermore, the Lords did not oppose the proposed adjournment so that the private negotiations were able to begin the following morning at Crewe House.

Balfour, Lansdowne and Lord Cawdor met Crewe, Birrell and Asquith, with the Archbishop of Canterbury attending at the King's suggestion. It soon became apparent, however, that no common ground could be reached over the question of teachers giving religious instruction. As Campbell-Bannerman wrote to the King that evening:

> The demands of the Opposition being that liberty to teach dogmas should be given (a) to head teachers as well as assistants, (b) in all schools, large and small, in town and country, (c) with or without the assent of the local authority, and these three

conditions being said to be each essential, there could evidently be no settlement. Such a scheme would imply the continuance of the present denominational schools, with the addition of a rent being paid for them. The purpose for which the Bill was introduced was the exact reverse of this, and therefore Cabinet cannot hope to save the Bill.[77]

In his speech to the Lords the next day, Crewe stated that only a few minutes of the meeting had been required to show that the negotiations had been undertaken merely 'to give an air of plausibility to the action of irreconcilables'.[78] Lansdowne, on the other hand, recorded privately that Crewe and Birrell were unwilling initially to negotiate any concession over the teaching of religious instruction although Birrell had suggested later that a partial concession might be granted if the remainder of the government's demands were complied with. The overall impression produced upon Lansdowne and his colleagues was that Crewe and his colleagues felt that 'they had already gone too far, and were inclined to draw in their horns rather than to advance further'.[79] Balfour also noted his belief that Crewe and Birrell had not revealed all their plans but what they had was unacceptable to him. What concerned him most was 'how far can they be squeezed; *and* when the utmost concessions have been wrung from them, ought these concessions to be accepted by the Leaders of the Unionist Party?' For him the provisions for Clause 3 and 4 schools were paramount and in his detailed analysis of possible concessions his conclusion was that not enough was likely to be gained to meet all his criteria.[80] The outcome was that Lansdowne moved that the 'Lords do insist upon their amendments' and it was carried by 132 to 52 votes, Devonshire and the Bishop of Hereford voting with the government. Hereford was depressed by the Lords' decision, writing to a colleague:

> I am just starting for home after looking on at our wreckage proceedings in the H. of L. It is, I think, quite possible that our Bishops and Balfour may all alike live to regret them. They are not specially gifted with that insight which is the gift of true prophecy.[81]

The next day the government informed the Commons that they would withdraw the measure and John Burns observed that Balfour was 'lucky to be away on sick furlough. The Rads would not have heard him'.[82]

Birrell, like many, was inclined to blame Balfour for the Bill's failure:

... It seemed to stink in his philosophical nostrils, and to perpetuate separation; whereas his ideal was Union on a broad basis of comprehension, without bothering about precise agreements. He blocked all the roads that might have led to settlement.[83]

And Lord Salisbury frankly admitted that Balfour had 'smashed the Bill' because he believed the Unionist Party was being too moderate and he was convinced that

the issue will not be the House of Lords v. the People, but Church v. Chapel, and on that basis they believe it is possible to reconstruct the Opposition as an effective force.[84]

The considerable resistance of the Catholics and Anglicans to the measure as well as the divisions rent among the government's Nonconformist supporters by Clauses 3 and 4 provided substance for this view. There were other factors involved, however, in the failure of the measure.

The Bill had lacked from the outset unanimous support within the Liberal Party and among its allies and this had been reflected in, and reinforced by, the lack of unanimity within the Cabinet. This point was made by Viscount Esher when he criticised the trend towards the drafting of government measures, including the Education Bill, by government departments with little reference to the Prime Minister. The result was, he claimed, 'the indecisive manner in which questions are dealt with when they come before Parliament, and when the Government is subjected to Parliamentary pressure'. Such a phenomenon tended to be compounded, he asserted, by the fact that Liberal governments were 'peculiarly liable to the complaint of indecision'.[85] This view appeared to be shared by John Burns who noted privately, 'Shake the nervousness out of this Cabinet and the remnant would be first class'.[86] While these factors contributed to the failure of the Bill, the fundamental problem remained the incompatibility of views held by the opposing parties, religious as well as political, plus the dominance of the Unionists in the Lords. By the end of 1906, the failure of the Education Bill and other measures had provided additional evidence of the need for reform of the Lords' powers if electoral democracy was to triumph and Campbell-Bannerman made it clear that he was not prepared to acquiesce to the manipulations of either Balfour or the Lords. He told the Commons:

... A settlement of this great question of education has been prevented, and for that calamity we know, and the country knows

311

on whom is the responsibility . . . .The resources of the House of Commons are not exhausted, and I say with conviction a way must be found, and a way will be found, by which the will of the people . . . will be made to prevail.[87]

Five years later, Campbell-Bannerman's vision was to prevail but, in the meantime, the government remained committed to achieving a fundamental shift in national educational policy. This goal was not to be the lot, however, of Birrell.

NOTES

1. Campbell-Bannerman Papers, Add MS 41211, J. Bryce to H. Campbell-Bannerman, 5 Sept. 1902.
2. Bryce Papers, UB 32, H. Campbell-Bannerman to J. Bryce, 23 Sept. 1902.
3. Campbell-Bannerman Papers, Add MS 41237, fos. 54–5, S.T. Evans, D. Lloyd George *et al* to H. Campbell-Bannerman, 31 Oct. 1902.]
4. F. Guinness Rogers, 'The Nonconformist Uprising', *The Nineteenth Century and After*, LIV (Oct. 1903), pp. 688–9.
5. Campbell-Bannerman Papers, Add MS 41237, fos.146–7, H. Campbell-Bannerman to Rev. Prof. A.J. Paterson, 13 Aug. 1903.
6. A.K. Russell, *Liberal Landslide: The General Election of 1906* (1973), pp. 31–4.
7. J. Wilson, *CB: A Life of Sir Henry Campbell-Bannerman* (1973), pp. 453, 461–3.
8. J.E. Miller, 'The Liberal Party and Education 1898–1908', unpublished MEd thesis, University of Liverpool, 1984, p. 71. I am grateful to Dr. Robin Betts for facilitating access to this source.
9. See R. Betts, 'Dr Macnamara and the Education Act of 1902', *Journal of Educational Administration and History*, 25, 2 (July 1993), pp. 119–20.
10. W.L. Guttsman, *The British Political Elite* (1963), p. 210; Miller, op. cit.
11. *The Times*, 23 Jan. 1906.
12. A. FitzRoy, *Memoirs* (1927), I, p. 278.
13. BP Add MS 49758, fo.92, A.J. Balfour to A. Balfour, 17 Jan. 1906.
14. Ibid., Add MS 49764, fo.144, J.S. Sandars to A.J. Balfour, 21 Jan. 1906; Sandars Papers, MS Eng hist c.751, fos. 121–2, M.E. Hicks Beach to A.J. Balfour, 25 Jan. 1906.
15. C. Wimbourne, 'Evangelicals and the Education Question', *The Nineteenth Century and After*, CCCXLIX (March 1906), p. 387.
16. Russell, op. cit., pp. 65,79.
17. *Free Church Year Book*, 1906 cited in E. Halévy, *A History of the English People: The Rule of Democracy* (1939), VI, I, p. 64.
18. Ripon Papers, Add MS 43542, fos. 21–2, J. Bryce to Lord Ripon, 4 Dec. 1902.
19. PRO ED 24/116, Cabinet Committee, 'Education Bill', 3 Jan. 1906.
20. PRO ED 24/110, 'Memo of a conversation held at the Hotel Metropole, Brighton, on Sunday, 28 January 1906, between D.L.G., A.H.D.A., and A.B'.
21. PRO ED 24/116, Cabinet Committee, Education Bill, Meeting of 30 Jan., p. 2.
22. In the minutes of the meeting, Morant converted the 90 per cent to four-fifths. See PRO ED 24/118 Morant's notes of the meeting and PRO ED 24/116, Cabinet Committee, Education Bill, Meeting of 30 Jan., p. 4.

23. FitzRoy, op. cit., p. 281.
24. PRO ED 24/116, Education Bill, Cabinet Committee, Meeting on 6 Feb., p. 3.
25. PRO ED 24/110, Archbishop of Canterbury to A. Birrell, 22 Feb. 1902.
26. PRO ED 24/118, A. Birrell, 'Memorandum concerning the Education Bill', 16 Feb. 1906, p. 3.
27. Ibid., p. 8.
28. Campbell-Bannerman Papers, Add MS 41213, fos. 339–40, Lord Crewe to H. Campbell-Bannerman, 28 Feb. 1906.
29. J. Burns Papers, Add MS 46324, Diary, 21 March 1906.
30. FitzRoy, op. cit., p. 287.
31. PRO ED 24/110, R.L. Morant to S. Provis, 30 April 1906.
32. W.S. Blunt, *My Diaries, Being a Personal Narrative of Events 1888–1914* (1932), p. 557.
33. *The Times*, 30 Jan. 1906.
34. FitzRoy, op. cit., p. 291. His informant on this occasion was Haldane.
35. Crewe Papers, R.L. Morant to Lord Crewe, 27 March 1906.
36. BP Add MS 49764, fo. 173, J.S. Sandars to A.J. Balfour, 7 March 1906.
37. Birrell Papers, J. Morley to A. Birrell, 9 April 1906; J. Burns Papers, Add MS 46234, Diary, 9 April 1904.
38. Trevelyan Papers, CPT 38, C.P. Trevelyan, 'Parliamentary Letter', 10 April 1906.
39. Ibid.
40. PRO ED 24/117, Lord Crewe to R.L. Morant, 16 Jan. 1906.
41. PRO ED 24/112, A. Lupton to A. Birrell, 7 June 1906.
42. Archbishop of Westminster, 'The Education Bill', *The Nineteenth Century and After*, CCCLI (May 1906), p. 721.
43. *The Schoolmaster*, LXIX (21 April 1906), p. 822.
44. Ibid., (5 May 1906), p. 930.
45. Campbell-Bannerman Papers, Add MS 41239, fo.84, H. Campbell-Bannerman to I. Hoyle, 24 April 1906.
46. BP Add MS 49729, fo. 226, Lord Lansdowne to A.J. Balfour, 5 April 1906.
47. Ibid., fos. 228–30, A.J. Balfour to Lord Lansdowne, 13 April 1906.
48. A. Birrell, *Things Past Redress* (1947), p. 188.
49. Ripon Papers, Add MS 43542, fo. 56, A. Birrell to Lord Ripon, 6 May 1906.
50. G.K.A. Bell, *Randall Davidson, Archbishop of Canterbury* (1935), II, p. 520.
51. PRO CAB 41/30/59, H. Campbell-Bannerman to H.M. King, 23 May 1906.
52. PRO ED 24/112, G. Hay Morgan to A. Birrell, 22 June 1906.
53. PRO CAB 41/30/66, H. Campbell-Bannerman to H.M. King, 20 June 1906.
54. This was the amendment which had received the prior agreement of Cardinal Bourne through Ripon's efforts. See Ripon Papers, Add MS 43542,fos. 59–60, Lord Ripon to A. Birrell, 14 June 1906.
55. G.W.E. Russell (ed.), *Sir Wilfrid Lawson* (1909), p. 275.
56. PRO ED 24/112, A.H.D. Acland to E. Pelham, 27 June 1906.
57. Ripon Papers, Add MS 43518, fos. 99–100, Lord Ripon to H. Campbell-Bannerman, 24 July 1906. Ripon believed that the government were willing to accept amendments to the clause in the Lords which would benefit the Catholics.
58. Ripon Papers, Add MS 43518, fos. 66–7, A. Birrell to Lord Ripon, 23 July 1906.
59. PRO ED 24/112, A.H.D. Acland to E. Pelham, 27 June 1906.
60. BP Add MS 49764, fos. 210–13, J.S. Sandars to A.J. Balfour, 8 Aug. 1906.
61. BP Add MS 49729, fos. 235–6, Lord Lansdowne to A.J. Balfour, 19 Aug. 1906.
62. Campbell-Bannerman Papers, Add MS 41239, fos. 148–51, D. Lloyd George to H. Campbell-Bannerman, 22 Oct. 1906.

63. PRO ED 24/120, C. Eaton, 'An Account of the Education Bill, 1906', p. 23.
64. *Annual Report*, I, 1906, pp. 160–61 cited in G.I.T. Machin, *Politics and the Churches in Great Britain 1869 to 1921* (1987), p. 287.
65. Arthur Ponsonby told Birrell that following her death, Campbell-Bannerman had only just begun to recover from the 'broken sleepless nights of the last six months'. Birrell Papers, MS 10 1–3 v.2, A. Ponsonby to A. Birrell, 11 Sept. 1906.
66. Birrell Papers, MS 10 1–3 v.2, Archbishop of Canterbury to H. Campbell-Bannerman, 27 Oct. 1906; H. Campbell-Bannerman to A. Birrell, 27 Oct. 1906.
67. *The Schoolmaster*, LXX (17 Nov. 1906), p. 858.
68. Crawford Papers, MS 24.30, 'Memorandum on 1906 Education Bill', p. 9.
69. J.D. Fair, *British Interparty Conferences: A Study of the Procedure of Conciliation in British Politics 1867–1921* (1980), pp. 64–6.
70. Birrell Papers, MS 10 1–3 v.2, H. Campbell-Bannerman to A. Birrell, 25 Nov. 1906.
71. H. Campbell-Bannerman to A.H.D. Acland, 27 Nov. 1906 cited in J.A.Spender, *The Life of the Rt. Hon. Sir Henry Campbell-Bannerman, G.C.B.* (1923), II, p. 300.
72. PRO CAB 37/85/92, A. Birrell, 'Note on Education Bill', 3 Dec. 1906.
73. J. Burns Papers, Add MS 46324, *Diary*, 5 Dec. 1906.
74. PRO CAB 41/30/79, H. Campbell-Bannerman to H.M. King, 12 Dec. 1906.
75. Bell, op. cit., p. 527.
76. A. FitzRoy, op. cit., p. 308.
77. PRO CAB 41/30/82, H.Campbell-Bannerman to H.M. King, 18 Dec. 1906.
78. A. FitzRoy, op. cit., p. 310.
79. Lord Lansdowne, 'Note of meeting in Mr. Balfour's room at the House of Commons on the evening of Dec. 18, 1906', cited in Lord Newton, *Lord Lansdowne* (1929), pp. 356–357.
80. BP Add MS 49729, fos. 272–89, A.J. Balfour, 'Memorandum', 18 Dec. 1906.
81. Bishop of Hereford to Canon Alexander, 20 Dec. 1906 cited in W. Temple, *Life of Bishop Percival* (1921), p. 191.
82. J. Burns Papers, Add MS 46324, Diary, 20 Dec. 1906. Balfour was suffering from an attack of influenza.
83. Birrell, op. cit., p. 191.
84. FitzRoy, op. cit., p. 310.
85. Viscount Esher to H.M. King, 20 April 1906 cited in M.V. Brett (ed.), *Journals and Letters of Viscount Esher* (1934), II, p. 161.
86. J. Burns Papers, Add MS 46324, *Diary*, 6 April 1906.
87. Cited in J.A. Spender, op. cit., pp. 311–12.

10

New lamps for old

The replacement of the ambassador to the USA had been exercising the minds of Grey, Campbell-Bannerman and the King during the autumn of 1906, and when Sir Charles Hardinge, the King's choice, declined to take the post he was asked to propose someone else. A sleepless night produced the solution – James Bryce. An expert on the American constitution, Bryce was prone to make 'long and rather dull speeches on commonplace subjects which I knew to be a trait that would be popular with the American masses' and he was married to a 'charming and agreeable wife'.[1] Bryce's attributes eventually gained him the post but his transfer left a vacancy at the Irish Office. Lord Balcarres had observed of Birrell, after the withdrawal of the Education Bill, 'He can have a rest now, unless they are cruel enough to send him to Dublin'.[2] On Christmas Day Campbell-Bannerman wrote to Birrell to express his thanks that 'you are both (mark the both: it is very necessary) ready to sacrifice yourselves on the altar of duty'.[3] In February 1907 Birrell crossed 'that odious Irish Channel' to become the next Chief Secretary of State for Ireland in the knowledge that Reginald McKenna had been appointed to succeed him at the Board of Education.

McKenna had gained prominence as a young MP for his attacks in the House on the 1902 Bill but Campbell-Bannerman had appointed him as Financial Secretary to the Treasury in 1905. When Birrell agreed to go to Ireland, McKenna was on Campbell-Bannerman's shortlist of two for the Presidency of the Board of Education, the other being Winston Churchill. John Morley's belief that Churchill 'as umpire between Church and Chapel, and haggling over Syllabuses with the Abp. and Dr. Clifford, would be both ridiculous and a *scandal*' reinforced Campbell-Bannerman's concern that Churchill was 'only a Liberal of yesterday, his tomorrow being a little doubtful'.[4] The position became McKenna's after Morley's suggestion of Loulou Harcourt was negated by Harcourt. McKenna was, one observer noted, 'the perfect administrative man, bringing a cool, mathematical judgment to bear on the affairs of Department or Government, and about most of them exasperatingly right'.[5] He wasted no time in applying his skills to the work of the Board of Education and within a few weeks had taken control of what was to become the Education (Administrative Provisions) Act (see Chapter 12) as well as formulating a replacement Bill for that of 1906.

This new, one-clause Bill was intended to be no more than a temporary measure so that it would not 'prejudice a wider settlement when opportunity serves'. Its underlying principle was a resurrection of the Court of Appeal judgment in the West Riding case, that is, it was intended to allow undenominational religious instruction to be funded from the rates but not denominational teaching. Where the latter was provided, the managers of the school were to pay the LEA the costs involved, which for the purposes of the Bill were taken to be one-fifteenth of the teacher's salary. McKenna believed that the Bill could be introduced under the ten-minute rule, occupy no more than half a day for its Second Reading and a day in Committee. None the less, he believed it should be introduced as soon as possible.[6]

Unexpected corroboration of his estimate of the amount of salary to be deducted for religious teaching was provided in a memorandum from Cardinal Bourne relating to training colleges. McKenna was delighted that Bourne's estimate matched his while the cardinal, in turn, was pleased by McKenna's comment that his Bill did not prevent teachers from giving religious instruction in schools; it was concerned only with who was to pay for it.[7] But when McKenna introduced the Bill on 26 February, under the ten-minute rule, the reception from the Nonconformists was not promising and the Anglicans were furious. Trevelyan thought that the Lords might accept the Bill, however, as they could then claim that in doing so they had removed all the grievances of the Nonconformists, a possibility he did not find attractive.[8]

Three weeks after the Bill's introduction the government faced the threat of new passive resistance, this time from members of the High Church party, should the measure be enacted. Anxiety existed among teachers also as to whether, if the Bill became law, the denominations would reimburse them for giving religious teaching. Ripon was worried by rumours in the press of impending alterations to the Bill but on 22 March Crewe confided to him 'I don't know what the prospects of the Bill are, but it is not likely to be stiffened'.[9] By now it was clear that the Bill had virtually no friends but many enemies. In addition, the failure of the 1906 Bill had drained some members of the government of much of their earlier commitment to resolving the education issue and they included Campbell-Bannerman, who by now

PUNCH, OR THE LONDON CHARIVARI.—February 27, 1907.

FOR THIS RELIEF NO THANKS.

Mr. R. M'Kenna (*the good fairy*). "MY POOR SUFFERER, I AM COME TO FREE YOU FROM YOUR FETTERS!"
Dr. Clifford (*still passively resisting*). "OH, DON'T SAY THAT! I DO SO *LOVE* BEING A MARTYR."

[It is stated that the new Minister of Education is to introduce a Bill that will remedy the grievance of the Passive Resister.]

9 'For this relief *no* thanks': A novel portrayal of an education policy-maker – Reginald McKenna in his new role as President of the Board of Education with Dr John Clifford as the apparently unwilling beneficiary. (Cartoon in *Punch*, CXXXII, 27 February 1907, p. 147)

was somewhat weary of the topic, as well as suffering from a decline in his health.[10] Furthermore, there was now another Education Bill before the House which, with its provision for the medical inspection and treatment of elementary school children, was more likely to engender public support. The government consulted the committee of Nonconformist MPs as to whether they would prefer the government to continue with McKenna's Bill or have a more comprehensive measure in the next Session, and, receiving support for the latter, withdrew the Bill in May.

When McKenna dined with the Webbs in July Beatrice observed that 'Office has hardened him – developed both capacity and cynicism'. Sidney was impressed by the rapidity of his mind and they both recognised 'his hard businesslike tone', although Beatrice conceded that he did have some goodwill, albeit 'of a somewhat common sort'. Their meeting had been arranged to discuss an old-age pension scheme but McKenna discoursed upon a new Education Bill, 'which he means to pass!' Voluntary schools were to be required to have the support of three-quarters of the parents, would be funded solely by the parliamentary grant and voluntary contributions but would be totally free from LEA control. When he stated that Cowper-Temple instruction would be 'swept away, and in its stead hymns, prayers and Bible reading' Beatrice found it difficult to understand precisely what he meant.[11] A month later, McKenna revealed his ideas for the new Bill to the Cabinet.

He stressed that these ideas were predicated upon a consideration both of the education system ultimately desired and the intermediate means by which it could be achieved. The ultimate system would be one, he postulated, in which every State school would be wholly under the control of an LEA, in which the LEA would have the 'unfettered right' of both appointing and dismissing teachers and in which there would be no distinctions between State schools. To achieve this meant increasing rather than lessening the gap in the dual system of schools. Apart from the transfer of voluntary schools to LEA control in single school areas, albeit at the discretion of the LEAs, McKenna intended that the remaining voluntary schools should 'contract out' and only receive the parliamentary grant, in return for which they would be completely outside the jurisdiction of the LEA.[12] The Cabinet's response went unrecorded but two months later McKenna informed Morant that he was asking Thring to draw up a draft Bill based on these proposals. Crewe told Ripon that when he had last seen McKenna 'he seemed confident that he would get all sections at any rate to acquiesce in his proposals'. Crewe thought this a sanguine hope but was sure that McKenna had no intention of departing from his main aim of 'allowing strictly denominational schools to continue with a grant . . . on condition of their going off the rates'. Crewe foresaw all the opposition this proposal was likely to generate but thought that perhaps it did offer 'the clearest way out of the wood'.[13]

On 18 November, McKenna presented the draft Bill to Cabinet and cited the pressure on parliamentary time in the forthcoming Session as the chief reason for the measure's brevity. He remained committed to the main goal of a uniform public elementary school system, that is only rate-maintained schools were to be council schools and there would be no religious tests for teachers although they could volunteer to give Cowper-Temple instruction. In single school areas voluntary schools were either to be compulsorily acquired by the LEA, but for which no rent would be paid, or if they retained their voluntary status they had to forfeit both rate and State aid. In the case of those transferred voluntary schools which possessed a 'tight trust', that is one in which the school buildings were to be used solely for educational purposes, then the trustees would retain access to the buildings at week-ends. Finally, education rates for capital expenditure would henceforward be levied equally over a county and a new system of grants payable by the Board to the LEAs would be introduced.[14] John Burns thought McKenna's presentation of his case had been put 'clearly and bravely' but observed that Lloyd George was not happy with the proposals, being 'rather fractious and hostile to McKenna'. He was reputed to have warned McKenna that with his 'contracting-out' arrangement for the voluntary schools the Bill would be 'heading straight for the rocks'.[15] Campbell-Bannerman, not only overworked but still ill, appeared 'rather bored at the futility of attempting to reconcile education with sectarian claims and sacerdotal domination', but McKenna was authorised to develop his draft in readiness for the next Session.[16] At the end of November, however, McKenna left the country for a six-week holiday in France, telling his friend Walter Runciman that he had 'absconded' because his 'enfeebled constitution' prevented his staying at his work any longer, 'I was nervous and stammery and found myself getting excited at Cabinets, and so I left'.[17]

When Crewe met Morant in early January he found him 'strong for contracting out' as the only solution for any settlement of the voluntary schools but had no new information on the Bill.[18] And when McKenna returned to London a fortnight later John Burns found him 'full of faith about his simple three point Bill' but Morant was excluded from his counsels.[19] Thus when Morant discovered that McKenna had arranged a committee meeting for early February, he complained to Thring, 'I have had no talk of any kind with McKenna about my points on the Bill . . . and I do not know quite what the purpose of the . . . meeting is supposed to be'.[20] The probable reason for this somewhat irregular situation is not difficult to find. When Birrell left the Board he had told Campbell-Bannerman that he felt sure that Morant, despite rumours to the contrary, had served the government faithfully.[21] McKenna, however, was not so sure, having found Morant a not totally willing ally in the preparation of the Education (Administrative Provisions) Bill (see Chapter 12). Furthermore, in August 1907 he had received a disturbing letter about Morant from an acquaintance in the Reform Club:

> The last achievement of your friend Morant . . . is to refer to yourself, in my hearing (I was unknown to him), and *in mixed company*, at dinner, as being an 'utterly colourless person who did not count'; and, specifically and particularly, as *'merely Asquith's jackal'*.[22]

Why Morant should have been so foolish as to make these views public is difficult to understand except possibly for a revealing comment he made later to a colleague:

> . . . It is not often that I let things 'worry' me. I am generally content with the feeling that one is doing one's best, even though it results in little: and that some good *trend* is manifesting itself. But the recent lack of honesty of purpose, and debasing of our machinery to basely political purposes, does tell on one gradually – in the direction of embitterment.[23]

He was to suffer for his indiscretion, as McKenna's behaviour towards him revealed, while his position as Permanent Secretary came under closer scrutiny. McKenna knew that Morant's lack of tact had, earlier in 1907, resulted in a conflict with Runciman (Financial Secretary to the Treasury) over the Board's budget estimates. It was perhaps not surprising, therefore, that by April 1908 Runciman was told, 'By Whitsuntide (surely) we should have something definitely arranged about Morant. At least I earnestly hope so'.[24] But in February 1908 McKenna had to concentrate on ensuring Cabinet support for his Bill.

The new draft of the measure was presented to the Cabinet on 17

February and gained their approval, after some discussion, two days later. The modifications McKenna had made demonstrated quite clearly that the only provision of facilities for denominational instruction in any public elementary school would occur in single-school areas provided this was agreed to at the time of the school's transfer to the LEA. The Bill also made it abundantly clear that teachers in council schools would not be required, but could volunteer, to give Cowper-Temple instruction. The contracting-out arrangement for voluntary schools remained but was now only applicable to schools with at least 30 children and not located in a single school area; at the same time the parliamentary grant would be increased to 47 shillings per child in average attendance. Five days later McKenna introduced the Bill to a House in which the Unionists awaited his announcements, one journalist believed, with 'more curiosity than concern'.[25] Gorst wrote to congratulate McKenna on his 'lucid, *business like*' speech, as did the eminent Nonconformist minister Guinness Rogers who acknowledged that the measure was not the 'Dissenting settlement' but felt that it was now important for both dissenters and churchmen to 'learn a give and take policy'.[26] One LEA administrator present in the House for the introduction felt the measure would provide LEAs with 'clear main principles which we have not had yet' but he was perturbed by Balfour's tirade against it.[27] Balfour's 'furious hostility', as one MP described his reaction, had included the comment that it would be impossible for him to promise the Bill 'either a smooth or easy voyage' so that the possibility of another strenuous battle over education loomed once more.

Sandars liked the Bill no better than his leader and he was worried also about the strong likelihood of there being no substantial Unionist opposition to it, for there were now definite signs of boredom among the party as far as education was concerned. He felt that 'a great many of our people would be glad to get this thorny subject out of the way'.[28] Similarly, the thought of a repetition of 1906 (and 1902) troubled many Liberal MPs, and only Robert Perks of the Nonconformist Liberal MPs condemned it outright. But when Dr John Clifford, although unhappy about the contracting-out arrangement, accepted the need for compromise, Perks reluctantly endorsed the Bill at a meeting of the Free Church Council Education Committee.[29] Members of the Church were not so ready to accede, however, to a compromise because for them the Bill was draconian. It not only threatened a potential loss in income for those voluntary schools which contracted-out but it also meant that those of their schools which were transferred to LEAs would lose either all or, in single school areas, most of their denominational teaching. A National Society pamphlet depicted the measure as

> . . . a policy of wholesale destruction of Church schools in the country districts; degradation and the prospect of destruction – immediate in the great majority of cases and rapid in almost all – of voluntary schools in towns . . . . This Bill is almost entirely negative in its working. It destroys much, but . . . it creates little or nothing . . . .Mr McKenna's scheme is confiscation naked and unabashed.[30]

The Archbishop of Canterbury was disappointed by the Bill also, not so much by its intentions as by the way it was proposed to achieve them. After perusing it for ten days he could not find any basis for a possible compromise since the measure would only 'accentuate rather than relieve our existing difficulties'.[31] This view was shared by many Catholics and a by-election defeat for the government at Peckham was attributed in part to Catholic defections.[32] McKenna's problems were to increase when the Bishop of St. Asaph, encouraged by Lloyd George among others, introduced an Education Bill into the Lords at the end of March.

Ostensibly utilising the aims of McKenna's Bill, St. Asaph proposed that *all* schools should be transferred to LEAs, with undenominational teaching provided at the expense of the LEAs. This would ensure, he claimed, that all schools were part of one system and under public control. Where he differed from McKenna was in his proposal that if parents desired them, denominational facilities would be provided on at least three days a week, and within school hours although the LEAs would not be responsible for the funding of this instruction nor would teachers be required to give it. Davidson felt happier with this measure, believing it to be closer to achieving the necessary compromise between the Church and Nonconformists, and so supported it in the Lords. Balfour, on the other hand, felt that the Church was making rather than gaining concessions and opposed it. One Anglo-Catholic, Lord Halifax, who was firmly committed to the goal of equal provisions for denominational and undenominational instruction, was beside himself with fury after he had listened to the Bill's introduction. He told his daughter that both St. Asaph and Davidson had not only made 'odious' speeches but neither of them were 'to be trusted for a single instant'.[33] Lansdowne's motion at the end of the reading, proposing the Bill's adjournment, was accepted by the Lords

NEW LAMPS FOR OLD

as a means of allowing negotiations to take place with the government. A few days later, however, events were to alter the future of both Bills.

On 12 February Campbell-Bannerman had suffered another heart attack and then was stricken with influenza. Confined to his bed in 10 Downing Street, he refused to believe that he would not recover but as time passed and his condition did not improve, it was only a matter of time before he would have to resign. After six weeks he accepted the inevitable and on 3 April sent his letter of resignation to the King, who was in Biarritz. Edward VII then took the unusual step of summoning Asquith to France rather than returning to London to appoint the new Premier. Seen off by McKenna at Charing Cross station on 6 April, Asquith returned four days later as the confirmed successor to Campbell-Bannerman and in the ensuing government reshuffle McKenna moved to the Admiralty while Runciman succeeded him at the Board of Education; McKenna, however, continued to maintain his responsibility for the Education Bill.

On the day of Asquith's return as Premier, McKenna had a meeting with Davidson and found him to be totally unhappy with the provision in the Bill that the head teachers of transferred voluntary schools would be unable to give denominational instruction. As he commented subsequently, 'the measure of recognition . . . given to the denominational principle is quite different in your plan from what it is under the St. Asaph plan'. Furthermore, he was unhappy with McKenna's proposed procedure for a conference which would include:

(1) A resolve on your part what to recommend;
(2) an endeavour on your part to obtain the individual concurrence of certain leaders in ecclesiastical matters;
(3) a conference under the Prime Minister's chairmanship at which those who had already committed themselves to you in private should commit themselves in the presence of one another with such result that the conference might be quoted as having agreed to particular arrangements.[34]

Thus as the time for the Second Reading of the Bill approached, it was becoming apparent that the measure was engendering very little support from either the Liberal Party, the religious bodies or the public at large. McKenna also had his hands full sorting out the problems left at the Admiralty by his predecessor, Lord Tweedmouth. After a Cabinet discussion on the Bill on 13 May, however, it was decided that in the Second Reading debate nothing would be said that might 'close the door to a future arrangement, if (as is not yet the case) the various parties and interests can be brought within a measurable distance of agreement'.[35] McKenna thus opened the Second Reading with a comparison of his and St. Asaph's Bills and argued that given their similarity some compromise should be possible. The Opposition's lack of response to this approach led the Cabinet to agree that the Premier should try 'to open the way to a general understanding' but the subsequent debate in the House was not promising. Trevelyan noted the 'curious contrast to the over-heated electric atmosphere' that had existed in 1906 and thought that 'the moderate man was beginning to tire of the strife of sects'.[36] The absence of many Members from the chamber supported his view and further debate on the Bill was suspended by the government. It now became the task of Runciman to try to produce a viable solution.

Runciman had already had a meeting with Morant to discuss the main points to be included in any new Bill and the outcome was a mixture of those points already contained in the McKenna and St. Asaph Bills. While the contracting-out of voluntary schools remained a key feature, the funding would now be such that the process would be 'a penalisation and not a privilege' and it would be available only to those schools not conducted on Protestant lines. Apart from this, the other major difference from McKenna's Bill was that Runciman envisaged facilities being available for denominational instruction on three mornings each week in LEA schools, albeit only as a result of parental demand and still subject to LEA approval although not finance. This instruction would be given at the same time as the Cowper-Temple teaching although the latter would be given on every morning of the week and could be given by the head teacher.[37] Runciman's approach to formulating the measure was altered, however, by the receipt of a letter from Lord Crewe enclosing some papers by the Bishop of Ripon signalling his willingness to introduce a Bill into the Lords or to establish a conference 'excluding extremists' if it would help.

Crewe drew Runciman's attention to the important fact that the bishop 'gives up the Head Teacher', adding that he was

> . . . a very good type of Liberal Churchman and carries considerable weight. As the Archbishop does, he lays special stress on the consolation to those who lose the Church character of their schools, especially in country districts, in feeling that the quid pro quo is given in the form of greater facilities in other places. The Archbishop has always said that if this could be shown

to be the case the whole moderate Church opinion would be captured.[38]

Reflecting on these views, and Davidson's professed desire to reach a compromise, Runciman decided to adopt a strategy of negotiation before finalising the Bill's contents. To this end, and before the Second Reading of McKenna's Bill, he sent memoranda containing the points agreed with Morant, but with different degrees of emphasis, to both Davidson and the Nonconformist leaders. Towards the end of May, Runciman met with them, separately, to discuss the points as the possible basis for a settlement.

The Nonconformists were not only cautious in their response but were clearly unhappy about the possibility of there being any denominational teaching in LEA schools. Davidson was cautious too but indicated that he might be prepared to make concessions if it would lead to a settlement and he accepted Runciman's point that McKenna's Bill would form the basis of the settlement. But when he received a new memorandum from Runciman, reputedly incorporating the points discussed during their meeting, he found little difference between the two memoranda and expressed his 'puzzled disappointment'. He was particularly perturbed by the fact that neither his view of the need for greater emphasis on parental demands for denominational instruction nor his desire for safeguards to ensure that hostile LEAs could not prevent denominational facilities from being allowed had been incorporated. Faced with an imminent meeting of his bishops, Davidson wanted reassurances from Runciman that these points had been accepted. Runciman refuted the imputation that he had gone back on his word and added the comment that they needed to trust each other.[39] News of their meeting reached Lord Salisbury and in some alarm he warned Balfour: 'The Government are very anxious to compromise on the Education Bill and so are many of your followers in the House. It is therefore a moment of great peril.'[40]

Balfour's response came in a speech a month later and it worried Runciman for

> . . . with unusual skill he sets up a complete series of demands which he knows *no government* could grant, stating thereon that the option is between these and continued war![41]

Runciman warned Davidson of the consequences for any possible settlement as far as the government and its supporters were concerned if Balfour's 'apparent attitude' was allowed to dominate the Church and the House of Lords. Davidson noted Runciman's warning but when he was holidaying in Italy during August he learned from Michael Sadler news of a campaign within the Church to oppose the Bill. He knew that he could not quash it for this would alienate 'our extreme and more uncompromising friends' but, at the same time, he did believe the campaign would help to indicate that the Church was not prepared to accept 'scraps' from the government.[42]

While Davidson remained in Italy there was little that Runciman could do in achieving a settlement with the Church and to the public, unaware of his negotiations, it looked as though McKenna's Bill was being allowed to lapse. Runciman thus found himself being criticised by some Nonconformists for the lack of progress. He reassured the Free Church Council that the government had not forgotten the education question yet could only comment that he was 'toiling quietly' and hoping to achieve 'by other means what we have hitherto failed to secure by frontal attack'.[43] At the same time Runciman wrote to Robertson Nicoll, editor of the *British Weekly* and a fervent supporter of the Nonconformist cause, complaining about the attacks coming from the Nonconformists, and stated that not only was he 'quietly negotiating' for a settlement but that he hoped to succeed.[44] It was not to be until October, however, before any further progress could be made.

Shortly before he met Davidson in mid-October, Runciman received a letter reporting a recent meeting of the National Education Association, which had been addressed by Kekewich on the ways a compromise could be reached with the Church. Kekewich's proposals had included denominational instruction by head teachers and the abolition of the Cowper-Temple clause but they had been rejected by the meeting since the first point was a major 'bone of contention' with the Church owing to the seminal importance of the head teacher's role for a school's character.[45] This point was not lost on Runciman for when he met Davidson the latter had not shifted his ground on this issue and, as in 1906, he insisted on the head teachers of voluntary schools being allowed to continue to give denominational instruction. The memorandum submitted by Runciman to the Cabinet after the meeting, outlining the possible basis for a settlement, showed that while there was concurrence in the majority of instances this was not so where the head teacher's role was concerned.[46] Davidson, in his account to his colleagues about the meeting, forecast that there would be opposition from some LEAs and teachers over the contracting-out option and the provision of facilities within council schools. He also identified the House of Lords as another possible source of opposition

THE TRAGEDY OF ROMEO AND JULIET.

JULIET (DAVIEZONE) to ROMEO (RUNCIMAN) *as they are torn apart by
infuriated friends.* "I have no joy of this contract to-night!
  It is too rash, too unadvised, too sudden;
  Too like the lightning, which doth cease to be
  Ere one can say 'It lightens.' Sweet, good night!

  This bud of love by Ingram's ripening breath
  May prove a beauteous flower when next we meet."
ROMEO. "Oh, blessed, blessed night! I was afeard,
  Being in night, all this was but a dream,
  Too flattering-sweet to be substantial!" [*Is hauled down.*

10 'The Tragedy of Romeo and Juliet': The doomed attempt by Davidson and
Runciman to reach a settlement over the 1908 Bill. (Cartoon in *Punch*, CXXXIV,
9 December 1908, p. 427)

and believed that if a successful settlement was to be reached the Lords should not be pressed. He advocated the remainder of the year being spent in private conference and negotiation as a means of breaking down resistance to a settlement.[47] Runciman, conscious of the pressure being exerted by the Nonconformists for results, could not afford to be so generous with time.

Another meeting between Davidson and Runciman in October, with Morant and the Bishop of Southwark also present, was used by Davidson to seek not only clarification on certain points but also to reinforce the Church's position on the importance of head teachers being allowed to give denominational instruction. Prohibition of this was seen to be, he claimed, 'a *very* serious difficulty'.[48] The Bishop of Southwark told Morant subsequently that there was another major stumbling block in the form of the urban voluntary schools, not least because of the amount of money which had been spent on them. The bishop floated the idea of rate maintenance in preference to contracting-out for if the latter position had to be adopted to preserve the schools, the Roman Catholics 'would revile us and hold us up to the scorn of our own people'. Though Morant was not very sympathetic, the bishop persisted with his proposal, arguing that the loss of urban as well as rural schools would be 'too great a double sacrifice' to be borne by the Church.[49] Morant told Thring, the Parliamentary Draftsman, that the negotiations to date had revealed only

> how many are the practical points on which breakdown is likely to arise, even though some agreement on rather vaguely worded points might be attained. And we have not yet seen the way in which this can be avoided.[50]

All now seemed to hinge on a meeting of the bishops at Lambeth on 27 October as it was still not clear whether they would veto the possibility of a settlement, agree to terms which would be impossible for the government to accept or push for a viable settlement.

The meeting revealed that although the bishops were agreed in principle to a settlement there were still considerable difficulties blocking its achievement, not least being the 'immense' sacrifice required of the Church. Davidson told Asquith that this burden would be accepted by some of the Church only if it would lead to a resolution of the religious controversy but there were others who were firmly convinced that this would not happen and that they would 'be opposed to our listening favourably to the suggestions made'. All he could provide at this stage, therefore, were the terms which he and his supporters were prepared to accept. They matched those in Runci-man's Cabinet memorandum fairly closely but Davidson observed that considerable discontent existed with the terms for contracting-out and stated that if 'reasonable fairness' was to be achieved by the settle-ment then the number of denominational schools in urban areas con-tracting-out 'must be considerable'. Furthermore, since many urban voluntary schools were educationally sound the terms of the contract-ing-out arrangement should be such that these schools would not be left in the position of 'a sickly and somewhat awkward excrescence, grudgingly tolerated on the outside of our national system of educa-tion'.[51] Asquith responded by arranging a meeting with Davidson and Runciman and this proved to be successful in that agreement was secured on all but two of the main points to be included in the Bill. Disagreement remained over the prohibition of the head teacher from giving denominational instruction and of an LEA being empowered but not required to ensure that facilities were made available in its schools. Morant decided, none the less, that Thring should produce a series of amendments to the McKenna Bill as soon as possible, warn-ing him that the wording of the amendments was crucial, for the points to be covered were the outcome of Runciman's negotiations with both the Nonconformists and the archbishop. Morant was worried that many of these points appeared inconsistent with the formulation of a clear policy for the Bill but this could not be prevented as Runciman considered them all to be vital.[52] A letter two days later from Clifford and six other Nonconformist leaders, however, revealed that these preparations might be premature.

Clifford and his colleagues had found Davidson's concessions to the government's proposals 'limited' at best, for nowhere could they find evidence that he was prepared to countenance the establishment of a truly national system of elementary education. Furthermore, his views about denominational facilities were seen as being both repugnant and coercive with respect to council schools. Unless Davidson changed his stance on these points they felt it would be pointless trying to negotiate a settlement.[53] Morant appears to have accepted their views at face value and told Runciman that there was now little chance of a Bill being passed. But when Maurice, Runciman's private secretary, attended a public meeting addressed by Clifford and others a few days later, his overall impression from the audience's response was that

> it did not look as if they would feel bound to get up much of an agitation hereafter if they woke up one morning to find you had passed your settlement through on to the Statute Book.[54]

Maurice believed the door to a settlement remained ajar and the next critical stage would be, therefore, Runciman's forthcoming meeting with the committee of Liberal Nonconformist MPs.

Runciman took great care in his address to this meeting to demonstrate the rationale underlying each stage of the negotiations since May. Ignoring the latest message from them, Runciman explained that the concessions by Clifford and the other Nonconformist leaders had been made on the basis that if the Church was to be expected to make a major sacrifice, 'we must ourselves advance in our position'. He portrayed in graphic terms the difficulties which had accompanied the negotiations with the Church before revealing that the only issues which remained outstanding were that of the head teacher giving denominational instruction and whether facilities in council schools should be optional or compulsory. Emphasising the point that unless agreement could be reached upon them there would be no settlement, he went on to argue that if there was not to be a wholesale contracting-out of voluntary schools there would have to be facilities granted within council schools: 'The more *bona fide* your facilities, the smaller will be the number of contracting-out schools.' Such a policy would mean, he claimed, that only some 600 schools would contract out rather than a possible 6000 if this policy was not implemented. Once this was achieved then it would be only a matter of time before pressure of finance would force the contracted-out schools into the state system. On the second issue of whether it should be optional or compulsory for LEAs to provide facilities Runciman felt the position of the Primate had to be considered. The concessions gained from him had to be balanced with the ones gained by him, and these had to be

> not a mere chance but something in black and white which is substantial. That is what he wants. And it is not only what he wants, but it is in order to save his own skin to a large extent, and I think we must consider his skin. Because I must say for him that he has played perfectly fair with me, and I do not want to take him in.[55]

Runciman believed that if agreement could be reached on these two outstanding points then the Lords would comply with the archbishop's views. This would leave Balfour as the only unknown factor in the equation but he was confident that he (Balfour) would be powerless to wreck the Bill in the face of Anglican and Nonconformist agreement. At the end of the meeting, and despite 'a decent show of reluctance and a respectable exhibition of conscientious scruples', Runciman, with a 'pocket full of proxies', received overwhelming support, even from Perks, who seconded the resolution supporting the government's efforts.[56] Asquith was able to write to Davidson the next day, therefore, and offer that 'if you will meet us over the Head Teacher, we will acquiesce in a statutory right of entry to all Council Schools'.[57]

Davidson's views had been affected, in the interim, by his chairing of a meeting of the Standing Committee of the National Society a few days previously. Seeking the Society's acceptance of the government's proposals as the best offer they would ever get, his arguments had been received by a long silence, eventually broken by speeches of 'mingled remonstrance, indignation and despair' from Lord Hugh Cecil, John Talbot, the Dean of Canterbury and Canon Cleworth, and consequently the Committee had resolved to adjourn for a week.[58] Lord Halifax, a key member of the Society, was absent from the meeting but when informed of the Archbishop's views he felt close to apoplexy:

> I nearly strangle with rage every time I think of the Archbishops and the Bishops generally. Oh the traitors! Some few remain, but for the rest I should like to put them all into a bag and make a parcel of them to Dr Clifford to clean his boots and brush his clothes.[59]

His reaction was to be expected but Davidson could not afford to ignore the general atmosphere of the meeting and his response to Asquith's offer was muted and hedged with requests for further clarification of the government's position. The government were thus still no wiser as to the chances of a settlement being reached and Runciman decided to consider the Catholics' views of the Bill.

The Catholic hierarchy had been upset by the government's firm request in September that a procession of the Consecrated Host should not take place in London during an international eucharistic conference. Ripon had acted on behalf of the government in the affair and had secured Bourne's reluctant acquiescence to the request but Ripon had resigned from the government shortly afterwards. Runciman continued to use him, however, as the channel by which to contact Bourne and sent him a note containing a warning that as Bourne refused to negotiate with the government until they removed Catholic disabilities he had 'to devise as generous terms for the English Catholics as we can without conference with their representatives'.[60] The message had the desired effect and a few days later Ripon reported that Bourne was prepared to discuss the Bill. At their meeting Runciman revealed the state reached in the negotiations with the Anglicans and Nonconformists and Bourne felt bound to reply that it appeared pointless to agree to anything until Runciman had actually finalised matters with the Anglicans. Privately he was alarmed by the amount of agreement that had already been reached for it looked as though the Catholics were in danger of becoming isolated. His concern was justified for Sandars believed the government's inquiries had satisfied them that 'they can safely ignore the R.C.s as an electoral quantity and that they may regret but they can disregard their protests'.[61] Sandars' view appeared to be confirmed when, a few days later, Runciman left a copy of the draft Bill with Davidson.

The draft did not please Davidson for, while it reflected in general the agreements reached, it also lacked the details about the conditions of contracting-out, the transfer of voluntary schools – including the headmaster's role in teaching denominational instruction – and the finances involved. He informed Asquith of his concerns but on the same day received a virtual summons from Runciman:

> It is necessary that we should know tonight by letter –
> (i) that you do not press the right to set up *new* contracted-out schools;
> (ii) and that rather than wreck the agreement, you will accept the head teacher's power to volunteer being limited to existing head teachers in existing denominational schools.[62]

Runciman added that if the archbishop responded favourably to these two items nothing would be left incomplete except the financial details and this, he added, 'we expect you to leave open'.

Davidson was aware that some of his colleagues believed he was now in danger of being outwitted by Runciman who was seen as having 'the wits of a sharp boy and is not overburdened with scruples'.[63] His reply pressed, therefore, for the missing details to be provided before he would give his assent and, furthermore, this would only be given in respect of the recommendations being considered by his fellow Churchmen. Asquith, alarmed that the chance of a settlement was in danger of foundering, asked Davidson to stipulate precisely the terms needed for his acceptance, which he did, stating that they were the Church's right to build new contracting-out schools; the right of a voluntary school headmaster to give denominational instruction in his transferred school and the power for LEAs to provide advisory committees with regard to denominational instruction. The government accepted them, and on 19 November Asquith informed the House that as a concordat had been reached with the Church and Nonconformists, McKenna's Bill would be withdrawn and a new one introduced the next day.

One of Runciman's friends believed that success was still possible, writing:

> I have a mental vision of you standing at the helm of a very fine schooner close-reafed [sic] to a hurricane of bigotry and narrow mindedness, but still clearing the sea of ignorance & successfully [breaking] off the lee shore which threatens to smash your Bill![64]

But Lord Balcarres, the Unionist Whip, held a different view:

> I doubt if this Bill can hope to pass in its present form . . . The broad observation is that it purports to be a compromise – but it accepts all from us and gives nothing in return – or to be more accurate the Bill devises elaborate and crushing methods of denying to us in substance those rights of which we shall only secure the shadow. . . . It is obvious the Archbishop has been duped. He is no lawyer, no draftsman; he is unaccustomed to deal with astute and unscrupulous ministers . . . [65]

Meeting the Bishop of London a few days later, Balcarres learned that a critical appraisal of the right of entry he had given the bishop had caused the archbishop 'to revise his opinion or rather to state that the Bill does not embody the undertakings he received'. The bishop also authorised Balfour to state in the Second Reading of the Bill that he (the bishop) would vote against the Bill owing to the illusory nature of the terms affecting school transfer, contracting-out and the right of entry.[66]

It was the financial allowances contained in the Bill that troubled Davidson most, and he told Runciman that the sum stipulated for contracting-out schools, that is from 47 to 50 shillings (per child in attendance) was totally inadequate. He commented also that throughout the negotiations Runciman had intimated that the government would be generous in the measure's financial terms and he had had 'implicit trust' in Runciman's statements. This trust had enabled him to resist the view of friends that he was 'a simple Simon negotiating with people who are not simple Simons at all'. For that trust to be retained he had to be assured that if it could be shown that the Bill would 'mean a general impossibility of contracting out' Runciman would revise the finances involved.[67] But Runciman's speech on the Second Reading of the Bill did not assuage the Primate's worries and he told him that '. . . both the contracting-out terms and the rent schedule for transfers, would *as they stand*, make your offer almost void. I think I can, with expert aid, make this clear to you'.[68] He proposed, therefore, that an appropriate amendment be drafted by the Board of Education to which he could respond. Runciman dispatched Morant to try to resolve this problem with Davidson and when a letter appeared in *The Times* from Bourne expounding the Catholics' grievances about the Bill's terms, including the proposed financial settlement, Runciman told one of his assistants to go with Morant, and whomsoever he thought necessary, to meet the Catholics' experts and to 'Make mincemeat of their figures'.[69] Although Morant was successful in both of these tasks, such actions by Runciman could not hold back the rising tide of opposition to the measure.

Hirst Hollowell found it distressing that a Liberal government had introduced a Bill containing the two 'anti-democratic principles of "right of entry" and "contracting out"'. He told Labour MP Ramsay Macdonald that his speech against the Second Reading had made him look to the Labour Party to reinforce opposition to the Bill and in this he sought the co-operation of the Labour Party with the Northern Counties' Education League, the NUT, the National Education Association and the Liberation Society. One goal would be a conference and demonstration in London against the Bill.[70] Hollowell's sentiments were shared by some teachers who looked to the Labour MPs to support amendments to minimise contracting-out, the right of entry and to provide a fair wage for teachers in contracted-out schools, for the 'proper safety and due interest of many teachers' were likely to be in jeopardy under the Bill.[71] Prominent members of the Church hierarchy, meanwhile, had taken their own steps to prevent a settlement being reached, and these had culminated in a petition to Davidson for the holding of a special meeting of the Representative Church Council. He had to accede to this, and the meeting was called for 3 December.

The day before the meeting, Runciman sent Davidson a long and detailed memorandum containing evidence which clearly refuted the calculations made by the Church's experts about the financial settlement contained in the Bill. At the same time, he indicated that the government was nevertheless prepared to make further financial concessions, the net effect of which would be that the government would bear five-sixths of the costs of contracted-out schools while the Church would only have to find one-sixth. He repeated these points in a speech that night in the House, and his comments received some support:

I cannot refrain from thanking you most warmly for your courageous and complete exposure of the 'cooked accounts' tonight. The Archbishop has been badly 'tookt in', as the Devonshire people say. If he is prepared to give up his innocently extravagant demands, and abide by his side of the agreement, then we can go on with dignity . . .[72]

The onus for achieving a settlement now appeared to rest with the Representative Church Council meeting.

Davidson tried to persuade the non-moderates present that their views of the Bill ignored the reality of what had been happening to their schools and cited as an example the fact that in the previous three years 550 Church schools had been closed with the loss of some 160,000 children to LEA schools. Responding to his own challenge, 'What about the Church's care for those children?', he claimed that the answer lay with the Bill, for under the terms of the settlement the Church would have the legal right of entry into every school in the country, and could thus reach all elementary school-age children. His argument fell on deaf ears, however, and the majority of the clergy and laity present remained resolutely opposed to the settlement while only a majority of the bishops supported him.

Fearing that this might be the likely outcome of the Church Council meeting, Runciman had written to Davidson on the day of the meeting stating that he still saw 'some glimmer of hope if you will agree that no more then 900 Church of England Schools shall contract-out and will show means by which this will be secured'. Davidson's answer had to be received, however, before the Cabinet meeting at 11 am the following morning.[73] The meeting was delayed until the afternoon so that Davidson's reply could be received. When it was, Davidson's comment that he could not see Runciman's suggestion removing 'the grave difficulties which seem to me to render some of your proposals inoperative', marked, John Burns noted, the 'end of compromises'.[74] In his reply to Davidson after Cabinet, Runciman made it quite clear that both the meeting and resolutions of the Representative Church Council had 'altered the whole situation', especially as an accepted amendment of the Bishop of Salisbury had proposed claims outside those previously agreed upon. The government had only been able to conclude that the Primate had not managed to secure 'adhesion to the terms on which the proposed settlement was based' and it had, therefore, decided to drop the Bill.[75] Three days later, Asquith announced the government's decision to the House and in the course of his tributes to Runciman, the archbishop and the Nonconformist leaders added the personal comment that he had never experienced 'a more heavy and thorough disappointment'.

Sandars saw the effect of the Bishop of Salisbury's resolution on the government as 'comic', adding, 'But it is all part of the burlesque which has been played throughout'.[76] Lord Ripon was uncertain, however, about the reason for the loss of the Bill, asking

> was it the result of a very Balfourian intrigue, or of weakness on the part of the Archbishop of Canterbury. In my own mind I favour the first explanation, coupled with the strange incapacity of the Anglican Clergy to understand the bearings of any political subject. Of course the only gains will be the friends of secular education.[77]

Runciman, in offering Asquith his resignation, stated that he had been, 'overbold, and the breakdown is I feel much more than a personal matter. Your administration does suffer because I have not succeeded'.[78] Privately, he told two correspondents his real feelings. To one he argued that he had done

> everything that was in my power to meet their views and finally by doubling the rent schedule and leaving them free in their post 1902 schools to drive as hard a bargain as they liked, to make the terms of transfer so liberal that they far exceeded the practice which has sprung up in the past four years. But it was no good when the Archbishop fell ill at the beginning of the week he became dependent for his technical information on the officials of the National Society, all of whom, with the exception of old Sir Francis Powell, were his inveterate enemies and deeply pledged against settlement.[79]

To the second, Lord Ripon, he added that he was, 'greatly grieved – and a little astonished at the short sightedness of many of the denomi-nationalists'.[80]

Asquith rejected Runciman's offer of resignation (although, significantly, he kept the letter) and claimed that he had been equally responsible for the outcome of the Bill. This generous comment not only reflected the magnitude of the forces arrayed against the Bill but demonstrably overlooked Runciman's cardinal error, after so much negotiation, in not indicating the level of the finances to be included in the Bill before it was published. By this failure, and by not providing the Board's analysis of the real expenditure to be faced by the Church until 2 December, Runciman had, although trying to preserve the government's position against excessive Church demands, unwittingly weakened Davidson's case against his vociferous colleagues and thus had contributed to the failure of the Bill. In this sense, Balfour's comment was apt:

> The Education Bill itself was the most remarkable piece of bungling on the part of both the Archbishop and the Ministry that ever was heard of. Even now I cannot discern what they were at or how they could ever imagine that negotiations so strangely conducted could have even a temporary chance.[81]

At the same time, Campbell-Bannerman's comment about the 1906 Education Bill's failure was still valid for 'if there had been only the Archbishop of Canterbury to deal with, a compromise could have been arranged'.[82] This had not been the case and now, six years after its enactment, the Welsh rebellion and three attempts at legislation by the Liberal government, the 1902 Education Act remained the legal basis of the nation's education system. The government decided that another attempt in the near future was not worth pursuing. This somewhat dismal achievement as far as educational policy reform was concerned was counterbalanced by two educational measures which had been passed in 1906 and 1907 and were to be of more lasting consequence and benefit as far as many of the nation's scholars were concerned.

NOTES

1. Lord Hardinge, *Old Diplomacy* (1947), pp. 131–2 cited in J. Wilson, *CB: A Life of Sir Henry Campbell-Bannerman*, p. 570.
2. Cited in J. Vincent (ed.), *The Crawford Papers: The journals of David Lindsay 27th Earl of Crawford and 10th Earl of Balcarres, 1871–1940 during the years 1892 to 1940* (1984), 21 Dec. 1906, p. 99.
3. Birrell Papers, MS 10.2, fo.8, H. Campbell-Bannerman to A. Birrell, 25 Dec. 1906.
4. Campbell-Bannerman Papers, Add MS 41223, fos.207–8, J. Morley to Sir H. Campbell-Bannerman, 1 Jan. 1907; Sir H. Campbell-Bannerman to A. Birrell, 25 Dec. 1906 cited in Wilson, op. cit., p. 590.
5. J.A. Spender, *Life, Journalism and Politics* (1927), p. 164.
6. PRO CAB/37/87/15, R. McKenna, 'One Clause Bill', 14 Feb. 1907.
7. Ripon Papers, Add MS 43640, fos. 66–7, R. McKenna to Lord Ripon, 23 Feb. 1907; Add MS 43545, fos. 106–7, Lord Ripon to Cardinal Bourne, 25 Feb. 1907.
8. Trevelyan Papers, CPT Ex 71, Political notes pre-1914.
9. Ripon Papers, Add MS 43552, fo.142, Lord Crewe to Lord Ripon, 22 March 1907.

10. A mild heart attack had occurred in Oct. 1906 and he was to suffer two more in 1907, one in June and the other in Nov. See Wilson, op. cit., p. 608.
11. B. Webb, *Our Partnership* (1948), pp. 384–5.
12. PRO CAB 37/89/78, R. McKenna, 'Suggestions for an Education Bill', 19 Aug. 1907.
13. Ripon Papers, Add 43552, fos. 183–4, Lord Crewe to Lord Ripon, 21 Oct. 1907.
14. PRO CAB 37/90/95, J. McKenna, 'Draft of an Education Bill', 14 Nov. 1907.
15. R.W. Perks to Lord Rosebery, 26 Nov. 1907 cited in G.I.T. Machin, *Politics and the Churches in Great Britain 1869 to 1921*, p. 290.
16. J. Burns Papers, Add MS 46235, *Diary,* 18 Nov. 1907.
17. Runciman Papers, WR 21, R. McKenna to W. Runciman, 3 Jan. 1908.
18. Ripon Papers, Add MS 43552, fo.189, Lord Crewe to Lord Ripon, 9 Jan. 1908.
19. J. Burns Papers, Add MS 46236, *Diary,* 24 Jan. 1908.
20. PRO ED 24/153, R.L. Morant to A.T. Thring, 25 Jan. 1908.
21. Campbell-Bannerman Papers, Add MS 41239, fos. 192–3, A. Birrell to H. Campbell-Bannerman, 22 Dec. 1906.
22. McKenna Papers, McKN 2/1,4, J.H. (?Anfallon) to R. McKenna, 28 Aug. 1907. It is perhaps significant that this was one of the very few of his papers McKenna did not destroy towards the end of his life.
23. Marvin Papers, MS Eng lett d 258, fos. 208–9, R.L. Morant to F.S. Marvin, 30 Dec. 1907.
24. Runciman Papers, WR 21, C.F.G. Masterman to W. Runciman, 1908.
25. *Glasgow Herald,* 25 Feb. 1908.
26. McKenna Papers, McKN 2/1, J.E. Gorst to R. McKenna, 24 Feb. 1908; J. Guinness Rogers to R. McKenna, 25 Feb. 1908.
27. McKenna Papers, McKN 2/1, C. [?] to R. McKenna, 26 Feb. 1908.
28. BP Add MS 49382, J.S. Sandars to Alice Balfour, 20 March 1908.
29. D.W. Bebbington, *The Nonconformist Conscience* (1982), pp. 149–50.
30. PRO ED 24/1909, National Society, 'Annotated edition of 1908 Education Bill', pp. 3–12.
31. PRO ED 24/153, Archbishop of Canterbury to R. McKenna, 10 March 1908.
32. Machin, op. cit., p. 290.
33. J.G. Lockhart, *Charles Lindley Viscount Halifax* (1936), II, p. 160.
34. PRO ED 24/153, Archbishop of Canterbury to R. McKenna, 11 April 1908.
35. PRO CAB 41/31/56, H.H. Asquith to H.M. King, 13 May 1908.
36. Trevelyan Papers, CPT 38, C.P. Trevelyan, 'Doings in Parliament', 27 May 1908.
37. PRO ED 24/14, R.L.Morant, 'Rough Preliminary Draft of Points for the Bill set out as desired by the President, Mr. Runciman, after Conversation, April 1908'.
38. Crewe MSS, C/43, Lord Crewe to W. Runciman, 24 May 1908.
39. Runciman Papers, WR 25, Archbishop of Canterbury to W. Runciman, 1 June 1908; W. Runciman to Archbishop of Canterbury, 2 June 1908.
40. BP Add MS 49758, fo.200, Lord Salisbury to A.J. Balfour, 5 June 1908.
41. Runciman Papers, WR 25, W. Runciman to Archbishop of Canterbury, 14 July 1908.
42. Sadler Papers, Archbishop of Canterbury to M.E. Sadler, 19 Aug. 1908.
43. Runciman Papers, WR 24(1), W. Runciman to T. Law, n.d.; Law was the Secretary of the Free Church Council.
44. Lord Riddell, *More Pages from My Diary* (1934), p. 3.
45. Runciman Papers, WR 24(1), J. Massie to W. Runciman, 9 Oct. 1908.
46. PRO ED 24/154, W. Runciman, Cabinet memorandum, 20 Oct. 1908.
47. PRO ED 24/153, Archbishop of Canterbury, Memorandum, 19 Oct. 1908.

48. Ibid., R.L .Morant, 'Notes of Conversation between the Archbishop and the Bishop of Southwark and Mr. Runciman and myself', 23 Oct. 1908.
49. Ibid., Bishop of Southwark to R.L. Morant, 26 and 29 Oct. 1908.
50. Ibid., R.L. Morant to A.T. Thring, 27 Oct. 1908.
51. PRO ED 24/1905, Archbishop of Canterbury to H.H. Asquith, 29 Oct. 1908.
52. PRO ED 24/153, R.L.Morant to A.T. Thring, 31 Oct. 1908.
53. Ibid., J.Clifford *et al.* to H.H. Asquith, 2 Nov. 1908.
54. Ibid., R.L. Morant to W. Runciman, 6 Nov. 1908.
55. Ibid., Notes of Runciman's talk to Committee of Nonconformist MPs, 9 Nov. 1908, p. 23.
56. BP Add MS 49765, fos. 186–7, J.S. Sandars to A.J. Balfour, 15 Nov. 1908.
57. PRO ED 24/1905, H.H. Asquith to Archbishop of Canterbury, 10 Nov. 1908.
58. G.K.A. Bell, *Randall Davidson Archbishop of Canterbury*, I, p. 534.
59. Hickleton Papers cited in Lockhart, *Charles Lindley Viscount Halifax 1885–1934*, II, p. 161.
60. Ripon Papers, Add MS 43640, fos. 176–7, W. Runciman to Lord Ripon, 12 Nov. 1908.
61. BP Add MS 49765, fo. 187, J.S. Sandars to A.J. Balfour, 15 Nov. 1908.
62. PRO ED 24/153, W. Runciman to Archbishop of Canterbury, 17 Nov. 1908.
63. BP Add MS 49765, fo. 186, J.S. Sandars to A.J. Balfour, 15 Nov. 1908.
64. Runciman Papers, WR 24, I, H. Warrington Smyth to W. Runciman, 7 Dec. 1908.
65. Vincent, op. cit., p. 117.
66. Ibid., p. 118.
67. Archbishop of Canterbury to W. Runciman, 21 Nov. 1908 cited in Bell, op. cit., p. 537.
68. Runciman Papers, WR 25, II, Archbishop of Canterbury to W. Runciman, 26 Nov. 1908.
69. PRO ED 24/153, W. Runciman to G. Murray, 27 Nov. 1908.
70. PRO Ramsay Macdonald Papers, 1152/145–6, J. Hirst Hollowell to R. Macdonald, 26 Nov. 1908.
71. PRO Ramsay Macdonald Papers, 1152/155–8, G. Jenks to R. Macdonald, 27 Nov. 1908. Jenks was Secretary of the Leicester Teachers' Association.
72. Runciman Papers, WR 24, I, J. Massie to W. Runciman, 2 Dec. 1908.
73. PRO ED 24/153, W. Runciman to Archbishop of Canterbury, 3 Dec. 1908.
74. PRO ED 24/153, Archbishop of Canterbury to W. Runciman, 3 Dec. 1908: Burns Papers, Add MS 46236, fo. 50, Diary, 4 Dec. 1908.
75. PRO ED 24/153, W. Runciman to Archbishop of Canterbury, 4 Dec. 1908.
76. BP Add MS 49765, fo. 193, J.S. Sandars to A.J. Balfour, 5 Dec. 1908.
77. Ripon Papers, Add MS 43640, fo. 188, Lord Ripon to W. Runciman, 5 Dec. 1908.
78. Runciman Papers, WR 302, W. Runciman to H.H. Asquith, 6 Dec. 1908.
79. Runciman Papers, WR 25, II, W. Runciman to H. Gresford Jones, 6 Dec. 1908.
80. Ripon Papers, Add MS 43640, fo. 191, W. Runciman to Lord Ripon, 8 Dec. 1908.
81. BP (Whittingehame), GD 433/2, M247, fo. 3, A.J. Balfour to A. Balfour, Dec. 1908 (Sunday).
82. FitzRoy, *Memoirs,* I (1927), p. 312.

11

And what of the children?

> The whole tendency of civilisation is . . . towards the multiplication of the collective functions of society. The ever-growing complications of civilisation create for us new services which have to be undertaken by the State.[1]

In 1897 the nation had celebrated with due pomp and circumstance the Diamond Jubilee of Victoria's accession to the throne. But it was not, as Halévy remarked, 'simply an act of almost religious homage paid to the person of the aged Queen, it was an act of homage to the Empire' and running through the celebrations was 'a gesture of defiance' to the other nations.[2] The age of the imperialist had reached its zenith in Britain although some of the more perceptive members of society were aware that amid all the displays of nationalism, chauvinism and confidence there were other, keener issues of state. Kipling's poem, 'Recessional', warned of the mortality of empires:

> Far-called, our navies melt away;
> On dune and headland sinks the fire:
> Lo, all our pomp of yesterday
> Is one with Nineveh and Tyre!
> Judge of the Nations, spare us yet,
> Lest we forget – lest we forget![3]

while Elgar's newly composed Imperial March, 'popular music for the popular mood', was subdued and reflective in many passages.[4] More of the nation were to be subdued and reflective two years later when, on Monday, 30 October 1899 – soon to be known as 'Mournful Monday' – the nation's press revealed the shattering news of a setback for the army in South Africa, only a fortnight after the outbreak of the war there.

The jingoistic expectation that the army would administer a short, sharp blow sufficient to quell the militant Boers was immediately deflated, as Bertha Synge recalled:

> I shall never forget last Tuesday in London, when the news of the missing battalions arrived about midday. Picture the news-

340

boys at the corners . . . . shouting 'Terrible Reverse of British Troops – Loss of 2,000'. Imagine the rush for papers as we all stood about the streets – regardless of all appearances, reading the telegrams with breathless anxiety. Carriages stopped at the corners for papers to be bought – bus conductors rushed with handfuls of pennies as deputation for their passengers. There was a perfect sea of newspapers and anxious faces behind – intense gravity prevailed . . . People walked along speaking in whispers and muttering, while ever echoed round the shrill and awful cry of 'Terrible Reverse of British Troops' . . .[5]

As catastrophe succeeded catastrophe in the conduct of the war, with the sieges of Ladysmith, Kimberley and Mafeking followed by the 'Black Week' of mid-December 1899, it became clear that not only the might of the British Army but also, by implication, the right of the British to control their vast empire had been challenged and found wanting by a handful of Boer farmers. These depressing results were to be compounded as the war continued for the next three years, not least being the revelation of a high rejection rate among army recruits. Arnold White's polemic, *Efficiency and Empire*, indicated that 60 per cent of recruits in Manchester had been rejected as being physically unfit and his figures were substantiated by those produced from Seebohm Rowntree's analysis of recruitment in Sheffield, Leeds and York.[6] These statistics provided extra fuel for the concerns and speculations blazing into speech and print about the state and fitness of the nation, not least the increasingly apparent view that Britain was no longer, economically, industrially or politically, *primus inter pares* among nations.

But the reverses of the Boer War and the associated problems of recruitment were, in some respects, only the culminatory stage in the generation of public unrest about the nation's health and physique for other, rather more enduring, phenomena had been claiming attention for some time. The first was the declining birth rate, apparent from the national returns available since the first were published in 1876 and continuing without any hint of a check. By 1899 the crude birth rate had dropped to 30.5 per thousand from 35.5 per thousand in 1876, a decrease of 14.1 per cent, and exceeded in Europe only by that of France.[7] The concern engendered by this decline was compounded by the high infant mortality rate which phenomenon had become more noticeable after the general death rate had declined by 15 per cent between 1860 and 1900 and the mortality rate for children between one and five years had dropped by a third in the same period.[8]

Furthermore, there had been an increase in the infant mortality rate since 1888, notably during the first three months of life, which had been on average 6.8 per cent but during the hot summers of 1898 to 1900 there had been an increased number of deaths arising from infant diarrhoea epidemics. Thus, not only were fewer children being born (overall) but those that were had less chance of survival. Social concern about these phenomena was exacerbated by the changes taking place in the size of families, with the most marked reduction being in social class I (landowners and professionals) and the least among social class VII (miners).[9] These statistics, when coupled to the high rejection rate recorded among army recruits at the outset of the Boer War and to contemporary concepts of intelligence related to social class, produced agitation and public remonstrances, especially among social Darwinists and imperialists. A belief grew in some sectors of society that the inevitable consequence of the racial degeneration demonstrated by these statistics would be not only the impairment of the nation's ability to maintain control over its empire but also the destruction of its chances in future international economic competition. T.J. Macnamara made no excuse for his public advocacy of drastic reform measures for children's health, acknowledging that it was 'rank Socialism' but contending that it was also

> first rate Imperialism. One of the ugliest thoughts which I ever have . . . is when I see rickety, haggard, little scraps of humanity ranging the gutters, or down-at-the-heel, broken, dilapidated men and women filling the Embankment seats, or strewing like wreckage the green sward of the Park. Because I am instantly haunted by the remembrance that each is a steward of the heritage of the British people. I believe in the British Empire. I believe in its mission among the peoples of the world. But I shudder for its future when I think of the condition of tens of thousands of those upon whose appallingly unfit shoulders the burden of its maintenance is falling.[10]

Other responses to the declining birth rate and the high infant mortality rates included attempts to make motherhood appear more desirable while, at the same time, overcoming the mothers' deficiencies which were blamed for infant mortality. Thus, as Davin has noted, 'moral blackmail, exploiting the real difficulties and insecurities of many mothers, underpinned their new status' while the new ideology ignored class differences.[11] Maternal ignorance tended to be seen, however, as predominantly the preserve of working-class

mothers and accusatory fingers were pointed at the morals and practices of these women, especially those in employment outside the
home, albeit conveniently overlooking the interrelated factors of
unemployment and poverty. Although developments in the natural and
social sciences during the second half of the century had provided a
better understanding of the developmental needs of individuals, the
current stress on the competitive nature of life in the international
community was coupled with the adherence by many to the social
policy promulgated by the New Poor Law of 1834. Poverty was seen
thus as the

> natural and inevitable condition of a system of wage labour, a
> vital incentive to industriousness and good behaviour. Pauperism
> on the other hand was the result of a defective character and an
> indolence which bred improvidence, drunkenness and vice.[12]

The pervasiveness, as well as one corollary, of these views was
apparent in the comments made about feeding starving schoolchildren
by Octavia Hill in a speech to the Charity Organisation Society in
1890:

> . . . It is no pleasure to this Society to urge the benevolent to hold
> their hands, it realises well how school teachers and managers
> must feel when children come hungry and neglected to school.
> But one must follow them to their homes to see the results of this
> wholesale feeding of them which is advocated . . . . I say I can
> imagine no course so sure to increase the number of underfed
> children in London as to the wholesale feeding of them by
> charity. I myself know family after family where the diminution
> of distinct responsibility increased drunkenness and neglect,
> where steady work is neglected and lost, training for work
> abandoned, house duties omitted, all because of our miserable
> interference with duties we neither can nor should perform, and
> in no way is this evil clearer to me than in the provision of free
> food for the apparently hungry . . .[13]

At the same time, there also an increasing and profound
pessimism among certain sectors of society about the quality of the
urban environment, a pessimism which was accentuated by the realisation that urban life, with all its problems, had become the norm for
the majority of the population.[14] Even many of the socialists of the
period found it especially difficult to relate to the plight and needs
of the poor, unskilled working class and joined in the call for their

physical removal to labour camps. In the somewhat fevered and critical perspective engendered by concern about the survival of the fittest, as the evidence about the physical state of the nation mounted so the lamentable plight of a substantial proportion of the nation's schoolchildren came under scrutiny.

The appointment of Dr James Kerr as Bradford's Medical Superintendent of Schools in 1893 led to an analysis of the physical condition of the city's working-class schoolchildren with the conclusion that the 'spread of contagious diseases in closely packed and poorly ventilated classrooms, and the dirty state of children's bodies, were . . . the indices of deprivation and impoverishment'.[15] His series of public examinations of the city's schoolchildren led him to the view that the factors paramount in the widespread existence of a 'defrauded childhood' were dirt and disease rather than hunger, a view which reinforced the professional evidence becoming increasingly available from throughout the nation. The magnitude of the problem was overwhelming: in London alone there were some 300,000 elementary school children whose homes were designated as 'very poor' in the survey conducted in 1890 by Charles Booth and of whom some 51,000 were habitually in need of food:

> Puny, pale-faced, scantily clad and badly shod, these small and feeble folk may be found sitting limp and chill on the school benches in all the poorer parts of London. They swell the bills of mortality as want and sickness thin them off, or survive to be the needy and enfeebled adults whose burden of helplessness the next generation will have to bear.[16]

An anthropometrical survey of 45,000 children conducted by the British Association between 1878 and 1883 had revealed distinct class differences in the physique of boys aged 11–12 years, where those in public schools were, on average, some five inches taller than their peer group in industrial schools. Similarly, a survey carried out by Dr Charles Roberts in 1873 of the weights of boys from different social classes had revealed a difference on average of 10lb between nine-year-old boys in a London charity school and those attending public schools, or 9 lb when the comparison was made between the London and rural schoolchildren: this difference increased to 16lb or 10lb, respectively, by the age of 12. These differentials did not decrease as the century drew to a close but remained well into the twentieth century. Thus, an examination of Liverpool schoolchildren in elementary and secondary schools undertaken by Dr A.S. Arkle in 1904 revealed that by the age of 14 the maximum discrepancy in average heights among boys was 6.5 in. and in weight difference 23.5lb; and again, these differences reflected the social class of the pupils. Dr Ralph Crowley's analysis of 2,000 Bradford elementary school children confirmed the earlier findings of Kerr, despite the reform measures introduced in the interim by the School Board urged on by Margaret McMillan.[17] And the health of the children of the poor was no better.

A survey of 1,000 board school children in London in 1892 had revealed that only 137 had sound teeth while the majority's were 'commonly green . . . standing in irritated and receding gums'. Another survey, four years later, revealed that 61 per cent of a sample of 8,125 children, also London board school children, lacked normal vision and these statistics were reinforced by the findings of surveys made in other urban areas.[18] These defects were, in many instances, accompanied by others, for example ringworm and skin diseases, anaemia, heart disorders, adenoids, rickets, etc., the majority of which were visible. Some of the other problems affecting the health of many children which were not so visible, were revealed by the above and other inquiries. Dr Arkle found some children wrapped in multiple layers of clothing during the winter months, including some who were 'absolutely stitched into their clothes' and this gave cause for concern about cleanliness. What he was not prepared for, however, was the large number of children who were underclad:

> One little fellow, who looked quite well-to-do, did not want to take his coat off, as he explained his shirt was in the wash. On investigation, I found a piece of linen about half the size of a handkerchief attached to his collar, and I fear that was all the shirt he had. It was a bitterly cold day – but not one stitch of underclothing had he on.[19]

Many elementary school teachers had to take precautions to safeguard their own health given the classroom environments they were working in including, as Lowndes recalled graphically:

> bags of sulphur sewn round the hems of the teacher's trailing skirt to prevent the vermin climbing, sidling, or leaping up.[20]

And they were not always sympathetic to the plight of their charges, as one of them remembered:

> Discipline in schools inevitably reflected the class pattern of society beyond the walls. Teachers were only too well aware

from the physique, clothing and cleanliness of their charges just how far each one stood from the social datum line. In spite of their compassion for the neglected and deprived (not always in evidence), some teachers publicly scolded the condition of their dirty and ill-dressed pupils, too often forgetting the poverty from which they came. It was difficult for a child to keep himself clean in a house where soap came low on the list of necessaries. Children of the quality they might reprimand but seldom punished; the rest were caned (it seldom amounted to much) with fair indiscrimination.[21]

Kerr's emphasis upon dirt and disease as the reasons for the 'defrauded' childhood endured by many elementary school pupils reflected his own research findings and approach but there were others who did not discount the significance of malnutrition for these children. Arkle's perceptive comments highlighted the deleterious effects of hunger on children:

Starvation acting on a nervous temperament seems to produce a sort of acute precocious cleverness. Over and over again, I noted such cases of children without an ounce of superfluous flesh upon them, with skins harsh and rough, a rapid pulse and nerves ever on the strain, and yet with an expression of the most lively intelligence. But it is the eager intelligence of the hunting animal, with every faculty strained to the uttermost so as to miss no opportunity of obtaining food . . . .On the other hand, with children of a more lymphatic temperament, starvation seems to produce creatures much more like automata. I do not know how many children I examined among the poorer sort, who were in a sort of dreamy condition, and would only respond to some very definite stimulus. They seemed to be in a condition of semi-torpor – unable to concentrate their attention on anything, and taking no notice of their surroundings if left alone.[22]

The need to alleviate malnutrition among children had been recognised 30 years earlier when individuals like Sir Henry Peek in Devon and the Rev. W. Moore Ede in Tyneside had established school meals. By the mid-1880s, their enterprise had been emulated in Bristol, Birmingham and London but the subsequent provision of meals was haphazard. The report of the Inter-Departmental Committee on Medical Inspection and the Feeding of Children noted in 1905 that there was still no widespread provision of meals by voluntary agencies in urban areas. Only in 38 of 137 borough councils, 55 of the 77 county borough councils and 22 of the 55 urban district councils, that is 42 per cent of the authorities, were meals being offered by these agencies. Peek and Ede had charged a halfpenny or a penny for their meals but had also given some on a free basis. The Charity Organisation Society became involved in the provision of some of the London meals but firmly believed in a 'user pays' philosophy as a means of ensuring that the meals had a 'non-demoralising' effect. This view was not confined to the Society and in many cases the quality of the meals offered reflected both the moral rectitude of the providers and a determination that only the very needy should eat them. Smith and Hurt have given details of the substantial variations among the meals provided by various organisations and for many children their nutritional benefits were dubious, especially as many of the meals consisted constantly of either a vegetable soup or very weak cocoa. By 1895 the meals provided in London had deteriorated so much in quality, mainly because of an attempt to make them financially self-supporting, that one witness before the School Board's inquiry into the situation stated that the poor vegetable soup offered was 'almost devoid of nourishment' and if taken by children constantly would lead to death from diarrhoea.[23] Although malnutrition existed among rural children the problem was not nearly so great as in the urban areas but there were other problems. Those children who took their lunches to school had the food usually wrapped in paper or in handkerchieves and if the weather was wet by the time the child had walked to school the lunch was often 'sodden and pulpy'. Furthermore, the only drink available in many schools, even in the winter, was cold water. But there were some rural schools where the managers or head teacher provided either a drink of cocoa, for example Gorsley in Gloucestershire or hot meals during the winter months, such as Siddington in Cheshire and Rousdon in Devonshire, charging between a penny and a penny halfpenny for the meal but on the whole these were isolated instances.[24] The existence of the provision in both urban and rural areas was indicative, despite the views of Kerr and others, of the significance of malnutrition as well as of dirt and disease in the warping of the lives of many children. The consequences of the continued neglect of these factors in the past was being illustrated in no uncertain manner to the nation by the Boer War as well as in their midst, if it cared to look. Before 1899, however, social reform was not a rewarding topic politically and there were only two politicians of significance committed to its achievement, Joseph Chamberlain and John Gorst, and only the latter was really interested in the plight of children.[25]

Gorst's credentials were substantial given, as has been noted earlier, his attendance at the Berlin Labour Conference in 1890, his membership of the Royal Commission on Labour (1891–94) and his well-publicised campaign in the early 1890s about the need for social reforms.[26] Equally important was the fact that he was, unlike most of his Treasury Bench colleagues, actually conversant with the conditions being endured by the poor members of the working class, and his weekly stays with the Barnetts at Toynbee Hall from 1892 onwards had reinforced and expanded this knowledge. His efforts to ameliorate these conditions made him a member of those social reformers whom G.R. Searle has termed the National Efficiency Movement and whose activities ensured that the components of the potential problem facing the nation were constantly brought under public scrutiny.[27] Their efforts were reinforced by those of other bodies and organisations – for example the *Lancet* and *Public Health* medical journals were actively involved in lobbying for educational reform.[28]

Gorst had taken up the case of children's welfare in the course of his annual Supply speech on education to the House in 1898. He had publicised the plight of half-time children (those who in one week worked, for example, in a factory in the morning and attended school in the afternoon and vice versa for the next week) as well as highlighting the problems arising in elementary schools from both poor attendances and children's malnutrition, all the time taking care to substantiate his claims with evidence from the reports of the inspectorate. The Liberal leader, Sir William Harcourt, praised his speech and added that it ought to have an 'immense influence' upon both the House and the nation. Both remained unmoved, however, *The Times* taking the opposite view and claiming that Gorst's speech

> ... was distinguished by that amazing and embarrassing candour which makes people sometimes wonder why he has so long remained either a member of the Ministry or a representative of the University of Cambridge. If an educational autocrat with the unfettered will and enthusiasm of the German Emperor were seated at Whitehall, we might, perhaps, look for a new heaven and a new earth. But Sir John Gorst can hardly hope that this mission is reserved for him . . . it is the primary duty of an English Minister to carry on the work of his department as a going concern.[29]

An unrepentant Gorst took up the cudgel again ten months later during his next Supply speech, this time concentrating upon the state of children forced to be wage-earners. Utilising the findings of a recent parliamentary return to substantiate his case, he made the point that they cast 'a very lurid light' on the social conditions of a large sector of the population, conditions that revealed 'a most difficult social problem' for the government and House to resolve.[30] The return recorded 144,000 children as being full-time pupils yet engaged also in working for wages, a figure which Gorst believed to be only the tip of the iceberg partly owing to the unrecorded children employed in casual or seasonal labour. None the less, the statistics reinforced the findings of Mearns and Booth but on a nationwide scale.[31]

Although the proportion of children in the labour force had been declining rapidly since 1881, just under a third of the children recorded in the return were ten years old or younger, with 131 children aged six or under. In this latter group there were children working up to 35 hours a week, peeling onions, working in a brick works, seaming hose or acting as a nurse girl, for wages of between a penny and three shillings and sixpence a week. Older children were employed for longer hours but not necessarily for greater financial reward, one Standard IV boy working 87 hours a week for two shillings and six-pence while a girl in Standard V worked for 72 hours a week for a wage of two shillings.[32] Gorst believed that the Return contained sufficient evidence to demonstrate that the 'educational welfare and even the bodily health of the children are evidently being sacrificed to parental selfishness or indifference' and provided a clear basis for ameliorative legislation but, only six months before 'Mournful Monday', his efforts met again with little response from the House.[33] As he was to comment later: 'People cannot deny these facts, but they are determined to ignore them. They shut their eyes to the monstrous folly of their system.'[34] The reason, he believed, was the competition for children between the education system and the labour market, the justification for the latter being derived from the nature of certain industrial processes, the recreational pursuits of the wealthy or parental poverty.

It was this latter point which caused substantial problems for Gorst and other social reformers, for a complete prohibition of child labour would have been financially devastating for many poor working-class families. The values held by some working-class parents compounded the issue as far as education was concerned, some arguing that their children should emulate their own career history; a view reinforced in some instances by the feeling of alienation produced by the middle-class values pervading the compulsory education institutions.[35] In some instances, as well, employment provided some children with a welcome break from the tedium of the rote and drill of the Code and the discipline of the school plus the chance to get closer to achieving the (relative) independence that came with full-time employment. Thus, while Gorst and others could rail against the iniquities practised by some employers and/or parents, they faced considerable resistance from them at any attempt to improve school attendance while curtailing child employment, not least in those strongholds of part-timers, Yorkshire and Lancashire. ILP trade unionists defended the part-time system, claiming that it was an economic reality of working-class life.[36] Unfortunately for the children of the nation, the exigencies of the Boer War were, in the short term, to deflect attention away from their plight, so much so that there was a real danger that those advances achieved by the social reformers would be completely lost.

A general mood of hostility had greeted critics of the nation's short-comings since the outbreak of the war and the so-called Khaki Election of 1900 had reflected the mood of jingoism pervading the nation. Mingled with it was the belief that imperialism and materialism were symbols of the nation's greatness and Searle has noted that for many Radicals the years of the Boer War were a period of 'black reaction' in which 'militarism, racialism, xenophobia, Caesarism, contempt for democracy and humanitarian aspirations' prevailed.[37] Some contemporary observers felt that the Liberal Party as well as the government were failing through lack of effort:

> . . . in the wider sphere of national politics the party of progress has fallen upon evil days. The champions fight as those that beat the air. Programmes adopted at one election are abandoned at the next. 'Social reform' is extolled in pompous phraseology, but when examined is often found to disappear in a maze of verbiage . . . . Meanwhile the problems themselves deepen in magnitude and gravity, and the opportunity for solving them in some peaceful and adequate manner becomes daily less favourable.[38]

The year 1901, however, marked the nadir for the social reformers because as the Boers remained undefeated so the mood of jingoism in the nation gave way to disappointment, disillusionment and uncertainty. The government soon found itself facing the first of an unprecedented series of by-election defeats before its own total defeat in the 1906 election. Canon Barnett sensed that a change of attitude was taking place and observed that the concept of decentralisation in government had suddenly become socially acceptable. The change had been accelerated by a plethora of articles published in 1902 examining the implications of a possible degeneration in the national physique, of which possibly the most famous was Major General Sir John Maurice's article, 'Where to Get Men', published in the *Contemporary Review*. The article not only provided an apparently official confirmation of the 60 per cent rejection rate among army recruits but also asserted that the cause for this unacceptably high rate lay in the living conditions endured by the working class.[39] Although the Inter-Departmental Committee on Physical Deterioration of 1904 subsequently refuted Maurice's interpretation of the recruitment statistics, 'national efficiency' suddenly became a socially accepted concept and the columns of the press began to burgeon with letters indicting the attitudes and inefficiency of the class comprising the nation's managers. As Stedman Jones has indicated, the perspective from which the casual labourer and his milieu was observed changed when chronic poverty was perceived to be an almost lethal threat to national efficiency, and in the resolution of which the State must act.[40] Gorst was not slow to utilise the changed mood in pressing for government action especially since he was now free, in 1902, as he put it somewhat ingenuously, from the chains of office.

In January 1903 he began a campaign of public speeches concentrating upon the necessity of providing meals for hungry elementary school children, confiding to Edith Marvin that one of the aims behind the campaign was to 'frighten Mr. Balfour and the rich; I say – see what you will come to, if you delay the moderate reform asked by us moderate people'.[41] Unswerving in his belief in Tory Democracy, Gorst pressed also for greater decentralisation of government services and wanted the power to rectify social ills to rest with local rather than central government. His most trenchant exposition of the need for decentralisation was made during the course of a biting article on the Conservative Party's role in social reform, the intensity of which led one commentator to exclaim that Gorst was 'unmuzzled and no mistake':

> Give up the dream of a benevolent central government, which is to do everything for the people – to diagnose the social disease, to invent and apply the remedies, and to superintend their operation. That may come hereafter in some future generation, but we are in a more primitive and elementary stage as yet . . . Let each county and municipal authority become absolutely and entirely, as it is already partially and imperfectly, responsible for the health and welfare of its own men, women, and children.[42]

351

The government, not surprisingly, had different views and had established, well before Gorst's campaign had begun, a Royal Commission into the physical training of Scottish children, mainly as a result of the efforts of Sir Henry Craik. One of the commissioners told Craik that when he had discussed the commission's terms with the chairman of a school board, the latter's approval was qualified by the comment that 'the feeding of the children will require to be improved'. Craik was later to tell Gerald Balfour that 'it soon became apparent to us all that something in the feeding way must be done'.[43] The emphasis of the commission's report revealed a preoccupation with the notion of physical degeneracy rather than physical training and, inevitably, a concern with provisions for the feeding of children. In this respect it mirrored the recently published findings of Seebohm Rowntree's analysis of life in York in which the condition of the working-class children demonstrably reinforced the view that childhood was an indicator of the state of the nation's physique. But the government was not prepared, given the financial, political and educational problems arising from implementation of the 1902 Act and the cost of the Boer War, to consider instituting an inquiry into children's health, knowing the likely costs that could result from it. They opted instead for a more general 'searching inquiry' into the physical condition of the people.

The initial term of reference was for a committee to make a

> preliminary enquiry into the allegations concerning the deterioration of certain classes of the population as shown by the large percentage of rejections for physical causes of recruits for the Army . . . with a view to the appointment of a Royal Commission and the terms of reference to such a commission if Appointed.[44]

But as Balfour and the Cabinet became increasingly divided over the merits of Tariff Reform, so the government gave up whatever genuine interest it may have had in social reform and passed the responsibility for an inquiry into physical deterioration directly to the existent committee, thereby pre-empting the creation of a Royal Commission. Furthermore, by settling the inquiry upon a committee of civil servants under the chairmanship of Sir Almeric FitzRoy, Secretary of the Privy Council and Devonshire's erstwhile colleague, the likely quality of their report was virtually vouchsafed.

FitzRoy had begun planning the committee's programme as soon as he had been appointed chairman by Devonshire in mid-August 1903 but its public announcement a fortnight later was completely over-shadowed by the political developments surrounding Tariff Reform, including the restructuring of the Cabinet. The committee's new terms of reference, viz:

(1) To determine, with the aid of such counsel as the medical profession are able to give, the steps that should be taken to furnish the Government and the Nation at large with periodical data for an accurate comparative estimate of the health and physique of the people; (2) to indicate generally the causes of such physical deterioration as does exist in certain classes; and (3) to point out the means by which it can be most effectively diminished[45]

were thus only briefly mentioned in the press. But FitzRoy was pleased with the membership of the committee, believing that some were 'first-rate', especially J.G. Legge, the Chief Inspector of Reformatory and Industrial Schools who represented the Home Office. Moreover, he was confident that he would have little difficulty in 'guiding' the team.[46]

The committee were diligent in their task, interviewing witnesses including Booth, Rowntree, Gorst and Macnamara and spending nine months on their inquiries, their report being published in July 1904. Some of the witnesses did not impress FitzRoy, including Major General Sir John Maurice, whose evidence he believed to be 'tainted by his tendency to generalise from single instances within his own experience, and to develop hearsay gossip into an elaborate indictment of the physical condition of the masses', and Charles Booth, who annoyed FitzRoy by refusing 'to commit himself to any definite steps of a legislative or administrative character arising out of the conclusions to which his investigations have conducted him'.[47] The HMI Dr Alfred Eicholz, on the other hand, made a positive impression with his 'wealth of information, conveyed with a resolute air of self-assured confidence that carried great weight' and FitzRoy was relieved to find his views as optimistic as Maurice's were pessimistic.[48] FitzRoy clearly welcomed witnesses who provided optimistic views but towards the end of the committee's meetings, he and four other members made an excursion one night into South East London under the direction of Dr Shirley Murphy, the LCC's Medical Officer of Health, and gained first-hand evidence of the shelters and lodgings provided for the poor. Among those visited, the Salvation Army's shelter in Southwark provoked in FitzRoy a peculiar touch of horror. In four rows, stretching away into an infinite perspective, appeared what on first sight one took for coffins, each with its occupant in some forced and unnatural attitude. Never did sleep visit suffering mortality in forms that stereotyped more cruelly the broken struggles of life. As we passed down the lines and flashed lanterns on the recumbent figures, not an aspect of human misery remained unrevealed; all the impotent terror, the haggard despair, the truculent brutality of the human animal in the lowest stages of degradation were there depicted; thought could hardly realise the waste of material so collected, the wrecks of existence thus for a moment drifted into some kind of haven . . .[49]

But when the report was published in July, the committee's general conclusion was that there was no sign of physical degeneration among the population.

This notwithstanding, the committee had recognised during the course of their investigations that there were certain outstanding areas of concern, one of which was the physical condition of schoolchildren. They did accept the overwhelming view of their witnesses that there was a need for a more comprehensive system of medical inspection and recommended that it should be made a duty upon all LEAs, albeit with the aid of central government funding. The children to be inspected should, in general, be limited to those attending 'that class of school which from its character and surroundings affords clear evidence of the type of which its scholars are composed'. In addition, the inspection should be carried out initially by the teachers, to reduce costs, and individual cases would be referred by them to the Authority's medical officer. But medical treatment of any complaint was seen to be a matter for the parents or, in the case of hardship, the 'proper authorities', for example, the Poor Law Board of Guardians. Clearly, the degree of State intervention was expected to be minimal.[50]

On the issue of the feeding of schoolchildren, Eicholz's evidence that a third of the children attending the Johanna Street Board School in Lambeth had to be fed by the school between October and March was accepted by the committee but his subsequent estimates of the proportion of unfed children in both London and Manchester (16 and 15 per cent respectively) were carefully compared with the views of other witnesses before being given a qualified acceptance. The committee acknowledged that the 'most uncompromising advocacy of public responsibility' for providing meals had been made by Gorst and Macnamara and conceded that the overwhelming consensus of their witnesses was that 'the time has come when the State should realise the necessity of ensuring adequate nourishment to children in attendance at school'. These points, and the accompanying evidence, notwithstanding, the committee remained opposed to the direct provision of meals by LEAs, preferring to believe that a combination of school management and voluntary agencies was sufficient to meet most cases. The schools would provide the facilities and the agencies the food, and this would constitute a compromise between 'the privileges of charity and the obligations of the community'. In those instances where direct LEA provision had to be made, the committee firmly believed that the relevant legislation would have to be amended 'to compel the neglectful parent to take his full share of responsibility . . . a few prosecutions to this end would have a most salutary and stimulating effect'. These changes would, it was felt, meet the points raised by the witnesses yet protect society from the 'consequences of the somewhat dangerous doctrine that free meals are the necessary concomitant of free education'.[51]

FitzRoy pronounced himself pleased with the reception accorded the report by the press:

> The London papers this morning have given some sixteen columns to it in all: *The Times, Standard*, and *Daily News* are loudest in its praise . . . *The Standard* lays stress upon the weight and moderation of the recommendations, and all are unanimous that the work has been done quickly and well, and should be productive of marked results in stimulating and educating the public mind. My friends in the Civil Service have also expressed themselves in terms of emphatic appreciation and I have every reason to be content with the general verdict.[52]

And the response he cherished most from his colleagues was that of Murray, the Permanent Secretary of Treasury, who congratulated him on having done a Royal Commission's work at a tenth of the cost. The *Manchester Guardian* was rather more critical in its review of the report, however, commenting that while the committee's observations were sensible, nearly all of them had been made before and felt, consequently, that no knowledgeable person on the subject would use 'this interesting but somewhat amateurish report for information'.[53] Given the plethora of evidence presented to them by persons well qualified to comment on the plight of the nation's poor, it was not surprising that in many ways the report duplicated the earlier findings of Booth, Rowntree and others. But while the report did increase public interest and discussion about the topics covered by it, this was mainly because the momentum for reform had been increasing before the report was published.

Increased coverage of the plight of poor children had appeared during 1903 in the medical press, the *British Medical Journal* making the same point about the deleterious effects of child labour that Gorst had made four years earlier.[54] A week before the publication of the report, a petition signed by 14,718 members of the medical profession asking for an appreciation of cleanliness, pure air, food and drink to be included in the curricula of elementary and secondary schools was presented to Lord Londonderry by a deputation led by Dr R. Farquharson MP, chairman of the House of Commons Public Health Committee. Londonderry's response was to hint that the Inter-Departmental Committee's Report would be more reassuring than some suspected and also to claim that the Board of Education had the matters of school hygiene and the teaching of hygiene well in hand, citing not only extracts from the Pupil-Teachers' Regulations but indicating that a forthcoming book from the Board on suggestions for teachers would contain the necessary and relevant advice.[55] He had clearly forgotten the apposite fact, given the demands of the petition, that Morant in his introduction to the new elementary school regulations published in May had responded to the public clamour by including the proviso that the elementary school curriculum should give the pupils 'every opportunity for the healthy development of their bodies, not only by training them in appropriate physical exercises and encouraging them in organised games, but also by instructing them in the working of some of the simpler laws of health'.[56] The Secondary School Regulations, no doubt reflecting the view that the social class of pupils in such schools obviated the need for such instruction, restricted the provision for the pupils' physical development to 'physical exercises'.

The Board of Education's immediate response to the report was to issue two circulars, 515 and 515A, to LEAs and to teacher training colleges respectively. The former emphasised the need for LEAs to implement a new system of physical exercises recently drawn up by the Inter-Departmental Committee on Physical Training and for them to establish evening and Saturday morning in-service training courses to acquaint teachers with the system. It was recommended that each class should spend between 30 minutes and an hour per week carrying out the exercises and that schools should also institute a system of taking physical measurements of their pupils. The training colleges were advised that their students needed to be made aware that in their future role they would not only be required to study and report on the physical capabilities of children under their care and training but also to understand that the physical exercises component of the curriculum was 'only part of a much larger question, viz. that of school and personal hygiene'.[57] Teacher trainees were thus to have sufficient practical experience in their training to be able to differentiate between children with normal health and physique and those without, as well as being able to recognise the symptoms associated with malnutrition and other aspects of ill-health. These points were reiterated in the Board's Annual Report where stress was put on the desirability of elementary schools 'imparting to the children who are destined to become the mothers and fathers of the race, the broad principles of healthy living'.[58]

Morant was also fortunate in that before he had resigned from the Department of Special Inquiries and Reports, Michael Sadler had commissioned Alice Ravenhill, a lecturer in hygiene employed by the West Riding of Yorkshire County Council, to prepare a report on the teaching of domestic science in the United States of America. Completed in 1903 the report was intended to be one in a projected series of special reports on school training in connection with domestic duties and its publication was originally to be delayed until the others were completed. Motivated by the belief that a woman's role lay in the home, Ravenhill's report chimed completely with the sentiments expressed in the report of the Inter-Departmental Committee that the ignorance and neglect of domestic duties were major contributory factors to the low standards of physical fitness and living conditions among the poor working class. Morant had no hesitation, therefore, in having Ravenhill's report published on its own shortly after the publication of the committee's report.[59] When he learned that a Conservative MP, Claude Hay, was about to introduce a resolution into the House for the provision by LEAs of school meals, the Board issued a memorandum summarising the findings of FitzRoy's committee on malnutrition among children and put great emphasis upon the role played by parental ignorance, especially with regard to the types and preparation of food suitable for children. The education of both parents and children was thus seen by the Board as the only effective solution for malnutrition. In the case of children there should be the

> compulsory teaching to the elder children (especially girls) in schools of such matters as the laws of health and hygiene, the proper use of food, and cookery; and also of enforced attendance

357

after school age at continuation classes for the purpose of continuing instruction in such subjects.[60]

The necessity of providing school meals was seen only as a short-term approach once such instruction as that advocated by the Board became effective and the Board's immediate response to the recommendations of FitzRoy's committee was to develop policy in accord with them but without committing themselves to the larger issues involved. This was to be an inadequate response, as events in the House soon made clear.

Gorst had first raised the possibility of government intervention for achieving social reform with Anson in the House on 28 March, asking how long it would be before the Board of Education would see its way to take some practical steps to ameliorate the condition of schoolchildren. Anson had stonewalled, claiming that until the Inter-Departmental Committee had reported, the Board (and the government) would not be in possession of the necessary facts.[61] But when notice of Claude Hay's resolution, supported by Gorst, reached the Cabinet they agreed that not only should it not be made a government division but that Anson should 'indicate the dangers which may easily follow on any plan for relieving parents of their plain duty at the expense of the rates'.[62] Anson dutifully did this but, at the same time, he indicated his belief that some settlement of the issue should be achieved. That it could only be through the use of voluntary agencies was made clear by Balfour a few weeks later in Cabinet when he stated that he (Anson) could make a speech, 'as sympathetic as he liked but on no account should there be any call on the rates for the feeding of children'.[63] For the social reformers, however, these responses were insufficient and efforts were made to force a more effective response from the Board and government, with Gorst and Macnamara as the chief movers to this end.

Gorst's first opportunity for raising the issues covered by the Inter-Departmental Committee Report came in a debate on Estimates on 10 August. He argued that the Report's recommendations about physical training not only supported the comments he and Macnamara had made a year earlier but could be implemented immediately by Anson. Anson would neither be pressured nor commit himself, however, only five days before prorogation and Gorst had to take his campaign to the country, telling Edith Marvin that he saw 'a prospect of an agitation all the autumn about feeding school children, with *The Times* and "respectable" people against it'. He acknowledged the reality of the problem facing him when he added, 'The worst is that we must for the moment appeal to "Charity" alone, as no authority can help us until Parliament gives power'.[64] His message to his audiences in Leeds and London, and in his letters to *The Times*, was consistent – that malnutrition and stunted growth were detrimental to a child attempting to benefit from schooling. The solution lay in the LEAs being granted the power to provide school meals. Macnamara had used the same theme in an article comparing the physical condition of working-class children in 1870 with those of the present. Contending that the poorer 20 per cent of schoolchildren were now in the 'most hopeless condition' with respect to food, clothing and housing, he reiterated the demand he had made as a witness before FitzRoy's committee, namely that LEAs should be empowered to supplement the efforts of voluntary agencies in feeding schoolchildren. While he made it quite clear that he was not in favour of totally free meals in instances where the parents could afford to pay for them, Macnamara did argue the case for State involvement in the feeding of children and also in those cases requiring medical inspection, clothing and adequate housing. The time had come for the abandonment of the principle of *laissez-faire* as far as the children and future of the nation were concerned.[65] Macnamara also argued, and won, this case before the NUT Executive in September – that the Union's forthcoming conference agenda should include a resolution to empower LEAs to provide meals.[66]

With the agitation over the issues contained in the Inter-Departmental Committee Report showing no signs of abating, Anson held a private conference at the Board of Education on the topics of school meals, medical inspection and special schools for children. The conference completely accepted the views of the Inter-Departmental Committee on school meals, including that of the LEA taking the necessary steps to recover the cost of feeding wherever possible. Anson argued, therefore, that free meals should either be provided in consultation with the relieving officer of the Poor Law Board of Guardians who, in the subsequent order for relief would include an order for the meals, or as the result of an 'adequate inquiry' by the teacher, school manager or school attendance officer. On the issue of medical inspection there was unanimous assent to the concept of an inspection when a child started school and on becoming an 'older scholar' but the question of cost, if the inspection was made compulsory, loomed large in Anson's mind. He raised the possibility, therefore, of local authorities employing their medical officers in such a way as to achieve an effective yet not costly system of examination. It was the costs, once more, plus the administrative difficulties of establishing special schools for children who had suffered educationally as a result of ill nurture, that also worried Anson. He believed, somewhat prophetically, that 'mainstreaming' (to use a late twentieth-century term) would be more appropriate, for any such child would benefit from the 'competition and stimulus of being with children of brighter intellect than himself'.[67] Armed with the decisions of this conference, Anson was most anxious that they should be included in the King's Speech for the opening of Parliament and discussed the idea with Balfour. Morant, learning of this, wrote to Balfour, ostensibly on Londonderry's behalf, to indicate his alarm about the possibility of a Bill, based on these proposals, having to provide local authorities with the power to raise a rate for the necessary expenditure involved, something that Balfour had barred in May. While ostensibly placing the decision in Balfour's hands, Morant added the rider that if Balfour stood by his earlier decision 'one does not quite see how any of Anson's proposals can be carried out'.[68] By the beginning of 1905 it became clear that on this particular issue Balfour did have settled convictions: the government's educational policy was to be firmly in line with the views expressed in the Inter-Departmental Committee's report.

The gulf which existed in society at the beginning of 1905 between those wanting to maintain a *laissez-faire* policy and those in favour of social reform was highlighted by an editorial in *The Times* castigating Gorst's campaign. Gorst's advocacy of school meals was seen as one of exaggeration and playing to his audience without due regard to the facts, as well as undermining the concept of parental responsibility:

> If he would consider the glee with which his proposal is hailed by those whose aim is to establish a condition of things in which the State is to do everything for everybody and nobody is to do anything for himself that he is disposed to shirk doing, he might perhaps begin to suspect that there is something to be said for the view which he has not taken the trouble to understand . . . .It is easy, showy, comforting – everything that the sentimentalist loves – to put hungry children on the rates and be done with it. But it is putting a premium upon laziness, meanness, and self-indulgence; and, at the same time, discouraging all who still endeavour to resist these degenerate vices . . . . It is a race of fatherless and motherless foundlings to which Sir John Gorst's proposals point.[69]

Gorst presumably viewed such criticism as supporting his contention about the nature of the controlling forces of society but they provided him with food for thought when he chaired the National Labour Conference on the State maintenance of children held in the Guildhall in London three weeks later.

Opening the meeting with some brief remarks, Gorst quickly dissociated himself from the resolution before the conference in favour of State maintenance of all children, indicating that he advocated State maintenance of necessitous children only. His view was reiterated by both Dr Jonathan Hutchinson and Macnamara, the latter moving an amendment calling for legislation to implement the recommendations of FitzRoy's committee. Macnamara tried to make the point that advocacy of total State maintenance could produce such a backlash among taxpayers that it might negate the achievements made to date in the campaign for school meals and medical inspection, but his views were listened to impatiently and the amendment was lost. The original resolution was passed and it was agreed that a deputation led by Gorst should meet with Balfour. *The Schoolmaster* believed that the conference had rejected moderate counsel and its headline for its account of the meeting read accordingly, 'Socialists Capture the Guildhall Conference'. The *Western Morning News* along with many other provincial papers decried the conference outcome, claiming that 'men who without blush or shame can make such a claim upon the State must have ceased to possess the attributes of humanity'.[70] Anson's response to the event was contained in a Cabinet memorandum at the beginning of February in which he acknowledged the impact of the debates both in and out of the House on the issue of school meals. Anson postulated formulating a measure 'to meet the necessities of the case without necessarily laying a burden upon the rates, and without making any concession to the demand formulated from some quarters for the State maintenance of children in our Elementary Schools'.[71] His memorandum, in essence almost a duplicate of the December conference summary, covered only the provision of school meals and he made it quite clear that he would only advocate such a provision if there was a complete cost-recovery programme accompanying it. Meals would be charged at a fixed rate, equivalent to the costs of the food, serving staff wages, and fuel and rent of the building. If LEAs tried to provide meals at a cost cheaper than this then he believed the Local Government Board should decide whether elected council members should be surcharged.

The Cabinet were not impressed by his arguments and Londonderry's memorandum a week later made it clear that they preferred the establishment of another inter-departmental committee. Not only would such a committee prevent them from having to accept 'outside persons pressed upon us, who might approach the subject with pre-conceived conclusions' but it would also allow them to fend off any 'premature or too far-reaching' proposals that might arise from the debate on the King's Speech, now that it was known Gorst was likely to use the debate to discuss the government's lack of response to the recommendations of the 1904 Inter-Departmental Committee. Londonderry wanted the new committee's terms of reference defined in such a way as to prevent them, on the one hand, from making pro-posals which the party would not accept, including rate aid for the universal provision of free school meals, while, on the other hand, from not being so narrowly restricted that the government could be accused of 'burking discussion' and taking no effective steps to pro-vide remedies for the problems under scrutiny. The main thrust of the draft terms he provided was for the committee to examine how existent powers could be used by local and central authorities to treat children not up to normal school standards yet not defective. He included alternative clauses covering the provision of school meals, the first of which dealt with 'the organisation of meals in special cases for such children, but not out of public funds' and this he favoured, as did Gerald Balfour, the new President of the Local Government Board. Anson preferred the second – 'for organizing or supervising the provision, by charitable agencies, of meals for children attending public elementary schools'. He believed that because the committee would, under this proposal, only be concerned with the way in which charity could be utilised, no danger could be said 'to lurk within' it – without this wider proposal it would be difficult to counter accusations that the committee's work was futile.[72] Four days later a revised draft of the committee's terms of reference, accommodating Anson and Londonderry's views, revealed the inclusion of medical inspection as well as school meals:

(1) To ascertain and report on what is now being done, and with what result, by Local Education Authorities in respect of medical inspection of children in Public Elementary Schools.

(2) And further to ascertain and report upon the methods employed, the sums expended, and the relief given, by various voluntary agencies for the provision of meals for children at public elementary schools, and whether relief of this character could be better organized, without any charge on public funds, both generally and with special regard to children who, without

being defective, are from malnutrition below the normal standard.[73]

Why this change had taken place is not clear but Anson, with the support of the December conference behind him, may have pushed for it. The Cabinet accepted the change, apart from insisting upon the excision of 'Local Education Authorities' from Clause 1, and a committee was formed by 9 March although publication of the news was delayed for a week. One possible reason for the delay may have been inter-departmental jealousy, FitzRoy referring to the 'slumbering hostility' of the Home Office and fears of the Local Government Board in connection with his own committee.[74] These may well have been exacerbated by the composition of the second committee with the Home Office not being represented and there being only one member from the Local Government Board. None the less, the delay was a tactical error given the barrage of questions being fired in the House by Gorst after he had learned that the government did not intend to legislate for either medical inspection or school meals, and his promise that he would press the matter on the House at every possible opportunity was being realised, to the embarrassment of the Front Bench.

Ably supported by Macnamara, Gorst had continually harassed Anson, and the President of the Local Government Board, Walter Long (and his successor Gerald Balfour), with questions designed to try to secure from the government the promise of rapid intervention to alleviate the plight of the children legally required to attend elementary school but physically unable to benefit from the schooling provided. The interchanges with Anson became quite acrimonious and revealed their dichotomy of views. Although he was a master in the art of stonewalling, Anson found himself increasingly under attack not only from Gorst and Macnamara but also from Keir Hardie, Will Crook and others over the Board's lack of action on destitute children. The continued reference in these sessions to Dr Eicholz's evidence to the 1904 Inter-Departmental Committee about the plight of the schoolchildren attending the Johanna Street School in Lambeth eventually forced Anson to visit the school. His response in the Commons to questions about his visit implied that there was nothing amiss with the children there apart from the fact that they might 'with advantage have been provided with a curriculum more suited to their capacities'.[75] This retort generated the celebrated visit to the school on 15 March 1905 by Gorst, Macnamara, the Countess of Warwick and Dr Hutchinson of the Great Ormond Street Children's Hospital.

Macnamara had obtained the prior consent of Sir William Collins, chairman of the LCC, for a visit, without notice, to a South London school by himself, Gorst and Lady Warwick, for the purpose of ascertaining, 'as far as we can, the conditions of the children in regard to lack of food'.[76] The inclusion of Hutchinson and their investigation of, rather than merely ascertaining, the children's condition was to produce a rather pedantic reprimand subsequently from the chairman of the Council's Joint Committee on Underfed Children, Sir Charles Elliott, but by then the aim of the visit had been achieved. Aided by the headmaster, Mr Wilkins, and Miss Griffiths of the girls' department, Hutchinson went from class to class and identified pupils suffering from malnutrition. The numbers selected by Hutchinson from each boys' class were staggering; 16 out of 40 in Standard I, 45 from 56 in Standard II and 47 from 57 in Standard III, etc., and fully supported Eicholz's evidence. Pupils who had come without breakfast that day were also identified and with that information Macnamara and his colleagues descended upon the Lambeth Board of Guardians, whom they knew to be meeting then, and had soon obtained their consent to relief being provided for these children.[77] The visit thus established a definite precedent whereby Boards of Guardians, when being given an application on behalf of certain children, were 'bound to send their relieving officer to inquire into the circumstances and, if found necessary, to give the required relief'.[78] Armed with this achievement, Gorst and Macnamara were able to exert more pressure in the Commons.

The day after the visit Balfour revealed, following a question from Gorst, the existence of the new Inter-Departmental Committee. It was to be a further four days before the members' names were released by Anson, knowledge of which caused Gorst to confide privately:

> I am disappointed in Morant. I hoped his administration would atone for the questionable methods by which he climbed to the head place, . . . but I am afraid it will not . . . . The Committee he has appointed with Simpkinson at its head, is a bare-faced expedient for hindering action while Parliament is sitting and will serve no purpose but delay.[79]

Pressure was maintained, accordingly, upon the occupants of the Front Bench and was directed towards enabling LEAs to refer to the Poor Law authorities for relief in circumstances similar to those at Johanna Street School. Anson gave way a little in a debate on 27 March when he indicated that he would consult the Local Government

Board but he did so in such a manner as to upset not only the Liberals but also some of his own party and the government emerged from the vote with a majority of only 56.[80] The introduction of two Private Members' Bills to provide school meals, as attempts to force the government into action, failed when Balfour refused to grant the necessary parliamentary time. But by the beginning of April, Gerald Balfour informed the House that he had been in discussion with the Board of Education and was considering what further steps to take with regard to relief provided by Boards of Guardians. Two weeks later, he announced that a circular was being prepared and he would have no objection to its being laid on the table of the House. The next day, however, brought an acceleration in progress when a debate on physical deterioration arose from Hay's resolution that

> local authorities should be empowered . . . for insuring that all children of any public elementary school . . . shall receive proper nourishment before being subjected to physical or mental instruction.[81]

Anson remained a stout defender of the government's policy despite the counter-arguments presented to him, and he took delight in deriding Gorst and Macnamara's visit to Johanna Street given the facts gathered by the Lambeth Guardians following their visit. 'Charitable people', he stated, 'were often misled by appearance' and claimed that this appeared to have happened on 15 March.[82] He did reveal to the House, however, that the Board of Education would shortly circulate the Local Government Board Order to LEAs so that they could ensure that schools identified daily the children in need of meals. To try to save the party from further embarrassment the vote on the resolution was made a non-party one, which was just as well, for it was carried by a majority of 63.

The issuing, nine days later, of the Relief (School Children) Order of 1905 empowering Poor Law authorities to provide relief for hungry schoolchildren was superficially a small achievement but, as Gorst had told Edith Marvin, the major obstacle to achieving substantial reform in child welfare was the total dependence upon charity until powers were provided by Parliament. The new measure, by providing for State intervention, represented a step in the effective breaching of repressive nineteenth-century attitudes to child welfare, and a tacit recognition of the rights of the child. At the same time, one Liberal MP's comments to Macnamara before the resolution was passed bore more than a modicum of truth: 'if . . . you succeeded in getting it passed, there would be an end of the matter. It would lead to nothing, and no more would be heard of it'.[83] Although by mid-1905 Balfour believed the government was good for another Session, subsequent events in the House were to prove him wrong, including his gamble when resigning in December. These political events, culminating in the landslide victory of the Liberals in January 1906, overshadowed not only what had been achieved in April but also the report of the Inter-Departmental Committee when it was published in November. Gorst's loss of his seat at Cambridge to a Tariff Reformer marked the end of his parliamentary career while Macnamara felt it politically expedient to forsake educational matters to a large extent in the new House after Birrell's ascendancy to the Presidency of the Board of Education. Thus the transformation of their victory into legislation fell to a new Labour MP, William T. Wilson.

The implementation of the Order was not a success, partly because many Boards of Guardians disregarded it completely or because of the friction engendered between the Guardians and the LEA in implementing an agreed scheme. While the LEAs did not want the children to suffer in their schooling from a lack of food, the Guardians approached the matter in a spirit of deterrence and ruthlessly pruned any lists of underfed children submitted by the LEA. By the end of 1906 the Order was, to all intents and purposes, dead.[84] Luck in the ballot for Private Members' Bills at the beginning of the new Parliament enabled Wilson, however, to introduce his Bill for the feeding of schoolchildren, a fact which took Morant completely by surprise. He told his counterpart at the Local Government Board, Sir Samuel Provis, that he had 'just heard that someone, I think a Labour Member, is going to introduce, this day week a Bill for sanctioning Free Meals for School children or something of that kind'. Morant added: 'I find that my President's mind is practically blank on the subject'.[85] But Birrell's apparent lack of knowledge was matched by the vagueness of Morant's perceptions, as revealed by the language used in his letter. Furthermore, the letter demonstrated that Morant was really unwilling to support such a measure and the brief on the subject prepared by Pelham, Birrell's secretary at the Board, mirrored this view. In his analysis of the 'socialistic', 'practical' and other views on the subject, Pelham warned Birrell that the feeding of schoolchildren by LEAs constituted a 'big socialistic step' which was not justified as there was no conclusive evidence that voluntary effort in this field had failed. The proposals of the recent Inter-Departmental Committee for the more effective organisation of these voluntary bodies, he contended, should be tried and evaluated before taking any other step. Fortunately for the needy children, Birrell ignored his officers' advice. In the Second Reading of the Bill on 2 March, Birrell indicated that as President of the Board he could not allow an LEA to ignore the physical plight of hungry children and, furthermore, he could not think of any greater service to posterity than to improve the standard of living of children. The government agreed, therefore, to provide the necessary parliamentary time for the measure. The pressure upon the parliamentary timetable meant that it was not until 21 December that the Bill reached the Statute Book and the final measure was permissive rather than compulsory as far as the role of LEAs was concerned.

The Act maintained the use of voluntary agencies in the feeding of schoolchildren by Clause 1, under which an LEA could associate with any committee (to be known as a School Canteen Committee) which would provide the food, in return for which the LEA would provide the staff and facilities for preparing and serving the meals. It was expected that parents who could pay for the meals should and failure to do so would lead to recovery of the sum as a civil debt. Only in the instance where there were insufficient voluntary contributions was it intended under the Act that an LEA should use rate money to provide the food; food that could be purchased within the limit of a halfpenny rate. Furthermore, the freedom of the LEAs to implement this proviso required the sanction of the Board of Education. As the Select Committee of the House which had considered the Bill stated in their report, the provision of school meals solely by an LEA had not been 'seriously suggested'.[86] None the less, LEAs did now possess the power to address the physical needs of children under their care in a more effective way than previously. Gilbert has claimed that Section IV of the Act ensured, by stipulating that parents who were unable to pay for their child's meals were not to be disenfranchised, that school meals could, in certain circumstances, be free and that proviso marked the beginning of the welfare state.[87] Hurt has pointed out that such a provision was not novel, however, for parents had been able to have voluntary school fees paid by the Poor Law Guardians since 1876 without the loss of their voting rights.[88] The significant feature of the Act, therefore, was that the rights and needs of the child were recognised as being distinct from those of its parents. The Board of Education's interpretation of the Act was not totally of this persuasion, however, as Circular 552 revealed.

Issued to guide LEAs in their implementation of the Act, the Circular acknowledged that this new educational measure could present opportunities 'of a most beneficial nature' provided its implementation was handled with 'full circumspection' and on carefully planned lines. The Board deemed such an approach to be necessary for while it would allow the 'earnest, yet wise' social reformer with unrivalled opportunities for overcoming some of the major problems afflicting children, it also would ensure that the State was not involved in 'undue intervention in parental responsibilities'. The Board's attitude thus veered more towards the views of the Charity Organisation Society than the spirit intended in Wilson's original Bill. This was substantiated by the advice about the charges for meals and the awarding of the Board's sanction. As far as the charges were concerned, the Board stated that they should be enforced, claiming that in instances where parents could not pay the full cost they would often be able to make some contribution:

> For reasons which need not be here stated, it is better that they should pay whatever their means permit, rather than that meals should be given free of cost.[89]

As far as an LEA obtaining its sanction for the use of rate funding for meals was concerned, the Board made it quite clear that this would not be given lightly. In each instance the Board would assess the information provided by the LEA with its application, the extent of the emergency to be met, the costs to be paid by the LEA and the basis upon which the LEA had reached its decision to apply. If it was satisfied that all these criteria had been met then sanction would be given but only on a temporary basis and it would be limited to the raising of a specific sum from the rates.

The requirements of the Board resulted in some LEAs adopting a daunting and rigorously investigative approach in ascertaining the plight of children as well as a minimalist provision for those ascertained to be in need. By 1911 only 128 LEAs had established school canteen committees, the other 198 LEAs being content to rely upon the efforts of the voluntary agencies. But even when school canteen committees were established, they could still face substantial ratepayer opposition while some of the committees maintained a very restricted view of their roles and these factors were reflected in the meals provided. Thus the breakfasts given by Gateshead LEA to 728 children consisted of porridge, milk and a bun, with the porridge heavily salted (to prevent gluttony), the milk thin and the buns stale.[90] There were additional problems associated with getting the meals, as one Burnley inhabitant remembered:

Two lads, brothers, were literally starving. We'd lots of thin lads in our class of 60. These two lads were so thin they got free meals. At a minute to noon, every day, they turned out, and walked a mile and a half down into town, in summer heat or winter snow, without coats. They went to a wooden hut where one or two women supervised two cauldrons. These lads, standing in the open, were each given a bowl and a chunk of bread. The bowl was first filled with a brown stew from one cauldron, and when this was drunk they got a ladle full of white stuff from the second cauldron. They cleaned the bowls out with pieces of bread and handed them back to the women. The lads then walked back to school.[91]

These and other problems arising from the implementation of the Act meant that it did not provide, in the short term, either a quick or complete resolution of malnutrition among elementary school children. While the number of meals provided nationwide by LEAs in the year 1909–10 had represented an increase over previous years, with rate expenditure upon them almost double that for the preceding year, in 1911 there was a 4.2 per cent decrease in the number of meals provided, and a seven per cent reduction in rate expenditure, despite the existence of a major strike in the coal industry during the year. Equally important was the fact that the number of children fed represented only the tip of the iceberg while the intermittent nature of the provision, not at weekends nor during the school holidays, meant that the benefits to the children were limited. And what the Board and the LEAs had overlooked in their implementation of the Act was the impact of their methods upon the recipients. Their methods might be understandable from a middle-class perspective but they required of working-class parents a willingness to bare their lives to outsiders as well as endure the social stigma attached to participation in the programme. For many parents this was too great a burden.[92] Oblivious to this, the Board appears to have been more disappointed that what it called the educative side of school meals, that is, the inculcation of cleanliness, courtesy and good manners, was not being attained as appeared in many instances, to judge from the reports of the inspectorate:

... the children come to and leave their places with a good deal more noise than is desirable or necessary. No attempt to teach orderly eating was made; there was a certain amount of actually disorderly conduct, throwing bits of food at each other and so forth. Grace was sung in a repulsively loud shout by many children.

In another centre

the meals were served in a very rough and ready fashion, a newspaper usually did duty for a table-cloth, and although I admit that I did not see any very flagrant cases of misbehaviour, no effort to teach manners, etc., was observed.[93]

Morant was unhappy about this and other aspects of the Act's implementation and believed that unless the provision of meals became an integral part of the School Medical Service, 'it may degenerate into a system of doles and be administered in a haphazard fashion on merely eleemosynary and sentimental lines'. Under the aegis of the School Medical Service, with due regard being paid to scientific organisation, medical and educational considerations, he believed the system could be improved so that 'wasteful and reckless expenditure can be prevented and full value, in the form of increased vigour and more effective education, be obtained for the expenditure of the Authority'.[94] His concept was implemented, albeit under his successor at the Board, Selby Bigge, but there was no substantial improvement in the near future. At best then, although the Act represented an advance from the *laissez-faire* attitude of the nineteenth century it also embodied the concept of the social service state rather than the welfare state – that is one in which minimum standards were applied to the poor as opposed to the application of optimum standards to the total population.[95] It was to take two world wars and a major economic depression before any substantial advance could be achieved and for the rights of the child as an individual to be fully recognised.

NOTES

1. W. Churchill, 11 Oct. 1906, *Complete Speeches*, 1, pp.675–6 cited in M. Bentley, *The Climax of Liberal Politics: British Liberalism in Theory and Practice 1868–1918* (1987), p. 112.
2. E. Halévy, *A History of the English People, 1895–1905* (1939), p. 40.
3. Rudyard Kipling, 'Recessional', 1897.
4. P.M. Young, *Elgar, O.M.* (1973), p. 79.
5. Milner Papers, Bertha Synge to Alfred Milner, 3 Nov. 1899.
6. G.R. Searle (ed.), A. White, *Efficiency and Empire* (1973), pp. 101–2; S. Rowntree, *Poverty, A Study of Town Life* (1901), pp. 216–21.
7. D. Dwork, *War is Good for Babies and other Young Children* (1987), p. 4.

8. C. Dyhouse, 'Working-Class Mothers and Infant Mortality in England, 1895–1914', *Journal of Social History*, 12, 2 (1978), p. 248.
9. F.B. Smith, *The People's Health, 1830–1910* (1979), p. 119.
10. T.J. Macnamara, 'The Physical Condition of the People' in 'Coming Men on Coming Questions', *Review of Reviews* (1905), p. 64.
11. A. Davin, 'Imperialism and Motherhood', *History Workshop Journal* (Spring 1978), pp. 13–14.
12. M. Langan, 'Reorganizing the labour market: unemployment, the state and the labour movement, 1880–1914' in Mary Langan and Bill Schwarz (eds), *Crises in the British State 1880–1930* (1985), p. 106.
13. H. Bosanquet, *Social Work in London 1869 to 1912: A History of the Charity Organisation Society* (1914), pp. 255–6.
14. See D. Reeder, 'Predicaments of City Children: Late Victorian and Edwardian Perspectives on Education and Urban Society' in D. Reeder (ed.), *Urban Education in the 19th Century* (1977), p. 77.
15. C. Steedman, *Childhood, Culture and Class in Britain: Margaret McMillan 1860–1931* (1990), p. 46.
16. M. Tabor, 'Elementary Education' in C. Booth (ed.), *Life and Labour of the People in London*, III (1892), p. 207.
17. A.S. Arkle, 'Medical Examination of School Children'; R.H. Crowley, 'The Physical Condition of School Children', papers presented to the North of England Education Conference, *School Government Chronicle*, 77 (12 Jan. 1907), pp. 76–81.
18. F.B. Smith, op. cit., pp. 175–81.
19. Arkle, op. cit., p. 77.
20. G.A.N. Lowndes, *Margaret McMillan, The Children's Champion* (1960), p. 55 cited in B.B. Gilbert, *The Evolution of National Insurance in Great Britain* (1966), pp. 118–19.
21. R. Roberts, *The Classic Slum* (1973), p. 138.
22. Arkle, op. cit., p. 78.
23. J.S. Hurt, *Elementary Schooling and the Working Classes 1860–1918* (1979), pp. 105–6:117–21; F.B. Smith, op. cit., pp. 179–80.
24. Report of the Inter-Departmental on Medical Inspection and the Feeding of School Children Attending Public Elementary Schools, *PP*, XLVII, [Cd.2779] 1906, pp. 54–8.
25. For a more detailed consideration of Gorst and Chamberlain's non-education reforming work see E.P. Hennock, *British Social Reform and German Precedents: The Case of Social Insurance 1880–1914* (1987); Gilbert, op. cit.
26. See J.E. Gorst, 'English Workmen and Their Political Friends', *The North American Review*, CLIX (Aug. 1894), pp. 207–17; W.T. Stead, 'Sir John Gorst', *Review of Reviews*, IV (July–Dec. 1891), pp. 575–85; S. Tooley, 'Labour and Social Problems: An Interview with the Right Hon. Sir John Eldon Gorst, M.P.', *The Humanitarian*, 1894 in *New Zealand Department of Labour Journal* (18 Aug. 1894), pp. 23–32.
27. G.R. Searle, *The Quest for National Efficiency: A Study in British Politics and Thought 1899–1914* (1971).
28. R. Lowe, 'Some Neglected Sources for Historians of Early Twentieth Century Education: The Medical Journals' in K. Dent (ed.), *Archives and the Historian of Education* (1975), pp. 16–23; P.W. Musgrave, 'Morality and the Medical Department: 1907–1974', *British Journal of Educational Studies*, XXV, 2 (June 1977), p. 136.

371

29. *The Times*, 18 June 1898.
30. *4 PD*, 70, c.833, 28 April 1899.
31. A. Mearns, *The Bitter Cry of Outcast London: An Inquiry into the Condition of the Abject Poor* (1883); C. Booth (ed.), *Life and Labour of the People in London* (1892).
32. *4 PD*, 70, c.837–8, 8 April 1899. See also L. Rose, *The Erosion of Childhood: Child Oppression in Britain 1860–1918* (1991), pp. 4–6.
33. Annual Report of the Committee of Council on Education, 1898–9, *PP*, XX, [c.9400] 1899, p. 14.
34. J.E. Gorst, 'School Children as Wage Earners', *The Nineteenth Century*, 46 (July 1899), p. 9.
35. S. Meacham, *A World Apart: The English Working Class 1890–1914* (1977), p. 174.
36. C. Steedman, op. cit., p. 43.
37. Searle (ed.), A. White, *Efficiency and Empire*, p. xxxix.
38. C.F.G. Masterman (ed.), *The Heart of the Empire: Discussions of Problems of Modern City Life in England* (1901), pp. vii–viii.
39. Miles [J.Maurice], 'Where to Get Men', *Contemporary Review*, LXXXI (Jan. 1902), pp. 78–86.
40. G. Stedman Jones, *Outcast London: A Study in the Relationship between Classes in Victorian Society* (1971), pp. 327–8.
41. Marvin Papers, MS Eng lett misc c.237, fos. 10–11, J.E. Gorst to E. Marvin, 27 Jan. 1903.
42. J.E. Gorst, 'Social Reform: The Obligation of the Tory Party', *The Nineteenth Century*, 53 (March 1903), p. 530.
43. Craik Papers, MS 7175, fo.128, H. Shaw Stewart to Sir H. Craik, 29 March 1902; BP (Whittingehame), GD 433/2, M 121, fo.3, Sir H. Craik to G. Balfour, 31 March 1905.
44. Report of the Inter-Departmental Committee on Physical Deterioration, *PP*, XXXII [Cd.2175] (1904), p. 1.
45. Ibid.
46. A. FitzRoy, *Memoirs,* I, p. 162. The other members of the committee were Colonel G.M. Fox, H.M.I of Physical Training, and H.M. Lindsell, Principal Assistant Secretary, from the Board of Education; Colonel G.T. Onslow, Inspector of Marine Recruiting; J. Struthers, Assistant Secretary, Scottish Education Department; Dr J.F.W. Tatham of the General Register Office and E.H. Pooley of the Board of Education as Secretary.
47. Ibid., pp. 175,179.
48. Ibid., pp. 175–6.
49. Ibid., p. 196.
50. Report of the Inter-Departmental Committee on Physical Deterioration, *PP*, XXXII, [Cd.2175] (1904), p. 65.
51. Ibid., pp. 69–72.
52. FitzRoy, op. cit., p. 214.
53. *Manchester Guardian*, 29 July 1904.
54. *British Medical Journal*, 25 July 1903, cited in Gilbert, op. cit., p. 87.
55. Londonderry Papers, L/D0/F/554, *Daily Telegraph*, 12 July 1904.
56. Code of Regulations for Public Elementary Schools, *PP*, LXXV, [Cd 2074] 1904, p. i.
57. Board of Education Circular 515A, 26 Aug. 1904 cited in *School Government Chronicle*, 72 (24 Sept. 1904), pp. 294–5.

58. Annual Report of Board of Education for 1903–4, *PP*, XXV, [Cd.2271] 1904, p. 16.
59. C. Dyhouse, *Girls Growing up in late Victorian and Edwardian England* (1981), pp. 92–4.
60. PRO ED 24/106, 'Summary of Inter-Departmental Committee Report'.
61. *4 PD*, 132, c.905–11, 28 March 1904.
62. CAB/41/30/15, A.J. Balfour to H.M. King, 18 April 1904.
63. BP Add 49787, fo.123, R.L. Morant to A.J. Balfour, 3 Dec. 1904.
64. Marvin Papers, MS Eng lett c.237, fos. 33–4, J.E. Gorst to E. Marvin, 20 Sept. 1904.
65. T.J. Macnamara, 'Physical Condition of Working-Class Children', *Nineteenth Century*, 56 (Aug. 1904), pp. 305–11.
66. 'Feeding the Hungry and Ill-fed Children', *The Schoolmaster*, 10 Sept. 1904, pp. 446–8.
67. PRO ED 24/590, 'Notes on Conference on Wednesday, 7 Dec.'.
68. BP Add 49787, fo.123–4, R.L. Morant to A.J. Balfour, 3 Dec. 1904.
69. *The Times*, 2 Jan. 1905.
70. *The Schoolmaster*, 28 Jan. 1905.
71. CAB 27/74, Sir W. Anson, Memorandum, 3 Feb. 1905.
72. PRO ED 24/590, Lord Londonderry, 'Underfed Children', 10 Feb. 1905, p. 3.
73. PRO ED 24/590, Lord Londonderry, 'Departmental Committee upon Underfed Children and Medical Inspection', 3 March 1905.
74. FitzRoy, op. cit., pp. 257–60.
75. *4 PD*, 143, c.455–6, 20 March 1905.
76. *School Government Chronicle*, 73 (15 April 1905), pp. 348–9; 'Underfed Scholars', *Morning Post*, 24 March 1905.
77. In the event only one child's parents out of the 60 visited applied for relief. Some of the pupils subsequently admitted that their parents knew the school would feed them if they did not provide breakfast and were quite happy to use this situation to their advantage. *School Government Chronicle*, 73 (15 April 1905), p. 349.
78. H.E. Gorst, 'Starving School Children', *Manchester Guardian*, 20 March 1905.
79. J.E. Gorst to Mrs E. Marvin, Marvin Papers, MS Eng lett c.237, fos. 46–9, 25 March 1905. The other committee members were Dr H. Franklin Parsons, Assistant Medical Officer of the Local Government Board; Cyril Jackson, Chief Inspector of Elementary Schools; Hon. Maude Lawrence, Chief Woman Inspector; Riversdale Walrond, Senior Examiner and E.H. Pelham, Secretary and Junior Examiner, all of the Board of Education.
80. *Manchester Guardian*, 28 March 1905.
81. *4 PD*, 145, c.531, 18 April 1905.
82. Ibid., c.561.
83. H.E. Gorst, op. cit.
84. M. Bulkley, *The Feeding of School Children* (1914), pp. 39–44.
85. PRO ED 24/107, R.L. Morant to Sir S. Provis, 23 Feb. 1906.
86. Report of Select Committee on the Education (Provision of Meals) Bills (England and Scotland), 1906, p. vi cited in M. Bulkley, op. cit., p. 49.
87. Gilbert, op. cit., p. 112.
88. Hurt, op. cit., pp. 123–124.
89. PRO ED 24/108, Circular 552 on 1906 Education (Provision of Meals) Act, p. 1.
90. F.B. Smith, op. cit., p. 181.
91. W.R. Mitchell, *Life in the Lancashire Mill Towns* (1984), p. 14.
92. Meacham, op. cit., pp. 208–9.

93. Report on the working of the Education (Provision of Meals) Act, 1906, *PP*, XVIII [Cd.5724], 1911, p. 276; Annual Report of the Chief Medical Officer of the Board of Education for 1911, PP, [Cd 6530], 1912–13, p. 723.
94. Report on the working of the Education (Provision of Meals) Act, 1906, *PP*, XVIII [Cd.5724] 1911, p. 273.
95. For a wider discussion of these concepts see A. Briggs, 'The Welfare State in Historical Perspective', *Archives Européennes de Sociologie* (1961), II, 2, pp. 221–58 and J.R. Hay, *The Origins of the Liberal Welfare Reforms, 1906–1914* (1975), pp. 11–12.

12

An indissoluble partnership?
The State, the child and health

The report of the Inter-Departmental Committee on Medical Inspection and the Feeding of School Children noted that while there did not appear to be any 'specific statutory provision' for LEAs to conduct medical inspections of school pupils, by 1905 85 LEAs had appointed school medical officers and in 49 of these authorities a definite system of inspection was operating. The variations in the prescription of the school medical officers' duties meant, inevitably, that the quality of inspection provided varied between these authorities; in the case of some small authorities, all the elementary school children were inspected whereas in the larger ones a sampling technique was usually the norm. But despite the revelations of these inspections only in a very few instances had medical treatment been provided, partly because free treatment was a socially and politically more contentious issue than inspection. The first Inter-Departmental Committee had been firmly opposed to treatment being provided by LEAs while Dr James Kerr, the LCC's school medical officer, forbade it on the grounds that free medical treatment might pauperise the parents. Another school medical officer, Dr Rhys Davies, pointed out that when he had been first appointed by a school board :

> I was expected . . . to ask the single question, 'Do these children suffer from any physical defect which interferes with their reasonable progress in school?' I was not expected to ask 'What is the cause of this defect?' nor the further question, 'How can I, as Medical Officer, treat these children?'[1]

It was not surprising, therefore, that among even these (relatively) progressive education authorities the rate aid required for their school medical services was minimal. In most county borough councils the average annual expenditure on inspection, including staff costs, was £100 to £150 per annum, that is a $\frac{1}{12}$d rate in Burnley and a $\frac{1}{15}$d rate in Halifax while at the urban district council level, the average expenditure was £50 per annum or between a $\frac{1}{15}$d rate in Keighley and a $\frac{1}{30}$d rate in Eastbourne. Even in London, where the annual salary costs for Kerr and his staff were £6783, the rate requirement was $\frac{1}{20}$d.[2]

The 1905 Inter-Departmental Committee noted their predecessor's injunction against treatment by LEAs, observing that the increased costs involved as well as the potential opposition from private practitioners might constitute major obstacles to such treatment. None the less, they were sufficiently moved by the evidence presented by their witnesses to comment that under the current system not only would the child of negligent parents continue to suffer but there were also many parents who wanted their child treated but could neither afford the loss of time from work nor find the means to do so. Consequently, they believed that

> . . . the results leave something to be desired, and that there is much opening for improvement. It is to be remembered that the Local Authority does not attempt treatment of the children's defects, it merely points out to the parent their existence, and except in very rare cases it has no power to force him to have the defect remedied. We have not sufficient data, upon which to base any estimate of the percentage of cases not receiving treatment; such percentage probably varies greatly from area to area, but we fear there is no doubt that it is a large one.[3]

Prevented by their terms of reference from making any recommendations the Committee were powerless to effect change and the impetus for that meant that it would have to come from outside the government, given the clearly demonstrated unwillingness of Balfour and the Cabinet to commit themselves to any substantial measure of social reform. The likelihood of a general election shortly after the Committee's report was published meant that the Liberals had an election campaign gift presented to them at the end of 1905 but, even so, they were in danger of having this stolen from them by the Labour movement.

In the autumn of 1905 the TUC had endorsed a resolution from Will Thorne of the Gasworkers' Union demanding the provision of free medical advice and inspection for all children and this aim became an integral component of the TUC's educational policy which had to be accepted and promoted by all parliamentary candidates endorsed by the Parliamentary Committee.[4] In addition, the ILP was mounting a campaign against the 1902 Act because of its rate aid provisions for voluntary schools and the abolition of the school boards as well as agitating against the inequalities prevalent within the education system, especially access to secondary and higher education for working-class children.[5] Morgan has characterised the ILP as the most important socialist movement in Edwardian England which 'influenced public life and public dialogue at an immense variety of levels'. Furthermore, ever since its inception in 1893 the party had been fully alive to the importance of the control of local government bodies as a means of implementing socialist practices, and this had included the school boards.[6] Lord Crewe recognised the danger of this situation and warned Campbell-Bannerman before the election that, 'the Liberal party is on its trial as an engine for securing social reforms . . . . It has to resist the I.L.P. claim to be the only friend of the workers'.[7] It could be argued that his warning was accepted by some politicians, to judge by Winston Churchill's speech in Glasgow, nearly a year after the election:

> . . . I look forward to the universal establishment of minimum standard of life and labour, and their progressive elevations . . . . I do not think that Liberalism in any circumstances can cut itself off from this fertile field of social effort . . .[8]

But if some Liberal MPs had discerned the political importance of advocating social reform, the actual impetus for implementing reforms in the field of child welfare came from outside that party as the Labour MP W.J. Wilson's Bill for providing school meals, albeit building on the earlier work of Gorst and Macnamara, demonstrated early in the life of the new Parliament. And the issue of school medical services was promoted by Margaret McMillan in her address to the annual conference of the ILP in the Spring of 1906.

She acknowledged the desirability of a universal ladder from the elementary school to the university but felt that the party was overlooking the rotten rungs at the bottom of it. Quoting statistics demonstrating the extent of the rottenness of these rungs, McMillan's impassioned delivery emphasised the importance of ensuring 'the proper health and proper development of all the bodily and mental faculties of the child' before other educational considerations.[9] While her message stilled the conference and gained her deep respect, her plea for the introduction of medical inspection throughout the nation's schools did not convince the party's leaders, especially Ramsay MacDonald and Keir Hardie. She tried privately to impose her views upon MacDonald and Hardie through correspondence, no doubt unhappy with Clause 35 of Birrell's recently published Education Bill which gave LEAs the power, subject to the sanction of the Board of Education, for 'attending to' the health and physical condition of elementary school children. This power was too vague for McMillan, who wanted medical inspection to be included and may have known from her contact with Morant that an earlier draft of the clause had contained this function.[10] Her lack of success in her attempts may have led her to join a group of women with diverse practical experience of school medical inspection methods, including Edith Marvin, to meet Birrell for lunch in the House of Commons in early July. The organiser of this meeting, Margaret MacDonald (wife of Ramsay) had warned Edith Marvin that she was not sure whether McMillan 'would think you quite definite enough to please her', but added :

> . . . we need not all say exactly ditto to each other. We all want Medical Inspection in the most efficient way possible. Miss Zimmerman is coming with us: she has experience of what should be avoided in Medical Inspection as it obtains in her school, and that will be very useful too as she is keen upon it but naturally wants it done effectively.[11]

McMillan does not appear to have felt that the meeting had achieved much, for a few weeks later, at her first attendance at the National Administrative Council of the ILP, she was 'Full of complaints about MacDonald and Hardie over her Physical Inspection Clause . . . [and] speaks rudely to them both'.[12] The reason for this disgruntlement may have been an amendment to Clause 35 of the Education Bill introduced by H.J. Tennant which, although it was intended to allow LEAs to carry out the medical inspection of children attending public elementary schools, was worded in almost a very similar manner to the original clause. Birrell's reaction, while perhaps acknowledging the impact of the lunch meeting arranged by MacDonald, was definitely a response to the House's support for the amendment, should have negated her feelings, however, for not only did he accept the amendment but he also altered the wording slightly so as to include the words 'medical inspection' and made the inspection a duty of LEAs.[13]

While McMillan was unhappy about the unwillingness of her Labour colleagues in the House to try to alter this part of the Bill, Morant was horrified by Birrell's action. He attempted to counter this 'unadvisable' amendment by postulating that neither LEAs nor the Board of Education had had sufficient experience in this area to enable such a proposal to be applied compulsorily henceforth. It was far better, he believed, that LEAs should only be enabled to implement medical inspection. Then 'no doubt at some future time what is now a power may be made a duty'.[14] The government, however, affirmed Birrell's judgement and were supported by memorials on the subject during the remainder of the Bill's passage, not least by one from the Amalgamated Society of Railway Servants.[15] The educational press took up the theme, citing examples indicative of the 'public readiness – impatience even – to act' in this area.[16] The failure of the Bill to reach the Statute Book appeared to remove consideration of the matter for some time but two events were to alter this. The first was McKenna's replacement of Birrell at the Board of Education and the second was the introduction on 21 February of a Private Member's Bill by Walter Rea, the Liberal MP for Scarborough, for the provision of vacation schools and for the medical inspection and treatment of public elementary school children.

McKenna has not been perceived by historians as an educational reformer, yet Beatrice Webb observed of him after her first meeting with him early in 1906 that while he lacked an exciting personality he appeared to be 'a genuine reformer of the ordinary kind'.[17] And he does appear to have demonstrated an interest in the issue of medical inspection almost immediately upon taking up his new post. Morant informed Provis on 19 February that his new chief was 'anxious on many grounds to reintroduce what became Part 2 of the late Education Bill'. At the same time he told T.J. Macnamara, the recently appointed Parliamentary Secretary to the Local Government Board, that the intention of McKenna's new Bill was to establish the medical inspection of schoolchildren as well as resolving the problems concerning teacher registration.[18] McKenna's Bill was introduced on 5 March, 11 days after Rea's.

Rea's Bill was, its author contended, an 'absolutely non-contentious measure', since it was derived verbatim from the two clauses of the 1906 Education Bill 'in the form in which it left this House and had the approval of every section of the House'.[19] He made it quite clear from the outset that his Bill was a safety measure, designed to circumvent the process known to the House as 'the massacre of the innocents'. In the event of pressure of business preventing the government from passing their own, similar measure he hoped his would still be there to ensure the establishment of a national medical inspection system.[20] In both aims he was supported by Balfour, on behalf of the Opposition, and by T. Lough, the Parliamentary Secretary to the Board of Education, for the government. Unfortunately for Rea this support was not enough for it was his Bill, and not McKenna's, which suffered from pressure of business. Having completed the Report stage, the Bill was set for the Third Reading on 18 June but, at the request of McKenna, the Bill was adjourned and thus fell victim to the Prime Minister's motion on 26 July that for the remainder of the Session government business should have priority. In spite of its short life, Rea's Bill was not without significance as will be seen later, but it is necessary to examine some of the events surrounding McKenna's measure.

It is clear from Morant's correspondence with Macnamara that the Bill, basically concerned with various administrative provisions, had been drafted and printed by 19 February, utilising wherever possible the relevant clauses of the 1906 Education Bill as amended by the House of Lords, including the one covering medical inspection. What is also apparent is that Morant had sent a copy of the measure to Anson, now the Opposition's spokesman on education. Acknowledging receipt of the copy, Anson noted the inclusion of some new items which, he thought, 'may need a little consideration' on the grounds that if the Bill was to be non-controversial 'we must make it really so'.[21] He told Balfour his views of the Bill, indicating what the new inclusions were. Discussing Clause 10, the one providing for medical inspection, he noted the unanimous support this proposal had received in 1906 and added as a rider, 'I suppose our zeal for 'social reform' has not cooled since'. He felt that the inspection should be made compulsory yet was concerned as to how it would be financed, for he did not want ratepayers to have to shoulder the full burden.[22] Balfour's reaction to this favourable evaluation was to ask Morant to see him '*if Mr McKenna thinks that a suitable course*, for discussion of the Medical Inspection Bill'.[23] McKenna raised no objection and Morant saw Balfour to discuss the points raised by Anson. The outcome, Morant informed Anson, was that

> . . . we should of course expect the Front Opposition to raise a protest; but this would not go so far as dividing against the Bill or against the Clause . . . .Mr Balfour seems to think that, without of course pretending that the Bill will go through sub silencie, it can properly be considered non-controversial, and so far as the Front Opposition Bench is concerned, will not be divided against nor talked about except perhaps the Rate burden of Medical Inspection.[24]

This agreement, or compact, when taken in conjunction with the debates in the House, reveals why Rea's Bill failed to reach its Third Reading.

Both Rea's and McKenna's Bills utilised the original Clause 35 of the 1906 Education Bill for the creation of a system of medical inspection by LEAs. Why then was Rea's killed? The explanation given to the House by McKenna was that it appeared that Rea was likely to accept some amendments to his Bill which he (McKenna) was unwilling to have foisted upon his Board. The reality appears, however, to have been an unforeseen statement made by Rea while countering an amendment to excise the main clause of his Bill. Captain Craig, the seconder of the amendment, raised the point that the wording of the clause providing for medical inspection 'covered far more than really appeared from the clause'.[25] He believed that what was intended was the provision of medical treatment as well as inspection, yet his objection was solely about the funding which would be required – not the principle of medical treatment. Anson, in rejecting the amendment (made by one of his backbenchers), made a similar point, stating that the only contentious aspect of medical treatment was the source of its funding, that is, the very point he had made to Balfour and the one acknowledged in the compact. Rea seems to have ignored the nuances of the points being made, however, perhaps being more concerned with the survival of his Bill, and made a categorical assurance that there never had been nor was there any intention 'of providing medical attendance for children of all ages'.[26] This statement was at variance also with the title of the measure which was 'To make provision for Vacation Schools and for the Medical Instruction and Treatment of School Children'. Only three weeks before this debate Morant had read an enquiry made by Birmingham's LEA, which had arisen from the Bill's perceived intention that an LEA 'should have full power to take whatever steps may be necessary in dealing with children medically after they have been medically inspected' and he felt that it raised an 'acutely controversial point'. But it was not about the principle of providing medical treatment, rather the amount of 'treatment to be provided free by LEAs'.[27] Rea's statement unwittingly yet effectively scuppered the wider potential of the clause made possible by the compact between Balfour and McKenna and the only way to revive that potential was to kill Rea's Bill.

The discussions in the Commons on Rea's Bill had revealed that Members on both sides of the House were aware that the wording of Clause 1 could be interpreted so as to allow medical treatment to be provided by LEAs. Furthermore, this view was not confined to the

House but, to judge from the Birmingham query, was held elsewhere. The claim has been made by Gilbert and others that the Second Reading debates of McKenna's Bill were notable for the conspicuous absence of debate about the aims of Clause 10. This is true, but not for the reason purported – that there was a deliberate attempt to mislead the House. Rather it was for the simple reason, as the Conservative MP for Tewkesbury, Michael Hicks Beach, indicated, that there was no objection to its general principles. Indeed, Anson, leading for the Opposition, dealt solely with matters of financial detail arising from the 13 clauses and this was the theme taken by the other major Opposition speakers, Sir Henry Craik and George Wyndham. The only threat to the creation of a national system of inspection and treatment came in the Report stage when Craik proposed an amendment which would have made inspection and treatment merely a power rather than a duty of LEAs, his concern being about the lack of government financial support for their implementation. In this he was bluntly opposed by Anson, who affirmed his belief in the government's measure as 'an important step' involving the 'laying on local authorities [of] a very serious duty'. Rather than reducing this step what was required, he stated, was additional 'machinery' in central government to ensure that the LEAs would carry out their duties as efficiently as possible.[28] McKenna's acknowledgement of Anson's proposal and his indication that the Board was in the process of forming a medical branch were sufficient to ensure negation of the amendment. The subsequent debate on the *treatment* of children and the likely costs demonstrated almost total support from the House. One of the Members for Cambridge University, S.H. Butcher, went so far as to state that in this particular regard the clause was 'very timid and very tentative' while Lane-Fox, in proposing an amendment to recover costs of treatment from parents, made it quite clear that 'he did not wish to prevent these [ailments] being dealt with'.[29] The Bill passed onto the Statute Book on 12 August.

The formulation and passage of the Bill does raise a question about the authorship of the School Medical Service which derived from the subsequent implementation of the Act. Clause 10's origins resided in Clause 35 of the 1906 Education Bill and this was freely admitted by Rea, McKenna and Morant. This clause only empowered LEAs to attend to the 'health and physical condition' of public elementary school children but for Tennant, and the majority of the House, this had been insufficient:

> The Bill was an Education Bill; it provided for education, and he

conceived that education presupposed health, mental and physical. Education in this country was compulsory and universal, and therefore the conditions upon which education depended ought to be compulsory and universal. We ought not to allow the local authorities to differ from the nation in a matter in regard to which the nation had already pronounced.[30]

Tennant's view that there should be a national, compulsory system of medical inspection reflected not only the mood of the House but also that of many in the nation, in which the new 'sociology' acknowledged 'the interdependence of individuals within the social organism'.[31] Although Tennant did not view inspection as synonymous with treatment what does emerge from the debates in the Commons, the educational press and the correspondence in the Board of Education files is evidence of a widespread feeling that treatment was accepted as a component of medical inspection. The first requisite, however, was the creation of a compulsory national system, and credit for acceptance of this concept must lie with Tennant rather than Morant. None the less, it was to be Morant and Dr George Newman who played the key roles in the interpretation and implementation of the policy contained within the Act.

It was only shortly before the Second Reading of McKenna's Bill that Morant had begun to consider the implications of the measure for the Board. He had hoped originally that the Local Government Board could be persuaded to assume responsibility for the organisation of the medical inspection and treatment but, as in the previous year over the issue of feeding children, he had been thwarted. In a confidential memorandum written in May, Morant indicated that the Board's role as far as implementation of the Act was concerned would only be advisory and limited to telling local authorities about the best methods for carrying out medical inspection, albeit providing the forms for recording the data collected, as well as the steps to be taken to treat any 'evils' revealed by the inspection. The memorandum revealed that his priorities lay with inspection and prevention rather than treatment for, as he told McMillan, while he could accept that 'what subjects are taught and how they are taught do not matter anything like so much nowadays as attention . . . to the physical condition of the scholars' he still preferred the 'Preventive side of this quasi-medical aspect of sociology' to McMillan's concern with what he termed the 'Therapeutic Remedial side'.[32] Successful implementation of this policy would be dependent, however, upon the staff employed by the local authorities and he acknowledged the existence of competing views about whether the work should be carried out by 'dedicated' school medical officers or come under the aegis of existent local authority medical officers of health.

Through his friendship with the Webbs, Morant was aware of Beatrice's views in connection with her membership of the Royal Commission on the Poor Law. Over dinner in late April the trio had discussed her ideas about the desirability of school-age Poor Law children coming under the aegis of the LEAs although infants would be the responsibility of the local medical officer of health:

> He agreed to both and was much pleased with the latter idea because it chimes in with his notion of taking the ordinary infants away from the school and placing them under the Public Health authority.[33]

But Morant told them that while he would like to move to the Local Government Board to supervise implementation of the Commission's recommendations, he was in the meantime being 'forced to start a medical department' because of the incompetence of that Board. Slightly alarmed that this could jeopardise the unity of their plans, the Webbs pressed on Morant the need for the new school medical officers coming under the medical officers of health in each local authority. And just to be sure that their ideas received full consideration, Beatrice saw McKenna at the Board shortly afterwards for 'a friendly chat', but found that he was worried about the possible increase in expenditure that would result if they were implemented. Morant, however, had accepted all the Webbs' ideas and thus rejected the idea of 'dedicated' school medical officers. As he informed Balfour, the reason for his choice lay with the fact that

> a desperate effort is being made in certain quarters to bring about an ad hoc organisation for Medical Inspection on the same principles as Elementary Education was treated until our great Act of 1902, which brought all the educational aspects of childlife more nearly into the same Local Authority's hands as the sanitary and some other aspects of childlife.[34]

While he did not see the county and county borough councils as the ideal local administrative organisation he much preferred them to *ad hoc* bodies for he remained convinced that little was to be gained if a single central authority had to deal with a variety of different kinds of local authorities. He also believed that the supporters of the *ad hoc* organisation emphasised treatment at the expense of preventative measures.[35] What was required to prevent this attempt to reintroduce *ad hocery* into the education system was, therefore, a director for the Board's new medical department who shared his views and who could help to achieve this ultimate goal of a unified health system.

In Morant's search for a suitable candidate, the Webbs played another seminal role, this time arranging for him to meet George Newman, the Medical Officer of Health for Finsbury, at one of their dinner parties. It was to Newman, whom she had known since 1900, that Beatrice had turned for supporting evidence when she had suddenly decided during the meetings of the Poor Law Commission that medical inspection and treatment should be made compulsory for all sick persons and that illness should be treated as 'a public nuisance to be suppressed in the interests of the community'.[36] On this occasion, Beatrice was using Newman as an expert on infant mortality which was correct in so far as he had had his views on the subject published, but also because his views closely matched hers and other Fabians. Newman was a firm proponent of the view that this mortality was primarily the result of the ignorance of working-class mothers and their employment in the workforce. In this he mirrored the Webbs' view that if the State was to provide relief 'for the maintenance of the home [it should be] conditional on the mother's abstaining from industrial work'.[37] Even after his retirement from office 40 years later, and despite all the evidence produced to the contrary, Newman remained convinced that sanitation, sub-standard housing and poverty were of secondary importance in infant mortality when compared with maternal ignorance, negligence and mismanagement.[38] Newman thus subscribed firmly to preventive measures to bolster motherhood, for example, schools for mothers, the provision of day nurseries as crèches, modification of the elementary school curriculum to include the teaching of mothercraft and infant hygiene, as the means to overcome not only infant mortality but also childhood ailments. And like the Webbs, Newman believed not only that if medical treatment had to be provided then parents should be expected to pay according to their means but that at the local government level all health professionals should be subordinate to the medical officer of health.

News of his possible appointment alarmed Margaret McMillan, not just because of Newman's views but also because of her knowledge of Morant's methods:

> I know Mr Morant's rule very well. I had it for 10 years, and I have learned something from it. No subordinate of Mr Morant's will be of any real value as the responsible agent of medical and

physiological reforms. The Doctor or Doctors I have in mind must be responsible only to the Minister & the public, & their greatest qualification . . . will be that they are entirely independent of Mr Morant and his rule . . . . PS Don't think I don't appreciate Mr Morant's cleverness and goodness. *I do.* Only I don't like to see men doing work they cannot possibly understand – and doing it authoritatively. *You* may be impressed by them. *I* am *not*.[39]

McMillan may have had her erstwhile colleague from Bradford, James Kerr, in mind when she wrote this note, not least, perhaps, because he had 'a dogged capacity of his own' as well as 14 years' experience of working among working-class children in Bradford and London schools. But Kerr was a strong proponent of the 'dedicated' school medical officer and his medical ideas were reinforced by his educational outlook, one of his maxims being that children should go to the 'highest grade school at which they were capable of making progress'.[40] By 1907 he was claiming that the development of school hygiene in England was largely due to his own efforts in the preceding 16 years. Kerr was supported by the BMA which not only opposed the existence of medical officers of health but was worried about the possible consequences for its members should a State health service develop. This support, let alone his views and bluff personality, was anathema to Morant and not surprisingly, given the similarity of Newman's views to his, the Webbs' permeation technique prevailed. At their dinner party of 17 July McKenna informed them, rather ingenuously, that he intended to appoint Newman 'as he had heard nothing but good of him'.[41]

There had been one other eligible candidate for the position besides Newman and Kerr and that was Alfred Eicholz, the HMI who had first brought Johanna Street School to the public view as a result of his evidence to the Inter-Departmental Committee on Physical Deterioration. This may have been a disadvantage as far as Morant was concerned although he did claim, when breaking the news to him of Newman's appointment, that

So long ago as August last year . . . political and other considerations necessitated that the first chief of whatever Medical Bureau might be started by this Board would have to be appointed from outside; and this still maintains.[42]

Morant did make the point to Newman, however, about the forthcoming press announcement of his appointment that it would be difficult to put in as much as I should like of your own personal qualification, without seeming to show too definitely the comparatively small list of personal qualifications in the same direction that are possessed by Dr. Eicholz. And it would be a pity to invite invidious comparisons in this way from the outside to his detriment.[43]

Eicholz was not excluded from the staff of the department, however, for he was the first to be appointed at the medical officer level and although Newman did not know him until then their subsequent working relationship led Newman to record that 'he made bitter waters sweet'.[44] Despite Newman's protestation that he did not 'quite see the use of a lady' on the staff, Dr Janet Campbell joined the department shortly after Eicholz and they were joined later by Dr Ralph Crowley, Kerr's successor at Bradford. In addition to this medical staff of four, the department's personnel included four HMIs of physical training.

Newman knew that Morant was 'under instructions' to ensure that the Act's implementation should be in 'wide and elastic' terms but at the same time he shared Morant's view about how the Act should be implemented.[45] Shortly before the public announcement of his appointment Newman told Morant that the press release should

bring together opposing forces and make them see that we not only mean business but that we have a wide and wholesome view of the whole problem. We are out on a big piece of work and we may do well not only to have comprehensive and unifying views but show them straight away from the beginning.[46]

This would require tact, as he indicated subsequently:

. . . we don't quite want to say we object to an *ad hoc* authority and the Kerr School. But we do want to hint at the general idea of the broad commonsense basis, and general outlook as compared with merely thumping children's chests idea. We want to show . . . that the Board is going to help at the general sanitary evolution, is going to establish an organic thing which will grow naturally, and is for unification of the whole health service of the State.[47]

At the same time, Newman believed that the staff of the new department should contain at least one member from the Kerr School, that is, 'the school doctor in the narrow sense – a specialist at inspection of children'.[48] The press release did reflect these points with an emphasis being made on the need for local authorities to employ existent methods of health administration rather than introduce 'new competing agencies'. But the explicit enunciation of the Board's policy came with the publication of Circular 576 in November.

There had been a critical reaction from certain sectors of the medical world to the announcement of Newman's appointment, not least from Archibald Hogarth, a former student of his now serving under Kerr. In a letter to the *British Medical Journal*, Hogarth had not only indicted both Birrell, for failing to keep his promise to Kerr of first refusal of the chief medical officer's position, and Morant, for telling Kerr subsequently that the idea of the Board having a medical department had been scrapped, but had also claimed that Newman's knowledge of school hygiene was non-existent.[49] Newman was furious on reading the letter but was counselled by Arthur Newsholme, Brighton's Medical Officer of Health, that as far as the *Journal* was concerned

> . . . you can't touch them with a long pole directly or indirectly. You shd not forget this. I am not advocating a malignant spirit: but all you can do with them after admitting Hogarth's letters is to leave them absolutely alone. Of course they must leave you & Morant alone.[50]

Accepting this advice, Newman took a great deal of care in drafting the Circular although it was only intended to be of a preliminary nature, even to the extent of sending drafts to various colleagues for their observations, including Newsholme. Their response was mixed and J.R. Kaye, the County Medical Officer for the West Riding of Yorkshire, commented cryptically that he had nothing but 'admiration for it as the work of an enthusiastic giant who plans out equally big jobs for those of us who are *not* giants and have other work to do already'.[51]

Kaye estimated that Newman's proposals would require in his area 50,000 medical inspections in 1908 and 1909 and they would rise to 100,000 annually after 1910. Since they had to be carried out on school premises during school hours and, where possible, in the presence of parents, the amount of subsidiary work involved in addition to the inspections would be 'enormous' while the total requirements would be 'more than a load'. Kaye believed that the large LEAs would prefer a 'little slower pace at first' but had no doubts that they would eventually meet Newman's goals.[52] This point was reinforced by another correspondent who argued that the LEAs would be rather frightened by the memorandum as now drawn . . . halting and timid bodies, and bodies that are just now very nervous of anything that sounds like socialism, would . . . be reached better in the first instance by a rather simpler circular.[53]

Newsholme was more supportive of Newman's proposals and felt the Circular would 'do a great good'. He counselled him not to spare himself in 'licking it into final shape: but don't let other people (exc. Morant) chop it about'. He did warn him that there would undoubtedly be protests from the medical profession but discounted their effect for 'it will be an ineffective trades-union effect, & *will be universally recognised as such*'.[54]

The final, published version of the Circular still emphasised medical inspection as the first priority for the LEAs, supporting this approach with the argument that the data to be collected were necessary for the planning of subsequent reforms. Newman was at pains to stress the educational and economic nature of the 1907 Act, the first because mental and moral improvement were a 'natural corollary' of physical improvement while the second arose from the decrease in inefficiency and poverty which would accompany the prevention of physical disabilities. He argued that if the Act was to be successfully implemented then the work of the medical officer and his assistants would have to 'extend over the whole external environment of the child', including visits to his/her home, and the co-operation of parents, in addition to that of the school nurses and teachers, would therefore be a critical component in the work of the medical officers. Morant appears to have seen this as the first step towards a broader approach, envisaging the medical inspections as

> the means of extending public action generally in regard to the medical and sanitary condition of the families whose children attend the Elementary Schools – and that word 'condition' must gradually include the home, and not be restricted to the school.[55]

At the same time, Newman took care to reinforce his and Morant's conviction that school medical officers should not regard themselves as working in an independent field but, rather, should be developing an organic relationship with the local medical officer of health and his staff, not least because this would bring *that* officer 'into closer touch with the personal hygiene of the population'.

The minimum number of inspections envisaged per child was three: one on or about the time of admission to school, the second at seven years of age and the third at ten or on leaving school. But for 1908, the first year of the Act's implementation, the inspections would be confined to school entrants and leavers, a concession no doubt based upon the warnings of Kaye and Cross, but they had to be carried out on school premises in school hours and with one or both parents of the child present. Schools would be required to maintain a confidential register of the results of the inspections while the school medical officer had to submit an annual report to both the LEA and the Board of Education. The Circular did also alert LEAs to the need for them to start formulating schemes for medical treatment for subsequent submission to the Board but a rider was included that medical treatment was to be deferred until the results of the first wave of inspections had been forwarded to the Board. A draft of the Circular had included the statement that LEAs should not provide medical treatment *per se* but refer cases to existing agencies, Newman's defence for this view being that such action by an LEA would tend to pauperise the patient but Morant had disagreed, seeing it as important that the LEAs should treat minor ailments. The final version of the Circular thus stated that the aim of the Act was practical and the LEAs should start to plan accordingly for the future establishment of school clinics 'for the amelioration of the evils revealed by medical inspection'. Since their planning would have to be guided by the data revealed by the medical inspections, in the interim the authorities were to provide treatment through 'such agencies as are conveniently available'.[56]

The idea of school medical officers carrying out the inspections listed in the Circular, as well as visits being made to the child's home, was strongly opposed by the British Medical Association who feared that the livelihood of its members, predominantly GPs, would be jeopardised.[57] Newman accepted that visits to the child's home represented the 'most ticklish point of all' but he remained committed to his goals. In the schedule of advice to supplement Circular 576, published two months later as Circular 582, he claimed that the chief difficulties facing LEAs over the Act's implementation were administrative rather than educational or medical, adding 'there is comparatively little dispute as to the end in view'.[58] None the less, he repeated his earlier procedure of sending copies of the first draft of the new Circular for comment to medical officers. He sought Morant's views on including Kerr in the correspondents, not as 'a question so much of policy and administration as of technique and though I can anticipate Kerr's criticisms it may save subsequent trouble'. Morant would agree only if the covering letter to Kerr made it quite clear that the Board was seeking neither 'his imprimatur on the schedule, or his concurrence'.[59] Their efforts were in vain, as Kerr made clear in a speech to members and officials of local education committees a few months later.

His scathing references to the absence of educationists in the Board as well as its stance of not advancing education were clearly directed, by implication, at Morant:

> In England education has been strangely neglected; it has been degraded to the position of a pawn in the game of politics. Like shadows Ministers come and go, apparently caring little knowing less of the real national educational progress, which to a very great extent has been controlled and even opposed by the red tape of officialism.

His comments about Newman, although not naming him, were no less caustic:

> School hygiene is (then) one of the most highly specialized branches of medical work, and the official writer who speaks of establishing this [school hygiene] 'on the broad basis of public health' gives us serious reason for doubting the extent of his knowledge or the value of his judgments in these matters.[60]

The tone and contents of the speech not only demonstrated the strength of Kerr's opposition to the Board's policy and personnel but also his own characteristics of being 'brusque and tactless'.[61] This speech, his overall manner and his bitterness at not gaining the position held by Newman were to have a practical consequence when Kerr refused to implement the Board's policy in London for the next four years. One prominent casualty of this conflict was Margaret McMillan, for her attempts to establish a school clinic in London were rebuffed by the LCC, but the major sufferers were the children of London since Kerr's action had little effect upon either Morant or Newman. The latter did feel moved to comment in his annual report for 1909, however, that the LCC's performance under the 1907 Act represented 'a failure "without parallel"'. And Kerr's action both alienated his previous ally, the BMA, and contributed to his removal by the LCC.[62]

A less strident and more telling criticism of the Board's policy was voiced privately by Gorst:

> We are going to put in force on Jan.1st a very stringent examination of the health of children when they first come to school, and I have accepted the office of Manager of the Schools here

391

[Letchworth], so that I shall see how it operates. We shall find about one-third of the children suffering from poverty and the remedial measures to be adopted are still left at large.[63]

Given this seminal point, it was apposite that in January 1908 Morant received a letter from Henry Hobhouse, chairman of the County Councils' Association Education Committee, raising a query about the Board's intentions concerning expenditure on medical appliances. Morant passed the query to Selby Bigge, the newly appointed Principal Assistant Secretary of the Whitehall division, who reacted cautiously knowing that the Board was unable to provide any grants-in-aid towards implementation of the Act because of the government's failure to make any financial provision for the School Medical Service. He advised Morant that the Board should stall and reply that it was not in a position to formulate the principles required for dealing with applications from LEAs for sanction to provide medical treat-ment. Morant concurred, noting that while Hobhouse loved 'putting conundrums: we must often evade being caught by them'.[64] None the less, Selby Bigge was set the task of clarifying the Board's position on medical treatment under the Act and he reported in May his belief that with the sanction of the Board the LEAs did possess 'very wide powers' for providing medical treatment of minor ailments either on school premises or in special rooms 'provided with special equip-ment'. Citing some of the interpretations expressed in the House during the Act's passage, Selby Bigge felt that the original intention had been for medical treatment to be limited to the 'minor ailments to which children are subject'. This notwithstanding, his conclusion was that the words of Section 13(1)(b) of the Act would allow an LEA greater exercise of their powers if it was willing to meet the costs involved.[65] Dismayed by these comments, Newman set about drafting some notes on 'means of amelioration' and the establishment of school clinics.

He contended that when the Board advised LEAs about providing medical treatment, it should reinforce the educational nature of the Act and stipulate that any treatment should, as far as possible, be a development of the preventative means of treatment. Thus, under current social conditions, the State's role was to be limited to pointing out diseases or defects in children and would leave treatment to the 'ordinary channels of therapeutics', especially those which would increase rather than decrease the sense of parental responsibility. If school clinics were established by an LEA, it was critical that the treatment they provided should neither pauperise parents nor be prejudicial to the interests of medical practice. He did acknowledge that children should be the clinics' first priority but that the treatment they received should be limited to that which 'fits the child for school life, or makes the child directly able to receive education which without such treatment the child would not be able to receive'.[66] But when Circular 596 was published in August, the majority of its content was devoted to a consolidation of the principles and practices of school medical inspection although it now reinforced the role to be played by school medical officers since they had been officially recognised, in the Elementary School Code for 1908, as personnel having specific functions within the elementary education system. Only the final quarter of the Circular was devoted to the Board's first policy statement on medical treatment by LEAs and eight suggestions considering the possible methods of treatment were made by the Board. These were:

(a) Improvement of the School Arrangements
(b) Exercise of Powers under Special Acts relating to School Children
(c) Co-operation with the Sanitary Authority
(d) Advice or Direction to Parents
(e) The School Nurse
(f) Provision of spectacles, &c
(g) Contributions to Hospitals, Infirmaries, Dispensaries, &c
(h) School Clinics.[67]

This priority listing of suitable 'treatments' revealed that in Newman's view, prevention still remained preferable to cure as far as the activities of the LEAs were concerned. It was only half way through the list, therefore, that the appointment of school nurses was suggested while the establishment of school clinics was consigned to the eighth, and final, suggestion and here the Board's approach closely followed the stringent practice adopted for the provision of school meals. Thus where the establishment of school clinics was contemplated by an LEA, the Board required the authority to submit detailed information not only as to the treatment which the clinic/s would provide but also its plans for ensuring that the children treated were only those for whom 'adequate provision' could not be made by either their parents, voluntary agencies or the Poor Law authorities.[68]

Gilbert has claimed that this Circular was the basic charter for the School Medical Service but at the time there was still considerable hostility from the medical profession to the possibility that public funds could be used to create 'a system of unfair competition with private practitioners'.[69] Furthermore, Newman's over-cautious approach meant that he harboured doubts as to the wisdom of insisting upon everything in the Circular's schedule. Morant, in a more positive vein, had thought that by using the new Elementary Code certain items could be insisted upon absolutely. Eicholz was even more emphatic and was in favour of insistence upon almost every item in the schedule, noting that through identification and treatment 'physical amelioration becomes possible and through neglect of them that deterioration remains wide spread and stereotyped'.[70] Support for Eicholz's view came from Ralph Crowley, soon to join Newman's staff, who told him that general practitioners were

> at length appreciating what is our chief function in regard to the public or rather it is being disclosed to us. A quite new world is opening and it has got to be possessed: it will not however come about with considerable shrieking from sundry Local Divisions of the B.M.A.[71]

Pressure for medical treatment also emerged as a result of a meeting Newman had with a deputation from the NUT led by the Conservative MP Ernest Gray. Leading the presentation, Gray stated that he would prefer to see medical treatment being provided rather than the 'collection of statistics' because he feared some LEAs would use the amount of work and staff involved in inspection as an excuse for not treating any defects revealed by the inspection. He argued also that teachers should not be involved in the inspection process since they were employed to teach and not carry out unpaid medical and clerical work, work which might bring them into conflict with some parents. Newman's response was to claim that the specific examples quoted by Gray and other members of the delegation were 'quite exceptional' when compared with his own observations, and he reiterated his view that the 1907 Act was an education Act, that Parliament had intended school hygiene to be an organic part of the education system and they must all help, therefore, to bring educational and medical matters 'into line'.[72] And despite these comments from Eicholz, Crowley and the NUT, all pressing for more positive moves to be made in the provision of medical treatment, Newman refused to abandon his cautious approach as was demonstrated when the first LEA annual report on medical inspection and treatment was received by the Board from Somerset County Council in November 1908.

Commenting on Somerset's schemes, Newman felt he had to urge 'great caution' upon the Board in any sanctioning of its schemes for medical treatment, advocating that it be limited to 'safe schemes' and only those applied to necessitous cases. The principles which guided his approach towards implementation of the Act became clear from his delineation of the guidelines to be used by the Board in cases of medical treatment. No scheme should be approved, he argued, which was likely

(a) to pauperise the parent;
(b) unduly to burden the Education Rate (that is, extravagant schemes);
(c) to saddle the State with responsibilities obviously belonging to the parent;
(d) to derange in any serious degree the practice of the medical profession.[73]

Thus, despite Morant's earlier intervention over the statements on medical treatment in Circular 576, Newman still retained an outlook which bore a remarkable resemblance to the views of the Charity Organisation Society. Morant had to intervene once more, therefore, making the point this time that the current situation was as it had been in 1870 with regard to elementary education, 'It could not stop at that. [3Rs] The development was irresistible, and will be so in this sphere too'. He was personally delighted with the Somerset Report and thought it reflected the most important development he had seen in either the work of the Board or Local Education Authorities for several years and he ordered it to be printed. He welcomed the steps taken by the county as a major advance in the rural sector and saw them as matching the work being done by the large urban authorities. He believed that in 20 years' time the Board would be able to look back on the establishment of medical inspection as the seeding of a well developed medical system for children:

> The next few years will, I believe show a vast development of the public conscience in regard to public health: and particular developments such as these now stated in Somersetshire will do very much to stimulate this, if carefully planned and continued.[74]

In the meantime, it was perhaps not surprising that when the statistics for the first year of operation of the School Medical Service became available, they revealed the impact of Newman's policy as well as caution on the part of many LEAs.

All but 21 of the country's 328 LEAs had had their schemes of medical inspection approved by the Board while 300 had appointed school medical officers. The Board had adopted a flexible approach to approval of the medical inspection schemes and sanctioned all which did not conflict with the general principles contained in Circular 576. Newman had been worried initially by the possible extravagance or parsimony of some LEAs' schemes when they were submitted to the Board but by the end of 1908 he was relieved to note that there were signs of moderation of both excesses. The provision of medical treatment also conformed very closely to Newman's ideal. Only one school clinic had been established, at Bradford, and only 55 LEAs were offering some form of treatment at a total cost of £3,400. Eight other authorities were making contributions to hospitals in order to secure treatment.[75] Medical inspection was thus the dominant form of activity and when requests were received by the Board from LEAs about the likely loading to be required of them in 1909 with respect to inspections Newman was inclined to reward them for their efforts during the first year of the system's implementation with 'a little sweet reasonableness rather than irritate them by undue burdens'. He claimed, however, that he could not decide which scheme to choose from those put forward by LEA medical officers as he and his department had had little time to see what had been going on in LEAs during 1908 because of the pressure of office work. It was thus left to Selby Bigge to advocate the additional inspection of 8–9-year-olds, on the simple basis that they were approximately half way between entrants and leavers. But as a corollary, Bigge argued for a more summary inspection of entrants since they tended to be 'nervous and troublesome and it is difficult to get anything worth having out of an inspection'. Morant was troubled by this observation because he had hoped that it would be with this very group that so much preventive work could be initiated in serious cases and provide 'so much educational influence on the mothers'.[76] Newman supported Selby Bigge by claiming that the defects exposed among school entrants were 'home-bred (and we cannot at present increase the burden on LEAs of grappling even indirectly with these)'. Morant could only write, in the margin of Newman's note, 'I think I care more about this side than almost any other, at present'; Morant was perhaps more than usually interested in this aspect because his eldest child, Basil, suffered from an affliction.[77] Any possible further progress on this matter was postponed for a year by Runciman, however, because of other rate demands being made on LEAs.[78]

A few months later, under the guise of merely 'thinking aloud' at the annual dinner of the Society of Medical Officers of Health, Morant was able to indicate that the LEAs had, in general, accepted the principles of the Board's policy and he believed that it could now be said that the School Medical Service had passed beyond the initial stage. Reacting to public criticisms that the State, through the institution of preventive measures being supported by the Board, was fostering socialism and interfering with the freedom of the individual, Morant claimed that there were certain aspects of life which required joint action by the community and while it had been recognised by society that education should be obligatory for the ultimate benefit of the community that perception was only just being reached with regard to health. In developing this theme he invoked one of Gorst's concepts – that the best way to attain any real improvement in a community was 'to interest the people themselves in the development of their own powers and will through the local authorities'. At the same time, he took care to reiterate his belief that prevention was preferable to cure and in connection with this made the point that 'every individual owed a duty to the community in the matter of his own health'. He conceded that although the Board's measures had enabled linkages to be made between the previously separate worlds of education and health, what was still required was to ensure that the new relationship could be harmoniously developed. Such a development, he claimed, needed a cautious approach if it was to succeed.[79] For his audience Morant's comment obviously referred to the continued antagonism being shown by the BMA to the Board's policies as well as to medical officers of health but Morant also knew that a new problem had just arisen which threatened to undermine the Board's policy on medical treatment, and that was the passing of the Local Government Board's LEA (Medical Treatment) Bill a few weeks previously.

The Act was designed to stimulate the establishment of school clinics, especially among recalcitrant local authorities, by providing the authorities with the legal right to recover from parents as a civil debt the costs incurred in medical treatment. While this was intended to help offset, in part at least, the demand clinics made on the rates, the significant point of the measure was that if a parent could not afford the costs then he/she would not suffer any civil penalty. This principle threatened to undermine the necessitous element fundamental to the Board's policy on treatment and raised the question of whether the Board should now make it a condition of sanctioning LEA plans for medical treatment that an LEA (a) established the necessary machinery to recover the costs of treatment from parents who could afford to pay and (b) the LEA informed parents of their financial liability before providing the medical treatment. At the time the measure was still before the House, Morant had written on an internal Board memorandum on its contents:

> It is for domestic circulation only, of course – and to be conspicuously marked Confidential. The less attention we draw to the Bill so far as the public are concerned, the better.[80]

Newman's reaction was, predictably, to urge caution:

> . . . we must proceed slowly and, as I understand the term, in a conservative manner, i.e. economically (by which I do not mean necessarily cheaply), constructively, using, as far as may be, voluntary agencies and the potentialities of the parents, and, doing it all at such a reasonably slow pace that real and steady growth, both in the conceptions and in the practice of the Authorities, is allowed for.[81]

He was unwilling to abandon the concepts embodied in the Circulars, especially those discouraging 'indiscriminate gratuitous medical aid'. Although Selby Bigge concurred with this last sentiment he did comment that apart from the slight, if any, moral effect produced by the recovery of costs from parents, the actual expenses involved made such an exercise not worthwhile on financial grounds. He believed that the new Act would not only boost medical treatment but an advantage would accrue to those who supported it 'on what may be called socialistic grounds'.[82] Well aware of this, Morant wanted to publish details of the medical treatment already being carried out, otherwise 'we shall stand to be blamed by the British Public'. Runciman concurred and the matter was speedily put in hand.

The Board's policy on medical treatment reached its Rubicon at the beginning of 1911, however, when the question was raised about the power of an LEA to prosecute a parent, under the Children's Act of 1908, for failing to provide the necessary medical treatment for a child.[83] Under the Act, 'a huge inchoate measure' designed to protect the legal rights of the child, Claud Schuster, the Board's legal counsel, argued that if an LEA was willing to provide the necessary treatment the parent must use it, even if he/she was unwilling to pay for it, or face prosecution. The result, he believed, would be that medical treatment would become compulsory and this had to be confronted by the Board, since they had

> pledged themselves to the doctrine under s.13 of the Act of 1907

that medical treatment is not compulsory. Strictly speaking, it would not be a departure from this pledge if it should turn out that it is compulsory in effect under a section in another Act of Parliament; but it would be very difficult to make the world at large see the distinction.[84]

The recent introduction of State-provided old age pensions highlighted the futility of the Board trying to retain its original policy and the medical treatment of schoolchildren by the State now became another unquestioned legal right of the child. Six years earlier Gorst had made the same point:

> The child's claim on its family is the first but not the only claim to which its birth in the world entitles it. In the second place, it has a claim upon society . . . . The law recognises the separate rights of children. In regard to protection of life and limb, they are placed on the same footing as adults.[85]

He had also formulated what the State's obligations should be in this regard for schoolchildren:

> Every child, on entering school, should be medically examined; the ailing ones classified; and their condition recorded. Treatment, medicine, appliances and diet should be prescribed for those that need medical aid; and the School Authorities should see that they obtain that which is ordered for them either from their parents or, if their parents fail, from the public.[86]

His efforts, as well as those of Macnamara, McMillan and the other members of the 'National Efficiency' movement, on behalf of the children of the nation, had finally achieved fruition, in theory if not completely in practice.

In his address to the Society of Medical Officers of Health in 1909, Morant had claimed that the School Medical Service had not only passed beyond the initial stage but that it was working 'both satisfactorily and efficiently'. This was an easy, yet convincing, claim for him to make as the LEAs had only just started to carry out the first medical inspections. But as time passed the development of the Service did not maintain these standards. It could be argued that Newman's cautious approach and emphasis, in conjunction with Morant, upon prevention rather than cure impeded rather than helped the quick and comprehensive development the plight of many children demanded yet, as in other aspects of the education system, it was the significant disparity between the LEAs which was the major causal factor. Newman had commented in the annual report for 1910 that the implementation of the Act had achieved something more than the amelioration of disease and disability and this was the manifestation

> of a great and worthy partnership – what has been well called, 'the joint obligation of an indissoluble partnership' – between voluntary and paid workers, between Local Authorities and Central Government, between the individual and the community, which whatever be its other fruits cannot fail of good result in bringing about a larger measure of that coordination and unification which is perhaps the greatest single need in the sphere of English local government.[87]

His comments were somewhat roseate compared with the reality of the situation, for it was at this stage a rather unbalanced 'partnership' caused, at least in part, by the absence of government funding for either the establishment or development of the Service and as the LEAs responded to the Circulars being sent out by the Board they found themselves having to bear virtually all the costs involved. Some LEAs restricted themselves, therefore, to the minimal requirements under the Act, and by 1910 Newman was forced to comment that in some areas

> the foundations of the administrative machinery still remain to be completed, and in all areas there is much solid building and good contriving yet to be done, particularly in the realm of treatment.[88]

One year later, there still remained 15 LEAs who had not completed their arrangements for providing a School Medical Service. Even at the basic level of implementation of the Act there were substantial differences among LEAs in the rigour of their inspections despite the wishes of a large number of parents that the inspection should be of a 'thorough and exhaustive nature'. While Salford found 1:162 pupils had ringworm, in neighbouring Manchester the proportion was 1:259, whereas in Bradford it was 1:82 but Swansea reported finding only 1:955.[89] In some instances the motives of the LEAs in providing treatment were not altruistic but financial for when pupils were absent from schools for long periods the LEA lost their per capita grants for them from the Board. In the case of body lice or ringworm infections not only were children now excluded from the schools by the school medical officers but the traditional treatments were time consuming; for the LCC this amounted to £5–6,000 a year in lost funding. Not surprisingly, then, some LEAs not only introduced medical treatment to try to reduce these financial shortfalls but found that the high costs involved in introducing X-ray treatment, £130-150, to treat cases of ringworm was more than repaid by the great reduction in time when compared with traditional treatment.[90] Some LEAs had established clinics after they had tried to carry out Newman's early injunctions to refer treatment to other agencies, such as the voluntary hospitals, for they had found themselves incurring the wrath of these agencies' because of the subsequent overloading of their facilities, for example, of the out-patient departments of hospitals, and some refused to treat children. By 1911 the total number of school clinics established stood at 56, with some providing only dental treatment, and only 82 authorities had received sanction to provide spectacles for children. Thirty-two LEAs had managed to reach an accommodation with hospitals, through financial grants, to treat children referred by the school medical officers. The quality of treatment, like that of inspection, thus varied considerably between adjoining LEAs as well as nationally because of these different ways of implementing the Act, as well as the variations in interpretation of the intention of the Act. Equally significant for many parents was the fact that their situation was little changed from that depicted by the Inter-Departmental Committee in 1905; and they could still afford neither the financial outlay required for some treatment nor the time lost through attending hospitals with their child while the repugnance and social disadvantages of applying for Poor Law assistance made that option unacceptable. Thus, of the children needing treatment, in many instances no more than a quarter received it.

When Morant left the Board in 1911 it could be argued that the School Medical Service was still well and truly in its initial stage as opposed to his statement of 1909. The subsequent development of the Service is beyond the purview of this study but it does need to be noted that the Ministry of Health Act of 1919 was of great significance, for under the Act all the powers and duties of the Board of Education with respect to the medical inspection and treatment of schoolchildren and young persons were transferred to the new Ministry of Health. And Morant, the Ministry's first Permanent Secretary, and Newman, its Chief Medical Officer, were responsible for the development of a unified health service for the nation. The organic relationship they had wanted to see develop between the school and wider community health services could now be ensured and their major goal of 1907 realised. The irony of this situation was that it was ultimately a consequence of Morant's enforced departure from the Board of Education.

NOTES

1. Report of the Inter-Departmental Committee on Medical Inspection and the Feeding of Children attending Public Elementary Schools, *PP*, XLVII, [Cd.2779] 1906, pp. 2, 9.
2. Ibid., p. 11.
3. Ibid., p. 31.
4. C. Griggs, *The Trades Union Congress and The Struggle for Education 1868-1925* (1983), pp. 151–2; B. Simon, *Education and the Labour Movement, 1870-1920* (1965), pp. 257–8.
5. C. Steedman, *Childhood, Culture and Class in Britain: Margaret McMillan, 1860–1931* (1990), pp. 169–70.
6. K.O. Morgan, 'Edwardian Socialism' in D. Read (ed.), *Edwardian England* (1982), p. 101.
7. Campbell-Bannerman Papers, Add MS 41213, fo. 337, Lord Crewe to Sir H. Campbell-Bannerman, 19 Nov. 1905.
8. W. Churchill, *Complete Speeches*, I, pp. 675–6 cited in M. Bentley, *The Climax of Liberal Politics* (1987), p. 112.
9. *Labour Leader*, 18 May 1906 cited in B. Simon, op. cit., p. 285. See also C. Steedman, op. cit., pp. 169–70.
10. For McMillan's contact with Morant see C. Steedman, op. cit., pp. 55–6.
11. Marvin Papers, MS Eng lett c.237, fo. 139, M.E. MacDonald to E. Marvin, 5 July 1906.
12. Diary of John Bruce Glaiser, 28 July 1906 cited in C. Steedman, op. cit., pp. 55–6.
13. *4 PD*, 160, c.1398, 16 July 1906.
14. PRO ED 24/117, Note by R.L. Morant: this appears to have been sent to Lord Crewe rather than to Birrell, thus indicating the magnitude of Morant's anger with Birrell over the issue.
15. PRO ED 24/112, R. Bell to A. Birrell, 24 Oct. 1906.
16. *School Government Chronicle*, 76 (15 Sept. 1906), p. 224.
17. B. Webb, *Our Partnership* (1948), p. 333.
18. PRO ED 24/128, R.L. Morant to Sir S. Provis, 19 Feb. 1907: R.L. Morant to T.J. Macnamara, 19 Feb. 1907.
19. *4 PD*, 170, c.426–7, 1 March 1907.
20. Ibid.
21. PRO ED 24/128, W.R. Anson to R.L. Morant, 27 Feb. 1907.
22. Ibid., W.R. Anson to A.J. Balfour, 27 Feb. 1907.
23. Ibid., W.M .Short to R.L. Morant, 28 Feb. 1907.
24. Ibid., R.L. Morant to W.R. Anson, 1 March 1907.
25. *4 PD*, 176, c.36, 14 June 1907.
26. Ibid., c.39.
27. PRO ED 31/151, R.L. Morant to R. McKenna, 30 April 1907.
28. *4 PD*, 180, c.912, 12 Aug. 1907.
29. Ibid., c.915–8.
30. Ibid., 160, c.1376–7, 16 July 1906.

31. M. Bentley, *Politics without Democracy 1815-1914* (1984), p. 327.
32. R.L. Morant to M. McMillan, 26 June 1907 cited in A. Mansbridge, *Margaret McMillan Prophet and Pioneer: Her Life and Work* (1932), p. 64.
33. B. Webb, *Diary*, 26, p. 2489, 27 April 1907.
34. Sandars Papers, MS Eng hist c.753, fo. 177, R.L. Morant to J.S. Sandars, 13 May 1907.
35. L. Brock in V. Markham, 'Robert Morant – Some Personal Reminiscences', *Public Administration*, XXVIII (Winter 1950), pp. 259–60.
36. B. Webb, *Our Partnership*, pp. 348–9.
37. A. Vinson, 'The Edwardians and Poverty: Towards a Minimum Wage?' in D. Read (ed.), *Edwardian England*, pp. 83–4.
38. G. Newman, *The Building of a Nation's Health* (1939), p. 258.
39. Ramsay MacDonald Papers, PRO 30/60 1151, M. McMillan to R. MacDonald, 11 May 1907.
40. See C. Burt and L. Fairfield in H.W.S. Francis, 'The Doctor as Educationalist: James Kerr :1861–1941', *The Medical Officer* (29 May 1970), pp. 303–4.
41. B. Webb, op. cit., pp. 385.
42. PRO ED 24/280, R.L. Morant to A. Eicholz, 28 Aug. 1907.
43. Ibid., R.L. Morant to G. Newman, 28 Aug. 1907.
44. Newman, op. cit., pp. 195–6.
45. Ibid., p. 458. Although Newman did not provide the source of these instructions it could have only been McKenna, thereby confirming Morant's observation that his political master knew what he wanted to obtain from this particular piece of legislation. See also Sandars Papers, MS Eng hist c.738, fo. 177, R.L. Morant to J.S. Sandars, 13 May 1907.
46. PRO ED 24/280, G. Newman to R.L. Morant, 8 Aug. 1907.
47. Ibid., 6 Sept. 1907.
48. Ibid.
49. B.B. Gilbert, *The Evolution of National Insurance in Great Britain*, pp. 136–7.
50. PRO ED 50/5, A. Newsholme to G. Newman, 17 Oct. 1907.
51. Ibid., J.R. Kaye to G. Newman, 29 Oct. 1907.
52. Ibid.
53. Ibid., E.R. Cross to G. Newman, 5 Nov. 1907.
54. Ibid., A. Newsholme to G. Newman, 17 Oct. 1907.
55. PRO ED 24/280, R.L. Morant to C.F.G. Masterman, 4 Nov. 1907.
56. Board of Education Circular 576, *PP*, XXIII, [Cd.4986] 1910, pp. 152–3.
57. PRO ED 50/3, British Medical Association Memorandum on Medical Inspection of Children, Dec. 1907.
58. PRO ED 50/6, Circular 582: Schedule for guidance of work of medical inspection laid down in Circular 576, and covering S.13 of the 1907 Education (Administrative Provisions) Act, p. 1.
59. PRO ED 50/6, G. Newman to R.L. Morant, 10 Jan. 1908: R.L. Morant to G. Newman, 10 Jan. 1908.
60. PRO ED 50/7, J.Kerr, 'The Medical Inspection and Treatment of School Children', 22 April 1908.
61. L. Fairfield in H.W.S. Francis, op. cit., pp. 303–5.
62. J.D. Hirst, 'A Failure "without parallel": The School Medical Service and the London County Council 1907–12', *Medical History*, 25 (1981), pp. 281–300; Gilbert, op. cit., pp. 139–43.
63. Fowlds Papers 2/5, J.E. Gorst to G. Fowlds, 20 Dec. 1907.
64. PRO ED 50/3, L.A. Selby Bigge to R.L. Morant, 24 Jan. 1908; R.L. Morant to

L.A. Selby Bigge, 3 Feb. 1908.

65. Ibid., L.A. Selby Bigge, Memorandum, 29 May 1908.
66. PRO ED 50/7, G. Newman, Rough Notes on the Question of Means of Amelioration and the Establishment of Clinics, for further consideration, 29 June 1908.
67. Board of Education Circular 596, *PP*, XXIII, [Cd.4986] 1910, pp. 163–5.
68. PRO ED 50/7, Circular 596, 17 Aug. 1908, p. 9.
69. Gilbert, op. cit., p. 145; *British Medical Journal* (18 July 1908), p. 41.
70. PRO ED 50/7, G. Newman to A. Eicholz, 16 June 1908; A. Eicholz to G. Newman, 17 June 1908.
71. Ibid., R.H. Crowley to G. Newman, 23 July 1908.
72. PRO ED 50/3, 'Memorandum of interview between Dr G. Newman and W.R. Davies and an N.U.T. delegation led by Ernest Gray MP', 22 Feb. 1909.
73. PRO ED 50/3, G. Newman, 6 Nov. 1908.
74. Ibid., R.L. Morant, 22 Nov. 1908.
75. Annual Report of the Chief Medical Officer of the Board of Education for 1908, *PP*, XXIII, [Cd.4986] 1910, pp. 42, 98, 105–6.
76. PRO ED 50/3, L.A. Selby Bigge to R.L. Morant, 6 April 1909; R.L. Morant to G. Newman, 9 May 1909.
77. Ibid., G. Newman to R.L. Morant, 11 May 1909.
78. Ibid., E. Maurice to R.L. Morant, 19 May 1909.
79. *Public Health*, 23 (Nov. 1909), pp. 66–8.
80. PRO ED 50/3, W.R. Barker, Draft Memorandum on 1909 L.E.A. (Medical Treatment) Bill, 29 Sept. 1909.
81. Ibid., G. Newman to L.A. Selby Bigge, 9 Nov. 1909.
82. Ibid., L.A. Selby Bigge to R.L. Morant, 10 Nov. 1909.
83. For details of the Act see B.B. Gilbert, op. cit., p. 153.
84. PRO ED 50/3, C. Schuster, Memorandum, 19 Jan. 1911.
85. J.E. Gorst, 'Children's Rights', *Living Age*, 246 (July 1905), p. 231. See also his book *The Children of the Nation* (1906), for a more detailed exposition of these rights.
86. J.E. Gorst, 'Physical Deterioration in Great Britain', *North American Review*, DLXXXIV (July 1905), p. 6.
87. Annual Report of the Chief Medical Officer of the Board of Education for 1908, *PP*, XXIII, [Cd.5426] 1910, p. 364.
88. Ibid.
89. Ibid., [Cd.4986], p. 33.; J. Hurt, *Elementary Schooling and the Working Classes, 1860-1918* (1979), p. 136.
90. Annual Report of the Chief Medical Officer of the Board of Education for 1911, *PP*, XXIII, [Cd.6530] 1910, p. 566; J. Hurt, op. cit., pp. 132–3.

13

The end of the beginning

I seem to have failed to learn what the cost can be of one moment's defective application of mind and imagination.[1]

The Liberal government's attempts at educational reform in 1906 had been focused on elementary education but both Birrell and Morant were aware of other pressing policy issues in the post-elementary education area. These included the development of the higher elementary schools, the contentious issues of access to, and the financing of, secondary education as well as teacher registration. Although Birrell had brought them to the Cabinet's attention in May it was to be the issue of the higher elementary schools, as a result of the publication in July of a report on these schools by the Consultative Committee, that precipitated a policy solution in secondary education. A preoccupation with the passage and fate of the 1906 Education Bill, however, meant that the various parties interested in these schools, especially the NUT and TUC, did not respond to the report until the end of 1906. It thus fell to McKenna to try to provide resolutions for what were, in fact, to become some of the most pressing issues for English education in the twentieth century. The contentious nature of the debates about these issues between the teachers and the Board, but especially Morant, has contributed, in part, to Grace's hypothesis that State–teacher relations in twentieth-century England may be characterised as one of trench warfare, utilising Gramsci's concept of a war of position. Gramsci used this term to denote the nature of the conflict between the State and other organisations and believed that at times passive resistance constituted the form of war but at others a war of movement or underground warfare were the dominant components. It was these features, rather than trench warfare, which marked the initial stages of the NUT–Morant conflict and it was to take several years before the trench stage was reached. None the less, as the conflict over teacher registration developed, Gramsci's rider, that 'in politics the "war of position", once won, is decisive definitely', was to become applicable.[2]

A few months after the publication of the new Secondary School Regulations in 1904 a discussion had taken place in the Secondary Branch of the Board about higher elementary schools. Opinion was divided over whether they should be allowed to continue and, if they were, whether their curriculum should be modified. The division was caused by a feeling of uncertainty about the schools' role in relation to the increasing number of secondary schools and how far they served, or could be made to serve, 'a distinct purpose which . . . a Secondary School does not serve'. Edmond Holmes and Headlam believed that the secondary schools should be available only to those likely to complete the four-year course stipulated in the regulations, while the higher elementary schools could cater for those pupils who would not stay until the age of 16 but might be induced to stay to 14 or slightly later. Leach and Mackail felt that it was difficult to tell which pupils were likely to stay on until 16, given the pull of employment openings, and this could create problems. Chambers suggested, when relaying these points to Morant, that a temporary investigating committee could be formed to collect the data needed to make a decision about the higher elementary schools' future.[3] Morant modified this plan and asked Bruce, the head of Secondary Branch, to draw up the terms of reference for the Consultative Committee, including 'the task of framing Differentia between H.E. Schls and Secy. Schls', although he added that he had little expectation of 'getting practical help from them'.[4] Shortly afterwards, Morant had an interview with Courtenay Hodgson, Secretary of the Cumberland LEA, about higher elementary schools and the possibility of establishing new ones in rural areas. Hodgson discussed the matter further with colleagues from neighbouring LEAs and submitted a memorandum of his findings to Morant a month later.

There appeared to be consensus among northern LEAs about the need for more post-elementary education provision within rural areas and that a curriculum based primarily on the Elementary Code should be developed to a higher standard, with the possibility of Latin, Greek or modern languages being offered subject to local circumstances. Hodgson envisaged these schools offering education up to the age of 16 years but was wary of possible competition that might arise with secondary schools and Morant told Bruce that if any action was to be taken 'it must be under Part III and not under Part II of the Education Act'.[5] Circulation of Hodgson's memorandum around the Secondary Branch staff resulted in considerable support for the ideas contained in it. Headlam observed that where attempts had been made in rural communities such as Stokesley (Cleveland) or Middleton-in-Teesdale to run a secondary school which was 'necessarily a rival to the elementary school', they had been unsuccessful. The possibility of expanding the elementary school to include curricular options for those pupils who required 'more than the ordinary course' received his enthusiastic endorsement as well as support from Fletcher and Mackail. Leach was more cautious, being concerned that the provision of subjects like Latin could be a disadvantage:

> Latin . . . is precisely the thing that in my experience they always inveigh against, and would keep them away. The Tom Tullivers are not attracted to it.[6]

Of equal concern to all was the funding of these schools and they were not sure whether Hodgson's proposal that old grammar school endowments be used was viable. Morant referred the matter to Selby Bigge who minuted that he did not think it either 'desirable or even feasible' to use endowments to supplement rate aid and government grants.[7] His comments acted as a damper on the enthusiasm for the venture but, this notwithstanding, the Board applied to Treasury for permission to change the terms of the Higher Elementary School Minute of 1900.

Outlining the reasons which had lain behind the creation of the Minute, the Board argued that the changes made to the education system following implementation of the 1902 Education Act, as well as the unsuitability of the predominantly scientific curriculum of these schools, had produced an unforeseen consequence. There had been

> an increasing tendency to put into secondary schools, receiving secondary schools grant from this Board, many pupils who cannot in fact stay to the end of the secondary school course. By this the standard of the secondary school is in these cases lowered and the intention of the Board's scheme of secondary school grants is not properly carried out.

To overcome this and the other problems connected with the current higher elementary schools, the Board proposed changes to the curriculum, the age of entrance (to be 12 years instead of 10) and the grants awarded to the schools. By these it was hoped that the schools would become more relevant for pupils who could not stay beyond the age of 15 but who required 'something wider and more advanced than the ordinary elementary school curriculum can afford, but shorter in duration than that of the secondary school'.[8] Treasury concurred with the proposals and the changes were promulgated shortly afterwards in the Code for 1905, albeit producing little impact upon the educational world at the time. This state of affairs was to change when the Consultative Committee produced its report one year later.

Morant's belief that anything satisfactory was unlikely to be achieved by the committee's report was reflected in Bruce's comment to members of the Secondary Branch that if during their interviews by the committee they were asked wide-ranging questions then 'we are all of us authorised to say exactly what we like as it has been explained to the committee that the Board will be in no way committed'.[9] This condition never became public knowledge; so when the report was published the Board found itself inextricably linked to the views contained therein. The Liberal MP J.H. Yoxall castigated the report for being 'caddish and snobbish' while in their rebuttal of its views the NUT claimed that the report was part and parcel of 'a deliberate policy . . . to keep exclusive the secondary schools and set up higher elementary schools for the masses'.[10] These negative comments have been reiterated subsequently by Simon who states that the report was unusual in that it was 'a completely frank statement of a class outlook in education, of the kind more usual in an earlier age before the extension of the franchise'. Taylor, on the other hand, believes that the report was intended to promote a rationalisation of the Code which was implicit in the provisions of the 1902 Act.[11]

Overall, the report certainly did appear to accept rather than react against the divisions existent within the post-elementary system and thus reinforced, rather then condemned, the stratifications of the nation's education system. This, it could be argued, was signalled by the comment that while the higher elementary schools prepared their pupils for the 'lower ranks of commerce and industry', the secondary school pupil was prepared for the 'higher ranks and for the liberal professions'. Another comment, that the home conditions of the higher elementary school pupil 'at best, do little to favour the ends of school education, and at worst are antagonistic', only damned the report further in the eyes of its critics. The palatability of such oft-cited comments was made more difficult because underlying them, unfortunately, there was more than a degree of truth. The harsh reality of the lives of many working-class children in Edwardian society mirrored the tyrannical effects of the still predominantly *laissez-faire* view held by society of both the economy and the welfare of its citizens. For many working-class parents, consequently

> . . . children old enough to work, yet still at school, represented
> a financial sacrifice many parents told themselves they could not

afford. . . . Economic necessity had bred a tradition decreeing that a child was 'educated' by the time he was twelve or thirteen. Further years in school wasted the youngster's time while depriving his family of much needed income.[12]

The committee could hardly be condemned, therefore, for the observation that

> at present the effects of the educational system . . . upon the ordinary life and thought of those classes for whom higher elementary schools more especially provide are of a limited kind, and that in consequence the cooperation of parents cannot yet be counted upon to go very far.[13]

Seen from this particular perspective the report's recommendations were somewhat more enlightened than the NUT was willing to acknowledge.

There was a general condemnation by the committee's witnesses of the elementary system for producing pupils who lacked, in the words of one witness, 'self-activity and resource'. The prevalent system of 'drill, chalk and talk', which Edmond Holmes was to indict a few years later in his seminal work *What Is and What Might Be*, was viewed with concern by the committee which advocated that a freer teaching methodology be adopted by the higher elementary schools so as to ensure greater self-help and self-education as goals for their pupils. They argued that the desired pupil outcome should be the possession of what they labelled 'general handiness', that is:

> adaptability and alertness, habits of observation – and the power to express the thing observed – accuracy, resourcefulness, the ability to grapple with new and unfamiliar conditions, the habit of applying one's mind and one's knowledge to what one has to do.

Acquisition of these traits (which bear more than a passing resemblance to those advocated in the late twentieth century for achieving intellectual flexibility and adaptability in students) had to be based upon a general education. The committee acknowledged that as the majority of the schools' pupils would enter their careers immediately upon leaving school, there would have to be some practical bias in the school courses. They preferred it to be essentially an encouragement of 'the practical way of looking at things, to encourage the attitude of mind which looks to practice for the illustration of theory and to theory for the explanation of practice', rather than specific vocational training as such.

The committee were aware, as has been stated, of the reality of life for prospective higher elementary school pupils. At the same time, they were not unconscious of the long-term beneficial effect education could have upon all classes of society:

> . . . as the conception of the purpose and value of education gradually penetrates more deeply into the structure of society as a whole so at the same time the conditions of home life in every class may come more and more into harmony with the ideals of school training.

If this could be achieved, then there was also the possibility that the parents would begin 'to demand the kind of education for their children which is really needed' but this possibility was threatened by the NUT. One of Headlam's correspondents observed that the union had been

> playing the democratic string very loud since the present government came in . . . I believe they are going to put themselves out of court by attempting to wreck the new Higher Elementary Schools.[14]

Why then, given the above views, was the NUT so hostile to the report? One reason lay not so much with the report as with the person they saw as its perpetrator – Morant. As will be seen later, by the time the report was published, Morant was on a virtual collision course with the NUT over the issue of teacher registration, with each being determined to thwart the other's intentions on this issue, and it was one in which the Consultative Committee had been involved. The Board's publication of a report by the committee in which there was a virtual wholesale condemnation of the teaching in elementary schools only added insult to injury as far as the NUT was concerned. The insult was made more unbearable because, once more, it contained more than a hint of the truth.

The elementary schools had been free for a decade from the tyranny of payment-by-results and had had greater freedom over their curriculum and teaching methods following the 1900 block grant system and the 1904 Code changes. Yet in many schools there had been no significant change in either the aims or methods of the elementary school teachers, the schools functioning in 1906 almost as they had in 1896. While this reflected, as Holmes pointed out, the corrosive effects of the payment by results system, none the less the very lack of significant change within the schools permitted criticism and with it, by implication, criticism of the elementary school teachers' advocate and mentor, the NUT. As recipients of the effects of the vitiating class divisions which permeated the teaching world and the consequent 'social estrangement between different grades of teachers', the elementary school teachers naturally looked to the NUT to ameliorate their condition. By denying higher elementary schools any chance of being designated secondary schools, the Consultative Committee's report served only to reinforce the existent status of elementary school teachers. This was an additional blow just at the time when the momentum for change, held out by teacher registration, appeared to be in danger of faltering. In such circumstances, the NUT appears to have decided that attack was the best form of defence, and had little compunction in condemning the report as another manifestation of the Board's élitist and class-based views of secondary education and, by implication, another Morantian scheme to subjugate elementary school teachers.

One outcome of the NUT's manoeuvre was that criticisms of the report were made in the House during McKenna's first defence of the Education Estimates in the Spring of 1907. E.H. Pickersgill, the Liberal MP for Bethnal Green, launched the attack with a criticism of the 'undemocratic spirit' and lack of interest in the concept of secondary education for all held by the Board's Secondary Branch. Claiming that the Consultative Committee's report represented an exposition of this particular spirit, Pickersgill scrutinised the current conditions of access to secondary education and, after highlighting the lamentable state of the scholarship system, indicted the Board for its imposition of fee charging on secondary schools.[15] McKenna carefully defended the fees policy but acknowledged the criticisms about the report and stated that the future composition of the Consultative Committee would be broadened. He then announced that he would be introducing a system of free places in secondary schools for elementary school pupils. This innovation, to take effect from 1 August 1907, was to be included in the new Regulations for Secondary Schools.

Having managed to obtain extra funds from the Chancellor of the Exchequer for secondary education, McKenna was able to introduce a two-tier system of grants to secondary schools. A new grant of £5 per pupil would be awarded to those schools which had a majority of representative managers, did not require religious tests of their staff or governing bodies and would offer at least 25 per cent of their places free to pupils from elementary schools. Schools which did not conform to these requirements would receive only the old grant of £2 per pupil. When he provided these details to the House, McKenna took care to stress both the minimal role allowed the Board in the control of secondary education and the fact that the provision of secondary education rested with the LEAs. He went so far as not only to ask Members to be lenient with the Board but also to state that its policy was to 'democratise the secondary schools in the sense of raising the level and securing for the humblest in the land the opportunity of education for their children in really good schools'.[16] While these policy changes and appeals redounded to McKenna's credit they made little impact upon the NUT. Furthermore, they did nothing to dampen that organisation's increasing hostility towards Morant as the issue of teacher registration became increasingly tortuous and contentious.

The impact of the mid-nineteenth century view that teaching as 'a profession . . . obtains but little respect from society, and confers no social advantages upon its members' had resulted in efforts by teachers' organisations to achieve the establishment of teacher registration. Such a register, it was believed, could redress this perspective by justifying their claim 'to be considered a body of professional men worthy of as much social regard as any other similar body'.[17] Subsequent, but unsuccessful, legislation to provide for teacher registration had led to parliamentary recognition of the need for such a register by the last decade of the century.[18] Realisation of the concept was accelerated by (a) the 1895 Bryce Report's recommendation that a single register for all teachers based upon both academic and professional qualifications should be established and (b) Gorst's occupancy of the Vice Presidency.

Gorst had accepted in principle the Bryce Report's recommendation on teacher registration but, faced with the educational and political complexities of the 1896 Education Bill, had had a separate Bill drafted for teacher registration. It incorporated Bryce's recommendation for a single register but differed in its advocacy of an autonomous registration council. Although the Teacher Registration Bill enjoyed considerable support, the failure of the larger measure led to its being withdrawn while the government pondered their educational legislation programme. It was not until 1899 that Gorst's Teacher Registration Bill resurfaced as part of the Board of Education Act. But, instead of the independent registration council, the new Act provided for the creation of a Consultative Committee charged with the framing of regulations for, and the maintenance of, a register of teachers, in addition to its other roles.

The committee's role in the formation of a teachers' register was 'greeted on practically all sides with favour', but its constitution was vague and a cause for public concern.[19] Michael Sadler had worried that the committee of 18 men appointed in 1900 might be 'ill contrived through the choice of flatterers and bigwigs rather than of men who have really tried to think the educational question out'.[20] Elementary school teachers were more worried by the predominantly secondary school or university backgrounds of the committee members, and Yoxall asserted that the NUT would renounce the committee for its unrepresentative membership.[21]

Undeterred by these criticisms, the Consultative Committee had soon started formulating the registration regulations and were showered with proposals from a variety of teacher organisations. The proposals revealed very clearly, however, the gulf that existed between elementary and secondary school teachers. The Teachers' Guild wanted entrance to the register to be easy initially, albeit with the proviso that the level of qualifications required be raised after a fixed period of time, but the Headmasters' Conference and the Training of Teachers' Joint Committee believed that the register should be solely for graduates. The NUT, on the other hand, made no secret of its determination for a single register, for many elementary school teachers believed a single register could provide them with the chance of achieving enhanced professional status as well as greater social mobility.[22] But if divisions existed between the teachers on this issue so too did they within the Board of Education.

The committee's draft proposals for registration had gained general approval from Kekewich but Gorst believed that the new registration body should be as independent as possible from both the Board and the Consultative Committee, at least for the first three years. At the same time, he wanted the Board to select at least half of the 12 members of the registration authority, fearing that if the Consultative Committee assumed this responsibility they might nominate 'some political member, like Acland, who would make mischief'. Devonshire, reportedly 'much perplexed' by the whole issue, concurred with Gorst's proposals.[23] An Order-in-Council of 6 March 1902 established a register whose structure was to be as recommended by the Consultative Committee except that it was to be administered by an autonomous Teacher Registration Council. This Gorstian amendment was to grate constantly on the committee in the future.

One strength of a teachers' register constantly alluded to from the outset had been that it would eventually result in the exclusion of incompetent teachers from the profession. The Bryce Report had seen this as the chief purpose for which registration was required, and the Consultative Committee's regulations reflected their concern about the necessary entrance requirements to ensure this aim. Although they were prepared to widen entry to registration they could not accept

> lowering the standards of their requirements to an extent that would have been necessary to admit all, or even the major part of the elementary teachers, as this would probably have rendered the Register unattractive to many teachers in secondary schools, and prevented registration from having a beneficial effect on the teaching profession.[24]

Accordingly, they proposed that the register should include two columns, A and B. Whereas the former would be for all certificated elementary school teachers, it was a requirement of registration under column B that a teacher should have spent either at least one year's probation in 'a recognised school (not being an elementary school)' or have taught 'at a recognised school or schools (not being an elementary school or schools)' in addition to having completed a degree and at least one year's teacher training in an approved institution. But when this regulation appeared in an Order-in-Council it provoked an outcry from elementary teachers' organisations.

The *School Board Chronicle* rebuked both the committee and the Board, for the regulation was seen not only as reflecting the bias of the committee members but also as perpetuating the Board's class-based policies as exemplified recently by the Cockerton Case and the Higher Elementary School Minute.[25] The Gateshead and District Head Teachers' Association bluntly condemned 'the exhibition of caste spirit in excluding Teachers in Primary Schools from column B of the register, solely because they are Teachers in Primary Schools'.[26] And at its Easter conference the NUT had emphatically condemned the 'injustice which will be inflicted on the Primary Teachers of the country by the introduction into the Register of two lists'.[27] The *Journal of Education*, on the other hand, viewed the regulation as a 'happy solution of a much vexed problem' while the wrath of the elementary school teachers was ignored by the Board, for the institution of the double column register had raised other problems once registration had begun.

The administrative problems which had developed by the autumn of 1902, including the 54 variations under which an applicant could claim to register under column B, had led to a meeting between the Board, the Registration Council and the Consultative Committee in an effort to resolve them. But their lack of success meant that by 1904 the Consultative Committee had, as drafters of the regulations, remained embroiled with their analysis of them and the principles upon which they were based. By then Morant was impatient for the committee to examine other pressing educational problems, including the higher elementary schools, and had favoured putting pressure on them to hasten their deliberations. Anson was more sensitive to the committee's hostility, arising from the Board's limitation of their powers, and urged caution:

> ... I don't like, in these official communications, to talk about 'pressure' and 'agitation'. We as a Board are only concerned with the reasonableness or unreasonableness of demands. I in the House of Commons may have to yield to 'pressure' and 'agitation' and suffer fools as gladly as I can. But upon us and the Consultative Committee the dry light of reason alone should shine.[28]

There were other obstacles, however, preventing the committee's completion of their labours.

The Registration Council's term of office was due to expire in 1905 but, more importantly, the council had now accepted the elementary school teachers' objections to the discrimination existent in the register. Consequently, the council did not wish to see the retention of column A 'as at present constituted', nor could it see any justification for the current waiving of the requirements of professional training for registration in column B.[29] Consideration of these two issues had to be passed to the Consultative Committee and it was not surprising that they felt, faced with this opposition to their regulations as well as the council's seeming inability to resolve the administrative problems confronting it, that the current situation vindicated their original view that registration should have been their responsibility. In their report they recommended the abolition of the Registration Council as from 1 October 1906, with the Board of Education assuming responsibility for all the financial aspects of registration while a sub-committee of their committee assumed responsibility for all other aspects of registration. At the same time they urged the Board to demonstrate its commitment to registration by administratively reinforcing the concept and suggested the insertion into the Secondary Schools Regulations of 'clauses requiring all Schools in receipt of grant to be staffed partly or wholly by "registered" teachers'.[30]

The Board's lack of response to this report appeared to reinforce its by now demonstrable lack of commitment to registration and both Frank Heath and Horace Mann, the committee's new secretary, warned Morant. Heath cited the 'dangerous possibilities involved' if the Board maintained this stance while Mann was more fulsome. He reported the committee's anxiety for a decision on their report, given the impending expiration of the Registration Council's term of office, and the fact that the registration regulations remained 'in a state of suspense and uncertainty as long as it is known that the Committee have reported (and presumably suggested changes) but that the Board have taken no action'. He maintained that the committee were tired of the whole registration issue, not just because of the amount of time it required, and the fact that it had not been a success, but because the Board had 'apparently shelved the report and the question in each case' reported on by them. Continued procrastination by the Board could only lead to a renewal of the 'old-standing feeling of hostility (which I understand the Committee have at times felt towards the Board) and even to increase this feeling if and where it still exists'.[31]

Morant remained unmoved so Heath tried again, this time supported by Bruce, the committee's former secretary. The latter argued that on the issue of registration the Board had now reached

> a parting of the ways, and must either let it be known that we don't believe in it and don't mind if it comes to naught, or else we must give it such backing as will make its success assured.[32]

Here he disagreed with Mann, who was convinced that

> If the profession cannot maintain it [a register] because the teachers are not yet sufficiently an organised and professionally spirited body of persons, I do not see personally why the Board should be called upon to protect it with their aegis.[33]

Mann's views were important for they appeared to reflect, at least in part, Morant's. Stipulating that the case for registration did not lead logically to the existence and maintenance of a 'professional' roll, but rather to the 'absorption of the teaching profession into the service of the State as State Officials', Mann declared that 'a register distinct from official records was . . . as you [Morant] believe . . . unnecessary'.[34]

This concept of teachers as civil servants accorded with the points Morant had made in 1898 about professionalism and the control of education, in both his Swiss education report and in a speech to the 'Education Club'. But Morant's concept of policy-makers did not include teachers, most especially elementary school teachers. As has

been seen, Morant was very critical of the limited standard of education of many elementary teachers and, more importantly, their absence
of culture so that implementation of his idea that these teachers should
be lower echelon civil servants rather than members of an autonomous
and fully professional body would have ensured that policy-making
would remain in the hands of a small number of picked, expert professionals in central government. His chosen tactic remained, therefore, procrastination, for if the Board could at least delay, if not
negate, the achievement of an effective teachers' register then the
possibility of a truly professional body challenging his views was less
likely. In this Morant had undoubtedly been aided, prior to 1906, by
the suspicion and wariness demonstrated by his political superiors
towards the role of the Consultative Committee *vis-à-vis* the Board's
powers. Gorst and Anson had constantly curbed any attempts by
the committee to increase its influence. Thus Anson had acquiesced
readily in 1905, when faced with the committee's report just before
the forthcoming General Election, to Morant's assessment of their
proposals as 'very far-reaching' and requiring not only 'much consideration . . . [but also] real change of policy'.[35] Anson had opted to
defer policy issues to the incoming President, concurring only with a
proposal that the Registration Council's life be extended for another
six months. Thus by the end of 1905, at the cost of the Board's partial
alienation of both teachers and the Consultative Committee, Morant
had been successful with his tactics. The change of government in
1906 was to present an opportunity for openly achieving his goal.

Early in March 1906, Frederick Storr of the Teachers' Registration
Council had received an invitation from Morant to a confidential
meeting on the future of the register. The invitation had cited the
council's view of the impossibility of the current situation *vis-à-vis* the
register, Morant adding 'this is what I have myself always felt'.
During their meeting Morant indicated his belief that the only future
for the register lay in its abolition, so that when Storr left he was convinced that '*alea jacta est*'. None the less, he felt that the abolition of
the register, with the implicit concomitant of making teachers civil
servants, would be bitterly opposed. He believed also that Morant's
analysis of the likely opposition to a register solely of secondary
school teachers was exaggerated.[36] But Morant was convinced that
such a register would be sheer anathema to the elementary school
teachers, observing that the NUT were 'specially setting themselves
against [it]'. Furthermore, since he believed the NUT were politically
strong enough to prevent its existence, Morant remained determined to

forestall their goal of a 'unified register with an absurd minimum' by not having a register, even if it meant 'we are in for a blazing row'.[37]

He received support for his views from R.D. Swallow and J.D. McClure, the honorary secretaries of the Incorporated Association of Head Masters, who indicated their association's strong opposition to a single-column register and a preference for two separate registers.[38] Passing their letter to Birrell, Morant minuted its significance as being a demonstration of the 'fundamental and irreconcilable divergence of view between Secondary and Elementary teachers'. Birrell accepted his comments and decided subsequently that while column A was 'perfectly useless' column B was not fulfilling the aims behind its establishment. The time had come, therefore, to terminate the register and a clause to this effect was inserted into the 1906 Education Bill.[39] Support for his action came from sections of the educational press, with their denunciations of the Consultative Committee's ideas as a 'hopeless tangle' and 'tinkering and botching and patching a Noah's ark contrived to hold every teacher' but opposition was not long in making an appearance.[40] The first came in a resolution from the Consultative Committee to Birrell, disclaiming any responsibility for the discontinuance of the register and requesting that the Board give their resolution immediate publicity. Then calls for the removal of Clause 36 of the Bill, which proposed the abolition of the register, were made during the passage of the Bill by a majority of teachers' organisations both individually and at a public meeting convened by the University of Oxford. Such was the magnitude of the opposition that Morant decided to publish a memorandum setting out his reasons for the necessity of the register's abolition.[41] His action was unsuccessful, for Clause 36 was amended in the Lords by Lord Monkswell, acting on behalf of the NUT and other teachers' organisations. The amended clause provided for the creation of a new registration council, 'representative of the teaching profession', charged with establishing and keeping a single-column register.

The demise of the Bill, and with it the loss of this particular victory, explains why the NUT's response to the Consultative Committee's report on higher elementary schools was delayed until January 1907 for by then it appeared that Morant's policies were in danger of succeeding. Being desperate to prevent this, they had seized on the report as a weapon with which to continue the attack against Morant. But Morant's actions and views were not only annoying the teachers: FitzRoy had had cause to castigate him personally in 1905 over some offence and had observed that Morant had begun to assume a *sic volo*, *sic jubeo* attitude within the Board. By 1907 this attitude had developed to such an extent that Morant was observed by some to be the 'tyrant of the Education Office'.[42] McKenna, as has been seen, was not prepared to accept this attitude or to ignore both the NUT's discontent and that which had generated Monkswell's action. Consequently, the amended Clause 36 of the 1906 Bill became section 16 of the 1907 Education (Administrative Provisions) Act.

Emboldened by this progress, meetings of representatives of 12 educational associations were held under the chairmanship of the Reverend Dr Gow, headmaster of Westminster School, to discuss plans for the new register and council. Working from the autumn of 1907, Gow's team drew up a scheme for membership of a Teachers' Registration Council by the end of February 1908 consisting of a council of 25 members, including five elementary school representatives, two representing technical institutions, six Crown appointees and a maximum of three co-opted members. The scheme was submitted to Morant for his consideration with a request that he receive a deputation to discuss it, but at the meeting Gow's deputation were dismayed by Morant's criticism of their failure to consider the representation of all the school teaching subject and kindergarten associations and teacher training colleges on the council. How, he queried, could the proposed council be considered to be truly representative of the profession in accordance with the terms of the Act? For each point made by the deputation, Morant had further, more detailed questions about the membership for them to consider. At the same time, he refused to consider the council as having any flexibility or autonomy for dealing with potential problems concerning membership that might arise. The only concession he made was to agree to the deputation's request that their scheme be published but, as events proved, not immediately as they had hoped. In a state of some disarray Gow's deputation withdrew to ponder Morant's reaction.

Morant was interviewed by Runciman on the issue in the intervening period and Morant used all his powers to try to convince Runciman that there was no obligation upon the Board to produce proposals for a new Registration Council. This view conveniently overlooked, however, the seminal role placed upon the Board in the issuing of an Order-in-Council necessary to ensure implementation of the 1907 Act's requirements. Morant's arguments had little effect and he was left in no doubt that Runciman viewed him as being 'destructive, and never constructive, and that I produced heaps of objections to everything: and . . . that I am therefore no use to you'. Morant tried subsequently to justify his approach on the grounds that a Minister 'must come to grief (as McKenna did) if he won't learn the utmost difficulties, before trying to solve them,'[43] but his comments fell on at least partially deaf ears.

In June Runciman became the subject of pressure arising from Morant's actions when he was asked on two separate occasions in the House what steps had been taken to continue the teachers' register. His reply to the trio of inquisitors – Anson, Butcher and Magnus – could only be that the Board was still waiting to hear from Gow's committee. It was not until 27 June that the committee's communication arrived. Part of the delay was caused by Gow, who was not only furious with Morant's treatment of him and the committee but was also convinced that the Board 'notoriously means to veto any proposal and he's not going to waste his valuable time'.[44] The committee's revised scheme refuted Morant's seemingly pedantic approach to the constitution of the registration council and reiterated the practical desirability of retaining a broad classification of teachers, that is, elementary, secondary and technical. Any other teachers' organisation not coming within one of these categories could be accommodated by the judicious utilisation of the Crown appointees and co-opted members. Morant's reaction was to publish a White Paper containing the original scheme of Gow's committee, his and Gow's correspondence as well as letters from certain teachers' organisations opposing the scheme, letters which Morant had drummed up. And as a sting in the tail, the paper included Morant's destructive analysis of the latest submission from the committee, in which he firmly laid the blame for the continued delay in establishing a council with the teachers' organisations and not with the Board.[45] Although he must have sanctioned the publication, Runciman took the precaution of soliciting other advice on the registration issue after the receipt of Gow's latest submission.

One of his consultants was Anson, who delineated what he believed to be the causes for the delay in the matter and, by implication, indicted Morant. He commented that it was easy enough 'to construe the words "representative of the teaching profession" in such a way as to make the creation of a Council impossible' but argued that such pedantry was unproductive. An Order-in-Council, he reminded Runciman, 'admits of modification, if unexpected difficulties arise, and what is wanted is to make a start'.[46] Morant also found himself the subject of a public attack by Gow in an article in *The School World*, in which Gow's frustration with Morant's pedantic approach to the council's membership was made manifest.[47] Trying to counter these attacks Morant presented Runciman with 20 letters opposing Gow's committee's proposals and, at the same time, he urged Runciman to make a public statement 'correcting the notion that is being widely disseminated that this Office is gratuitously hindering progress in regard to the new Registration Council'.[48]

These activities merely goaded Gow further, and he now charged Morant with generating the letters of opposition solely for his own purposes. Gow's charge, plus his failure to circulate an earlier reply from Morant to the rest of the committee, led one of his committee, aware of the danger for the negotiations of personal antagonism, to request that he state that his views were only personal.[49] Morant, confident that his tactics were proving effective, told an old acquaintance, Sir Hubert Parry, that he had been able 'to successfully resist' the 'very strong pressure' from the secondary school associations, Parliament and 'other pressure' by demonstrating the absence of a really united professional opinion on the issue, despite 'being violently abused by them for this factious opposition on my part'.[50] But one month later he had to go on the defensive.

In January 1909 the *Christian World* reported that Morant had been

> mercilessly attacked from all quarters at the annual meeting of the IAHM. Mr J.H. Yoxall MP was present by invitation, and joined in the attack. Thus we had the spectacle of both elementary and secondary teachers – united for once – saying some very straight things about the real power at the Board of Education. The trouble was about the Teachers' Register. All classes of school teachers have come to the conclusion that SIR ROBERT MORANT is determined to smash any and every attempt to set up a Teachers' Registration Council and a Register of Teachers .... It is so seldom that teachers attack officials that the event is noteworthy'.[51]

What was equally important apart from this closing of ranks among elementary and secondary teachers was the fact that the topic was now being covered by the daily press and was no longer confined to the educational world. A somewhat dispirited Morant believed that the registration issue had become 'an infernal question', and he acknowledged that his earlier obstructive tactics 'cannot get a hearing now'. His view was reinforced when Gow curtly informed him that his committee, 'instead of having a bit of a scrap with you, has resolved to hold a conference of all educational societies'. Morant then learned that Runciman was going to be pressed by the teachers' associations 'on the ground that I am needlessly obstructing the whole thing'. He was still determined, he told Parry, to persist with his demonstration of the 'insoluble difficulties involved in arriving at a satisfactory Council', but urged him to keep this confidential as 'it would never do to let it be known that I had offered such views'.[52]

Morant's policy seemed to be justified when Gow's committee decided suddenly to disband because of the lack of unanimity among the teachers' organisations over their proposals for the registration council. But Morant's relief was short-lived, for the struggle was taken up by the Federal Council of Secondary Schools' Associations under a new chairman, James Easterbrook of Owen's School, Islington. Easterbrook, noted as 'a strong man' by Morant, arranged with other major teachers' associations, including the NUT, for a conference of teachers' associations to be held on 13 November at the Clothworkers' Hall. Learning that delegates from 37 teachers' associations would be attending, Morant asked if two Board officers could attend in order for the Board 'to obtain a more comprehensive expression of the views of the Teaching Profession on this subject than has ever yet been possible'.[53] Easterbrook agreed and hoped that Morant would be one.

Each speaker at the conference was limited to five minutes, and Easterbrook made it quite clear that if they were to achieve anything from the day then the final decision about the new registration council's constitution would have to be left to a higher authority. This was accepted, but in fact there was hardly any need for his warning as the conference displayed remarkable unity on the council's composition (voting 33:4 in favour), tenure, a scheme for the first council and a definition of the term 'teacher' for the purposes of the register – all passed unanimously. Morant, accompanied by Bruce, was faced with the spectre of a teaching profession fully united in their determination to achieve the establishment of registration and their own registration council. The *Morning Post* hoped that Morant had 'left the meeting a wiser and sadder man' as a result of having witnessed the unity present at all times.[54] Morant remained obdurate, however, convinced that the conference's rejection of some ATTI amendments to the council's membership reflected the absence of true unity and representation of all the profession in the new scheme. More than a year was to pass before he considered the matter again, leading the *Morning Post* to argue that progress would not be achieved 'as long as the personnel of the Board of Education remains as it is'. The *Yorkshire Post* reported the very bitter feeling now being manifested against the

Board because of its lack of activity on the issue.[55] At Runciman's behest, Morant held three meetings with selected teacher organisations during March 1911. In the course of these meetings he skilfully attempted to sow seeds of doubt as to both the effectiveness of the register structure laid down in the 1907 Act and the practicality of the council scheme proposed by the Clothworkers' Hall conference. This *volte face* over the 1907 Act's requirements, which had formed the basis of all his previous criticisms, plus his account of these meetings, published as another White Paper in June 1911, were interesting in revealing the considerable stress he was now under. In his account, Morant did not provide evidence to substantiate the contentious items he claimed arose from the discussions, giving instead a very subjective perspective, for example, 'I cannot recall any specific statement, but the impression left on my mind. . .' or 'so far as I could judge'. More importantly, he contended that the teachers were now no longer interested in the establishment of a register as their first priority, being more concerned with the creation of a professional teachers' council. He was quite happy for such a proposal to go forward, believing that its role lay with the unification of the profession rather than with the creation of a register also, and the possibility thereby of a truly autonomous profession. He recommended that the government 'take note of the changed situation . . . and to do whatever is possible to give practical expression to so important a wish'.[56]

Completely ignoring his previous statements that the Board could not be involved in the drafting of any proposal involving registration, Morant informed Runciman that there would be little difficulty in his [Morant] amending the Clothworkers' Hall conference resolution on the council's composition to make it 'really representative' of the whole profession. For him this required the inclusion of university representatives, although it increased the council membership by nearly 40 per cent. Arguing that the council would not be too large to arrive at effective decisions, Morant conveniently ignored the fact that university representation had been deliberately excluded from the con- ference's scheme for the council, so as to 'enable a Council to get to work with a clear mind and without waste of time in futile discussions as to scope'.[57] Morant's amendment had the potential to sabotage the conference's scheme, so that it can only be concluded that while yield- ing to the teachers, Morant was still hoping to win his war of position.

The important point was that Morant had had to yield, his responsi- bility for the Board's inactivity on the issue having become more transparent and more untenable with the passage of time. If Morant had intended his yielding to be a means of assuaging the teachers' wrath he was not successful. His views and handling of the issue had succeeded as had no other in achieving both the unification and opposition of all teachers. Their resulting strength had led to Morant's seemingly impregnable position within the Board becoming increasingly vulnerable after 1906. That by 1909 he was without the protection afforded by the usual anonymity of the Civil Service reflected the magnitude of the teachers' success, as well as an absence of support from his political chief.

Runciman had kept Morant at arm's length when he had become President, refusing to see him for other than very brief discussions during the first month. This action, which Morant claimed had 'well nigh broken my energy for working the Office', was continually reinforced by Runciman, so that three years later Morant was complaining about 'the dreadfully small amount of time that I've been able to get with you, for talking out the many big things now in our hands needing direction and decision or guidance'.[58] If Runciman had not forgotten the hostile interview in 1907 with Morant before he became President, this continued action not only affirmed who was in control of the Board but also his dislike for Morant's methods, a feeling no doubt reinforced by his receiving a continuous stream of complaints about them. One complainant had put his view succinctly: 'In two and a half years three Presidents, three Secretaries, three Bills, but Morant remains'.[59] Arthur Acland had found Morant's interventions in the Consultative Committee's work intolerable, being incensed by one in 1909:

> . . . Morant presumes to say it will be more convenient for us to take a stranger now. I presume to be a better judge on that subject than Morant . . . . The plea that Wood alone can work out officially our Evening School recommendations is of course all Morantian moonshine.[60]

The President of the Board of Agriculture, Lord Carrington, had had to rebuke Morant over the charges he had made against another civil servant although he refrained from discussing the 'irregular manner in which the subject has been brought forward or to the language you have thought fit to use with regard to one of His Majesty's Civil Servants'.[61] Cyril Jackson sought Runciman's help to ease relations between the Board and the LCC, making the point that 'personal grudges might have embittered our relations . . . Morant has a determination to attack me always and everywhere'.[62] But the growing litany of complaints against Morant was not limited to either individuals or the teachers' organisations for some LEAs, including Leeds, had found grounds for critical comment.

In May 1905 James Graham had been appointed the Secretary for Higher Education in Leeds and he had welcomed the opportunities provided under the 1902 Act for an LEA to develop and control the educational institutions under its authority. In similar vein, he and the city's Education Committee had welcomed the 1907 Secondary School Regulations for providing, by its requirement that schools receiving the new, higher grant had to possess a majority on their governing bodies of elected members, the possibility of greater public control of secondary education. But the system of direct control exercised by the LEA over its secondary schools by the higher education sub-committee had impressed neither the inspectorate in 1905 nor the Board, both believing the head teachers, in the absence of governing bodies for their schools, lacked the necessary access to the Education Committee. Leeds was not unique in its arrangement but it appears to have been chosen as a test case by the Board when it refused to comply with the Board's set of model articles for the governance of secondary schools sent to every LEA in 1908. The reason for this is not difficult to discern: Morant undoubtedly saw this and similar LEAs as depriving the secondary schools of that autonomy which he had so strongly advocated.

The city's argument was that under the 1902 Act they had the power to supply and control secondary education and should be free, therefore, to determine the best scheme for their schools. The Board's model articles were inappropriate as well as revealing the Board's ignorance of 'the actual working conditions of educational administration under large Local Education Authorities'.[63] The Board had conceded that the city could use its sub-committee instead of individual boards of governors but insisted upon compliance with the model articles, as required under Article 22 of the 1907 Regulations. Runciman made an oblique reference to the problem in a speech in the House in July 1910, commenting on the 'over-control of [local] officials', and this was followed by a letter from the Board in which reference was made to the possibility of a reduction of the Board grant to the city.[64] Graham was incensed by this treatment and received support from the authority to resist the Board's attempt to treat the LEA as an endowed grammar school rather than a local government body. Three months later, Morant was forced to apologise to Graham and the city for the Board's 'misapprehension of a cardinal fact', that is, that the LEA's Director/Secretary of Education was also the secretary of all governing bodies within an LEA and thus could not be construed as a barrier between the governing body and headmaster of any school under an LEA's aegis. The Board was willing, therefore, to accept the LEA's arrangements. This admission must have been galling for Morant, but even more so was the fact that Runciman had to be informed of the mistake. Although he accepted full responsibility for it, his admission just at the onset of the Holmes Circular affair can have done little to improve relations with his political chief.[65]

By the time the Holmes Circular affair started in February 1911 it confirmed what many had already observed, being 'only a flash revealing (on the *expede Herculeum* principle) . . . what has been continually going on'.[66] It is perhaps not surprising, therefore, that throughout his presidency of the Board, Runciman appears to have wanted to divest himself of Morant: a feeling which strengthened as each year passed. Shortly after he became President, Runciman entertained hopes that Morant could be persuaded to go to the Local Government Board to take on the reorganisation of the Poor Law in 1909. Morant was ambivalent about the move and Burns was not willing to have him, despite the best efforts of Masterman and the Webbs. As the individual complaints about, and the teachers' hostility towards, Morant increased, so other avenues of transfer were explored including the possibility of his becoming a Commissioner on the Development Commission. This did not materialise, despite Lloyd George's support, partly because Morant had clashed with the Commission during 1909, to such an extent that the Commission were left in a 'consuming rage'.[67] At the beginning of the 1911 Session, therefore and despite the impending introduction of a new Education Bill, Runciman tried to press Morant to take three months' leave, and even offered him a free sea voyage, but to no avail. As events turned out, this proved to be an unwise decision by Morant.

On 5 December 1908 Frank Emerson of Wimbledon had responded to an advertised vacancy, stating that he was 'considered intelligent, and of good address, and I am not afraid of work'. He was given a simple examination to complete by the prospective employer but the results were lamentable. More importantly, they found their way to Runciman who asked Edmond Holmes, the Chief Inspector for Elementary Education, to comment upon them. Holmes' reply was a résumé of the defects of the elementary education system which, although 'less mechanical and unintelligent than it was 20 years ago . . . . is still deeply tainted with . . . defects'. He contended that the

HMIs were doing what they could to improve the system but frequently 'in the teeth of opposition from Local Authorities and Local Inspectors'. In addition, he observed, it appeared very difficult for the HMIs to make any impression upon the teachers and he was not in the least surprised that employers criticised the products of the elementary schools as being worse than those of two decades ago.[68] What he did not tell Runciman was that he had sent a questionnaire to all the HMIs designed to ascertain the backgrounds and calibre of LEA inspectors and discover whether they were a 'help or hindrance' to the HMIs. By the autumn of 1910 the results had been received and correlated, and they were incorporated into a confidential memorandum by Holmes on 6 January 1911.

Holmes's analysis of the results was brutally frank as far as the majority of LEA inspectors was concerned. Many of them had been elementary school teachers, and Holmes argued that because they had been successful under the payment-by-results policy, they were wedded to 'the days of schedules, percentages, uniform syllabuses, cast-iron methods, and the rest'. These characteristics, which he labelled 'vicious', were compounded by the generally 'uncultured and imperfectly educated' nature of their owners and it was not surprising, therefore, that most of the local inspection in cities and large towns constituted a hindrance rather than a help to progress. He believed that the only hope for the future lay with the local inspectorate being filled by men 'of real culture and enlightenment', arguing that the £500 per annum being spent on one Oxford man by East Sussex LEA was of greater benefit than the £900 being expended by the Durham LEA on three ex-elementary teachers.[69] Unfortunately for Holmes, Morant (who had approved the publication and distribution of the memorandum) and Runciman, a copy of the document found its way to the offices of the National Association of Education Officers within a fortnight. The Association, aware of the discrepancy between the views expressed in the memorandum and Runciman's 'public democratic pronouncements on educational matters', told Runciman that they possessed a copy. They requested that the memorandum be withdrawn and that he receive a deputation on the issue. Runciman's refusal to meet these requests met with the response that the Association could no longer feel it necessary for individual members to respect the document's confidentiality.[70] One month later, Samuel Hoare, the Conservative MP for Chelsea, raised the matter in the House.

Hoare, before he had seen the memorandum, asked Runciman if a circular had been issued from the Board in 1910 in which the inspectorate were advised to try to influence the appointment of LEA inspectors. Runciman replied that the Board had not given, nor would give, such advice. But when Hoare, who had been an LCC councillor from 1907 to 1910 and chairman of the authority's higher education sub-committee, subsequently received a copy of the document from a 'Conservative colleague of mine in the LCC', he showed it to Lord Balcarres, his party's Chief Whip. Balcarres immediately recognised the circular's 'considerable Parliamentary value', and Hoare found himself plunged into a controversy which, he recalled later, 'reverberated further than I had intended'.[71]

On 22 March, in the Education Supply debate, Hoare reopened the issue of the memorandum and, quoting extracts from it verbatim, argued that it represented evidence of the Board's ongoing attempts to interfere with the autonomy of LEAs. Much worse, however, was the fact that this policy document not only could potentially deprive elementary school teachers of the 'plum' positions in their careers but also represented a secret crusade against elementary teachers. He asked Runciman why the document had not been withdrawn and what guarantee would be given that the policy had been abandoned.[72] Runciman's reaction was 'a display of temper rarely witnessed on the Treasury bench' in which, 'apparently with a view to crushing this Debate by vehemently striking the [dispatch] box in front of him' and using language of 'indecent violence', he managed to alienate many in the chamber.[73] Denouncing Hoare as a receiver of stolen property, which he must have obtained from 'raking about among . . . musty waste paper baskets', Runciman dissociated himself totally from Holmes's views, commenting that he was not 'going to go out of my way to defend the views of everybody who serves under the Board of Education on every educational subject'.[74] This negation of a Minister's traditional role in such circumstances meant that Runciman's subsequent claim that not only did he support elementary school teachers gaining administrative or inspectorial positions with either LEAs or the Board but that Holmes's views in no way represented the policy of the Board, made little impact upon the hostile House. Lord Hugh Cecil claimed that Runciman 'seeing the storm has thrown his subordinate over, with all the expedition that Jonah was thrown to the whale', a view shared by Holmes:

> . . . in order to be able to throw me overboard Runciman had to
> misstate the facts. Anyone who read my speech would imagine
> that I had issued the (so-called) circular on my own initiative and

without consulting the Board. As a matter of fact the *Board* issued the circular (which was really not a circular, but a minute from me to Selby Bigge) on *their* initiative and without consulting *me*![75]

Holmes, a Buddhist, was prepared on a personal level to 'bow low before the blast, In patient, deep disdain', but felt that for the honour of the Civil Service he should strike back at the apposite moment. Runciman and the Board, having been caught, as Lord Hugh Cecil had commented, 'in undress' and observed 'as it were in an unguarded hour', were more concerned with defusing a situation which possessed the potential 'to set in motion against the Government the whole political strength of that powerful body the National Union of Teachers'.[76]

Runciman's first action was to issue a minute, authorising Morant to retrieve as many copies of the memorandum as possible. A very long and partly abject memorandum from Morant admitted responsibility for both authorising the publishing of the memorandum and for not having brought it to Runciman's attention. At the same time he defended, in principle, both his and Holmes's actions and criticised, by implication, Runciman for not telling the House the truth of the matter.[77] Runciman, in turn, castigated Morant for not telling him this before the debate and added that he had never been 'so badly "let in"', and "let in" I must remind you not over Holmes' language but over what appears to be the control I exercise over my department'.[78] As a step towards regaining that control he issued a second minute requiring that all material to be printed in the future should receive clearance initially from the Parliamentary Secretary and in those cases where a document was based on personal views it was to be headed by a prominent disclaimer indicating that it did not reflect Board policy. He took care in the House during the next few days to exonerate Holmes while indicating Morant's admittance of error. But when asked to consider the possibility of Morant being sacked for his error, Runciman responded by stating that like his two predecessors as President 'I have had most loyal assistance from the Permanent Secretary, the Inspectors, and the other officers of the Board'.[79]

At least one official at the Board believed that Runciman was to blame for the Holmes memorandum affair getting out of hand:

> The fact is, he lost his temper and would not get up the details. Had he kept calm and narrated the exact truth which he had not troubled to learn – he could have carried the House with him.[80]

Morant made virtually the same point in a subsequent note to Runciman when he pointed out that he had begged him to tell the House of his [Morant's] involvement in the publishing of the memorandum 'as it had *not* been made plain there on Tuesday [21 March]'. Furthermore, he added:

> You will, I am sure, bear me out that I have always throughout the past five or six weeks in which this matter has been under your consideration in the Office, told you quite plainly of my share in the business, particularly that the distribution of the circular to the particular 100 Inspectors was with my sanction. I have *always* made this quite plain to you in our talks since you and I first got on to this matter. And, as you know, *I* had not the *least* desire to burk or conceal this. On the contrary I should have wished a *full* description of the genesis of the document to have been given to the House *in reply to Hoare on Tuesday*.[81]

Interestingly, Claud Schuster, one of Morant's confidants, felt that Runciman had not shirked any of his responsibilities as he had never denied them in the House, and he had, moreover, 'stood loyally by his subordinates'. His correspondent, R.P. Hills, a barrister, did not agree, although he was willing to concede that perhaps Runciman's behaviour was not intended and may have been 'merely another instance of his maladroitness'. This notwithstanding, he believed Runciman should have defended rather than abused the memorandum, for to all intents and purposes it was an authorised Board document and the views in it 'circulated as they were without contradiction or qualification, must in general have been in accord with [the] Board's views, even though the Board did not intend at the moment to put them into effect'. Runciman's abandonment of his officials gained no sympathy:

> After all, Runciman is Minister for education, and his duty is to preach right principle whenever he gets the chance, certainly when acts of his officers are definitely challenged. Instead of this, he throws his officers to the dogs, declares he cannot understand how Holmes penned such phrases, that they were not a happy crowd etc, that Morant is not to be censured only because he has already expressed regret for an error. Let him damn Morant and Selby Bigge as much as he likes in private (if he is in a position to do so, which I doubt), but let him defend them in public.[82]

Hill's view was held by a majority but Runciman's actions, put, as only he could then, into the context of the strained relationship with Morant during his presidency and the problems that remained unresolved because of the latter's views, not least teacher registration, are understandable. He had, albeit somewhat belatedly, defended Morant and this condemned him in the eyes of some.

One Scottish Liberal supporter relayed, in no uncertain terms, the views of party supporters about the Holmes affair:

> . . . the general opinion is that the Permanent officials rule the roost. *You must know* that Morant is a creature of Balfour's and is doing all in his power to thwart Liberal policy and were you the strong man we took you to be, Morant would have got his walking ticket. The Liberals want no favours but by Heaven we will have fair play.[83]

Arthur Guttery, General Secretary of the Primitive Methodist Society, made a similar point, writing that:

> It is not *your* administration of which we complain, but that of your officials. We believe you are not faithfully served and yet must hold you responsible.[84]

John Massie, a friend of Runciman's but also the chairman of the National Education Association, found it embarrassing to have to relay the message agreed by his members, given Runciman's defence of Morant in the House:

> But perhaps I may put it in this form. Whatever Morant's merits may be, I am sure there will never be any confidence, on the part of Liberal educationalists, in the permanent staff of the Board of Education as long as Morant is head; and no loyal defence of yours will modify their distrust.[85]

Similar views had been expressed in some sections of the press including the *Westminster Gazette*, under the editorship of Harold Spender. Runciman took exception to Spender's leader on his comments in the House but Spender was not moved, claiming that he had been 'scrupulously fair, and courteous to yourself' and found it difficult to comprehend how his comment that 'better arrangements must be made so that permanent officials shall not deal with important questions of policy unknown to the Board of Education' could be construed as being unfriendly.[86] A more sympathetic line was taken by H.W. Massingham, editor of the *Nation*, for although he reprimanded

Runciman for his performance in the House it was Morant who emerged as the real culprit:

> What we want to know is whether he [Morant] pursued it, or allowed Mr Holmes to pursue it, without consulting Mr Runciman, who, on this hypothesis, was kept in ignorance of a vital procedure on the part of his staff . . . .if these questions are answered in a sense unfavourable to Sir Robert Morant, Mr Runciman must either dispense with his services or pass over an act of grave injury to his own policy perpetrated by an officer whose single duty was to pursue it.[87]

Massingham regarded Runciman as part of the 'centrepoint of Liberal power and activity' (the other members being Lloyd George, Churchill and McKenna), so he explained his reasons for this approach to Runciman, stating that he was

> impenitent on the Morant business. I think him not holdable by the Deity Himself when he wants to do a thing; and I think he has done things against successive heads of the Department (not yourself) which are against all my educational views and tendencies. I dare say the Holmes business was a little exaggerated; but it was surely a big *assumption*.[88]

It was the NUT, however, that grasped the memorandum most firmly as a powerful weapon in their war with Morant.

Only three days after the Hoare–Runciman clash the NUT president, Marshall Jackson, brandished the new weapon via the columns of *The Times*, but it was Yoxall who applied it, in a speech at Burton-on-Trent, along with the Higher Elementary Schools Report and teacher registration, to make a forceful denigration of the Board's attitudes and policies towards elementary education since 1903.[89] The union then rushed out a series of six pamphlets, 'The Protest Series', emphasising the perceived class bias of the Board, the Civil Service and Oxbridge. These were followed by a mass demonstration in the Albert Hall on 13 May to protest against the conspiracy of the Civil Service and the slander of teachers in the memorandum. Hoare declined an invitation to attend, citing a previous engagement, but those who did come repeated the denunciations of both caste in the Civil Service and of Morant.[90] And like a terrier engaged with its victim, the NUT refused to release its hold and became locked in combat with Morant; visitors to Morant's office at the time could not but help noticing that a copy of Kipling's poem 'If' was fixed to one wall.[91] Unfortunately, as in many conflict situations, subsequent actions revealed that rationality had been replaced by prejudice in the case of his opponents and the appearance of a new Education Bill in May served to illustrate the point.

The Education (School and Continuation Class Attendance) Bill was an attempt by Runciman and the Board to legislate on some of the findings released in 1909 of investigations by both the Consultative Committee – into attendance at continuation schools – and a departmental committee on the working of the Employment of Children Act. The departmental committee, examining in particular the half-time system, had recommended that children under 13 years old be totally exempt from employment. In this recommendation they were giving official cognisance to the unanimous view of the 1908 TUC that the time had 'long since arrived for the abolition of the half-timer'.[92] The numbers of half-timers had been slowly dwindling during the previous two decades so that by 1907 there were some 47,360 compared with 175,437 in 1890. The Consultative Committee's report was critical also of the employment undertaken by large numbers of children while they were still school pupils. The fact that only one in four of the two million adolescents aged between 14 and 17 years received any form of continuation education was condemned by them as 'a tragic waste of early promise'.[93] The Education Bill proposed, therefore, the abolition of the half-time system, the extension of compulsory attendance at school to 14 years (or beyond by local option) and the possibility of attendance at continuation classes until the age of 16 years. Included also was a consolidation and clarification of legislation regulating school attendance including, under Clause 20(2), an attempt to try to ensure that children could complete the post-elementary courses offered by preventing broken final school terms. Through these reforms the Board hoped that

> the gradually wakening consciousness of the nation can, by successive stages, complete and elaborate a system which may finally direct and guide the child from its earliest years to the threshold of manhood.[94]

Unfortunately for the TUC, a ballot by the Cotton Operatives Amalgamation in 1909 had destroyed the unanimity which had prevailed at the Congress the previous year on the abolition of the half-time system, a majority of the Amalgamation's members voting to retain the system. This result affected the views of the Bill held by MPs representing those areas with substantial numbers of half-timers but the most vehement opposition to the Bill came from Massingham. He, in turn, was supported by the NUT.

Massingham argued that the two reforms, abolishing half-timers and extending the age of attendance, and requiring at most a single-clause Bill, had been buried among 22 other clauses. This unnecessary complexity, plus the inclusion of contentious reforms of the school attendance laws, was guaranteed, he claimed, to hamper the Bill's chances of passing through a House preoccupied with the Parliament Bill. Furthermore, the Bill was not one demanded by the Liberals but represented instead the culmination of Morant's policy of 'delimiting' the elementary school:

> The bureaucracy has been at work again, and a Liberal Minister of Education has once more been coerced or befooled by his autocratic and reactionary officers . . . .Liberal Ministers have again and again tried to legislate, but each time their Bills have been ruined by having the crevices and the schedules stuffed with ingenious 'educational reforms' . . . .at all times it has been a steady, pitiless delimitation of the 'elementary' school, the 'elementary' scholar, the 'elementary' teacher, and the law of 'elementary' education. When is this nightmare to cease?[95]

There was truth in Massingham's comments about the Liberal Party's reaction to the measure, for Runciman discovered that he faced substantial opposition from the MPs representing Lancashire and the West Riding of Yorkshire, where the majority of half-timers were located, including requests that he proceed more slowly with the changes. This opposition 'from quarters, which could not but be seriously considered', coupled with a Cabinet reshuffle in October, resulted in no progress being made with the Bill and it was withdrawn later in the year. But Massingham's other assertions were faulty and revealed more about his feelings for Morant than constituting an objective assessment of the proposals on educational grounds. It was to take Morant's removal from the Board and a world war before these progressive aims were incorporated successfully into legislation.

As the summer of 1911 proceeded, more and more resolutions were forwarded to the Board from around the country by LEAs and branches of teachers' organisations, all condemning what was now labelled the Holmes–Morant Circular. A full inspection by HMIs of the upper departments of Birmingham's elementary schools, followed by a severe condemnation in their report of some of the practices observed, did not ease matters. It not only annoyed Birmingham's

LEA but was seized upon by *The Schoolmaster* as proof that Holmes' memorandum was indeed official Board policy because in Selby Bigge's covering note to Morant on that document he had suggested such a practice as a possible means of improving elementary school teachers' practices.[96]

In September Runciman learned that preliminary arrangements were under way as a precursor to a Cabinet reshuffle. As far as he could ascertain he was unlikely to be moved from the Board, no doubt due to the Holmes memorandum, for although Asquith had considered the possibility of his going to the War Office earlier in the year this idea had been dropped. Runciman was adamant that he was 'not going to drift' and was prepared to resign his office, for to stay on would be a 'waste of time'.[97] In mid-October he was both surprised and depressed to receive the offer of the Presidency of the Board of Agriculture, accompanied by reasons which Asquith stated 'seem to me very strong'. Aware of the sideward rather than upward nature of the offer, Runciman was reluctant to accept a move that might conceivably prejudice his chance of a higher office that might become vacant in the near future. He told Asquith he was prepared to accept the offer, if he (Asquith) would bear in mind his reservations, and asked if the announcement was to be made soon for, if so, 'should I close up at the Board of Education this week?'[98] Asquith made no promises and Runciman decided to comply, no doubt realising the weakness of his position as well as remembering that Asquith had retained the letter containing his offer of resignation in 1908.

Just before Asquith's offer was made, Runciman had received a long letter from Morant asking him not to accede to a request from the NUT for a deputation to present itself at the Board on the difficulties associated with the evening school regulations, until the union ceased its continued attacks through *The Schoolmaster* upon 'the good faith and loyalty of the Board's Permanent Officials'.[99] The NUT had made a bitter attack in July on the administration of registers for evening and art classes by Chambers, now the head of the Technical Branch. *The Schoolmaster* attacked Chambers' apparent lack of qualifications for his present post in a pastiche of the Holmes memorandum:

> How 'complete' is the detachment of this officer from experience of the special work which he has to supervise is shown by his record. To be 'Chancellor's English Essayist' was something, no doubt; to have written 'The Medieval Stage' and 'The Tudor Revels,' and edited the poems of Donne, the poems of Vaughan, Early English Lyrics and the 'Red-Letter

Shakespeare,' shows a fine literary taste, no doubt. But how does all that qualify a man to direct, control, and administer the Royal College of Art, and the whole State-aided system of art and science teaching in the country?[100]

Chambers was, according to Dover Wilson, Morant's 'able lieutenant' and had been responsible for organising the administrative system and structure of the Board after 1903, a fact which, as has been mentioned, Morant had acknowledged. The NUT's vilification of Chambers could only have been interpreted by Morant, therefore, as a means of attacking him by a different avenue. Chambers, a 'painfully shy man; a shyness interpreted as Oxford hauteur by ruffled deputations from the provinces', was upset by the attack. He had refused to receive the deputation since he had been unable to reply to the NUT's accusations and this had produced Morant's appeal to Runciman.[101] Runciman was too preoccupied with his departure from the Board, however, to become involved with the issue. So keen was he to leave, as his acceptance of Asquith's offer revealed, that his Private Secretary had to prevail upon him to see if he could get Morant's salary raised, as showing approval of his long service, since 'it would make all the difference to his peace of mind here to find he really was appreciated. He is one of those who rather need to be told it often'.[102] Runciman penned Morant a gracious letter instead, the receipt of which produced the result forecast by Maurice, but he would not make a decision about the deputation, leaving that to his successor, J.A. Pease.

As soon as Pease had taken up the presidency, Morant tackled him on the topic, reiterating the points he had made to Runciman about the NUT's attacks on the Board's personnel and objecting very strongly to the NUT's sustained attack upon his professional integrity. He also stated that on personal grounds he could not continue to see

one's fair name dragged in the mire . . . one's name rendered synonymous with dishonour and cowardice throughout the teaching profession . . . on unwholly untrue grounds.

Did he not have the right

even though a Civil Servant, to the preservation of one's good name, if only for one's children's sake, if (as each Minister under whom I have served here cordially states) one has done nothing to forfeit it?[103]

Pease's reply the next day informed him that the NUT deputation would be seen on 12 December. Twenty-four hours later, Lloyd

George announced to the House that Morant would be the Chairman of Insurance Commissioners once the National Insurance Bill became law.

When Tim Healy had interjected during Lloyd George's announcement that it was a good opportunity to get rid of Morant from the Board, Lloyd George had rebuffed him with a virtual catalogue of Morant's strengths as an administrator. But *The Schoolmaster* could not resist a final blow at its adversary, however, and claimed that Morant's skill constituted, in reality, an 'inner presence of some permanently stupid or thwarting influence'. Stating that under Morant's reign the Board had become known as 'the sink' within the Civil Service, the editorial stated that his departure reflected the strength of public opinion organised by the NUT.[104] Morant was infuriated by this final smear and wrote Pease a lengthy minute refuting the claims and emphasising the effects upon the morale of the Board's staff if Pease acquiesced and received the NUT deputation. Even the suggestion that he might institute a libel action, to bring the NUT 'to their knees' if it was politically impossible to achieve a cessation of the attacks and an apology, fell on deaf ears.[105] On 29 February 1912 an Order-in-Council created a new Teacher Registration Council and a single register. Robert Morant's war of position had been irretrievably lost, bringing to an end the crucible years in English educational policy formulation.

NOTES

1. Runciman Papers, WR 44, R.L. Morant to W. Runciman, 25 Oct. 1911.
2. Q. Hoare and G. Nowell Smith, (eds), A. Gramsci, *Selections from Prison Notebooks* (1978), pp. 229–39.
3. PRO ED 24/185, E.K. Chambers to R.L. Morant, 12 Oct. 1904.
4. Ibid., R.L. Morant to W.N. Bruce, 20 Oct. 1904.
5. PRO ED 24/40, R.L. Morant to W.N. Bruce, 28 Nov. 1904. Part III covered elementary and Part II secondary education.
6. Ibid., A.F. Leach to W.N. Bruce, 10 Jan. 1905.
7. Ibid., L.A. Selby Bigge to R.L. Morant, 13 March 1905.
8. Ibid., J. Bromley to H.M. Treasury, 19 April 1905.
9. Headlam-Morley Papers, Acc 727, Box 33, W.N. Bruce to J.W. Headlam, 28 Nov. 1905.
10. Cited in B. Simon, *Education and the Labour Movement 1870–1920* (1965), p. 267.
11. Ibid., p. 264; W.Taylor, 'Higher Elementary Schools and Social Change', *Research and Studies*, 21 (Nov. 1961), pp. 73–4.
12. S. Meacham, *A World Apart: The English Working Class 1890 to 1914* (1977), pp. 72–3.

13. PRO ED 24/185, Board of Education, Report of the Consultative Committee upon Questions Affecting Higher Elementary Schools, 1906, p. 23.
14. Headlam-Morley Papers, Acc 727, Box23, A.S. Lloyd to J.W. Headlam, 19 July 1906.
15. *4 PD*, 171, c.91–3, 13 March 1907.
16. Ibid., 174, c.1056, 15 May 1907.
17. J. Simpson, 'On the Expediency and the Means of Elevating the Profession of Educator in Public Estimation' in *The Educator* (1839), p. 425 cited in H. Silver, *Education and the Social Condition* (1980), p. 171; PRO ED 10/131, J.D. McClure, 'Registration of Teachers: Historical Summary', Teachers' Registration Council, Paper 1, pp. 1–2.
18. For further details see P.H.J.H. Gosden, *The Evolution of a Profession* (1972), pp. 235–44.
19. PRO ED 24/8, R.L. Morant, 'Précis of opinions recently expressed by persons or bodies of weight on the Board of Education Bill', 1899, p. 10.
20. Sadler Papers, Eng lett misc c.551, fos. 179–82, M.E. Sadler to Sir M.T. Sadler, 26 March 1901.
21. Lady C. Jebb, *The Life and Letters of Sir Richard Jebb* (1907), pp. 354–5.
22. See A. Tropp, *The School Teachers: The Growth of the Teaching Profession in England and Wales from 1800 to the Present Day* (1957), pp. 172–9 and B.H. Bergen, 'Only A Schoolmaster: Gender, Class, and the Effort to Professionalize Elementary Teaching in England, 1870–1910', *History of Education Quarterly*, 22, 1 (Spring 1982), pp. 1–21.
23. PRO ED 10/131, G.W. Kekewich to J.E. Gorst and the Duke of Devonshire, 25 June 1901; J.E. Gorst to the Duke of Devonshire, 4 Oct. 1901; R. Walrond to R.L. Morant, 16 Oct. 1901.
24. Ibid., Consultative Committee to G.W. Kekewich, June 1901.
25. *School Board Chronicle*, 67 (8 Feb. 1902), p. 133.
26. PRO ED 10/58, Gateshead and District Head Teachers' Association to Board of Education, 1 March 1902.
27. Runciman Papers, WR 5, H.J. Bryan to W. Runciman, 2 May 1902; PRO ED 10/131, NUT Circular to Parliamentary Correspondents, 16 April 1902.
28. PRO ED 10/147, W.R. Anson to R.L. Morant, 30 Dec. 1904.
29. PRO ED 10/47, Memorandum from Teachers' Registration Council to Board of Education, 17 Feb. 1905.
30. Ibid., Consultative Committee to Board of Education, 18 May 1905; PRO ED 10/95, Annual Report of the Consultative Committee for 1905; PRO ED 10/131, H. Mann to R.L. Morant, 12 Oct. 1905.
31. PRO ED 10/131, F. Heath to R.L. Morant, 11 Oct. 1905; H. Mann to R.L. Morant, 12 Oct. 1905.
32. PRO ED 10/47, W.N. Bruce to R.L. Morant, 24 Nov. 1905.
33. PRO ED 10/131, H. Mann to R.L. Morant, 12 Oct. 1905.
34. Ibid.
35. Ibid., R.L. Morant to W. Anson, 3 Dec. 1905; W. Anson to R.L. Morant, 4 Dec. 1905.
36. Ibid., R.L. Morant to F. Storr, 7 March 1906; F. Storr to R.L. Morant, 18 March 1906.
37. Ibid., R.L. Morant to R.D. Swallow, 24 March 1906.
38. Ibid., R.D. Swallow and J.D. McClure to R.L. Morant, 2 April 1906.
39. PRO ED 10/132, A. Birrell to Sir W. Hart Dyke, 4 April 1906.
40. *Educational Times* (2 April 1906), pp. 161–2; *Journal of Education*, April 1906.

41. PRO ED 10/132, R.L. Morant, 'Memorandum on the Registration of Teachers and the Abolition of the Register', 8 June 1906.
42. A. FitzRoy, *Memoirs* (1927), I, p. 231; Grier Papers, File 23, R. Fitzgibbon Young to L. Grier, 21 Jan. 1953. The observer was Professor Sir Samuel Dill.
43. Runciman Papers WR 21, R.L. Morant to W. Runciman, 22 May 1908.
44. PRO ED 10/132, R.P. Cholmely to H.F. Heath, 12 July 1908. Cholmely was President of the Assistant Masters' Association.
45. Ibid., R.L. Morant, 'Scheme for a New Teachers' Registration Council proposed to the Board of Education by the Representatives of Certain Educational Associations', 8 July 1908.
46. Ibid., W. Anson to W. Runciman, 28 June 1908.
47. *The School World* (Aug. 1908), pp. 281–3.
48. PRO ED 10/132, R.L. Morant to W. Runciman, 19 Oct. 1908.
49. Ibid., J. Gow to R.L. Morant, 23 Nov. 1908; J. Wertheimer to J. Gow, 30 Nov. 1908.
50. Ibid., R.L. Morant to Sir H. Parry, 9 Dec. 1908.
51. *Christian World* (14 Jan. 1909).
52. PRO ED 10/132, R.L. Morant to Sir H. Parry, 4 Feb. 1909; J. Gow to R.L. Morant, 5 Feb. 1909.
53. Ibid., R.L. Morant to J. Easterbrook, 8 Nov. 1909.
54. *Morning Post* (15 Nov. 1909).
55. Ibid., 21 Dec. 1910; *Yorkshire Post* (26 Dec. 1910).
56. PRO ED 10/132, R.L. Morant to W. Runciman, 'Report of Three Informal Conferences Concerning the Proposed Teachers' Registration Council and the Proposed Teachers' Register', 12 June 1911, [Cd.5726], p. 12.
57. PRO ED 10/132, 'Notes as to Registration', 1909, p. 3.
58. Runciman Papers, WR 21, R.L. Morant to W. Runciman, 22 May 1908; WR 44, R.L. Morant to W. Runciman, n.d. but 1911.
59. BP Add 49765, fos. 186–7, J.S. Sandars to A.J. Balfour, 15 Nov. 1908.
60. Runciman Papers, WR 28, A.H.D. Acland to F. Acland, 3 May 1909. Morant had replaced Wood as the committee's secretary on the grounds that he was too expensive.
61. Ibid., Lord Carrington to R.L. Morant, 6 April 1909. Not surprisingly Carrington refused adamantly to accept Morant into that department in 1911.
62. Ibid., WR 44, C. Jackson to W. Runciman, 27 Jan. 1911.
63. Leeds Education Authority, Higher Education Sub-Committee, 'Memorandum on Model Articles of Government', Jan. 1909 cited in L. Connell, 'Administration of Secondary Schools: Leeds v Board of Education', *Journal of Educational Administration and History*, V, 2 (July 1973), p. 27.
64. W.R. Meyer, 'James Graham *versus* the Board of Education', *History of Education Society Bulletin*, 51 (Spring 1993), p. 23.
65. DES File 59/3820Y, N.E. Worcester to E.J.R. Eaglesham, May 1960.
66. Runciman Papers, WR 44, J. Massie to W. Runciman, 20 April 1911.
67. Ibid., WR 35, F.S. Hopwood to W. Runciman, 3 Jan. 1910.
68. Ibid., WR 28, E.G.A. Holmes to W. Runciman, 3 Feb. 1909.
69. Ibid., WR 46, Memorandum by Mr.E.G.A. Holmes on the Status, Duties, &c., of Inspectors employed by Local Education Authorities, pp. 1–2.
70. Templewood Papers, I 6, H.G. Maurice to W.P. Donald, 9 Feb. 1911; W.P. Donald to W. Runciman, 18 Feb. 1911; Runciman Papers, WR 46, H.G. Maurice to W.P. Donald, 22 Feb. 1911.
71. Templewood Papers, XX.2, Typed MSS of unfinished book 'At home and

abroad: The great divide', pp. 121–2. Hoare's LCC friend has never been identified but in view of his earlier comments to Runciman, Cyril Jackson would certainly have had grounds for such an action. Cross, however, suspects that it may possibly have been Hoare's brother-in-law, Henry Lygon. See J.A. Cross, *Sir Samuel Hoare, a Political Biography* (1977), p. 20 et seq.

72. *5 PD*, 23, c.275–280, 22 March 1911.
73. *Daily Mail*, 22 March 1911; 5 PD,23, c.307, 21 March 1911.
74. *5 PD*, 23, c.281–3, 21 March 1911.
75. Ibid., c.287, 21 March 1911; Marvin Papers, MS Eng lett misc c.261, fo. 72, E.G.A. Holmes to F.S. Marvin, 26 March 1911.
76. *Morning Post*, 23 March 1911.
77. Runciman Papers, WR 46, R.L. Morant to W. Runciman, 23 March 1911.
78. Ibid., W. Runciman to R.L. Morant, 24 April 1911.
79. *5 PD*, 24, 11 April 1911, c.419.
80. Marvin Papers, MS Eng lett d.261, fos. 64–5, F.M. Dale to F.S. Marvin, 23 March 1911.
81. Runciman Papers, WR 46, R.L. Morant to W. Runciman, n.d. but 25 March 1911.
82. PRO ED 24/102, Schuster Papers, C. Schuster to R.P. Hills, 3 May 1911; R.P. Hills to C. Schuster, 10 May 1911.
83. Runciman Papers, WR 46, J. Gibson to W. Runciman, 1 April 1911.
84. Ibid., A.T. Guttery to W. Runciman, 19 April 1911.
85. Ibid., WR 44, J. Massie to W. Runciman, 20 April 1911.
86. W.Harris, *J.A. Spender* (1946), p. 97; *Westminster Gazette*, 23 March 1911.
87. *Nation*, 25 March 1911.
88. Runciman Papers, WR 46, H.W. Massingham to W. Runciman, 21 April 1911; A.F. Havighurst, *Radical Journalist: H.W. Massingham (1860–1924)* (1974), p. 123.
89. *Manchester Guardian*, 1 April 1911.
90. Runciman Papers, WR 46, A.D. Sanderson to H.G. Maurice, 15 May 1911; *The Schoolmaster* (20 May 1911), pp. 1029–34.
91. B.M. Allen, *Sir Robert Morant: A Great Public Servant* (1934), p. 262.
92. Simon, op. cit., p. 291; E. and R. Frow, *The Half Time System of Education* (1970), pp. 66–7; C.Griggs, *The Trades Union Congress and the Struggle for Education 1868–1925* (1983), pp. 39–48.
93. Board of Education, Report of the Consultative Committee on Attendance at Continuation Schools, [Cd. 4757] 1909, p. 215.
94. PRO ED 24/1909, Schuster Papers.
95. *Nation*, 3 June 1911, 'The Board of Education and the Liberal Party', pp. 349–50.
96. *The Schoolmaster*, 'Birmingham in Thrall', LXXX (29 July 1911), p. 17.
97. McKenna Papers, McKN 3/22, No. 3, fos. 78–9, W. Runciman to R. McKenna, 1 Oct. 1911.
98. Runciman Papers, WR 302, H.H. Asquith to W. Runciman, 14 Oct. 1911; W. Runciman to H.H. Asquith, 18 Oct. 1911.
99. PRO ED 24/102, R.L. Morant to W. Runciman, 13 Oct. 1911.
100. *The Schoolmaster* (15 July 1911), p. 101.
101. Dover Wilson Papers, MS 14357, fo. 98; PRO ED 24/102, J. Yoxall to R.L. Morant, 15 Sept. 1911.
102. Runciman Papers, WR 44, H.G. Maurice to W. Runciman, 20 Oct. 1911.
103. PRO ED 24/102, R.L. Morant to W. Runciman, 13 Oct. 1911; R.L. Morant to

J.A. Pease, 26 Nov. 1911.
104. *The Schoolmaster* (2 Dec. 1911).
105. PRO ED 24/102, R.L. Morant to J.A. Pease, 3 and 7 Dec. 1911.

Epilogue

Between 1908 and 1909 Robert Morant was faced with the possibility of being offered a transfer from the Board of Education to other positions within the Civil Service and, at one stage, he had indicated that he would be prepared to move because he believed that under the prevailing social and political conditions he had achieved as many reforms in education as were possible. Three years later, however, two independent yet critical assessments of the Board's policies and reforms, were published by two previous members of that department, Edmond Holmes and Sir John Gorst. Holmes' assessment was contained in the first half of his book, *What Is and What Might Be*, and was a forthright condemnation of the aims and practices of the system from which he had only recently retired. Gorst's equally condemnatory comments, made in one of his last public statements about the state of the system, included the claims that in most elementary schools the children were still drilled rather than educated while secondary and tertiary education remained fettered by medieval systems. The time was ripe, he declared, for

> a drastic revolution in the red-tape methods by which education is tied and bound, and the tyranny of the Board of Education over local authorities could now be relaxed or altogether removed.[1]

Was Morant's implication that the nation's education system was in better shape in 1911 than in 1895 justified, or were Holmes's and Gorst's criticisms valid? In many respects, both views were, for as Michael Sadler once said, an education system is a living thing and thus there is the danger, when trying to ascertain the impact of certain educational policies upon the education system, of producing simply a frozen representation of an ever-changing organism. In addition, there is usually a significant difference between the aims envisaged by policy formulators, and encapsulated in a specific measure, and the reality of their implementation as achieved via a variety of educational institutions and individuals, let alone the possible effect on the system at the same time of other significant influences – for example, social, financial or political. As Sadler commented, 'we should not forget that the things outside the schools matter even more than the things inside the schools, and govern and interpret the things inside'.[2]

In parts of the elementary sector the positive effects of the policy changes implemented since 1895 were noticeable. Sutherland has stated that by 1895 it was possible to discern a more child-centred approach within the elementary schools; by 1911 that approach had been furthered by the liberating effect of the 1900 block grant upon the curriculum as well as the influence of the aims contained within the 1904 Code of Regulations. The schools now had a series of clearly defined, broad interrelated educational aims, as well as the freedom to implement them in a manner best suited for each school and group of pupils. A recent analysis by Rose of the recollections of a significant cohort (444) of ex-elementary school pupils born at the turn of the century reveals that between 50 and 85 per cent of them, depending on their social class, enjoyed their schooling while a similar proportion also liked their teachers. Unfortunately, Rose does not analyse the data in more precise detail, for example, what proportion of the cohort attended elementary school before or after 1900, but the testimony of some of the pupils in these schools after 1900 is remarkably positive and imbued with the telling point made by one of them: 'School, even though a sterile place as compared with today, was still an oasis in a grim social situation'.[3] That is not to say that all schools had responded in equal manner to the policy changes; many had not, but a love of learning still existed among some of their pupils and this was developed by some of the staff who were 'kindly, human and even gifted teachers'.[4] The policy changes did, however, allow such teachers to flourish rather than constrain them as had been the usual case in the era of payment by results. The Board claimed, in its annual report for 1910–11, that the changes made to the elementary school curriculum after 1903 had produced a situation where

> The child's life in school is being brought into closer relation with his life out of school . . . the teacher of to-day uses the materials and experiences with which the children are familiar in every-day life . . . . At the same time, the influence of the school is spreading more and more widely over the whole sphere of the child's interests and activities. The school concerns itself with his bodily as well as his mental and moral development, with his amusements as well as with his labours; it teaches him to use his hands as well as his head, to play as well as to work.[5]

But if such changes could be said to support Morant's view, they did not negate those of Gorst and Holmes, for the majority of the children were still being taught in a regimented fashion, and for some pupils this was abhorrent. One perceptive pupil noted that the arrival of the HMIs at his school (after 1911) still produced marked changes among the teaching staff, for 'they suddenly became more anxious, patient, friendly . . . all canes disappeared'.[6] In addition, the numbers of pupils in a class still remained overwhelmingly large, with 50 or 60 remaining the norm in many urban schools, while the teaching resources were limited and gender discrimination continued to exist within the curriculum, to the marked disadvantage of girls.[7] Social class and parental or social expectations also remained an impedance as far as the educational development of many children was concerned. Consequently, these children remained severely hampered in their access to higher levels and types of education. One example was the continued existence of half-timers, albeit more so in certain parts of the nation than others, despite the TUC's opposition to what it labelled a 'survival of barbarism', and this reflected not only the strong resistance from employers determined to retain their cheap labour but also the views of those parents who

> don't want to be cleaned, enlightened, inspected, drained . . .
> They don't want compulsory thrift, elevation to remote standards of virtue and comfort, irritation into intellectual or moral progress.[8]

By 1911, then, the elementary school sector reflected continuity and change or, as Sadler put it, 'It reflects, while it seeks to remedy, the failings of national character'.[9] The potential for change, synonymous with progress, was aided by the reforms to teacher training introduced after 1903; but for many Edwardian children the changes did not appear fast enough and it was their successors rather than they who benefited from them. None the less, the changes introduced, not least those pertaining to school meals and medical inspection and treatment, did recognise that the rights of the child would no longer be ignored by the State, even if this was not the case as far as some parents were concerned. This achievement represented a significant move away from the debilitating effects of the *laissez-faire* attitude which had so marred education in the previous century.

If the elementary school curriculum and teaching methodologies in 1911 represented an advance on what had prevailed in 1895, unfortunately a similar situation did not prevail widely among the nation's established secondary schools. The prescription contained within the 1904 Secondary Regulations did help, however, to initiate a leavening of the imbalance within the curriculum which the weight of tradition combined with social class had engendered. This was aided by the power of LEAs under the 1902 Act to develop secondary education in their areas and by 1911, of the 862 grant-aided secondary schools in England 352 were being administered by these authorities. The regulations also recognised the seminal importance of a broad-based education being given before specialisation, a concept most successfully applied now to virtually the whole school population, up to the age of 18, in Japan but unfortunately still not fully realised in England, mainly for social and political, rather than educational, reasons. This innovation, coupled with the 1907 Free Place Regulations, did, however, make an impact upon the Edwardian working and lower middle classes. By 1911 the proportion of ex-elementary school pupils attending the 862 grant-aided secondary schools was slightly in excess of 60 per cent.[10] The financial relief provided under the Free Place Regulations may have contributed to this but the main cause was the increasing realisation among the working class that the 'new' secondary education provided a means for acquiring social mobility:

> Technical knowledge might raise a worker to the rank of foreman but it was secondary education in the mould cast by Robert Morant and A.J. Balfour which was more likely to provide the social mobility needed to join the ranks of the white collared workers.[11]

This factor was fuelled, in turn, by the increasing demands from commercial, business and government departments for more clerical workers – for example, in 1911 the total number of clerks in employment represented a 37.5 per cent increase on the number employed in 1901:

> To be a member of the 'salaried staff' as opposed to a wage earner not only meant that you could not be given one hour's notice of dismissal as was common with many manual workers but were also usually guaranteed greater job security in general . . . whilst many craftsmen and 'semi-skilled' workers often despised 'pen pushers' they were nevertheless keen for their youngsters to attend secondary school so that they might obtain one of these 'secure' jobs.[12]

This phenomenon was reinforced by the fact that nearly 16 per cent of the clerks were aged between 15 and 20 and employers preferred to employ someone who had completed a secondary school education.

One problem facing many parents of the working and lower middle classes keen for their children to receive this type of education was the limited number of schools and places offered under the Free Places scheme. In 1911 the total number of pupils in the 862 secondary schools was 88,256 but the total population of 12- to 17-year-olds was estimated to be nearly 3,400,000. In 1908 Morant had initiated a re-organisation of the Technical Branch of the inspectorate and had placed it under Chambers' command with Frank Pullinger as the Chief Inspector. One recruit to the branch remembers Pullinger 'pouring' into his ears

> Morant's dream of an industrial democracy. In such a demo-cracy, young persons would find that part-time day continuation schools could provide meaning for the work they did with their hands.[13]

But the idea of the continuation school, while possessing the potential to provide a partial alleviation of the problem of access to post-elementary education, could only remain a second best to full-time secondary education. Morant's transfer from the Board of Education meant that his concept had to pass to his successor, Selby Bigge, for possible implementation. That this did not become possible until the passing of the 1918 Education Act not only reflected the prevalent social views about education but also Selby Bigge's role as Permanent Secretary. Although the number of secondary schools con-tinued to increase, the rate of increase was both slow and insufficient to meet parental demands and it was not surprising that 'secondary education for all' soon became the dominant educational goal for many.

If both the elementary and secondary sectors of the education system represented a mixture of continuity and change before 1911, the one area in which the implementation of policy changes had wrought a wholesale change, which was not only visible but also ben-eficial, was that of educational administration. Under the reforms initiated since 1895, and culminating in the Board of Education Act and the 1902 Education Act, the nation now possessed a coherent and rational system of educational administration for the first time in the history of its system. The considerable variations of educational pro-vision which had existed between various localities under the *ad hocery* of the nineteenth century had been minimised by passing local control of the nation's schools to bodies with resources sufficient to provide more uniformity of development and standards and thereby prevent children from being disadvantaged solely through reason of location. The dissolution of the school boards had not resulted in the loss of local control of education; in fact it was reinforced under the new LEAs, not least by virtue of their having the voluntary schools also under their aegis. Furthermore, the size and the resources of the major LEAs meant, as Gorst had intended, that the local government of education could resist any possible tyranny by, or unreasonable demands of, central government upon the schools, which ensured that there would be also, in reality, a dual partnership in the governance of the nation's schools.

Sutherland has carefully differentiated between policy-making and innovation, rightly pointing out that the two are not necessarily synonymous given that some policies can be conservative or restrictive. And in her study of policy-making in elementary education in the 25 years up to 1895, she discovered that the majority of civil servants in the Education Department were not involved in the educational innovations of the time, either because of personal disinclination or institutional arrangements, the notable exception being Kekewich. The major responsibility for innovation, then, lay with the politicians and the local education bodies.[14] This represents a significant contrast with policy-making in the next 16 years where it was much more a combination of civil servants and politicians as the formulators of innovation, with local authorities coming to the fore only once more after 1911. In part, this was due to some of the policies introduced but it was also due to the different personnel involved as well as the different political situation, especially before 1906. Thus Kekewich's role as an innovator within the civil service was taken over initially by Sadler who, in turn, was replaced by Morant, who then brought in Bruce, Chambers, Mackail, Selby Bigge and, finally, Newman as co-innovators. But it is clear that the rather conventional image of this period, with Morant portrayed as a 'statesman in disguise', is a somewhat flawed one, partly because of the considerable input of his colleagues in the Board of Education, as he acknowledged, and also because of the significant contribution to policy formulation made by certain politicians, notably Gorst, Devonshire, Balfour and McKenna.

Before 1902, the politicians were clearly in the ascendant as far as both policy-making and innovation were concerned, with Devonshire making notable contributions to both the Board of Education and 1902

Acts while Balfour's role in guiding the passage of the 1902 Bill was equally significant. It is, none the less, difficult to concede to Balfour the position of an innovator, for his motivation was based primarily on politico-religious rather than educational grounds, while his views about elementary schools, and the welfare of the children attending them, were reactionary. The contrast between Balfour (and his uncle, Lord Salisbury) and Gorst on educational matters was so great that it was not surprising that Gorst had to make all the running as far as trying to achieve educational innovation was concerned. His dogged commitment to decentralisation, despite considerable personal and political ostracism both within and without the government, as well as to a wider concern with the welfare of the child rather than being based solely upon academic considerations, revealed a progressive outlook which would not be constrained by short-term considerations, as the sacrifice of his political career demonstrated. In many ways, Gorst was not only the perfect foil for Morant's increasing dominance during the latter stages of this period but he was also the source of some of the ideas about reform, for example, teacher training, and the physical health and welfare of children, for which Morant has traditionally received considerable credit.

Between 1903 and 1906, it is clear that while Morant and his colleagues assumed the pre-eminent role in both educational innovation and policy-making, they were still subject to considerable political control exercised by Balfour and also to political interference – for example, by Lloyd George in the case of the Welsh rebellion. After 1906, policy formulation reverted primarily to the politicians, with Morant and his colleagues having to work within parameters established for them, as well as having to contend with conflict about control of the system with those LEAs which were keen to develop the autonomy granted them by the 1902 Act. This change was not only demonstrated by the contents of the three abortive Education Bills but also in the passage and implementation of the 1906 and 1907 Education Acts. In these last two examples, Morant was outflanked by the politicians and forced to implement measures he was not interested in, initially at least. To his lasting credit as an administrator, his methods of implementation were designed not to curtail but to allow development, albeit incremental rather than dramatic, of the systems established by these measures.

Allowing for the contributions made during this period by other civil service personnel to policy formulation, it cannot be denied that Morant stood head and shoulders above them, and not only because of his physical height. But if, as has been stated, the concept of him as a statesman in disguise is flawed, what were his signal achievements during this period? He once claimed that he had reached the pinnacle of his powers with the passing of the 1902 Education Act but such a claim rather overlooks the contributions of Gorst, Devonshire and Balfour, although it has to be acknowledged that the provisions for secondary education were his. In reality, his major contributions were made in the three years after the passing of the Act with the organisation of the Board of Education undoubtedly a singular achievement. This is not to deny the importance of the reform of teacher training and the revised regulations for both elementary and secondary schools, which have been cited previously, but the creation of a well designed and run central government body was of vital importance to the establishment of a truly functional dual system of educational governance. It was imperative for the development of the education system as a whole that the left hand of central government did know what the right hand was doing. In achieving this, he not only realised his aims as embodied in his Swiss Report but also revealed his great strength as an administrator; few others could have achieved what he did so well in such a short period of time.

No education system can be perfect, by virtue of the very nature of its constituent parts and also because of the conflicting views in any society of what constitutes education. Even so, it would be difficult to overlook the lamentable state of some of the components of the late-nineteenth-century education system of England and Wales or the fact that the administrative and educational principles which guided that system no longer fully met the needs of either society or the children in the schools. Despite the conflicts which attended them, and the inevitable flaws contained within them, the policy changes introduced between 1895 and 1911 were sufficient not only to achieve the necessary break with the past but also to reform the education system sufficiently so as to permit substantial and progressive development during much of the twentieth century. The reasons for these changes should not be forgotten, especially as the policy changes currently being made appear to bear out Hegel's dictum:

> What experience and history teach us is this – that people and governments never have learnt anything from history, or acted on principles deduced from it.[15]

NOTES

1. *The Times*, 27 Nov. 1911.
2. M.E. Sadler, 'How Far Can We Learn Anything of Practical Value from the Study of Foreign Systems of Education?', Address to the Guildford Educational Conference, 20 Oct. 1900 cited in E.J. Higginson, *Selections from Michael Sadler: Studies in World Citizenship* (1979), p. 49.
3. T. Dan Smith cited in J. Rose, 'Willingly to School: The Working-Class Response to Elementary Education in Britain, 1875–1918', *Journal of British Studies*, 32 (April 1993), p. 127.
4. R. Roberts, *A Ragged Schooling* (1979), pp. 146.
5. Board of Education Annual Report for 1910–1911, *PP*, XXI, [Cd.6116] 1912–13, p.292.
6. Roberts, op. cit., pp. 148–9.
7. See C. Dyhouse, 'Good Wives and Little Mothers: Social Anxieties and the Schoolgirl's Curriculum, 1890–1920', *Oxford Review of Education*, 3, 1 (1977), pp. 21–35.
8. C.F.G. Masterman, *The Condition of England* (1901), p. 116.
9. Sadler, op. cit., p. 49.
10. Board of Education Annual Report for 1910–1911, *PP*, XXI, [Cd. 6116] 1912–13, p. 297.
11. C. Griggs, *The TUC and the Struggle for Education 1868–1925* (1983), p. 117.
12. Ibid.
13. J. Dover Wilson, *Milestones on the Dover Road* (1969), p. 67.
14. G. Sutherland, *Policy-Making in Elementary Education, 1870–1895* (1973), pp. 341–6.
15. Cited in G.B. Shaw, *The Revolutionist's Handbook* (in *Man and Superman*) (1903), p. 228.

Select Bibliography

MANUSCRIPT SOURCES

1. *Official Papers*

(i) Public Record Office

Cabinet Papers
CAB 24; CAB 27; CAB 37; CAB 41.

Education Department/ Board of Education Papers
ED 10; ED 11; ED 12; ED 14; ED 23; ED 24; ED 31; ED 50; ED 53; ED 114.

(ii) Department of Education and Science

File 56/1518Y

2. *Private Papers*

Bodleian Library, Oxford:
A.H.D. Acland Papers.
Asquith Papers
Bryce Papers
Harcourt Papers
John Johnson Collection
Marvin Papers
Milner Papers
Sadler Papers
Sandars Papers
Selborne Papers

British Library:
A.J. Balfour Papers
Burns Papers
Campbell-Bannerman Papers
Cross Papers
Gladstone Papers
Mary Gladstone Drew Papers
Hamilton Papers
Passfield Papers
Ripon Papers
H. Spender Papers

Cambridge University Library:
Crewe Papers
Templewood Papers

Chatsworth, Derbyshire:
Devonshire Papers

Churchill College, Cambridge:
Chandos Papers
Lord R. Churchill Papers
Esher Papers
Headlam-Morley Papers
McKenna Papers

Duke University, North Carolina:
Kekewich Papers

Durham County Record Office, Durham:
Londonderry Papers

Eastbourne Public Library:
Browning Papers

Gloucestershire Record Office, Gloucester:
Hicks Beach Papers

Greater London Record Office:
Barnett Papers

Hatfield House, Hertfordshire:
Salisbury Papers (Third and Fourth Marquess)

Hereford and Worcester Record Office, Hereford:
James Papers

House of Lords Record Office, London:
Ilbert Papers

Lady Margaret Hall, Oxford:
Grier Papers

Lambeth Palace, London:
Benson Papers
Davidson Papers
Riley Papers
Temple Papers

National Library of Scotland, Edinburgh:
Craik Papers
R.B. Haldane Papers
Dover Wilson Papers

Public Record Office, Kew:
Anson Papers
J.R. MacDonald Papers
Schuster Papers

Scottish Record Office, Edinburgh:
A.J. Balfour Papers (Whittingehame),

BIBLIOGRAPHY

Thailand National Archives, Bangkok:
Scott Papers

University Library, Auckland:
Fowlds Papers

University of California Library, Los Angeles:
Sadler Papers

University Library, Newcastle upon Tyne:
Runciman Papers
C.P. Trevelyan Papers

In private hands:
Gorst Papers
Jebb Papers
Morant Papers

PARLIAMENTARY PAPERS

(i) Hansard's Parliamentary Debates, Fourth and Fifth Series

(ii) Reports of Commissioners, Committees, Departments, etc:
The annual reports of the Education Department, Department of Science and Art and the Board of Education, in addition to circulars issued by the Board, were a major source of published official material. The other major reports used were:

Report of the Royal Commission on the Working of the Elementary Education Acts, England and Wales, *PP*, 1887, XXIX [C.5056]; 1888, XXXV [C.5485].

Report of the Royal Commission on Secondary Education, *PP*, 1895, XLIII [C.7862]; XLIV [C.7862–I]; XLV [C.7862–II]; XLVI [C.7862–III]; XLVIII [C.7862–V].

Report of the Committee appointed to inquire into the Distribution of Science and Art grants, *PP*, 1897, XXXIII [C.8417].

Education Department, Special Reports on Educational Subjects, 1896–97, 1, R.L.Morant, 'The French System of Higher Primary Schools', *PP*, 1897, XXV [C.8477].

Report of the Departmental Committee on the Pupil–Teacher System, *PP*, 1898, XXVI [C.8761]; XXVI [C.8762].

Higher Grade Board Schools and Public Secondary Schools (Statistics), *PP*, 1898, XXV [C.8447].

Parliamentary Return of the Joint Memorandum on the Relations of Primary and Secondary Schools to one another in a National System of Education, *PP*, 1898, XXV (381).

Education Department, Special Reports on Educational Subjects, 3, R.L. Morant, 'The National Organisation of Education of All Grades as Practised in Switzerland', *PP*, 1898, XXV [C.8988].

Board of Education, Special Reports on Educational Subjects, 9, M.E.Sadler, 'The

Unrest in Secondary Education in Germany and Elsewhere', *PP*, 1902, XXVII [Cd. 836].

Headlam, J.W., 'Report on the Teaching of Literary Subjects in Some Secondary Schools' in General Reports on Higher Education; with Appendices for the Year 1902', *PP*, 1903, XXI [Cd.1738].

Papers relating to the resignation of the Director of Special Inquiries and Reports, *PP*, 1903, LII [Cd.1602].

Board of Education, Code of Regulations for Public Elementary Schools, *PP*, 1904, LXXV [Cd.2074].

Board of Education, Regulations for Secondary Schools, *PP*, 1904, LXXV [Cd.2128].

Report of the Inter-Departmental Committee on Physical Deterioration, *PP*, 1904, XXXII [Cd.2175].

Report of the Inter-Departmental Committee on Medical Inspection and the Feeding of Children attending Public Elementary Schools, *PP*, 1906, XLVII [Cd.2779].

Report on the working of the Education (Provision of Meals) Act, 1906, *PP*, 1911, XVIII [Cd.5724].

General Report on the Instruction and Training of Pupil–Teachers, 1903–7, *PP*, 1907, LXIV [Cd.3582].

Annual Report of the Chief Medical Officer of the Board of Education for 1908, *PP*, 1910, XXIII [Cd.4986].

Annual Report of the Chief Medical Officer of the Board of Education for 1909, *PP*, 1910, XXIII [Cd.5426].

Annual Report of the Chief Medical Officer of the Board of Education for 1911, *PP*, 1912–1913, XXI [Cd.6530].

Board of Education, Report of the Consultative Committee on Attendance at Continuation Schools, *PP*, 1909, XVII [Cd. 4757].

Report of the Royal Commission on the Civil Service, *PP*, 1912, XV [Cd.6535].

CONTEMPORARY NEWSPAPERS AND PERIODICALS

Christian World
Church Quarterly Review
Daily Mail
Edinburgh Review
Educational Times
Fortnightly Review
Glasgow Herald
Journal of Education
Manchester Guardian
Monthly Review
North American Review

BIBLIOGRAPHY

Picture-Politics
Public Health
Punch
Review of Reviews
School Board Chronicle
School Board Gazette
School Government Chronicle
Teachers' Review
The Contemporary Review
The Morning Post
The Nation
The Nineteenth Century and After
The Schoolmaster
The Speaker
The Spectator
The Times
The Times Educational Supplement
Westminster Gazette
Westminster Review

BOOKS, PAMPHLETS, THESES AND ARTICLES

(Place of publication is London, unless otherwise stated.)

Abdy, J., and Gere, C., *The Souls* (1984).
Abel, E.K., 'Canon Barnett and the First Thirty Years of Toynbee Hall', unpublished PhD thesis, University of London, 1969.
— 'Middle-Class Culture for the Urban Poor: The Educational Thought of Samuel Barnett', *Social Service Review* (Dec. 1978), pp. 596–620.
— 'Toynbee Hall, 1884–1914', *Social Service Review* (Dec. 1979), pp. 606–31.
Acland, A., *A Devon Family: The Story of the Aclands* (1981).
Acland, A.H.D. and Llewellyn Smith, H. (eds), *Studies in Secondary Education* (1892).
Adamson, J.W., *English Education 1789–1902* (Cambridge, 1964).
Allen, B.M., *William Garnett: A Memoir* (1933).
— *Sir Robert Morant :A Great Public Servant* (1934).
Andrews, L., 'The School Meals Service', *British Journal of Educational Studies*, XX, 1 (Feb. 1972), pp. 70–5.
Anonymous, 'The Education Act, 1902: How to Make the Best of It', *Fabian Tract* No. 114 (March 1903).
Archer, M.S., *Social Origins of Educational Systems* (1979).
Armytage, W.H.G., *Four Hundred Years of English Education* (Cambridge, 1964).
— *A.J.Mundella: The Liberal Background to the Labour Movement* (1951).
Asaph, A.G., 'Educational Concordats', *The Nineteenth Century*, 55 (Jan. 1904), pp. 40–6.
Ashby, E. and Anderson, M., *Portrait of Haldane* (1974).

Balfour, A.J., *Chapters of Autobiography* (1930).
Balfour, Lady Frances, *Ne Obliviscaris*, 2 Vols (1930).

Banks, O., 'Morant and the Secondary School Regulations of 1904', *British Journal of Educational Studies*, III (1954), pp. 33–41.
— *Parity and Prestige in English Secondary Education: A Study in Educational Sociology* (1963).
Barnard, H.C., *Were Those the Days? A Victorian Education* (1970).
Barnett, H.O., *Canon Barnett*, 2 Vols (1918).
Baron, G., 'The Teachers' Registration Movement', *British Journal of Educational Studies*, II (May 1954), pp. 133–44.
Bassett, A.T., *The Life of John Edward Ellis* (1914).
Batho, G., *Political Issues in Education* (1989).
Baumann, A.A., *The Last Victorians* (1927).
Bayley, S.N., 'Life is too short to learn German: Modern languages in English elementary education, 1872–1904', *History of Education*, 18, 1 (1989), pp. 57–70.
Bebbington, D.W., *The Nonconformist Conscience* (1982).
Bell, G.W.K., *Randall Davidson Archbishop of Canterbury*, 2 Vols (Oxford, 1935).
Benson, A.C., *The Life of Edward White Benson, sometime Archbishop of Canterbury*, 2 Vols (1900).
Bentley, M., *Politics without Democracy, 1815–1914* (1984).
— *The Climax of Liberal Politics: British Liberalism in Theory and Practice 1868–1918* (1987).
Bergen, B.H., 'Only A Schoolmaster: Gender, Class, and the Effort to Professionalize Elementary Teaching in England, 1870–1910', *History of Education Quarterly*, 22 1 (Spring 1982), pp. 1–21.
Betts, R., 'Winston Churchill and the Presidency of the Board of Education, 1906–7', *History of Education*, 15, 2 (June 1986), pp. 89–93.
— 'Robert Morant and the Purging of H.M. Inspectorate, 1903', *Journal of Educational Administration and History*, XX, 1 (Jan. 1988), pp. 54–9.
— 'Dr Macnamara and the Education Act of 1902', *Journal of Educational Administration and History*, 25, 2 (July 1993), pp. 111–21.
Birchenough, C., *History of Elementary Education in England and Wales from 1800 to the Present Day* (1927).
Birrell, A., *Things Past Redress* (1947).
Bishop, A.S., *The Rise of a Central Authority for English Education* (Cambridge, 1971).
Bland, H., 'After Bread, Education', *Fabian Tract No. 120* (1905).
Blake, R., *The Conservative Party from Peel to Churchill* (1970).
Blake, R. and Cecil, H. (eds), *Salisbury: The Man and his Policies* (1987).
Blunt, W.S., *My Diaries: Being a Personal Narrative of Events 1888–1914* (1932).
Booth, C. (ed.), *Life and Labour of the People in London* (1892).
Bosanquet, H., *Social Work in London 1869 to 1912: A History of the Charity Organisation Society* (1914).
Boyce, D.G. (ed.), *The Crisis of British Unionism: The Domestic Political Papers of the Second Earl of Selborne, 1885–1922* (1987).
Brennan, E.J.T., 'Educational Engineering with the Webbs', *History of Education*, I, 2 (June, 1972), pp. 174–99.
— (ed.), *Education for National Efficiency: The Contribution of Sidney and Beatrice Webb* (1975).
Brereton, C., 'Revolution at the Board of Education', *Monthly Review*, 15 (June 1904), pp. 55–66.

Brett, M.V. (ed.), *Journals and Letters of Viscount Esher*, 2 Vols (1934).

Briggs, A., 'The Welfare State in Historical Perspective', *Archives Européennes de Sociologie*, II, 2 (1961), pp. 221–58.

Briggs, A. and Macartney, A., *Toynbee Hall: The First Hundred Years* (1984).

Brooks, R., *Contemporary Debates in Education: An Historical Perspective* (1991).

Bulkley, M., *The Feeding of School Children* (1914).

Burnett, J. (ed.), *Destiny Obscure: Autobiographies of Childhood, Education and Family from the 1820s to the 1920s* (1984).

Carruthers Gould, F., *Froissart's Modern Chronicles* (1902).

— *F.C.G.'s Froissart's Modern Chronicles 1902* (1903).

— *Political Cartoons 1903* (1904).

— *Political Cartoons 1906* (1907).

Channing, F.A., 'The Liberal Solution of the Education Problem', Northern Counties' Education League Pamphlet, April 1901.

Chester, D.N., 'Robert Morant and Michael Sadler', *Public Administration*, XXIX (1950), pp. 109–15.

— 'Morant and Sadler – Further Evidence', *Public Administration*, XXXI (1953), pp. 49–54.

Clarke, P.L.P., 'The Education Act of 1902', unpublished Ph.D. thesis, University of London, 1964.

Clifford, J., 'Primary Education and the State', *The Contemporary Review*, 69 (March, 1896), pp. 441–56.

Clyne, J. R., *Memoirs: 1869–1924*, 2 Vols (1937).

Connell, L., 'Administration of Secondary Schools: Leeds v Board of Education', *Journal of Educational Administration and History*, V, 2 (July 1973), pp. 25–32.

Craik, H., *The State in Its Relation to Education* (1914).

Cross, C., *The Liberals in Power, 1905–1914* (1963).

Cross, J.A., *Sir Samuel Hoare, a Political Biography* (1977).

Cruickshank, M., *Church and State in English Education* (1963).

— 'A Defence of the 1902 Act', *History of Education Society Bulletin*, 19 (Spring, 1977), pp. 2–9.

Cunningham, H., *The Children of the Poor. Representations of Childhood since the Seventeenth Century* (Oxford 1991).

Daglish, N.D.,'The Educational Work of Sir John Gorst', unpublished Ph.D. thesis, University of Durham, 1974.

— ' "How Half-Civilized People Ought to be Managed": John Gorst, Education and the Waikato Maoris 1860–1863', *Durham and Newcastle Research Review*, IX, 45 (Autumn 1980), pp. 135–44.

— 'The Morant–Chulalongkorn Affair of 1893–94', *Journal of Educational Administration and History*, XV, 2 (July 1983), pp. 16–23.

— 'Planning the Education Bill of 1896', *History of Education*, 16, 2 (1987), pp. 91–104.

— 'The Politics of Educational Change: The Case of the English Higher Grade Schools', *Journal of Educational Administration and History*, XIX, 2 (1987), pp. 36–50.

— 'Robert Morant's hidden agenda? The origins of the medical treatment of school-children', *History of Education*, 19, 2 (1990), pp. 139–48.

— 'Robert Morant and Teacher Registration – a war of position?', *Journal of Educational Administration and History*, XXIII, 2 (July 1991), pp. 25–37.

— 'Sir John Gorst as an educational innovator: a reappraisal', *History of Education*, 21, 3 (Sept. 1992), pp. 259–76.

Dale, R., 'Education and the capitalist state: contributions and contradictions' in M. Apple (ed.), *Cultural and Economic Reproduction in Education* (1982).

Davies, J.J., 'The new Minister of Education and his work', *Westminster Review*, 144 (Sept. 1895), pp. 332–6.

Davin, A., 'Imperialism and Motherhood', *History Workshop Journal* (Spring 1978), pp. 9–65.

Dent, H.C., *The Training of Teachers in England and Wales 1800–1975* (1977).

Diggle, J., 'A Study of the Ministers Responsible for Education 1856–1944', unpublished M.Ed. thesis, University of Manchester, 1963.

Dover Wilson, J., *Milestones on the Dover Road* (1969).

Dugdale, B.E.C., 'Arthur James Balfour and Robert Morant', *Quarterly Review*, 260 (Jan. 1933), pp. 152–68.

— *Arthur James Balfour*, 2 Vols (1939).

Dutton, D.J., 'The Unionist Party and Social Policy 1906–1914', *Historical Journal*, 24, 4 (1981), pp. 871–84.

Dwork, D., *War is Good for Babies and other Young Children* (1987).

Dyhouse, C., 'Social Darwinistic Ideas and the Development of Women's Education in England, 1880–1920', *History of Education*, 5 , 1 (Feb. 1976), pp. 41–58.

— 'Good Wives and Little Mothers: Social Anxieties and the Schoolgirl's Curriculum, 1890–1920', *Oxford Review of Education*, 3, 1 (1977), pp. 21–35.

— 'Working-Class Mothers and Infant Mortality in England (1895–1914', *Journal of Social History*, 12, 2 (1978), pp. 248–62.

— 'The Condition of England 1860–1900' in L. Lerner (ed.), *The Victorians* (1978), pp. 70–89.

— *Girls Growing up in Late Victorian and Edwardian England* (1981).

Eaglesham, E.J.R., *From School Board to Local Authority* (1956).

— 'Morant on the March (1895–1901): A Great Administrator's Earlier Educational Assumptions' in G.Z.F. Bereday and J.A. Lauwerys (eds), *Yearbook of Education* (1957), pp. 220–7.

— 'Planning the Education Bill of 1902', *British Journal of Educational Studies*, IX, 1 (Nov. 1960), pp. 3–24.

— 'Implementing the Education Act of 1902', *British Journal of Educational Studies*, XI, 2 (May 1962), pp. 153–75.

— 'The Centenary of Sir Robert Morant', *British Journal of Educational Studies*, XII, 1, (Nov. 1963), pp. 5–18.

— *The Foundations of 20th Century Education in England* (1967).

Edmonds, E.L., *The School Inspector* (1962).

Education Group (Centre for Contemporary Cultural Studies), *Unpopular Education: Schooling and Social Democracy in England since 1944* (1981).

Egremont, M., *Balfour* (1980).

Elliott, A., 'The Bradford School Board and the Department of Education, 1870–1902: Areas of Conflict', *Journal of Educational Administration and History*, XIII, 2 (July 1981), pp. 18–23.

Ensor, R.C.K., *England 1870–1914* (Oxford, 1936).

458

Evans, P.W., 'The Contribution of Arthur Herbert Dyke Acland to Education Administration and Policy Making in England and Wales', *History of Education Society Bulletin*, 50 (Autumn, 1992), pp. 43–54.

Evans, R.A., 'The University and the City: The Educational Work of Toynbee Hall, 1884–1914', *History of Education*, 11, 2 (1982), pp. 113–25.

Evans, W. and Claridge, M.A., *James Hirst Hollowell and the Movement for Civic Control in Education* (Manchester, 1911).

Fair, J.D., *British Interparty Conferences: A Study of the Procedure of Conciliation in British Politics 1867–1921* (Oxford, 1980).

— 'From Liberal to Conservative: The Flight of the Liberal Unionists after 1886', *Victorian Studies*, 29, 2 (Winter 1986), pp. 291–314.

Fairbairn, A.M., 'The Policy of the Educational Bill', *The Contemporary Review*, 69, (June 1896), pp. 761–74.

Fairhurst, J.R., 'Some Aspects of the Relationship between Education, Politics and Religion from 1895–1906', unpublished D.Phil thesis, University of Oxford (1974).

Feuchtwanger, E.J., *Disraeli, Democracy and the Tory Party* (Oxford, 1968).

Fitch, J.G., 'The Higher Grade Board Schools', *The Nineteenth Century*, XLIX (Feb. 1901), pp. 321–31.

FitzRoy, A., *Memoirs*, 2 Vols (1927).

Foster, R.F., *Lord Randolph Churchill* (Oxford, 1982).

Francis, H.W.S., 'The Doctor as Educationalist: James Kerr: 1861–1941', *The Medical Officer*, 29 (May 1970), pp. 303–5.

Fraser, P., 'The Liberal Unionist Alliance: Chamberlain, Hartington, and the Conservatives (1886–1904', *English Historical Review*, 77 (1962), pp. 53–78.

— *Joseph Chamberlain: Radicalism and Empire, 1868–1914* (1966).

Frow, E. and R., *The Half Time System of Education* (Manchester, 1970).

Garnett, W., 'A Retrospect: How the County Council became the Local Education Authority for London', *Educational Record* (April 1929), pp. 746–60.

Garvin, J.L., and Amery, J., *The Life of Joseph Chamberlain*, 5 Vols (1933/1951).

Gathorne Hardy, A.E., *Gathorne Hardy, First Earl of Cranbrook*, 2 Vols (1910).

Gautrey, T., *'Lux Mihi Laus': School Board Memories*, n.d.

George, W.R.P., *Lloyd George: Backbencher* (Llandysul, 1983).

Gilbert, B.B., 'Sir John Eldon Gorst and the Children of the Nation', *Bulletin of the History of Medicine*, XXVIII (1954), pp. 243–51.

— 'Sir John Eldon Gorst: Conservative Rebel', *The Historian*, XVIII, 2 (Spring 1956), pp. 151–69.

— 'Health and Politics: The Physical Deterioration Report of 1904', *Bulletin of the History of Medicine*, 9 (1965), pp. 143–53.

— *The Evolution of National Insurance in Great Britain: The Origins of the Welfare State* (1966).

— *David Lloyd George – A Political Life: The Architect of Change 1863–1912* (1987).

Gordon, P., *The Victorian School Manager* (1974).

— 'Katharine Bathurst: A controversial woman inspector', *History of Education* 17, 3 (1988), pp. 193–207.

Gordon, P. and White, J., *Philosophers as Educational Reformers* (1979).

Gordon, P., Aldrich, R. and Dean, D.W., *Education and Policy in the Twentieth Century* (1991).

Gorst, H.E., *The Fourth Party* (1906).
— *Much of Life is Laughter* (1936).
Gorst, J.E., 'English Workmen and Their Political Friends', *The North American Review*, CLIX (Aug. 1894), pp. 207–17.
— 'Settlements in England and America' in J.M. Knapp (ed.), *The Universities and the Social Problem* (1895).
— 'Prospects of Education in England', *North American Review*, 163 (Oct. 1896), pp. 427–37.
— 'School Children as Wage Earners', *The Nineteenth Century*, 46 (July 1899), pp. 8–17.
— 'The National Control of Education', *Popular Science Monthly*, 60 (1902), pp. 49–57.
— 'The Education Bill', *The Nineteenth Century*, 52 (Oct. 1902), pp. 576–90.
— 'Social Reform: The Obligation of the Tory Party', *The Nineteenth Century*, 53 (March 1903), pp. 519–32.
— 'Governments and Social Reform', *Fortnightly Review*, 83 (May 1905), pp. 843–55.
— 'Children's Rights', *Living Age*, 246 (July 1905), pp. 230–37.
— 'Physical Deterioration in Great Britain', *North American Review*, DLXXXIV (July 1905), pp. 1–10.
— *The Children of the Nation* (1906).
Gosden, P.H.J.H., 'The Board of Education Act, 1899', *British Journal of Educational Studies*, II (1962), pp. 44–60.
— *The Development of Educational Administration in England and Wales* (Oxford, 1966).
— *The Evolution of a Profession* (Oxford, 1972).
Gourvish, T.R. and O'Day, A. (eds), *Later Victorian Britain, 1867–1900* (1988).
Graves, A.P., *To Return to All That* (1930).
Graves, J., *Policy and Progress in Secondary Education* (1943).
Gray, E., 'The New Education Bill: A Criticism', *Fortnightly Review*, 69 (1901), pp. 1068–78.
Grier, L., *Achievement in Education* (1952).
Griffith-Boscawen, A.S.T., *Fourteen Years in Parliament* (1907).
— *Memories* (1925).
Grigg, J., *Lloyd George, The People's Champion 1902–1911* (1978).
Griggs, C., *The Trades Union Congress and the Struggle for Education 1868–1925* (Sussex, 1983).
Gullifer, N., 'Opposition to the 1902 Education Act', *Oxford Review of Education*, 8, 1 (1982), pp. 83–98.
Guinness Rogers, F., 'The Nonconformist Uprising', *The Nineteenth Century*, LIV (Oct. 1903), pp. 677–89.
Guttsman, W.L., *The British Political Elite* (1963).

Haldane, R.B., *An Autobiography* (1929).
Halévy, E. *History of the English People: Epilogue: 1895–1905* (1939).
— *History of the English People: The Rule of Democracy* (1952).
Hamer, D.A., *Liberal Politics in the Age of Gladstone and Rosebery: A Study in Leadership and Policy* (Oxford, 1972).
Hamilton, Lord G., *Parliamentary Reminiscences and Reflections*, 2 Vols (1916).

Hance, E.M., 'Elementary Education in England' in *Subjects of the Day: No.1: State Education* (1890), pp. 25–43 .

Harris, J., *William Beveridge: A Biography*, Oxford (1977).

— 'The Transition to High Politics in English Social Policy, 1880–1914' in M. Bentley and J. Stevenson (eds), *High and Low Politics in Modern Britain* (Oxford, 1983), pp. 58–79.

— 'Political Thought and the Welfare State 1870–1940: An Intellectual Framework for British Social Policy', *Past and Present*, 135 (May 1992), pp. 116–41.

— *Private Lives, Public Spirit; A Social History of Britain, 1870–1914*, (Oxford, 1993).

Harris, J. and Hazlehurst, C., 'Campbell-Bannerman as Prime Minister', *History*, 55 (1970), pp. 360–83.

Harris, W., *J. A. Spender* (1946).

Havighurst, A.F., *Radical Journalist: H.W. Massingham, 1860–1924* (Cambridge, 1974).

Hay, J.R., *The Origins of the Liberal Welfare Reforms, 1906–1914* (1975).

Hazlehurst, C., 'Asquith as Prime Minister, 1908–1916', *English Historical Review*, 75 (July 1970), pp. 502–31.

Hendrick, H., *Child Welfare, England 1872–1989* (1994).

Hennock, E.P., *British Social Reform and German Precedents: The Case of Social Insurance 1880–1914* (Oxford, 1987).

Henson, H.H. (ed.), *A Memoir of the Rt. Hon. Sir W. Anson* (Oxford, 1920).

Heward, C., 'Men and women and the rise of professional society: the intriguing history of teacher educators', *History of Education*, 22, 1 (1993), pp. 11–32.

Hicks Beach, Lady Victoria, *Life of Sir Michael Hicks Beach*, 2 Vols (1932).

Higginson, J.H., *Selections from Michael Sadler: Studies in World Citizenship* (Liverpool, 1979).

— 'Michael Sadler and the German Connection', *Oxford Review of Education*, 16, 2 (1990), pp. 245–53.

— 'My Life in the History of Education: II: Rescuing Sadleriana', *History of Education Society Bulletin*, 52 (Autumn 1993), pp. 39–40.

Hirst, J.D., 'Vision Testing in London: A Rehearsal for the School Medical Service', *Journal of Educational Administration and History*, XIV, 2 (July 1982), pp. 23–9.

— 'A Failure "without parallel": The School Medical Service and the London County Council 1907–12', *Medical History*, 25 (1981), pp. 281–300.

— 'The Growth of Treatment through the School Medical Service, 1908–18', *Medical History*, 33 (1989), pp. 318–42.

Hoare, Q. and Nowell Smith, G. (eds.), *A. Gramsci: Selections from Prison Notebooks* (1978).

Hobhouse, H., 'Secondary Education in England', *Edinburgh Review*, CLXXXIX (Jan., 1899), pp. 149–66.

Holland, B., *The Life of Spencer Compton, Eighth Duke of Devonshire, 1833–1908*, 2 Vols. (1911).

Hollis, P., *Ladies Elect: Women in English Local Government 1865–1914* (1987).

Holmes, E.G.A., *What Is and What Might Be* (1911).

Holmes, G.M., 'The Parliamentary and Ministerial Career of A.H.D. Acland, 1886–97', *Durham Research Review*, IV (Sept. 1964), pp. 128–39.

Honey, J.R. de S., *Tom Brown's Universe. The Development of the Victorian Public School* (1977).

461

Horn, P., *Education in Rural England 1800–1914* (1978).
— 'The education and employment of working-class girls, 1870–1914', *History of Education*, 17, 1 (1988), pp. 71–82.
— *The Victorian and Edwardian Schoolchild*, (Gloucester, 1989).
Hughes, K.M., 'A Political Party and Education: Reflections on the Liberal Party's education Policy, 1867–1902', *British Journal of Educational Studies*, VIII, 2 (Nov. 1960), pp. 112–16.
Humphreys, R.E., 'James Bryce and the Advancement of Secondary Education', *Gleanings for Tomorrow's Teachers* (symposium produced for the triennial celebrations of Christ Church College, Canterbury, 1971), pp. 19–36.
Hunt, F. (ed.), *Lessons for Life: The Schooling of Girls and Women, 1850–1950* (Oxford, 1987).
Hurt, J.S., *Elementary Schooling and the Working Classes 1860–1918* (1979).
Hutchinson, H.G.,(ed.), *The Private Diaries of the Rt.Hon. Sir Algernon West, G.C.B.* (1922).
Hyndman, M., *Schools and Schooling in England and Wales: A Documentary History* (1978).

Jackson, P., *The Last of the Whigs: A Political Biography of Lord Hartington, later eighth Duke of Devonshire* (1994).
Jay, R., *Joseph Chamberlain; A Political Study* (Oxford, 1981).
Jebb, Lady Caroline, *The Life and Letters of Sir Richard Jebb* (1907).
Jenkins, R., *Asquith* (1964).
Johnson, N.E. (ed.), *The Diary of Gathorne Hardy* (Oxford, 1981).
Jones, A., *Lyulph Stanley: A Study in Educational Politics* (Waterloo, Canada, 1979).
Jones, G.E., 'The "Welsh Revolt" Revisited: Merioneth and Montgomeryshire in Default', *The Welsh History Review*, 14, 3 (June 1989), pp. 417–38.
Judges, A.V., 'The Educational Influence of the Webbs', *British Journal of Educational Studies*, X, 1 (Nov, 1961), pp. 33–48.

Kang, H-C., 'Equality of Educational Opportunity: Ideas and Politics, 1900–1918', *British Journal of Educational Studies*, XXXII, 1 (Feb. 1984), pp. 58–77.
Katz, M., 'From Bryce to Newsom; Assumptions of British Educational Reports, 1895–1963', *International Review of Education*, XI, 3 (1965), pp. 287–302.
Kazamias, A., *Politics, Society and Secondary Education in England* (Philadelphia, 1966).
Kekewich, G.W., 'The Church and the Education Act', *The Contemporary Review*, LXXXIII (June 1903), pp. 779–86.
— 'The Amendment of the Education Acts', *The Contemporary Review*, LXXXIV, (Oct. 1903), pp. 457–68.
— *The Education Department and After* (1926).
Kipling, R., 'Recessional' (1897).
Koss, S., *Asquith* (1976).

Langan, M. and Schwarz, B. (eds), *Crises in the British State 1880–1930* (1985).
Lawn, M., *Servants of the State: The Contested Control of Teaching 1900–1930* (Sussex, 1987).
Lawn, M. and Grace, G.R. (eds), *Teachers: The Culture and Politics of Work* (Sussex, 1987).

Lawson W., and Carruthers Gould, F., *Cartoons in Rhyme and Line* (1905).

Lawton, D. and Gordon, P., *H.M.I.* (1987).

Lawton, R. (ed.), *The Census and Social Structure* (1978).

Leese, J., *Personalities and Power in English Education* (1950).

Lerner, D., *The Passing of Traditional Society* (New York, 1958).

Lilley, R.C., 'Attempts to Implement the Bryce Commission's Recommendations – and the consequences', *History of Education*, 11, 2 (1982), pp. 99–111.

Lockhart, J.G., *Charles Lindley Viscount Halifax 1885–1934*, 2 Vols (1936).

Lowe, R., 'Some Neglected Sources for Historians of Early Twentieth Century Education: The Medical Journals' in K. Dent (ed.), *Archives and the Historian of Education* (1975), pp. 16–23.

— 'The Divided Curriculum: Sadler, Morant and the English Secondary School', *Curriculum Studies*, 8, 2 (1976), pp. 139–48.

— (ed.), 'New Approaches to the Study of Popular Education, 1851–1902', *History of Education Society Occasional Publication*, No.4 (Spring, 1979).

— 'Robert Morant and the Secondary School Regulations of 1904', *Journal of Educational Administration and History*, XVI, 1 (Jan, 1984), pp. 37–46.

Lowndes, G.A.N., *The Silent Social Revolution*, Oxford (1965).

Lucy, H., *A Diary of the Home Rule Parliament, 1892–1895* (1896).

— *A Diary of the Unionist Parliament, 1895–1900* (1901).

— *The Balfourian Parliament, 1900–1905* (1906).

— *Memories of Eight Parliaments* (1908).

— *Nearing Jordan* (1916).

— *The Diary of a Journalist* (1922).

McBriar, A.M., *Fabian Socialism and English Politics, 1884–1918* (Cambridge, 1962).

— *An Edwardian Mixed Doubles: The Bosanquets versus the Webbs; A Study in British Social Policy 1890–1929* (Oxford, 1987).

McCulloch, G., *Philosophers and Kings: Education for Leadership in Modern England* (Cambridge, 1991).

Machin, G.I.T., *Politics and the Churches in Great Britain 1869–1921* (Oxford, 1987).

Mackay, R.F., *Balfour: Intellectual Statesman* (1985).

Mackenzie, N. (ed.), *The Letters of Sidney and Beatrice Webb*, 3 Vols (1978).

Macnamara, T.J., 'The local support of education', *The Nineteenth Century*, XL (Dec. 1896), pp. 919–24.

— 'The Government and the London Education Problem', *The Contemporary Review*, LXXXIII (Feb. 1903), pp. 153–67.

— 'Physical Condition of Working-Class Children', *The Nineteenth Century*, LVI (Aug. 1904), pp. 307–11.

— 'The Physical Condition of the People' in 'Coming Men on Coming Questions', *Review of Reviews* (1905), pp. 46–64.

— 'For and Against the Education Bill', *The Nineteenth Century*, CCCLI (May,1906), pp. 705–11.

— 'The Lords and the Education Bill', *The Nineteenth Century*, CCCLV (Sept., 1906), pp. 478–84.

Machray, R., 'The Prime Minister at Whittingehame', *Pall Mall Magazine*, XXIX (March 1903), pp. 347–56.

463

Malcolm, I., *Lord Balfour: A Memory* (1930).

Mallet, C., *Herbert Gladstone: A Memoir* (1932).

Mansbridge, A., *Margaret McMillan Prophet and Pioneer: Her Life and Work* (1932).

— *The Trodden Road: Experience, Inspiration and Belief* (1940).

Markham, V., 'Robert Morant – Some Personal Reminiscences', *Public Administration*, XXVIII (Winter 1950), pp. 249–62.

— *Friendship's Harvest* (1956).

Marsden, W.E., *Unequal Educational Provision in England and Wales: The Nineteenth Century Roots* (1987).

Marsh, P.T., *The Discipline of Popular Government: Lord Salisbury's Domestic Statecraft 1881–1902* (Sussex, 1978).

— *Joseph Chamberlain: Entrepreneur in Politics* (Yale, 1994).

Masterman, C.F.G. (ed.), *The Heart of the Empire: Discussions of Problems of Modern City Life in England* (1901).

Masterman, L. (ed.), *Mary Gladstone (Mrs. Drew): Her Diaries and Letters* (1930).

Mathieson, M., and Bernbaum, G., 'The British Disease: A British Tradition?', *British Journal of Educational Studies*, XXXVI, 2 (July 1988), pp. 126–74.

Matthew, H.C.G., *The Liberal Imperialists: The Ideas and Politics of a Post-Gladstonian Elite* (1973).

Meacham, S., *A World Apart: The English Working Class 1890–1914* (Harvard, 1977).

— *Toynbee Hall and Social Reform 1880–1914: The Search for Community* (Yale, 1987).

Meyer, W.R. 'James Graham versus the Board of Education', *History of Education Society Bulletin*, 51 (Spring 1993), pp. 20–32.

Middleton, Earl of, *Records and Reactions 1856–1939* (1939).

Midwinter, E., *Nineteenth Century Education* (1970).

Miles [J. Maurice], 'Where to Get Men', *The Contemporary Review*, LXXXI (Jan. 1902), pp. 78–86.

Miller, J.E., 'The Liberal Party and Education 1898–1908', unpublished M. Ed. thesis, University of Liverpool, 1984.

Milner, Viscountess, *My Picture Gallery, 1886–1901* (1951).

Mitchell, W.R., *Life in the Lancashire Mill Towns* (Clapham, 1984).

Morgan, K.O. (ed.), *Lloyd George: Family Letters 1885–1936* (1975).

— *Wales in British Politics, 1868–1922*, 3rd edition (1991).

Morris, A.J.A., *C. P. Trevelyan 1870–1958: Portrait of a Radical* (Belfast, 1977).

Müller, D.K., Ringer, F., and Simon, B. (eds), *The Rise of the Modern Educational System* (Cambridge, 1987).

Munson, J.E.B., 'The London School Board Election of 1894: A Study in Victorian Religious Controversy', *British Journal of Educational Studies*, XXIII, 1 (Feb. 1975), pp. 7–23.

— 'The Unionist Coalition and Education 1895–1902', *Historical Journal*, 20, 3 (1977), pp. 607–45.

Musgrave, P.W., 'Morality and the Medical Department: 1907–1974', *British Journal of Educational Studies*, XXV, 2 (June 1977), pp. 136–54.

Musgrave, T., *Edwardian Childhood* (Oxford, 1981).

Musgrove, F., 'Middle-Class Education and Employment in the Nineteenth Century', *Economic History Review*, NS 12 (1959–60), pp. 99–111.

BIBLIOGRAPHY

— 'Middle-Class Education and Employment in the Nineteenth Century: A Rejoinder', *Economic History Review*, NS 14 (1961), pp. 320–29.

National Education Association, 'Save the Higher Grade Schools', *Special Leaflets, Higher Grade Schools*, No.5 (1900).
Newman, G., *The Building of a Nation's Health* (1939).
Newton, Lord, *Lord Lansdowne* (1929).

O'Day, A. (ed.), *The Edwardian Age: Conflict and Stability, 1900–1914* (1979).
Ostrogorski, M., *Democracy and the Organisation of Political Parties*, 2 Vols (1902).

Paz, D.G., 'The Composition of the Education Committee of the Privy Council, 1839–1856', *Journal of Educational Administration and History*, VIII, 2 (July 1976), pp. 1–9.
Perkin, H.J., 'Middle-Class Education and Employment in The Nineteenth Century: A Critical Note', *Economic History Review*, NS 14 (1961), pp. 122–30.
— *The Rise of Professional Society; England since 1880* (1989).
Pierce, G.O., 'The "Coercion of Wales" Act, 1904' in H. Hearder and H.R. Loyn (eds), *British Government and Administration* (Cardiff 1974), pp. 215–33.
Pile, W., *The Department of Education and Science* (1979).
Pugh, D.R., 'The 1902 Education Act: The Search for a Compromise', *British Journal of Educational Studies*, XVI, 2 (June 1968), pp. 164–78.
— 'The Church and Education: Anglican Attitudes 1902', *Journal of Ecclesiastical History*, XXIII, 3 (July 1972), p. 219–32.
— 'English Nonconformity, education and passive resistance 1903–6', *History of Education*, 19, 4 (1990), pp. 355–73.

Quinault, R.E., 'Lord Randolph Churchill and Tory Democracy, 1880–1885', *The Historical Journal*, 22, 1 (1979), pp. 141–65.
— 'Joseph Chamberlain: a Reassessment' in T.R. Gourvish and A. O'Day (eds), *Later Victorian Britain, 1867–1900* (1988).
— 'Asquith's Liberalism', *History*, 77 (1992), pp. 33–49.

Ramsden, J. (ed.), *Real Old Tory Politics: The Political Diaries of Robert Sanders, Lord Bayford, 1910–35* (1984).
Read, D., *Edwardian England 1901–1915* (1972).
— (ed.), *Edwardian England* (1982).
Reeder, D. (ed.), *Urban Education in the 19th Century* (1977).
Rempel, R.A., *Unionists Divided, A. Balfour, J. Chamberlain and the Unionist Free Traders* (Newton Abbot, 1972).
Rich, R.W., *The Training of Teachers in England and Wales during the Nineteenth Century* (1933).
Richards, N.J., 'Religious Controversy and the School Boards 1870–1902', *British Journal of Educational Studies*, XVIII, 2 (June, 1970), pp. 180–96.
Richter, M., *The Politics of Conscience: T.H. Green and His Age* (1964).
Riddell, Lord, *More Pages from My Diary* (1934).
Ridley, J., and Percy, C., *The Letters of Arthur Balfour and Lady Elcho* (1992).
Roach, J., *Secondary Education in England 1870–1902: Public Activity and Private Enterprise* (1991).

Roberts, R., *The Classic Slum* (1973).

— *A Ragged Schooling*, Glasgow (1979).

Roberts, R.D. (ed.), *Education in the Nineteenth Century* (Cambridge, 1901).

Robinson, W., 'Pupil teachers: the Achilles heel of higher grade girls' schools 1882–1904?', *History of Education*, 22, 3 (1993), pp. 241–52.

Rogers, A., 'Churches and Children – A Study in the Controversy over the 1902 Education Act', *British Journal of Educational Studies*, VIII, 1 (Nov., 1959), pp. 29–51.

Rose, J., *The Edwardian Temperament, 1895–1919* (Ohio, 1986).

— 'Willingly to School: The Working-Class Response to Elementary Education in Britain, 1875–1918', *Journal of British Studies*, 32 (April 1993), pp. 114–38.

Rose, L., *The Erosion of Childhood : Child Oppression in Britain 1860–1918* (1991).

Rowland, P., *The Last Liberal Governments: The Promised Land, 1905–1910* (1968).

Rowntree, S., *Poverty, A Study of Town Life* (1901).

Russell, A.K., *Liberal Landslide: The General Election of 1906* (Newton Abbot, 1973).

Russell, G.W.E. (ed.), *Sir Wilfrid Lawson* (1909).

Rutherford, J., *Sir George Grey, KCB, 1812–1898: A Study in Colonial Government* (1899).

Sacks, B., *The Religious Issue in the State Schools of England and Wales 1902–1914* (Albuquerque, 1961).

Sadler, M.E., 'Sir Arthur Acland', *The Oxford Magazine* (21 Oct. 1926), pp. 13–14.

Sadleir, M., *Michael Ernest Sadler 1861–1943: A Memoir by his Son* (1949).

Sandars, J.J., *Studies of Yesterday by a 'Privy Councillor'* (1928).

Sanderson, M., *Educational Opportunity and Social Change in England* (1987).

Scott, R.P. (ed.), *'What is Secondary Education?' and Other Short Essays* (1899).

Searle, G.R., *The Quest for National Efficiency: A Study in British Politics and Thought 1899–1914* (Oxford, 1971).

— (ed.), *A.White , Efficiency and Empire* (Sussex, 1973).

Selby Bigge, L.A., *The Board of Education* (1927).

Shannon, R., *The Crisis of Imperialism* (1974).

— *The Age of Disraeli, 1868–1881: The Rise of Tory Democracy* (1992).

Sharp, P.R., 'The Entry of County Councils into English Educational Administration, 1889', *Journal of Educational Administration and History*, I, 1 (1968), pp. 14–22.

Shaw, G.B., *The Revolutionist's Handbook* (1903).

Silver, H., *Education and the Social Condition* (1980).

— *Education, Change and the Policy Process* (1990).

Simon, B., *Education and the Labour Movement 1870–1920* (1965).

— 'The 1902 Education Act – A Wrong Turning', *History of Education Society Bulletin*, 19, (Spring 1977), pp. 9–14.

Simon, B. and Bradley, I., *The Victorian Public School* (1975).

Simpson, L., 'Imperialism, National Efficiency and Education, 1900–1905', *Journal of Educational Administration and History*, XVI, 1 (Jan. 1984), pp. 28–36.

Smith, F., *A History of English Elementary Education 1760–1902* (1931).

Smith, M., 'The Evaluation of Curricular Priorities in Secondary Schools: regulations, opinions and school practices in England, 1903–4', *British Journal of Sociology of Education*, 1, 2 (1980), pp. 153–72.

Smith, F.B., *The People's Health, 1830–1910* (1979).

Sneyd-Kynnersley, E.M., *H.M.I. Some Passages in the Life of one of H.M.Inspectors of Schools* (1910).

— *H.M.I.'s Notebook or Recreations of an Inspector of Schools* (1930).

Soloway, R., 'Counting the Degenerates: the Statistics of Race Deterioration in Edwardian England', *Journal of Contemporary History*, 17 (1982), pp. 137–64.

Spencer, F.H., *An Inspector's Testament* (1938).

Spender, H., *Life, Journalism and Politics* (1927).

Spender, J.A., *The Life of the Rt. Hon. Sir Henry Campbell-Bannerman, G.C.B.*, 2 Vols (1923).

Stanley, L., 'Reopening the Education Settlement of 1870', *The Nineteenth Century*, XXXVIII (Dec. 1895), pp. 915–30.

— ' The New Education Bill', *The Contemporary Review*, 69 (May 1896), pp. 741–60.

— 'The Position of the Education Question', *The Contemporary Review*, 72 (Nov., 1897), pp. 649–59.

— 'Higher Elementary Schools', *The Contemporary Review*, 78 (Nov. 1900), pp. 643–52.

Stedman Jones, G., *Outcast London: A Study in the Relationship between Classes in Victorian Society* (Oxford, 1971).

Steedman, C., *Childhood, Culture and Class in Britain: Margaret McMillan, 1860–1931* (1990).

Steedman, H., 'Michael Sadler and the Campaign for an Educational Council, 1893–1903', *Research in Education*, 2 (Nov. 1969), pp. 76–87.

Stephenson, G., *Edward Stuart Talbot, 1844–1934* (1936).

Sutherland, G. (ed.), *Studies in the Growth of Nineteenth-century Government* (1972).

— *Policy-Making in Elementary Education 1870–1895* (Oxford, 1973).

Tabor, M., 'Elementary Education' in C. Booth (ed.), *Life and Labour of the People in London*, III (1892), pp. 204–46.

Taylor, A.I., 'The Church Party and Popular Education, 1893–1902', unpublished D. Phil thesis, University of Cambridge, 1981.

— 'The Cockerton Case Revised: London Politics and Education 1898–1901', *British Journal of Educational Studies*, XXX, 3 (Oct. 1982), pp. 329–48.

— 'Lord Salisbury and the Politics of Education', *Journal of Educational Administration and History*, XVI, 2 (July 1984), pp. 1–11.

— '"An Early Arrival of the Fascist Mentality": Robert Morant's Rise to Power', *Journal of Educational Administration and History*, XVII, 2 (July 1985), pp. 48–62.

— 'The Cecils and the Cockerton Case: High Politics and Low Intentions', *History of Education Society Bulletin*, 37 (Spring 1986), pp. 32–43.

— 'Lord Cranborne, the Church Party and Anglican education 1893–1902: from politics to pressure', *History of Education*, 22, 2 (1993), pp. 125–46.

Taylor, R., *Lord Salisbury* (1975).

Taylor, W., 'Higher Elementary Schools and Social Change', *Research and Studies*, 21 (Nov. 1961), pp. 70–5.

Temple, W., *Life of Bishop Percival* (1921).

Thompson, P., *The Edwardians: The Remaking of British Society* (1977).

Tooley, S., 'Labour and Social Problems: An Interview with the Right Hon. Sir John Eldon Gorst, M.P.', *The Humanitarian* (1894) in *New Zealand Department of Labour Journal*, 18 (Aug. 1894), pp. 23–32.

Toulmin, G., 'First Impressions of Parliament', *Pall Mall Magazine*, XXVII (Aug. 1902), pp. 514–19.

Tropp, A., *The School Teachers: The Growth of the Teaching Profession in England and Wales from 1800 to the present day* (1957).

van Hall, R.W., 'The Unionist Party, Arthur Balfour and Social Reform 1900–1905', unpublished Ph. D. thesis, University of South Carolina, 1975.

Vincent, J.R., '"A Sort of Second-Rate Australia": A Note on Gorst and Democracy, 1865–8', *Historical Studies (Australia and New Zealand)*, 15 (1973), pp. 539–44.

— (ed.), *The Crawford Papers: The Journals of David Lindsay 27th Earl of Crawford and 10th Earl of Balcarres, (1871–1940) during the years 1892 to 1940* (1984).

Vincent, J.R. and Cooke, A.B., *The Governing Passion: Cabinet Government and Party Politics in Britain, 1885–86* (Brighton, 1974).

Waddington, R., 'The Voluntary School Problem', *The Westminster Review*, 146 (July 1896), pp. 88–94.

Ward, L.O., 'Joseph Chamberlain and the Denominational Schools Question', *Journal of Educational Administration and History*, V, 2 (July 1973), pp. 21–4.

Ware, F., *Educational Reform: The Task of the Board of Education* (1900).

Watts, M.R., 'John Clifford and Radical Nonconformity, 1836–1923', unpublished D. Phil thesis, University of Oxford, 1967.

Webb, B., *Our Partnership* (1948).

Westminster, Archbishop of, 'The Education Bill', *The Nineteenth Century and After*, CCCLI (May 1906), pp. 719–23.

Whitbread, N., 'The early twentieth-century secondary curriculum debate in England', *History of Education*, 13, 3 (1984), pp. 221–33.

Widdowson, F., *Going up into the Next Class: Women and Elementary Teacher Training 1840–1914* (1983).

Wiener, M.J., *English Culture and the Decline of the Industrial Spirit 1850–1980* (1981).

Wilkinson, M.J., 'The Office of Special Inquiries and Reports: Educational Policy Making under Michael Sadler', *History of Education*, 8, 4 (1979), pp. 275–91.

Wilson, J., *CB: A Life of Sir Henry Campbell-Bannerman* (1973).

Wimbourne, C., 'Evangelicals and the Education Question', *The Nineteenth Century and After*, CCCXLIX (March 1906), pp. 387–400.

Wrigley, E.A., *Nineteenth-century Society: Essays in the Quantitative Methods for the Study of Social Data* (1972).

Wynne Evans, L., *Studies in Welsh Education: Welsh Educational Structure and Administration 1880–1925* (Cardiff, 1974).

Young, K., *Arthur James Balfour: The Happy Life of the Politician, Prime Minister, Statesman and Philosopher, 1848–1930* (1963).

Young, P.M., *Elgar, O.M.* (1973).

Yoxall, J.H., 'The Education Bill and the Minute', *Picture-Politics* (July–Aug. 1901), p. 11.

— 'Our Educational Dux', *New Liberal Review* (Dec. 1901), pp. 680–86.

Z. M., 'Maude Lawrence', *Macmillan Dictionary of British Women's Biography* (1982).

Zebel, S.H., *Balfour: A Political Biography* (Cambridge, 1973).

Index

Abney, W. de W., 92, 95–6, 99, 100, 115, 124, 219, 228

Acland, A.H.D., 2, 6, 12–14, 20–3, 35, 42, 52, 56, 62, 93, 95–6, 134, 138, 175, 221, 228, 281, 283–4, 287, 298, 301, 413, 424

Acts of Parliament and Bills:

Board of Education Act (1899), 71, 84, 88–101, 106, 108, 113, 121, 125, 128, 202, 226, 230, 412, 446–7; Children's Act (1908), 398; Education Act (1870), 3–4, 6, 15, 40, 45, 48–9, 50, 52, 54, 144, 154, 254, 290; *see also* Cowper-Temple Clause; Education Code (1890) Act, 110, 122; Education Act (1891), 62; Education Act (1901), 142–3; Education Act (1902), 54, 142–68, 201, 204, 207, 209, 211, 216, 218, 224, 226, 230, 233, 236, 241–3, 247–8, 251–5, 259, 266, 268, 271–2, 275, 277, 281–6, 291, 295, 300–2, 307, 309, 315, 337, 352, 376, 407–8, 425, 445–6, 448–9; Education (London) Act (1903), 207, 248–52; Education (Defaulting Authorities') Act (1904), 261–2, 267–76; Education (Feeding of School Children) Act (1906), 366–70, 377, 448; Education (Administrative Provisions) Act (1907), 316, 318, 320, 379–83, 387, 391–2, 394–5, 398, 400, 419, 423, 448; Education Act (1918), 446; Endowed Schools Act (1869), 125; LEA (Medical Treatment) Act (1909), 397; Local Government Act (1888), 5, 13, 146–7, 241; Local Taxation (Custom and Excise) Act (1890), 13, 128; London Government Act (1899), 241; Technical Instruction Act (1889), 13, 73, 123, 125–6, 137, 144; Voluntary Schools Act (1897), 58–66, 70; Welsh Intermediate Education Act (1889), 13; Education Bill (1896),

42–56, 64, 70–1, 74, 79, 128–9, 131, 134, 143, 145, 147, 152, 161, 190, 195–6, 412; Education Bill (1901), 142, 144, 151; Education Bill (1906), 277, 286–311, 315–16, 337, 378–82, 405, 418–19, 448; Education Bill (1907) (McKenna's), 316–24, 448; Education Bill (1907) (Rea's), 379–81; Education Bill (1908), 324–337, 448

Africa, South, 136, 177, 198, 285, 340; *see also* Boer War

Anglicans, *see* Church of England

Anson, Sir William, 121, 135, 160, 172, 178, 183–4, 193, 197, 201, 204–5, 220–1, 234, 236, 415, 417, 420; and 1903 Education Act, 245–6, 248–51; and opposition to 1902 Act, 258, 262–5, 268–75; and child welfare, 358–65, 381–2

Arkle, Dr A.S., 344–6

Asquith, H.H., ix, 1, 52–3, 70, 138, 149, 206, 283–4, 309, 320, 323, 328–9, 331–2, 336, 435–6

Association of School Boards, 106, 115

Balcarres, tenth Earl of, 304, 315, 333, 428

Balfour, A.J., ix, 27, 33–4, 43, 91, 113, 115–16, 121, 124, 125, 131, 133, 142, 205, 245, 252, 276–7, 283, 285, 321–2, 325, 330, 333, 336–7, 351, 358, 360–1, 364–6, 376, 379–81, 384, 431, 445, 447–9; on Duke of Devonshire, 29, 131; and voluntary schools, 40; planning of 1896 Bill, 41–3, 47–51, 53–5, 56–7; and 1897 Act, 58–66; and 1901 Bill, 131, 133, 135–8; 1902 Act, 142–68, 172–4, 175–6, 180–97, 242, 255–6, 282; becomes PM, 177–8; and 1903 Act, 244, 251; and opposition to 1902 Act, 254, 260, 265–6, 268–73; opposes

For Product Safety Concerns and Information please contact our EU
representative GPSR@taylorandfrancis.com Taylor & Francis Verlag GmbH,
Kaufingerstraße 24, 80331 München, Germany

Batch number: 08153774

Printed by Printforce, the Netherlands